D0630712

THE STUDENT ENGAGEMENT HANDBOOK: PRACTICE IN HIGHER EDUCATION

THE STUDENT ENGAGEMENT HANDBOOK: PRACTICE IN HIGHER EDUCATION

EDITED BY

ELISABETH DUNNE
University of Exeter, Exeter, UK

DERFEL OWEN
University of Exeter, Exeter, UK

United Kingdom • North America • Japan
India • Malaysia • China

Emerald Group Publishing Limited
Howard House, Wagon Lane, Bingley BD16 1WA, UK

First edition 2013

Copyright © 2013 Emerald Group Publishing Limited

Reprints and permission service
Contact: permissions@emeraldinsight.com

No part of this book may be reproduced, stored in a retrieval system, transmitted in any form or
by any means electronic, mechanical, photocopying, recording or otherwise without either the
prior written permission of the publisher or a licence permitting restricted copying issued in the
UK by The Copyright Licensing Agency and in the USA by The Copyright Clearance Center.
Any opinions expressed in the chapters are those of the authors. Whilst Emerald makes every
effort to ensure the quality and accuracy of its content, Emerald makes no representation
implied or otherwise, as to the chapters' suitability and application and disclaims any warranties,
express or implied, to their use.

British Library Cataloguing in Publication Data
A catalogue record for this book is available from the British Library

ISBN: 978-1-78190-423-7

ISOQAR certified
Management System,
awarded to Emerald
for adherence to
Environmental
standard
ISO 14001:2004.

ISOQAR
REGISTERED
Certificate Number 1985
ISO 14001

INVESTOR IN PEOPLE

This book is dedicated to three people who have passed away, before their time, during the period of writing this Handbook. Each has — in their own way — influenced so much of the experience and thinking behind its creation.

Ian King, who was a friend and mentor to Derfel as a student and in later life. Ian's passion and work to promote student engagement and to improve students' unions will have had an impact, in one way or another, on every student in the United Kingdom.

Jenny Wren, who was a friend to both of us. She was a creative, enthusiastic, inspiring and natural teacher; she always wanted the very best for her students and engaged with them in so many innovative ways, always striving for improvement.

Richard Dunne, who taught Elisabeth so much, supported her passion for learning and learners over several decades, and gave her the confidence to be at the forefront of educational practice and change.

Contents

List of Contributors   *xi*

Introduction   *xv*

PART 1: VANTAGE POINTS ON STUDENT ENGAGEMENT
Elisabeth Dunne and Derfel Owen   *1*

1. Haven't We Seen It All Before? Historical Themes in Student Engagement
   Derfel Owen   *5*

2. Towards a New Vision for University Governance, Pedagogies and
   Student Engagement
   Stefan Popenici   *23*

3. A Relational and Multidimensional Model of Student Engagement
   Ian Solomonides   *43*

4. What Does Student Engagement Mean to Students?
   Alex Ratcliffe and Andrew Dimmock   *59*

5. Staff Perceptions of Student Engagement
   Gwen van der Velden   *77*

PART 2: A NEW ERA — THE POLICY AND QUALITY CONTEXT
FOR STUDENT ENGAGEMENT
Elisabeth Dunne and Derfel Owen   *93*

6. Harmonisation and the Bologna Process: A Driver for
   Student Engagement?
   Alex Bols   *97*

7.   Student Engagement in Private Sector Higher Education
     Sue Rivers and Thomas Willans   *111*

8.   Trusting Dialogue for Engaging Students
     Carmen Werder and Erik Skogsberg   *133*

9.   Student Engagement in Practice: Ideologies and Power in Course
     Representation Systems
     Rebecca Freeman   *145*

10. Students Engaged in Academic Subject Review
     Derfel Owen   *163*

11. Meaningful Engagement with Disabled Students
     Aaron Porter   *181*

     **PART 3: STUDENT ENGAGEMENT WITH THE COMMUNITY: THE
     UNIVERSITY AND BEYOND**
     Elisabeth Dunne and Derfel Owen   *197*

12. Meanings of Engagement to Part-Time, Working Students in Higher
     Education
     Julie Wintrup, Kelly Wakefield and Elizabeth James   *201*

13. Student Engagement Through Volunteering
     Lorraine McIlrath and Lorraine Tansey   *221*

14. 'Giving to Sport': Community Engagement Within and Beyond the
     Curriculum
     Lucy Spowart and Mike Tripp   *237*

15. The Creative Campus: Empowering the University Community to Change
     Spaces
     Ian Bride, Louise Naylor and Carin Tunåker   *255*

     PART 4: STUDENTS TAKING RESPONSIBILITY FOR THEIR LEARNING
     Elisabeth Dunne and Derfel Owen   *271*

16. Student Engagement in and Through Orientation
     Sharon Pittaway and Timothy Moss   *275*

17. Peer Education
    Marcia Ody and William Carey   291

18. 'We Need Support Too': Providing Postgraduate Peer Support
    Jacques van der Meer, Lucy Spowart and Simon Hart   313

19. Reflection as a Strategy to Enhance Students' Engagement in their
    Learning
    Janet Strivens and Rob Ward   331

20. Breaking Down the Walls: Engaging Students with the Development
    of their Intercultural Competencies
    *Christine Hardy, Sean Prince, Viola Borsos, Christopher
    Demirjian, Ji Kim, Nga Mok and Oliver Roman-Worsley*   349

21. Reframing Diversity and Student Engagement: Lessons from Deaf-Gain
    Peter Felten and H-Dirksen L. Bauman   367

22. Engaging Students Through Assessment
    Kay Sambell   379

           **PART 5: STUDENT ENGAGEMENT IN CURRICULUM DESIGN
                              AND DELIVERY**
                     Elisabeth Dunne and Derfel Owen   397

23. Active Participation in Learning: Students Creating their
    Educational Experience
    Joan Walton   401

24. Engaging Students for Professional Practice in Global Health
    Manisha Nair and Emma Plugge   421

25. Students as Digital Change Agents
    *Malcolm Ryan, Emma Franklin, Tanbir Galsinh, Dale Potter, Jenny Wren,
    Mark Kerrigan, Antony Coombs and Simon Walker*   437

26. Students and Staff Co-creating Curricula: An Example of Good Practice
    in Higher Education?
    Catherine Bovill   461

27.   Students as Partners: A Three-Layered Approach for Enhancement
       Stuart Brand, Luke Millard, Paul Bartholomew and Paul Chapman   477

              **PART 6: STUDENT ENGAGEMENT IN DISCIPLINE AND
                          PEDAGOGIC RESEARCH**
                       Elisabeth Dunne and Derfel Owen   493

28.   Deliberative Democracy for Curriculum Renewal
       Amani Bell, Lyn Carson and Leanne Piggott   499

29.   Students as Co-Researchers: A Collaborative, Community-Based Approach
       to the Research and Practice of Technology-Enhanced Learning
       Sue Timmis and Jane Williams   509

30.   Students Engaging with Change
       Elisabeth Dunne, Jackie Bagnall and Barrie Cooper   527

31.   Catalysing Multiple Forms of Engagement: Student–Staff Partnerships
       Exploring Teaching and Learning
       Alison Cook-Sather   549

32.   Practical Approaches to Student Engagement through Community-Based
       Research and Learning
       Eileen Martin and Catherine O'Mahony   567

33.   Student as Producer: Radicalising the Mainstream in Higher Education
       Mike Neary   587

Conclusion   603

About the Authors   637

Index   653

List of Contributors

Jackie Bagnall	University of Exeter, Exeter, UK
Paul Bartholomew	Birmingham City University, Birmingham, UK
H-Dirksen L. Bauman	Gallaudet University, Washington, DC, USA
Amani Bell	University of Sydney, Sydney, Australia
Alex Bols	1994 Group of Universities, London, UK
Viola Borsos	Nottingham Trent University, Nottingham, UK
Catherine Bovill	University of Glasgow, Glasgow, UK
Stuart Brand	Birmingham City University, Birmingham, UK
Ian Bride	University of Kent, Canterbury, UK
William Carey	University of Manchester, Manchester, UK
Lyn Carson	University of Sydney, Sydney, Australia
Paul Chapman	Birmingham City University, Birmingham, UK
Alison Cook-Sather	Bryn Mawr College, PA, USA
Antony Coombs	University of Greenwich, London, UK
Barrie Cooper	University of Exeter, Exeter, UK
Christopher Demirjian	Nottingham Trent University, Nottingham, UK
Andrew Dimmock	University of Exeter, Exeter, UK
Elisabeth Dunne	University of Exeter, Exeter, UK
Peter Felten	Elon University, NC, USA
Emma Franklin	University of Wolverhampton, Wolverhampton, UK
Rebecca Freeman	University of Warwick, Coventry, UK
Tanbir Galsinh	University of Wolverhampton, Wolverhampton, UK

Christine Hardy	Nottingham Trent University, Nottingham, UK
Simon Hart	University of Otago, Dunedin, New Zealand
Elizabeth James	University of Southampton, Southampton, UK
Mark Kerrigan	University of Greenwich, London, UK
Ji Kim	Nottingham Trent University, Nottingham, UK
Eileen Martin	Queens University Belfast, Belfast, UK
Lorraine McIlrath	National University of Ireland, Galway, Ireland
Luke Millard	Birmingham City University, Birmingham, UK
Nga Mok	Nottingham Trent University, Nottingham, UK
Timothy Moss	University of Tasmania, Hobart, Australia
Manisha Nair	University of Oxford, Oxford, UK
Louise Naylor	University of Kent, Canterbury, UK
Mike Neary	University of Lincoln, Lincoln, UK
Marcia Ody	University of Manchester, Manchester, UK
Catherine O'Mahony	National Academy for the Integration of Research, Teaching and Learning, Ireland
Derfel Owen	University of Exeter, Exeter, UK
Leanne Piggott	University of Sydney, Sydney, Australia
Sharon Pittaway	University of Tasmania, Hobart, Australia
Emma Plugge	University of Oxford, Oxford, UK
Stefan Popenici	University of Melbourne, Melbourne, Australia
Aaron Porter	Independent Higher Education Consultant, UK
Dale Potter	University of Exeter, Exeter, UK
Sean Prince	Nottingham Trent University, Nottingham, UK
Alex Ratcliffe	University of Exeter, Exeter, UK
Sue Rivers	BPP University College of Professional Studies, London, UK
Oliver Roman-Worsley	Nottingham Trent University, Nottingham, UK
Malcolm Ryan	University of Greenwich, London, UK
Kay Sambell	Northumbria University, Newcastle, UK

Erik Skogsberg	Michigan State University, Lansing, MI, USA
Ian Solomonides	Macquarie University, Sydney, Australia
Lucy Spowart	Plymouth University, Plymouth, UK
Janet Strivens	University of Liverpool, Liverpool, UK
Lorraine Tansey	National University of Ireland, Galway, Ireland
Sue Timmis	University of Bristol, Bristol, UK
Mike Tripp	University of St Mark & St John, Plymouth, UK
Carin Tunåker	University of Kent, Canterbury, UK
Jacques van der Meer	University of Otago, Dunedin, New Zealand
Gwen van der Velden	University of Bath, Bath, UK
Kelly Wakefield	University of Southampton, Southampton, UK
Simon Walker	University of Greenwich, London, UK
Joan Walton	Liverpool Hope University, Liverpool, UK
Rob Ward	Centre for Recording Achievement, Wigan, UK
Carmen Werder	Western Washington University, Bellingham, WA, USA
Thomas Willans	Coventry University, Coventry, UK
Jane Williams	University of Bristol, Bristol, UK
Julie Wintrup	University of Southampton, Southampton, UK
Jenny Wren	University of Exeter, Exeter, UK

Introduction

Defining Student Engagement

Look up the term 'student engagement' and you will find a confusing array of definitions and associated concepts. It is used in the same breath as student participation, involvement, commitment, effort, time on task or motivation. It is associated with teamwork, leadership, community or civic engagement, democracy, with partnership, co-creation and collaboration, with developing new relationships between staff and students, and with students as customers. It is linked to institutional strategies and interventions and student satisfaction, to pre-induction, induction and transition programmes, to retention, continuation and completion. It is linked to curriculum design and is claimed to be promoted by a variety of modes of teaching or learning, as well as by the nature of assessment and feedback provided for learners, to the role of peers as mentors, or to the power of technology to promote engagement. It is about working 'with' students, not providing 'for' students. It is discussed in terms of underpinning personal identity, emotion and individual cognitive performance, or student success, or institutional success; engagement is linked to national and institutional improvement strategies, to students having a 'voice', to enhancement, to validity, reliability, and quality. Different forms of engagement are reported: active engagement, fluctuating engagement, disengagement, effective engagement.

This book provides a series of descriptions to disentangle concepts, to put meat on the bones of the words, and to highlight both emerging theory and practical approaches to engaging, and engaging *with*, students. It is intended for researchers and teachers in higher education, for university and national policy makers and strategic decision-makers worldwide. It gives the most up-to-date view available of what student engagement is perceived to mean to those involved in higher education — from researchers to students — and discusses the challenges, the pitfalls and the overall benefits and excitements of genuine student engagement. Chapters have been contributed from experts in the field from across the world, and include researchers and experienced practitioners, many of whom are working at the forefront of thinking and practice. Ironically, direct student voices are rarely apparent in texts on the 'student voice' or on student engagement. Student voices are 'listened to' by researchers and institutions and then collated and interpreted by these groups, rather than students themselves being encouraged and enabled to take on this responsibility. There is much to be learned from students and much to which they can contribute directly if given the opportunity. So we have deliberately sought to include contributions from students working in collaboration with academic practitioners.

So why is such a book of importance? First, there can be little room for doubt that student engagement is an all-pervasive term used in higher education across the world and it is therefore worthy of attention. Second, student engagement is universally perceived as 'a good thing', focused generally on what must be central to higher education — learners and learning. An 'engaged' student is likely to be a successful student (Trowler & Trowler, 2010). Student engagement does not align well with conceptualisations of passive learners or students as empty vessels to be filled, but with students actively and deliberately engaging with their formal and informal learning in the broadest sense — in their academic learning and how it is delivered and made available to them, in their relationships with their teachers and peers, in their learning environments, in learning about, working with, or representing their peers, in the quality processes of their institutions, or in developing practices and responsibilities within their local communities and beyond. As outlined in a wide-ranging and ambitious Student Life Strategy by the University of Tennessee:

> The mission of the Division of Student Life is to foster the intellectual, cultural, social and emotional development of students by providing a climate conducive to learning and personal growth, enabling them to become fully productive members of the Global Community.
>
> To achieve this mission we will engage all students in meaningful co-curricular opportunities to promote retention and persistence toward graduation. (University of Tennessee, 2011)

Undoubtedly, there is a need to better understand the variety of interpretations and conceptualisations that constitute 'student engagement' since otherwise it has the potential to become a valueless hotchpotch of words and activities, with little shared meaning. Trowler and Trowler (2010), in their comprehensive review of student engagement, provide a warning:

> It is clear that the term 'student engagement' carries a number of quite diverse meanings. The danger is that people run the risk of talking past each other when discussing how to enhance student engagement within their institution, thinking they are talking about the same thing when in reality they are not. (Trowler & Trowler, 2010, p. 225)

Developing shared meanings and understandings is all the more important since there can also be little doubt that 'student engagement' is the catch phrase of the moment in UK higher education, as well as being prevalent worldwide. It follows on from other such buzz phrases: 'student satisfaction', 'the student experience', 'the student voice'. Student engagement is enshrined within Government papers in the United Kingdom; it is advocated in the policy of numerous national bodies from the Quality Assurance Agency (QAA, 2009) to the Higher Education Academy (HEA, 2010, 2013) and the National Union of Students (NUS, 2010); it is ubiquitously written into university strategy plans; it is on the tip of the tongue of every university senior manager; it is the topic of workshops, seminars and conferences. As outlined by the national press (*The Guardian*, 2011):

> Every university, HE association, umbrella group or think tank worth its salt has taken it [i.e. student engagement] on: the Higher Education Academy (HEA) suggests it is essential for student retention and success, the Equality Challenge Unit (ECU) encourages HEIs to go beyond their legal obligations and engage disabled students in facilities, curriculum and assessment design. The Quality Assurance Agency for Higher Education (QAA) has developed an entire strategy that will see them 'actively engaging students as a primary stakeholder community in shaping and developing quality assurance and enhancement activities'. (2011)

A very different view of engagement is proposed by an Australian university, where it is the students' engagement with the institution that is seen as all-important:

> Monash University adopted a strategy to increase student engagement. The strategy involved setting up a call centre for the purpose of contacting recent Monash University graduates who had not completed the graduate destination survey and course experience questionnaire surveys to explain the significance of the graduate feedback to the institution. (Nair, Adams, & Mertova, 2008)

In the USA, student engagement is similarly clearly linked to the National Survey of Student Engagement (NSSE) which has allowed a detailed, longitudinal study, from 1999, on the quality of students' educational experiences, More than 537,000 students from 751 institutions in the United States and Canada completed the survey for 2011 alone, and the findings will be used for widespread institutional enhancement and change. However, despite the title of 'student engagement', the surveys are far more about student 'satisfaction', enabling the identification of institutional activities that lead to improved performance and the drawing of lessons to inform improvement. There may be links or possibly correlations between engagement and satisfaction, but they are not the same thing. Further, although the student voice is central to these surveys — and the power and importance of this voice should not be underestimated — and student feedback is central to institutional development and change, this is not the same as students themselves taking responsibility for institutional responses and progress; nor is it directly concerned with any individual's learning and development.

Kuh (again from the United States) suggests that the concept of student engagement is clear-cut, and relates to the effort and time that individual students put into learning alongside the effectiveness of curriculum delivery and of the feedback they receive from teachers:

> The engagement premise is straightforward and easily understood: the more students study a subject, the more they know about it, and the more students practice and get feedback from faculty and staff members on their writing and collaborative problem solving, the deeper they come to understand what they are learning and the more adept they become at managing complexity, tolerating ambiguity, and working with people from different backgrounds or with different views. (Kuh, 2009)

This relationship between student behaviours and effective teaching may not be as straightforward as Kuh suggests, and more recent discussion suggests that student engagement is less easily understood; indeed it is characterised by complexity. In a 'whole person' view presented by the New Zealand Council for Educational Research at their 2009 student engagement conference it is postulated that:

> Improving learning involves engaging the minds, hearts and imaginations of young people. It requires us to have faith in our students and to show them respect. It means building on what they already know and believe, what they care about now, and what they hope for in the future, so that they become active and committed lifelong learners. This mix of behaviour, emotion and cognition is known as student engagement. (New Zealand Council for Educational Research, 2009)

The UK website for the RAISE network (Researching, Advancing and Inspiring Student Engagement (RAISE), 2010) builds on this yet further:

> Student engagement is about what a student brings to Higher Education in terms of goals, aspirations, values and beliefs and how these are shaped and mediated by their experience whilst a student. Student engagement is constructed and reconstructed through the lenses of the perceptions and identities held by students and the meaning and sense a student makes of their experiences and interactions. As players in and shapers of the educational context, educators need to foster educationally purposeful student engagement to support and enable students to learn in constructive and powerful ways and realise their potential in education and society. (2010)

The Higher Education Context

Just these few examples serve to highlight the difficulty of defining student engagement, and many more illustrations will be given throughout this book. However, each of the three above quotes is clear in valuing the impact of engagement for each and every student as a tolerant, committed and aspiring learner of the future. Importantly, conceptualisations of engagement are increasingly linked to what it means to be a student in the changing world of higher education at this moment in time, and what it might mean in the world ahead.

Current changes to higher education suggest a far less secure and straightforward future for students than that enjoyed be their forerunners: more students will be studying part-time (already more than one in three students studies part-time and one in six is from overseas), more will be studying online, there will be more 'pick-and-mix' degrees, with students gaining credits at different universities, possibly within different countries, and possibly with gaps for employment, and more will be living in their own or their parents' homes. In addition, there are warnings about the precariousness of university finances in the new fees climate and the risk of students increasingly becoming 'consumers', more interested in gaining credit than in learning, and determined that their requirements will be met. University leaders have also warned that market forces could adversely impact on four areas that are currently key to higher education policy and delivery: social mobility, student choice, subject mix and institutional viability.

Such change does not pertain to the United Kingdom alone. Universities worldwide are in a state of flux. Overall, there has been an unprecedented global surge in the numbers of young people going to university. Among the developed OECD countries, graduation rates have almost doubled since the mid-1990s. Whereas the United Kingdom is squeezing investment in universities; other countries — the United States, France, India and China — are spending more and expanding fast. In 1998, there were only about a million students in China. Within a decade, it has become the biggest university system in the world. The number of Chinese undergraduates in the United States has tripled in just three years, to 40,000, making them the largest group of foreign students at American colleges. There are currently more overseas students taking UK degrees in their own countries than there are overseas students coming to study in the UK, and there are more students studying UK degrees abroad than there are UK students in total, but the culture of this market is changing — western universities will no longer be able to depend on their pivotal position. For example, a plan to bring more overseas students into China is part of the country's drive to internationalise its economy and become a 'knowledge power'. In addition, the growth of the private degree provider is a widespread phenomenon. In the United States several large corporations are taking a growing chunk of not only their own domestic market, but also of the international market.

On top of this, the economic climate worldwide will be influencing perceptions of the value of higher education. According to the McKinsey Centre for Government:

> Worldwide, young people are three times more likely than their parents to be out of work. In Greece, Spain, and South Africa, more than half of young people are unemployed, and jobless levels of 25 Per cent or more are common in Europe, the Middle East, and Northern Africa. Around the world, the International Labour Organization

estimates that 75 million young people are unemployed. Including estimates of under-employed youth would potentially triple this number.
This represents not just a gigantic pool of untapped talent; it is also a
source of social unrest and individual despair... If young people who
have worked hard to graduate from school and university cannot
secure decent jobs and the sense of respect that comes with them,
society will have to be prepared for outbreaks of anger or even violence. The evidence is in the protests that have recently occurred in
Chile, Egypt, Greece, Italy, South Africa, Spain, and the United States
(to name but a few countries). The gap between the haves and the
have-nots in the OECD is at a 30-year high, with income among the
top 10 percent nine times higher than that of the bottom 10 percent.
(Mourshed, Farrell, & Barton, 2012)

So how does this new and shifting world relate to student engagement? Why is
there such an interest in this topic? Why has it become so important in discussions
across the world? Is it more important now than ever before? Above all, what does
student engagement really mean, and for whom? To what extent can there be a global definition, and do definitions shift — or need to shift — along with political and
societal change? This book addresses just such questions and issues, with each of
the six parts addressing a different vantage point, from conceptualising in theoretical terms what 'student engagement' means, to the many ways in which it is played
out in practice.

What is noticeable, certainly in the United Kingdom but also more widely, is
how the emphasis in meaning is shifting; conceptions of student engagement are
increasingly related to significant changes in the way that the role and responsibilities of students are perceived, and the way in which they relate to their institutions
and wider educational bodies. Over the past decade, the concept of the 'student
voice' has become prevalent, along with the many ways that this can be meaningfully captured (Czerniawski & Kidd, 2011). There is no doubt that institutional listening to student voices is essential, but it is often related to more passive means of
engaging; that is students offer feedback but are not engaged in the decision-making
processes beyond that point, they are not responsible for the changes that come
about as a result of that feedback, indeed they may often not know what changes
are made within institutions as an outcome. However, from as long ago as 1998, the
European Students' Union (then named ESIB − the European Student Information
Bureau) called for students not only to become engaged in decisions about their
educational provision and, engaged in the processes of 'shaping and developing'
their educational experiences:

Education in the twenty-first century will face a lot of old problems,
but we need to keep in mind that new and unexpected situations will
arise as well. Students shall face these problems and they will find
new, creative solutions fitting the spirit of the age. We students ask
for recognition of our sense of responsibility for our own education...

Students as adults should participate in the organization of their education at different levels. We are participants rather than clients in higher education. Decisions made on national and regional levels influencing higher education or students' social life cannot be taken without consulting us. Students have a common interest and therefore demand a share of responsibility in decision-making bodies. Close co-operation between students and staff is — therefore — of vital importance and could be developed further through this shared responsibility. (ESU, 1998)

This kind of view is increasingly pervading the rhetoric and literature on student engagement and is increasingly filtering into practices, and it is one which is keenly supported by the authors of this book. It reflects more than an interest in and regard for student feedback. In the words of an enthusiast from the school setting in the United States (Fielding, 2006):

Imagine... a place where all adults and students interact as co-learners and leaders, and where students are encouraged to speak out about their schools. Picture all adults actively valuing student engagement and empowerment, and all students actively striving to become more engaged and empowered. Envision school classrooms where teachers place the experiences of students at the center of learning, and education boardrooms where everyone can learn from students as partners in school change.

Such a vision is not impossible for higher education: a place where student engagement means far more than paying attention and being motivated in class, far more than offering feedback on learning experiences, but encompasses students taking responsibility for co-creating and taking ownership of their own educational environment, culture and ethos, working 'with' people and institutions rather than being engaged 'by' them. And through that process, students learn about far more than disciplinary knowledge; they learn about the fundamentals of knowledge-creation, of pedagogy, of democratic decision-making processes and institutional change and the wider context in which they study and live. These are the students who are truly engaged, who will have the potential to be the leaders of the future and who will be better equipped for an uncertain world ahead. (Fielding, 2006)

The UK HEA (2012) in its *Dimensions of Student Engagement* document states, in more down-to-earth fashion, but strongly supporting the new vision of student engagement:

Student engagement encompasses ways in which students become active partners in shaping their learning experience. This ranges from students influencing national policy on learning and teaching, to students developing their own individual learning agendas. In between there are examples of students engaging in institutional and departmental discussion on curriculum design and delivery. (HEA, 2012)

It is essential to keep this kind of optimism and vision, but the pathway is not necessarily easy. As is a recurring matter of discussion in the following chapters, not only does achieving student engagement require time and energy on the part of the institution, the staff and the students themselves, but it is currently perceived as being undermined by the more recent consumerist attitude to education worldwide. An example of such change can be seen in the rhetoric of the NUS. In 2008, Porter — then Vice President for Higher Education, NUS — argued that:

...the relationship in learning between students and academics transcends the customer-provider contract; the opportunities to make the institution and its provision better are so much greater, through the active participation of learners, than anything a business can gain from its customers.

Shortly after, as President of the NUS, Porter quotes evidence that:

...an increasing number of students want to put forward their views about how and what they are taught and assessed. Different students will want to engage in different ways and therefore HE needs to open up the fora through which they can do that. (Porter, 2010a)

Yet, just two years later, and with a marked change in tone, Porter (2010b) claims: '...*the student vitriol directed against the rise in fees will be poured on their universities*'. In the fees-paying environment that England has entered, students are encouraged to consider themselves customers, entitled to value for money:

I will not stand by and let [student] interests fall into second place behind old-fashioned thinking and approaches, no longer fit for purpose in that world. (Porter 2010c)

Hence there seems to be something of a dilemma or tension: a culture that, largely due to the huge rise in fees in the United Kingdom, is becoming increasingly consumer-like and demanding, counteracted by calls for increased student engagement in their educational environment and in the ways in which learning is delivered, managed and quality assured. Indeed it has been suggested that 'growing interest around student engagement is motivated by an attempt to find an antidote to the "students as consumers" philosophy' (Anyangwe, 2011). Whatever the truth of this, Greatrix (2011) argues that what '... the student as consumer concept fails to capture is the essence of what really makes a high quality education for students?' This is the very purpose of the Handbook: how does student engagement relate, in multi-faceted ways, to the best possible learning experience for all in higher education and how can this be achieved at the practical level? Student engagement is at the heart of this quest, both at the level of how Universities engage with their students and the education of their students, and how students engage with their education.

The Contents of the Student Engagement Handbook

The six parts of the book and the individual chapters within them have been designed to give a broad overview of student engagement from multiple perspectives, including the bits 'in between' of the HEA quote above, and taking into consideration the shifting vision of higher education in a rapidly changing world. Topics are presented in a variety of formats, from think-pieces, to descriptions, to evaluative case studies, and they cover both curriculum-driven initiatives and activities beyond the curriculum. Each chapter will serve the overall purpose of clarifying meanings, highlighting new and effective practices and offering insights to others to develop evidence-led change, building on the inspirations, practicalities and evaluations of authors from across the world. There is an emphasis on research-led and critical analysis but, above all, authors are enthusiasts for student engagement, administrators and practitioners with stories about their personal interests, involvement and endeavours, immersed in ideas and activities for improving the student learning environment. Importantly, although some chapters are set in specific disciplines, no initiative described is discipline-specific, and all could be transferred to any higher education context.

Overall, the book is not designed to present definitive definitions and models. It is designed to add to the reader's overall understanding of some of the background and practices relating to student engagement, and to present a few of the many philosophies and passions that underpin significant activities in this area. Above all, it is designed to provide informed ideas that can be used to develop practice in any context, and to support others to bring about change, whether on the scale of a single module or across an institution or beyond.

The sequence of the book covers a series of vantage points from the theoretical, to the socio-economic and policy and quality context that is underpinning current change, and from more traditional conceptualisations to those that provide a new vision for collaborative endeavour, engaging students in the development of the higher education community. The majority of contributions are from UK authors but there is a good range from across the world: from Australia, New Zealand, the United States and Ireland, all of which contribute to a common goal in understanding and giving meaning to student engagement in its many forms.

Part 1 includes historical, theoretical and empirical conceptualisations, specifically to gain different vantage points from practitioners and students, and setting the scene for the rest of the book. Part 2 outlines a number of themes within current and developing policy and quality issues in higher education that impact on students and heavily influence how institutions are expected to manage student participation and engagement. Part 3 demonstrates how student engagement with the community, both within and beyond the university, is far broader than the everyday curriculum, encompassing the formal workplace, volunteering and the development of learning spaces, Part 4 suggests how the positive facilitation of learning can motivate and engage students in their individual learning and development, and highlights how aspects of the learning environment — forms of assessment, peer support and the nature of the students themselves — can all impinge on students' ways of working and how they engage in their educational processes. Part 5 reviews ways in which students can be actively involved in curriculum design and delivery, working in partnership with academics to improve the learning experience for all. Finally, Part 6 demonstrates innovative means for encouraging students to engage collaboratively in both discipline and pedagogic research, so that the research process perceived as fundamental to higher education becomes accessible to students as well as academics.

Given the almost overwhelming interest in this topic — an interest that has increased significantly since the first conceptualisation of the Student Engagement Handbook — it has to be said that these chapters just serve to skim the surface of all that is being achieved in the name of student engagement. However, they catch the spirit of the moment, the richness and complexity, the excitement and diversity, the passion for individual learning and learners and the development of personal identities alongside institutional and national strategy, the variety of activities alongside the development of more formal models that allow us to understand and be more explicit about what student engagement means, what it is in practice, and how we can promote it for the benefit of all learners in higher education.

Elisabeth Dunne
Derfel Owen
Editors

References

Anyangwe, E. (2011). Is student engagement a panacea for consumerism in HE? *Guardian Professional, Higher Education Network*. Retrieved from http://www.guardian.co.uk/higher-education-network/blog/poll/2011/oct/24/student-engagement-panacea

Czerniawski, G., & Kidd, W. (2011). *The student voice handbook: Bridging the academic/practitioner divide*. Bingley, UK: Emerald.

ESU. (1998). *ESIB's statement on Higher Education towards the next century and the UNESCO World Conference*. Retrieved from http://www.esu-online.org/news/article/6065/151/

Fielding, M. (2006). Leadership, radical student engagement and the necessity of person-centred education. *International Journal of Leadership in Education*, 9(4), 299–313.

Greatrix, P. (2011). University isn't just a business — And the student isn't always right. *Guardian Professional, Higher Education Network*. Retrieved from http://www.guardian.

co.uk/higher-education-network/higher-education-network-blog/2011/mar/14/students-as-consumers

HEA. (2010). *Framework for Action: Enhancing student engagement at the institutional level.* Retrieved from http://www.heacademy.ac.uk/assets/documents/studentengagement/Frameworkforaction_institutional.pdf

HEA. (2012). *Dimensions of student engagement.* Retrieved from http://www.heacademy.ac.uk/resources/detail/studentengagement/Dimensions_student_engagement

HEA. (2013). *Students as Partners.* Retrieved from http://www.heacademy.ac.uk/students-as-partners-work

Kuh, G. D. (2009). High impact activities: What they are, why they work, who benefits?. In C. Rust (Ed.), *Improving student learning through the curriculum.* Oxford, UK: Oxford Brookes University Centre for Staff and Learning Development.

Mourshed, M., Farrell, D., & Barton, D. (2012). *Education to employment: Designing a system that works.* McKinsey Center for Government.

New Zealand Council for Educational Research. (2009). *Engaging young people in learning: Why does it matter and what can we do?* Retrieved from http://www.nzcer.org.nz/about-nzcer/75th-conference-events/student-engagement-conference

Nair, C., Adams, P., & Mertova, P. (2008). Student engagement: The key to improving survey response rates. In *Quality in higher education* (Vol. 14, Number 3). Oxford: Routledge.

NUS. (2010). *Student Engagement Toolkit.* Retrieved from http://www.nusconnect.org.uk/campaigns/highereducation/student-engagement/toolkit/

Porter, A. (2008). The importance of the learner voice. *The Brookes eJournal of Learning and Teaching, 2*(3). Retrieved from http://bejlt.brookes.ac.uk/article/the_importance_of_the_learner_voice/

Porter, A. (2010a). *Interview with QAA.* Retrieved from www.qaa.ac.uk/podcasts Accessed on June 6, 2013.

Porter, A. (2010b). Wrong direction. *Times Higher Education,* December 9–15.

Porter, A. (2010c). Presentation to quality in higher education group meeting, November, London.

Quality Assurance Agency for Higher Education (QAA). (2009). *Outcomes from institutional audit – Student representation and feedback arrangements.* Retrieved from http://qaa.ac.uk/reviews/institutionalAudit/outcomes/series2/students09.pdf

RAISE. (2010). *Working definition of student engagement.* Retrieved from http://raise-network.ning.com/

The Guardian. (2011). *Are students the consumers of higher education?* Retrieved from http://www.guardian.co.uk/higher-education-network/blog/2011/dec/14/marketisation-best-bits

Trowler, V., & Trowler, P. (2010). *Student engagement evidence summary.* New York, NY: Higher Education Academy.

University of Tennessee. (2011). *Student life strategic plan 2011–2016.* Retrieved from http://studentlife.utk.edu/forms/StudentLifeStrategicPlan.pdf

PART 1: VANTAGE POINTS ON STUDENT ENGAGEMENT

Elisabeth Dunne and Derfel Owen

As indicated in the Introduction, there are numerous competing meanings, definitions, conceptualisations and assumptions relating to student engagement.

Krause (2005) suggests that student engagement:

> ...has become a catch-all term most commonly used to describe a compendium of behaviours characterising students who are said to be more involved with their university community than their less engaged peers. (p.3)

Such a compendium is complex. 'Student engagement' is becoming ever increasingly discussed worldwide, the 'university community' takes many forms, and the parameters are constantly shifting. The chapters throughout this book begin to highlight that complexity of behaviours. Yet it is apparent that moving towards a coherent and simple definition, or a model, is not easy and is not currently well supported by research. Trowler and Trowler (2010) highlight that research on student engagement in the United Kingdom is rarely robust, due to the lack of longitudinal surveys and analysis of institutional features that are prevalent in the United States and, to some extent, Australia. However, even where there is systematic research, an issue has been that the term 'student engagement' has been used somewhat uncritically and without challenge. Recently there has been a move to re-consider meanings and to conceptualise theoretical models that will enable a deeper understanding of what it means to be an engaged student.

One of the key players in this arena is Bryson with his work on clarifying the concept of student engagement by reviewing the many existing paradigms and models. Bryson and Hardy (2011) offer a review of recent conceptualisations of student engagement, again stressing the difficulty and complexity of pinning down exactly what it means, and acknowledging that their own definition has changed and developed over time.

> Previous attempts to capture a map of all the elusive complexity of the meta-construct of student engagement have not succeeded and tend to be coloured by the philosophical stance of the cartographer ...

> Indeed any scientific model that proposes that it can neatly be divided into antecedents/influences, how the individual makes sense of it all (the psychological), and outputs/consequences has too much of an element of linearity and discreteness to it to adequately represent the holistic reality of the individual. (Bryson & Hardy, 2011, p.19)

Bryson and Hardy also suggest that part of the difficulty lies in: 'the paradigmatic definition of SE that is dualistic i.e. what both students and institutions do. That also creates confusion between SE as an outcome and SE as a process. Although we understand that of course it is the interactions of these (and some other aspects too) that are important, we propose that in seeking conceptual clarity, we should separate them into: Engaging students and Students engaging' (p. 17).

The first four chapters that make up Part 1 of this handbook are important in that to some extent they set the scene for the descriptions and discussions throughout the book. They develop the ideas of the Introduction in more detail, exploring this problematic topic by presenting further analysis of some key ideas, illustrating how the economic context is currently impacting on student engagement and demonstrating how theoretical approaches are being developed to support a more developed understanding of student engagement. The chapters specifically range over a set of vantage points: the past and the present, the practical and the theoretical, the global and the personal, and including the academic view alongside the voice of the student. Each chapter also shows the intricate interweaving of the two strands of engaging students and students engaging.

The first chapter takes an historic angle on student engagement, asking the question, 'Haven't we seen it all before?' In so many ways, the topic of student engagement is nothing new. The same issues have been prevalent over generations of students. Students have always engaged in their education through multi-faceted approaches. The purpose of higher education has been discussed throughout the centuries. The power relationships between staff and students have oft been challenged. In so many ways, the needs and wants of students have not changed. What is different today is the sheer volume of students: 130 million in higher education now, set to be 262 million by 2025 (Maslen, 2012). This prompts a new question; not whether we've seen it all before, but what can student engagement possibly mean for this number of people, from so many backgrounds? How can any definition be meaningful? Set in the context of the somewhat difficult economic times worldwide, Chapter 2 discusses the impact that such an environment can have on student engagement within higher education, and the difficulties of maintaining a strong sense of motivation and engagement with learning when institutions are driven by market forces and consumer attitudes. The tensions and stress points of the constant expansion in student numbers are considered from multiple viewpoints. Nonetheless, there are ways in which a passion for knowledge and a love of learning can be maintained.

Chapter 3 describes the development of a model of engagement that begins to respond to these complex issues by putting the individual student at the centre of their learning. The model puts a 'sense of being' and a 'sense of transformation' at the very heart of education; the focus is on the 'self', with every student having an individual sense of being and the potential for learning being a transformational experience. Chapter 4 extends this idea further by presenting a very personal and detailed account of what engagement beyond the curriculum means to two students at a particular university, what their community is to them, why they engage with it, and to what extent this aligns with the institutional stance on student engagement. Their sense of 'being' and of 'self' as 'engaged' students is evident throughout their story of involvement in academic representation. Chapter 5 takes a different — but extremely important — angle, looking at staff perceptions of student engagement, an aspect that is rarely considered in discussions or research. Again questions are asked: how comparable are staff and student views, or is there, in fact, a significant mismatch in perceptions, a mismatch which is perhaps increasing within the current climate of consumerism. Is there a challenge to the collegial view of engagement, and that sense of 'being' and of 'transformation', if academic success and satisfaction is perceived by students to be transactional, dependent on teachers and teaching behaviours rather than on the engagement, effort and motivation of the individual student.

None of these chapters encapsulates a definitive sense or meaning of student engagement, but each of the perspectives allows a glimpse of possibilities and problems, set within a particular context or way of thinking, and cumulatively enabling more understanding of the complexity of the topic from different vantage points.

References

Bryson, C., & Hardy, C. (2011). Clarifying the concept of student engagement: A fruitful approach to underpin policy and practice. Paper presented at the HEA Annual Conference, 5–6 July, Nottingham.

Krause, K.-L. (2005). *Understanding and promoting student engagement in university learning communities*. Retrieved from http://www.cshe.unimelb.edu.au/resources_teach/teaching_in_practice/docs/Stud_eng.pdf

Maslen, G. (2012). Worldwide student numbers forecast to double by 2025. *University World News*, Issue No 209.

Trowler, V., & Trowler, P. (2010). *Student engagement evidence summary*. New York: Higher Education Academy.

Chapter 1

Haven't We Seen It All Before? Historical Themes in Student Engagement

Derfel Owen

Abstract

By extracting some of the themes and messages that have featured throughout this book, this chapter explores the historical context for student engagement in higher education. The changes that are taking place in global higher education: internationalisation, massification, the social media revolution, professionalization of staff and the systematisation of quality assurance regimes are all affecting and challenging conventional models of higher education, but are they affecting the relationships between university and student?

Student engagement has emerged in recent years as a catch-all term that presents part of the solution to some of the challenges presented by these changes and some of the potential benefits. If you look up the term, you will find an array of definitions and associations with various university strategies and activities. In these contexts it is often put forward as a new solution or innovation to help alleviate challenges or to drive forward solutions. This chapter argues that student engagement and participation has been central to higher education since its inception, and that while the contexts have changed, the debate about the value of student engagement and the roles and responsibilities of students have not.

1.1. Introduction

Much of the historical research on the establishment and evolution of universities is focussed on modern Europe, but it is helpful to look beyond those foundations, at scholarly communities in the medieval Europe and to go as far back as the sophist movement of ancient Greece to identify the seeds of student engagement. 'Universities' in ancient Greece are unrecognisable in the context of the modern

The Student Engagement Handbook: Practice in Higher Education
Copyright © 2013 by Emerald Group Publishing Limited
All rights of reproduction in any form reserved
ISBN: 978-1-78190-423-7

Humboldtian University. However, the pre-eminence of Pythagoras, Plato, Aristotle, Demosthenes and many other Greek sophists in any discussion of science, society or philosophy shows that the values and practice of research, scholarship, curiosity and exploration were esteemed and nurtured as far back as the sixth century BC. The oldest institutions of higher education were arguably started on the island of Kos, Greece, in about the fifth century BC by Hippocrates. These schools primarily taught medicine but also covered topics concerning the nature of humanity and the universe. A group called the Pythagoreans, who were followers of the Greek philosopher and mathematician Pythagoras (c. 580−500 BC), started the first communities of higher education in Italy. They taught philosophy and mathematics in Greek. The great Greek philosophers Socrates (470−399 BC), Plato (c. 428−348 BC) and Aristotle (384−322 BC) carried on this tradition (Walden, 1912).

It is not until early middle ages, with the establishment of the University of Bologna by papal charter, that we start to see a consolidation and articulation of what a university is for and the communities that coexist within it (Grendler, 2002). Cardinal Newman's seminal text 'The Idea of a University' some time later in 1852 then begins to develop an understanding of the relationships that exist between learning and learners and teaching and research. Following this publication and throughout the late 19th and 20th century the nature, value and purpose of higher education have been extensively explored, but perhaps without a serious and direct focus on student engagement.

While direct exploration or analysis of student engagement is absent from the early texts and later analysis of these periods, a reading of the various accounts from and of the period reveal patterns of behaviour and interaction that demonstrate a more complex relationship between students and their 'university' than might be assumed. This chapter draws on a range of sources to explore themes in student engagement that have emerged in different periods and to establish whether there are lessons that can be learnt from those contexts.

The historical themes of leadership, consumerism and community explored in this chapter are selected because they are recurrent throughout this book. The Introduction to this handbook outlines the challenges to global higher education (Dunne & Owen, 2013) that raise expectations of consumerism and marketisation. It is this expectation that has driven many of the examples that are detailed in this book. In their case studies, analyses and conclusions, many authors have devised and adopted approaches that require student leadership, as partners, co-producers or change agents etc. Finally, questions of the students' role in the university community are posed and explored in many places. The intention in this chapter is to explore whether this is anything new, or have we been here before?

1.2.   Student Leadership

In the current global context, where the roles and attitudes of students are in flux, we should think of student leadership in terms of activism both at national and institutional levels. In popular consciousness, scenes of student leaders protesting against national governments and international organisations have become familiar. Dating back to the 1968 student uprising in France and the campaigns against the Vietnam War in the United States throughout the 1960s (Schwartz, 2008), organised student movements have had a high profile with visible leadership and structures. Student leadership attracted the attention of the world in June 1989 when students in China flooded Tiananmen Square in Beijing to mourn the death of a former Communist Party leader and to voice their concerns over inflation, their limited career options postgraduation and corruption (Nathan, 2001). The scenes of protest that were shown around the world, and the subsequent brutal massacre of protestors by the government, drew attention to student leadership and activism that has continued to this day, where students are at the forefront of protests against economic management of Western governments.

While this sort of protest draws public attention it should not be assumed that this is the extent of student leadership. Other chapters in this book will explore student representation structures at institutional, national and international levels; but it is sufficient to say that student leadership structures, aligned with opportunities to engage with the national and institutional governance structures in higher education, give voice to student views and allow opportunities for students to lead debate and decision making about higher education (Smith, Locke, Scesa, & Williams, 2009). Equally, it should not be assumed that this sort of high profile, attention grabbing student activism, organisation and leadership is a new phenomenon, in fact these traditions date back to the earliest records and throughout the history of higher education.

1.2.1.   Collective Organisation

In his comprehensive study of the Universities of Greece, Walden (1912) extracts from letters and chronicles of the time significant evidence that students would self-organise into corps, closely aligned with their sophist lecturers.

> Attached to each sophist was a sort of corps, or incorporated student body, composed of those students who, having sworn allegiance to the sophist's cause, attended his lectures as his regularly enrolled pupils. Each of these corps had its own student leader and expected of its members mutual co-operation in upholding and promoting the interest of its teacher. (Walden, 1912, pp. 296–298)

These corps professed loyalty to their professors and would actively promote the interests of their corps to other students and townsfolk (Capes, 1922, pp. 97–99). Though these corps were prone to sycophancy and were mainly motivated to promote their professors, they clearly demonstrate characteristics of student organisation and leadership that would become prevalent as higher education institutions became more established. It is not until the establishment of the medieval universities of Bologna and Padua do we learn more about student self-organisation and leadership. This time, the circumstances were different:

> The Universitates or guilds which were formed in the Studium
> Generale of Bologna were associations of foreign students ... in an
> Italian city state these foreign students had neither civil nor political
> rights; they were men "out of their own law," for whom the govern-
> ment under which they lived made small and uncertain provision.
> Their strength lay in their numbers, and .... They early recognised the
> necessity of union if full use was to be made of the offensive and
> defensive weapons they possessed. (Rait, 1918, p. 13)

These guilds were therefore different in nature, they afforded protections to foreign students that were not natives of the city states and rights that the authorities
would be willing to recognise because of the financial, intellectual and numerical
strength of their membership (Rait, 1918). As well as establishing students' rights in
their locality, these 'guilds' acted as governing bodies for their universities; a sort of
'student republic, free from the trammels of external control and served by a lecturing force, elected by and responsible to the student body' (Cobban, 1975, p. 194).

After this, it is interesting to note that the role of students and the contribution
they make to university life receives very little attention. Whereas early texts and
records of higher education appear to recognise the criticality of students' active
engagement in higher education, until the 19th century there appears to have been
little thought given to this. Indeed Cardinal Newman, in his 'The Idea of a
University' does not talk of students as though they are relevant contributors to
university life, but rather refers to them as passive recipients of knowledge.

> A University may be considered with reference either to its Students
> or to its Studies; and the principle, that all knowledge is a whole and
> the separate Sciences parts of one, which I have hitherto been using in
> behalf of its studies, is equally important when we direct our attention
> to its students. Now then I turn to the students, and shall consider the
> education which, by virtue of this principle, **a University will give
> them** .... (Newman, 1852, p. 99) *(my emphasis)*

Those final words 'the education which ... a University will give them' reflect a
shift that had occurred from the active student corps of Ancient Greek society
through to collective social bargaining in the early medieval universities to students
being passive recipients of the knowledge owned by universities and academics.
There is no reference in Cardinal Newman's work, or in the other major works of
the time, to student organisation or leadership (Bonner, 1995).

It is not until the 20th century that we start to see a more serious consideration
of the role of students and their role as part of an academic community. In this
more recent period there does not appear to be a standard pattern or form of
student organisation. Throughout the 19th century, student organisation mainly

took the form of radical political activism that will be discussed in the next section; however, Anderson (2004, pp. 275–279) argues that during this period a number of models of student organisation began to emerge in Europe:

- The German model: focussed on small, closed organizations, with an intense social life, but rather hostile to co-operation with each other on a university basis.
- The corporate model: taking hold in Northern Europe in those countries with strong corporate traditions, these maintained a wide range of university-wide activities with open rather than selective membership.
- The social/residential elite model: largely based in the very traditional collegiate universities such as Oxford and Cambridge. These began to resemble closely knit private clubs with their own private languages, initiation ceremonies, and the ongoing influence of former members in acting as pressure.
- The Latin model: exclusive student organisations were weak; students tended to integrate with the wider life of the town or city, centred characteristically on cafés, theatres and dance halls.

To some extent, these models are still identifiable in Europe, the United States and elsewhere. It is in the United Kingdom, combining the corporate and social/residential elite models above, where student organisation has become most explicitly established. The first students' union was founded at the University of St Andrews in 1864, and progressively each university incorporated an independent student representative body into their statutes. This was recognised in law in the Education Act 1994 when membership of the students' union became automatic for all students attending university. However, in many higher education sectors, students' unions, governments or guilds (or equivalent) are commonplace. In recognition of this, a transnational organisation, the European Students' Union, was established in 1982 to represent and advocate and the collective views of 47 members from 39 countries (ESU, 2013).

1.2.2.   Activism and Protest

As outlined earlier, political activism is a most visible form of student leadership. In recent decades, since the late 1950s, students have led or been at the forefront of many national and international movements; most recently in Europe against the European Union and fiscal austerity measures.

This activism, however, as recorded by Schachner (1938, pp. 203–206) is not a recent phenomenon. There were student riots and anti-student protests even within the medieval universities. In 1229, a violent and extended student riot at the University of Paris resulted in the deaths of a number of students. Students at the university were highly privileged and subject to different laws to those of the townsfolk. This led to confrontation with city authorities and the university authorised the city guard to punish students after a confrontation. When the city guard responded with a heavy hand that led to the deaths of a number of students, the academic community and students all went on a strike that lasted for almost two years (Rashdall, 1936).

This sort of violent organised protest was prevalent throughout the early development of universities in Europe:

> The notion of student power is a crucial one for an understanding of university development in the pre-Reformation era. Organised student protest is virtually coeval with the emergence of universities in southern Europe where it became endemic .... Revolutionary student activity in the medieval situation was rarely aimed against the established social order: it was either a defence mechanism or was channelled towards the winning of increased student participation within University structures. (Cobban, 1975, p. 163)

Student-led radicalism would re-emerge following the French Revolution, but throughout the 19th century, their protests were brutally repressed and outlawed (Anderson, 2004).

As student radicalism reasserted itself and was allowed to flourish in the more liberal democracies of the 20th century, it should not be assumed that this was a comfortable experience for universities. The behaviour of students and their drift towards 'institutional masochism' was not welcome; as student violence became commonplace, universities began to pander to their needs and supporting their extra-curricular demands. But this could not be maintained and it was argued that, contrary to expectation, this was not fostering and nurturing student independence, it was in fact undermining it (Barzun, 1969, pp. 71–76).

1.2.2.1. Channelling students' energy

This triggered a period of consideration about the leadership role students should properly play in University governance. In a major speech in 1966, the chancellor of New York State University had the following to say:

> Maturity of the student can be nurtured as we draw him into the orbit of decision making on the campus .... Such decisions have to do with academic programs, with adaptations or expansion of calendars, with regulations relating to student life, with experimentation and innovative change.

> Granted that the student lacks experiences with most or all of these matters, he is the one who contributes to making them succeed or fall. And so, although he is in no position to make the deciding judgements as to what should be done, he can participate in the process that brings about such judgements. (Gould, 1966)

Clearly, Gould felt that steps needed to be taken both to recognise and make explicit the important contribution students could make to the university, but also to encourage a more mature and responsible approach from students to their responsibilities as members of the academic community.

This point of view was not shared universally. In 1978 Brubacher, an eminent American professor and educational philosopher, made an impassioned plea against drawing students too closely into the decision making of universities:

> To what degree does the acceptance of the student into the learned community entitle him or her to a meaningful role in its government? Many, especially student activists, have called for "participator democracy" in academic affairs. On the Jeffersonian thesis that all governments derive their just powers from the consent of those governed.
>
> Neither college nor university is a political community. Its business is not government but the discovery, publication, and teaching of the higher learning. Its governance is based not on numbers or the rule of the majority, but on knowledge.
>
> The student is transient. Four years is too short a time to become familiar enough with the higher learning to make competent judgements about its dissemination .... Furthermore, the engagement of students in the onerous task of government would deflect their energies from what should be the principal investment of their time, the acquisition of a higher education. (Brubacher, 1978)

So even though students had finally reacted to the organisational side-lining that they had experienced in recent centuries and made their voices heard, there was still some considerable debate and discomfort about the value and nature of their contribution. This is a debate that has still not been resolved.

1.3. Students as Consumers

Consumer behaviour by students has in recent years become a major concern and consideration for universities. Streeting and Wise (2009), van der Velden (2012) and Popenici in Chapter 2 (Popenici, 2013) of this book argue that this is a recent phenomenon, a response to massification of higher education, changing relationships between government and state and the imposition of student fees (particularly in the United Kingdom, but equally valid in other nations too). This debate has been particularly vivid recently in the United Kingdom, as the government has sought to reform public services to introduce further elements of consumer choice and increases to the direct cost to students of their education through the fees they pay.

In a comprehensive review of the values of educational engagement (described as participation) versus consumerism (described ad acquisition) Coffield (2008) set out the following characteristics (Table 1.1).

Table 1.1: Coffield's review of the values of educational engagement.

	Acquisition	**Participation**
Goal	Individual enrichment	Community building
Learning	Acquiring facts	Becoming a participant
Student	Recipient, customer	Apprentice, peripheral participant
Teacher	Deliverer, provider	Expert, dialogue partner
Knowledge	Possession, commodity	Aspect of practice
Knowing	Having, possessing	Belonging, participating

However, these concerns have been echoed through the history of higher education. In the 1960s, as higher education expanded rapidly in the United States, many thoughtful pieces were written about the role of students. Parsons (1968), in a sociological analysis of higher education governance wrote:

> It is sometimes rather intemperately asserted that the academic system should be run exclusively for the benefit of students. This would, however, conflict with the multifunctional character of academia; the relation of students to academia is, in fact, quite complicated ....
>
> ... Students have long had the status of "membership" in the university that clearly distinguished them from the customers of a firm in the usual market context. Students must be "admitted" to a college or graduate school; the graduate to become "alumni", which is by no means a status of negligible importance. Their membership constitutes a presumptive status of a "citizenship" in the academic community .... Students are thereby coming to be treated more as responsible adults and less as "wards" of the institution. (Parsons, 1968, pp. 183–187)

He goes on to explain:

> There seem to be two other major contexts of change, both involving student-faculty relations far more than one just mentioned. These concern the teaching-learning process and the "government" of the institution, respectively. They are closely interdependent, but distinct. With respect to the first, the faculty seems to have two bases of superiority or "precedence", and correspondingly of responsibility, that cannot be shared in a completely egalitarian fashion with all students. The first, particularly salient in the academic sphere, concerns the superior competence gained by their technical training and experience. If there were no substantial differences on this score, it would be difficult to legitimise the process of formal education at all. The alternative to some form of institutionalised faculty "precedence" would seem to be a populist ideal of complete equality of all participants.

> To assert the necessity of faculty "precedence" is not to impugn the students' academic freedom, which is the freedom to be instructed ... . The student's academic freedom also includes the basic right to question what he is taught within the framework of orderly procedure.
>
> The second basis of the precedence of the faculty member over the student is a consequence of the former being typically a teacher and researcher on a career basis, not just for the several years of studentship. His personal commitments give him far larger stake in the academic enterprise than has the average student. Hence he is entitled to larger "say" than is the student. (Parsons, 1968, pp. 183–187)

This thoughtful analysis sets out the complex relationship between student and academic and university long before massification, globalisation and commercialisation were part of the higher education lexicon.

This concern about the commodification of higher education might not, however, have been at the forefront of Cardinal Newman's thinking when writing The Idea of a University. Pontificating on the reasons for the church establishing universities, he said:

> When the Church founds a University, she is not cherishing talent, genius, or knowledge, for their own sake, but for the sake of her children ... with the object of training them to fill their respective posts in life better, and of making them more intelligent, capable, active members of society. (Newman, 1982)

This seems to adopt a very patriarchal and condescending view of the student, attending university in order to receive wisdom, to be trained by the experts. He does, however, recognise their ongoing value and contribution to society. This would actually be borne out by surveys of student opinion dating back to medieval ages that 'the normal student ambition was to gain lucrative employment within the safety of the established order' (Cobban, 1975, p. 165).

Despite this, there is evidence that Newman's forefathers had higher expectations of their students. Documenting the history of the medieval universities, Wieruszowski notes the following lamentation from Cardinal Jacques de Vitry, Bishop of Acre and member of the College of Cardinals, in 1228 dwelling on the low state of morality among students:

> Almost all the students at Paris, foreigners and natives, did absolutely nothing except learn and hear something new. Some studied merely to acquire knowledge .... Very few studied for their own edification or that of others. (Wieruszowski, 1966)

He may or may not have shared Parsons' vision of shared ownership between students and the academic community, but he clearly believed that students had a higher responsibility that they were not living up to. Indeed it could be said that by studying 'merely to acquire knowledge' they were behaving, 800 years ago, in the consumerist, transactional manner that is so feared today by Streeting and Wise, van der Velden, Popenici and many others around the world.

An additional characteristic expected of the student consumer, as opposed to the engaged student as partner, that is not set out in Coffield's analysis, is that of an empowered shopper, willing and able to take their 'custom' elsewhere. The reforms set out by the UK coalition government in 2010 clearly anticipated this behaviour as a response to the changes (BIS, 2010).

However, this behaviour anticipated by the government is not an unfamiliar challenge in higher education. Walden (1912) notes the concerns of the philosopher Libanius:

> That teachers were often deterred from punishing their pupils by the fear of losing their patronage is clear enough. Libanius says that the defection of students from one sophist to another was in the time of his youth a thing almost unheard of; a few had been known to transfer their allegiance, but the action had been considered dishonourable, and the students who engaged in it had been shunned by nearly all their friends. In his later life, however, hardly a day passed without its example of such defection. Sometimes the student went around the sophists swearing allegiance to each in turn. (Walden, 1912, p. 325)

Even without the pressures of a more consumerist society and high student fees, students understood and used the power of their patronage; this practice was known as apostasis. The sophists even went as far as to agree contracts with their students that set out expectations and their, or their parents, rights to complain and appeal:

> Any father who was dissatisfied with the sophist under whom he had placed his son was to have the privilege of examining his son or of having him examined by competent persons, in order to determine if the sophist was neglecting his duty. If there was apparent evidence that the sophist was neglecting his duty, then the father might enter a formal complaint against him and have the case tried before a board of his own selection, composed of teachers and non-teachers ... such a contract, we learn, was made and put in force. (Capes, 1922, p. 97)

Earlier in this chapter, I quoted Brubacher arguing that students should not be distracted into university governance. However, he seems to have understood the complexity of the relationship 'As consumers of HE, students want some degree of influence in deciding on the curriculum and on the appointment, promotion, and dismissal of faculty. This demand is not without justification'. Even when rejecting the case, the validity is recognised. It appears that categorisation of the role of students is not so straightforward, and is a matter that has perplexed and challenged higher education, for centuries.

1.4. Students as Part of the Community

1.4.1. A Constitutional Presence

The size and scale of most universities mean that, in one way or another, they form a self-governing community with students and academics coexisting and developing rules of engagement to ensure that stability is maintained and a learning culture fostered, these rules will be captured in a governing document, such as a constitution or charter. This provides an important reference point for members of the community so that they can know and understand their rights and responsibilities.

Recent innovations have sought to clarify and crystallise what had been presumed by the government not to exist before. In the United Kingdom, the Beer/Porter report for the Government on Student Charters mapped out plans for all UK universities to have a jointly owned charter (BIS, 2011) that would 'establish clear mutual expectations and help monitor the student experience and how relationships are working'. This was a new initiative, but the report clearly and explicitly recognises that the formal role of students as members of the university had been established before. Indeed, the 1994 Education Act asserted the rights and authorities of students and their representative bodies.

In the United States, it has become commonplace for universities to have an honour code (Olsen, 2008). A quick glance at some university websites indicates that there are many competing claims for the origin of this system. The University of Maryland claims that it 'pioneered the concept of "modified" honor codes' in the 1980s (University of Maryland, 2013). The College of William and Mary on the other hand argue that none other than Thomas Jefferson pioneered the concept when he was the governor of Virginia in 1779, but this is challenged by the University of Virginia, which claims to have 'the nation's oldest student-run honor system' (University of Virginia, 2013).

A rather tragic story is told by the University of Virginia of how honour codes are supposed to have originated:

> This tradition of student self-governance began with an incident in the University's early years. On the night of November 12, 1840, a masked student shot and killed John A. G. Davis, a popular professor of law. Sobered by the incident, the students agreed to a plan whereby they "vouched" for one another by agreeing to report misbehavior. In the same spirit, University faculty established an "honor pledge" on examinations, agreeing to trust students when they pledged that they had "neither received nor given assistance" on their schoolwork. (University of Virginia, 2013)

It will probably never be possible to pin down the exact origins of the honour codes. However, this might not be useful, as there are traces further back of efforts to codify the constitutional roles and responsibilities of students. For example, the constitution of the University of Orleans in 1389 contained reference to the shared responsibility of 'doctors' and 'students' for the administration of their colleges (Rashdall, 1936, pp. 145–148). Equally the constitution of the University of St Andrews, confirmed by King James I in 1432, bestowed rights and responsibilities to its students as well as professoriate (Rashdall, 1936, pp. 298–299).

It may therefore be that the formalisation of student participation is not a new, or even recent development. As set out earlier in this chapter, the collective student body had made its presence felt and been noticed for centuries, this had also been absorbed into formal constitutional structures of universities.

What might be more noteworthy is the apparent abdication by students of their responsibilities, or more likely their exclusion by the academic community. For even though their roles, rights and responsibilities have been codified for centuries, it was an early act of academics to seek to exclude students, ensuring that 'real power was lodged with the professorial body':

> ... the Masters succeeded in reducing the student-vote in the University to a mere fiction would seem to have been the doctrine that the consent of the Regent Masters of Art was required for any vote involving the expenditure of money. (Rashdall, 1936, volume II, pp. 298–299)

It is only in recent years that these voting rights and authoritities have been reasserted. Perhaps this is because recognition of the consumer rights of students has served to remind universities that students should be integrated as members of the academic community. Without the introduction of fees and transparency about expenditure; 'Regent Masters' and their equivalents could still be arguing that their judgement and votes are more equal than those of the students.

1.4.2. Initiation and Entry

Universities are often portrayed as incubators of tight-knit groups of students with their own peculiar rules of entry and engagement. In popular culture, particularly American TV shows and films involving young adults, it is common to feature 'Frat houses' or 'sororities' that students join. These often show the traits of student leadership discussed earlier in this chapter. Another feature of this is the initiation ceremony, the 'rite of passage' into university or a particular group within a university that serves as a formal point of entry where student membership is achieved and recognised by their peers.

These ceremonies are often secretive in nature and involve the ritual humiliation of new applicants to join a group. Individual occasions are often drawn to the attention of national press and media and lead to condemnation. Again this is not a recent challenge; a comprehensive catalogue of American Fraternity houses by Baird records an offence in 1875 at the University of Pensylvania where members of the 'Sharswood Club' were forced to return their charter 'for the alleged reason that the prescribed initiation ceremony was puerile and unworthy of the dignity of men seriously engaged in professional study' (Baird, 1905).

Such events have led to numerous public and internal inquiries and in some cases led to the outlawing of initiation ceremonies but with little success (Graebner, 1987). There may, however, be something more deeply engrained about this practice as it is not a new phenomenon. There is evidence that initiation ceremonies involving public humiliation have been common for millennia; the following description was written by Olympiodorus of initiation rites in ancient Greece (translated in Walden, 1912):

> When now a young man arrives ... he is made the object of jest and banter by all who wish to take part in the sport. The purpose ... to humble the conceit of the new student and to bring him at once under the authority of the corps ... the proceeding looks most frightful and cruel ... the victim is marched in procession through the market-place to the public bath. Those who form the escort arrange themselves in a double line, two by two, with a space after each couple and so conduct the youth to the bath. When they come near, they begin to jump and to shout at the top of their voices ... at the same time they batter the door and terrify the young man with the noise.

Once that ordeal is over, the new student is received as one of their own.

These rites and ceremonies are by no means pleasant or justifiable in their cruelty and behaviour; however, they are not a recent phenomenon, students have behaved in such ritualistic ways for centuries, performing elaborate and extreme ceremonies in order to initiate their new peers into their community. In fact, Barzun argues forcibly in his historical account of American universities that the existence of initiation ceremonies was not the problem, but their lack of formality as part of the university experience (Barzun, 1969, pp. 63–65). Similarly Joan Abbott in her exploration the effect of class on student society gave a more socially constructive explanation, she recognised that student-staff relationships are clear and prescribed:

> Relations of student with those who are not students within the institution are regulated .... Staff-student relations are constrained by the hierarchical ordering of positions, and expectations of behaviour are institutionally circumscribed .... (Abbott, 1971, p. 372)

However, student-student relations are not prescribed, and the hierarchies of intellect, experience and age are not clearly explained anywhere and must therefore be asserted somehow:

> In terms of authority structure – in return for the rewards of belonging to the group – members must submit to a more pervasive supervision ... he will undergo an intense period of reorientation. (Abbott, 1971, p. 372)

> Sub-groups develop their own culture and membership rule as halls of residence, fraternities, and sororities. In this case, lateral and social concentration accentuates membership, and group solidarity is encouraged by marks of status, by separation of years and by often arduous initiation rites which increase a sense of belonging. Thus by distancing themselves from other groups within the institution ... these groups are able to socialise their members more easily. (Abbott, 1971, p. 375)

The 'ordeal' described by Olympiodorus may be quite unpleasant, and it does not appear that these ceremonies or rite of passage have become any more comfortable today, but they are not a new challenge, they are a means by which to socialise, induct and engage students with their new community, ones that emerge when organic or formal structure and hierarchies are not present. This is a challenge that universities are still trying to resolve.

1.4.3.   *Engaging the Wider Community*

Universities have a significant impact on their local communities; their physical presence alone makes a visual impression but equally the integration of students with the local population will change the dynamic of a local community. A great deal of attention is paid to this at times of growth, when communities might feel under threat, or at times of tension when the different aspirations and experiences of students and the local community will be in conflict. These tensions are well documented and historic. When universities started to be established across mainland Europe in the middle ages, town and city folk did not respond well. Students and academic staff were often victims of physical abuse and this led to conflict (Rait, 1918; Rashdall, 1936). Indeed it became one of the core presumptions of university life that tensions and violence would periodically erupt between students and 'the people of the town'. In a rather cynical account of student behaviour in modern American universities, Barzun describes students thus:

> Students will fight on slight or non-existent pretexts ... at Jefferson's New University of Virginia in 1825 the faculty petitioned for a police force to protect them from personal danger. Down through the nineties *(there were)* recurrent, ugly problems of discipline. (Barzun, 1969, p. 64)

The chapters in this book authored by O'Mahoney and Martin and McIlrath and Tansey give extensive and detailed accounts of student civic engagement. This is seen as great strength of universities and in particular is seen as very positive way to extend the university mission to engender wider communities. A report from the representative body for UK universities in 2010 showed that universities invested heavily in their local communities; students in particular invested almost 3.5 million hours to voluntary work in the community (Universities UK, 2010).

These traditions of student volunteering extend back to the 1960s and have coincided with a significant change in attitudes to universities and students. This a welcome development that demonstrates that while the reasons for tension (social segregation, class division etc.) may persist, the actions taken to mitigate those tensions can lead to productive outcomes.

1.5. Conclusions

In the space of one chapter, it is impossible to do justice the entire history of student engagement with its many facets and complexities. By exploring a few themes of student engagement that feature significantly in this book and drawing historical analogies, it is clear that patterns and challenges of student engagement may not be entirely new. We may be entering new, uncharted territory in higher education with global competition, marketisation and massification challenging the ways in which universities operate; but some themes will be constant. The role of students will be one of those. The historical evidence drawn upon in this chapter covers almost 2500 years of history, but some of the quotes and examples could be transposed to any date. For example, the word of the Bishop of Acre bemoaning student moralism in the 13th century could quite easily be heard in the offices of any university today. Current questions about the role of parents in the current fee paying, 'consumerist' environment (Redmond, 2008) could be answered by looking back at the ancient Greek universities with their student contracts and academic appeal panels.

It may be that we are anticipating a groundswell of student agitation and activism in response to globalisation and the cost of university, but these debates are not new. The thoughtful comments by Gould, Parsons and Brubacher show that deep thinking has been applied to the role of students for almost 50 years in Western universities, but again this should not be assumed as new. In the middle ages, clear efforts were made to codify the role of students, although academics pulled in the opposite direction and devised creative ways to exclude students from decision making and debate that were not corrected until the 19th century.

Even in some of the more troubling aspects of student engagement, where students embarrass themselves and the academic community by enacting their rite of passage and initiation ceremonies in order to 'admit' new students, we are not experiencing anything new. In fact, as noted by Barzun, we may just be seeing the manifestation of the complex relationship students have with their academic community. None of this makes our current challenges and efforts less burdensome, but it does give a sense of perspective. We've been here before.

References

Abbott, J. (1971). *Student life in a class society*. Oxford: Pergamon Press Ltd.

Anderson, R. D. (2004). *European universities from the enlightenment to 1914*. Oxford: Oxford University Press.

Baird, W. M. R. (1905). *Baird's manual of American college fraternities* (6th ed.), New York, NY: The Alcolm Company.

Barzun, J. (1969). *The American university*. London: Oxford University Press.

BIS — UK Government, Department of Business, Innovation and Skills. (2010). *Students at the heart of the system*. Retrieved from https://www.gov.uk/government/uploads/system/uploads/attachment_data/file/32409/11-944-higher-education-students-at-heart-of-system.pdf

BIS — UK Government, Department of Business, Innovation and Skills. (2011). *Final report of the student charter group*. Retrieved from http://www.bis.gov.uk/assets/biscore/higher-education/docs/s/11-736-student-charter-group.pdf

Bonner, T. N. (1995). *Becoming a physician: Medical education in Britain, France, Germany and the United States, 1750–1945*. New York, NY: Johns Hopkins University Press (digital version) Retrieved from http://books.google.co.uk/books/about/Becoming_a_Physician.html?id=uNPtywo-EOcC&redir_esc=y

Brubacher, J. S. (1978). *On the philosophy of higher education*. San Francisco, CA: Jossey-Bass, Inc.

Capes, W. (1922). *University life in ancient athens*. New York, NY: G. E. Stechert & co. Retrieved from http://archive.org/details/universitylifein00capeuoft

Cobban, A. B. (1975). *The medieval universities: Their development and organisation*. London: Methuen & Co Ltd.

Coffield, F. (2008). *What if teaching and learning really were the priority?* London: Learning and Skills Network.

Dunne, E., & Owen, D. (2013). Introduction, *The student engagement handbook*. Bingley: Emerald Group Publishing Ltd.

ESU — The European Students Union. (2013). Retrieved from http://www.esu-online.org/about/members/. Accessed on June 4, 2013.

Gould, S. B. (1966). *The role of the student in the life of the university*. Chancellor of New York State University; Speech to the National Association of Student Personnel Administrators.

Graebner, W. (1987). Outlawing teenage populism: The campaign against secret societies in the American high school, 1900–1960. *The Journal of American History*, *74*(2), 411–435.

Grendler, P. F. (2002). *The universities of the Italian renaissance*. Baltimore, MD: Johns Hopkins University Press.

Nathan, A. J. (2001). The Tiananmen papers. *Foreign Affairs*, *80*(1), 2–48.

Newman, J. H. (Cardinal) (1852). *The idea of a university*. New York/London. Longmans.

Olsen, P. R. (2008). *And out of the corner of my eye...* New York Times. Retrieved from http://www.nytimes.com/2008/01/06/education/edlife/notebook.html?scp=1&sq=college%20of%20william%20and%20mary&st=nyt&_r=0

Parsons, T. (1968). The academic system: A sociologist's view. *The Public Interest*, *13*, 183–187.

Popenici, S. (2013). The widening gap between higher education and student engagement. In E. Dunne & D. Owen (Eds), *The student engagement handbook*. Bingley: Emerald Group Publishing Ltd.

Rait, R. S. (1918). *Life in the medieval university*. Cambridge: Cambridge University Press Retrieved from http://www.gutenberg.org/files/20958/20958-h/20958-h.htm#page013

Rashdall, H. (1936). *The universities of Europe in the middle ages.* (F. M. Powicke & A. B. Emden, Ed., 1895, 2nd ed.). Oxford: Oxford University Press.

Redmond, P. (2008). *Here comes the chopper.* London: Guardian Newspapers. Retrieved from http://www.guardian.co.uk/education/2008/jan/02/students.uk

Schachner, N. (1938). *The medieval universities.* London: Allen and Unwin Ltd.

Schwartz, P. (2008). *1968: The general strike and the student revolt in France.* Retrieved from http://www.wsws.org/en/articles/2008/05/may1-m28.html

Smith, B., Locke, W., Scesa, A., & Williams, R. (2009). *Report to HEFCE on student engagement.* Centre for Higher Education Research and Information. Retrieved from: http://www.hefce.ac.uk/media/hefce/content/pubs/2009/rd0309/rd03_09.pdf

Streeting, W., & Wise, G. (2009). *Rethinking the values of higher education – consumption, partnership, community?* Gloucester, MA: Quality Assurance Agency for Higher Education .Retrieved from http://www.qaa.ac.uk/Publications/InformationAndGuidance/Documents/Rethinking.pdf

Universities UK. (2010). *Universities: Engaging with local communities.* Retrieved from http://www.universitiesuk.ac.uk/highereducation/Documents/2010/EngagingLocalCommunities.pdf

University of Maryland. (2013). *Student honour council history.* Retrieved from http://www.shc.umd.edu/SHC/History.aspx

University of Virginia. (2013). *The code of honor.* Retrieved from http://www.virginia.edu/uvatours/shorthistory/code.html

van der Velden, G. (2012). *Student engagement: Whose education is it anyway?* Gloucester, MA: Quality Assurance Agency for Higher Education. Retrieved from http://www.qaa.ac.uk/Publications/InformationAndGuidance/Documents/talking-about-quality-student-engagement.pdf

Walden, J. W. H. (1912). *The universities of ancient Greece.* London: George Routlege and Sons Ltd.

Wieruszowski, H. (1966). *The medieval university: Masters, students, learning.* New York, NY: Anvil Books.

Chapter 2

Towards a New Vision for University Governance, Pedagogies and Student Engagement

Stefan Popenici

Abstract

Drawing on recent empirical and theoretical studies, this chapter critically examines the role of social, culture and economic factors in shaping and opening possibilities for educational transformations of universities and student engagement. Considering the impact on higher education of rising inequality, unemployment, underemployment and youth marginalization, this study explores risks and opportunities for change of teaching, research and student participation in higher education. Underlining the need to explore alternative designs for a sustainable future, this paper investigates trends and challenges for policy makers and education providers alike. Exploring the vision about what an engaged student could be like in an alternative scenario for higher education this study suggests a common set of general policy goals and pedagogical directions for the future.

2.1. Contextual Determinants of Student Engagement

Higher education is central to social and economic progress and remains, more than ever before, a priority for governments and economic policies. Countries around the world are registering the rapid expansion of higher education and this presents a number of great opportunities for the future. Access to higher education is also marked by rapid expansion and there has been no general decline in enrolments, funding or public funding in public tertiary education in Organisation for Economic Co-operation and Development countries (OECD, 2009). Significantly more young adults are now enrolled in higher education compared with 15 years ago, accounting for a more than a quarter of 20–29 year-olds. The rapid increase in student

The Student Engagement Handbook: Practice in Higher Education
Copyright © 2013 by Emerald Group Publishing Limited
All rights of reproduction in any form reserved
ISBN: 978-1-78190-423-7

numbers comes with opportunities and new challenges for the assurance of quality. In Education Today 2013: the OECD Perspective underlines that:

> Countries have shared the very rapid expansion of higher or tertiary education, which means that instead of this being an experience enjoyed by a privileged minority, it has now become even the majority experience of each new cohort. (OECD, 2012)

From 1995 to 2010, enrolment rates among 20−29 year-olds increased by over 10 per cent across countries in the OECD. The number of people with a tertiary degree has grown rapidly in OECD countries over the past decade — and even more rapidly in the non-OECD G20 countries. This represents significant progress for countries and for the world economy, and benefits of university education for individuals are underlined in a variety of well-documented studies across the world. However, nearly a third of university students still fail to graduate (OECD, 2009; OECD, 2010a, b; OECD, 2013) and financial, economic, social and political uncertainties are having a significant destabilizing potential.

Alongside the expansion, the increasing numbers of graduates unable to find jobs suitable for their qualifications and the increasing rate of graduate unemployment have significant implications for students, faculty and the future of universities. For example, data released by the US Bureau of Labor Statistics reveals that 48 per cent of employed US university graduates are in jobs that require undergraduates. Moreover, the projected future growth in the number of graduates exceeds the actual or projected growth in high-skilled jobs, which may lead in future years to an increase of numbers of graduates affected by underemployment and unemployment (Vedder, Denhart, & Robe, 2013).

In addition, the next decade will be unpredictable and filled with challenges for universities. A need for change in higher education is evident, given the emerging disconnect between an expansion of expectations and goals and the capacity of universities to secure the resources to finance them. Governance models adopted by many universities in the last decades impact on sustainability of universities, systems of higher education and the future of students. In a piece entitled 'Colleges' Debt Falls on Students After Construction Binges', the *New York Times* offers the following introduction to what happened to many universities around the world in the last decade:

> Some call it the Edifice Complex. Others have named it the Law of More, or the Taj Mahal syndrome. A decade-long spending binge to build academic buildings, dormitories and recreational facilities — some of them inordinately lavish to attract students — has left colleges and universities saddled with large amounts of debt. Oftentimes, students are stuck picking up the bill. (Martin, 2013)

In an accelerated trend, universities have adopted the unique vision of a market paradigm, and the principal field of reference for educational policies has shifted to profits and marketability. Students worldwide are placed in a reality of ever-increasing costs for postsecondary studies, a fast-widening gap between rich and poor, inequality and alarmingly high levels of unemployment, underemployment, and social and economic marginalization of youth and university graduates. The US Department of Education reports that tuition costs have increased an average of 15 per cent within just the last two years, and student debt is reaching unprecedented levels. Problems are exacerbated since, in the biggest economy of the world, half of young people cannot find a job, and since 2009 over 50 per cent of all new jobs across all sectors of the US economy have been low-paid temporary positions. Young people take the vast majority of these positions, and those taking the higher education pathway accumulate insurmountable amounts of student debt. With some of the best universities in the world, the United States reported over $1 trillion in outstanding student loan debts at the end of 2012 and an alarming rate of delinquent loans (FED, 2012). In other words, an alarming number of graduates cannot pay back their loans and this impacts directly on their credit records, job prospects, family life and health. The most significant shift is that it is increasingly visible across society that a graduate diploma is no longer a safe and aspirational investment.

Herein lies a serious problem. It is obvious that no one can enjoy the satisfaction of going into debt in order to secure profits and competitive advantage for an institution. Students are able to see when their money matters more than their ideas, learning and effort. We simply cannot expect student engagement when it is evident that students are just a practical source of subsidy for the spending binge of some university administrators, or are supporting the 'Taj Mahal complex' outlined earlier.

The global financial crisis has increased the pressure on graduates with unprecedented amounts of student debt and new constraints on national budgets to fund colleges and universities. Higher education is struggling to cope with ideological contradictions, having to answer the imperative of quality assurance, student engagement and academic rigour, while following a model of commercialization and profitability. These imperatives are in practice on a collision course and — as explored in this chapter — lead to unsustainable models for student engagement and quality assurance. Students are placed in-between these conflicting values and practices while they face the increasing possibility of expecting unemployment or underemployment.

In February 2012, the European Central Bank President Mario Draghi warned European countries that the 'traditional social contract is obsolete' and austerity is the only solution (Blackstone, Karnitschnig, & Thomson, 2012). The social contract metaphor is especially important as democratic societies place at the core of their political and social values the idea of freedom and equality. For this reason, most systems of higher education and universities have a remarkable history of resistance to class privilege in education, or discrimination or restriction of access to higher education on economic or class grounds. The disintegration of the social contract, announced by one of the most influential European figures, seems to be accentuated by the fading visibility of social models that embed values aligned with student engagement and intrinsic motivation for learning. It is hard to imagine functional, prosperous and thriving universities in a society in turmoil, marked by youth and student protests. Problems associated with youth unemployment, underemployment and marginalization are raising the concern of political leaders across the world. In May 2013, the German Finance Minister Wolfgang Schaeuble went as far as to warn that failure to win the battle against youth unemployment could tear Europe apart, having the potential to spark a revolution (Melander & Vinocur, 2013). Social and economic trends, especially youth unemployment and underemployment, have a central relevance for educational policies and institutional strategies for the future.

It is important to consider the fact that universities are placed in an intertwined relation with all economic, social and cultural influences and changes in that society. Higher education retains the power to determine the fabric of society and decisively contribute to economic progress and competitiveness (Universities UK, 2011). Higher education is determined itself by the social and cultural contexts of students, by economic challenges and political decisions. This is why universities have strong reasons to be concerned about inequality, and about the new forms of exclusion and poverty affecting youth and its graduates. Dealing with these concerns is made all the more complex by changing influences impacting on universities in many countries.

Higher education systems in countries such as the United Kingdom, Italy, Netherlands, Portugal or Australia are already affected by funding cuts (EUA, 2013). The impact of changes imposed by the economic tensions, as well as by new possibilities opened by technology (e.g. Massive Open Online Courses) may mean that universities will engage in strong competition to attract students, particularly those students with the best grades. Therefore, universities have to prepare for a future where they will be thoroughly scrutinized by current and potential students, parents and social partners (e.g. employers), with unprecedented intensity. In this new context, student engagement and quality of teaching, facilities, community involvement and real opportunities opened up for graduates will secure their own progress and future. It is important to note for universities that student engagement remains determined to a vast extent by students' connection with the wider economic, social and cultural contexts that determine their lives and future. Students are also social beings, people with family ties, with friends and former school classmates, neighbours and acquaintances and their stories determine their relation with university studies, motivation and commitment.

In this context, student engagement is a powerful driver of quality assurance, so long as it involves dialogue and a complex understanding of the wider social, cultural and economic context determining interactions in education, and not just information on the student's experience. If students see that people in their generation, and many university graduates, are now unemployed, underemployed, or not in employment, education or training (NEETs), we just have to imagine the impact on student motivation for learning and engagement will be. In the United Kingdom, the ACEVO Commission on Youth Unemployment reflected on the type of financial costs involved by youth unemployment and marginalization:

> The human misery of youth unemployment is also a time-bomb under
> the nation's finances. We have done new research on the cash costs of

youth unemployment. Even we were surprised. At its current rates, in 2012 youth unemployment will cost the exchequer £4.8 billion (*more than the budget for further education for 16- to 19-year-olds in England*) and cost the economy £10.7 billion in lost output. But the costs are not just temporary. (ACEVO, 2012)

Eurostat, the statistical office of the European Union, reported that only 34 per cent of Europeans aged between 15 and 29 were employed in 2011 (Eurostat, 2013). Globally we see the same trend, with youth paying the highest price for economies' mistakes, corruption and the adoption of unsustainable models for both economy and society. The International Labour Organization reports on this international trend:

> Globally, the youth unemployment rate has remained close to its crisis peak in 2009. [...] Nearly 75 million youth are unemployed around the world, an increase of more than 4 million since 2007. Medium-term projections (2012–16) suggest little improvement in youth labour markets. By 2016, the youth unemployment rate is projected to remain at the same high level. (ILO, 2012)

Youth unemployment involves immense financial cost for economies, but it is equally important to keep in perspective the long-term effects on civic engagement, the potential for social disruption and the impact on the symbolic space and motivations for current and future generations. When almost 70 per cent in your peer group cannot find a job or confronts daily social and economic marginalization of youth, facing daily the effects of the reality of growing inequality between affluent classes and the middle class it is realistic to assume that these realities have a considerable impact on motivation and engagement for university students (Eurofound, 2012). In a recent study released by OECD, Trends Shaping Education 2013, it is documented that 'despite increasing affluence, income inequality has been growing on average in OECD countries in the last 25 years' (OECD, 2012). As reflected in this comprehensive analysis, the situation impacts directly on student participation, access and equity in higher education. We may argue that this also affects students' levels of motivation for study and the uncertainty of the labour market presents the potential to undermine their commitment to academic work.

In the current context, rising inequality also poses the fundamental question to students if the path to individual socioeconomic success requires an educated mind. This line of inquiry links to levels of student motivation and engagement, and consequently to retention and success. In a public report released in 2013 by Oxfam International, we find a vivid picture of the reality of a rising tide of inequality around the world:

> In the US the share of national income going to the top 1 per cent has doubled since 1980 from 10 to 20 per cent. For the top 0.01 per cent it has quadrupled to levels never seen before. [...] This is not confined to

> the US, or indeed to rich countries. In the UK inequality is rapidly returning to levels not seen since the time of Charles Dickens. In China the top 10 per cent now take home nearly 60 per cent of the income. Chinese inequality levels are now similar to those in South Africa, which are now the most unequal country on earth and significantly more unequal than at the end of apartheid. Even in many of the poorest countries, inequality has rapidly grown. (Oxfam, 2013)

Growing inequality presents serious implications for students' motivations, engagement and success in higher education. There is the evident effect on equity and restriction of access to higher education for students from disadvantaged backgrounds. However, low participation rates, retention and success for students from low socioeconomic status (SES) backgrounds in higher education are determined earlier than the point of entry into university. To take just one example we can think about implications of one set of evidence provided by the OECD Programme for International Student Assessment (PISA). In 2009, PISA conducted a worldwide study on reading and literacy with the participation of 470,000 15-year-old students. The analysis of this vast amount of data reveals also that socioeconomically disadvantaged students are less engaged in reading than socioeconomically advantaged students (OECD, 2010a, b). Research has consistently shown that engagement and proficiency in reading and writing effectively opens the path towards upper levels of education and lifelong learners. Implicitly, research also documents that low reading and literacy skills have direct implications on dropout rates. A key risk factor for dropping out of school is reading achievement level, and in a world environment with high demands for reading comprehension, vocabulary and literacy skills, students from low socioeconomic backgrounds are significantly more likely to fail or withdraw from university as a result of disadvantage experienced early in their lives (Chowdry, Crawford, Dearden, Goodman, & Vignoles, 2013).

We approach here the complex concept of student engagement in a comprehensive perspective, where student experience is just a part of the interconnected web of influences determined by a student's relationship with the community, economic realities, local culture as 'webs of significance' (Geertz, 1973), curriculum and cultural constructs (Bruner, 1996). Students' imaginations represent in this context a crucial part of motivations for learning and one of the strongest determinants of student's academic and emotional engagement.

Consistent research in student engagement has shown that motivation is one of the main pillars of the learning process. Motivational theorists in psychology developed in the last decade socio-cognitive and socio-ecological models to explain student engagement and motivation for learning. These approaches focus on the influence of social environments, such as family and friends, as important constructs in students' behaviour. These constructs have the power to determine the way students relate to learning and impact on the intellectual performance in the classroom (Bandura, 1986; Mitchell, 1992; Popenici, 2010; Ryan & Deci, 2000; Toshalis & Nakkula, 2012). Motivation and engagement provide energy, drive and direction and fuel students' resilience required to effectively tackle academic work. This is why we have to look at students' motivations, understand the key role of emotions and how their imagination is captured by heroes and role models, symbolic representations and narratives of the society where universities promise that they will have a future.

2.2.   University Governance and Student Engagement

Another important development with implications for student engagement is represented by the impact of the widespread belief of the last decades that markets and profits left to their own devices lead to prosperity and universal well-being. This paradigm is leading worldwide to practices and realities that are inconsistent with academic values, and may even contribute to the erosion of the public perception of higher education as a trustworthy institution. The primacy of profits and sacrificing vision for efficiency was also strengthened through the influence of international organizations regulating commercial policies. An important event is the adoption in 1995 in Marrakesh of the General Agreement on Trade in Services (GATS). This international commercial agreement marks the official inclusion of higher education as part of trade services sectors. In effect, the World Trade Organization adopted an official agreement for international trading of higher education services in the conclusions of the 'Millennium Round', the title of multilateral trade negotiations initiated in Seattle in 1999.

The impact of these steps is profound and the primacy of the market was adopted in a place where this principle does not easily belong. The intrusion of the market as the governing principle has changed the profound cultural and organizational structure of universities and produced a hybrid form of corporate governance in academia. Michael Sandel, in revealing what undergirds this process in 'What Money Can't Buy: The Moral Limits of Markets', claims:

> The most fateful change that unfolded in the last three decades was not an increase in greed. It was the expansion of markets, and of market values, into spheres of life where they don't belong …. The reach of markets, and market oriented thinking, into aspects of life traditionally governed by nonmarket norms is one of the most significant developments of our times. (Sandel, 2012)

Sandel argues that this is a destructive change for at least two main reasons, inequality and corruption: 'Putting a price on the good things in life can corrupt them'. Inequality, complex forms of corruption and an underlying lack of vision and economic, civic and social sustainabilities became evident in higher education in the last years with a decline of academic rigour and widely reported funding problems for universities. This complex context is again marked by youth discontent, linked by many with the significant problem of graduate underemployment and unemployment (Arum & Roksa, 2011; OECD, 2011; Pascarella, Blaich, Martin, & Hanson, 2011).

Rising inequality is evident and well documented, and it became impossible not to notice that students worldwide blame the injustice of the broken social contract promoted by the current system. The market-oriented management that was thrust into higher education involves multiple corrosive effects on academic values and pedagogical practices. The academic community has been undermined and weakened by the pervasive influence of the market and the neoliberal economic philosophy that configures it.

One of the most damaging consequences for student engagement is visible across the higher education sector in most Western countries, where a crude understanding of profitability cost-effectiveness in the university governance is leading to faculty disengagement and dissolution of academic ethos within universities. Gradually, some influential higher education systems (e.g. Australia, United States) adopted what is known as 'casualization', a general policy of downsizing tenure staff and adopting the practice of short-term contracts or even temporary teaching jobs limited to the time required to deliver one course. This phenomenon has reached unprecedented levels in some parts of the world. In Australia, an open letter signed in 2012 by 68 senior staff at the University of Sydney said that 'higher education is already the country's second-most casualized industry, after catering'. The Australian Government Review of Higher Education (the Bradley Review) reported that 40–50 per cent of all teaching in Australian universities is conducted by sessional, casual staff (DEEWR, 2008). In the United States, the American Association of University Professors announced that the tenure system has 'all but collapsed' and now represents approximately only 30 per cent of academic staff. In the United Kingdom, the University and College Union signals the unprecedented pressure on academic staff and runs a national 'anti-casualization committee'.

Frank Donoghue, Professor at Ohio State University and the author of 'The Last Professors: The Corporate University and the Fate of the Humanities', notes that poorly paid adjuncts with heavy teaching loads 'don't have a reason to be loyal to the universities they work for and not much reason to be loyal to the students'. The fact is that globally contingent and precarious faculty represent now the absolute majority of the academic workforce. This does not always have to be problematic, but there are risks that this impacts not only on staff loyalty to the institution, as observed by Donoghue. Perhaps the academic ethos of the institution is also undermined, with a direct impact on the individual capacity to teach and build the intellectual connections with students that are paramount for engagement and motivation for learning.

Faculty — the force within universities that can decisively influence students' engagement or disengagement — is placed under the coercive pressure of casualization and restriction of autonomy and academic freedom (Lorenz, 2012). Teaching and most important learning interactions with students run the risk of taking place in the context of undermined involvement, loyalty to the institutions and personal insecurity.

2.3. Students' Imaginations, Motivations for Learning and Academic Engagement

Students are actors in socially and culturally constructed worlds that make sense through what Vygotsky (1978) called 'semiotic mediation', relating various signs and relationships, dynamics of power and social interactions to certain meanings. Students relate to the world they experience in the living of their lives, and this also determines their position towards the significance of learning and their levels of engagement. The profound significance for learning is that academic life can be seen as a mediated action with meanings associated by students in a social context. This is why the ethos of universities, the teaching practices, the faculty and the learning arrangements have a crucial importance in student's involvement in academic life.

The focus on the concept of student engagement seems to be unnecessary if we take into consideration that universities place at the core of their message the promise to offer students the ideal environments for learning and study. The visibility of this issue across research and educational policies reveals not only the complexity of what stays behind the label of 'student engagement', but reveals that what needs to be part of the everyday life within most institutions of higher education is a difficult goal to achieve. Policy makers struggle to find solutions for attrition rates and to engage low-performing students, demotivated or unprepared to learn, entering higher education with poor time management or low levels of literacy and numeracy. Extrinsic motivation is volatile, with an external locus and transitory capacity to support student academic work, interest and respect for knowledge, learning and research.

There is a vast array of theories, concepts, methodologies, and analytical approaches to research and explain student engagement and the most recent reveal the complexity of this topic and the importance of contextual determinants, social and cultural variables, time and space. However, the closest theoretical framework to the analysis in this chapter is the overarching theory of self-determination (SDT), a 'macro theory of motivation' suitable for providing a comprehensive framework to data and research relevant to the complex problem of student engagement. Reeve offers in 2012 a perfect working definition of student engagement through an SDT perspective:

> all students, no matter their age, gender, socioeconomic status, nationality, or cultural background, possess inherent growth tendencies (e.g. intrinsic motivation, curiosity, psychological needs) that provide a motivational foundation for their high-quality classroom engagement. (Reeve, 2012)

In other words, students with self-determination decide themselves to engage with their studies, based on their personal values, aspirations, beliefs and interests. Intrinsic motivation, curiosity and psychological needs (such as companionship and the sense of belonging) play a crucial role (Ryan & Deci, 2000). Students' imaginations determine their engagement in learning, scholarship and academic activities.

Therefore, family, social and cultural contexts, self-understandings and the influence of dynamic symbolic structures within society shaped by role models, especially those to which one is emotionally attached, determine student engagement or disengagement. These in turn determine students to choose between personal engagement in academic life, or to disregard or simply reject learning opportunities (Dean & Jolly, 2012).

As noted before, the vision of the future can represent a real and significant concern for current and prospective university students, though it seems to be overlooked in general by universities and administrative offices for 'student well-being'. Two nationwide research studies are relevant to this issue. In February 2013, Toronto District School Board (TDSB) released findings from the largest youth census conducted in Canada. Around 103,000 students from grade 7 to 12 participated in the census. The findings on social and emotional well-being are especially relevant since part of this cohort will be enrolled in the upper levels of education, including colleges and universities. Results reveal that a large percentage of youth is concerned about the future:

> TDSB conducted a similar survey of students in 2006, but new revelations emerged from questions on emotional well-being included in the 2011 survey. Those results revealed that one in three high school students feel like crying, three in four worry about the future, and 47 per cent feel they aren't able to overcome difficulties. (Hammer, 2013)

Imagining the future was also the focus of the largest research study conducted on students' role models and motivation for learning. Results of this study reveal a surprising map, with implications for curriculum alignment and the importance of academic ethos and learning contexts in universities. It also reflects that the predominant symbolic spaces in society and youth prospects capture students' interest and imagination.

This was also the focus of nationwide research conducted in Romania involving a representative sample of all students enrolled in general and vocational forms of lower secondary education (Popenici, 2010). Selecting this cohort was especially relevant as this level is either 'terminal ' (i.e. preparing students for entry into working life) and/or 'preparatory ' (i.e. preparing students for upper secondary education). Results reveal a map of representations that describe how students imagine their future, their models for life and their relation with institutional and informal education.

Taking into consideration that the relationship between individuals' identities, attitudes, behaviours and role models is not a simple determinist correlation, this study aimed to map students' imaginations and see how their role models influence engagement and disengagement, and motivations for learning. A first surprising finding of this study is that over 88 per cent of students indicate that they have a role model and clearly identify these 'heroes' as a source of motivation and inspiration for their life. Mass media is the main source of role models. Dominant heroes are not linked to school's symbolic space. Moreover, learning and education are disconnected from models of socioeconomic success. In other words, values attached to contemporary heroes are separated from education, learning and academic culture, as the perception is that their success is linked to other values. In findings consistent for all groups, regardless of location, socioeconomic status or family background, young people in this study reveal that the path to a better life is rarely determined by education and academic excellence. In addition, educators do not seem to be interested in students' aspirations, dreams and ideals in life.

The ways in which students imagine their futures determine motivations for learning, engagement, the quality of their achievements and resilience towards academic work. The ability to imagine the possibilities of hypothetical future scenarios shapes human resiliency and relates to optimism or anxiety. Scenarios of our future can determine how we perceive and interact with the world (Fortunato & Furey, 2011). The possible scenario of underemployment or unemployment, or a future of debt bondage and missed opportunities, may stay as a source of anger and frustration for students in many countries across the world. It is the reason for youth riots and massive student rallies in Chile or Canada, and students' involvement in the Occupy Movement in the United States and Europe (Berrett, 2011; Schrader & Wachsmuth, 2012) highlight that the current economic context, inequality and a worrying perspective of the future capture students' imaginations. It is a futile exercise to approach students' engagement, and learning and teaching strategies unless grounded in the analysis of socioeconomic and cultural contexts, their contemporary heroes and everyday life events.

The impact of technologies in higher education is significantly linked with changing trends that are affecting teaching, learning, and creative inquiry in higher education. Perhaps the most important aspect of the rapid evolution of new technologies in learning and teaching is the unprecedented flexibility and transparency offered to students across the world. Learning analytics, for example, provide new and powerful tools for universities to design bespoke solutions for student learning, community participation and relevance of degrees for the labour market. The paradigm of openness, easy access to data and academic resources, and ever increasing transparency bring important opportunities for universities to align with student needs. At the same time, this unprecedented transparency and variety of choices for learning pathways represents a challenge for many universities to compete for students and use ICT to enhance student engagement and continuously improve their learning experience.

There is no doubt that the rapid evolution of new technologies will change the landscape of higher education worldwide. This trend will open new opportunities for learning and teaching, but there are some inherent risks. If technological solutions are adopted to cut costs and increase profits, not for pedagogical purposes, they will always work against student engagement and may hinder results. The need for a balanced view on the use, power and potential of new technologies in higher education needs to be taken into consideration. In the 1990s the American writer George Gilder predicted that cities would disappear as 'leftover baggage from the industrial era'. In a prediction that was enthusiastically accepted, he detailed how new technologies would make communication so simple and accessible that people and businesses would have no need to be near one another. Therefore, he concluded, cities will slowly dissolve as people spread across rural areas. However, the 'death of the cities' never eventuated and urbanization is rising at an unprecedented pace (Popenici & Kerr, 2013). Higher education should involve the power of critical reflection and see what serves the interest of the student and consider decisions beyond temporary hype and naive enthusiasms. If technology comes first for a university, learning and teaching having to come second, students may find this an impediment rather than a help for their learning.

The overall challenge ahead for higher education is to find alternative ways to capture students' imaginations and fuel their curiosity and capacity for effort in the search for knowledge. Many universities are building on the idea that we cannot look at a sustainable future with a system that values seat time and student numbers rather than love for learning, student engagement and the university's contribution to the world. There are numerous examples suggesting that this approach leads to remarkable results both in student results and university's general outcomes. This also reflects that the challenge of tomorrow is to avoid to succumb to the trap of grade inflation and lowering standards for 'students as customers', and focus on creating a system able to engage students in an equitable manner. This pedagogical approach can nurture educated minds for creative, responsible and knowledgeable citizens.

2.4.   The Future: Rethinking the Context for Student Engagement

Universities are urged to respond to heightened and almost insurmountable expectations for the good reason that they serve the public interest in shaping the future of societies, culture, workforce and economies. At the same time, there is an almost universal acceptance that these institutions should be subjected to the rigours of the market. Consequently, the pattern of reducing public funding for higher education, while pressuring universities to be more profitable, has been globally adopted. In succumbing to these pressures, there is the constant risk that academic rigour and quality will be too often traded off to secure student satisfaction and revenues for the institution (Bok, 2003). Degradation of labour conditions within universities and the impact of this on the fabric of academic culture involves long-term repercussions on the nature and context of the relationships between students and universities (Baltodano, 2012; Gilbert, 2013; Ryan, Burgess, Connell, & Egbert, 2013).

The consumerist pattern of thinking that is structuring neoliberal policies of university governance are already questioned, not only as they fail to achieve their promises, but as a result of new demands from society, citizens, employers and students (Brady, 2012; Giroux, 2002). It is no longer easy to answer with ideological stands when a prolonged economic crisis requires new and complex solutions. It becomes obvious that it is important to rethink the new social, economic, ecological and cultural contexts and admit that education affects everyone's life in ways that go beyond what can be measured by market earnings, profit balances and economic growth.

It may also be important for universities to focus more on the type of symbolic messages they send to their students. Consistency with stated values, reflected in practices and stories about their institutions, can shape how students relate to their own tasks and responsibilities. There are numerous examples, but we can take that of Florida Atlantic University in the United States, which firmed a deal in the first months of 2013 to rename its football stadium after a private prison corporation. Bob Libal, the executive director of social justice group Grassroots Leadership, was quoted by the *New York Times* commenting on this decision:

> It's startling to see a stadium will be named after them. It's like calling something Blackwater Stadium. This is a company whose record is marred by human rights abuses, by lawsuits, by unnecessary deaths of people in their custody and a whole series of incidents that really draw into question their ability to successfully manage a prison facility. (Bishop, 2013)

These decisions may seem trivial and marginal, but they build in fact a narrative that is not only misaligned but antagonizes academic values. This may also impact on how students relate to university and their learning as they build a different type of relationship with their universities and academic tasks when they feel that the system is becoming more commercial. If everything is for sale, why it is not acceptable for a student to buy a paper or plagiarize? How students experience university plays a major role in their academic engagement, quality of learning and success.

The utilitarian trend in higher education may not be sufficient to provide solutions for the uncertain future of universities and for the challenges ahead. Most universities are facing increasing pressures to reinvent and build sustainable models, which are able to engage students and open up for new possibilities associated with their degrees. These sustainable models have, at their core solutions, to actively involve students in an academic culture focused on the profits of learning, not markets. The risk of producing masses of graduates holding a devoid diploma or credentials depleted of value goes far beyond the risk of financial bankruptcy. It already becomes obvious that the great demands of the future involve the requirement to generate insightful questions and innovative solutions for the great social, economic, cultural and ecological challenges ahead of us. Rather than judging a university degree simply through the prism of immediate financial benefits of first jobs, governments, policy makers, parents and students will realize that a university degree is worthwhile if it opens to a lifetime of growth and change, participative citizenship, and new opportunities opened by responsible and informed decisions.

There are students who are intrinsically motivated to learn and this is what they do in any context or institutional arrangement. However, the majority will not genuinely engage in the complex and strenuous path to academic scholarship and discovery if it is obvious that they (and their professors) are regarded to a large extent as revenue sources. This is first and foremost a failure of imagination: policy makers and university administrators have to engage themselves in empathic reasoning to design solutions for student engagement fitted to the specific realities and contexts of their institution. This complex task requires bespoke solutions and courageous decisions.

Exercising our imaginative ability is essential to put ourselves in the position of students and make the effort to see the world as they see it. This exercise opens an understanding of what students' lives are like and how changes of various sorts affect them. In Cultivating Humanity (1998) Nussbaum advocated the need to train our 'narrative imagination'. In combining the use of imagination with knowledge and actual experience we have the potential to overcome the limitations of our own narrow world views and 'venture beyond our local settings'. Taking this position we can see that — facing an uncertain future — students need to imagine that the university does not just tolerate them, but considers students the most important component of academic life, an integral part of a culture oriented to learning and discovery. They find in these environments opportunities to debate, collaborate with, and learn from scholars in very different fields. We solve the problem of student engagement when we engage their imagination, the most powerful structure for the passion and love for learning, for curiosity and discovery. This opens an important discussion on general directions of our future.

Nussbaum, in 'Cultivating Humanity', observes a detail of essential importance:

> Our campuses educate our citizens. Becoming an educated citizen means learning a lot of facts and mastering techniques of reasoning. But it means something more. It means learning how to be a human being capable of love and imagination. (Nussbaum, 1998)

Unless universities take note of this, they continually run the risk of losing relevance and turning into an assembly line designed to produce 'narrow citizens' who have a devalued credential. The complacent and mediocre institutions of higher education will slowly disappear as society needs imaginative and innovative citizens, capable to move forward thriving societies, venture into unfamiliar spaces with an unabated desire to explore the unknown, fitted to deal with continuous change and new challenges. Economies and employers also find that increasing control and restricting imaginations may serve an ideology, short-term interests and profits, but it cannot produce a culture capable of providing innovative solutions and sustainable results. Importantly, it does not lead to creating adaptable employees with initiative, critical thinking, knowledge, creativity and responsibility. The 'skills gap' debate — currently polarized between positions of employers interested in hiring exceptional employees with minimum payments and the outraged reaction of youth — will gain more consistency as a new field of research when it provides data able to inform this important discussion. The fact is that both sides agree that the future requires new skills, creativity and flexibility, in-depth knowledge and imagination.

The current polarization between high-quality knowledge-driven academic cultures and profit-oriented institutions presents the risk of a parallel existence of a gray area, where ephemeral providers will struggle to cope with tremendous challenges and elite institutions. Quality of learning and teaching, commitment to a curiosity-driven research and scholarship — less limited by short-term interests of the industry — already exists at the core of great disparities in funding and the capacity to attract resources. In 2012, top universities proved to be a magnet for consistent donations: Stanford University raised an unprecedented $1.035 billion, Harvard University $650 million and Yale at $544 million in fund-raising. An explanation comes from Ann E. Kaplan, director of the Voluntary Support of Education Survey in the United States:

> Stanford has been doing a remarkable job .... They have some very big ideas, and they're good at capturing people's imagination, thinking about what they can do and what they could be. (Lewin, 2013)

This example underlines the capacity of some universities to build the sense of social responsibility and commitment to education in their graduates. It may also present an alternative to the type of financial arrangements that impact on academic values and narratives associated with the university. Higher education may soon be compelled to deny the primacy of the market and shift the emphasis to education, not on the purchase of credentials. It is crucial for its future to recapture the imagination of students and faculty as this maintains the potential to enthuse students with passion for learning, knowledge and discovery. This involves a balanced model of governance — realistic about efficiency, but far from glorifying the illusory profitability of precarization — with a focus on the value of learning and academic ethos. This new model takes at the core the importance to recognize the value of diversity, including the diversity of models for university governance with a continuous exploration of options, of different pedagogical models and paradigms. Adapted to a dynamic and fast changing reality this paradigm of intellectual and managerial flexibility involves a genuine and firm commitment to academic freedom, academic values and a shift of focus towards creativity, imagination and academic constancy. It involves also a fundamental shift towards a comprehensive view of student engagement, taking into consideration intrinsic motivations and changing cultural and socioeconomic realities affecting our students.

In this current complex context, it becomes more evident why universities are compelled to place a new emphasis on insightful, original and imaginative policy models for student engagement. However, this is determined by a vast web of variables of personal, social, economic and cultural contexts, complex motivations, family narratives and symbolic constructs, learning environments, meanings and symbols attached to education and students' future. Since student engagement is perceived as an exceedingly complex issue for analysis, policies will aim to create not only comfortable and engaging learning environments, but also an ecology of equitable agreements between the university and the student and new pedagogies. These new pedagogies can redesign teaching through a focus on the engagement of students' imaginations through discovery, in learning how to do things and collaborate for new ideas and solutions. In emphasizing through innovative collaborative projects the way knowledge can have an impact on the world may lead to a new focus on applied research conducted by students and faculty and external partners (e.g. industry, community groups).

Where will this new context of sociocultural, economic and political changes lead universities when students will be graduating into a world of tremendous turbulence and uncertainty? What is the vision for the future engaged student and what do we need to do to turn this into the living reality of our universities? First of all, we can expect that the marketization of universities may evolve fast from crude forms of taylorism and New Public Management (Bok, 2003; Lorenz, 2012) to flexible managerial models and horizontal structures of decision and collaboration. These are already adopted by innovative corporations, such as Google, and present a model of innovative research, experimental approached and strong investments in their own human capital. This evolution can replace ruthless and destructive practices of control and human resources management adopted by many universities with sustainable models oriented to build excellence and staff loyalty. In itself, this shift can turn institutions of higher education into hotbeds of ideas for reimagining higher learning, research and collaborations with students, stakeholder and social partners. New approaches of teaching can be better aligned in the new paradigm with student contexts and needs.

We share the opinion that the most important mission for universities will be to nurture creativity and stimulate innovation. This may come not only from the need to prepare students for a globalized world, fast changing demands and challenges on the labour market, but to answer the increasing demand of the labour market to independent, creative, engaged and adaptable individuals. Transforming the educational experience so that it is meaningful to students and answering the need to nurture imagination and creativity brings the potential to make innovative teaching a high priority for practice and research in universities across the world. It involves making the classroom more socially connected and international through technological opportunities, building both on students' independence and connectivity. The interaction with the world and a more comprehensive view of students as individuals placed in very different contexts than those familiar to their teachers will adjust our teaching more effectively. This can be achieved through a more widespread use of experimental hubs for research and innovation and idea incubators, where students and faculty can actively collaborate with partners from industry, community groups or international collaborators.

Many universities will also need to build a new narrative for their contract with students, strengthening the complex fabric of an academic milieu conducive to student engagement. There are already many institutions able to offer exceptional case studies and ideas for this direction, but these isolated examples may turn into a generalized trend as a result of increasing demands from social partners, employers and students themselves. Placing student needs in balance with academic standards and the importance of building a deeply personal love for learning, this change of direction will help many universities cross the troubled waters ahead. The road ahead for universities will be determined by institutional capacity to instill the love for learning, responsibility and the curiosity of educated minds. Institutions of higher education will be differentiated by their capacity to build engaged and knowledgeable citizens, creative individuals committed to wide participative collaborations, locally and globally. Those universities that stay consistent with their mission and values, while also equating change and challenges with the opportunity to improve, will be the ones that move forward successfully into the future.

References

Arum, R., & Roksa, J. (2011). *Academically adrift: Limited learning on college campuses.* Chicago, IL: The University of Chicago Press.

Baltodano, M. (2012). Neoliberalism and the demise of public education: The corporatization of schools of education. *International Journal of Qualitative Studies in Education, 25/4,* 487–507.

Bandura, A. (1986). *Social foundations of thought and action: A social cognitive theory.* Englewood Cliffs, NJ: Prentice-Hall Inc.

Berrett, D. (2011). *Intellectual roots of wall street protest lie in academe.* The Chronicle of Higher Education. Issue: October 16, 2011. Retrieved from http://chronicle.com/article/ Intellectual-Roots-of-Wall/129428/. Accessed on June 22, 2013.

Bishop, G. (2013). *A company that runs prisons will have its name on a stadium.* The New York Times, February 19. Retrieved from http://www.nytimes.com/2013/02/20/ sports/ncaafootball/a-company-that-runs-prisons-will-have-its-name-on-a-stadium.html. Accessed on February 24, 2013.

Blackstone, B., Karnitschnig, M., & Thomson, R. (2012). Europe's Banker Talks Tough. *Wall Street Journal,* February 24, 2012. Retrieved from http://online.wsj.com/article/ SB10001424052970203960804577241221244896782.html. Accessed on June 18, 2012.

Bok, D. C. (2003). *Universities in the marketplace: The commercialization of higher education.* Princeton, NJ: Princeton University Press.

Brady, N. (2012). From 'moral loss' to 'moral reconstruction'? A critique of ethical perspectives on challenging the neoliberal hegemony in UK universities in the 21st century. *Oxford Review of Education, 38*(3), 343–335.

Bruner, J. S. (1996). *The culture of education.* Cambridge, MA: Harvard University Press.

Chowdry, H., Crawford, C., Dearden, L., Goodman, A., & Vignoles, A. (2013). Widening participation in higher education: Analysis using linked administrative data. *Journal of the Royal Statistical Society, 176*(2), 431–457.

Dean, K. L., & Jolly, J. P. (2012). Student identity, disengagement, and learning. *Academy of Management Learning & Education, 11*(2), 228–243.

Eurofound. (2012). *NEETs — Young people not in employment, education or training: Characteristics, costs and policy responses in Europe.* Luxembourg: Publications Office of the European Union.

European University Association. (2013). *EUA's public funding observatory — spring 2013.* Retrieved from http://www.eua.be/Libraries/Governance_Autonomy_Funding/EUA_ PFO_report_2013.sflb.ashx. Accessed on June 23, 2013.

Eurostat. (2013). *Euro area unemployment rate at 11.8 per cent.* EuroIndicators — January 8, 2013 News Release. Retrieved from http://epp.eurostat.ec.europa.eu/cache/ITY_PUBLIC/ 3-08012013-BP/EN/3-08012013-BP-EN.PDF. Accessed on January 9, 2013.

FED. (2012). *Quarterly report on household debt and credit — November, 2012.* Federal Reserve Bank of New York, NY: Research and Statistics Group.

Fortunato, V. J., & Furey, J. T. (2011). The theory of mindtime: The relationships between future, past, and present thinking and psychological well-being and distress. *Personality and Individual Differences, 50*(1), 20–24.

Geertz, C. (1973). *Thick description: Toward an interpretive theory of culture.* New York, NY: Basic Books.

Gilbert, D. A. (2013). The generation of public intellectuals: Corporate universities, graduate employees and the academic labor movement. *Labor Studies Journal, 38*(1), 32–46.

Giroux, H. (2002). The corporate war against higher education. *Workplace, 9*, 103–117.

Hammer, K. (2013). Survey of 103,000 students, grade 7 through 12, gives rare look into their lives. *The Globe and Mail*, February 12. Retrieved from http://www.theglobeandmail.com/news/toronto/survey-of-103000-students-grade-7-through-12-gives-rare-look-into-their-lives/article8485352/. Accessed on February 14, 2013.

ILO. (2012). *Global employment trends for youth 2012.* Geneva: International Labour Office.

Lewin, T. (2013). Report says Stanford is first university to raise $1 billion in a single year. *The New York Times*, February 20. Retrieved from http://www.nytimes.com/2013/02/21/education/stanfords-fund-raising-topped-1-billion-in-2012.html. Accessed on June 24, 2013.

Lorenz, C. (2012). If you're so smart, why are you under surveillance? universities, neoliberalism, and new public management. *Critical Inquiry, 38*(3), 599–629.

Martin, A. (2013). Colleges' debt falls on students after construction binges. *The New York Times*, December 13, 2012. Retrieved from http://www.nytimes.com/2012/12/14/business/colleges-debt-falls-on-students-after-construction-binges.html. Accessed on February 12, 2012.

Melander, I., & Vinocur, N. (2013). *Germany Fears Revolution If Europe Scraps Welfare Model.* Reuters, May 28, 2013. Retrieved from http://uk.reuters.com/article/2013/05/28/uk-europe-unemployment-idUKBRE94R0VC20130528. Accessed on June 23, 2013.

Mitchell, J. (1992). Interrelationships and predictive efficacy for indices of intrinsic, extrinsic and self-assessed motivation for learning. *Journal for Research and Development in Education, 23*(3), 149–155.

Nussbaum, M. C. (1998). *Cultivating humanity: A classical defense of reform in liberal education.* Cambridge, MA: Harvard University Press.

OECD. (2009). *Higher education to 2030, globalisation* (Vol. 2). Paris: OECD Publishing and Centre for Educational Research and Innovation.

OECD. (2010a). *Education at a glance 2010 OECD indicators.* Paris: OECD Publishing.

OECD. (2010b). *PISA 2009 results: Learning to learn student engagement, strategies and practices* (Vol. III). Paris: OECD Publishing.

OECD. (2011). *Divided we stand: Why inequality keeps rising.* Paris: OECD Publishing.

OECD. (2012). *Education today 2013: The OECD perspective.* Paris: OECD Publishing.

OECD. (2013). *Trends shaping education 2013.* Paris: OECD Publishing.

OXFAM. (2013). *The cost of inequality: How wealth and income extremes hurt us all.* Oxfam Media Briefing, 18 January 2013, Ref: 02/2013. Retrieved from http://www.oxfam.org/sites/www.oxfam.org/files/cost-of-inequality-oxfam-mb180113.pdf. Accessed on February 20, 2013.

Pascarella, E. T., Blaich, C., Martin, G. L., & Hanson, G. M. (2011). How robust are the findings of academically adrift? *Change: The Magazine of Higher Learning, 43*(3), 20–24.

Popenici, S. (2010). Contemporary heroes and students' motivation for learning. In K. Egan & K. Madej (Eds.), *Engaging imaginations and developing creativity* (pp. 159–176). Newcastle upon Tyne: Cambridge Scholars Publishing.

Popenici, S., & Kerr, S. (2013). *What undermines higher education — and how this impacts employment, economies and our democracies.* Charleston, SC: CreateSpace.

Reeve, J. (2012). A self-determination theory perspective on student engagement. In S. L. Christenson, A. L. Reschly & C. Wylie (Eds.), *Handbook of research on student engagement* (pp. 149–172). New York, NY: Springer.

Ryan, S., Burgess, J., Connell, J., & Egbert, G. (2013). Casual academic staff in an Australian university: Marginalised and excluded. *Tertiary Education and Management, 19*(2), 161–175.

Ryan, R. M., & Deci, E. L. (2000). Self-determination theory and the facilitation of intrinsic motivation, social development, and well-being. *American Psychologist, 55*, 68–78.

Sandel, M. J. (2012). *What money can't buy: The moral limits of markets.* New York, NY: Farrar, Straus and Giroux.

Schrader, S., & Wachsmuth, D. (2012). Reflections on occupy wall street, the state and space. *City, 16*(12), 243–248.

The ACEVO Commission on Youth Unemployment. (2012). *Youth unemployment: The crisis we cannot afford.* London: ACEVO.

The Department of Education, Employment and Workplace Relations, Australian Government — DEEWR. (2008). *Review of Australian higher education: Final report.* Canberra: Commonwealth of Australia.

Toshalis, E., & Nakkula, M. J. (2012). Motivation, engagement, and student voice. *Education Digest, 78*(1), 29–35.

Universities UK. (2011). *Driving economic growth. Higher education — a core strategic asset to the UK.* Retrieved from http://www.universitiesuk.ac.uk/highereducation/Documents/2011/DrivingEconomicGrowth.pdf

Vedder, R., Denhart, C., & Robe, J. (2013). *Why are recent college graduates underemployed? University enrollments and labor-market realities.* Washington, DC: Center for College Affordability and Productivity. Retrieved from http://centerforcollegeaffordability.org/uploads/Underemployed/percent20Report per cent202.pdf

Vygotsky, L. S. (1978). Internalization of higher psychological functions. In M. Cole, V. John-Steiner, S. Scribner, & E. Souberman (Eds.), *Mind in society: The development of higher psychological processes.* Cambridge, MA: Harvard University Press.

Chapter 3

A Relational and Multidimensional Model of Student Engagement

Ian Solomonides

Abstract

Student engagement is broadly conceptualised in current research and application according to three dimensions: behavioural, cognitive and emotional, with some authors also including a social-cultural perspective. The current primacy of behavioural and cognitive models of student engagement, characterised by the National Survey of Student Engagement (NSSE) and its derivatives, is challenged, seeking to redress the balance by including more affective aspects of engagement. This chapter reviews contemporary representative research, critically examining the findings against the author's empirical research before setting out an alternative model of student engagement that places a Sense of Being *and a* Sense of Transformation *at the heart of student engagement, about which other foci of attention rotate. The model illustrates a variety of phenomena that students focus on at various times during their experience of 'engagement' and consequentially the elements policy-makers and practitioners might seek to enhance in order to support student engagement.*

3.1. Introduction

Much of the contemporary literature on student engagement focuses on the interplay between behavioural, cognitive, affective and socio-cultural dimensions at the level of the individual learner. In this chapter the present primacy of behavioural and cognitive models of student engagement characterised by the National Survey of Student Engagement (NSSE) and its derivatives is challenged, seeking to redress the balance by including more affective aspects of engagement and concepts of engagement established from discussions with learners. The chapter reviews contemporary representative research, before describing the history of the development of

The Student Engagement Handbook: Practice in Higher Education
Copyright © 2013 by Emerald Group Publishing Limited
All rights of reproduction in any form reserved
ISBN: 978-1-78190-423-7

an alternative model of student engagement that places a *Sense of Being* and a *Sense of Transformation* at the heart of student engagement, about which other aspects of engagement rotate. The model illustrates a variety of phenomena that students focus on at various times during their experience of engagement with learning and consequentially therefore on some of the elements policy-makers and practitioners might seek to enhance in order to support student engagement described in this way.

3.2.   Context and Background

Living and working in Australia means that the author is exposed to a localised application of student engagement, which at present is broadly focusing on quality assurance based on the annual cross-sectional surveying of students against conceptual items that are deemed proxies for quality learning and teaching. Having previously lived and worked in the United Kingdom, the author has a long-standing interest in the enterprise of higher education and particularly the ways in which students and teachers experience various phenomena therein.

Understanding experience and producing taxonomies or models that seek to order that experience lay at the heart of phenomenography, an approach to research that typically involves the interpretation of interview data to describe the essential variation in the ways people subjectively experience and live out a phenomenon such as studying for an assignment. Phenomenography was developed and brought to prominence in higher education most notably through the groundbreaking work of Ference Marton (1981, 1986) and Roger Säljö (1996) in the establishment of the now familiar concepts of *deep* and *surface approaches to study* and related *conceptions of learning*. The author's research is located in this phenomenographic tradition in that the object of the research is the relationship between the subjects (in this case students) and the phenomenon (in this case 'engagement'). Consequently, the models presented in this chapter seek to describe the elements that make up the essence of that phenomenon and its underlying structures.

Previous works by the author and colleagues (Reid & Solomonides, 2007; Solomonides & Martin, 2008; Solomonides & Reid, 2009; Solomonides, Reid, & Petocz, 2012) have analysed students' and teachers' responses from interviews about their experiences if learning and teaching. This has led to the presentation of an alternative model of student engagement to that associated with the norms of engagement that underpin instruments such as the NSSE. In the continual quest to understand and improve the experiences of students in higher education, this alternative model is re-presented.

Student engagement has become the focus of attention, applied in differing ways, in a variety of countries and sectors, for very different reasons. No single description of these differences will satisfy the various stakeholders, practitioners, researchers and commentators on the subject, posing a challenge both to finding common ground and to making comparisons between initiatives. Student engagement has become a ubiquitous and enigmatic phenomenon, interpreted and applied in a variety of ways across different higher education contexts and sectors. At the same time, in the United Kingdom at least, there is much focus on the experiences of students and what that means in terms of their contested position as 'consumers' of education. One of the forefathers of the student engagement movement in North America, Robert Pace, almost anticipated the current debates and rhetoric around consumption versus production in higher education when he said:

> Excellence, efficiency, productivity, accountability — these are all common words in much of the rhetoric about higher education today. But more often than not, the rhetoric has been one sided …. It assumes that the student is buying a product and therefore entitled to value for that product. It is a curious line of thinking because actually a student at a later point in time is the product! (Pace, 1982, p. 3)

Pace had earlier developed the College Student Experiences Questionnaire — still used today — and which informed the later development of the NSSE. Underpinning both these instruments is the belief that involvement, or engagement, is identifiable through survey item responses and that levels of engagement are related to participation in particular curricula and extra-curricular activities. A problem, if there is one, is the way in which those activities have been conceptualised and what, if anything, has been left out that might otherwise afford a richer description of engagement and greater utility in focusing effort by policy-makers and individual teachers. It is to this end that the author's current work is applied.

3.3.   Student Engagement in Australia and the United Kingdom

Engagement research in Australia has tended to focus on individual or academic engagement in learning as opposed to engagement or participation with or in the administration of the university, curriculum development, or co-creation of resources and knowledge as tends to occur in the United Kingdom. This may be a function of the prominence (in the United Kingdom) of, *inter alia*, a national survey of student satisfaction (as opposed to a survey of engagement) and the publishing of the outcomes together with league tables, compulsory student unionism and increased awareness of students' experiences as determining choice, retention and so on. In the United Kingdom, student engagement appears to be a much more inclusive concept both in philosophy and application, suggesting it is about 'supporting both the transactional and the transformational interests of students' (see van der Velden, 2012 and Chapter 5 of this volume). Taking that approach there have been some impressive initiatives in what might be deemed constructivist approaches to participation driven through a strong promotion of group and individual identity, agency, choice and partnerships. In some cases this has been significant enough to inspire whole of institution strategy (c.f. University of Lincoln, 2012) or a manifesto for action (c.f. NUS, 2012), both framing engagement within political economics and promoting radical reimagining of the relationship between the university, the student and learning.

In Australia, however, the agenda has been significantly influenced by the introduction of the Australian University Survey of Student Engagement (AUSSE) (ACER, 2008) and associated drive for aligning engagement measures with quality assurance determinations (Coates, 2006a). The AUSSE was introduced to Australia under the offices of the Australian Council for Educational Research in 2007 (Coates, 2010). The antecedents to the AUSSE are found in the National Survey of Student Engagement that emerged in the United States in 1998 following work by the National Center for Higher Education Management Systems, Colorado, and the Postsecondary Research and School of Education at Indiana University. The NSSE has now been developed for use as a cross-sectional survey instrument in the United States and Canada, in South Africa as the South African Survey of Student Engagement (SASSE) (Strydom, Kuh, & Mentz, 2010), in Australia as mentioned (Coates, 2006b), and in China as the National Survey on Student Engagement-China (NSSE-C) (Ross & Cen, 2012).

At the time of writing there are no known substantial uses of the NSSE in the United Kingdom, so the author notes with interest the work currently sponsored through the Higher Education Academy exploring the '... viability of using items derived from the National Survey of Student Engagement (NSSE)' (with benchmarking across nine institutions) and the subsequent *Cognitive Review of Student Engagement* with the intention of

> ... an evaluation of student understanding and validity of a selection of Student Engagement items derived from the NSSE, across a range of institutional, subject and student characteristics, to inform development of the items, and institutional understanding of results. (HEA, 2013, p. 2)

This most recent development described above would appear to herald a significant interest in the use of NSSE type surveying within the UK sector. Prior to this there have been several Student Engagement Research Projects also funded through the Higher Education Academy. Of these, notable for their focus on NSSE type surveys are those at Warwick (Taylor, Koskela, & Lee, 2011) and Worcester (Scott, 2011). Earlier there had also been an exploration into using a NSSE type instrument at Reading and a report produced in which Creighton, Beasley, and Jeffreys (2008) reflect:

> Alas the NSSE model was not adopted for a UK-wide survey, where the student as a customer-to-be-satisfied approach was taken instead.

Nonetheless, at conferences on research into Higher Education, many wistfully ponder what such a survey would have shown at their own institution.

In Australia, the principal survey of student experience has for many years been the Course Experience Questionnaire (the CEQ) (Ramsden, 1991), but it is applied in such a way and without some of the original scales that correlate most with deeper approaches to study, and by association, quality of learning achieved. The CEQ's original utility as a proxy measure of the quality of student learning is somewhat compromised and further impediments to its application (it is sent to Australian students after they have graduated) include achieving a sufficient response rate to discriminate at various levels of the academic endeavour (faculty, discipline, programme, etc.); its timing in the student life cycle meaning results lag behind the cohort it drew data from; and, the biasing of result based on other factors such as whether or not the respondent secured a job that satisfies them.

The UK National Student Survey (NSS) also has some inherent issues leading Gibbs (2010) to conclude:

> There have been no recent studies to confirm the original findings concerning relationships between features of courses, student responses and learning outcomes in current contexts. There have been no direct studies of the validity of the NSS in relation to its ability to predict educational gains. There have been no studies that demonstrate that if evidence-based practices are adopted, and NSS scores improve, this will be associated with improved educational gains. For that kind of evidence we have to look to measures of student engagement.

Gibbs (2010) goes on to suggest that as a process variable, student engagement is one of the few that can be clearly shown to have a link to educational gain by the student, usually through application of the 'seven principles of good practice' identified by Chickering and Gamson (1987) that in part inform the NSSE items and sub-scales. The principles are as follows: encourages contact between students and faculty, develops reciprocity and cooperation among students, encourages active learning, gives prompt feedback, emphasises time on task, communicates high expectations, and respects diverse talents and ways of learning. Chickering and Gamson note, 'While each practice can stand alone on its own, when all are present their effects multiply. Together they employ six powerful forces in education: activity, expectations, cooperation, interaction, diversity, and responsibility' (p. 3). Later, Pascarella and Terenzini (1991, 2005) synthesised many of the studies and data associated with student progress through, and success in, higher education. In validating the seven principles and other practices they concluded that '… institutions should focus on the ways they can shape their academic, interpersonal, and extracurricular offerings to encourage student engagement' (2005, p. 602).

3.4.   Agendas and Tensions

It is timely then to reflect and consider how the student engagement agendas have moved since the development of these highly valid principles and the wistful comment cited earlier by Creighton et al. (2008). The work reported in this chapter leads the author to conclude that perhaps, despite the ground-swell support for NSSE type surveys across the globe, we need to be careful before placing too much emphasis on results as proxies for quality in learning and teaching. Moreover, the underlying norms associated with the NSSE and its derivatives mean that the survey items 'measure' engagement as conceptualised against pre-determined pedagogic practices, rather than, or perhaps as well as, how engagement is experienced by students.

Sectors applying NSSE type surveys have by and large adopted a more positivistic approach and concept of engagement, largely predicated on measures of student behaviour and teaching practices. As already alluded to these behaviours and practices are well articulated in the literature following the work of Pace (1979, 1982), Astin (1977), Chickering and Gamson (1987), Tinto (1987) and others who tended to focus on issues such as effort and involvement, as well as pedagogic practices. Critically, much of these practices were centred on what the student does — described by Pace as '… once students got to college, what counted most was not who they were or where they were but what they did' (Pace, 1982, p. 20). Astin (1984) also focused on effort in describing involvement in academic life suggesting that it was the '… amount of physical and psychological energy that the student devotes to the academic experience' (p. 518), further suggesting that the learning that was achieved by each student was mediated and moderated by elements such as the student's involvement in general university life and their peer-to-peer relationships.

The elements above are reflected in the NSSE. The NSSE is a survey instrument that includes a series of items against which the students rate themselves or their perception of some provision in the curriculum or campus. There are five benchmarks within the NSSE: level of academic challenge; active and collaborative learning; student—staff interaction; enriching educational experiences; and a supportive campus environment. A sixth benchmark, work integrated learning, was added to the Australian version. As has already been established, many of the concepts and practices on which the NSSE and AUSSE are built have sound empirical and theoretical foundations. Many, such as the seven principles would, if enacted, transform the experience of students in higher education for the better in terms of quality of learning outcomes.

However, in attempting to measure them in a comparative survey across a number of countries one starts to run the risk of creating an inevitable tension between the potential of engagement as best pedagogic and learning practices, and the measurement of engagement through a survey with inherent norms about learning and teaching. In other words, what norms of teaching and learning are measures of student engagement based on and therefore what behaviours do they implicitly reinforce? Are these measures and norms sensitive to the ways in which students live out the intersections between life, learning and work across different countries and contexts (Voerman & Solomonides, 2012)? Moreover, in using outcomes from measurements such as the NSSE in setting policy or strategic direction are we running the risk of seeing, '... targets that seem measurable become exciting tools for improvement' such that, 'when a measure becomes a target, it ceases to be a good measure'[1] (Strathern, 1997, p. 308)? Strathern is in part evoking the work of Keith Hoskin (1996) and the '... "awful idea of accountability": inscribing people into the measurement of objects'. This is particularly troublesome in the knowledge that some applications of student engagement data are driven from an ideology that 'locates students in higher education primarily as consumers, and is based on neoliberal thinking about the marketisation of education. From this perspective student engagement focuses primarily on ensuring consumer rights, hearing the consumer voice and about enhancing institutional market position' (HEA, 2010, p. 3).

Returning to what might be described as 'academic engagement' — meaning the relationship the student has with his or her learning and the things that support or hinder that relationship — and taking an holistic view of engagement, suggests some tensions and paradoxes. In an earlier study (Solomonides & Martin, 2008), teaching staff and students were quizzed as to their conceptions of engagement, learning, and teaching. The findings suggested that staff tended to see engagement from an epistemic viewpoint, while students leaned more towards the ontological. Staff tended to focus on effort, the evidence for which was students being prepared, active, critical, inquisitive and constructivist. Staff also provided an unsolicited list of deficits or things that students did that was contrary to engagement, being passive, detached, apathetic, alienated, unfocused and distracted. Students on the other hand talked about wishing to have confidence, happiness, imagination and self-knowledge. The students also described the conditions that supported these things, being clear objectives, goals, feedback, resources and seeing the benefits of what they were doing within a broader context. It could be argued that the staff and students were conceptualising engagement along two broadly similar but somewhat misaligned themes. Staff tended to focus on the cognitive and conative factors (as well as deficits) associated with engagement, while students tended to refer more to the emotive and affective while focusing on personal and creative identity. These different 'ends' of engagement are illustrated in a quote from Harris, Bolander, Lebrun, Docq, and Bouvy (2004, p. 1):

> Academic engagement is defined as engaging in the activities of a course programme with thoroughness and seriousness. Indicators of academic engagement are cognitive (organising and planning his/her own work, entering deeply into learning on his/her own), affective (being motivated, persevering, taking pleasure in the course, being interested), conative (giving the necessary energy and time) and relational.

---

[1]This is also known as 'Goodhart's Law' after Charles Goodhart, former Chief Advisor to the Bank of England who stated, 'Any observed statistical regularity will tend to collapse once pressure is placed upon it for control purposes' (Goodhart, 1983, p. 96).

Both students and staff tended to see engagement as an outcome of the learning experience as well as a process to be encountered but there was some variance in the quality of this engagement. This aligns somewhat with the ideas of Csikszentmihalyi (1990) and positive psychology; as one staff interviewee put it:

> Wanting to do what they're doing; doing work for the sake of getting it right or learning from it, not for the mark, being prepared to find it fun. Erich Fromm's book 'To Have and to Be' talks about the 'being mode' of doing things, which fits with this — there's a description (fairly early on?) of a being-mode student and a having-mode student. Csikszentmihalyi's idea of 'flow' is a description of serious involvement, and while that isn't student (or most people's) everyday experience, the characteristics of possible flow tasks or activities he gives: clear goals, immediate feedback, matching skills and abilities: chance of completing task, open-ended task — no matter how good you get, it's always possible to go further, are things that could be built into the student experience. I think students can experience flow when working on essays or design work or other creative stuff, which is demanding, but going well. (Solomonides & Martin, 2008, p. 15)

In other words students immersed in such a process would have levels of concentration and engagement where the 'self' would be forgotten (Debold, 2002). Engagement (at least academic engagement) was therefore a process to be gone through before achieving engagement as an outcome; there would be no 'thrill without the drill' as it were. This was described as a threshold, and has alignment with the work of Meyer and Land (2005) inasmuch as there was a liminal space between process and outcome that had to be negotiated if students were to achieve these high levels of involvement: 'Engagement is a broad term … liminality offers less predictability, and appears to be a more "liquid" space, simultaneously transforming and being transformed by the learner as he or she moves through it' (Meyer & Land, 2005, p. 380). Moreover, this view of a move from the transitional to the transformative is a theme in the literature (van der Velden, 2012) and the work of authors such as Barnett (2004, 2005, 2007) and Dall'Alba and Barnacle (2007) when describing practices and processes that lead to students negotiating the liminal space on the way to epistemological transitions, and ontological transformations (Meyer & Land, 2005, p. 386). What was appearing through this work was a description of a multi-faceted, multi-dimensional concept of engagement with learning, a view confirmed by Krause and Coates (2008) and explored by Kahu (2011), Leach and Zepke (2011) and others.

3.5. Developing a Model of Student Engagement

Earlier work (Reid & Solomonides, 2007; Solomonides & Reid, 2009) also explored the dimensions of engagement, concentrating on the perspective of the learner. This led on to the development of an empirically based model of engagement, referred to here as relational and multidimensional.

Figure 3.1 represents an earlier version of a model of engagement based on the findings from interviews with students of architecture and design. The 81 students were studying creative, design and studio-based courses in the United Kingdom and Australia. That study (Reid & Solomonides, 2007) illustrated a core feature that many students reported and described in interviews, that is a *Sense of Being*, which as the model implies is central to the nature of engagement and is a hub, about which other structural elements rotate — much like a wheel — or that may be referred to in the understanding of 'self'. It describes the personal relationship the student has with each of the elements or spokes of the wheel and relates to the various but essential aspects of being a design student. In the context of a productive discipline like design, *Sense of Artistry* referred to the ways in which students reported a need to be doing something that had utility, involved production, or the aesthetic. *Sense of Being a Designer* spoke the way in which design students saw themselves as part of or initiates into the profession of design, while *Sense of Being within Specific Contexts* was described as being part of a particular context, here a community of learners responding creatively to the tasks at hand. *Sense of Transformation* evokes the way *Sense of Being* is transformed through learning or as the 'self' is transformed through the experience of becoming in this case, a designer; ultimately engagement and creativity are perceived as integral components of

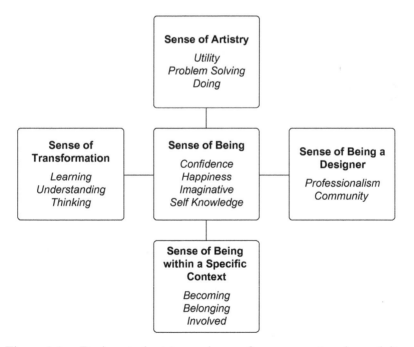

Figure 3.1:   Design students' experience of engagement and creativity.

commitment to transformative learning, the production of objects and identity all predicated on a robust *Sense of Being* (Reid & Solomonides, 2007, p. 35).

While the model satisfied a need to understand academic engagement, it was specific to creative disciplines. It did however identify the centrality of *Sense of Being* as an ontological rather than epistemological expression, thus differentiating itself from the other paradigms of engagement that tended to focus on the studious activities of the learner and his or her effort. The emphasis here was much more on affective relationships within students' learning and the innate ways in which student may be relating to formal and informal learning. Affect and ontology relative to student engagement have been described by several authors (c.f. Barnett, 2004, 2005, 2007; Barnett & Coate, 2005; Dall'Alba & Barnacle, 2007; Mann, 2001), while a sense of self, belonging and relatedness is also established in the literature (c.f. Deci & Ryan, 2000; Mann, 2001). Similarly, transformation is also referred to in the literature (c.f. Meyer & Land, 2005) and it became clear that transformation was critical not only to integrating knowledge and experience but also to the process of integrating the various outcomes of learning with the student's *Sense of Being*. Consequently a second model was developed to indicate the alignment and centrality of *Sense of Transformation* and *Sense of Being* and to articulate the other elements in a more generic way that might enable others to make sense of it specific to their own discipline contexts. This second version is shown in Figure 3.2.

In Figure 3.2 it can be seen that *Sense of Transformation* and *Sense of Being* are now located at the hub of the model and the other elements have been reconceptualised in such a way as to make them applicable to higher education more broadly. *Sense of Being a Designer* becomes *Sense of Being a Professional*; *Sense of Artistry* becomes *Sense of Discipline Knowledge*; and *Sense of Being within a Specific Context* is now *Sense of Engagement*. Listed alongside each of the elements are references to publications indicative of the dimension described, hence, for example, the central hub represents the transformative nature of the relationship the student has with study that affects the 'self' as suggested by Barnett (2007, p. 28):

> Such an invocation of a relational account of the student in her educational setting has merit on its side, but it is also misleading. It sets off the student from her settings …. We do not properly understand the student as separate from her educational settings, even if related to her educational settings. Rather, we understand the student more properly as being *in* her educational settings. The question is: what is the nature of that being?

Here, the idea of relationship is not so much the transactional, rather the ontological nature of being a student or a learner within discipline *x*, *y* or *z*. In other words it is as much, if not more, about the nature of being than it is about knowledge as the outcome of engaging in studies in higher education, or as Dall'Alba & Barnacle put it, 'knowing and being are interdependent' (2007, p. 681), and further that:

> An ontological turn provides a way of addressing a number of shortfalls in current higher education programmes. These include:

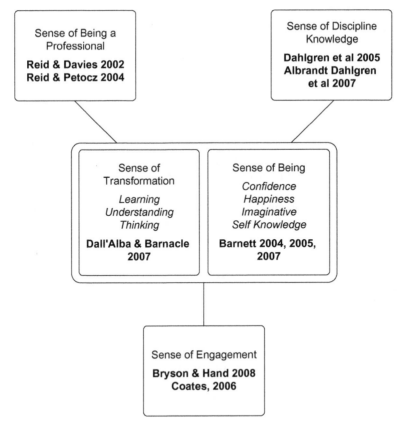

Figure 3.2:   A relational and multidimensional model of student engagement.

decontextualisation of knowledges from the practices to which they relate, emphasis on a narrow conception of knowledge rather than learning, overemphasis on the intellect, and a focus on epistemology at the expense of ontology. [...] epistemology must be in the service of ontology in higher education programmes. The task is incomplete with mere knowledge acquisition. Instead, higher education programmes need to re-orient their focus by assisting students to integrate knowing, acting and being. In so doing, emphasis is placed on learning and its enhancement, not on knowledge in itself. (p. 686)

The model in Figure 3.2 is described as relational and multidimensional. Multidimensional because as has already been argued there are a number of dimensions that students attend to and are more or less in focus within their experience of learning, and relational, in that there is a deep transformative relationship between these dimensions and the student's *Sense of Being* so that *Sense of Being* and *Sense of Transformation* are in a dynamic relationship with the other elements conceptualised more generically than in Figure 3.1 as

- *Sense of Being a Professional* incorporating and representing the ways in which students relate to the broader professional community and as initiates into the various rituals and practices of that community and the discipline (Reid, Dahlgren, Petocz, & Dahlgren, 2011; Reid & Davies, 2002).
- *Sense of Discipline Knowledge*, which is the legitimate activities, skills and knowledge of the discipline itself and described as rational/substantive (having utility within the discipline or transferable between contexts), and ritualistic (the context-free exchange value of knowledge) (Dahlgren, Reid, Dahlgren, & Petocz, 2008; Reid et al., 2011).
- *Sense of Engagement* meaning the freedom that is required for learners to engage creatively with the task in hand and thus to become more aware of the epistemology and ontology of the subject and adopt moral and philosophical stances relative to it (Bryson & Hand, 2008).

3.6. Concluding Comments

As implied by the evolving nature of the model, it is a work in progress and as such does not claim to be a unifying theory of student engagement. Nor could it be, given the variety of applications now subsumed under the student engagement concept, ranging from identity and belonging to the time and effort devoted to study to participation in administration and decision-making. The model was developed from analysis of interviews with students in higher education but does not claim to represent all students in all disciplines and conditions in higher education — it is for the reader to consider if and how it may apply in their own context. What the model does, however, is to gently challenge the predominance (in the United States and Australia at least) of a construct of engagement as a proxy for quality learning, based on behavioural norms and measures at the potential expense of socio-cultural and affective dimensions that may ultimately be more important. The model attempts to broaden the concept of engagement with learning into something more holistic. Through empirical research (c.f. Leach & Zepke, 2011; Solomonides et al., 2012) or critiques of the literature (c.f. Hagel, Carr, & Devlin, 2012; Kahu, 2011) there is a steady emergence of writing that increasingly accommodates the affective dimensions of engagement as lived by the student and attempts to be more sensitive to the intersections between life, learning and work.

Already we are seeing 'engagement' put to work in a number of ways. It has realised political, social, economic and technical ends. When conflated with student experience, it includes hygiene factors that might simply be expected, but the absence of which might contribute to disengagement — such as availability of carparking or access to other facilities, amenities and opportunities for recreation. This is a tension that needs to be resolved, for while it makes conceptual sense to think of engagement or experience in these holistic ways, by doing so we conflate so many contributors to engagement together that the most critical factors may be masked by other, less critical elements. This also runs the risk of the concept being applied to divergent, possible contradictory aims, and the ability or not of institutions to deal with issues such as part-time versus full-time education, online versus on-campus engagement and transactional versus transformative. Focus also quickly turns to policy, whether as a reaction to outcome data, a defined standard to be met or an expected reference point against which to chart progress. This brings a new risk whereby it is possible that 'Student engagement has thus become a quality control indicator and, accordingly, subject to formal quality assurance mechanisms, rather than a subject of meaningful dialogue' (Baron & Corbin, 2012, p. 765). In other words there is a great deal of rhetoric around the concept with both prosaic and exceptional applications to practice:

> So, to recap: student engagement is widely viewed as desirable by government, by universities and by individual academics. Yet students appear to spend less time at university and to be less engaged with their studies, their institutions, teaching staff and fellow students. In response, pressures are being placed by government upon universities, and, in turn, by universities upon organisational units and individual teachers, to raise student engagement. This is unlikely to succeed, however, unless engagement is approached holistically, as the evidence is strong that academic and community engagement run in parallel. [...] We would note a final paradox: while universities are pushing for schools and academics to improve student engagement, many of their practices may have actively contributed to an environment of disengagement. (Baron & Corbin, 2012, p. 767)

This is a curious thing, for the benefits of 'engagement' in its broadest forms are clear. The principles that underpin some of the survey instruments are unquestionable, and yet in attempting to measure them for the sake of improvement we have inadvertently evoked Goodhart's Law.

The Australian experience is such that at the time of writing, and after much promotion, the AUSSE has not been widely adopted for use across the sector. This may be a function of its method of introduction, its voluntary but commercial status, both, or some other yet to be identified reason within the context of Australian higher education. With this in mind it will be most interesting to see how, if at all, elements of the NSSE are imported into the UK context or elsewhere, under whose control, to what ends and with what impact.

References

ACER (2008). *Attracting, engaging and retaining: New conversations about learning.* Melbourne: Australian Council for Educational Research.

Astin, A. W. (1977). *Four critical years. Effects of college on beliefs, attitudes, and knowledge.* San Francisco, CA: Jossey-Bass.

Astin, A. W. (1984). Student involvement: A developmental theory for higher education. *Journal of College Student Personnel, 40*(5), 518−529.

Barnett, R. (2004). Learning for an unknown future. *Higher Education Research & Development, 23*(3), 247−260.

Barnett, R. (2005). Recapturing the universal in the university. *Educational Philosophy and Theory, 37*(6), 785−797.

Barnett, R. (2007). *A will to learn: Being a student in an age of uncertainty.* Maidenhead, UK: Open University Press and Society for Research in Higher Education.

Barnett, R., & Coate, K. (2005). *Engaging the curriculum in higher education.* Maidenhead, UK: Society for Research into Higher Education and Open University Press.

Baron, P., & Corbin, L. (2012). Student engagement: Rhetoric and reality. *Higher Education Research and Development, 31*(6), 759−772. Retrieved from http://dx.doi.org/10.1080/07294360.2012.655711

Bryson, C., & Hand, L. (2008). *Aspects of student engagement — SEDA special 22.* London: Staff and Educational Development Association.

Chickering, A. W., & Gamson, Z. F. (1987). Seven principles for good practice in undergraduate education. *American Association of Higher Education Bulletin, 39*(7), 3−7.

Coates, H. (2006a). The value of student engagement for higher education quality assurance. *Quality in Higher Education, 11*(1), 25−36.

Coates, H. (2006b). *Student engagement in campus-based and online education: University connections.* Abingdon, UK: Routledge.

Coates, H. (2010). Development of the Australasian Survey of Student Engagement (AUSSE). *Higher Education, 60*(1), 1−17.

Creighton, J., Beasley, S., & Jeffreys, P. (2008). *Reading Student Survey 2008.* Reading, UK: University of Reading.

Csíkszentmihályi, M. (1990). *Flow: The psychology of optimal experience.* New York, NY: Harper & Row.

Dahlgren, L. O., Abrandt Dahlgren, M., Hult, H., Hård af Segerstad, H., Johansson, K., Handel, G., … Bayer, M. T. (2005). Students as journeymen between cultures of education and working life . Retrieved from http://www.hewl.net/HPSE_CT-2001-0068__final_ju.pdf

Dahlgren, M. A., Reid, A., Dahlgren, L. O., & Petocz, P. (2008). Learning for the professions: Lessons from linking international research projects. *Higher Education, 56*(2), 129−148.

Dall'Alba, G., & Barnacle, R. (2007). An ontological turn for higher education. *Studies in Higher Education, 32*(6), 679−691.

Debold, E. (2002). Flow with soul: An interview with Dr. Mihaly Csikszentmihalyi. *What is Enlightenment, 21.* Retrieved from http://www.enlightennext.org/magazine/j21/csiksz.asp

Deci, E., & Ryan, R. (2000). The what and why of goal pursuits: Human needs and the self-determination of behavior. *Psychological Inquiry, 11*(4), 227−268.

Gibbs, G. (2010). *Dimensions of quality.* York, UK: Higher Education Academy. Retrieved from http://www.heacademy.ac.uk/assets/York/documents/ourwork/evidence_informed_practice/Dimensions_of_Quality.pdf

Goodhart, C. A. E. (1983). *Monetary theory and practice: The UK experience.* London: Macmillan.

Hagel, P., Carr, R., & Devlin, M. (2012). Conceptualising and measuring student engagement through the Australasian Survey of Student Engagement (AUSSE): A critique. *Assessment & Evaluation in Higher Education, 37*(4), 475−486.

Harris, R., Bolander, K., Lebrun, M., Docq, F., & Bouvy, M. T. (2004). *Linking perceptions of control and signs of engagement in the process and content of collaborative e-learning.*

Paper presented at the Network Learning Conference. Lancaster, UK, April 2004. Retrieved from http://www.networkedlearningconference.org.uk/past/nlc2004/proceedings/symposia/symposium10/harris_et_al.htm

HEA. (2010). *Framework for action: Enhancing student engagement at the institutional level.* York, UK: The Higher Education Academy. Retrieved from http://www.heacademy.ac.uk/assets/York/documents/ourwork/studentengagement/Frameworkforaction_institutional.pdf

HEA. (2013). *Higher Education Academy call to tender: Cognitive review of student engagement survey items.* York, UK: The Higher Education Academy. Retrieved from http://www.heacademy.ac.uk/assets/documents/postgraduate/Cognitive_Review_of_Student_Engagement_Survey_Items.docx

Hoskin, K. (1996). The 'awful idea of accountability': Inscribing people into the measurement of objects. In R. Munro & J. Mouritsen (Eds.), *Accountability: Power, ethos and the technologies of managing* (pp. 265−282). London: International Thomson Business Press.

Kahu, E. R. (2011). Framing student engagement in higher education. *Studies in Higher Education.* 1−16. iFirst Article. Retrieved from http://dx.doi.org/10.1080/03075079.2011.598505

Krause, K.-L., & Coates, H. (2008). Students' engagement in first year university. *Assessment and Evaluation in Higher Education, 33*(5), 49−505.

Leach, L., & Zepke, N. (2011). Engaging students in learning: A review of a conceptual organiser. *Higher Education Research & Development, 30*(2), 193−204. Retrieved from http://dx.doi.org/10.1080/07294360.2010.5097

Mann, S. J. (2001). Alternative perspectives on the student experience: Alienation and engagement. *Studies in Higher Education, 26*(1), 7−19.

Marton, F. (1981). Phenomenography — describing conceptions of the world around us. *Instructional Science, 10*(1981), 177−200.

Marton, F. (1986). Phenomenography: A research approach to investigating different understandings of reality. *Journal of Thought, 21*(3), 28−49.

Meyer, J. H. F., & Land, R. (2005). Threshold concepts and troublesome knowledge (2): Epistemological considerations and a conceptual framework for teaching and learning. *Higher Education, 49*(3), 373−388.

NUS. (2012) *A manifesto for partnership.* London, UK: National Union of Students. Retrieved from http://www.nusconnect.org.uk/resourcehandler/0a02e2e5-197e-4bd3-b7ed-e8ceff3dc0e4/

Pace, C. R. (1979). *Measuring outcomes of college: Fifty years of findings and recommendations for the future.* San Francisco, CA: Jossey-Bass.

Pace, C. R. (1982). *Achievement and the quality of student effort: Report to the Department of Education.* Washington, DC: Department of Education.

Pascarella, E. T., & Terenzini, P. T. (1991). *How college affects students: Findings and insights from twenty years of research.* San Francisco, CA: Jossey-Bass.

Pascarella, E. T., & Terenzini, P. T. (2005). *How college affects students, Vol. 2: A third decade of research.* San Francisco, CA: Jossey-Bass.

Ramsden, P. (1991). A performance indicator of teaching quality in higher education: The course experience questionnaire. *Studies in Higher Education, 16*(2), 129−150.

Reid, A., Abrandt Dahlgren, M., Petocz, P., & Dahlgren, L. O. (2011). *From expert student to novice professional.* Dordrecht, NL: Springer.

Reid, A., & Davies, A. (2002). Teachers' and students conceptions of the professional world. In C. Rust (Ed.), *Improving student learning theory and practice — 10 years on.* Oxford: The Oxford Centre for Staff and Learning Development.

Reid, A., & Petocz, P. (2004). The professional entity: Researching the relationship between students' conceptions of learning and their future profession. In C. Rust (Ed.), *Improving student learning: Theory, research and scholarship* (pp. 145–157). Oxford: The Oxford Centre for Staff and Learning Development.

Reid, A., & Solomonides, I. (2007). Design students' experience of engagement and creativity. *Art Design and Communication in Higher Education, 6*(1), 25–39.

Ross, H., & Cen, Y. H. (2012). Reinterpreting quality through assessing student engagement in China. In I. Solomonides, A. Reid, & P. Petocz (Eds.), *Engaging with learning in higher education* (pp. 383–412). Faringdon, UK: Libri.

Säljö, R. (1996). Minding action — conceiving of the world versus participating in cultural practices. In G. Dall'Alba & B. Hasselgren (Eds.), *Reflections on phenomenography — towards a methodology?* Goteborg, Sweden: Acta Universtatis Gothoburgensis.

Scott, I. (2011). *Student engagement final report: Survey of student activity and engagement.* York, UK: The Higher Education Academy.

Solomonides, I., & Martin, P. (2008). All this talk of engagement is making me itch. In C. Bryson & L. Hand (Eds.), *Aspects of student engagement — SEDA special 22* (pp. 13–19). London: Staff and Educational Development Association.

Solomonides, I., & Reid, A. (2009). Understanding the relationships between student identity and engagement with studies. *The Student Experience, Proceedings of the 32nd HERDSA Annual Conference.* Darwin, Australia, 6–9 July 2009 (pp. 388–397). Retrieved from www.herdsa.org.au/wp-content/.../HERDSA2009_Solomonides_I.pdf

Solomonides, I., Reid, A., & Petocz, P. (2012). *Engaging with learning in higher education.* Faringdon, UK: Libri.

Strathern, M. (1997). 'Improving ratings': Audit in the British University system. *European Review, 5*(3), 305–321.

Strydom, J. F., Kuh, G. D., & Mentz, M. (2010). Enhancing success in South Africa's higher education: Measuring student engagement. *Acta Academica, 42*(1), 259–278. Retrieved from http://www.sabinet.co.za/abstracts/academ/academ_v42_n1_a10.html

Taylor, P., Koskela, J., & Lee, G. (2011). *Student engagement final report: Shaping history.* York, UK: The Higher Education Academy.

Tinto, V. (1987). *The principles of effective retention.* Paper presented at the Maryland College Personnel Association Fall Conference, Prince George's Community College. Largo, MD. Retrieved from http://fyesit.metapress.com/content/k1r37016u2864123/fulltext.pdf

University of Lincoln. (2012). *Student engagement strategy 2012–16.* Retrieved from http://studentengagement.blogs.lincoln.ac.uk/files/2012/09/Student-Engagement-Strategy-For-Consultation.pdf

van der Velden, G. (2012). Student engagement: Whose education is it anyway? *Talking about quality, 3.* Quality Assurance Agency for Higher Education, Gloucester, UK. Retrieved from http://www.qaa.ac.uk/Publications/InformationAndGuidance/Pages/student-engagement.aspx

Voerman, A. & Solomonides, I. (2012). Discourse and dialogue in student engagement. In I. Solomonides, A. Reid & P. Petocz (Eds.), *Engaging with learning in higher education* (pp. 414–439). Faringdon, UK: Libri.

Chapter 4

What Does Student Engagement Mean to Students?

Alex Ratcliffe and Andrew Dimmock

Abstract

This chapter will explore what 'student engagement' means for students at the University of Exeter. The objectives and priorities of Exeter's own 'Student Engagement Strategy' define the term as predominantly relating to student initiatives and activities that occur outside the curriculum. This is in contrast to how many other higher education institutions approach and define the term. Exeter's definition and approach to 'student engagement' are discussed alongside students' definitions of the term. Both authors draw on their own experience as 'engaged students' in order to pursue a key question: what activities comprise 'student engagement' at Exeter? We discuss how committee organisations and local culture shape the appearance and nature of 'student engagement' at this University and ask what truly motivates a student to participate and volunteer within their university when it is not a compulsory requirement in order to complete their course? We argue that student motivation to engage rests on a combination of cultural expectation, temptation, self-interest and altruism.

4.1. Introduction

There is no clear or uniform definition of the term 'student engagement'. It is an umbrella term that covers a vast range of areas and activities that seek to actively include and integrate students within a university community. This chapter aims to explore what the term 'student engagement' means to students at the University of Exeter in the United Kingdom. The national Quality Assurance Agency recognises Exeter's approach to and association with the term. Exeter's own particular institutional definition of the term is explored through the objectives and priorities set in its own 'Student Engagement Strategy'. These objectives and priorities indicate that

The Student Engagement Handbook: Practice in Higher Education
Copyright © 2013 by Emerald Group Publishing Limited
All rights of reproduction in any form reserved
ISBN: 978-1-78190-423-7

Exeter takes a different approach to the term than the trend that Dr Chris Garrett (2011) summarises and represents in the United States. Garrett defines 'student engagement' as a phenomenon confined to the curriculum. Exeter's own institutional definition is discussed in relation to how students at Exeter actually define the term themselves. The divergence and commonalities between the samples of primary student definitions are identified and explored. As a closer examination into how students truly perceive the term both authors explain what motivated them as students to actively participate and engage with their university.

4.2.   The University of Exeter

The University of Exeter is a medium-sized research-intensive university that teaches and supports some 18,000 students in the South West of the United Kingdom. Exeter is part of the Russell Group for high-performing UK universities and has consistently been ranked highly in national league tables for student satisfaction (University of Exeter, 2012a). Exeter offers a wide range of undergraduate and postgraduate degree programmes in the Sciences, Social Sciences, Arts and Humanities.

'Student engagement' is a term that is externally associated with Exeter. The Quality Assurance Agency is an external body that audits and reviews the quality and standard of teaching and provision for students across the UK higher education sector (Quality Assurance Agency, 2012a). The QAA defines student engagement as being 'all about involving and empowering students in the process of shaping the student learning experience' (Quality Assurance Agency, 2012f). The published 'QAA Institutional Review of the University of Exeter' in April 2012 notes that one of Exeter's fundamental areas of good practice lies in its ability to engage students innovatively and on so many levels:

> The review team saw evidence of student engagement in sector-leading projects such as Students as Change Agents and in a wide range of College and university-level committees and processes. (Quality Assurance Agency, 2012b, p. 15)

The published QAA Institutional Review mentions the term 10 times in relation to Exeter (far more than other contemporaneous QAA university reviews).[1] The term is overwhelmingly used in relation to the provision and support that allows students to express their voice and contribute input into the running, organisation and governance of the University (QAA, 2012b, pp. 8, 9, 10, 15). The QAA deploys

---

[1]In the QAA Institutional Reviews for the University of Buckingham (Quality Assurance Agency, 2012c), the University of Wales: Trinity St David (Quality Assurance Agency, 2012d) and the University of Leeds (Quality Assurance Agency, 2012e), the term is not once deployed in the published review reports.

the term in relation to how Exeter approaches its own governance, quality assurance processes and decision making (QAA, 2012b).

4.3. The Approach at Exeter

Exeter's own definition and approach to 'student engagement' plays a crucial role in shaping and setting the expectations of its own students. Before we can explore what 'student engagement' means to students we need to establish the wider context and use of the term within higher education and then compare that to how the term is understood and used at Exeter. A student's perception and understanding of what 'student engagement' means is strongly shaped by the policies and structures that they find themselves living and acting within. This section explores some of the core policies and committees that serve to embed 'student engagement' within the culture and every day running of the University. Exeter's own 'Student Engagement Strategy' is an internal document that provides the most direct and holistic consideration of the term and its associated activities and groups.

Similarly to the QAA (above) the UK Higher Education Academy (HEA) supplies a similar definition of the term and emphasises the role of students as 'active partners in shaping their learning experience' (Higher Education Academy, 2013). The Higher Education Academy is a national organisation that aims to support excellence in learning and teaching at UK universities through sharing knowledge and good practice. Both the QAA and HEA provide far ranging definitions that allow the term to be used to describe student involvement and empowerment across a whole university: both within and outside the curriculum.

Writing in the US context, Garrett approaches 'student engagement' as a term that describes a quality of learning. Garrett's (2011) paper 'Defining, Detecting, and, Promoting Student Engagement in College Learning Environments' assembles and summarises various definitions of the term 'student engagement' from colleagues and scholars from around the world. Garrett and his own academic colleagues at Oklahoma City University define the term through exploring the actions and processes that allow teaching staff and students to enthusiastically and innovatively interact with each other and with their ideas (Garrett, 2011, p. 3).

> Students are engaged when they show one or more of the following behaviours or actions: involvement in class discussions, participating in learning activities, asking questions, responding to other comments, marking in their texts, debating, bringing questions and problems to class that were discovered by reading out-of-class, writing response papers, emailing or posting discussion thread questions and comments to the instructor or others, blogging, re/searching independently, making connections with other texts and writers, and probing deeply into a text or a research problem. (Garrett, 2011, p. 6)

Garret's definition of the term is more focused and specific than that given by the QAA and HEA. Garrett discusses 'student engagement' as a phenomenon that occurs within the academic sphere: either within the classroom or around the ideas and arguments that are approached within a taught course. Garrett makes no reference to 'student engagement' as a term that encompasses activities in either the wider university community (outside the academic course and its content) or the running of the administration and governance of a university. However, at Exeter 'student engagement' is explicitly linked to activities and initiatives that do not directly relate to the content and ideas expounded within a student's programme of study. The difference between Garrett's approach and Exeter's approach to the term can largely be explained by the fact that Exeter's 'Student Engagement Strategy' was written by administrative and professional services staff from the Student's Guild and Academic Services division within the University. As a result the term at Exeter tends to reflect the activities and projects that are more familiar to non-academic staff.

Exeter approaches 'student engagement' as a method through which it can develop and improve the experience that a student has during their time at University. The Exeter 'Student Engagement Strategy' was written and circulated in time for the first cohort of students paying the increased university tuition fee of £9,000 per annum. The improved student experience that increased 'student engagement' aims to deliver is a saleable feature for Exeter in an increasingly competitive market place. Outside Exeter, both Birmingham City University (BCU) and Lincoln University (LU) run student inclusive initiatives that actively aim to involve and empower students. The Student Academic Partners scheme at BCU employs students to work as 'equals' alongside staff on defined projects that aim to improve the student experience (Birmingham City University, 2010, p. 3). The Student as Producer scheme at LU supports students to carry out and produce their own research alongside the taught curriculum (Lincoln University, 2010). Both these initiatives explicitly aim to involve and empower the learning experience of students. However, neither university use the term 'student engagement' to brand or categorise these schemes. The principles of 'student engagement' as defined by the QAA and HEA can be found in activities and initiatives that are not labelled under the term. Exeter has latched onto the term 'student engagement' and actively uses it more than many other UK universities.

It is important to note that Exeter's strategy identifies that 'student engagement' is closely linked to student 'satisfaction' (University of Exeter & Students' Guild at the University of Exeter, 2011, p. 6). The 'Student Engagement Strategy' approaches 'student engagement' as the means by which Exeter can maintain and improve the quality of its student experience. The prominence of student satisfaction, increased employability and the central involvement of the Students' Guild within the strategy closely link Exeter's approach to recommendations made in the 1994 Group's 2007 Policy Report 'Enhancing the Student Experience' (1994 Group, 2007). The 1994 Group is a collection of medium-sized research-intensive teaching universities within the United Kingdom that share similar goals and good practice

(1994 Group, 2013). Until August 2012 Exeter was a member of that university block. The report identifies four key areas that allow small-to-medium sized research-intensive universities to enhance the experience of their students: promoting and maintaining a shared community ethos; producing exceptionally employable graduates; making students partners in learning; and joining up the student journey from pre-arrival to graduation (1994 Group, 2007, p. 27−39). Nowhere within the report is the term 'student engagement' directly deployed or discussed. However, when we compare it with the priorities and focus of Exeter's 'Student Engagement Strategy' it becomes apparent that Exeter seeks to achieve success in improving the 'student experience' via increased 'student engagement'. The committees and initiatives included in the 'Student Engagement Strategy' seek to break down barriers and include students within the wider university community via input into decision making, leading committees, arranging events and activities, and through employment on campus.

The 'Student Engagement Strategy' is an internal document which states that Exeter aims to increase levels of student involvement across the board and to market the University as a sector leading provider of enticing and stretching extra-curricular activities for its students (University of Exeter & Students' Guild at the University of Exeter, 2011, p. 1). It sets out a mission to remove barriers to engagement; increase incentives and rewards for students who engage outside the classroom; expand the 'Change Agents' scheme (see below); increase and support student engagement at discipline level; and develop 'student engagement' as a brand that positively defines and sells the Exeter student experience (University of Exeter & Students' Guild at the University of Exeter, 2011, p. 3−11).

The strategy initially defines student engagement through a model of categorisation that maps out five different 'categories' of engagement (local terminology is defined below):

1. Bystanders: "students who attend University but do not engage with the wider or academic community."
2. Participants: "students who participate in Guild Societies, [Athletic Union] Clubs, volunteering, providing feedback etc."
3. Organisers: "students who sit on organising committees of Guild Societies and Clubs, support events, are employed by the University."
4. Leaders: "students in leadership positions in Guild Societies, [Athletic Union] Clubs, [Student Staff Liaison Committees] etc."
5. Change Agents: "students actively leading change, Guild elected officers, external political engagement." (University of Exeter & Students' Guild at the University of Exeter, 2011, p. 1)

Category one identifies the least 'engaged' group of students and category five identifies the most 'engaged' group of students. The strategy goes on to state: 'we do not expect all students to engage at the higher levels in this model, however we aim for 100% of students to be active participants in University life and to be encouraged and supported to progress to higher levels of engagement' (University of Exeter & Students' Guild at the University of Exeter, 2011, p. 2).

If we unpack the above categories of 'engagement' four key points emerge:

1. 'Attending' university is the lowest level of 'engagement'. The strategy aims to encourage all students to be at least 'participants'. Therefore according to this strategy 'bystander' is not a desirable type of student for Exeter. The key differentiator between 'bystander' and 'participant' above is that as a 'participant' a student is willing to voice their opinion and take part in extra-curricular activities. Although feedback is explicitly mentioned as an example of participation, it is not necessarily linked to the curriculum. This strategy does not directly address participation within the classroom or with the academic work within a programme. This focus sends a message to both staff and students about the type of activities that are categorised under the term 'student engagement' (versus Garrett, 2011 above).

2. 'Student engagement' at Exeter is ostensibly linked to four core organisations within the University: Students' Guild elected sabbatical officers[2]; student societies[3]; Student–Staff Liaison Committees[4]; and the Athletic Union.[5] All of these groups (bar the Athletic Union) are organisations and committees that sit solely or partially within the Students' Guild.

    The Students' Guild co-wrote Exeter's 'Student Engagement Strategy', which helps us to understand why so many of the initiatives and activities classed as 'student engagement' are often non-academic. The Students' Guild does not

---

[2]The Students' Guild is the student union organisation attached to the University of Exeter. It is a registered charity that possesses its own permanent staff, mission statement and commercial enterprises. The Students' Guild mission states: 'we exist for students at Exeter. We offer support, advice, representation, entertainment and other activities that will enhance your student experience here' (Students' Guild at the University of Exeter, 2012a).
[3]There are over 150 student societies within the Students' Guild. These societies support the promotion and facilitation of activities ranging from the Arts through to Internationalisation. In 2011–2012 these societies possessed over 8000 registered student members from Exeter (Students' Guild at the University of Exeter, 2012b). Each society is run by a committee of democratically elected student representatives. They are primarily funded and supported by the Students' Guild. Students have to register and pay to be members of these societies.
[4]Student–Staff Liaison Committees (SSLCs) are committee groups that aim to 'facilitate greater communication between students and staff' and encourage 'student contribution at all levels of decision-making concerning unreserved business' within the University (University of Exeter, 2012b, p. 1). The SSLC is a forum where students can raise issues, questions and concerns to members of staff.
[5]The Athletic Union (AU) is a University organisation that "is responsible for student sport clubs … competitive fixtures, recreational pursuits and local, regional, national and international competition" (University of Exeter, 2012c). The AU possesses a democratically elected student president who works alongside University staff and student committee members to manage athletic and sport provision for Exeter staff, students and external customers.

teach or carry out research in the academic fields that the University covers through its degree programmes. The Student—Staff Liaison Committees (SSLCs) do deal with academic issues, but these are more likely to be with the speed and quality of feedback on returned assessments and the books available in the library rather than a debate or engagement with academic ideas and arguments. The student academic societies are more likely to arrange social events and trips abroad than to engage directly with the teaching offered on a particular course. The Students' Guild plays an important role in supporting and embedding the vast array of extra and co-curricular engagement that occurs at Exeter. Hence 'student engagement' at Exeter is defined and shaped by the multitude of student committees which arrange and lead the campaigns, events and social activities that occurs within the wider university community.

3. The highest categories of 'engagement' in the 'Student Engagement Strategy' identify students who lead others. The culmination of the model is a 'Change Agent'. A 'Change Agent' is briefly defined as a student who leads change within the university; works as an elected sabbatical officer for the Students' Guild; or work as someone who engages with external political movements (University of Exeter & Students' Guild at the University of Exeter, 2011, p. 1). 'Change Agents' is an extra-curricular programme that Exeter launched in 2008. The initiative offers students support and guidance in identifying and researching project areas for future improvement in the running and everyday life of the University (Dunne & Zandstra, 2011, p. 2). The scheme provides a defined avenue for engaging students and allowing them to lead and help to deliver change and improvement in their wider university community.

It could be argued that the model's approach to 'student engagement' is in essence elitist. The strategy states that 'we do not expect all students to engage at the higher levels in this model' (University of Exeter & Students' Guild at the University of Exeter, 2011, p. 2). The model is visually presented as a flow diagram that starts with 'bystanders' and culminates with 'Change Agents'. The model reflects that the activities associated with student engagement serve to provide an opportunity for a core and small group of student leaders to be trained and supported. The first two categories of 'engagement' cater for a large number of students, but the final three categories reflect the provision that is made for a small and defined group of students to become 'super-engaged'. For example, many 'Change Agents' already sit on society committees and hold leadership roles within the Students' Guild.

4. The employment of students by the University is classed as a form of 'student engagement'. The strategy states that 'research shows that extensive student employment on campus improves student retention, satisfaction and achievement as well as supporting integration into the academic community' (University of Exeter & Students' Guild at the University of Exeter, 2011, p. 6). This marks another divergence between Garrett's approach to the term and Exeter's approach. Garrett does not include student employment within his definition of 'student engagement' (Garrett, 2011, p. 6). There are very few employment opportunities for undergraduate students to become involved in teaching or

academic research. However, the Learning and Teaching in Higher Education Programme does allow postgraduate students the opportunity to teach and lead courses of undergraduate students (University of Exeter, 2013a). Undergraduate students are more often likely to be employed on campus in retail, hospitality or customer services roles.

The Student Campus Partnership scheme is an intern scheme that promotes and facilitates both disciplines and departments within the University to employ current students in part-time roles. The staff who run the scheme promote that an 'intern will bring an injection of enthusiasm; provide existing team members with the chance to be involved with training and supervision; and help staff to better understand the student audience' (University of Exeter, 2013b). There are staff at Exeter who recognise that the University can greatly benefit from incorporating its students into its departments and teams. 'Student engagement' via student employment offers many individual university departments the opportunity to inject new ideas into their teams as well as help them to better understand their primary customer base.

To summarise, the categories of 'engagement' within Exeter's 'Student Engagement Strategy' emphasise how Exeter predominantly uses the term 'student engagement' to denote student participation in extra-curricular activities. Many of these activities are facilitated and managed by the Students' Guild. Elected and selected committees of motivated students play a central role in shaping what 'student engagement' looks like at Exeter and how it is channelled and structured. Exeter views 'student engagement' as an avenue through which a finite and select group of individuals are given an opportunity to lead others and lead change within the University. In addition, 'student engagement' provides students with important management and organisational skills.

4.4. Student Definitions

Having reviewed how the institution approaches the term 'student engagement', we were interested to consider how students address and define the term at Exeter. Current student perceptions of the term are addressed alongside how students are likely to perceive it in the future due to changes instigated by Exeter's 'Student Engagement Strategy'.

Despite 'student engagement' being an important area of concern for Exeter strategy, the term itself is not widely used, or immediately recognised, by the majority of students studying at Exeter. The term carries far more meaning with administrative university staff than it does with students (or indeed with many academic teaching staff). In the light of this, interviews were carried out to ascertain what students understood the term to mean. A range of undergraduate and taught postgraduate students from all years and across a range of disciplines were asked the following question: what do you understand the term 'student engagement' to mean? There was no single uniform or trending definition. The following samples reflect the breadth of response:

A. Claire (fourth year undergraduate History and Spanish student):

> 'Student engagement' to me can be considered on two levels. Firstly, on a more 'local' level: I think of it as students engaging with each other, co-operating and working together, entering into discussion and using each other as resources to better their understanding and knowledge of their subjects. On a second, 'wider' level: I believe student engagement refers to students questioning and challenging the University, addressing a range of issues from how modules are taught, to how departments are run, to the options available in the food outlets, and so on. Student engagement is the interaction between students and the University whereby students voice their concerns and opinions: be they positive or negative. Only through comprehensive student engagement do I believe students can get the most of their education and the best 'service' from the University. Equally, only through student engagement do I believe the University can benefit from the wealth of ideas staff and students alike have for the constant development and progression of the University.

Claire places great emphasis on the student voice being able to contribute to the running and improvement of the University. At the time of the response Claire was an elected representative for the Students' Guild who was committed to report and champion her peers' views and issues back to the Student's Guild and the University. Claire could quite easily fit into categories 2, 3, 4 and 5 of Exeter's 'Student Engagement Strategy' model (University of Exeter & Students' Guild at the University of Exeter, 2011, p. 1). Claire fits the model very well as an example of an 'engaged' student within the wider university community.

B. Helen (fourth year Classics with Study Abroad student):

> I think 'student engagement' refers to the University's initiative to increase students' awareness of opportunities within the Colleges and in the University, such as years abroad, post-graduate study, graduate schemes and employability. It aims to create better communication between staff and students, as students are often unaware of the extra opportunities offered by the University.

Similarly to Claire, Helen defines the term in relation to her own status within Exeter. In particular, Helen places an emphasis on studying abroad for a year as part of a degree. Helen understands 'student engagement' to denote an increased student involvement with the potential opportunities that studying at Exeter can offer. Helen had extended her original 3-year degree programme to include a year studying abroad. Helen views her own decision to embark on this opportunity as an example of what it means in practice to be an 'engaged' student.

C. Chris (second year Ancient History student):

> I feel that in order to really be engaged you have to have real drive to go above and beyond the call of a normal student. To me student engagement is not just attending lectures and doing the work set: it is an active participation in activities that do not count to your degree.

Chris' response supports Helen's interpretation in that strong emphasis is placed on a student carrying out an activity that is not immediately compulsory for the certified completion of his or her degree programme. Chris asserts that 'student engagement' raises a student from being just a 'normal student'. Chris touches on the idea that by being 'engaged' you can differentiate yourself from the crowd. This understanding of the term is discussed further below.

D. Andrew (postgraduate taught Politics student):

> I consider 'student engagement' to be both academic and voluntary. I think some students fail to 'engage' with the degree, do the bare minimum and often get away with it.

E. Alex (third year Mathematics student):

> the idea of students captivated by involvement.

Both Andrew and Alex touch on a strong theme that runs throughout 'student engagement' at Exeter. There is a strong cultural expectation that students will be involved in extra-curricular and non-compulsory activities alongside their degree programme. Andrew makes a sharp comment that 'some students fail to "engage" with the degree, do the bare minimum and often get away with it'. There is an assumed expectation here that students should be doing more than the 'bare minimum' of requirement to complete their degree programme. Student societies, sports teams and committees are heavily promoted by both the Students' Guild and the University in the first few weeks of each new academic year. New students find themselves surrounded by assertions and enticements that engaging with a certain activity will secure them friends and improve their time at Exeter. Alex captures a more positive definition that students at Exeter are 'captivated' by being 'involved'. 'Involvement' can be interpreted as both engaging with the degree course *and* with extra-curricular activities.

F. Charlotte (third year undergraduate Theology student):

> when a boy studying at university proposes to a girl who is also studying at university.

Charlotte offers a response that is both flippant and understandable. The phrase 'student engagement' is principally a piece of institutional jargon. For the vast majority of students the phrase does not immediately conjure up an obvious and accepted definition. It is only when individual students start to reflect on it at greater length that they start to deploy examples of activities and instances that they have been involved in themselves and believe fit the term.

These definitions reflect the breadth of interpretation and lack of precise consensus in what the term means when approached out of context. The overriding commonality between all these definitions is that on the whole the student defines the term in relation to their own status and position within the University.

However, 'student engagement' is a term that appears to be gaining increased currency with students at Exeter. As part of the 'Student Engagement Strategy' Exeter has increased the amount of staff whose core remit is to explicitly promote and facilitate activities and initiatives branded as 'student engagement'. In 2011 Exeter appointed a central and full-time Student Engagement and Participation Development Manager. One of this position's core roles was to oversee the creation and implementation of the above discussed cross-institutional and co-authored Students' Guild and University 'Student Engagement Strategy'. A key element of the strategy seeks to explicitly and locally embed student engagement within each of Exeter's academic colleges (University of Exeter & Students' Guild at the University of Exeter, 2011, p. 2).

In the summer of 2012 three of Exeter's five academic colleges appointed recent graduates as Student Engagement Officers. Two of the fundamental areas that these officers support are SSLCs and the 'Change Agents' initiative. On a structural level 'student engagement' is a term that students at Exeter are starting to see as a member of staff's core remit and workload. There are two immediate consequences to this. First, employing members of staff who explicitly work on and support 'student engagement' suggests to the student that it is an area of weight and worth. Second, by possessing active and visible 'Student Engagement Officers', students are invited to question and learn what the tagline 'student engagement' means. The increased presence of individuals who work directly with students and employ the term 'student engagement' on a day-to-day basis within the academic colleges will expose an increased number of students to the term and its associated activities.

There has at times been a lack of consensus between staff over the remit that the term covers. This new 'student engagement' staffing model holds the potential for an increase in the sharing of good practice and the coordination of joint initiatives across colleges. If there are commonalities and increased consistency in remit and activities under this brand, then the institution as a whole can more effectively market and sell the term to staff, students and external stakeholders. If there are too many variances and divergent interpretations, then it becomes confusing for not only the staff involved but also the primary target audience: students.

To conclude, 'student engagement' is not a term that is widely used or debated by students at Exeter. If students are asked to consider the term then their primary instinct is to relate the term to their own status and level of involvement within the University. Students primarily identify the term to mean participation in extra-curricular activities and opportunities that reside outside the compulsory requirements of a degree programme. However, because each student is different and they 'engage' with Exeter on so many different levels, the 'student' definition of the term is colourful, divergent and varied. The introduction of 'Student Engagement Officers' within the academic colleges is likely to promote 'student engagement' as a particular term in its own right in the future. The notable discrepancy between Exeter's own definition of the term and the students' definition lies in the inclusion of paid employment within the classed categories of 'student engagement'. Generally speaking students would not automatically class paid employment as an example of 'student engagement'. None of the student responses to define the term mentioned paid employment on campus as a form of 'student engagement'. This phenomenon is most likely a consequence of the well-established culture for student volunteering at Exeter. Very few of the committees and societies that sit within the Students' Guild are paid positions. It is an established institutional and peer expectation that students do not require payment as an incentive to organise and take part in activities that can be social and rewarding in their own right.

4.5. Student Motivations

In this section we both draw on our own personal experiences as 'engaged students' to discuss what motivates students at Exeter to become 'engaged'. Outlined and explored below are three key motivators: establishing a 'unique' identity; group and peer expectation; and the desire to gain new skills and experiences. Financial motivation is also examined as a fourth contributing (but very rarely driving) factor that colours and shapes what 'student engagement' means to students at Exeter.

Both authors were involved in a wide range of activities associated with the University community during their 4 years of study at Exeter. Through listening to our peers' concerns and voicing those concerns to the Students' Guild and the University we both actively engaged with academic representation. Academic representation allowed both of us to hold leadership roles in chairing committees of student representatives. Outside the academic sphere, we were both Community Wardens for the University. As Community Wardens we were employed to offer advice and support to students who lived in private accommodation off campus. The role required us to actively engage with the wider city and to help organise events that would bring student and local non-student residents together. As a Student Ambassador, Andrew visited secondary schools to promote and inform children about the benefits and opportunities to study at university.

Both of us were involved in the above activities predominantly during the final two years of our study. Neither of us particularly engaged with sports clubs and our bias of interest was focused on academic representation. None of these activities were a compulsory requirement to be carried out in order to complete our respective degree programmes. So why did we both raise our hands to so many optional extra-curricular activities?

1. *Group identity*

   'Student engagement' involves the membership of a defined community. There are around 18,000 students studying at Exeter each academic year (University of Exeter, 2013c). As students we found ourselves surrounded by a daunting and vast number of peers. 'Student engagement' was one way that we could seek to define and establish ourselves within that large mass. One of the most powerful motivators that urged us to join one society or group over another was the desire to both fit in and stand out. To take an example, neither Andrew nor I were inclined to join the rugby team; we are both slight and not particularly athletic. The rugby team would not have been the right group or type of activity for us to successfully slot in. Both authors lacked the inclination or prior sporting experience to feel that they would be able to fit in. Whether those assumptions were correct or not they undoubtedly played a strong part in defining the area of the University that we chose to engage with. By choosing the activities and groups that we did we made a conscious decision to align ourselves with a particular group of students and associates. Through the membership of certain groups and committees we were differentiating ourselves not so much from 'non-engaged students', but rather from students who 'engaged' *differently*.

2. *Expectation*

   There is a certain level of expectation at Exeter that during your time of study you will be involved on some level with a voluntary or non-curricular activity. The sheer volume and loud presence of activities and opportunities made it hard for us not to engage. Family and friends convinced us that we really should take part in order to make the most of our time at university. Once we started engaging with particular activities it became harder to say 'no' to taking on further responsibilities. Both authors started as academic representatives and then went on to chair committees of academic representatives. Making friends with both staff and students made it easier and more appealing to say 'yes' to taking on roles with increased responsibility and workload. Neither author was forced to become involved with academic representation, but once we had taken on the commitment it became harder to step away and reduce our involvement without good reason. The opportunities and activities that we engaged with initially required small demands that increased and provided further possibilities for deeper involvement over time.

3. *Self-interest*

   Both authors made a value judgement that taking part in all of these activities would *probably* serve to benefit us in the future. Chairing SSLCs allowed both of us to meet new people and contribute something back to our university community. Exeter is structured into academic colleges, which contain individual disciplines. Student representatives from each programme within a college sit on an SSLC that allows them to raise issues and provide feedback to university staff. The committees possess at least one senior academic member of staff and a member of administrative staff. Both authors were voted by their peers to set the agenda and chair the meetings of the SSLC.

Why did we put ourselves forward to be chairs? Both authors had been junior representatives on SSLCs. It felt like a natural progression to continue and expand our role within a department that we felt close to and valued being a part of. Alex states: 'Personally, I was seriously considering studying a PhD after my MA and I had identified the SSLC as an avenue through which I could network with members of staff and learn more about an area in which I could potentially be working in in the future. I saw this as an opportunity to learn more about higher education and to accrue a set of skills that I would not directly develop within my academic degree programme. Being able to voice student issues and concerns back to my discipline's department was a result of my acceptance of the position, but in brutal honesty that had not been the initial driver behind my decision. Taking up the position of an SSLC chair was an action that I believed would enable me to get the most out of my time at Exeter and prepare me for a life after graduation'.

4. *Financial incentive*
Exeter's 'Student Engagement Strategy' clearly states that paid employment with the University constitutes a form of 'student engagement' (University of Exeter & Students' Guild at the University of Exeter, 2011, p. 7). As a Student Ambassador for the University, Andrew travelled to local schools to deliver widening participation sessions. Andrew would explain the opportunities and benefits that Exeter could offer applicants from specific backgrounds. The role paid around £7.00 per hour. Although Andrew was being paid to perform this role he was still making a valuable contribution back to the institution. Increasing the number of students from varied and less privileged backgrounds is viewed as a worthy and moral activity to engage in. Andrew was also able to use his position as a current student to deliver sessions and talks based around his own experiences. As a 'Student' Ambassador Andrew was able to give a more direct, honest and convincing portrayal of university life to his younger target audience.

The pay was not the primary motivation for Andrew. When delivering outreach sessions in local schools, ambassadors were usually expected to schedule a visiting time; adapt the material provided to the time available and progress of the group; travel to and from the school; and complete a feedback form for Exeter. Andrew did not do all of that for the hour and a half's worth of pay that he received per visit. Payment was a valued result, but the satisfaction of talking to younger children and advertising the wealth of opportunities available to them was far more motivational.

'Student engagement' is closely defined by the factors that motivate students to take part in initiatives and activities within the wider University community. University is both daunting and overpopulated by a mass of initially similar individuals. 'Student engagement' allows a student to access a group identity and group culture that comforts them and serves to define them within that larger group. The expectation and assumption that students will want to interact and engage with certain activities and opportunities serves to tempt and convince students that they are making the most of their time at Exeter. The more you volunteer and commit the harder it becomes to say 'no'. 'Student engagement' is a social activity that makes connections, colleagues and friends. Chairing committees, arranging events and leading on projects are all valuable skills that students feel they need in order to succeed later in life. Financial motivation does contribute to the definition and scope of 'student engagement', but in the majority of cases it rarely drives or causes it.

Both authors agree that we found it hard to justify why we *shouldn't* be involved outside our degree programme. We each studied a humanities and social sciences degree; on average our contact hours per week were far lower than students who studied science, technological, economic or mathematics based degrees. The considerable amount of free time, and free choice of what to do with that time, provided us with an opportunity to satisfy the above motivations. Many students have no choice but to focus the majority of their effort and time on the direct requirements of their academic degree programme. However, in our cases we were keenly aware that we had the available time and necessary dedication to take on extra commitments. The activities and initiatives that we were able to take part in improved and expanded our student experience. By feeling more involved and valued we felt more satisfied that we were making the most of the opportunities and support available to us. In this sense our experience supports the assertion in Exeter's 'Student Engagement Strategy' that there is a positive correlation between increased engagement and student satisfaction (University of Exeter & Students' Guild at the University of Exeter, 2011, p. 6).

4.6.   Conclusion

On the whole, students at Exeter define the term within the boundaries and activities that the Students' Guild and the University set and provide. However, there is no single or unifying consensus between students on where emphasis should be placed in understanding the core meaning of the term. The term 'student engagement' is still only used on a regular basis by a defined and limited group of administrative and academic staff. As a result, when students define the term they first do so by relating it to their own personal status, position and experience within the University. The appointment of Student Engagement Officers will most likely serve to increase the volume of both staff and students who are exposed to the term and the activities and initiatives associated with it. The most noticeable discrepancy between how the institution and its students define the term is the inclusion of student employment within its scope. There is a long established culture of volunteering at Exeter and most students would not think to immediately include student employment (on campus or for the University) as a form of 'engagement'.

Understanding student motivation behind engagement is an important element in defining how students perceive the activities and initiatives associated with the term.

By joining a committee or a particular society students are able to define and align themselves with a particular group of other students. 'Student engagement' allows a student to define and mould their own identity within a large body of ostensibly 'similar' students. There is a cultural and peer expectation at Exeter that students will volunteer and engage with their wider University community. 'Student engagement' also allows an individual student to accrue new skill sets and network with friends and members of staff. The activities and initiatives pinned to the term serve to cater to a set of needs that are not fully satisfied within the classroom or the content of an academic degree programme. The role of financial reward is generally a valued result, rather than a primary driving factor behind students choosing to work for the University. If financial incentive was the driving factor then students would be able to pursue easier and less demanding work outside the University community. Free time outside of a student's course requirement is also an important factor in defining the frequency and the manner in which students engage with their university.

For both authors 'student engagement' had a positive impact on our student experience. The opportunities that were provided to us catered for what motivated us as students within a wider university community. They allowed us to grow and develop outside our academic degree programme. There is a danger that a student can become too involved with the extra-curricular at the expense of the curricular. Both authors knew friends and peers who poured more energy and creativity into running charitable events and initiatives than they did into their own degree. However, one of the results of increased 'student engagement' is student empowerment. Students are treated as valued partners within a university community and they are given the power to decide how they wish to balance and structure their time at university. This is a vital skill that all students need to be able to master when they leave home and full-time education.

The extra-curricular bias of Exeter's 'Student Engagement Strategy' and the discrepancy between how Exeter approaches the term in comparison to academics such as Garrett reflect how there is potential in the future for Exeter to expand its understanding and use of the term into the curriculum. This is not to say that academics currently do not actively engage and involve their students with the content and assessment of a particular academic field. In many respects 'student engagement' is a re-branding of existing and on-going practice. Although the multitude of interpretations and the expanse of the term's conceivable remit can cause headaches for both staff and students alike, it is a potent 'buzzword' that carries powerful connotations. The phrase places a responsibility on universities and students' unions to actively ensure that their students are not passive consumers. In order to 'engage' with students, you have to entice and include them in their own learning and the wider university community. The term rightfully recognises the obligation that a university has to deliver a varied and valuable degree experience to a fee paying student. If universities are to achieve this, then they have to offer an enhanced educational package that expands and improves on the structured and rigid taught curriculum in primary and secondary education. Involving students with the running, organisation and development of their own university empowers and stretches them. It offer a valuable experience and supports the development of a more active skill set that will allow them to succeed as graduates.

References

1994 Group. (2007, November). *Enhancing the student experience. Policy statement.* Retrieved from http://www.1994group.ac.uk/documents/public/SEPolicyStatement.pdf

1994 Group. (2013). *About us.* Retrieved from http://www.1994group.ac.uk/aboutus

Birmingham City University. (2010). *Creating the learning community through academic partners.* Retrieved from http://www2.bcu.ac.uk/docs/media/celt/SAP_Brochure_Spreads.pdf

Dunne, L., & Zandstra, R. (2011). *Students as change agents.* Bristol: Escalate Subject Centre for Education: Higher Education Academy.

Garrett, C. (2011). Defining, detecting, and promoting student engagement in college learning environments. *Transformative Dialogues: Teaching and Learning Journal, 5*(2), 1–12. Kwantlen Polytechnic University.

Higher Education Academy. (2013). *Student engagement.* Retrieved from http://www.heacademy.ac.uk/student-engagement

Lincoln University. (2010). *Student as producer: Home.* Retrieved http://studentasproducer.lincoln.ac.uk/

Quality Assurance Agency. (2012a). *About QAA.* Retrieved from http://www.qaa.ac.uk/Pages/default.aspx

Quality Assurance Agency. (2012b, April). *University of Exeter — institutional review by the Quality Assurance Agency for Higher Education.* Retrieved from http://www.qaa.ac.uk/InstitutionReports/reports/Documents/RG977_University_of_Exeter.pdf

Quality Assurance Agency. (2012c). *University of Buckingham — institutional review by the Quality Assurance Agency for Higher Education, August.* Retrieved from http://www.qaa.ac.uk/InstitutionReports/reports/Documents/RG1041Buckingham.pdf

Quality Assurance Agency. (2012d, June). *University of Wales: Trinity St David — institutional review by the Quality Assurance Agency for Higher Education.* Retrieved from http://www.qaa.ac.uk/InstitutionReports/reports/Documents/RG978TrinityE.pdf

Quality Assurance Agency. (2012e, February). *University of Leeds — institutional review by the Quality Assurance Agency for Higher Education.* Retrieved from http://www.qaa.ac.uk/InstitutionReports/Reports/Documents/RG855UniversityofLeeds.pdf

Quality Assurance Agency. (2012f). *Student engagement.* Retrieved from http://www.qaa.ac.uk/Partners/students/student-engagement-QAA/Pages/default.aspx

Students' Guild at the University of Exeter. (2012a). *About us.* Retrieved from http://www.exeterguild.org/about/

Students' Guild at the University of Exeter. (2012b). *Societies.* Retrieved from http://www.exeterguild.org/societies/#arts

University of Exeter. (2012a). *Brief profile.* Retrieved from http://www.exeter.ac.uk/about/facts/profile/

University of Exeter. (2012b). *Code of good practice — Student/Staff Liaison Committees. Teaching and quality assurance manual.* Retrieved from http://admin.exeter.ac.uk/academic/tls/tqa/Part%209/9Eliaison.pdf

University of Exeter. (2012c). *Sport — Athletic Union.* Retrieved from http://sport.exeter.ac.uk/studentsport/au/

University of Exeter. (2013a). *Learning and teaching in higher education programme*. Retrieved from http://as.exeter.ac.uk/lthe/

University of Exeter. (2013b). *Student campus partnerships*. Retrieved from http://www.exeter.ac.uk/careers/employers/internships/scp/

University of Exeter. (2013c). *Student headcount summary*. Retrieved from http://www.exeter.ac.uk/about/facts/studentheadcountsummary/

University of Exeter & Students' Guild at the University of Exeter. (2011). *Student engagement strategy*. Internal Document, University of Exeter, UK.

Chapter 5

Staff Perceptions of Student Engagement

Gwen van der Velden

Abstract

The purpose of this chapter is to give an insight into current staff perception of student engagement against a policy background which stimulates and strengthens the influence of the student voice. Concepts of types of student engagement are evaluated such as consumerism and supplyism, and collegial and transformational engagement as opposed to transactional staff and student interests. This is a conceptual paper, based on a general review of literature, examples of student engagement in practice and vignettes of staff discussions about student engagement. The author describes a preference by academic staff for collegial (reciprocal) engagement between staff and students, but notes the obstacles that staff and students put in the way of achieving this. Noting the challenges that current terminology around student engagement holds, the author re-introduces a different conceptual approach to staff and student engagement based on earlier work by other authors. The practical implication of these new concepts is a more amenable platform for staff–student engagement with educational as well as organisational aspects of the learning experience. The evaluation of vignettes as in this chapter would benefit from further testing in a broad range of institutional contexts. Research on staff perceptions is remarkably absent in the literature, but this chapter gives a conceptual framework allowing such research to take place in future.

5.1. Introduction

This chapter concentrates on perceptions of student engagement commonly held by academic staff. It aims to disentangle co-existing conceptual interpretations of student engagement as student consumerism or staff–student partnerships (collegial engagement). Apparently contradictory views of academic practitioners as brought out in research literature and case studies are questioned and put into a context of recent UK policy developments, which appear to encourage a particular bias

The Student Engagement Handbook: Practice in Higher Education
Copyright © 2013 by Emerald Group Publishing Limited
All rights of reproduction in any form reserved
ISBN: 978-1-78190-423-7

towards consumerist student engagement. Specific attention is given to vignettes of evaluated teaching innovations and academic practices which illustrate academic views. Throughout the vignettes of staff perceptions of student engagement, a tension between consumerist demand and collegial desire remains palpable. An alternative conceptual approach is offered which allows staff to avoid the limiting nature of the existing polarised student engagement debate. As the vignettes illustrate, academics can perceive institutional and external focus on student engagement as forcing them to take either the side of students and compromise academically or to stay true to academic values and standards and undermine student satisfaction. Instead of trying to balance such a contradictory tension, it is proposed that students and staff can engage constructively, while respecting differing interests, if alternative interpretations of student expectations (transactional and transformational) are adopted.

5.2.   Commonly Held Perceptions: Consumerism, Supplyism and Collegial Values

Student engagement as a concept has been present in higher education for a good number of years and is understood in a myriad of ways (Trowler, 2010). Although there is a richness of understanding to be derived from the different paradigms or theories that consider student engagement, this chapter takes a close look at the narrow area of staff perceptions of student engagement in relation to learning and teaching, mostly at the level of the discipline and the classroom — virtual or otherwise. Evaluating the literature, this appears to be a rare area of focus. The majority of research undertaken concentrates on student views, on outcomes for students or institutions, or on philosophical, cultural and political considerations behind student engagement. It is remarkable that any literature on staff views consists almost entirely of individual staff evaluating their experience of consumerism or engagement in their daily academic work (Delucchi & Korgen, 2002; Eliophotou-Menon, 2003; Gvaramadze, 2011; Kahu, 2011). Quantitative or even qualitative evaluation of staff perceptions beyond the individual level is rare and difficult to access.

Within the community of academic practitioners, engagement by students is most commonly interpreted in relation to the psychology of individual learning: the level at which students engage with their studies in terms of motivation, the depth of their intellectual perception or simply studiousness. Engaged students are viewed as taking ownership for their own learning, working together with staff on ensuring academic success and accepting the role of engaged and willing apprentice to an academic master with a shared interest in academic success for students.

Much of the literature concentrates on this angle of student engagement, and in particular the way students engage and how staff can influence this, such as Solomonides, Reid, and Petocz (2012) or Bryson and Hand (2007). In that sense, student engagement takes on a role based on the values of the Collegium, along the lines of this concept as described by McNay (1995) or Van der Velden (2012a, 2012b).

Yet now that especially in England the roles and the power balance between institutions, government and the student body are changing as a result of substantial policy and student fee changes (BIS, 2011), many staff fear that a less collegial type of engagement by students may become more prevalent in higher education.

Long debated, but relatively rarely researched concerns focus on a consumerist type of engagement within a commodified educational system. In a consumerist situation, the member of staff may still have the academic success of the student in mind, but is also likely to experience pressure to achieve student satisfaction (measured through surveys or otherwise) for the duration of the learning process and avoid dissatisfaction with teaching performance particularly. In such a scenario, the academically passive consumerist student may be aiming to 'receive' a high score for their assessed activity while seeking to ensure that sufficient 'value for money (fees)' has been acquired while on the course. In essence, the shared interest between the student and academic staff is limited and there are several interests which can differ greatly and may be oppositional in nature. Consumerism suggests that students' actions do not concentrate on engagement with academic matters as they would in a setting of collegial engagement, but on negotiation of the process of achievement of desirable course results, and those results themselves (Van der Velden, 2012a, 2012b). In a sense, although the student remains engaged with the process of education in order to acquire the results they have (financially) invested in, that active engagement is not academic. The student−staff relationship becomes based on meeting the expectations of the person who pays and thus a consumerist supply−demand concept is introduced. As Mwachofi et al. note, 'The burden is on the vendor to provide customer satisfaction' (Mwachofi, Strom, Gilbert, & Cohen, 1995). The result of this type of engagement is seen as negative. Naidoo and Jamieson state that '… the reconceptualization of the complex relationship between students and teachers to that of "service provider" and "customer" is likely to be corrosive of both sides of the relationship' (Naidoo & Jamieson, 2005).

In the daily practice of teaching, the corrosive nature of consumerism can take the form of a distinct mismatch between student expectations on staff and vice versa, resulting in a dissatisfying and educationally undesirable state of affairs for both parties. The vignette below is an example of consumerism as it can play out in the classroom, as described in a published article by Delucchi and Korgen (2002). Especially noteworthy in this article are the efforts that the authors have made to investigate not just what the existing ethos of the students is, but also what these same students would like it to be, with surprising and perhaps encouraging results.

5.2.1.   *Vignette 1: Consumerism*

Delucchi and Korgen describe consumerism as an inversion of the responsibility for academic success from the student onto their teachers. In 2001 they explored the nature of student engagement of 195 sociology students in a single institution in the United States. They used a survey to test the level of engagement of students by identifying the number of hours spent on study in comparison to formally awarded credits (an indication of expected study hours), by asking students to compare themselves to students with 12 different types of approach to their studies and by investigating views on the relationship between tuition fees paid and an entitlement of academic success. Students reported to invest fewer hours in their studies than were formally expected, identified themselves with student views that related closely to consumerism and ascribed a high relevance to their contribution of tuition fees to the quality and outcomes of their education. Particularly remarkable results were the expectation of just over half of the students that 'It is the instructor's responsibility to keep me attentive in class'. Two fifths of students agreed with the statement 'If I am paying for my university tuition, I am entitled to a degree' (Delucchi & Korgen, 2002).

Although the authors found that the majority of students identified themselves with engagement types closer to the consumerist ethos, they also established that those same students would much prefer to be more alike the types with a stronger collegial ethos.

While speaking out strongly against the level of consumerism they found, the authors conclude that students are likely to be better served by institutions that are more demanding and expect a higher level of academic engagement of them despite consumerist student feedback. Such institutions instil in their students from induction stage onwards an acceptance of a sense of insecurity about the educational ups and downs of learning. Instead, they reported that the more common reaction to student demands was to increase the level of entertainment within lectures. Colleagues appeared to accept that many students were looking for the route of least effort to achieve a pass grade and to respond to scores on 'rate your professor' type questionnaires.

The Delucchi and Korgen research shows in a relatively stark manner the difference between the interests of staff towards academic integrity in their teaching, against the acceptance of consumerist realities. It equally illustrates the tension between the consumerist realities for students, against their own ideals for a more academic achievement inspired approach. There is no joint interest in education, and both parties view each other as responsible for the success (or failure) of the educational experience, but against their own separate definitions of success.

5.2.1.1. The staff version of consumerism

Aside from illustrating student consumerism and staff and students' desire for an alternative educational ethos to inform teaching and learning, this vignette also indicates how staff perceive they have become the sole responsible party for the educational process. Korgen and Delucchi — and others — clearly view this as troublesome and wish students to re-engage with taking responsibility for their own learning and academic success. The next vignette shows a different ethos that staff may embrace, whereby the staff — again — own the educational process, but where this ownership is not the result of student consumerism. Instead it is driven by staff's own values and expectations in relation to the education they provide. In this approach, staff expect students to engage according to traditional academic expectations, but will rarely make these expectations explicit. This is an educational ethos where power and control lie fully with the staff that 'supply' the teaching. Though such a level of empowerment may seem deliberate and favourable for staff, the result is not generally viewed by the same staff as desirable. Students disappoint by not living up to expectations and the one-way communication, that is often typical for this approach, does not lead to a sense of achievement or satisfaction for either party. It is not uncommon that staff take this approach even when trying to improve the student experience, with a genuine view to enhance student engagement.

5.2.2. Vignette 2: Supplyism

A practical example of the search for positive student engagement at the discipline and classroom level is the change management process that took place in a single-discipline school[1] where strong dissatisfaction with the learning experience of students was exposed by annual student survey results since 2006. In 2008, the school sought advice from an external professional to explore ways of enhancing teaching practices. A core part of the agreed change process was to support staff in moving from teacher-centred approaches to student-centred approaches, while counterbalancing concerns regarding conceding to consumerist student demands or 'pandering and molly-coddling' (anonymous staff quote). A number of discussions took place within the school around the co-ownership of the education between teacher and learner. Co-ownership of education opposed the traditional and, for the department, more comfortable model of a teacher-centred concept of education. Education was seen as a supply of knowledge to students who were increasingly deemed to be unable to receive and process that knowledge 'in the expected and time-honoured manner' (anonymous staff quote). In the context of reflecting on the nature of the relationship between students and their learning, it is noteworthy that the traditional didactic approach was — almost like consumerism — one of a clear supply and demand chain. Staff featured in the supply role, while students received their education. Hence, the supply side strongly holds the control over the educational experience, with no influence by the demand side.

The open comments gathered through the survey listed student views which were interpreted as 'consumerist'. Students wanted much more feedback, preferably personalised and written rather than verbal. More access to staff was requested, more clarity about assessments, a faster return of marked work and, above all, a better teaching performance in particular units. The feedback was viewed by staff as overly demanding and this saddened many of them who felt there had been a time when students were more motivated and engaged during their study. During discussions with the school leadership, concepts of staff and students sharing academic interests

---

[1]This case study took place in an engineering based subject within a research intensive, pre-92 institution. Nomenclature in relation to the university's organisation and provision has been changed to allow for anonymity.

through engagement were explored, leading to an understanding of the educational process as an interaction, co-owned by staff and students. As a result, working groups were established that consisted of both staff and students and which concentrated on specific academic aspects of the educational experience, such as assessment and feedback, project supervision, tutoring arrangements and supporting lab-based learning. These groups advised the department on their learning and teaching practices, leading to on-going, often small and sometimes larger changes. The head of the school also invested in improving the communication with students, primarily to create a sense of joint departmental belonging between staff and students. A dominant part of this communication was responding to student feedback and discussing the organisation of the environment for student learning. In time, the relationship between staff and students changed, allowing more room for the student voice, and less room for the instructive approach of some of the teaching staff.

In 2010, three institutional colleagues who were external to the school undertook a review of the school's organisation and management of the student learning experience. Several interviews took place with students and staff, and separately with the head of the school and course leaders. The focus groups with each year cohort separately illustrated a stark difference between those students who had experienced the school 4 or 5 years ago (depending on study trajectory) and those who were in their first or second year. Fourth and final year students recognised that the school's ethos was changing, and yet they reported a strong dissatisfaction with the way in which their views had been dismissed in the past. These students still identified their education as something the staff owned. They did not feel part of the school and described communication as a top-down affair. More recently started cohorts did not recognise this distance and reported that the staff had an interest in their learning and communicated with them in an inclusive manner, suggesting a shared responsibility for educational success. This was experienced as highly motivating.

In this vignette, a student satisfaction survey — that is often viewed by staff as an instrument of consumerism — brought to the fore a tension between teaching-centred staff interests and a relative disengagement of the student body. In particular, this vignette describes a form of engagement with students that may be referred to as supplyism. The approach is not new to learning and teaching in higher education. Many traditional pedagogical approaches are highly teacher-centred with relatively little reference to student learning. The most traditional example is the taught unit (course) that is only supported by lectures leading to an exam, with little interaction and no feedback along the way. Without allowing students any interaction with either the intellectual or the social delivery of the desired learning, it is perhaps not surprising that students do not appear 'engaged'.

5.2.2.1. A return to collegial values
Both consumerism and supplyism are forms of engagement where very little joint interest between students and staff exist. This is in essence what much of the current student engagement discussions concentrate on. Yet when asked, both staff and students are far more interested in an approach where there is a more common interest,

usually around the interest in the subject of learning or the wider discipline, but also a genuine interest from both parties in successful student learning.

An alternative approach, then, is what was described earlier as 'collegial engagement', but is sometimes also referred to as reciprocal engagement or working in staff–student partnership. In a situation where a high level of collegial engagement can be found, staff and students each have concepts of success which have a substantial amount of overlap: student and staff members interact with the shared aim of enabling successful learning, and achievement of academic understanding and insight by the student. A prime example of this is the often highly collegial process of successful PhD supervision, but this approach can work equally well at other levels of education, as illustrated in the third vignette.

5.2.3. Vignette 3: Collegial Engagement

Under the name of 'VALUE' (Value Added Learning in University Education), a retention programme was initially created in 2001 to support first year students at risk of failure or underachievement at the University of Kent (Sellers & Van der Velden, 2003). In the form of a summer school, students and staff engage in a programme of learning and social activities designed to address subject-specific learning, key and study skills development.

The extra-curricular programme takes place in three parts: before the end of first year examinations, during the summer vacation (at a distance) and at the start of the students' second year. Student and staff interests in the programme align to a large extent: both reported to seek increased students' academic achievement and a considerable level of shared focus was on developing a sense of social belonging for students in the academic environment. Students spend some time initially setting out what commitment they intend to make to the programme and how they would like to engage with the staff to achieve their academic goals. Many of the activities during the programme are designed jointly with students and as a result some unusual activities sometimes take place, such as building temples from borrowed and negotiated bricks or joining comedy versions of 'highbrow' theatre events with a view to make theatre plays, cultural debate and critiques accessible.

Each time these and more traditional sessions combine academic learning with learning skills development and an enhancement of social belonging within the university culture.

> In our retention Summer School, this was done by creating a three-way partnership. Students, academic staff and student learning advisors were all involved in choosing the methods and content of teaching.'(p. 12) and 'Students are part of setting the direction, content and methods of the programme, even though we do not provide individual learning paths, but use group learning in the majority of our activities.' (Sellers & Van der Velden, 2003)

The communication methods described are — after initial recruitment — entirely dependent on two-way communication and students and staff negotiating a shared ownership of the educational processes and activities.

In 2012, this programme still continued despite the external funding having disappeared and there being little or no recompense for academic staff participation. It records a high level of success, with over 95% of students on the programme being retained in higher education. Uptake has grown from 40 students in 2001 to just under 280 students in 2010, with demand annually outstripping the supply of places. Staff and student feedback has shown that the collegial approach to the design and delivery of the programme is paying dividends — both academically and in terms of staff and student satisfaction.

5.2.3.1. Staff and students sharing interests

In short then, within a consumerist ethos where students have come to represent 'demand' and staff have come to function as suppliers of the commodity of education, there is much distance between respective interests, that is reciprocity between staff and students decreases in a consumerist context (Mintz & Hesser, 1996). In a context of more collegial engagement, staff and students engage through a shared interest in achieving academic success allowing forms of partnership within the educational context. As such, parallels could be drawn between the traditional collegial ethos of higher education in which student engagement is believed to be prevalent, against modern corporate institutions where student consumerism may more easily be anticipated and responded to.

5.3.   Two Contentious Areas of Student Engagement

In recent years, driven by national surveys on student satisfaction, published league tables and in anticipation of higher level student fees in England (Naidoo, Shankar, & Veer, 2011), many universities have increased their efforts to strengthen the relationship between students and their institution. Alongside actual changes in the governance and quality management of learning and teaching (Little, Locke, Scesa, & Williams, 2009; QAA, 2011a), institutions have introduced partnership statements, or student charters (De Beer & Porter, 2011). These statements of intentions and expectations between staff, students, the students' union and the institution often use terminology related to some form of engagement between the different stakeholders, such as co-ownership of the student experience, co-production of education and curriculum or more generically, partnership. The creation of charters is mostly undertaken by student representatives or students' unions together with staff from educational development units or members of the senior management team. Consultation and approval processes ensure in formal terms that due consideration, and ultimately approval of such statements, is given by the representatives of the academic community — these days both academic staff and students.

And yet, a partnership approach which describes the nature of engagement of staff and students in all aspects of study may not be strongly supported by individual teaching staff. Some report hesitance about charters becoming 'terms and conditions' and thus restrictive, while others note not to recognise the language used to express the intentions of the partnership and view a charter as descriptive for staff. Moreover, teaching staff may wish to work with students from an ethical intention of reciprocity in the classroom, but are not at ease with such an approach being stipulated by management or the students' union, both of which are seen to be removed from the core teaching experience of staff.

Core to these reservations is teaching staff's interpretations of how far partnership may reach. Kay, Owen, and Dunne (2012) describe four tiers of involvement of students' engagement in relation to quality enhancement. In relation to discipline-based teaching staff, this may perhaps be translated to mean student involvement in the development and improvement of teaching and the curriculum. The first tier is that of evaluator: influencing improvement and development through surveys and feedback. At this tier, engagement is reactive, with students responding to the teaching owned and delivered by staff. The next tier is that of observer, where students engage in learning- and teaching-related meetings, while the decision making remains firmly the responsibility of the staff and institution. Students may be more proactive and able to contribute ideas, but no ownership of decisions or outcomes is shared between staff and students. At the third tier students are recognised as experts. Within the decision making processes students gain a respected voice and ample influence. More importantly, students' opinion are of direct influence on enhancement and development processes, while at the fourth and final tier, students become full partners and members of a community of academic practice.

This tiering illustrates the gradual nature of developing student engagement and partnership outside the classroom. From a staff point of view, the model describes how control, influence and decision making affecting the educational process gradually become more 'shared' with students (Boland, 2005). In responding to this gradual change of power and control, comparisons could be made with discussions about shared governance in higher education between administrative powers and the academic community (Brundrett, 1998; Lapworth, 2004). While the academic staff community increasingly embraces student participation in quality enhancement activities, and seeks to encourage collegial engagement out of a genuine interest in students' success, that same process of change further diminishes the level of control and independence staff have. The perceived encroachment on academic influence and autonomy may help to explain why staff can express their eagerness to embrace a collegial engagement approach, but can be hesitant to formalise such approaches in governance terms or in relation to academic judgement aspects. Specifically the latter is seen as a domain that is solely the responsibility of academic staff, and this area of academic autonomy and freedom from interference is enshrined in most university policy. The vignette below gives an insight into the nature of staff reservations on the issue.

5.3.1.   Vignette 4: Student Engagement and Academic Autonomy

This vignette describes discussions that took place in a strongly collegial university where the majority of educational provision is campus based and full time. The author has witnessed similar discussions in two further universities and is aware, from taking part in national learning and teaching policy consultation activities, that the arguments made by academic staff resonate with considerations elsewhere.

During discussions regarding the involvement of students in curriculum or programme development teams and programme approval panels, opinions became divided around questions of academic judgement and autonomy. At the heart of the issue lay the question whether students can meaningfully take part in setting the curriculum at both discipline and unit or course levels.

Some staff felt that in the case of mature learners, who were professionals or experienced employees in the field of their formal — usually postgraduate — studies, they were well positioned to comment on the content of the curriculum. Therefore, many staff took no issue to such students taking part in the evaluation and ultimately approval of programme or unit proposals. Few staff, however, were positive about the prospect of undergraduate students taking on such responsibilities. Objections were varied, ranging from the view that students ought to have graduated before they are in a position to have a sufficient level of mastery of the discipline to concerns regarding the potential undermining of the role of academic judgement by staff.

The discussion regarding academic judgement was substantial. Early on, one of the senior staff pointed at long standing policy stating that, in the case of summative assessments, 'academic judgement cannot be questioned' — a common piece of academic policy across the higher education sector in the United Kingdom. Reference to this policy was not made lightly, and staff argued with some level of passion that academic judgement was a matter for academics only, was not a mere 'rule' but a core academic principle. The staff set out how the enshrined inviolability of academic judgement related to the independence and autonomy of academics and their institutions and that in the United Kingdom, at least, academic independence and freedom is at the heart of the value of higher education within society.

Student representatives who were also present at this discussion took little issue with these views. Representing both postgraduate and undergraduate students, their opinion could be summarised as wishing to have a voice on issues of teaching and teaching quality, organisation of teaching, resource and facilities availability, and any aspect directly relating to the student experience, but not academic content of the curriculum. Instead, students felt strongly that more recognition was due for the students' ability to make judgements about good teaching as well as learning. In a separate discussion, one experienced student representative noted that although it is true that students are not 'qualified' to judge teaching, not all staff are either, but at least all students appear well qualified to comment on the experience of learning within the teaching context they encounter. Clearly these remarks led to further discussion among academics and students.

As a result of the debate, the academic team in question — consisting of staff and students — ultimately decided to include a strong student representation onto programme development as well as approval panels under full membership arrangements (i.e. with all members having voting rights). Explicitly excluded from this was the involvement of students in the approval of academic content and curriculum. Remarkably, the students' union subsequently declined to join the institutional level committee that oversees the approval of new programmes, while involvement in unit approval was taken up.

5.3.1.1. Limits of student engagement

Whether inviolability of academic judgement, academic freedom and the autonomy of institutions are all based on entirely the same principle is debatable, but this is not the issue here. The vignette illustrates a limitation of acceptance by staff of student engagement and partnership based on accepted inequalities in their respective roles. A clear incongruence is identified here between staff expertise and student expertise, and on this aspect, staff and students found mutual acceptance of a lesser level of student influence. Not all universities share this view, and in some universities students are fully involved in shaping and making judgements about the academic content of the curriculum. However, it remains a point of discussion and hesitation for many academic staff.

Similar discussions have taken place in relation to strategic direction setting, both at institutional level and discipline level. Student representatives' participation in formal senior committees (councils, governing boards and senate or similar) is now accepted in almost all higher education institutions. By contrast, institutional student representatives — in the United Kingdom mostly elected and then appointed full time for a year — report that representation in the governance arrangements nearer the discipline level is much more contested. Academic staff who are content with student involvement in setting teaching policy appear less supportive when considering student representational involvement in the management of a department and its teaching. Perhaps this again relates to both the issue of felt academic independence (Eliophotou-Menon, 2003) as well as the earlier raised issue of pre-existing sensitivity regarding shared governance and diminishing levels of autonomy and control (Katz, 2003). Noteworthy perhaps is that this formal governance representation at institutional level is less common in higher education provision based in further education institutions, and this is an area where further development can reasonably be expected in the coming years.

5.4. A Different Paradigm of Student Engagement

A new balance of engagement between staff and students is evolving as student representation and an active consideration of the student voice becomes more common practice throughout all levels of higher education. The reasons for this strengthening of the student voice are contradictory forces. Although massification of higher education and the introduction of national consumerist policies and higher student fees promote consumerism, it is notable that institutions, academics and students are looking to rekindle the appreciation of collegial engagement — albeit with reservations regarding involvement in core academic decision making.

Yet while this process takes place, staff share concerns about the apparently increasing nature of demand by students. Such demands often relate to organisational aspects such as contact hours, access to facilities, resources and staff. Such consumerist expectations by students are now supported by national policy to have explicit and high expectations on a good number of measurable aspects of higher education. Based on market considerations, Lord Browne (BIS, 2011), who headed up a major England Higher Education Review, as well as the Higher Education Minister David Willetts (2011) have promoted the publication of institutional performance indicators to inform prospective students' choice. Information such as student satisfaction survey data, graduate destination data, methods used for summative assessment, fee and bursary information as well as accommodation costs are publicly provided in a manner which encourages direct comparison between universities and courses (Unistats, 2012). Institutions are asked to provide increasing amounts of information regarding the quality of learning and teaching, including from 2013, information about the teaching qualifications or training that staff have undertaken in support of their teaching. While this highly statistical approach to evidencing teaching quality informs student expectations, it appears to ignore their equal interest in academic progress and success and thus staff perceive this approach as encouraging students' consumerist attitudes.

Wedged between such consumerist pressures and collegial intentions, perhaps both staff and students could benefit from an alternative conceptual approach to understanding student engagement and the staff–student relationship. Based on the study of a number of institutional cases, Johnson and Deem (2003) separate aspects of the student experience that relate to organisation and management of resources, facilities, opportunities and the physical context of the student experience from the core academic, social and learning development students undergo when entering university life. Lizzio and Wilson (2009) summarise this as a differentiation between transactional and transformational aspects of the educational process.

Extending this conceptualisation into the current higher education context, instead of considering the dichotomy of consumerism and engagement, student interests might more usefully be separated into transactional and transformational expectations. Within the context of learning, transactional expectations relate to those aspects where a physical or organisational transaction effectively takes place. These matters can be organised and managed and clarity can be given on what can be expected and ought to be delivered. Transformational aspects of learning are less tangible, measurable or quantifiable. Instead, transformational interests relate to the process of change that students undergo during their studies in terms of social, intellectual and cultural development and learning. Outcomes such as attitudinal change, opinion forming, mastering a discipline and understanding key concepts and theories change the intellectual position of the student and this social and academic transformation is what staff and students can jointly, positively, relate to as core to the academic process of study.

By introducing these concepts, it is possible for staff and students to recognise that while there can be a strong and positive collegial engagement on shared transformational interests within the daily academic context, there can simultaneously be differing interests around transactional aspects. The negotiation regarding transactional aspects can then become part of a different and separate process of engagement and development than those addressing transformational aspects. The transformational aspects remain firmly within the academic realm, such as the classroom or the tutorial where staff and students continue to engage on academic matters without the interference of a potentially adversarial climate of differing transactional interests. This approach could address the staff perception that a consumerist student ethos conflicts with efforts to jointly achieve shared academic interests.

5.5. After These Rocky Changes

It is impossible to predict how the student engagement, and consumerism versus partnership debates will ultimately settle. There are considerable differences between institutional contexts and their desire or ability to shape the way they engage with their student body, with consequent effects on how staff can develop their relationship with students. And yet, core values of academic autonomy will no doubt continue to exist, while students and their representatives will gain ground within the context of institutional governance. There is ample debate to follow with staff, students, institutions and policy-makers taking different positions in relation to student engagement. Within the context of such opportunity and potential, it appears desirable to overcome the narrow and polarising position of typifying student engagement as either consumerist or partnership based. This will allow the complexity of mutual and contradictory staff and student expectations to come to the surface, while constructive progress towards academic transformation can continue to be made.

Acknowledgements

Thanks are due to audience members at keynotes and seminars where aspects of this chapter were presented. The feedback given and questions posed have strongly influenced the author's thinking, as have the on-going critical discussions about consumerism, the state of higher education, and research into policy developments with Dr Rajani Naidoo, Dr Colin Bryson, Professor Paul Blackmore and Dr Camille Kandiko. Nadine Grimmett is to be thanked for her patience with my text editing needs. Most importantly, appreciation is due for the unnamed staff and students from various universities and organisations who have been described in the vignettes or who in their work and discussions have generously given the author valuable insights into staff and student perceptions of engagement.

References

BIS. (2011). *Students at the heart of the system: Consulting on the future of higher education.* London: Department for Business Innovation and Skills. Retrieved from http://c561635. r35.cf2.rackcdn.com/11-944-WP-students-at-heart.pdf

Boland, J. A. (2005). Student participation in shared governance: A means of advancing democratic values? *Tertiary Education and Management, 11*(3), 199−217.

Brundrett. (1998). What lies behind collegiality, legitimation or control? An analysis of the purported benefits of collegial management in education. *Educational Management Administration & Leadership, 26*(3), 305.

Bryson, C., & Hand, L. (2007). The role of engagement in inspiring teaching and learning. *Innovations in Education and Teaching International, 44*(4), 349−362.

De Beer, J., & Porter, A. (2011). *Student charters: Final report.* London: Department for Business, Skills and Innovation.

Delucchi, M., & Korgen, K. (2002). "We're the customer — we pay the tuition": Student consumerism among undergraduate sociology majors. *Teaching Sociology, 30*(1), 100−107.

Eliophotou-Menon, M. (2003). Student involvement in university governance: A need for negotiated engagement. *Tertiary Education and Management, 9*, 233−246.

Gvaramadze, I. (2011). Student engagement in the Scottish quality enhancement framework. *Quality in Higher Education, 17*(1), 19−36. doi: 10.1080/13538322.2011.554310

Johnson, R., & Deem, R. (2003). Talking of students: Tensions and contradictions for the manager-academic and the university in contemporary higher education. *Higher Education, 46*(3), 289.

Kahu, E. R. (2011). Framing student engagement in higher education. *Studies in Higher Education, 1*−16.

Katz (2003). Academic democracy: Pursuing faculty involvement in collegiate governance. *Planning and Changing, 34*(1), 2−18.

Kay, J., Owen, D., & Dunne, E. (2012). Students as change agents: Student engagement with quality enhancement of learning and teaching. In I. Solomonides, A. Reid & P. Petocz (Eds.), *Engaging with learning in higher education* (pp. 359−380). Faringdon, UK: Libri.

Lapworth, S. (2004). Arresting decline in shared governance: Towards a flexible model for academic participation. *Higher Education Quarterly, 58*(4), 299−314.

Little, B., Locke, W., Scesa, A., & Williams, R. (2009). *Report to HEFCE on student engagement.* London: Centre for Higher Education Research Information, Open University.

Lizzio, A., & Wilson, K. (2009). Student participation in university governance: The role conceptions and sense of efficacy of student representatives on departmental committees. *Studies in Higher Education, 34*(1), 69−84.

McNay, I. (1995). From the collegial academy to the corporate enterprise: The changing cultures of universities. In T. Schuller (Ed.), *The changing university?* Buckingham: Open University Press.

Mintz, S. D., & Hesser, G. W. (1996). Principles of good practice in service learning. In B. Jacoby (Ed.), *Service-learning in higher education* (pp. 26−52). San Fransisco, CA: Jossey-Bass.

Mwachofi, N. w., Strom, M., Gilbert, P., & Cohen, H. (1995). Reflections on the 'student as consumer' metaphor. *Teaching Forum (The Undergraduate Teaching Improvement Council — UW System)*, *16*, 1−3.

Naidoo, R., & Jamieson, I. (2005). Empowering participants or corroding learning? Towards a research agenda on the impact of student consumerism in higher education. *Journal of Education Policy*, *20*(3), 267−281.

Naidoo, R., Shankar, A., & Veer, E. (2011). The consumerist turn in higher education: Policy aspirations and outcomes. *Journal of Marketing Management*, *27*(11−12), 1142−1162. doi: 10.1080/0267257x.2011.609135

QAA. (2011a). *Outcomes from institutional audit — student representation and support*. Gloucester: Quality Assurance Agency.

Sellers, J. G., & Van der Velden, G. M. (2003). Supporting student retention. In B. Smith (Ed.), *Continuing professional development series* (Vol. 5), York: Higher Education Academy.

Solomonides, I., Reid, A., & Petocz, P. (Eds.) (2012). *Engaging with learning in higher education*. Faringdon, UK: Libri.

Trowler, V. (2010). *Student engagement literature review*. York: Higher Education Academy.

Unistats. (2012). *Unistats compare official course data from universities and colleges*. Retrieved from http://unistats.direct.gov.uk/find-out-more/key-information-set. Accessed on 10 November 2012.

Van der Velden, G. M. (2012a). Institutional level student engagement and organisational cultures. *Higher Education Quarterly*, *66*(3), 227−247.

Van der Velden, G. M. (2012b). Student engagement: Whose education is it anyway? *Talking about Quality*. Retrieved from http://www.qaa.ac.uk/IMPROVINGHIGHEREDUCATION/ DEBATE/Pages/default.aspx

Willetts, D. (2011). *David Willetts: You ask the questions*. Mortarboard. Retrieved from http://www.guardian.co.uk/education/mortarboard/2011/oct/10/david-willetts-live-online? commentpage = 5#start-of-comments. Accessed on 26 October 2011.

PART 2: A NEW ERA — THE POLICY AND QUALITY CONTEXT FOR STUDENT ENGAGEMENT

Elisabeth Dunne and Derfel Owen

As previously outlined, the demand for higher education has grown exponentially in recent years. Developed economies have fuelled an appetite for higher qualifications in the workforce and developing economies have exported students to learn and gain qualifications. The OECD (2008) highlighted the demand and capacity challenges faced by the global sector in higher education:

> Education plays a crucial role by training a country's workforce in all fields, from teachers equipped to give a good basic education to statisticians and policy analysts monitoring capacity development. Many developing countries do not have enough tertiary education places or staff to meet domestic demand. And in spite of progress in recent decades, many will have to continue to expand their systems if they are to catch up with richer economies.

This demand has had a considerable impact on the student body with greater numbers, diverse backgrounds, a multitude of routes into higher education, and widespread internationalisation, but also has impacted dramatically on the policy requirements for student provision, with accompanying expectations for new modes of engagement by students. Part 2 will evaluate some of the major changes that have taken place in global higher education over the past few years, and the way in which those higher education providers and sectors have adapted to engage and involve students to shape their responses to emerging challenges and opportunities, and how providers have successfully engaged students in different contexts.

One response to globalisation and massification has been efforts to harmonise higher education policies and practice across regional blocks. The European Higher Education Area (EHEA) has made significant strides towards the goal of harmonisation. One of the many features of the this process, commonly known as the Bologna process, has been the strong focus on student engagement, both in terms of input the process of harmonisation and the aspirations and expectations contained. Chapter 6 explores that contribution, discussing how students managed to gain a seat at the negotiations and the impact it has had on student engagement in Europe.

Another response to globalisation is the need to expand the number of providers of higher education. In the United Kingdom this has led to the Government actively encouraging more 'private' and for profit providers into the sector. Chapter 7 takes a look at developments in the United Kingdom, from the perspective of one of the new higher education providers, and explores the sort of relationship these providers can and should have with their students and whether it is very different from public providers. As higher education continues to change and respond to global demands, it is important that the quality of education is not diminished. Many people will have views and perspectives on what good quality looks like and it is important that their voices are heard and are able to promote change. Chapter 8 sets student engagement in that context, identifying the important expertise that students have to offer. At the authors' University, there is a deep-rooted philosophy on what it means to be a student in HE, well-rehearsed over many years, and how students can impact on change.

No matter where a higher education institution operates, a culture of quality assurance and management is paramount to success and the legitimacy of claims of higher learning. The principle of peer review and evaluation is deeply instilled in higher education and supports a culture of deep self-reflection and criticism. This culture is sustained by a number of quality management processes within and across institutions that engages the whole academic community, including students. The QAA (2011) has stated that:

> Students are partners in quality assurance, and are experts not only on their own learning but also on issues of governance, policy and practice. We seek to harness that expertise in every aspect of our work.

This builds on research conducted by the European Network of Quality Agencies in 2006 that concluded:

> Students have increasingly become involved in the improvement and enhancement of their own learning experiences. Whether it be through providing feedback on the courses they have taken, contributing to the development of learning and teaching in their subject area, participating in university decision making processes, or representing student views in any number of ways through a student union or other representative body — students' voices are today being heard loudly and clearly and, ever more often, their views are being taken seriously.

A number of common practices have emerged in institutions to support a culture of quality management and improvement that is explored throughout this book. Chapter 9 takes a critical and evaluative look at the ideologies, practice and narratives that support that support those systems as well as the way in which power is distributed.

As well as creating new or additional systems and structures to engage students and give them opportunities to have their voice heard, Universities will seek to extend invitations for students to be involved in existing structures, opening the door to systems and decision making structures that may have previously been closed. Chapter 10 looks at the experiences of a number of UK universities when seeking to engage students as members of internal academic review teams. It highlights some of the misconceptions about working with students and some of the ways in which challenges can be overcome. Sometimes changes to the quality culture in higher education are driven from outside. In response to changing perceptions of disability, a number of countries have changed their legislative frameworks to ensure that disability is not discriminated against. In higher education this has been marked; it is in the interests of all universities to make sure their students are supported to achieve to the best of their ability. Chapter 11 evaluates the approaches taken by a number of UK universities to adapt their policies and practices to ensure disabled students are not excluded.

To retain a level of consistency of principle and practice, serious exploration has taken place about the role of students in sustaining quality cultures, concluding that students ought to play a full and active role as peers in the processes that have been developed. Part 3 will explore the impact and effectiveness that these quality management and improvement processes have on the student experience, how they drive institutional student engagement practices, and how they engage directly with students.

References

European Network of Quality Agencies (ENQA). (2006). *Student involvement in the processes of quality assurance agencies.* Helsinki: European Association for Quality Assurance in Higher Education.

OECD. (2008). *Cross border higher education and development.* Paris: OECD. Retrieved from http://www.oecd.org/dataoecd/24/48/39997378.pdf

Quality Assurance Agency (QAA). (2011). *Strategy 2011–14.* Gloucester: Quality Assurance Agency for Higher Education. Retrieved from http://www.qaa.ac.uk/AboutUs/strategy11-14/Pages/commitments.aspx

Chapter 6

Harmonisation and the Bologna Process: A Driver for Student Engagement?

Alex Bols

Abstract

Higher education systems across Europe have changed almost beyond recognition since 1999. Moves to create a European Higher Education Area have motivated radical changes to degree structure and length, an emphasis on outcomes rather than inputs and renewed focus on quality of provision. In all these reforms students and student engagement have been at the core.

Under the framework of the 'Bologna Process', 32 ministers from across Europe said back in 2001 that the input of 'students as competent, active and constructive partners in the establishment and shaping of a European Higher Education Area is needed and welcomed' (Prague Communiqué, 2001). Since 2001, student representatives have become part of the official structures and had a significant impact on the policy agenda. The reforms also placed student engagement as central to change at a local and national level: 'ministers affirmed that students should participate in and influence the organisation and content of education at universities and other higher education institutions' (ibid.).

This chapter will look at student engagement in these European policy-making structures and the impact that these European reforms have had on student engagement at the national level. It draws on evidence from European and national organisations, as well as in-depth interviews with student representatives involved in the Bologna Process.

6.1. Introduction

The year 2001 is most regularly associated with Space Odysseys, but it was also a seminal point in another journey, that towards student engagement in higher

The Student Engagement Handbook: Practice in Higher Education
Copyright © 2013 by Emerald Group Publishing Limited
All rights of reproduction in any form reserved
ISBN: 978-1-78190-423-7

education policy-making across Europe. A journey which began with a ministerial summit in Prague in May 2001 is still on-going. The ultimate destination, where students are actively considered as partners at all levels in higher education, is still far off, but a significant distance has already been travelled. In part the speed and pace of change has been driven by the pressure resulting from a process that, when I raise it at conferences in the United Kingdom, is either little understood or not even heard of — the 'Bologna Process'.

In this chapter I will examine the ways in which the Bologna Declaration, and the subsequent 'process', has impacted upon student engagement in both practical and policy terms. From an initial absence of students being involved in the first ministerial gathering, I will look at how students have become increasingly engaged, and influential, in the process itself and how this has had an effect more widely on higher education policy across Europe. I then consider the impact that the process had on a specific country, the United Kingdom, through a case study of the involvement of students in institutional review quality assurance panels in England, Wales and Northern Ireland. I go on to suggest that there has been an additional unintended consequence of the process, which has helped enhance student engagement, in that it has resulted in the creation of national unions of students in some European countries where they did not previously exist. Finally I consider whether the process has had a wider impact on student engagement outside Europe.

6.1.1.   *How Bologna Interprets Student Engagement*

Student engagement is often considered as a spectrum (HEA, 2011), and can refer to anything from an individual student engaging with their own learning all the way to involvement in national and European policy-making through student representation. In the context of this chapter I am particularly focusing on student engagement in higher education decision-making, whether through representation at the local, national or European level or through quality-assurance processes. It is, however, worth mentioning that the process itself increasingly addresses students through what it calls 'student-centred learning' and its emphasis on the importance of learning outcomes.

I will draw on my own experiences of the European and UK student movement, bringing in my own reflections on various events and policy changes during the last decade. I have also interviewed a number of the Chairs of the European Students' Union during this time, and I draw on their thoughts and perspectives in this chapter.

6.2.   How Bologna Gained Traction

In 1999, at the oldest European university, Università di Bologna, 30 ministers of higher education from across Europe came together to sign a declaration committing themselves to creating a European Higher Education Area by 2010. Over the years, there have been many similarly ambitious declarations that sink without trace within years, if not months. So what was different about the Bologna agreement?

Bologna was one of those serendipitous moments when the aims of various countries and organisations come together. A succession of national reports[1] provided the impetus for the meeting of the United Kingdom, France, Germany and Italy at Paris-Sorbonne Université in 1998 to discuss reforming their higher education systems. These reports called for major reforms to higher education systems, not least to enhance the global competitiveness of universities. This desire for reform of higher education across Europe, and the necessity for an external driver to help push the pace of reform, helped create the initial impetus for the meeting in Bologna a year later, where the number of participants expanded from the initial 4 to 29.

The year 1999 saw the end of the decade of the first major war on European soil since 1945. The year 1999 was itself a contentious year. NATO bombed Yugoslavia in the aftermath of the Kosovo conflict, amidst rumours of ethnic cleansing. The shockwaves that this sent through political elites should not be understated. The extension of the invitations to the Bologna ministerial summit beyond the boundaries of the European Union was a recognition of the role of education as a means of increasing understanding between nations.

Even the background for the initial Bologna Declaration does not really explain how the process gathered such momentum over the following decade. The bursting of the dotcom bubble and the resulting economic uncertainty between the Bologna Summit in 1999 and the Prague Summits 2 years later gave rise to calls for the EU to be more than just an economic and political union and for it to have a greater focus on the wider societal benefits. Education fitted well within this narrative, as the declaration put it 'the importance of education and educational co-operation in the development and strengthening of stable, peaceful and democratic societies is universally acknowledged as paramount, the more so in view of the situation in South East Europe' (Bologna Declaration, 1999). Placing increased emphasis on this process, and giving it new impetus through the involvement of higher education institutions and students, was a logical next step.

The Bologna Declaration had been signed by the ministers of higher education, which was appropriate given the highly centralised nature of some European higher education systems. However with some highly autonomous university systems, such as in the United Kingdom, any ambition to make a European Higher Education Area a reality could only ever be possible by engaging universities. This was rectified at the 2001 Prague ministerial summit with the incorporation of the newly formed

---

[1]In the United Kingdom (Dearing Report, 1997), Italy (Martinotti, 1997), France (Attali, 1998) and Germany (HRK, 1996).

European Universities Association[2] (representing rectors' conferences, such as Universities UK, and individual universities) along with EURASHE (representing colleges of higher education, and their representative bodies such as Guild HE).

It was not just universities that were invited to be involved in 2001. ESIB — the National Unions of Students in Europe — was also approached. ESIB (which became the European Students' Union (ESU) in 2007) is the European umbrella organisation of national students' unions. It was this engagement of students in policy-making at the European level, along with the incorporation of the importance of student representation in the text of the Communiqué itself, that gave a real boost to student engagement across Europe.

Involvement in the process was important as a legitimising factor for ESIB at the European level. There was growing concern within ESIB at the time about a threat to their recognition as the main representative voice of European students. In particular the European Commission was increasing its dialogue with other interdisciplinary student organisations, such as the Erasmus Student Network and AEGEE (Association des Etats Généraux des Etudiants d'Europe). As Martina Vukasovic (ESIB Chair 2002 and Executive Committee 2001) put it, it was 'no longer a play off between ESIB, AEGEE and ESN' as a result of the 'recognised status' in the Prague Communiqué, and this was 'further consolidated' by the 'firming up of the Bologna Process structures between 2001−3'. This background gave both organisations, EUA and ESIB, motive to focus on the Bologna Process as a way of establishing and strengthening their own organisational positions. So the climate was right for the Bologna Process to flourish and student engagement within it.

6.3. Involving Students in European Policy-Making

In many ways the Bologna Process itself reflects the evolution of student engagement in higher education policy more generally. The Sorbonne Declaration (1998) was an entirely ministerial meeting, in Bologna (1999) some students managed to get themselves invited, in Prague (2001) the Communiqué explicitly mentioned that ESIB should be 'consulted in the follow-up work' and by 2003 in Berlin were involved as 'consultative members' (Berlin Communiqué, 2003, p. 8). Over subsequent summits, it could be argued that ESIB became increasingly involved and influential, acting as a driving force for pushing forward and shaping the reforms.

---

[2]The European Universities Association (EUA) was established in 2001 out of the merger of Association of European Universities (CRE) and the Confederation of EU Rectors Conferences. Confederation of EU Rectors Conferences was an organisation bringing together the national representative bodies of vice-chancellors, such as Universities UK, from across the EU. Association of European Universities was a grouping of individual European universities.

This shift in the engagement of students between Bologna and Prague was noted in ESIB's Student Göteborg Declaration in 2001, which said in the preamble:

> In June 1999, ESIB and its members, the national unions of students, had to invite themselves to the ministerial meeting on 'A European Higher Education Area' in Bologna. Two years later, at the Prague Summit, ESIB was a keynote speaker. (ESIB, 2001)

This was the successful outcome of a deliberate strategy by ESIB to get itself officially involved in the Bologna Process.

In 2000, ESIB set up an *ad hoc* expert Committee on Prague, the stated aim of this group was 'to be strongly involved in the process of the creation of the European Area of Higher Education' and 'to prepare for the Prague ministerial summit in 2001' (ESU, 2012, p. 23). Over the following 18 months there was a twin-track approach. National unions lobbied their ministries for ESIB to be involved in the process, with the French Education Minister Jack Lang being a particular ally. At the same time the Committee on Prague developed a position on the European Higher Education Area with member national unions of students and worked constructively in various meetings of civil servants associated with the preparation of the summit. By the time of the Prague Summit, the engagement of students was seen as something that would enrich the process. This was demonstrated by the language of the Prague Communiqué that 'students as competent, active and constructive partners in the establishment and shaping of a European Higher Education Area [are] needed and welcomed'. However, there is also something double-edged about a phrase that implies involvement is reliant on students being competent, active and constructive and that if they do not meet these high standards then their right to involvement could be withdrawn.

The 2003 Berlin ministerial summit confirmed that student involvement was more than contingent. The Berlin ministerial communiqué established the Bologna Follow-Up Group; this included representatives of the Ministries of each member country as well as the European representatives of universities and students. This formalisation of the policy-making structures gave students a central role in the development of the European Higher Education Area.

It was in the interest of both EUA and ESIB to make an impact which would consolidate their position as European organisations. It was this motivation, along with their interest in the issues, that meant the student representatives came along well prepared focused on their key goals. Ligia Deca (ESU Chairperson 2008−10) observed:

> During my time ESU made it a strategy to be involved in every Bologna Follow-Up Group structure there was, with the idea that the voice of students had to be heard for all EHEA topics. This helped a lot in having all the information, actually nobody apart from the Secretariat and the BFUG Chairs had all the information that ESU had.

6.4.   Impact of Student Engagement in Bologna

Student engagement had a considerable impact on the Bologna Process. The purpose of student engagement is not just representation but rather how this representation can be used to make a real difference to the experience of students. This principle is best summed up by the former President of the National Union of Students (NUS), Digby Jacks, in 1974:

> Representation must never be seen, except in strategic and practical terms, as an end in itself. Too many union officers see it as a question of communication and merely sitting on the appropriate committee. The purpose of representation is to secure educational and social change. (Jacks, 1974)

Even through a basic text analysis it can be seen that there is a significant shift in emphasis between the 1999 Bologna Declaration and the 2001 Prague Communiqué. In particular it is possible to see the themes being raised by students through the Student Göteborg Declaration feeding through into the Prague Communiqué. Martina Vukasovic emphasised:

> A number of issues were put on the agenda, student participation being the first one of course (with the help of some allies – some national governments and the Council of Europe primarily), higher education as a public good and public responsibility (closely related to ESIBs work on GATS (General Agreement on Trade in Services) and again in cooperation with Council of Europe, EUA and some national governments), social dimension and the focus on obstacles to mobility other than academic/recognition issues.

Over the next decade of the process these key themes continued to be developed by ESIB. Following the Prague Summit, ESIB organised two Bologna Seminars. The first, in February 2003 with the Greek Ministry of Higher Education, aimed to articulate what was meant by the 'social dimension' raising questions of access to higher education. This trend was noticeable in the shift in attitudes from 1999 to 2003. In 1999 the ministers emphasised the primary importance of the competitiveness of the European Higher Education Area, whereas by 2003 the ministers said, 'The need to increase competitiveness must be balanced with the objective of improving the social characteristics of the European Higher Education Area, aiming at strengthening social cohesion and reducing social and gender inequalities both at national and at European level. In that context, the ministers reaffirm their position that higher education is a public good and a public responsibility' (Berlin Communiqué, 2003).

The second event, organised with the Norwegian Royal Ministry of Education alongside the Council of Europe in June 2003, addressed student participation in governance. The outcomes of the seminar called for:

> Further involvement of students [...] at all levels of decision making, this involvement should not only be legally permitted but effectively

encouraged by providing the means necessary for active participation both in the formal and informal approaches. (EHEA, 2003)

This was reflected in the ministerial communiqué arising from summit in Berlin in September 2003 (p. 5) which included the forward-looking statement that 'students are full partners in higher education governance', something not codified in the United Kingdom till the Student Engagement chapter of UK Quality Code was agreed in 2012.

This engagement in the policy-making structures at the European level has continued, and deepened, over the past decade. Allan Päll (ESU Chair 2011–12, Vice-Chair 2009–11) argued:

> Students' participation in the process has been of high influence. […] ESU's input has been valued in drafting Bologna policy of late and the eventual communiqués reflected most of the ESU priorities. One could simply look at the text 'copied' to the Communiqués from the statements of ESU, whether internal or external. (ESU, 2010)

Ligia Deca also added that the 'biggest achievements' of ESU in recent years were:

> … the adoption of the 20% by 2020 mobility benchmark in the Leuven/ Louvain la Neuve Communiqué (2009), following two years of intense lobbying and an alliance with the European Commission on pushing this through. This target only became adopted by the EU Council two years later (2011). Another success for European students was the clear formulation of student centred learning as a priority for the EHEA, as well as the agreement of its definition in the sense ESU gave in its T4SCL project. (ESU, 2010)

6.5. Bologna as a Driver for Student Engagement

The Bologna Process has also been a driver for promoting student engagement in higher education policy-making more widely. This was not the case from the start. The original declaration made little mention of student engagement: the only mention of the word 'student' was to preface 'mobility'. The Bologna Declaration was more concerned with the wider outcomes of education and the processes for achieving a European Higher Education Area.

The follow-up ministerial summit two years later in Prague changed matters, in part due to the active engagement of ESIB in the lead-up to the summit with their Göteborg Declaration. This Student Göteborg Declaration:

> … stressed that students, as competent, active and constructive partners, must be seen as one of the driving forces for changes in the field

of education. Student participation in the Bologna process is one of the key steps towards permanent and more formalised student involvement in all decision making bodies and discussion for a dealing with higher education on the European level.

This language was very much reflected in the Prague Communiqué, the outcome of the 2001 ministerial summit. The Communiqué used the 'competent, active and constructive partners' language, going on to stress that student engagement 'in the establishment and shaping of a European Higher Education Area is needed and welcomed'. The ministers went on to reinforce that students 'should participate in and influence the organisation and content of education at universities and other higher education institutions'. At the 2001 summit institutions were also accepted as members of the process by the ministers and so were implicitly also signing up to this statement. The EUA trends report in 2001 had a section on 'the role of students in the creation of the European Higher Education Area'.

Student engagement and representation continued to feature in the ministerial communiqués over the next decade. The Budapest—Vienna ministerial summit (2010) was clear that 'We fully support staff and student participation in decision-making structures at European, national and institutional levels.' Ligia Deca (ESU Chair 2008–10) described this student involvement as going beyond just what was written in the Communiqué:

> ESU was more involved in the preparations for the Leuven/Louvain la Neuve conference (2009 ministerial summit) and especially the (2010) Budapest/Vienna conference, where its opinions were taken into account in designing the programme, invited speakers and global student movement representatives.

The inclusion by the EUA (in their 2001 trends report) of information about how students are engaged at a national level was a symbolic moment in this process. This was registered in the next trends report and in the stocktaking reports for the ministerial summits. These trends/stocktaking reports provided a scorecard for how each country was doing, measured against various action lines. While there was no legal requirement for each country to implement the Bologna action lines, there was a peer-pressure effect generated by presenting the trends/stocktaking report to the ministerial summits and the regular meetings of civil servants through the Bologna Follow-Up Group meetings.

Allan Päll (ESU Chair 2011/12) reinforced this by saying that the Bologna Process 'has transformed the structures of higher education, it has given more say to student representative bodies than ever before'. He went on to say that the journey towards student engagement has not always been an easy one. He emphasised that too many countries have taken an 'a la carte approach' to implementing the Bologna recommendations. Ligia Deca reinforced this: 'ministers acknowledged in writing that the critical voices of the students and academics should be taken into account as they signal profound problems with national Bologna Process implementation.'

Päll went on to say that

> after the wave of student dissatisfaction that hit Europe through occu-
> pations and protest between 2008 and 2010, partly asserting blame on
> the process, we got ministers to admit the lack of communication in
> the Budapest-Vienna declaration. But Bologna still went quiet as the
> overwhelming feeling left from Vienna was that EHEA is now open,
> so the crucial moment was missed and the discussion and real push
> for involvement at did not go any deeper, to the institutional level.

While the Bologna Process benefited initially from the impetus generated by being a useful external driver to push through government reforms, in the longer term it became seen as a negative influence used to justify unpopular reforms.

6.6.   Case Study: England, Wales and Northern Ireland

It can be difficult in a UK context to point to specific changes as a result of the Bologna Process. It has sometimes been remarked that Bologna is just adopting the UK system, not least by the minister reassuring the UK press after returning from signing the declaration. One reform has a strong claim to have been brought about by external pressure created by the Bologna Process: the inclusion of student members in the Institutional Audit/Review in England, Wales and Northern Ireland.

The expectation that students should be included in external assessment procedures was embedded in the *European Standards and Guidelines for Quality Assurance in the European Higher Education Area* (ESG) (ENQA, 2005). The *Guidelines*, which were first published in March 2005, included in section 2.6.7 the standard that 'external assessment by a group of experts, including, as appropriate, student member(s)'.

While there have been student members of institutional review teams in Scotland since 2002, there was a significant amount of resistance from institutions in the rest of the United Kingdom. This was sometimes based on the perception that students should not be part of the external reviews, as they were not 'peers' in a peer review process. This was raised in a paper prepared by the Quality Assurance Agency for Higher Education (QAA):

> Traditionally, external panels have consisted of experts who are the
> most highly qualified in the academic world, that is, professors. A
> consideration when including students on the panels, therefore, is
> whether they should be considered experts like the other panel mem-
> bers, or have another, special status, for example, as stakeholder
> representatives. (QAA, 2008)

Following the ministers' adoption of the ESG in Bergen in 2005, there was increasing pressure in the rest of the United Kingdom to include student members on institutional review panels. This was evident at the 2007 ministerial summit. The summit was held in London and so increased the embarrassment to the hosts when the level of student engagement in quality assurance was one of the few areas that did not receive a dark green[3] on the stocktaking report (DfES, 2007). By October that year QAA had released a consultation outlining their rationale for introducing student members onto institutional audit panels and a timescale for implementation. The following January (2008) a Director from the QAA was quoted in the *Times Higher Education*, a UK specialist higher education magazine, as saying, 'The model of introducing student membership of institutional audit teams is increasingly becoming the norm across Europe' (Attwood, 2008).

Even at this point there was a last-ditch attempt to slow down the reform. The QAA Circular Letter (February 2008, CL01/08) noted that the 'QAA Board has now considered the responses received and has agreed that we should postpone the introduction of any change, to allow sufficient time to consult further with the sector around these important issues.'[4] This was in part due to the feedback from Universities UK and Guild HE raising concerns about 'the impact of implementing any change in the middle of an audit cycle'. This would have meant any change being held off until 2011.

It was therefore timely that the QAA was reviewed by the European Network for Quality Assurance (ENQA) in early 2008 as part of their cycle of reviews of national agencies. In their July report on the eligibility of the QAA for membership of ENQA, they were particularly scathing of the lack of student reviewers. In paragraph 60 of their report (ENQA, 2008), they state:

> The Panel has noted that QAA is not yet fully compliant with the expectations of the Standard relating to inclusion of a student member on external assessments. Whilst this procedure has for some time proved successful in Scotland, it has not yet been fully introduced in England, Wales and Northern Ireland. The Panel believes this development to be an entirely appropriate aspect of good practice. The Panel suggests that delaying the introduction of such aspects of good practice until the beginning of a new review cycle might unduly hinder the evolution of QAA and should be avoided, unless consistency of judgement about institutions is likely to be substantially compromised.

Their judgement was that the QAA were therefore only 'Substantially compliant' — one of only two judgements in the whole report not to be 'fully compliant'. QAA included students as observer members of institutional audit panels from early 2009, and as full members of institutional review panels in 2010. It says on the QAA's own website: 'Student reviewers quickly settled into the role and provided an anchor at the heart of the review process for the student experience, as well as contributing to the team spirit and the general operation of the review process. Since then, we have never looked back' (QAA, 2012).

6.7.   A Driver for Establishing National Unions

Students' unions can often develop at the local university level of their own accord, partly out of a desire to come together with other students for clubs, social activity and representation. It is, however, often an external driver that brings these local students' unions together to form a national union of students.

If we look at national students' unions across Europe there was a proliferation of unions being formed in the early 1920s. After the First World War, coming out of the peace movement, the International Students' Bureau was created. Membership of this organisation was only available to national organisations, and so several national students' unions were established, including VSS-UNES-USU Switzerland (1920), SFS Sweden (1921), SYL Finland (1921) and NUS UK (1922). There were similar moves after the Second World War, as the International Students' Bureau became the International Union of Students and national unions were established in countries such as Austria in 1946.

Since the signing of the Bologna Declaration, and the increasingly important role of ESIB within the structures of the Bologna Process, many national unions of students have been set up. This has been particularly true in Eastern Europe, with national unions established in Bulgaria, Lithuania and Slovenia in the early 2000s. Interviewed in 2012, Martina Vukasovic (ESIB Chair 2002) agreed:

> I think [this is true] in particular in the countries that had rather poor tradition of student participation in general. In Serbia as well as in other ex-Yugoslav countries, students' unions actively used Bologna Process documents and explicit references to student participation there to push forward more student participation on the national level.

As the Bologna Process spread further east over the next decade, national unions were created in countries such as Azerbaijan, Armenia, Albania and Georgia. Interviewed in 2012, Liga Deca (ESU Chairperson 2008–10) said:

> In Armenia a new national student union was set-up following ESU's visibility in the Bologna Process and the country study visit conducted there in 2008 by ESU with Open Society support. Azerbaijan also set-up a national student union following (at least formally) the model promoted by ESU through its Ljubljana Declaration. Kazakhstan is another country example which got to acknowledge the need for student participation following the interactions with ESU in the frame of the Bologna Process.

The Bologna Process also acted as an external driver for the development of a national union outside Eastern Europe. Both Portugal and Spain developed national unions during the 2000s due to a desire to engage with the process and there have been several attempts, as yet unsuccessful, by the Greek Ministry of Education to re-establish their national union to ensure active engagement.

This pressure to create a national union of students has come from a number of directions: first to enable local students' unions to have a voice within the structures of the Bologna Process, particularly in those European countries where Bologna is a major national issue responsible for radically reforming their higher education systems. This desire for engagement at the European level meant it was necessary for them to come together to form a national union to become members of ESIB/ESU.

However, this desire to see strong national unions also came increasingly from universities and ministries. There was a growing recognition during this period of the value of student representation. Regular constructive work at European events such as Bologna Follow Up Group meetings, seminars and ministerial summits demonstrated the value and importance of student representation at a national level.

6.8. Bologna as a Global Driver

While the concept of a European Higher Education Area has had a significant impact within Europe, there is also increasing interest in the process from across the globe. The first policy forum, held in Leuven/Louvain-la-Neuve in 2009 alongside the ministerial summit, had representatives from Australia; Brazil; Canada; P.R. China; Egypt; Ethiopia; Israel; Japan; Kazakhstan; Kyrgyzstan; Mexico; Morocco; New Zealand; Tunisia and the United States, along with the International Association of Universities and other international and non-governmental organisations.

At the recent ministerial summit in Bucharest (May 2012), the first session at the parallel policy forum was 'The Bologna Process — a catalyst for reform in other regions?', and it included speakers from the International Association of Universities, Thailand, Argentina and the United States. The resulting statement acknowledged 'the importance of [the] active participation of the academic community — students, faculty, staff and institutional leadership — in the governance and development of higher education responsive to societal change and economic needs'.

In 2009 there was a Canadian symposium (organised by the Association of Universities and Colleges Canada) looking at 'The Bologna Process and Implications for Canada's Universities'. The report noted in its conclusions that 'Bologna demonstrates that any successful continuing reform process requires both political will and resources from leaders in government and institutions, and engagement from students, faculty and staff' (AUCC, 2009, p. 14).

It is still too early to say whether the Bologna Process will have a significant impact on higher education reform outside Europe, particularly in the context of encouraging student engagement. But there is certainly a case to be made that in many of these countries, which have varying levels of student representation and engagement, simply witnessing the effective engagement of students in the process during the ministerial summits and policy forums, and the emphasis placed on it in the text of the ministerial Communiqués, will encourage a degree of reflection on the situation in their own countries.

6.9. Conclusions

Student engagement has been at the heart of the moves to create the European Higher Education Area almost from the start. Student representatives, despite being excluded from the early stages of the process, managed to get themselves invited into the structures and from there have gone from strength to strength in helping to both lead and shape the policy agenda.

Student engagement has ensured that student concerns have been central to the process, including making student mobility a reality, focusing on student-centred learning and emphasising the public good of higher education.

The process has driven student engagement more widely as a result of the importance given to student representation in the text of the ministerial statements themselves. This constant reinforcing of the importance, and benefits, of student engagement has been given an added dimension through countries being held to account through the regular stocktaking reports presented to ministers. This has resulted in increased importance being placed on student engagement and many national changes, the inclusion of students on institutional review panels in external review by the Quality Assurance Agency in England, Wales and Northern Ireland for example. The process has had other, perhaps unintended, consequences, such as the establishment of several national unions of students across Europe. This has enabled students in those countries to be able to engage with the European higher education policy-making processes and also with university and ministerial representatives.

The policy forums, and the interest in the process outside Europe, have begun to have an even wider impact. It will be interesting to monitor whether the Bologna Process will have a sustained impact beyond the boundaries of Europe, but it has already made a significant impact across the continent. However, it is important to keep in mind the warnings from Allan Päll that, while Bologna has been a driver for student engagement, this is not guaranteed if the process itself begins to lose its connection with those who support it, and students feel disenfranchised from the core discussions.

References

Attali, J. (1998). *Pour un modèle européen d'enseignement supérieur* [Toward a European higher education model]. Paris: Stock.

Attwood, R. (2008). *QAA to enlist students to audit quality. Times Higher Education.* Retrieved from http://www.timeshighereducation.co.uk/story.asp?storycode = 400130. Accessed on 10 January 2008.

AUCC. (2009). *The Bologna Process and implications for Canada's universities.* Retrieved from http://www.aucc.ca/wp-content/uploads/2011/05/bologna-report-20091.pdf. Accessed on 4 February 2013.

Berlin Communiqué. (2003). *Realising the European Higher Education Area.* Retrieved from http://www.ond.vlaanderen.be/hogeronderwijs/bologna/documents/MDC/Berlin_ Communique1.pdf. Accessed on 20 January 2013.

Bologna Declaration. (1999). *The Bologna declaration of 19 June 1999.* Retrieved from http://www.bologna-bergen2005.no/Docs/00-Main_doc/990719BOLOGNA_DECLARATION. PDF. Accessed on 20 January 2013.

Dearing, R. (1997). *Higher education in the learning society.* National Committee of Inquiry into Higher Education, Leeds. Retrieved from http://www.leeds.ac.uk/educol/ncihe/. Accessed on 7 October 2013.

DfES. (2007). *Bologna Process stocktaking, London.* Retrieved from http://www.ond.vlaanderen. be/hogeronderwijs/bologna/documents/WGR2007/Stocktaking_report2007.pdf. Accessed on 4 February 2013.

EHEA. (2003). *Summary and conclusions.* Oslo seminar on student participation in governance in higher education. Retrieved from http://www.ehea.info/Uploads/Seminars/030612-14 SummaryConclusions.pdf

ENQA. (2005). *Standards and guidelines for quality assurance in the European Higher Education Area.* Retrieved from http://www.enqa.eu/files/ESG_3edition%20(2).pdf. Accessed on 4 February 2013.

ENQA. (2008). *Report of the panel appointed to undertake a review of the Quality Assurance Agency for Higher Education (UK) for the purposes of full membership of the European Association for Quality Assurance in Higher Education (ENQA).* Retrieved from http:// www.enqa.eu/reviews_reports.lasso. Accessed on 7 October 2013.

ESIB. (2001). *Göteborg student declaration.* Retrieved from http://ebookbrowse.com/student-goteborg-declaration-pdf-d53726075. Accessed on 20 January 2013.

ESU. (2010) Time for a new paradigm in education: Student centered learning (abbreviated T4SCL). Retrieved from http://www.esu-online.org/projects/archive/scl/

ESU. (2012). *ESU turns 30.* Retrieved from http://www.esu-online.org/asset/News/6068/30th-Anniversay-Online.pdf. Accessed on 20 January 2013.

Haug, G., & Tauch, C. (2001). *Trends in learning structures in higher education (II).* Retrieved from http://93.188.136.109/educacion/udg/uni/documentos/TrendsinLearning StructuresinHigherEducationII.pdf. Accessed on 7 October 2013.

HEA. (2011). *Spectrum of student engagement.* Retrieved from http://www.heacademy.ac.uk/ resources/detail/studentengagement/Dimensions_student_engagement

Hogenschulrektorenkonferenz (HRK). (1996). *Internationalisierung der Hochschulbeziehungen im Zusammenhang mit dem Socrates/Erasmus-Programm* [Internationalization of university relations in connection with the Socrates/Erasmus program]. Bonn: Dokumente zur Hochschulreform.

Jacks, D. (1974). *Quoted on NUS website.* Retrieved from http://www.nusconnect.org.uk/ news/article/nus/3043/. Accessed on 27 November 2012.

Prague Communiqué. (2001). *Towards the European Higher Education Area.* Retrieved from http://www.ond.vlaanderen.be/hogeronderwijs/bologna/documents/MDC/PRAGUE_ COMMUNIQUE.pdf. Accessed on 15 April 2013.

QAA. (2008). Student membership of audit and review teams: Learning from the Nordic experience. Retrieved from https://www.qaa.ac.uk/events/smart08/StudentPaper2.asp July 2008

QAA. (2012). QAA website. Retrieved from http://www.qaa.ac.uk/Partners/students/reviews/ Pages/Student-reviewers.aspx. Accessed on 15 November 2012.

Chapter 7

Student Engagement in Private Sector Higher Education

Sue Rivers and Thomas Willans

Abstract

This chapter aims to review how student engagement is achieved in UK private sector higher education and to explore what can be learned from this. It particularly considers student engagement from the perspective of the student voice and participation in the institution.

A review was conducted to identify key themes in the literature and practice and to examine approaches in a number of private sector institutions. The chapter considers the various ways in which private sector institutions engage with their students, using BPP University of Professional Studies (BPP) as an example and drawing upon interviews conducted with Carl Lygo, Vice Chancellor, and Laila Heinonen, Chief Executive of Students, BPP. From examining practice in the publicly funded sector, a framework was devised for assessing student engagement in private sector higher education institutions (HEIs) based on categorising approaches as 'narrow' or 'wide'.

It was clear that private sector HEIs adopt both narrow and wide approaches to student engagement; however, where narrower approaches were employed they tended to be applied extensively and inclusively. A number of examples of good practice in the private sector were identified that the sector as a whole could learn from, especially in terms of specific ways of closing the feedback loop and using students as leaders of change.

The framework devised from this review is a useful tool for assessing the type and extent of student engagement in higher education (HE) generally. The private sector has much to learn from the publicly funded sector in this field and vice versa. In particular, both can learn innovative and different ways of enhancing the student experience.

The Student Engagement Handbook: Practice in Higher Education
Copyright © 2013 by Emerald Group Publishing Limited
All rights of reproduction in any form reserved
ISBN: 978-1-78190-423-7

7.1.   An Introduction to Private Sector Higher Education

Commentators appear to agree that there is significant, and rapidly increasing, demand for higher education worldwide, but a serious lack of global supply, and that private sector provision in the United Kingdom and worldwide has grown to meet this demand (Lygo, 2012; Middlehurst & Fielden, 2011). Indeed, according to Middlehurst and Fielden (2011, p. 3), throughout the world, the number of students in private institutions is growing faster than in publicly owned and funded ones and this is because governments simply cannot afford to pay for the higher education that is required, so the private sector is expanding to meet the demand. Levy (2011, p. 1) claims that, by way of best estimate, private sector higher education now accounts for over 31 per cent of global enrolment. What he terms 'this explosion' has overwhelmingly occurred in developing countries; thus, in Latin America 49 per cent of its enrolment is in the private sector and in Asia the figure is 36 per cent, although Asia has by far the largest actual numbers of students in this sector (Levy, 2008, 2010).

China provides an interesting example. There has been a significant overall expansion of higher education in China in the past few years, with gross enrolment rates from 9.8 per cent in 1998 to 23.3 per cent in 2008. By the end of 2008, over 29 million students were enrolled in tertiary institutions, making China's higher education system the largest in the world (Liu & Wang, 2010). What may not be so widely known, however, is the growth in private sector provision there. In 1997, twenty private higher education institutions (HEIs) provided formal programmes to 14,000 students (about 0.9 per cent of all regular HEIs and 0.4 per cent of total enrolments). In 2003 a law was passed promoting so-called *minban* education (people-run colleges, i.e. private institutions), and the number of private HEIs subsequently increased, reaching 638 by 2008 — approximately 28 per cent of the nation's total (Liu & Wang, 2010). Europe, with a smaller private sector than the global norm, is also seeing growth especially in central and eastern Europe. Estonia, Georgia, Poland and Latvia passing 20 per cent of private enrolment (Universities UK, 2010). Apart from the Netherlands (13%), France (14%) and Spain (10%) (Universities UK, 2010: 61) there is much less growth elsewhere in Europe e.g. Germany has only 3-5 per cent privately enrolled students.

The United States is world renowned for the extent and prestige of its private higher education, with some of its most highly acclaimed institutions, such as Harvard, Yale and Stanford, being outside of the public university sector. At the middle of the twentieth century, the private sector accounted for half of all the US enrolments, and, since then, it has remained consistently at around or just under a quarter (Levy, 2006). However, by 2009 a slight steady increase in the proportion of private sector enrolments from 22.7 per cent in 1997 to 27.5 per cent was noticeable (see Table 7.1).

The United Kingdom has traditionally had almost the opposite situation, with its most prestigious universities, Oxford and Cambridge, being part of the publicly funded sector. However, the recent growth in private providers in the United Kingdom led the Higher Education Statistics Agency (HESA) to carry out a survey

Table 7.1: Number and total HE enrolment at public and private (profit and non-profit) HEIs.

	1997			2008			2009		
	China[a]	United States[b]	United Kingdom[c]	China[a]	United States[b]	United Kingdom[c]	China[a]	United States[b]	United Kingdom[c,d]
Total public HEIs (number)	2200	1707	175	1624	1676	164	n/a	1672	164
Private HEIs (number)	20	2357	n/a	638	2733	n/a	n/a	2823	65
Total public and private HEIs (number)	2220	4064	n/a	2263	4409	n/a	n/a	4495	229
Percentage of HEIs that are private (per cent)	0.9	58.0	n/a	28.2	61.9	n/a	n/a	62.8	28.4
Total enrolment (million)	3.5	14.5	1.8	29.1	19.1	2.4	n/a	20.4	2.5
Private enrolment (number)	14000	3.3M	n/a	3.93M	5.1M	n/a	n/a	5.6M	38000
Percentage of higher education students at private HEIs (per cent)	0.4	22.7	n/a	13.5	26.7	n/a	n/a	27.5	1.5

n/a – not available.
[a]Chinese data: (Liu & Wang, 2010).
[b]US data: National Centre for Education Statistics (NCES, 2000, 2012).
[c]UK data: Higher Education Statistical Agency (HESA, 1999, 2009, 2010).
[d]UK data: Survey of private and for profit Higher Education providers (HESA, 2011).

of private providers in 2009–10 (HESA, 2011). This is needed as HESA's focus is upon the publically funded institutions, best classified as Government-dependent private tertiary institutions (Universities UK, 2010), with only one private provider, the University of Buckingham, included; hence only 2009–10 data is included in Table 7.1. The survey revealed that there were 37,738 students studying at higher education level at 65 private providers (see Table 7.1). The UK private sector therefore accounts for only 1.5 per cent of the total higher education student population. However, most of these students, some 27,896, were studying business, management, law or accounting and this amounted to a more significant 6.6 per cent of the total 422,365 Business and Administrative Studies and Law students in 2009 (HESA, 2010).

There has been a history in the United Kingdom of small private education institutions (such as colleges) providing tuition for degree programmes, mainly in disciplines such as business, law, computing, hospitality and tourism and management, with the degrees being conferred by other institutions with degree awarding powers. Often the students were part-time or studied by distance learning (e.g. the College of Estate Management in Reading offered property-related undergraduate and master's degree programmes conferred by the University of Reading or the Open University). These institutions often had relatively modest student numbers, typically no more than 2,000 students (Middlehurst & Fielden, 2011, p. 4) and frequently also provided other non-degree programmes (e.g. diplomas, individual modules and short courses). The University of Buckingham was the first (and until recently the only) private institution in the United Kingdom to have secured full university title (in 1983), enabling it to offer research-based degrees, such as PhD and DPhil as well as taught degrees, such as BA, BSc and LLB. Buckingham is probably the smallest UK university with around 1000 students. It prides itself on providing traditional, small-group, Oxbridge-style teaching alongside the best of the new technology in a community of many different nationalities in which honours degrees are achieved in 2 years (Pemberton, 2010; University of Buckingham, 2012).

A more recent development has been the granting of taught degree awarding powers to privately funded institutions in England. Such powers are granted by the Privy Council on the advice of the Quality Assurance Agency (QAA) after a rigorous process (e.g. in the case of Ashridge Management School, the process took almost 6 years from submission of original application to admitting students onto the new programmes (Lockett, 2012)). Applications are judged against a number of criteria 'designed to establish that the applicant is a well-founded, cohesive and self-critical academic community that can demonstrate firm guardianship of its standards' (Morgan, 2012b). In outline, the applicant must normally be able to demonstrate:

- the effectiveness of its regulatory and quality assurance arrangements
- that it has had no fewer than four consecutive years' experience, immediately preceding the year of application, of delivering higher education programmes
- a minimum proportion/number of students in higher education (BIS, 2004, p. 5).

Interestingly, the process specifically includes structured discussions with staff and students — an early requirement for a form of student engagement (BIS, 2004, p. 8).

There is a major movement towards private providers gaining such degree awarding powers (such as Ashridge Management School and the College of Estate Management), University College status (ifs University College) or University title (including BPP University, The University of Law and Regent's University London).

While many of these private institutions have charitable status, Middlehurst and Fielden (2011, p. 8) note the emergence of for-profit providers in the private sector, whether with or without their own degree awarding powers. For example Pearson, a large educational publisher, is now offering a Business and Enterprise degree validated by Royal Holloway College, University of London from September 2012 (Matthews, 2012).

The UK higher education sector today is undergoing significant change and consequent turmoil: those institutions previously largely publicly funded are now adjusting to an era of publicly provided student loans. In addition, changes in the rules governing university title have enabled smaller publicly funded (and often relatively specialist) institutions such as Bishop Grosseteste in Lincoln and Newman in Birmingham (both former teacher training colleges) to join their ranks. Meanwhile, in the private sector, English institutions previously reliant on others to provide accreditation for their awards (such as the College of Estate Management and Regent's College) are obtaining their own powers to do so and some have become universities such as Regent's University London. There is a sense that what was previously a public versus private sector divide is now reforming into large versus small; broad versus specialist institutions in which the experience, and hence the voice, of students as *funders* is becoming increasingly important.

7.2. A View of Student Engagement in UK HEIs

There appears to be no single agreed definition of 'student engagement'. According to the QAA (2012c, p. 2), the meaning has evolved over time and has been applied to a number of different things; however, they narrow it down to two principal areas:

- improving the motivation of students to engage in learning and to learn independently
- the participation of students in quality enhancement and quality assurance processes, resulting in the improvement of their educational experience.

Trowler (2010, p. 3) offers a similar concise, definition:

> Student engagement is concerned with the interaction between the time, effort and other relevant resources invested by both students

and their institutions intended to optimise the student experience and enhance the learning outcomes and development of students and the performance, and reputation of the institution.

These forms of student engagement can be traced back to the 1980s to the work of Astin (1984) who focused upon student involvement, defined as the amount of 'physical and psychological energy that the student devotes to the academic experience' (Astin, 1984, p. 297). Astin (1984) argued that student involvement improves student learning; therefore university policy needs to increase student involvement. Trowler (2010) recognised this and suggested that student engagement gained momentum from the 1990s onwards.

Some twenty-first century key milestones and influences have been:

• the advent of the National Student Survey (NSS) in 2005: this gave national prominence and league table status to feedback from students about aspects of their higher education experience, making it an influential factor in student and parental choice of higher education provider, and giving HEIs an imperative to ensure that as many eligible students as possible engage in giving this feedback while also elevating the importance of delivering a good student experience;
• the creation of 74 HEFCE funded Centres of Excellence in Teaching and Learning (CETLs) in 2005–10: a £115 million investment in learning and teaching enhancement in the public sector (e.g. Assessment for Learning, Northumbria University). As their name implies, CETLs focused upon teaching and learning rather than student engagement. However, Taylor and Wilding (2009) recognised that some CETLs (such as the Reinvention Centre for Undergraduate Research run by the University of Warwick and Oxford Brookes University) were focused upon student engagement in that they involved students as researchers in partnership with postgraduate, postdoctoral and academic researchers, emphasising the role of students in the production of knowledge.

The private sector was not involved in either of these important developments at the time; for example, CETLS were open only to HEFCE (publicly) funded HEIs. This meant that public and private sector HEIs were not able to enhance learning together through the CETLs or to be compared on the basis of their student feedback. This will now happen with private universities such as BPP entering the NSS.

7.2.1.   A Narrow Approach

One aspect of student engagement, therefore, can be seen as involving students in assuring the quality of their higher education experience. This can encompass mechanisms such as obtaining student feedback (e.g. through questionnaires) and having student representation on committees. It is what Trowler (2010, p. 10) terms 'engagement with structure and process'. According to the QAA (2012c, p. 2) it is widely accepted that the views of students, individually and collectively, should inform quality systems with the purpose of improving the student educational experience both for current and future cohorts. While there is space for HEIs to determine the exact means within their own institutional context, it is expected that they will ensure that arrangements exist for the effective representation of the collective student voice at all organisational levels, and that these arrangements provide opportunities for all students to be heard (QAA, 2012c, p. 7).

Little, Locke, Scesa, and Williams (2009, pp. 15–18) found that student feedback questionnaires are widely used in HEIs, at institution-wide level (92 per cent) and module/unit level (87 per cent) in addition to the National Student Survey of final year students. They also found that, within HEIs, student representation on institution-level committees is near universal, either through elected current students or student union officials. Other significant findings were that:

- just over half of HEIs operate Student–Staff Liaison Committees (SSLCs) — mostly at departmental or school level
- over half of HEIs have a student liaison officer — very often originally connected with student retention strategies, but increasingly seen as a 'neutral conduit between faculties and "the centre"
- the most common informal process was tutors and lecturers having an open door policy, whereby students could get access to them outside timetabled meetings or sessions.

However, Little et al. (2009, pp. 55–57) found that there was a tendency for institutions to feel that what they call 'the basic model for student engagement' (student feedback questionnaires and student representation systems) was reasonably or very effective, whereas a common issue was failure to 'close the feedback loop' by letting students know how their views (provided through surveys and student representatives) had been taken into account and what action had been taken as a result. The authors also found that while that 'basic model' is similar across the sector, actual practice varies both between institutions and within institutions and there was room for improvement in this model itself as well as going beyond the basics; for example they found evidence that greater engagement is achieved when students themselves lead on investigating issues which affect their learning experience and they also identified a lack of effective monitoring processes in some institutions.

7.2.2. A Wider View

In the QAA's (2012c, p. 6) view HEIs should create an environment that proactively encourages students to engage fully. This may point to a definition of student engagement that goes beyond collecting feedback and ensuring student representation. Indeed, in pursuing the idea of a 'fuller' kind of student engagement, Trowler (2010) identifies two further themes in the literature:

- individual student learning — including students' degree of interest in their learning and involvement in creating it [student engagement with learning]

Figure 7.1:   Involvement to engagement.

- issues of identity — e.g. instilling a sense of belonging for individuals and for marginalised groups [inclusively engaging everyone in learning].

This is reflected in institutional language, with HEIs seemingly now moving away from talking about 'student involvement' and 'student feedback' to terms such as 'student empowerment' and 'students as partners' (Coventry University), students as 'change agents' (University of Exeter) and 'students as producers' (University of Lincoln). There is, then, a sense in which we have moved on from the more passive 'filling in happy sheets' approach to the notion of students actively participating in curriculum development, having a say in what and how they learn and having a more powerful voice in key decision-making activities, such as institutional governance. Students are now being recognised as having a valuable contribution to make; not only is their 'buy in' to change being sought as stakeholders, but they are also being asked to lead it. This movement from involvement to engagement is depicted in Figure 7.1.

The move from student involvement to active engagement seems to parallel developments in pedagogy, especially the move away from viewing academic staff as 'the sage on stage' delivering didactic lectures to passive recipients, to becoming a 'guide on the side', facilitating the learning of active, self-directed learners (Laurillard, 2007), and who may be members, along with academic and support staff, of a community of practice (Wenger, 1998).

Trowler (2010, pp. 4, 5) goes further, seeing engagement as more than involvement or participation, rather as requiring feelings and sense making as well as activity, something along similar lines to the model of Bloom, Engelhart, Furst, Hill, and Krathwohl (1956) of cognitive, psychomotor (behavioural) and affective (emotional) engagement, making the difference between whether students attend sessions, skip them or disrupt them. Accordingly, Trowler (2010, p. 7) contrasts the act of linking engagement with learning and its outcomes with merely viewing it as involving and empowering students in the *process* of shaping the learning experience.

One particular, and sometimes controversial, aspect of a broader view of student engagement is the concept of 'the student as consumer'. Little et al. (2009, p. 8) remark on the increasing marketisation of higher education and claim that continuing drives to greater public accountability (the so-called 'new public management') have prompted renewed institutional efforts to ensure that student voices, as consumers and stakeholders, are listened to and their messages acted upon as appropriate. They argue that if students are consumers, logically they should have a voice (*ibid.*, p. 13).

Furedi (2009) points to growing consumerist behaviour in students, such as a culture of student complaints, which he feels marks a reversal of roles between teachers and students:

> The authority of the customer trumps that of the service provider. Therefore, it is the opinion of the students and not the academic that determines the position of a university in the league table. Accordingly, if students assess their experience positively, then their university is judged to be a wonderful place of learning.

Little et al. (2009, p. 8) feel that listening to the student voice, so that students' perspectives are taken into account, with view to enhancing the collective student learning experience underpins many institutions' rationales for student engagement, but institutions seem to place rather less emphasis on student engagement in terms of being central to creating cohesive learning communities of teachers and learners (*ibid.*, p. 42). They therefore suggest that the effectiveness of student engagement should be regularly monitored and reviewed (*ibid.*, p. 44). Significantly, therefore, Coventry University has a Pro-Vice-Chancellor (Student Empowerment) and a key aim in its Teaching Learning and Assessment Strategy is as follows:

> To improve students' satisfaction by empowering them as participants in a community of learning where staff and students work together to learn, create, solve problems and research. (Coventry University, 2011, p. 1)

Initiatives such as 'The Student as Producer' (University of Lincoln, 2012) emphasise the role of the students as collaborators in one of the fundamental functions of higher education: knowledge production. The scheme encourages students to become involved in learning and research and, in this way, to collaborate with academics in producing knowledge and meaning. Undergraduate students have the opportunity to work alongside staff in designing and delivering their teaching and learning programmes, and in the production of work of academic content and value. Similarly, the increasing use of peer review in assessment and the growth of Peer-Assisted Learning (PAL) schemes marks a trend towards viewing students as mentors or facilitators of the learning of others, acknowledging that they have experiences to offer by way of guidance and support to others (akin to 'expert patient' initiatives in the field of health). This is echoed in Exeter, where, according to Dunne and Zandstra (2011, p. 4), despite the genuine attention to student feedback and the efforts of the university to engage with students, there was a missing element: the direct involvement of students in actually bringing about change. Students from across the university therefore contributed to a 'Students as Change Agents' initiative, carrying out a series of research projects on their learning and teaching environment, selecting concerns raised through SSLCs, and providing recommendations and solutions to improve their experience (Dunne & Zandstra, 2011, p. 2). In their review of undergraduate students as researchers within

CETLs, Taylor and Wilding (2009) adopt the approaches of McCulloch (2009) and McMillan and Cheney (1996), arguing that the metaphor of the 'student as *consumer*' is at odds with that of the 'student as *producer*' (or specifically co-producer) of knowledge and is an incomplete understanding of a student. It may be argued that private sector HEIs are embracing student engagement and yet are also both familiar and comfortable with concepts such as the student as consumer, customer or funder, and use these terms interchangeably. Perhaps the key thing is that whatever form of words is used reflects the importance of allowing the student voice to be heard.

7.2.3. Assessing Student Engagement

By way of summarising the approaches to student engagement identified in his section, it is useful to encapsulate these into a framework (Table 7.2) against which the practice adopted by particular institutions, such as the various private sector institutions examined in Section 7.3, can be assessed.

Table 7.2: A framework for assessing student engagement.

Approach	Specific examples
Narrow 'Engagement with structure and process'	Student feedback questionnaires Student representation on institutional committees Role of Students' Union (or equivalent) Student−Staff Liaison Committees (SSLCs) Student Liaison Officer Informal processes, e.g. Tutor 'Open Door' policy

Wider
Engaging students with
  their learning
	An institutional ethos of proactive and inclusive
	  engagement
	Relevant and appropriate institutional language,
	  e.g. student empowerment
	A focus on service/acknowledging students as
	  customers or stakeholders, e.g. heeding the
	  student voice
	Acknowledging students' experience and expertise
	  in learning and research, e.g. Peer-Assisted
	  Learning schemes
	Encouraging students to participate in shaping their
	  learning experience, e.g. using students as agents
	  of change
	Ability not just to collect student feedback but to
	  act on it and to 'close the feedback loop'

7.3. Student Engagement in the Private Sector

Commentators point out the advantages of having private providers in higher education in the United Kingdom, such as catering for unmet demand for student places, providing value-for-money for tax-payers and investors and offering competition for publicly funded providers to drive up quality (Middlehurst & Fielden, 2011, pp. 8, 9). There has also generally been favourable coverage of other aspects of the student experience in the private sector, such as the small class sizes, the strong vocational and professional focus, the use of practitioners as teachers, and the emphasis on employment-related skills in close alignment to the needs of employers (pp. 8, 9, 27). Indeed, Aaron Porter, former president of the National Union of Students (NUS) has remarked on the market research approach taken by private providers:

> I've been really quite astounded and amazed by the attention to detail that some of the private providers have gone to in researching the student experience and conducting proper market research on how to deliver on that experience. (Quoted in Morgan, 2012a)

Lygo (2012) also points to the innovative approaches that private HEIs have offered, such as shorter overall degree programmes:

> … traditional UK universities have taught over three academic years, with the teaching terms in each year lasting as little as 24 calendar weeks. Private HEIs have offered students the ability to study the 72 weeks within two calendar years. This reduces the cost to the student, since they are not out of the job market for three years nor are they racking up additional student living expenses. (Lygo, 2012, p. 29)

In a climate of increased tuition fees and mounting student debt, the private sector may offer an alternative to a traditional full-time campus-based university experience and, in this sense, may be engaging with the issues that really matter to students, such as finance, flexibility and employment. This is illustrated by the case (cited by Lygo, 2012) of one student who had originally planned to go to a prestigious traditional university to study history and had scored one A and four A* grades at 'A' level. However, she chose to take up an opportunity to work 4 days a week at a law firm which sponsored her to take a part-time law degree at BPP University College (now BPP University), where she studies 1 day per week. She will still complete her degree in 3 years, as she works through the normal university holidays and during evenings. She said:

> 'It is fantastic. Obviously, there is a lot of work in the evening, but the opportunities it has given me are brilliant. I am so glad I have done it. I thought I might miss out on university life, but this is the

best of both worlds and I am learning so much quicker on the job.'
(Whitwam, 2012)

The private sector may well be accustomed to concepts such as 'the student as consumer', recognising the importance of seeking and acting upon student opinion and delivering a good standard of service along the way as well as ultimate success. Private sector students and their representatives seem to relate to this:

> I am comfortable with institutions referring to their students as customers; I think it is particularly important, with the rise in fees, that institutions recognise that students are investing a lot of money in their education, and it is therefore important to ensure that the 'customer/student' has a valuable educational experience. (Heinonen, interviewee; Rivers, interviewer, personal interview, 2012)

One interesting example of the student as consumer concerns the early days of the University of Buckingham, the United Kingdom's first private university:

> In the founding of a new university it is particularly important to establish good working relations with the students, and I was asked to chair a Student Liaison Committee. It was to be expected that, as fee payers, their wish list would be quite extensive, and dealing with it did require a good deal of diplomacy. Some early requests that were catered for included a dispensing machine for condoms, a tennis court, and gymnasium equipment. Recreation was clearly going to be an antidote to study. (Pemberton, 2010)

According to Lygo, student engagement is much wider than 'just handing out happy sheets', you need to get closer to what the student is doing and be able to give them much better advice, for example on what next to study; you need to understand their patterns better and help them (Lygo, interviewee; & Rivers interviewer, personal interview, 2012):

> Whatever label you give it, the behaviour of students has all the hallmarks of consumerism, such as being very demanding of good service, and it's how you respond to it that matters. Not doing so means that your product is going to die! You need to be really on top of your game in terms of student engagement and giving a good experience or you will be badmouthed in social media — this is the power of the consumer where the Consumer is King — it's like feedback on steroids! (Lygo, interviewee; Rivers, interviewer, personal interview, 2012)

However, Lygo acknowledges that the private sector has not always been innovative in the area of student engagement and may have placed more emphasis on informal approaches rather than formal mechanisms (Lygo, interviewee; Rivers, interviewer, personal interview, 2012). Nevertheless, there is evidence that when the private sector focuses on student involvement, it does so in a very thorough and appropriate way as evidenced by an NUS leadership visit to BPP:

> They were quite surprised when they found out that each Small Group Session has a student representative — many other institutions have one rep per year group, we have many more student reps which gives us a much wider sample of student opinion across all programmes. (Lygo, interviewee; Rivers, interviewer, personal interview, 2012)

Regent's University London (a London-based independent higher education provider, catering mainly for international students) evidences 'basic' student engagement processes using periodic surveys, questionnaires and student representative committees:

> ... Student feedback questionnaire systems are in place to provide us with your feedback concerning modules and programmes. Institutional surveys are conducted periodically. Alternatively you can feedback comments through your student rep to the appropriate committees/meetings. (Regent's College, 2012b)

In addition it places emphasis on *ongoing* student representation and feedback:

> It is expected that students will give informal feedback on an ongoing basis as and when appropriate, perhaps via your Tutor, Personal Tutor/Academic Advisor or Programme Director ... (Regent's College, 2012b)

It is significant that Ashridge (an independent, self-financing institution specialising in leadership and management education for postgraduate and post-qualification students) was praised in its Institutional Audit for the 'feedback-hungry' culture and responsiveness to matters raised by students as a feature of good practice (QAA, 2011). The ifs University College (the only specialist provider of professional financial education with taught degree awarding powers) has developed a framework for student feedback which includes programme-level focus groups, mechanisms for gathering feedback from students, representation at postgraduate level and working with the full-time class representatives to further enhance student engagement (ifs, 2011).

It is interesting that the QAA praised Ashridge for its feedback culture, despite the lack of training for student representatives:

> There is no formal induction or training provided to students because of the seniority and maturity of the majority of students and the

openness of the institution to feedback. Any student on the programme is welcome to attend the board meetings. The minutes are
shared on e-sites for other students to view. The audit team saw examples both at programme and institutional level of issues raised at
boards of study being rapidly addressed. The audit team considered
that the culture of feedback that exists at Ashridge for both staff and
students is a constant and valued feature, where both parties learn
from each other. (QAA, 2011, p. 8)

By contrast, Greenwich School of Management (a private college with 60 per
cent international students) failed to meet two of the three criteria in its
Institutional Review (QAA, 2012b). The quality of student learning opportunities
was said to require improvement to meet UK expectations and the enhancement of
student learning opportunities did not meet UK expectations. The college was specifically recommended top:

Develop a formal system for the training and support of student
representatives in order to enable them to contribute more effectively
to quality assurance processes across the institution. (QAA, 2012b)

However, while Ashridge had been operating since 1959 and focused on experienced students, Greenwich School of Management, although commended for its
support for international students (Morgan, 2012c), did not have the same level of
experience or maturity as an institution and may not have fully appreciated the
standards required of UK HEIs.

Although it may be unusual to find student engagement initiatives in the private
sector, such as that exist in Exeter and Lincoln, there is evidence of a willingness to
interpret student engagement in such a wider sense. For example the Mission
Statement of The School of Psychotherapy and Counselling Psychology at Regent's
University London includes an aim to 'facilitate an emotional engagement on the
part of the student with the subject matter under consideration' (Regent's College,
2012a).

Furthermore, the Institutional Review of Ashridge mentioned a culture of undefended learning spaces, in that distinction between faculty and students in the quality assurance of programmes was blurred (QAA, 2011, p. 8), suggesting that there
was a partnership between students and staff in this regard. In BPP, the Chief
Executive of Students (this role is explored in more detail later) acted as a change
agent by leading on the development of an institution-wide Personal Tutor Policy.

According to Lygo, although there was a well-developed policy already operating
in the Law School, the newer schools were not following it and students saw an
opportunity to redraft the whole policy not just adopt the Law School one (an
approach which was supported by a report from Aaron Porter). The Chief
Executive of Students was given the responsibility to drive it forward — it was
almost entirely student led (Lygo, interviewee; Rivers, interviewer, personal interview, 2012).

7.3.1. Assessing Student Engagement in the Private Sector

It is clear that there are a number of examples of distinct approaches to student engagement practice in the private sector. Applying the framework developed in Table 7.2, it is interesting to note that while the private sector institutions examined generally appear to adopt many of the 'narrow approaches', as would be expected throughout the higher education sector, a number of them apply these in a noticeably extensive and inclusive way, taking them to a broader level ('narrow plus'). Examples include:

- the open, 'feedback-hungry' culture of Ashridge
- the framework for student feedback adopted by the ifs School of Finance
- the strong focus on closing the feedback loop through the use of action logs in ifs University College
- embracing the concept of students as fee payers who demand good service in the University of Buckingham and BPP
- giving student representatives responsibility and accountability and using them as agents of change, for example the role of the Chief Executive of Students in initiatives such as the Personal Tutor Policy in BPP
- regarding students as partners in learning, such as Ashridge's culture of 'undefended learning spaces'.

7.4. A Case Study of Student Engagement at BPP University of Professional Studies

BPP UC traces its origins back to the establishment of BPP Law School in 1992, and is a wholly owned subsidiary of BPP Holdings Limited, which was formed in 1976. The institution was granted UK degree awarding powers by the Privy Council in 2007, attained University College status in 2010 and University title in 2013. It has a number of professional body accreditations and affiliations and also has Highly Trusted Status with the UK Border Agency (BPP University College, 2013). In 2011–12 BPP UC had 6,780 full-time equivalent (FTE) students in two Schools, BPP Law School and BPP Business School, of whom 5,808 were studying full time and 1,944 studying part time (QAA, 2012a). An unusual feature of BPP is its highly distributed nature, as it has 15 approved Learning Centres in different locations in the United Kingdom (BPP, 2013).

7.4.1. The Role of Chief Executive of Students

The aim of this role is to help improve the overall student experience and to represent the interests of students to the institution. The Chief Executive of Students is a former BPP student who reports directly to the Vice Chancellor of the institution.

This ensures that the students' view is at the heart of BPP and that the institution listens to students' feedback and actions are taken to make improvements.

Specific duties of the Chief Executive of Students include:

- to conduct focus group sessions with BPP students and attend SSLC meetings throughout the year across all programmes at all study centres to gain students' feedback on issues relating to any aspect of their educational experience. The Chief Executive of Students presents this feedback to executive officers of BPP highlighting areas of good practice and areas where change is recommended.
- to represent student opinion at formal committees, including the School Board meetings, the Education and Training Committee, the Learning, Teaching and Assessment Enhancement Committee, the Academic Council, the Academic Regulations and Awards Committee and the Student Assessment, Retention and Achievement Committee, and to act as an independent voice for BPP's students.
- to take an active role in feeding into new initiatives within the institution that will have a direct impact on students and, where necessary, to form or lead working groups with faculty (academic staff), deanery and senior management to work on specific areas of improvement that the students have identified and make recommendations for change.

The Chief Executive of Students has *de facto* acted as a change agent, contributing to and leading on many improvement initiatives; examples of such projects which the post holder has worked on in collaboration with students include:

- creating and implementing the Personal Tutor Policy; creating the Personal Tutor Handbook
- improving the pre-arrival information received by new students
- introducing a portfolio of graduation prizes
- developing a University wide Hardship Fund
- creating and providing training and guidance to student representatives
- incorporating student feedback to help enhance the prospectuses
- relaunching the student newsletter
- establishing and/or organising student events such as an annual BPP Summer Ball, the 2011 London Freshers' Fair, Christmas party and other events
- facilitating and organising the student representative elections
- running a number of focus groups with students, for example, to inform new programme development, improve the prospectuses and improve pre-arrival information
- regularly analysing and reporting student feedback to Committee and Board Meetings.

In addition, the Chief Executive of Students has worked in productive partnership with key stakeholders in the institution on major cross-institutional enhancement and change initiatives, for example recent projects led jointly with the Associate Dean (Student Learning Enhancement) to create a new Student

Engagement Policy and to design and implement a new student induction programme, which the recent QAA Institutional Review Report affirmed as 'a helpful
enhancement to student engagement'(QAA, 2012a, p. 16). In the Chief Executive of
Students' own words:

> The list of improvement initiatives that I have contributed to in the
> last year have really shown how effective this role can be, and shows
> that the institution has really valued and embraced this role by both
> allowing me to lead on some initiatives and make changes as well as
> inviting me to actively contribute to many projects across the institu-
> tion .... I am able to work on projects in response to student feedback
> truly highlighting the fact that BPP value this role and are happy for
> whoever is in the position to work on the areas for improvement iden-
> tified by the student voice (Heinonen, interviewee; Rivers, interviewer,
> personal interview, 2012).

7.4.2. *The Role of the Students' Association*

The Students' Association has developed a number of channels for students to communicate their feedback in addition to the surveys and SSLCs that the institution
provided prior to the Association's launch in 2011. The newly structured student
representation system and formation of the Association has developed as a strong
mechanism to channel the student voice.

7.4.2.1. Student Voice Representatives
The Student Voice Representatives is the collective name for the students who sit on
internal academic committees and boards. Their role is to represent the students'
views at the University as a whole during discussions at board/committee meetings.
Members of the board/committee invite them for their views on any matters arising
on the agenda that have an impact on the student experience, and there is a regular
student voice item on each agenda which is an opportunity for the Student Voice
Representatives to raise any issues affecting the student body.

The Student Voice Representatives form the National Students' Council meet
once per term to discuss issues arising from student feedback and decide on issues
to take forward to committee/board meetings.

Recent development to the Student Voice Representatives roles is as follows:

- Elections — a lot of effort has been made to publicise the student elections, to
  encourage a number of students to put themselves forward for the positions and
  other students to vote, to ensure top quality candidates are selected for the
  positions.
- Training — The Chief Executive of Students worked closely with the Learning
  and Development team to create a substantial full-day face-to-face training session to induct the Student Voice Representatives into their roles. This has been

imperative in ensuring that they champion the student voice effectively and represent student views from across the institution.

- Regular meetings — one of the biggest things we have learned from the first year of launching these roles is how effective and important it is to arrange regular meetings of the Student Voice Representatives to share the student feedback they have collected and their experiences on the committees as well as giving them an opportunity to read through student feedback and identify common issues. In response to this we have formed the National Students' Council, which is a regular termly meeting of all the Student Voice Representatives and the Chief Executive of Students to discuss student voice issues and identify areas for improvement.

7.4.3.   Student–Staff Liaison Committees

The SSLCs are a mechanism by which students and staff can communicate and obtain feedback about all aspects of the BPP experience including the programme, facilities, student welfare, careers and administration. SSLCs are made up of student representatives from every tutor group on all programmes at BPP, who are elected at the start of the year. These representatives meet with staff in order to raise issues or concerns, suggest improvements and offer feedback on new initiatives. The minutes of the meeting specify attendees and must take the form of a tabulated action plan containing information on the issue raised, the response, the person tasked to take action and the timescale for doing so. The minutes are sent to the Programme Board and to the School Board.

The SSLCs are a very powerful mechanism to collect qualitative feedback from students. With one student in every tutor group being an SSLC rep, this means that 5 per cent of the student population are student representatives; currently that is approximately 300 students. One of the reasons why the SSLCs are so effective in enhancing the student experience is because feedback is collected directly by the programme management team which are able to respond to changes quickly and hear any issues 'fresh' from the students, giving them an opportunity to identify issues early, before they develop, as well as being able to discuss the issues with students in depth.

7.4.4.   The Annual Student Written Submission

BPP had its Institutional Review with the QAA in autumn 2012, and in preparation the student representatives were tasked with preparing a Student Written Submission. The aim was to give students an opportunity, through their representatives, to give the QAA review team an impression of what it is like to be a student at BPP. The institution has valued this report so highly that it decided to continue with this process, beyond the confines and requirements of the QAA, and to make this part of the process of obtaining feedback from students by instituting this as an annual report from students to be submitted to the Vice Chancellor. In this way key aspects of feedback from students can be raised directly with the Vice Chancellor who has the opportunity and authority to action these, thus closing the feedback loop.

7.5. Summary and Conclusions

In summary, there is increasing global demand for and lack of supply of higher education which has influenced the growth in private sector provision worldwide. The United Kingdom has a history of private institutions providing some higher education programmes, previously usually accredited by another HEI. An increasing number of such private institutions have now been granted their own degree awarding powers, some achieving University title.

Although there is no single agreed definition of 'student engagement' in practice, there is a narrower aspect (often evidenced by mechanisms for collecting student feedback and ensuring student representation on key bodies) and a wider one (e.g. concerned with engaging students with their learning). In the UK private sector there may be a considerable emphasis on student involvement (feedback and representation) and this is often dealt with particularly well and in great depth. While there may not be so many obvious examples of engagement initiatives, there is wide acceptance of the concept of the 'student as consumer' and a willingness to harness the power of the student voice in order to deliver change and enhancement.

The private sector has much to learn from the publicly funded sector in the field of student engagement, especially in terms of initiatives such as student empowerment. However, there is evidence that the private sector has adapted and built on concepts such as 'students as change agents' for its own context; for instance, the Chief Executive of Students in BPP has a prominent and highly influential role in which she or he acts as a leader in significant change initiatives across the institution and this appears to be a more directly action-orientated and influential role, the figurehead role played by many Students' Union Presidents in public sector HEIs. The Chief Executive of Students' role is also significant because it acts as a link between collecting student feedback and carrying out consequent changes in partnership with the student body and key stakeholders, thus closing the feedback loop which has been an issue for some publicly funded HEIs. A number of other distinctive examples of student engagement have also been identified in private sector institutions which would be equally relevant to the publicly funded higher education sector. These include the establishment of an annual Student Written Submission in BPP and tracking the use of student representation action logs in ifs University College for continuous improvement, both of which are also useful tools in closing the feedback loop. Ashridge was praised for its transparency in sharing on e-sites minutes of Board Meetings for students to see, so feeding back the outcomes of any issues.

In reality, however, the private sector is still to find full acceptance in UK higher education, although it is certainly its intention to be an equal partner and to share its good practice; for example BPP University College is actively engaged in the Higher Education Academy and Leadership Foundation for Higher Education's Change Academy, is a consultee on key QAA proposals for change and its staff engage in communicating their practice through conference presentations and publications as well as influencing in roles such as External Examiners and QAA Institutional Reviewers. It is important that the sector as a whole opens its mind to the fact that there is good practice in the private sector. It should actively encourage initiatives, like those described above, which are likely to allow and encourage private sector institutions to communicate and share good practice, on the basis that we have a common interest in providing a high-quality experience for all students, wherever they choose to study.

Acknowledgements

The authors gratefully acknowledge the contributions of the following people in developing this chapter: Carl Lygo (Vice Chancellor, BPP University), Laila Heinonen (Chief Executive of Students, BPP University), Simon Atkinson (Associate Dean, Teaching Enhancement, BPP University) and Tim Stewart (Dean of Learning and Teaching, BPP University).

References

Astin, A. W. (1984). Student involvement: A developmental theory for higher education. *Journal of College Student Development, 25*, 297–308.

Bloom, B. S., Engelhart, M. D., Furst, E. J., Hill, W. H., & Krathwohl, D. R. (Eds.) (1956). *Taxonomy of educational objectives: The classification of educational goals; Handbook: Cognitive domain.* New York, NY: David McKay.

BPP. (2013). BPP University of Professional Studies 'About Us' section of website. Retrieved from http://www.bpp.com/university-college/1/about-bpp-university-college

College of Estate Management. (2012). *College of Estate Management granted degree awarding powers.* Retrieved from http://www.cem.ac.uk/news-events/news/college-of-estate-management-granted-degree-awarding-powers.aspx

Coventry University. (2011). *Coventry University Teaching Learning and Assessment Strategy 2011–2015.* Coventry University.

Department for Business Innovation and Skills (BIS). (2004, August). *Applications for the grant of taught degree awarding powers, research degree awarding powers and university title, guidance for applicant organisations in England and Wales.* London: BIS.

Dunne, E., & Zandstra, R. (2011). *Students as change agents, new ways of engaging with learning and teaching in higher education.* ESCalate/Higher Education Academy.

Furedi, F. (2009, 4 June). Now is the age of the discontented. *Times Higher Education.* Retrieved from http://www.timeshighereducation.co.uk/story.asp?sectioncode=26&storycode=406780&c=2

HESA. (1999). *Students in higher education institutions 1998/99.* Cheltenham, UK: Higher Educational Statistical Agency.

HESA. (2009). *Students in higher education institutions 2008/09.* Cheltenham, UK: Higher Educational Statistical Agency.

HESA. (2010). *Students in higher education institutions 2009/10.* Cheltenham, UK: Higher Educational Statistical Agency.

HESA. (2011). *Press release 159 — survey of private and for-profit providers of higher education in the UK 2009/10.* Cheltenham, UK: Higher Educational Statistical Agency. Retrieved from http://www.hesa.ac.uk/index.php?option=com_content&task=view&id=2086&Itemid=310

ifs. (2011). *Student representation workshop, October 2011.* London: ifs. Retrieved from http://www.ifslearning.ac.uk/qualifications/additionalpheinformation/professionalhighernewsletter/February2012/Studentrepresentationworkshop.aspx

Laurillard, D. (2007). *Rethinking university teaching: A framework for the effective use of learning technologies* (2nd ed.), Abingdon: Routledge Farmer.

Levy, D. (2006). *An introductory global overview. The private fit to salient higher education tendencies.* PROPHE Working Paper 7. University at Albany (SUNY). Retrieved from http://www.albany.edu/dept/eaps/prophe/working_papers.html#WP7

Levy, D. (2008). The enlarged expanse of private higher education. *Die Hochscule, 2,* 19–35.

Levy, D. (2010). *East Asian private higher education: Tendencies and policy options.* Washington, DC: The World Bank.

Levy, D. (2011). *The decline of private higher education.* PROPHE Working Paper 16. University at Albany (SUNY). Retrieved from http://www.albany.edu/dept/eaps/prophe/working_papers.html#WP16

Little, B., Locke, W., Scesa, A., & Williams, R. (2009). *Report to HEFCE on student engagement.* Bristol, UK: HEFCE.

Liu, J., & Wang, X. (2010). Expansion and differentiation in Chinese higher education. *International Higher Education, 60,* 7–8. Retrieved from https://htmldbprod.bc.edu/prd/f?p=2290:4:0::NO:RP,4:P0_CONTENT_ID:111091

Lockett, M. (2012). Case study D: Ashridge & TDA [Format of slides]. *Graduate Education UK, Winter Conference 2012.* Retrieved from http://www.ashridge.org.uk/website/IC.nsf/wFARATT/Case%20Study:%20Ashridge%20and%20Taught%20Degree%20Awarding%20Powers/$file/Ashridge%20DAP%20Case%20Study%20for%20UKCGE%2010.02.2012.pdf

Lygo, C. (2012). *A private education in times of austerity? Blue skies: Thinking about the future of higher education* (2012 ed.), London: Pearson. Retrieved from http://pearsonblueskies.com/2012/a-private-education-in-times-of-austerity/

Matthews, D. (2012, 14 August). Pearson launches College with Royal Holloway Degrees. *Times Higher Education.* Retrieved from http://www.timeshighereducation.co.uk/story.asp?storycode=420860

McCulloch, A. (2009). The student as co-producer: Learning from public administration about the student-university relationship. *Studies in Higher Education, 34*(2), 171–183.

McMillan, J., & Cheney, G. (1996). The student as consumer: The implications and limitations of a metaphor. *Communication Education, 45,* 1–15.

Middlehurst, R., & Fielden, J. (2011). *Private providers in UK higher education: Some policy options.* London: HEPI. Retrieved from http://www.hepi.ac.uk/466-1969/Private-Providers-in-UK-Higher-Education–Some-Policy-Options.html

Morgan, J. (2012a, 12 March). Enigma variations. *Times Higher Education.* Retrieved from http://www.timeshighereducation.co.uk/story.asp?storycode=419175

Morgan, J. (2012b, 27 July). Degree powers for Regent's College welcomed by Willetts. *Times Higher Education*. Retrieved from http://www.timeshighereducation.co.uk/story. asp?storycode = 420708

Morgan, J. (2012c, 20 September). QAA critical of met alternatives. *Times Higher Education*. Retrieved from http://www.timeshighereducation.co.uk/story.asp?storycode = 421194

NCES. (2000). *2000 Digest of education statistics*. Washington,DC: National Center for Education Statistics. Retrieved from http://nces.ed.gov/programs/digest/d00/dt245.asp

NCES. (2012). *Advance release of selected 2012 digest tables*. Washington, DC: National Center for Education Statistics. Retrieved from http://nces.ed.gov/programs/digest/ 2012menu_tables.asp

Pemberton, J. (2010, 29 November). Buckingham University: From pigsties to glory (blog by John Pemberton). Retrieved from http://buckinghamuniversity.blogspot.co.uk/

QAA. (2011). *Institutional audit of Ashridge. April 2011*. Retrieved from http://www.qaa.ac. uk/InstitutionReports/reports/Documents/RG794Ashridge.pdf

QAA. (2012a). *Institutional review of BPP University College of Professional Studies, December 2012*. Retrieved from http://www.qaa.ac.uk/InstitutionReports/reports/ Documents/RG1082-BPP.pdf

QAA. (2012b). *Institutional review of Greenwich Management School, June 2012*. Retrieved from http://www.qaa.ac.uk/InstitutionReports/Reports/Pages/IRENI-Greenwich-School-Management-12.aspx

QAA. (2012c). *UK quality code, Chapter B5 Student engagement*. Retrieved from http://www. qaa.ac.uk/Publications/InformationAndGuidance/Documents/Quality-Code-Chapter-B5.pdf

Regent's College. (2012a). *Mission statement of The School of Psychotherapy and Counselling Psychology*. Retrieved from http://www.spc.ac.uk/about_spcp/mission_statement.aspx

Regent's College. (2012b). *Student handbook — student Representation and Feedback*. Retrieved from http://www.regents.ac.uk/schools/academic_registry/student_handbook/ student_representation.aspx

Regent's College. (2012c). *Students' Union guide*. Retrieved from http://www.regents.ac.uk/ pdf/StudentUnionGuideOnlineV4.pdf

Taylor, P., & Wilding, D. (2009). *Rethinking the values of higher education — the student as collaborator and producer?* Undergraduate Research as a Case Study. Retrieved from http://dera.ioe.ac.uk/433/2/Undergraduate.pdf

Trowler, V. (2010). *Student engagement literature review*. York: Higher Education Academy.

Universities UK. (2010). *The growth of private and for-profit higher education providers in the UK*. Research Report. Universities UK.

University of Buckingham. (2012). *About us (about Buckingham and history)*. Retrieved from http://www.buckingham.ac.uk/about

University of Lincoln. (2012). *Student as producer*. Retrieved from http://studentasproducer. lincoln.ac.uk/

Wenger, E. (1998). *Communities of practice, learning meaning and identity*. Cambridge: Cambridge University Press.

Whitwam, L. (2012, 8 March). Minding the gap; college fair shows students the world is still their oyster. *Huddersfield Daily Examiner*. Retrieved from http://www.thefreelibrary.com/ MINDING + THE + GAP percent3B + College + fair + shows + students + the + world + is + still + their...-a0282398180

Chapter 8

Trusting Dialogue for Engaging Students

Carmen Werder and Erik Skogsberg

Abstract

This chapter describes the development of a culture of dialogue at Western Washington University, suggesting how such a culture can engage students not only as participants, but as co-inquirers in studying and enhancing higher education. The Teaching-Learning Academy (TLA) is a campus-wide dialogue forum on learning that gives all students an opportunity to engage with their institution and includes students, faculty, staff and community members. Now in its thirteenth year, the TLA has proved to be a kind of seminar for building mutual trust in dialogue, with students participating for credit or simply as volunteers. Dialogic classroom spaces explicitly honour the plurality of voices and views that make up multi-vocal meaning. Alexander (2008) identifies five essential attributes of a dialogic classroom: that it is 'collective', 'reciprocal', 'supportive', 'cumulative' and 'purposeful'. These attributes of dialogic teaching resonate with the dialogic principles that have emerged from the TLA. Assessment data show that this dialogue has resulted in a number of outcomes that include changes in participant attitudes, teaching and learning practices, and institutional initiatives. Student participants frequently report having a stronger sense of connection to the institution and to their own education after participating in TLA. The majority of student participants also report a surprising change in attitude towards faculty and staff.

8.1. Introduction

They talk about the people, but they do not trust them; and trusting the people is the indispensable precondition for revolutionary change. A real humanist can be identified more by his [or her] trust in the people, which engages him [or her] in their struggle, than by a thousand actions in their favor without that trust. (Freire, 1970, p. 60)

The Student Engagement Handbook: Practice in Higher Education
Copyright © 2013 by Emerald Group Publishing Limited
All rights of reproduction in any form reserved
ISBN: 978-1-78190-423-7

Who would contest the value of engaging students in their own education? Apparently no one. In fact, efforts to elicit student voices appear to be burgeoning. An initiative like 'Student Voices on the Higher Education Pathway' (*Public Agenda*) — part of the Bill & Melinda Gates Foundation's Postsecondary Success project in the United States — is one of the many deliberate efforts to listen to what college students have to say about their experiences as consumers. Another example comes from the Center for American Progress (billed as an independent educational institute) which recently published a report demonstrating their watchdog efforts to advocate for students, noting:

> Many for-profit colleges have been abusing the trust students place in them by misrepresenting the educational services they offer and over-charging for substandard educational experiences. (Morgan & Hoskimima, 2011)

This report cites students protesting rising tuition costs and increasing student debt and, like many of these initiatives, elicits student voices as higher education users, rather than as learners. Furthermore, as editors Dunne and Owen (Introduction) note, 'student voices are "listened to" by researchers and institutions and then collated and interpreted by these groups, rather than students themselves being encouraged and enabled to take on this responsibility.' Too often we do not trust the students to represent their own views — unmediated — as part of a wider dialogue.

8.2.   Our Story with Dialogue

Trust in dialogue has long been at the centre of what we co-authors believe about engagement in higher education. This trust has spanned a now 10-year relationship that began with Erik as a student in Carmen's course, eventually seeing Erik become a student co-facilitator in that same course, and then co-presenting at conferences across the country about student voices in higher education, and now as continued colleagues. While Erik pursues his PhD in English Education at Michigan State, Carmen directs the Learning Commons at Western Washington University including the Teaching-Learning Academy (TLA), a campus-wide dialogue forum on learning. Our decade-long relationship has resulted in our so embracing the concept and enactment of dialogue that we wonder how students — or anyone — can be *engaged* without the presence of dialogue in their academic and personal relationships. Conscious of the persistent inclination to represent students' views, we have regularly sought to engage student voices in active dialogue: challenging, shaping, helping us better understand our work and beliefs in higher education. We've constructed dialogic spaces on campus, in our classrooms, and have attempted to model (in our regular collaboration with each other) dialogic engagement across our work.

Sustaining this dialogue has taken an ongoing, active effort to reassert our belief in dialogue itself: both for us and for others.

Of course, we acknowledge that our call for cultivating a culture of dialogue is not a new one. As an example, peace activist Tom Atlee has pointed to the essential presence of a culture of dialogue in both realizing and transcending democratic ideals. In that same call, Atlee invokes the Dalai Lama's global invitation in 1997 in a speech in Prague, urging 'the promotion of a culture of dialogue ... as an important task of the international community'. While calls such as these have foregrounded the value of dialogue in promoting social justice and democracy, what we hope to do is highlight how dialogue has grounded our student engagement efforts both as a communication model and as an epistemological perspective. In this chapter, we will outline some of our attempts to develop and extend a culture of dialogue that has been at the centre of our work, and suggest how such a culture of dialogue can engage students not only as participants, but also as co-inquirers in studying and enhancing higher education.

Recently, we found ourselves in a kind of test situation when we were invited to put together a plenary at a conference that would communicate just what we believed about the role of students in the larger scholarly movement known as the Scholarship of Teaching and Learning (SOTL) and in higher education writ-large. As of now, we found ourselves moving, almost instinctively, towards a now familiar process. After working together over the course of 10 years (though many of those from a distance) and having presented at various conferences about our work, we jumped at the chance, and knew from the beginning the form we wanted this keynote to take: a dialogue. We decided to enact our keynote as a dialogue with one another and our audience, building the emergent content in real-time in front of our participants, first verbally, second digitally via a Google.doc, and finally inviting the participants into the shared space to join us in thinking about opportunities for student engagement through dialogue at their own institutions. Setting out with a loose structure, we were open to what could come about as our voices and ideas met one another, changing understandings as we communicated both the content of our work as well as the form that this work has taken through the nature of our talk with one another. In preparing for this keynote, we were regularly reminded of how much trust it takes to engage in this manner, as we had multiple moments when we wondered: how would our audience respond?

Would they view this back-and-forth exchange as a serious display of scholarly knowledge? As these questions loomed larger for us as the symposium approached, we consistently came back to trust, reminding one another to trust in our own voices and connected knowledge building *through* dialogue, as we had through our work over the years. This choice to trust in dialogue itself embodies much about our beliefs in how student engagement should manifest itself in higher education. This belief reflects a shared commitment to the value of each other's voices and views, and has forever rendered us engaged co-inquirers. While we do not know for sure if our audience at this recent symposium ended up believing in the potential of dialogue to completely transform higher education, they were willing to go along, and continued engaging in the digital space of the Google.doc even after our plenary session ended. The exchange also reinforced for us the trust we had built up over the years in our shared seeking of understanding as fellow travellers on a learning journey (Huber & Hutchings, 2005).

8.3. Dialogue as Essential Communication Mode for Engagement

So where did this bedrock belief in dialogue begin forming for us? We can trace its foundational layer back to our participation in a campus-wide dialogue forum on teaching and learning at our then common home institution: Western Washington University. Western Washington's initial commitment to engaging student voices in a broader dialogue resulted from the Carnegie Academy for the Scholarship of Teaching and Learning (CASTL)'s invitation to participate in a Campus Conversations programme in 1998. However, that initial conversation on our campus did not include student voices. About 15 faculty (including Carmen) participated in responding to questions posed by CASTL about our current learning culture. It was only in the process of explaining the initiative to the faculty senate that the question arose from a member of the college of education: 'Sounds good, but what about students?' The then Vice-Provost of Undergraduate Education paid close attention to the question and followed up by creating a summer Faculty Fellowship for the SOTL, which Carmen received. One of the results of that alliance was the creation of the Teaching-Learning Academy (TLA), a campus-wide dialogue forum that includes students, faculty, staff, and even community members. Now in its thirteenth year, the TLA has proven to be a kind of seminar (or perhaps even a seminary) for building our mutual trust in dialogue.

We have outlined the 'conversational principles' of the TLA previously (Werder, Ware, Thomas, & Skogsberg, 2010), but will summarize them briefly here:

- Create structured informality
- Provide for shared ownership
- Ensure reciprocal benefits
- Invite broad-based and proportional representation
- Recognize individual and collective expertise and contributions (pp. 18, 19).

The TLA continues to enact these principles with practices such as introducing ourselves using a personal experience or idea (rather than departments and titles), endorsing a set of agreements, deciding together on a common question to study for the whole academic year (we take a whole academic quarter to formulate this BIG question), enlisting students from a communication practicum to facilitate the smaller dialogue groups, and compiling highlights from across the four TLA sessions and sending them out to all participants for response on the off-meeting weeks. This series of highlights (much like the Google.doc created in our plenary) serves as a record of our past dialogue as well as becoming the basis of the next dialogue round, and then becomes part of a legacy that we pass on to the next

TLA participants. Like dialogue itself, these conversational principles and practices are always evolving, though some of the basic tenets, such as working towards a flattened hierarchy (a sisyphusian enterprise in the academy), continue to hold steady.

Since students can participate in the TLA for one credit in 'Applied Communication' (with no pre-requisite) or as part of a practicum for an upper-level civil discourse class (with only First-year Comp as a pre-requisite), or simply as volunteers — they come from various disciplines and with varying levels of engagement. Many start participating simply to earn 300-level credit (often with an urgency in order to satisfy a graduation requirement of having at least 45 upper-level credits), and approximately 20 per cent of the participants are general studies majors (many of whom were not able to gain admission into preferred majors and often have not received personalized advising). As a result, many participants bring strong feelings of disenfranchisement, but the majority of them leave saying that the experience in TLA dialogue causes them to feel more connected with the university and with their own education. For example: Olaf, a general studies major, remarked at one of his last TLA sessions just before graduating several years ago, that he had begun every morning for the previous 3 years, saying to himself, 'I hate school,' but since participating in the TLA, he had noticed that others were interested in what he had to say and was feeling unfamiliar pangs of regret at not being able to continue in the dialogue. (He actually came back to a few TLA sessions after graduating.)

While many students like Olaf come into the TLA dialogue seriously disillusioned with their undergraduate experiences, many others come with generally satisfactory attitudes towards the institution. And yet even these students report significant shifts in their levels of engagement after participating. For example, Daniel Espinoza-Gonzalez (2013) chronicles his journey of 'finding value' in voicing his views during his first quarter of TLA dialogue. After candidly expressing his experiences of being a student of colour (which implied some critique of the institution), he realized that one of the people listening particularly closely to him happened to be the university president's wife. In reflecting on that experience, he observes that he 'had never felt so acknowledged and appreciated by people (he) barely knew' and calls it a 'pivotal point' in his undergraduate experience which empowered him to seek out leadership positions (including in the campus Ethnic Student Center). Stories from students like Olaf and Daniel suggest the transformative influence of simply being heard.

Assessment data (from quarterly closing surveys) show that the TLA dialogue has resulted in a number of outcomes that include changes in participant attitudes, teaching and learning practices, and institutional initiatives. Student participants frequently report having a stronger sense of connection to the institution and to their own education after participating in TLA. The majority of student participants also report a surprising change in attitude towards faculty and staff, commenting on how they 'care' about student learning. Interestingly, faculty, staff, and community participants also report being surprised by how much students 'care' about their own learning and about teaching. Of course what effect this enhanced attitude towards one another has on learning is harder to track. But student participants repeatedly report two behavioural changes likely to enhance their learning as a result of participating in the TLA dialogue:

1. a willingness — even a new enthusiasm — to go to office hours when they did not go before or only went if they were desperate;
2. a willingness and a new inclination to ask questions in class when they did not or hesitated to do so before.

TLA also has a high positive recidivism rate, with many participants returning for multiple quarters to participate without any course credit (which points to their enhanced engagement as well). While some 'repeat offenders' say they return because TLA dialogue has resulted in explicit institutional change initiatives, such as the creation of a TLA-sponsored Reflective Garden, improvements to the general educational programme, and refinements to the Library's new Learning Commons, many say they come back because they appreciate 'being heard'. And they frame that appreciation in terms of being heard not simply as students, but as respected members *in* dialogue with one another. As one TLA student participant recently commented in a closing reflective comment about the process:

> ... helping each other in the creation of our BIG questions ... has made us a strong dialogical community ... one that has the potential to create a supportive and intellectually developing community because it gives people a chance to share their thoughts fearlessly and feel truly involved.

8.4. Dialogue as Essential Epistemology in Student Engagement

Moreover, we are eager to point out that participation in the TLA did not simply school us in the benefits of dialogue as a communication mode. The TLA opened a pathway into understanding dialogue as essential epistemology (Werder, Thibou, & Kaufer, 2012). In fact, our choice to engage in dialogue with one another in front of that plenary audience was built on a mutually shared commitment to dialogue-as-epistemology built across time in our work together connected to TLA. Our experience in the culture of the TLA represents the foundation for much of our work for student engagement, not only because it has provided us a model for talking and listening to each other, but even more importantly because it has enabled a way of knowing that continues to influence how we think about ourselves, as well as our relationships to each other, and to knowledge itself. Based on a fundamental distinction between discussion and debate with their primary emphasis on finding the one best answer and persuading others of it, and dialogue, with its primary emphasis on finding shared meaning (Ellinor & Gerard, 1998), the TLA relies on a social construction of knowledge. By recognizing the expertise of all participants, the TLA has taught us how to enter into a culture of dialogic thinking where we co-construct and discover shared meaning together.

One 'repeat offender' who has participated in the TLA for 3 years (2 years as an undergraduate and now as a graduate student in history) — Mason — characterizes the cognitive nature of dialogue in commenting on a closing reflection (email correspondence, 15 March 2003) that 'it allows for all opinions to be shared and heard' and leads to an understanding that 'there is never one right answer to a problem because it has to be looked at from all angles. Dialogue lets a person or people come to an ever-changing and relevant solution and ... this is how great changes are made in this world, by absorbing all opinions and not just one almighty answer.' Mason's comment reflects what many students say in their closing surveys each quarter: Experiencing an ongoing dialogue with multiple perspectives becomes a way of thinking. The TLA culture then represents the most important precursor for how we think about engagement for students (and for everyone really). Our work emerges out of a shared epistemology that values one another's voices and what emerges when these voices meet in mutual respect, trust and seeking for shared understanding of the knowledge we co-construct. It is not merely the mechanical implementation of a communication format or a pedagogical method to fill our schedules and assuage our need to hear our individual voices, but a deeply held belief in knowing together *through* talk that engages us. Freire importantly makes this distinction, pointing out that 'dialogue is a way of knowing and should never be viewed as a mere tactic to involve students in a particular task .... I engage in dialogue not necessarily because I like the other person. I engage in dialogue because I recognize the social and not merely the individualistic character of the process of knowing' as cited in Macedo's Intro to Freire (Freire, 2012, p. 17). We enter into dialogue with one another because we trust in what we can know together through mutual engagement.

This conviction that dialogue is epistemic highlights a belief that contrasts with narratives of engagement that render students as consumers to be 'engaged' for quality control and profit. Initiatives such as the Student Voices on the Higher Education Pathway seem to offer a narrative that focuses more on issues such as time-to-degree and customer satisfaction, rather than engaging student voices on the pathway of reconceptualizing higher education. It is a narrative of engagement that talks much about 'success' in terms of measures such as retention and persistence. For example, the Public Agenda website highlights how special attention was paid 'to examining how some students succeed, why some do not, and what students think could have helped them be more successful.' In this narrative, success would most readily be framed as whether or not students graduate and whether or not they would be willing to give testimonials about the quality of the experience.

While we have data to support a strong persistence rate in the TLA (*aka* 'positive recidivism'), rather than speaking so much about success using such traditional measures as numbers of students participating over time, we propose talking more about *significance* — that is, to what extent do students say their voices influence their own educations and to what extent do their views help us construct the questions we're asking about higher education. As one first-year student observed in a

TLA session, 'I just want to matter' — a comment to which several others (including faculty and staff) quickly responded, 'me too'. Certainly, this collective desire to 'matter' goes far beyond questionnaires about quality control and customer satisfaction, instead it requires an ongoing dialogue about what that means for each of us and how to realize it in higher education, perhaps especially for those of us working to preserve a liberal arts education. In a recent virtual dialogue, the Vice-President for Academic Affairs at The Evergreen State College in Washington State observed that 'mattering' might well serve as a good tagline for the state-wide initiative to sustain a liberal arts and sciences education (personal correspondence, 22 March 2013). And in an era of declining budgets and increasing tuition across many of our institutions, we believe students can *live* this opportunity to matter through dialogue and the shared construction of what higher education will mean to all of us in the years ahead. Taking this approach, students are actively engaged because they are integral to the future of higher education beyond an alumni satisfaction survey.

We see engagement in higher education as essentially an active, dialogic process across all stakeholders, but especially students. Furthermore, instead of the inquiry being led by professors and administrators from the top of the academic hierarchy, or by non-profit or for-profit organization CEOs, we want students not only to think with, and alongside, us, but also to help facilitate the dialogue. We want students to help ask the right questions and help frame the real challenges so that we don't blithely go about answering the wrong questions or solving beside-the-point problems. We want to engage them as they engage us — allowing all of us to be engaged *actors* in our educational institutions. Paulo Freire (1970) has aptly characterized these shifts in educational approaches, posing them against his well-known summation of the authoritative, monologic 'banking model', breaking down strict roles and boundaries through a dialogic relationship with education and our students:

> ... the teacher-of-the-students and the students-of-the-teacher cease to exist and a new term emerges: teacher-student and students-teachers .... Here, no one teaches another, nor is anyone self-taught. People teach each other, mediated by the world, by cognizable objects within banking education that are 'owned' by the teacher ... the problem-posing educator constantly re-forms his reflections in the reflections of the students .... The students — no longer docile listeners — are now critical co-investigators in dialogue with the teacher. (Freire, 1970, pp. 80, 81)

By honouring the dialogic nature of our classrooms and scholarship, we then become co-inquirers with our students. Otherwise, we risk silencing the plurality of voices present in our institutions, and ending up with an incomplete picture of optimal teaching–learning structures and of the scholarship we need to shape them (Werder, Winter 2013). For higher education to realize its fullest potential, for students to be actively engaged in our institutions and the thinking behind them, we must work alongside our students, and with a full recognition of the dialogic spaces in which we work. And we must trust them and the dialogic process itself to engage us all. Because after all, isn't this building of knowledge in dialogue with the voice of another really at the heart of the scholarly enterprise?

8.5.   Remembering Scholarship as Engaging Dialogue

Through research, we question and answer our way to knowledge by responding to educational discourses spoken long before us. As Kenneth Burke invited us to think about scholarship: 'Imagine that you enter a parlour. You come late. When you arrive, others have long preceded you, and they are engaged in a heated discussion ....' And once you have caught its tenor, you join it (Burke, 1941, p. 110). Only, we would replace the language of 'discussion' with dialogue to highlight, as Ellinor and Gerard (1998), the focus on 'divergence' — on an opening up understanding with multiple views, rather than on 'converging' on the *one* best answer. And it is through idiosyncratic epistemologies of comprehension and composition, disciplinary 'languages,' methodologies or theoretical frameworks, citations or systems of peer review we regularly respond to the voices of others. Applebee (1996) sees this process as the ideal, 'Janus-Like' nature of knowledge production: the organic 'knowledge in action' which speaks back to what calls it into being, rather than a static 'knowledge-out-of-context' which silences response, becoming out of touch with its prior living roots, and ignoring the true nature of how it came to existence (pp. 1–20). We see knowledge in this manner, allowing us to be open to a multiplicity of voices and perspectives that can respond to our views, continuing the dialogue and invoking a long tradition of the Bakhtinian (1981) dialogic and what we would hope is 'culture of dialogue' in education towards engagement for all.

Bakhtin (1981) contends that any 'utterance of a speaking subject serves as a point where centrifugal as well as centripetal forces are brought to bear', combining 'the processes of centralization and decentralization, of unification and disunification' (p. 272). Theories of dialogism figure individuals as composed of a self, surrounded by related others, where each is constantly becoming 'made and unmade' through relationship. Thus, through language, spoken dialogue between people 'is composed of an utterance, a reply, and a relation between the two'. It is out of this relation that meaning emerges (Holmquist, 2002, pp. 28–38). We are who we are and speak what we speak because of what others speak and believe. It is out of our relations through difference that anything we hold has meaning; knowledge is constructed through a back-and-forth dialogue between utterances, ideologies and meanings. This dialogue is central in a world where knowledge is constructed, and 'refinement of meaning is what education is centrally about' (Bakhtin as cited in Alexander, 2008, p. 25). We contend that this process of meaning making is what education is about, and through our embodied, dialogic embracing of it, we stand to truly engage our students as active co-constructors of our institutions and larger scholarly missions. We shouldn't engage students just for their tuition dollars or long enough to connect them to what *we* deem most important, but because we see them as essential partners in the important meaning making that can happen at the university.

Furthermore, we need not engage students as co-inquirers on a limited range of topics. Intergroup Dialogues, which originated out of a desire for diversity training, and which have been happening at a number of US higher education institutions since the early 1990s (Maxwell, Nagda, & Thompson, 2011), demonstrate the value of dialogue to bring together members of diverse social and cultural groups for the sake of promoting social justice. These Intergroup Dialogues have taken hold in many of our colleges and universities partly because they highlight the importance of a particular communication goal: understanding differences in contrast to erasing them. The movement also foregrounds the need for trained facilitators: confirming that dialogue is a distinctive communication mode that cannot be left to chance; it needs facilitators who understand its primary goal to achieve shared meaning and who have the capacities and skills to facilitate the process. The Intergroup Dialogue initiative provides one helpful model of critical dialogue that, while focused on dialogue across racial and gender differences, can point the way to important practices for creating a broader culture of dialogue. This dialogic approach, especially when it is understood as both a communication mode and an epistemology, can serve to engage students in all dimensions of their learning. Moreover, when dialogue is understood as both communication channel and episteme, it has the potential to engage them long after they leave the university, especially if they have opportunities not only to engage in dialogue but also to facilitate it.

8.6.   Trust and Enactment: Recommendations for Engaging Dialogue

To honour the dialogic nature of our institutions, teachers and students should pay primary attention to building upon the distinctive transaction of voices responding to classroom texts and co-constructing knowledge and understanding. Dialogic classroom spaces explicitly honour the plurality of voices and views that make up multi-vocal meaning, amplifying the unique interplay of student voices that respond to classroom work, and building knowledge and understanding together (Heintz, Borsheim, Caughlan, Juzwik, & Sherry, 2010) (Nystrand, Gamoran, Kachur, & Prendergast, 1997). Alexander (2008) identifies five essential attributes of a dialogic classroom: that it is 'collective' in how teachers and students choose to cooperatively tackle classroom work, 'reciprocal' in the manner teachers and students choose to listen to one another, 'supportive' of the variety of viewpoints that come up and with the common purpose of reaching understanding together, 'cumulative' in that teachers and students collectively construct meaning out of all the ideas present, and 'purposeful' due to the deliberate way teachers construct dialogic instruction to meet their educational goals. These attributes of dialogic teaching resonate with the dialogic principles that have emerged from the TLA. And they find counterpoint in the more traditional 'rote' and 'recitation' structures of traditional classrooms less apt to honour the multiple — especially student — voices and perspectives present (pp. 28–39). Could we use these terms to also describe how we have (or want) to go about engaging our students? Might we identify an explicit acknowledgement of the roles that student voices play in our daily classroom work and research? If we do not acknowledge student voices in this dialogue, then we silence an important interplay, and miss an essential relationship at the core of discourse in our classrooms, research and the academy. For those of us committed to student engagement, this acknowledgment of student voices in the interplay is essential. In fact, we contend, this trust in dialogue with students as co-inquirers is where engagement begins.

We acknowledge that our call here is nothing short of a major cultural shift, no doubt happening amidst what is oftentimes a history of glacial change in higher education. However, we can tell you from experience that this change is immensely worth the wait and effort as it creates a healthier, sustainable culture for faculty and students. Our own institutional work oftentimes took many stages to complete and is still currently evolving as we welcome more 'converts' into the fold. As a model of how to communicate and learn together across multiple stakeholders on and off campus, the TLA has proven effective and at least one other school that we know of (Eastern Michigan University) has replicated its dialogue format. But creating a campus-wide dialogue structure is not the only way to enact dialogue. While not able to provide you with a 'sure-fire' formula to immediately implement on your campus, we can at least offer three principles that have regularly guided our own institutional work:

1. Consistently *listen* to student voices, not as customers to be satisfied, but as co-inquirers who bring expertise about their own learning.
2. Be obsessive about inviting *all student voices* into all spheres of influence in university life, not just the high achieving, pre-designated student leaders.
3. Enter into dialogue with students as a *relational* dynamic, not simply as a way of talking and listening, but as a way of building human connections with each other and with knowledge itself.

Trusting in dialogue as a way of engaging students could even lead to believing in it as a way of engaging our humanity in the world together.

References

Alexander, R. (2008). *Towards dialogic teaching: Rethinking classroom talk* (4th ed.), North Yorkshire, UK: Dialogos.

Applebee, A. (1996). *Curriculum as conversation: Transforming traditions of teaching and learning*. Chicago, IL: University of Chicago Press.

Atlee, T. (n.d.). *Building a culture of dialogue (among other things)*. The Co-Intelligence Institute. Retrieved from http://www.co-intelligence.org/CIPol_CultrOfDialog.html

Bakhtin, M. M. (1981). *The dialogic imagination: Four essays*. Austin, TX: University of Texas Press.

Burke, K. (1941). *The philosophy of literary form: Studies in symbolic action* (3rd ed.), Berkeley, CA: University of California Press.

Ellinor, L., & Gerard, G. (1998). *Dialogue: Rediscover the transforming power of conversation.* New York, NY: Wiley.

Espinoza-Gonzalez, D. (2013, Winter). Finding value in my voice. *Diversity & Democracy,* *26*(1). Retrieved from http://www.aacu.org/diversitydemocracy/vol16no1/espinoza-gonzalez. cfm

Freire, P. (1970). *Pedagogy of the oppressed* (2012 Anniversary ed.), New York, NY: Continuum.

Freire, P. (2012). *Pedagogy of the oppressed* (30th anniversary ed.). New York, NY: Continuum International Publishing Group.

Heintz, A., Borsheim, C., Caughlan, S., Juzwik, M. M., & Sherry, M. B. (2010). Video based response & revision: Dialogic instruction using video and web 2.0 technologies. *Contemporary Issues in Technology and Teacher Education, 10*(2), 175–196.

Holmquist, M. (2002). *Dialogism: Bakhtin and his world* (2nd ed.), New York, NY: Routledge.

Huber, M., & Hutchings, P. (2005). *The advancement of learning: Building the teaching commons.* Stanford, CA: Jossey-Bass.

Maxwell, E., Nagda, B. A., & Thompson, M. C. (2011). *Facilitating intergroup dialogues: Bridging differences, catalyzing change.* Sterling, VA: Stylus.

Morgan, J. M., & Hoskimima, T. (2011). *Including more student voices in higher education policy making: Rising tuitions and student debts mean rising stakes for college students.* Center for American Progress. Retrieved from http://www.americanprogress.org/ wpcontent/uploads/issues/2011/11/pdf/student_voices.pdf

Nystrand, M., Gamoran, A., Kachur, R., & Prendergast, C. (1997). *Opening dialogue: Understanding the dynamics of language and learning in the English classroom.* New York, NY: Teachers College Press.

Public Agenda. (n.d.). Student voices on the higher education pathway: Preliminary insights and stakeholder engagement considerations. Retrieved from http://www.publicagenda. org/pages/student-voices-higher-education-pathway. Accessed on 23 March 2013.

Werder, C. (2013, Winter). Democratizing teaching and learning through real dialogue across differences. *Diversity and Democracy, 16*(1). Retrieved from http://www.aacu.org/diversity-democracy/vol16no1/werder.cfm

Werder, C., Thibou, S., & Kaufer, B. (2012). Students as co-inquirers: A requisite threshold concept in educational development? In C. King & P. Felten (Eds.), *Threshold Concepts in Educational Development: The Journal of Faculty Development* [Special Issue], *26*(3), 34–38.

Werder, C., Ware, L., Thomas, C., & Skogsberg, E. (2010). Students in parlor talk on teaching and learning. In C. Werder & M. Otis (Eds.), *Engaging student voices in the study of teaching and learning* (pp. 16–31). Sterling, VA: Stylus.

Chapter 9

Student Engagement in Practice: Ideologies and Power in Course Representation Systems

Rebecca Freeman

Abstract

Student engagement involves whole institutions in a range of activities. This chapter draws upon recent research conducted in a Post-92[1] and a Russell Group[2] institution in order to consider how individuals within higher education make sense of student engagement within their own context, how power relationships are defined and the implications for practice.

Drawing upon data from a series of interviews, observations and analysis of current policy this chapter explores some of the different narratives around 'student voice' in higher education. Taking course representative structures as a case study of a common form of student engagement in the United Kingdom, the chapter highlights some of the ways in which students, academics and senior managers understand their role in student engagement activities and the ways in which they enact these roles in practice. The importance of acknowledging the differences in power held by individuals involved in student engagement is discussed and the chapter concludes with implications for institutional student engagement policy and practice.

9.1. Introduction

Student engagement with the evaluation of their learning experience takes place in a variety of ways in the UK higher education system. Student representative systems,

---

[1]An institution awarded University status in the Further and Higher Education Act 1992.
[2]A group composed of 24 leading research intensive institutions.

The Student Engagement Handbook: Practice in Higher Education
Copyright © 2013 by Emerald Group Publishing Limited
All rights of reproduction in any form reserved
ISBN: 978-1-78190-423-7

module evaluations, the National Student Survey (NSS),[3] student complaints and student engagement in governance are all implemented in some format in the majority of institutions. These different structures for engagement have developed over time and have become more prevalent since the introduction and subsequent increase of tuition fees (Browne, 2010; HEFCE, 2003a, 2003b). Alongside the changes to the funding system, formal structures for student engagement have become increasingly prominent and subject to external promotion and guidance. Recently the development of the Quality Assurance Agency (QAA)[4] Student Engagement chapter within the Quality Code (QAA, 2012) has provided a 'definitive reference point' for UK higher education institutions, setting out expectations for the way in which student engagement, including representation, is undertaken. These developments highlight a number of different ideologies evident in policy which have a bearing on student engagement including students as consumers due to the payment of tuition fees; accountability to students and the public; and an emphasis on enhancement.

While research has been conducted to evaluate the student experience at universities it has tended to be primarily quantitative in nature and large-scale (e.g. the NSS, Student Barometer[5] and institutional satisfaction surveys). Surveys of this nature are distributed to students and focus on student experiences. These surveys generate a large quantity of data, serving to identify student satisfaction with particular institutional activities. While providing a useful overview of satisfaction for league table and management decisions, surveys tend to provide only a limited understanding of the complexity of students' experiences. Surveys of this type also fail to identify the experience of the academics and senior managers with whom students interact through representation and other engagement activity.

Student engagement in higher education is complex, can mean different things to different people and is underpinned by a range of different, and at times, competing ideologies. Recent course representation research (Carey, 2013; CHERI, 2008) has demonstrated that by talking to those involved in course representation, a richer understanding of engagement can be developed. The research undertaken in this study aimed to provide an alternative to the large-scale quantitative studies. By observing and talking to the individuals involved in student engagement (students, academics, students' union representatives and senior managers) the research aimed to generate a rich, nuanced understanding of the complex relationships that occur in order to deepen understanding of the concepts and relationships that influence representation in practice.

---

[3]A government-funded annual survey of final year undergraduate students across the United Kingdom.
[4]The government-funded body that oversees standards and quality in UK institutions.
[5]A UK-wide survey of students' experiences.

9.1.1. Research Outline

In order to generate a rich data set a critical-interpretative approach was adopted for the study. The interpretative lens sought to generate a deep understanding of the approach and practice of individuals and organisations, while the critical lens focused on the nature of power and ideologies in the data in order to establish the complexity of engagement in practice.

The research outlined in this chapter sought to establish:

- the ways in which individuals (students, students' union representatives, academics and managers) make sense of student engagement;
- how individuals behave in practice, and whether their actions are faithful to the way in which they articulate engagement;
- whether the range of ideological concepts held and enacted by individuals (such as students as consumers, democracy and enhancement) are coherent or whether they contain contradictions;
- how power relates to student engagement;
- and whether the range of different ways in which people understand their own participation has implications for the effectiveness of student engagement structures.

The research was based on a comparative case study model in order to consider the impact of structures for student voice in different contexts. The data were collected between 2011 and 2012 in two institutions, one Post-92 institution with a high proportion of part-time and work-based students and one Russell Group institution with a majority full-time student population. In order to develop an understanding of whether practices and ideologies differed between subject disciplines, students and academics from the Departments of English and Engineering were studied at each institution.

Within the case studies student voice structures were considered at the macro (government, university and students' union policies and practice), meso (senior managers' interpretation and implementation of these policies) and micro (students and academics interpreting, understanding and engaging within student voice structures) levels. This format enabled an understanding of the ways in which high-level student engagement structures influenced an individual's understanding of the purpose of representation and his or her personal role.

Fairclough's (2001, pp. 97, 98) model for the analysis of discourse (Critical Discourse Analysis (CDA)) was drawn upon throughout the study as an approach for unpicking the underlying assumptions, concepts and ideologies within the text. Fairclough (1993) suggests that language is not neutral; the way people talk and write reveals traces of particular assumptions, understandings and dynamics of power. Several forms of data relating to course representative systems were analysed to identify ideologies and power dynamics using CDA including:

- interviews with senior managers, academics and students (Post-92; four students, three academics, three senior managers and Russell Group; five students, five academics, two senior managers);

- observations of course representative committees within the sample departments;
- documents relating to student representation such as students' union produced student representative handbooks.

A selection of quotes and excerpts from the data is included in this chapter to illustrate the range and complexity of ideologies, experiences and relationships. The excerpts are selected to represent the range of ideologies drawn upon by the respondents to varying degrees, in different contexts and institutions, in order to demonstrate some of the dynamics of student engagement in practice. While the sample size is small, the depth of the data is intended to enrich understanding of the complexity of engagement.

9.2.   Exploring Ideologies

In 2008 a study funded by the Higher Education Funding Council for England (HEFCE) found that institutions held a number of distinct perspectives on the purpose of student engagement (CHERI, 2008). Deriving data from a series of interviews with institutional and students' union staff, the report found three common rationales which institutions used to justify their approaches to student engagement. These rationales included 'enhancing the student experience', which recognised students as customers and valued choice; 'listening and being responsive', which sought student opinion in order to 'nip problems and issues in the bud'; and less commonly, a 'learning communities' rationale, which sought to engage students as owners or co-producers of their education (CHERI, 2008). The report served to demonstrate the complex and subjective ideologies drawn upon by individuals designing and participating in student engagement.

Evident throughout the interviews and observations were a number of different ways in which individuals made sense of their role in student engagement. Participants were asked 'why' they were (or were not) involved in student representation. A number of these ideologies are outlined and the related literature explored in this section.

9.2.1.   Representation and Students as Consumers

The notion of students as consumers had pervaded the ways in which students and academics spoke about their experiences of representation. While many spoke to reject consumerism, almost all respondents engaged with it on some level. There was a perception that the purpose of student representation was at least in part a process linked to 'customer satisfaction', the customers in this context being the students.

The notion of students as consumers or customers has developed as a discourse since the introduction of tuition fees in 1998 (Gibbs, 2001; Lomas, 2007; McCulloch, 2009). The ideology positions the university as 'the provider of products and services' and students as consumers of provision and support placing students in a relatively passive role (McCulloch, 2009, p. 171).

Observations of student representative meetings presented a number of examples in which students might be viewed as behaving as consumers, for example:

> A couple of people talked about paying for hand-outs. We got one hand-out at the beginning of the year for one module and that was free and the second one at the start of this term we had to pay for. It wasn't very much but I think for a lot of people it was the principle — that we are paying for our fees — we just wondered why fees couldn't cover it? It was only a pound but these people were quite annoyed. (Year 2 Student, Student Representative Meeting, English, Russell Group)

The nature of students as fee-payers had pervaded the way in which students felt that they should be treated by their department in terms of the provision of resources.

The study showed that among management, the discourse of improvement, enhancement and student satisfaction was often seen as a consumer activity concerned with ensuring value for money for students. These discourses reflected some of the areas in which the government has expressed interest, exemplified by the data shared with prospective students through the Key Information Set (KIS)[6] (UCAS, 2012):

> That [student voice for improvement and enhancement] certainly is strong and I think that's to do with — that would come under the consumer and the tuition fees thing — you know teaching rooms that are fit for purpose, the resources that should be available in the library, the technologies involved in teaching — that they should be reasonably up to date. All that certainly is coming through very clearly. But contact hours is more of a priority than the latest form of teaching — so the more traditional idea of education persists strongly — the sort of resistance to the mass university. (Senior Academic Management, Russell Group)

The notion of consumerism is often seen as a passive transaction between institutions and students. Hartley (2007, p. 633) extends the reach of the ideology to other themes in education, suggesting a more sophisticated management of student consumers. Hartley suggests that the discourse around choice and personalisation that is popular in UK education illustrates the 'appropriation by policy-makers of consumerist and marketing discourses (which appeal to the emotions and to the 'self')'

---

[6]Comparable sets of information about undergraduate courses designed to meet the information needs of prospective students.

(Hartley, 2007, p. 633). Referring to the rise of discourse around choice and perso-nalisation in schools, Hartley (2007) and Fielding (2008) suggest that the concepts have become a rhetoric of empowerment which disguises increasing managerialism in education (Fielding, 2008, p. 59). Modularisation, semesterisation and the concept of self-directed learning (Gibbs, 2001, p. 87) are seen as ways in which students are, on the face of it, empowered to choose while also being constrained. As Fielding suggests, personalisation is preoccupied:

> With individual choosers, with little if any, account being taken of the claims of wider allegiance and the common good. Yet, this fore-grounding of choice, whether at a classroom level or in its systematic expression through multiple pathways, masks the deep dishonesty that ignores the many barriers to choice within the system, whether through ability labelling or entry requirement. (Fielding, 2008, p. 59)

The idea that student representation is part of a series of institutional structures that served to enable engagement, while concurrently constraining the ways in which this could take place, was supported in the interviews. Academics and man-agers spoke about 'managing expectations' and presenting students with a series of choices, which they had the potential to influence, but which were ultimately owned and designed by the institution. As one academic articulated:

> One of the things we are constantly engaged in is — and there's never an end to this of course — is talking to students about the conse-quences of an alternative arrangement. And that extends to quite small pragmatic arrangements as well. We're very happy to listen and say ok you don't like the look of this; the alternatives are x, y and z. Let's explain to you the consequences of those alternatives now. And then let us know what you think. (Senior Academic English, Post-92)

A number of examples of the 'management of student expectations' were evident when students requested provision that had not previously been offered by the department or university, such as access to marked exam papers or changes to library policies. Students tended to accept the explanation of the constraints offered by staff in these meetings, understanding that this was the way that things were done, certain actions could not be resourced or that processes were not feasible.

9.2.2.   Accountability

The idea of accountability and 'rights' was present in a number of the interviews. Academics in particular felt that the formal university processes were underpinned by a philosophy of accountability to students. The HEFCE's Strategic Plan at the time of the introduction of increased fees stated, 'students increasingly see themselves as consumers, entitled to agreed standards of provision and to full information about the quality of what is provided' (HEFCE, 2003b). This emphasis on accountability to 'stakeholders' (e.g. students, parents and the wider public) and the notion of entitlement was followed by the strengthening of approaches to monitoring quality on a national level through the Quality Assurance Agency, the Office of the Independent Adjudicator and the introduction of the National Student Survey (NSS).

At the Post-92 institution, one academic talked about the way in which accountability informed formal processes. Issues identified through formal representation routes were viewed as official and therefore were more likely to be acted upon than informal requests from students that occurred outside these structures. The official nature of student representative meetings gave students legitimacy:

> I'm not sure that it ever gets acted upon if it's less formalised. Sometimes if a student comes with a specific issue then a member of staff may choose to say 'OK, let's go the office together, let's sort this out now, bang, bang, done. They may say 'Send me an email' and then it gets sorted out once the facts are written down, depends how complex and what the issue is of course. They may say 'Oh, go and see so and so'. They may just nod and smile and do nothing about it. (Senior Academic Engineering, Post-92)

The students interviewed remarked that they felt that the concept of holding the university accountable was important, but felt that in practice their influence was limited to a small range of areas within student representation systems. Students recognised that they were able to hold academics and the university to account at some level, but that student satisfaction formed one of many influences on university policy and practice. One student spoke about an issue that he felt could not be addressed through the representation system. He felt he had the right to hold academics to account, and that current practice was unjust, but he was aware of multiple agendas to which academics worked, which limited his capacity to hold them fully accountable.

> The most annoying thing is that we don't get feedback at all sometimes and they take quite a long time to do it which is quite disconcerting because you put a lot of work into certain pieces of work — a certain assignment and then you expect an equal return but more often than not academics are too busy with their research and like getting [the university] high up in the league tables so they don't give you timely feedback. (Year 1 Student Representative Engineering, Russell Group)

There was a misalignment evident between staff perceptions of the importance of accountability to students through formal structures and the recognition by students that their capacity for holding staff accountable was limited.

9.2.3. *Democracy*

Most student representation systems maintain some relationships with democratic processes. Elections in some format are usually held at the start of the year and a quota of student representatives from each course is usually in place. One academic described their understanding of the democratic organisation of student representation as follows:

> They have access to all sorts of members of the department from their personal tutor or their seminar tutor up to the head of department without making it sound too hierarchical but they can express themselves to a whole range of different people depending on the nature of the issue. They elect their members. They stand for — if they want to be a rep they propose themselves and then if they want to chair it and the committee elects its own members — that sort of thing. That sounds pretty democratic to me ... it's up to them how they organise themselves and represent themselves. (Senior Academic English, Russell Group)

Students' unions also engaged with the ideologies of democracy as an ideal, although they felt that it often did not align with the way that student representation operated in practice:

> The university should be a community not necessarily a hierarchical or managerial organisation, although it is. I think student voice is important to maintain the community aspect in terms of the student direction for institutions. Students should have a voice in that. (Student Union Officer, Russell Group)

Early student engagement in the United Kingdom emerged from political engagement with institutions and traditionally approaches to representation in UK universities have drawn upon ideas of democracy to enable students to influence university policy and practice (Ashby & Anderson, 1970). At the heart of this ideology is the notion that students have the *right* to participate in the management of higher education as *citizens* (Fielding, 1973, 2004a). The concept also relates to ideas of equality and social justice allowing all the opportunity to elect or stand for a position as a representative (Furlong & Cartmel, 2009; Gorard & Smith, 2010).

The idea of a democracy was popular among a number of academics who linked ideas of democracy with the notion of collegiality, which they believed to be an important but undervalued concept within an effective institution:

> If one thinks of the original purpose of universities which was I suspect, sharing knowledge and experience, we have become much more hierarchical, managed and to be in a less managed world — I mean a world which some long serving academics will wistfully speak of is

collegiality as though it is something which has been lost and that's not far from democracy. (Director of Learning and Teaching, Post-92)

Despite the nostalgia around democracy, student and staff respondents did not feel that in practice representation was particularly democratic. For academics, democratic practice was undermined by the competing agendas that informed representation. For students, democracy was undermined by the differences in the power held by academics and students:

> [Democratic] I wouldn't say so. Because I'd say you are still reporting things to the department and then the department decide what to do with the things that are reported. So you have the power to say this is an issue but you don't have the power to do anything about it yourself. (Year 3 Student Representative English, Russell Group)

A contradiction was apparent between the ideals of democracy and the ways that students experienced representation in practice. Democracy, while recognised as an important ideology by many respondents, was widely dismissed beyond the organisation of representation through elections and encouraging representatives to engage with peers.

9.2.4. Development of Identity

The importance of students *feeling* ownership of the learning experience was emphasised by a number of academic respondents who felt that the development of student voice, identity and confidence was an important role of a representation system. The development of student 'voice' is explored by Barnett (2007). Barnett distinguishes between two types of 'voice' — the pedagogical, embodied voice, which is described as the 'capacity or willingness of the student to give voice to her thoughts or feelings', and the voice of the student as a critical being through which the student can express the authentic self. Barnett suggests that for real, life-shaping learning to take place a student must realise both 'types' of voice. A number of academics viewed student participation in representation as an opportunity for students to develop confidence and self-esteem thus laying the foundations for students to feel part of their institution:

> A buy in. If students have had a say and they've said 'This could be better' and we have made it better then they say 'Thank you' and feel that they've been a little bit of it rather than just subjects that we teach at. Passive learner to something more active, which is important on societal level as well as the personal level. You've got to be able to make a difference in the world. Leave footprints in the sands of time as it were. That's important in a self-esteem, self-view fashion. (Senior Academic Engineering, Post-92)

This echoes the discourse around student self-esteem and well-being which is increasingly prevalent in education and notions of 'student satisfaction' (Ecclestone, 2004; Ecclestone & Hayes, 2008). Ecclestone (2004) suggests that while activities concerned with identity and well-being in education may, on the face of it, appear empowering for students, they may in fact serve to disempower individuals by lowering expectations of 'people's capacity for resilience and autonomy' (Ecclestone, 2004, p. 112). Ecclestone sees the increasing focus on well-being (e.g. provision of student support, counselling and opportunities for engagement) as a phenomenon which 'both legitimises and extends institutional and government influence over people's psychological and emotional states' (Ecclestone, 2004, p. 112). As such student engagement becomes a route through which institutions are able to manage students' emotional selves in order to 'keep students happy'.

There was some evidence of the tensions around student well-being among students. A number of students spoke about representation as an outlet for frustrations, describing their participation as a cathartic experience. However, some students recognised that only certain frustrations could be legitimately aired within representative forums:

> To some extent, this thing serves to relieve some of the pressure and frustration you might feel. For instance as an individual if you have your own issues that impact upon the quality of your time here, you can't really do much to express them if they're personal concerns ...
> (Year 1 Student Representative Engineering, Russell Group)

There was a sense that while some participants acknowledged identity development as a driver for representation, some students felt that this development was constrained within the boundaries of what were regarded by academics and institutions as legitimate areas for discussion. For example student feedback relating to criticisms of named lecturers were seen by students and academics as 'out of bounds'.

The varying ideologies outlined above illustrate a few of the ways in which students and staff viewed and understood their role in representation. A number of different, and at times competing, ideologies were present and it was evident that these influenced individuals' perceptions of representation and the ways that they engaged. A range of areas that included institutional policies and discourses, experiences, training, handbooks, and discussion of the nature of higher education in the media informed respondents' ideologies. Individuals drew upon these ideas in complex ways explicitly and tacitly to develop their own, unique understanding of engagement.

9.3.   Perceptions of Power

A theme, which occurred throughout the interviews and observations, was that of power. Power dynamics between students, staff and senior managers (and internally within those groups) were seen to influence the engagement of all groups with representation.

Fielding (2004b) argues that issues of power are intrinsically linked to student engagement. Working primarily on student engagement in primary and secondary education, his research provides a useful lens through which to consider engagement practice in higher education. Fielding questions the nature of student engagement asking of formal student voice structures, are we

> carving a new order of experience? Or are we presiding over the future entrenchment of existing assumptions and intentions using student or pupil voice as an additional mechanism of control? (Rudduck & Flutter, 2000, cited in Fielding, 2001, p. 100)

Fielding (2004b) identifies three ways in which voices can be used by those in power — through *accommodation*, in which voices are reassured and reconstructed; *accumulation*, in which voices are used to provide knowledge which strengthens the *status quo*; and *appropriation*, in which voices are used to legitimise the dominant group's position. Aspects of these were evident within the data, which highlights some of the potential complexities of representation.

Analysis of student representation handbooks was conducted and served to illustrate some of the power dynamics evident in the formal processes as described by universities and students' unions. The manner in which representation is described in official documentation sets a framework for what is seen as legitimate and expected within an institution. While a range of factors (e.g. departmental cultures, training, and the confidence of individual academic convenors) informed the way in which representation was carried out in the different contexts, the 'official' process in the form of a representation 'handbook' set out the formal standards for representation.

The students' union and the institution jointly oversaw the system at each of the institutions studied. At both of the institutions, the students' union produced and distributed a handbook, which set out the aims, process and procedures for representation. Students were also offered training by the students' union. There were a number of power dynamics evident in the handbooks, which positioned students, academics and senior managers within the system. Individuals and student representative committees could, of course, chose to reject their given roles but in most interviews and observations the processes were broadly adopted at face value. Links to institutional quality processes and the consequent potential for review by the QAA served to further strengthen compliance.

The formal language of university administration was adopted within the handbooks rather than a more neutral, plain English tone. Terms such as 'feedback loops', 'academic concerns', 'agreed actions', 'transferable skills' and 'enhancement' presented a formal institutionalised vocabulary. The description of the process underlined the 'official' nature of the system and defined the nature of the transactions that could legitimately take place. The use of formal language to describe otherwise familiar activities professionalised the remit of student representation committees and emphasised institutional ownership of processes.

Systems were described in ways that focused on the practical role of the student representative, staff member and the institution rather than their role in relation to learning or the emotional or political components of representation. The focus in the handbooks was on *what* people were required to do rather than *why* they should do it. Individuals could develop their own understanding of engagement, or discuss the purpose within course representative training, but the exclusion within the documentation may have presented the impression that formally, the practical process was valued over the experiences of the participants.

The handbooks set out the different roles within the process for students and staff. The verbs used to describe the student role within the handbooks were largely mechanistic. For example:

> *To report* agreed action back to students
> *To read* minutes and ensure you *follow up* on any actions *allocated* to you (Russell Group)
>
> *Read and respond* to emails and other communication from the Students' Union
> *Signpost* University and Union services that may be of use to students (Post-92)

In contrast, the responsibilities listed for staff at the Russell Group institution were focused more on managerial processes:

> *Ensures* that SSLC concerns and requests are *considered* at staff meetings ...
> *Assists* the Chair and Secretary in the *organisation* of agenda items ...

The verbs used for students and for staff respectively create a hierarchy of responsibility. Students are required *to do* certain things while staff members are responsible for *ensuring* that things happen. This underlines subtle but important differences in the allocation of power and responsibility within the process which may inform the way in which individuals participate, and their perception of their ownership of the process.

The subtle differences in roles outlined within the handbook were illustrated in practice in the following account from an academic. There was a clear perception that in order to be a 'good' representative, students must act within the guidelines set out in the handbook. The text at the end of the statement mirrors some of the language present in the handbook of the institution:

> I think the student rep system is pretty good if the student does it properly. You're very reliant on the student. But we have excellent students. They're not there to represent their thoughts; they're there to represent students, they hold meetings and take it forward. (Senior Academic Engineering, Post-92)

The academic clearly understood that students should play the approved representation role, and felt that they did this well. The interviews with students suggested that students also held opinions about how well staff performed their role in student representation processes, but did not feel able to articulate these opinions to staff. The formal aspects of the process consequently had a greater impact in defining the role of the student than of the academic.

A number of staff also highlighted a sense of frustration when students did not play by the formal rules of engagement as set out by the institution. Institutions provided a range of opportunities for students to engage, but were often frustrated by a real or perceived lack of student participation and at times annoyed when students chose to evaluate experience through alternative routes, for example online or through protest. Where this occurred, it underlined some of the hierarchies of power within institutions, highlighting institutional perceptions of *legitimate* evaluation:

> And students are equally members of the public if you like. They are members of this university and we all have a responsibility. It's as simple as that really. If they don't tell us, then I think they've got a cheek to turn round afterwards and say it was awful. (Pro-Vice-Chancellor, Post-92)

Students acknowledged and demonstrated a level of frustration about the constraints of their engagement within formal systems, understanding that they held little or no power within student representation systems without the support of academics:

> I've found at times that the tutors aren't always that good at listening to problems that are brought up. Like if it's more of 'oh no, we don't think that's enough of a problem' it's quite easy to dismiss it I think. I do think that is an issue. Like there have been times when people have brought up problems and the Department has just been very 'oh well, we can't change that. (Year 3 Student Representative English, Russell Group)

Some academic respondents recognised the professionalisation of student representatives through guidance and training and felt that it had influenced the way in which interactions took place within meetings. Differing views emerged as to whether or not this was a positive sign of students understanding their formal role or whether they had become, to use Fielding's (2004b) term, *accommodated* into the system to the extent that they were no longer comfortable representing student views directly:

> I mean they're so well trained strangely, that it is very common now for reps to speak at [student representative committees] as if they are academics. It's almost as if they have crossed the divide. They've so fully understood the nature of the business and this is an interesting one. Is this a criticism of where this has led? They've so fully

understood the nature of the business that they've almost stopped speaking directly for the students if you like. (Senior Academic English, Post-92)

This comment summarises behaviour that was observed in student representative meetings. There were a number of instances in which students distanced their own views from those of their peers when raising issues that they felt might not be palatable to academic committee members. This trend was also present in research by Carey (2013, pp. 81, 82) who identified that some students felt embarrassed about raising particular issues or relayed the probable outcome to peers before raising an issue with staff.

Students recognised that their role as a representative allowed them a certain power but, at times, demonstrated a reluctance to jeopardise this by expressing unpopular views:

They'll sit on the student board. They have said before; 'I'm just going to say this opinion isn't my opinion, I actually think this is not a problem but this is my attitude towards it, this is what's coming from the student body. (Senior Academic Engineering, Post-92)

One of the fundamental ideals of representation in each institution was that students were elected by their peers and represented the views of a particular group. These ideas had their foundations in democracy. Within the interviews, however, there was widespread recognition that current course representation systems had only a tenuous relationship with democracy. Many representatives were uncomfortable with the requirement, whether due to a lack of feedback from peers, the discomfort felt when representing unpopular views or the restrictions placed on the expression of their own personal opinions.

9.4.   Conclusions and Implications for Practice

The power dynamics experienced by individuals, alongside the various ideologies drawn upon by those engaged in representation, highlight the complex picture in which course representation occurs. While these complexities have implications for practice, they do not necessarily devalue student engagement through representation. Most participants were pleased to be involved in representation processes and felt that many aspects of the structures worked. Students, while recognising the power dynamics in play, felt that changes were often made in response to their engagement and few regretted their involvement. Similarly, academics clearly valued the opportunity for engagement, listened to what students had to say and engaged actively in discussion.

In considering the implications for practice, a number of ways in which course representation was *not* discussed in formal documentation were identified in order to understand those aspects, which were implicitly, not formally, valued by institutions. Some of these aspects are hard to measure, quantify or define. They do not fit easily with the standard university style, but in order to ensure that policy supports engagement between students and staff, it is important to find a vocabulary for engagement with these aspects. Within the handbooks and individual descriptions of the process, there was very little about:

- interpersonal relationships between staff and students and how these might develop;
- development of the student as an independent learner or constructor of knowledge;
- university management and how representation fits into strategic university priorities and agendas;
- general culture, and how students and academics feel they are positioned;
- why people might want to be involved, beyond gaining experience for their CV.

The following three suggestions are offered as points for consideration by those involved in course representation who may want to explore practice in their context and consider approaches for maximising the value of engagement (Freeman, 2014, forthcoming):

1. *Increased awareness of the ideologies informing engagement*
   One of the aims of this research was to highlight the range of different influences that inform student representation. Institutional processes are not neutral and neither are the participants involved in these structures. To engage in collective activity without acknowledging the ideological purpose of structures and the individual understandings of those engaging with representation can lead to tensions, confusion and frustrations. By acknowledging the range of ideologies, individuals are able to act more knowingly with systems and to better understand their own engagement.

2. *Acknowledgement of power*
   It was clear in all of the interviews with students taking part in representation systems that they were distinctly aware of the power differential between themselves and university staff. The discourse observed in the handbooks and meetings reinforced these differences through language and behaviour. What resulted was often a sense of frustration among students who, while appreciating aspects of the system, fundamentally understood that they were one of many voices and thus had little power. Students' ideas required the support of academics to be taken forward. Students were pragmatic about this and they understood the context and the competing, influencing agendas, but because this was not discussed it remained an unspoken constraint rather than something that could be discussed or challenged.

3. *Developing a shared ideology*
   Many of the interview respondents remarked that taking part in the study was their first opportunity to articulate to others the methods through which they

made sense of the systems in which they engaged. No one respondent drew upon a single ideology; instead they pieced together their experiences and understandings to construct their own way of viewing the processes. In the recent QAA document universities in partnership with their student body are asked to 'define and promote the range of opportunities for any student to engage in educational enhancement and quality assurance' (QAA, 2012, p. 4).

A collaborative process of defining and promoting shared ideologies and understanding of what representation is about in a particular context is important for transformational discussion. This should take place at the lowest structural level that is appropriate for an institution, within course representative committees as well as between institutions and students' unions. For students and staff to share their understandings of what the student representation system should be, within their own individual context, could enable a heightened awareness of where ideologies differ and ensure a foundation of shared understanding.

The research identified a number of complex and at times competing ideologies that were drawn upon both explicitly and tacitly by individuals engaging in student representation systems. Senior managers, academics and students interpreted their own engagement in relation to a wide range of discourses and ideologies and were influenced by a range of tensions and contradictions. The extent to which individuals consciously engaged with these ideologies differed by respondent. The ideology of the student as consumer, for example, was explicitly addressed by most respondents, who recognised the notion as popular and contentious. Engagement with other ideologies such as well-being and democracy was more implicit, and often woven into examples and experiences.

The complexity of engagement with representation did not mean that students and staff saw the process as negative. In practice, most respondents felt that the student representation system was positive and productive, providing the time and structure for valuable discussions to take place. However, at times the mix of ideologies and failure to acknowledge differences in power limited engagement. A greater understanding and exploration of practice within different contexts could serve to ensure that the value gained through engagement in representation is maximised for individuals and institutions.

References

Ashby, E., & Anderson, M. (1970). *The rise of the student estate in Britain*. Cambridge, MA: Harvard University Press.

Barnett, R. (2007). *A will to learn: Being a student in an age of uncertainty*. Maidenhead, UK: Open University Press.

Browne, L. (2010). *Securing a sustainable future for higher education*. London: Brunswick Group.

Carey, P. (2013). Representation and student engagement in higher education: A reflection on the views and experiences of course representatives. *Journal of Further and Higher Education, 37*(1), 71−88.

CHERI. (2008, 11 June). *Study into student engagement.* Centre for Higher Education Research and Information. Retrieved from http://www.open.ac.uk/cheri/pages/CHERI-Projects-HEFCEstudentengagement.shtml. Accessed on 28 October 2012.

Ecclestone, K. (2004). Learning or therapy? The demoralisation of education. *British Journal of Educational Studies, 52*(2), 112−137.

Ecclestone, K., & Hayes, D. (2008). *The dangerous rise of therapeutic education*: London: Routledge.

Fairclough, N. (1993). Critical discourse analysis and the marketization of public discourse: The universities. *Discourse and Society, 4*, 133−168.

Fairclough, N. (2001). *Language and power.* Harlow: Pearson.

Fielding, M. (1973). Democracy in secondary schools: School councils and 'shared responsibility'. *Journal of Moral Education, 2*(3), 221−232.

Fielding, M. (2001). Beyond the rhetoric of student voice: New departures or new constraints in the transformation of 21st century schooling. *Forum, 43*(2), 100–110.

Fielding, M. (2004a). 'New wave' student voice and the renewal of civic society. *London Review of Education, 2*(3), 197−217.

Fielding, M. (2004b). Transformative approaches to student voice: Theoretical underpinnings, recalcitrant realities. *British Educational Research Journal, 30*(2), 295−311.

Fielding, M. (2008). Personalisation, education and the market. *Soundings, 38*, 56−69.

Freeman, R. (2014, forthcoming). *Student voice: New forms of power and governmentality in higher education.* Birmingham: University of Birmingham.

Furlong, A., & Cartmel, F. (2009). *Higher education and social justice.* Maidenhead, UK: Open University Press.

Gibbs, P. (2001). Higher education as a market: A problem or solution?. *Studies in Higher Education, 26*(1), 85−95.

Gorard, S., & Smith, E. (2010). *Equity in education: An international perspective.* Palgrave Macmillan.

Hartley, D. (2007). Personalisation: The emerging 'revised' code of education? *Oxford Review of Education, 33*(5), 629−642.

HEFCE. (2003a, 4 September). *Collecting and using student feedback on quality and standards of learning and teaching in HE.* Retrieved from http://www.hefce.ac.uk/pubs/rdreports/2003/rd08_03/. Accessed on 28 February 2009.

HEFCE (2003b). *Strategic plan: 2003−2008.* Bristol, UK: HEFCE.

Lomas, L. (2007). Are students customers? Perceptions of academic staff. *Quality in Higher Education, 13*(1), 31−44.

McCulloch, A. (2009). The student as co-producer: Learning from public administration about the student-university relationship. *Studies in Higher Education, 34*, 171−183.

QAA (2012). UK quality code of higher education. Part B: Assuring and Enhancing Academic Quality. Chapter B5: Student Engagement, pp. 1−16.

Rudduck, J., & Flutter, J. (2000). Pupil participation and pupil perspectives: Carving a new order of experience. *Cambridge Journal of Education, 30*, 75−89.

UCAS. (2012). *Unistats.* Retrieved from http://unistats.direct.gov.uk/. Accessed on 22 November 2012.

Chapter 10

Students Engaged in Academic Subject Review

Derfel Owen

Abstract

A significant feature of quality assurance systems is the cyclical periodic review of academic programmes. The process for doing this varies enormously in different countries and across universities; it will depend on culture, legislative and regulatory issues. This chapter focuses on student engagement in period subject review processes in the United Kingdom, drawing comparisons with systems throughout Europe.

Naturally, readers of a book on student engagement will be inclined to presume that students can and should be engaged in all processes; however, there can often by cultural, procedural and philosophical objections and obstacles to their involvement. Drawing on evidence from interviews with students and senior academic and administrators from nine UK higher education institutions, this chapter explores some of those challenges and ways in which they can be overcome.

10.1. Introduction

A recent report to the European Commission stated:

> Every institution should develop and implement a strategy for the support and on-going improvement of the quality of teaching and learning, devoting the necessary level of human and financial resources to the task, and integrating this priority in its overall mission ... (European Union, 2013a, 2013b, p. 64)

The Student Engagement Handbook: Practice in Higher Education
Copyright © 2013 by Emerald Group Publishing Limited
All rights of reproduction in any form reserved
ISBN: 978-1-78190-423-7

This echoes a requirement in the European Standards and Guidelines for Quality Assurance in the European Higher Education Area:

> ... institutions should develop and implement a strategy for the continuous enhancement of quality. The strategy, policy and procedures should have a formal status and be publicly available. They should also include a role for students and other stakeholders. (ENQA, 2009, p. 7)

Approaches of this kind are clearly important, and in the United Kingdom we have had quality assurance procedures to review teaching for several decades. In particular, the purpose of these processes has been to review the standards of programmes and the quality of support for student learning. These processes have been built on the core academic principle of peer review, where eminent and experienced academics with current or very recent experience of the activity or work being reviewed (in this case, providing or assessing higher education) form teams (QAA[1], 2013) who will seek evidence to make judgements about the standards and quality of a university's education. However, what has been historically lacking from these review team are students. The student voice had been taken into account through various forms of feedback, but students themselves had not been included in the 'peer community' as team members.

In 2007 the UK Quality Assurance Agency for Higher Education (QAA) began to explore options for including student members on its institutional audit and review teams (QAA, 2008a). This proposal was controversial (Attwood, 2009) and involved some extensive consultation and negotiation with universities before it was possible to introduce these new ways of working. Many universities objected to the very idea of students having anything to contribute to judgements about standards and quality:

> Auditors are or should be senior academics or administrators who can engage on equal terms with senior management in institutions. However well prepared and trained, students can never be peers in that sense. I believe that there is a real risk that audit will be devalued. (Brown, 2008)

Others raised practical objections about the time commitment required, the amount of work expected of panel member or the amount of trust that could be placed in students to handle confidential information. Of equal interest to critics of the proposals was the 'cost-benefit' analysis of these proposals, as though student views and experiences could be weighed and balanced off on a spreadsheet. It seemed to me at the time that these were unfounded concerns; fears that a system that had become familiar would be challenged by the introduction of student views

---

[1]The Quality Assurance Agency for Higher Education, a UK-based agency responsible for safeguarding standards and improving the quality of UK higher education.

were clouding an opportunity to discuss the value and expertise students had to offer and how to best get the most out of them. Given that one of the reasons this proposal was seriously considered at the time was because a number of English universities had started to engage students in their own internal review processes (QAA, 2008b), I set out to gather evidence from those universities who had taken the leap and included students as members of their own internal review teams to see if their experiences could allay fears of those who had raised objections.

The evidence presented in this chapter is based on qualitative information that I gathered from a series of interviews with students and senior academic and administrative staff at nine universities. The purpose was to gain an understanding of the challenges and benefits of involving students as members of academic subject review teams. The research outlined here specifically sought to establish the following:

- Are students up to the job of being academic subject reviewers?
- How do you recruit and select the most appropriate students to be reviewers?
- What training and support is required to make sure students are effective reviewers?
- Are students effective in the role and do they add value?

These issues were explored because they reflect the concerns raised by universities with QAA at the time (QAA, 2008a).

At some universities, students, academics and administrative staff were involved together in the interviews; at others only senior administrative staff were present. This format enabled a consideration of the challenges faced by all stakeholders in understanding and supporting the role of students. Selections of quotes from the interviews are included in this chapter to illustrate the range of perspectives and experiences. The excerpts are selected to represent the range of perspectives. While the sample size is small, the depth of the evidence is intended to enrich understanding of the context and value of student engagement.

This chapter analyses that data to explore some of the challenges and solutions that had been identified by the nine participating universities: the University of Exeter, The University of Manchester, Sheffield Hallam University, Queen Mary University of London, Royal Holloway University of London, London School of Economics, University of Liverpool, De Montfort University, and Aston University. This was a highly diverse group of institutions, with different experiences of engaging students and a broad range of subject specialisms. Students had been involved in review processes at these universities for varying lengths of time. One institution had included student members within its internal review teams for over 15 years. Another was trialling student membership at the time of interview. Other universities' experience varied within this range.

10.2. Are Students Up to It?

It seemed strange that universities would be raising objections to student membership of audit and review teams based on a view that they might be capable of doing the job. This at the same time as they were branding UK university graduates as the most employable in history:

> Skills and attributes that will help graduates get jobs and manage their careers over a lifetime are being developed as part of the broader higher education experience. This is now more important than ever, as universities — and their graduates — will be key to the UK's growth path out of recession. (Trainor, 2009)

However these concerns were raised, and it could be argued that skills for employment in industry are not necessarily the same skills required to be an effective peer auditor or reviewer. So I sought to gather information about how students had performed in these roles.

10.2.1. Role of Students as Team Members

The universities interviewed had clear policies and procedures for internal review that outline the role of review teams. In every instance, students were included as full and equal members of review teams with the same remit as other members. However, in some cases there were some restrictions. One institution had a line in its policies stating that students are 'not to have a detailed input on the curriculum'. Another institution offers non-prescriptive guidance on issues students might deal with: 'The representative from the Guild of Students is primarily concerned with the student experience and should ideally be given the opportunity to explore this, as appropriate, during the visit.' This does not appear to cause tension between team members, as the student member's knowledge and experience is particularly relevant in this area. The remaining seven universities do not make any special provisions for student members of review teams.

Typical comments:

> 'If students are going to play a full and equal part in the process we don't think it's necessary or useful to single them out for specific instructions/remits.' (Deputy Vice-Chancellor)

> 'We've found that student reviewers are fully and equally capable of engaging with the review process, so we haven't seen the need to cut them off from certain aspects of review'. (Senior Administrator 1)

So these universities took a principled view that including students on an equal basis was important to ensure they got the most out of the process. This was a fundamentally important starting point: in principle at least, students were welcomed to review teams and held, in the main, equal status to other reviewers, their ability to contribute the potential to offer expertise and insight to the process was accepted.

10.2.1.1. Leadership and chairing

There did, however, appear to be less consistency of practice when it came to leadership of review teams. All universities reported that a senior member of academic staff was appointed to lead and chair the entire review. As chair they would lead the process and act as principal liaison for the school/department under review, the review team and the institutional quality assurance office. Some universities' procedures allow individual review team members to chair different sessions of the review day. At three universities students would regularly take responsibility for chairing/facilitating meetings with students. One institution's guidance document for periodic review explicitly stipulated that the student team member will chair meetings with students. All three universities reported that this works well and that having the student member chair these meetings appears to put the students at ease from the outset.

Typical comment:

> I'm not sure it matters who chairs the meetings. They tend to be quite relaxed and all the reviewers will ask questions and follow line of enquiry. Perhaps we should get students to lead the introductions, but we don't do this for any of the other reviewers. (Senior Administrator 1)

Feedback from reviewers and students confirmed that a student presence on review teams helped put students who met the teams at ease. This ensured that students meeting the teams contributed fully to the process and helped break down communication barriers that might exist between academic reviewers and students.

Typical comments:

> Sometimes situations arise where reviewers and students do not connect very well, this can be because of differences in language or perspective. There are some obvious instances where having students on review teams has helped to ease these difficulties. (Academic Dean, former chair of review team)

> When I was a member of review team I chaired the meeting with students and I think it helped a lot, the students seemed to be reassured when I said I was the education officer at the students' union. A bit like having 'one of them' on the team. (Student 1)

10.2.2. Students' Understanding of Quality Assurance Information and Documents

The type and volume of information prepared for review teams varies slightly across universities, as does the level of detail contained in documents.

In all review procedures that were discussed during these interviews, the university procedures require a self-evaluation document (SED) from the school or department under review and for further documentation and evidence to be available and accessible to the review team as required. Two universities reported that they had particular arrangements for gathering the views of students ahead of the review. This is so they can be read and digested alongside the SED and other documents to inform the review team's understanding of the student learning experience in that department. At one of the two universities these views are gathered by a member of staff from the quality assurance office, who meets a group of students at a focus group to gather views on their learning experience and comments on the SED. Their feedback is analysed and reported back to the review team. The other institution asks the student member of the review team to carry out a similar exercise, meeting with student representatives at the particular school and gathering their views to present to the full review team.

Feedback from student members of review teams suggests they do not have difficulty understanding the documentation they receive. Their contributions throughout the review process also suggest they have little difficulty digesting information and forming lines of enquiry and judgements based on them. In some instances it was reported that students have often made a greater effort to digest and understand the documentation they receive, probably to compensate for the fact that they have less experience than other reviewers.

Typical comment:

> Once they get into the swing of it, student reviewers have no difficulty analysing the information, coming up with questions or using the evidence in the paperwork to back up judgements. (Senior Administrator 2)

Three universities reported that students occasionally, particularly if participating in their first review, are daunted by the documentation, citing its volume and the language and terminology used as particular problems. Where this happens, the quality assurance officer responsible for the review or other members of the review team usually provides support, as they would with all new reviewers.

Typical comments:

> We're always worried about first time students because they're sometimes daunted by the amount of information they are bombarded with for a review, especially when the language is also quite dense! This often happens with new reviewers so we make sure we book in some time to take them through it (the documentation and review process). They soon come round. (Senior Administrator 1)

> We always make sure we brief new reviewers, this is no different for students, but it is a bit repetitive because we're always working with a different student. (Senior Administrator 3)

> I actually found the information quite interesting. I wasn't sure what to do next, but reading it and getting an idea of how everything worked was really informative. (Student 2)

The majority of universities reported that students regularly make constructive and useful comments on documentation in advance of the review. Students suggest and pursue their own lines of enquiry, requesting additional documentation and information where necessary.

10.2.3.   *Time Commitment*

The time commitment expected from reviewers — taking a number of factors into account such as reading documentation, preparatory meetings, training, the review meetings and reporting — ranged between two and two and a half days. Whether working with students' union (SU) officers[2] or student representatives, all universities reported that students could broadly be relied upon to fulfil their entire commitment as reviewers and were willing to give up the time necessary to fulfil their duties. The majority of universities reported that students are very conscientious about their duties and that they have not experienced any serious difficulties with attendance. One institution, which works with student representatives rather than SU officers, reported some occasional difficulties with students having to drop out at short (3—4 weeks) notice because the assessment timetable had changed.

Typical comments:

> This is where real life kicks in, things happen and change. While we always stress the value and importance of them taking part, students can always decide that something else is more important. We can't force them to take part like we can staff who have contracts. So there are occasions when they drop out. (Deputy Vice-Chancellor)

> Students do drop out, most usually for very good reason that are out of their control, but we cope with that. We find someone else or get them to send us comments, questions and feedback that they would still like to be included. (Senior Administrator 4)

All universities reported that great care is taken to ensure sufficient notice is provided to review team members, and to ensure that reviews do not take place at times that are inconvenient for reviewers (academic and student) and for the schools/departments under review. Two universities working with SU officers reported occasions when SU officers had been elected and did not want to participate in review activities. This created some initial difficulties, but the universities' quality assurance officers worked with the SUs to find other solutions or officers to take their place.

---

[2]Each publicly funded university in the United Kingdom is required by law to have a students' union, the vast majority are led by full time, paid elected officers who serve for 12 months on sabbatical from their studies.

10.2.4. Student Role in Making Judgements, Commendations and Recommendations

This was a major concern raised by universities during QAA's consultation (QAA, 2008a), because there was concern that students may not take the consequences of judgements seriously, or that some judgements might be appropriate for them to make (e.g. relating to resources or student support) but other may be inappropriate (e.g. relating to academic standards). At each of the universities interviewed, student members of review teams play a full and equal role in making judgements, commendations and recommendations.

10.2.5. Student Role in Reporting

Arrangements in seven of the nine universities mean that the review secretariat (provided by the institution's quality assurance office) take notes throughout the review and prepares the report based on the lines of enquiry and judgements made by the review team. This report is circulated to all members of the review team for comments and to suggest amendments. Reviewers do not often make suggestions for changes, though one institution reported that student members of review teams were particularly keen at this stage and would often make several constructive contributions to drafts.

> We're quite used to review teams disappearing at the end of the review day and not hearing anything more from them, from their perspective, the job is done. Strangely though, some of the students I've worked with come to life at the end and comment extensively on my drafts. (Senior Administrator 4)

Arrangements for periodic review at another institution allow the school or department to write their own reflective report on the review, drawing on the judgements and comments of the review team to inform a reflective analysis and action plan for their school or department. Once this report is prepared, a draft is sent to the review team for comment. As with other universities, reviewers rarely make substantive suggestions for improvement. One institution asked individual reviewers to take responsibility for drafting sections of the report, based on their lines of enquiry and judgements. These sections are gathered by the secretariat and compiled into a full report, which is then circulated to the entire team for comment. Student members write the sections relating to the student learning experience and could be relied upon to produce clear, concise and timely reports.

10.3. Recruitment and Selection

A more practical objection was that recruiting and selecting the 'right kind' of student would be difficult and cumbersome. But this did not feel right to me, any process of review or audit is going to require a system for recruiting and selecting people with the right skills and experiences to do the work. With students, once their role was clarified, it seemed obvious that a university could recruit candidates to fulfil that role.

During these interviews, all universities reported that ensuring student members of their review teams are capable, willing and able to participate in institutional processes for quality assurance and enhancement is critical when considering which students to involve. The majority of universities (six) use officers from their SUs. This would normally be the officer with responsibility for academic matters, although two universities ask their SUs to occasionally use other officers.

A number of reasons were given for and benefits of using SU officers as members of review teams, mainly focused on the fact that SU officers will have a greater understanding and insight into the institution's quality assurance policies and procedures:

- They also serve on senior institution decision-making bodies, such as senate, academic board or learning and teaching committees. As a result they develop an insight into the nature and strategic priorities of the institution, as well as into the diversity of teaching and learning and devolved management structures.
- Student officers receive training for their SU roles from union staff and their predecessors. This training covers their involvement in periodic review and ensures they learn about the quality assurance process from an officer who has participated in a review. Two universities reported that incoming officers will occasionally shadow a review with their predecessor to get a feel for the process.
- The quality office has regular contact with SU officers and forms a relationship with them that lasts throughout their year in office. This helps to maintain reliable dialogue throughout reviews.
- SU officers are in regular touch with students from across the institution at various stages of their studies; they have a broader and deeper understanding of the student perspective when contributing to meetings and team decisions.
- According to one university, its SU officers participate in various networks and regularly share information and good practice from their own institution with other officers, and vice versa. Student officers bring this knowledge and insight to review teams, which adds depth to their contribution.

Typical comments:

> We have an excellent relationship with our students union and we always include their representatives in everything we do, so it seems quite logical that they should sit on internal review teams. (Pro Vice-Chancellor)

> It's part of the sabbatical officer's job role to sit on review teams so we don't have to worry about recruiting and persuading them to take part. They get very good support and training from their predecessors,

which means they are well prepared for taking part when the time comes. (Academic Dean, former chair of review team)

A typical challenge raised by three universities was that very occasionally officers are elected to SU posts and find that participation in institutional quality assurance processes is not a priority for them. The university then finds it difficult to engage these officers meaningfully in the periodic review process. This was not a situation that occurred regularly, but each of the three universities had experienced this difficulty at some stage and had worked with the SU to overcome the problem. In some instances the SU would co-opt another officer to take their place, and one institution was thinking of changing its periodic review policies in order to include non-sabbatical students on panels.

Typical comment:

> On one occasion, the education and welfare officer was singularly focused on welfare issues and did not appear to want to engage with academic matters. This hadn't happened before and hasn't happened since but it did mean we missed out on the student contribution for a while. (Senior Administrator 6)

Three universities reported that they do not use SU officers as members of internal review teams. Instead they work with the SU to recruit and train students interested in serving on review teams to act as representatives at departmental and faculty level.

These universities explained that they are not opposed to the principle of using sabbatical officers on internal review teams, and occasionally do if a review takes place at a time that is inconvenient for students (e.g. out of term time or during peak assessment periods). In these instances both the SU and institution felt that there is greater value in using students who are not SU officers, as they bring a uniquely student-focused perspective, which is not compromised by involvement in decisions about institutional-level policies and strategies. In these instances, the student members always have experience of serving as school, department or faculty representatives. This gives them some grounding and understanding of decision-making structures and matters relating to quality assurance and enhancement.

The process of recruiting students to participate is usually fairly informal. The SUs communicate with their network of representatives to inform them of upcoming reviews, and ask for expressions of interest. A novel approach was taken by one institution where they advertised and offered an opportunity for student representatives to attend a training session focused being an effective auditor/reviewer. Based on their performance at that training session, the university and SU would collect a bank of student reviewers who would be suitable to join review teams. Another SU recruits separately for each review, with the students' union requesting expressions of interest, then meeting each of the applicants separately for an interview and then selecting appropriate representatives. On average the SUs reported that between 8 and 15 students per review express an interest in participating.

Typical comment:

> 'We have no objection to sabbatical officers being members of review teams but since we started including students on teams the SU has always nominated student representatives from faculty committees. This has always worked very well and the calibre of students we have on teams is very high.' (Senior Administrator 3)

10.4. Training and Support

If any participant in quality assurance activity is going to be successful, it is important that suitable training and support is put in place. It was proposed that students would require entirely new and different forms of training and support in order to be successful in their roles. This seemed at odds with experiences of student engagement in other parts of the sector, and so it was important to understand how universities had trained and supported students to be successful reviewers, whether new approaches were needed or whether existing systems could be built upon and adapted.

None of the universities reported that they have formal training structures for reviewers. All indicated that the quality office (or equivalent) provides direct support for reviewers to ensure they understand the institutional context and the documentation they are provided with for the review. The universities that use student representatives rather than SU officers reported that the SU provides support and training to complement or replace support provided by the quality assurance office.

In two instances the SU provided formal structured training, as opposed to reactive support and guidance. These training programmes usually consisted of group exercises looking at mock documents and working through typical scenarios and lines of enquiry. Feedback from student reviewers indicated that this form of informal, activity-based training was very useful.

Typical comment:

> I attended a training session with the Union, there were eight of us involved in some mock exercises and role play. Three of us got to go forward to be on reviews, the training had been really helpful because it helped us to understand what was going to happen .... The others (not chosen) will have had a good opportunity to develop skills I suppose. (Student 3)

The support needs of students throughout the review processes tended to be similar across the universities, and were very similar to the support needs of new academic reviewers. Support required by students usually included:

- explaining the process and procedures involved in internal review;
- institutional context for quality assurance and enhancement;

- assistance to understand the language and terminology used in documentation;
- assistance to identify relevant sections of departmental or school policies to explore and test evidence presented in SEDs.

Typical comments:

> I hadn't done anything like this before, I didn't know what to expect in terms of the meeting that I would be attending or all the stuff we would have to read, so some advance notice would have been helpful. (Student 2)

> I've been doing these for years, I still don't think I've perfected the art. I didn't get any training at first and it was tough going, but I just had to throw myself into it ... student are game, they'll get the swing it in the same way. (Academic Dean, former chair of review team)

While it was surprising that few universities had training structures in place, it was reassuring to know that students coped well with the same level of training and support as other (more experienced) academic reviewers.

10.5. Value and Effectiveness

A more challenging and legitimate concern raised about student engagement in audit and review activity, in my view, was whether it would add value to existing arrangement. It seemed glib to argue that their presence would make the process more transparent, or just to make sure that students had input to every decision. It was therefore important to demonstrate that students could and did have a positive impact on and made a difference to the process.

10.5.1. Effectiveness

Across the board it was felt that student members of internal review teams play a full, professional and effective role when carrying out their duties. They interact well with other reviewers, engaging in discussion on various issues and do not always limit themselves to contributing on issues related to the student learning experience.

Students often propose new and additional lines of enquiry based on documentation and meetings with staff and students.

Typical comments:

> I want to say that I haven't been able to tell the difference, but that might sound like they haven't had an impact. What I meant is that students have joined teams and contributed as much as other panel

> members. It would be very strange not to have them there now. (Pro Vice-Chancellor)

> I think students have made a difference. They ask the obvious question that nobody has thought of, or just cut through some of the crap and remind us that we're here to educate students. (Senior Administrator 2)

Student members can usually be relied on to ask pertinent and penetrating questions that help the review team's understanding of particular issues. Where students experience difficulty in pursuing a line of enquiry or getting to the crux of a matter when meeting with staff, other team members feel quite comfortable stepping in to assist. Conversely student team members will assist other reviewers when they are meeting with students.

> Being part of a team is just that in my view. There are 6 of us on that panel and we all have something to add. We're all clever people, but some things make sense and some things don't, so we just talk through them. There have been times when a student has been a bit confused by some obscure acronym or process that is mentioned ... I've just explained what it is and we get on with it ... other times, I've listened to student feedback and not been 'down with the lingo' so having a student there as an urban dictionary has helped! (Academic Dean, former chair of review team)

10.5.2. *Added Value*

Every institution reported that including students as members of internal review teams was an important feature of their approach to student participation. A number of universities reported that student participation at this level reinforced their commitment to listening to students and dealing with them as partners in the development of the institution. The universities' views were that students are active participants in their own education and are part of the academic community, able to impact on the design and delivery of their own programmes. It was also widely commented that student membership of review teams added to the students' perception and understanding of their role in the wider college community.

Some universities also commented that including students on review teams raises the profile of internal reviews among students and, therefore, raises the level of interest in the process.

Typical comments:

> The more we involve students, the more they will feel part of what we do. (Deputy Vice-Chancellor)

> The centrality of students as partners in the strategic development and improvement of the university is very important to us, and so

their participation on internal review panels is essential. (Senior Administrator 7)

Students are part of the wider academic community and having them on review teams reinforces that message. We want them to contribute to development of the whole university, not just their own course, and this is one way for them to do that. (Academic Dean, former chair of review team)

A number of universities reported that internal review processes are an important element of effective quality assurance and enhancement, and should have a major impact on improving the learning experience of students across universities. Including students on review panels adds to the perception of legitimacy regarding this element of quality assurance and enhancement. This was a key consideration when the universities included student members on review teams.

Typical comments:

It's important that students feel confident in the processes we put in place to listen to them and to improve their experience. A student presence on university bodies, in this instance periodic review teams, does reassure students that their views and priorities will be taken seriously. (Senior Administrator 5)

I actually felt that I was able to make a difference ... not just because the process is important, but because I was able to say stuff that is important to student ... (Student 3)

If I hadn't been there, I'm sure it would have gone fine, but I know afterwards some of the students we met were saying that they were pleased someone was on the panel to make sure their feedback was listened to ... some of them even asked if they could take part themselves next time. (Students' Union Officer)

Issues of language and the appropriateness of quality assurance and enhancement terminology when communicating with students were raised by some universities. They observed that students, who may themselves have had difficulty coming to terms with the language and terminology at first, are particularly effective at framing or rewording questions during meetings with students, who then understand what the review team is asking them.

Typical comment:

It is sometimes quite apparent that the students review teams meet are very nervous and struggle to understand the questions being asked of them. Student reviewers are very effective at diffusing these situations by either suggesting alternative wordings for questions in advance of the meeting, or by rewording questions during meetings. (Academic Dean, former chair of review team)

It was also noted that a number of student reviewers commented on the language of final review reports, suggesting changes and improvements to make them more accessible to interested students.

Many universities noted that student members of review teams possess valuable expertise on and insights into the student experience. As current or recent students they are able to empathise with the various issues that impact on their learning experience. Universities also reported that student reviewers add an important perspective regarding quality assurance and standards, based on their learning experience.

Typical comment:

> You could put it like this, students bring additional expertise on the learning experience and an additional perspective on matters related to quality and standards. (Pro Vice-Chancellor)

Students who take part in reviews develop a much clearer understanding of institutional processes and priorities and their impact on individual schools and departments. This gives them a fuller picture of the diverse nature of their institution and, therefore, greatly improves their ability to contribute to wider discussions about institutional policies and practices.

10.6.   Lessons and Conclusions

The evidence contained in this chapter shows that students have a valuable contribution to make to academic subject reviews when they receive clear guidance and support throughout the process. Many of the chapters in this book talk about new and innovative initiatives that were student led, student focused or built around a desire to engage students. This chapter talks about a process of change where it was proposed that students are added or more deeply involved in an existing process. It was difficult for many universities to be comfortable with this, because quality assurance processes take time to establish and to gather buy-in, it is therefore unsettling when proposals are made to change them. However, the experience retold in this chapter explains that many fears about engaging student can be allayed if challenged directly with evidence and other successful experiences. It is now quite common for UK universities to include students as members of their internal quality review teams and interest in replicating this is growing in Europe.

The experience of universities shows that current students are capable and willing to participate in academic subject review activities. Those students who participate have experience of engaging in discussions about quality, standards, and learning and teaching at school and/or institutional level. Universities that used student representatives as members of review teams found that informal methods of communicating with students — such as advertising via email and using networking websites — proved to be the most successful recruitment methods. Where school and faculty student representatives were selected to sit on review teams, a selection stage was built into the recruitment process to ensure suitability; this proved successful as it reinforces the status of the role and also gives student clarity about what is expected of them.

Formal training for internal reviewers was not widespread, and where it was provided to students it was on a small scale. However, informal support for students grappling with the volume, language and terminology of review was a regular feature of universities' processes.

All the universities included in this analysis treated students as full and equal members of their review teams, with the same responsibility for the review and its judgements as other team members. In two instances some additional guidance was provided to students to indicate areas where they may or may not wish to pursue lines of enquiry. These instances were intended as guidance rather than restrictions and did not cause confusion for review teams. Universities reported that having student members of review teams helped to relax students attending meetings and break down communication barriers. This was particularly true when student members of review teams chaired meetings with students and led the questioning.

Universities reported that student members of review teams make every effort to digest information presented to them in advance of a review, conscientiously contribute to discussions and suggest lines of enquiry. It is clear that a number of students are daunted by the volume of documentation and the language and terminology contained within them. This reinforces the point that ongoing support and advice is a crucial ingredient in making student engagement a success.

In all internal review processes covered in this chapter, students play a full and equal part in forming judgements, commendations and recommendations. There is little evidence of reporting to draw upon. At one institution where students do produce their own sections of reports, no challenges or difficulties had been experienced. Where reports are written by the secretariat to review teams, students regularly make constructive contributions and comments and suggest amendments.

References

Attwood, R. (2009). *20% say 'no' to student auditors*. London: Times Higher Education. Retrieved from http://www.timeshighereducation.co.uk/news/20-say-no-to-student-auditors/408853.article

Brown, R. (2008). Quoted in *QAA to enlist students to audit quality*. London: Times Higher Education. Retrieved from http://www.timeshighereducation.co.uk/400130.article

ENQA. (2009). *Standards and guidelines for quality assurance in the European higher education area*. Retrieved from http://www.enqa.eu/files/ESG_3edition%20(2).pdf

European Union. (2013a). *Improving the quality of teaching and learning in Europe's higher education institutions*. Retrieved from http://ec.europa.eu/education/higher-education/doc/modernisation_en.pdf

European Union. (2013b). *Report of the High Level Group on the modernisation of higher education.* Retrieved from http://ec.europa.eu/education/higher-education/doc/modernisation_en.pdf

QAA. (2008a). *Student membership of institutional audit teams and QAA strategy on student engagement — intermediate correspondence.* Retrieved from http://www.webarchive.org.uk/wayback/archive/20110627101921/http://www.qaa.ac.uk/news/circularLetters/CL0108.asp

QAA. (2008b). *Student membership of audit and review teams.* Retrieved from http://www.webarchive.org.uk/wayback/archive/20110627101832/http://www.qaa.ac.uk/events/smart08/default.asp

QAA. (2013). *Definition of peer review.* Retrieved from http://www.qaa.ac.uk/AboutUs/glossary/Pages/glossary-p.aspx#p20

Trainor, R. (2009). Quoted in *'Employability' seen as vital by business — new CBI/UUK report.* Retrieved from http://www.universitiesuk.ac.uk/highereducation/Pages/CBI_UUK Report.aspx

Chapter 11

Meaningful Engagement with Disabled Students

Aaron Porter

Abstract

This chapter examines student engagement through the specific lens of engagement with disabled students, building on, examining and analysing the findings from the Higher Education Academy's project on meaningful student engagement. The project included 10 participating institutions across England and Wales, drawn from different parts of the sector, which advanced specific projects to support and develop their engagement with disabled students. While there are specific challenges and opportunities to engaging with disabled students, the principles which underpin successful engagement translate to other hard to reach groups of students, and indeed the student population more widely. The chapter identifies some common forms of effective practice and measures of impact across the 10 institutions, and highlights a tension between the definition that institutions developed for 'student engagement' and how activity was implemented. The key disconnect centred around the definition referring to 'active partnership' and the concept of 'power being in the hands of the students', whereas activity tended to take a more traditional form such as ensuring students were members of committees and that relevant representatives were consulted. This is an important component of meaningful student engagement, but is not quite the active partnership that was referred to in the definitions set out by institutions.

11.1. Background

Student engagement has received a great deal of attention in recent years. This has seen institutional focus on the student voice increase, particularly in the development of more sophisticated systems of student representation. In addition, the establishing of the National Student Survey (NSS) (launched in 2005) for final-year undergraduates has helped both institutions and students' unions to identify crucial

The Student Engagement Handbook: Practice in Higher Education
Copyright © 2013 by Emerald Group Publishing Limited
All rights of reproduction in any form reserved
ISBN: 978-1-78190-423-7

issues for students in relation to learning and teaching, as well as establishing a comprehensive benchmark for departments and institutions to measure and track their performance and improvement. The Higher Education Academy (HEA) has also run comprehensive experience surveys for postgraduate students through the Postgraduate Taught Experience Survey (PTES) and the Postgraduate Research Experience Survey (PRES).

Successive governments have sought to encourage institutions to focus on the ways in which they engage students. Student engagement was explicit in the Higher Education White Paper, *Students at the Heart of the System* (BIS, 2011), published by the Coalition Government in June 2011. The HEA have also undertaken a range of activities in relation to student engagement under the Students as Partners banner, including joint events with the National Union of Students (NUS), 10 research reports undertaken by institutions examining student engagement in a UK context (HEA, 2011) and support to the Student Learning & Teaching Network (SLTN). The HEA has also worked jointly with the NUS to support student-led teaching awards, which have stimulated student engagement, as well as a focus on and promotion of high-quality teaching and learning.

More recently, as part of the agenda of the Coalition Government to put power in the hands of students, there has also been a drive to make more information available to prospective students, notably through the introduction of Key Information Sets (KIS), which provide a standardised set of information including contact time, assessment methods, student satisfaction and graduate employability. Institutions are also revamping Student Charters, in Wales this is mandatory, which is being seen as an opportunity to set out the tripartite relationship of engagement between the institution, student body and students' union.

11.2. A View of Disability

Within the initiatives outlined above, it is not clear to what extent explicit attention has been given to the involvement of disabled students, or whether they are actively engaging in new ways of working as an outcome on the focus on student engagement. Nor is it clear whether there have been any specific impacts for disabled students. However, through the past decade, studies of disability in education have grown 'into a recognised field of educational study as scholars and practitioners have come to value social interpretations of disability (Gabel, 2005). Social interpretations are of considerable importance in changing perceptions of disability in a cultural background that still generally equates disability with individual tragedy, and a professional environment that reflexively construes disability within a medical-type framework of individual deficit and dysfunction (Danforth and Gabel, 2006). Finkelstein (2001) explains: '... at the personal level we may talk about acquiring an impairment being a personal tragedy, but at the social level we should talk about how the restrictions that we face are, and should be interpreted as, a crime. It is society that disables us and disabled people are an oppressed social group' (p. 2). This view clearly has implications for how disabled students are perceived in higher education, the way in which they are valued, and how they engage alongside, and with the broader university population. The Quality Assurance Agency (QAA) reiterate this 'social' view:

> In determining whether or not a person is disabled, reference is often made to the social model of disability which suggests that people with impairments are disabled by social, attitudinal or environmental barriers. The advisory group … considered this to be a key principle … and wished to emphasise that institutions should attempt to work towards an inclusive environment in which quality of provision and the best possible experience for all learners is pursued. (QAA, 2011, p.18)

At the current time, much of the study relating to education and disability resides in the context of schooling rather than higher education, and much focuses (even if taking a more social vantage point) on aspects such as failure in the education system and dropout (see, e.g., Reschly & Christenson, 2006). However, students who have gained a place in higher education have already shown themselves to be successful as learners, and there is far less academic research in this arena. There is much good practice reported in the provision of support for disabled learners, in the use of teaching and assessment methods that actively include disabled students, and in the design of the physical environment in ways that support access (QAA, 2009), and one positive aspect that has been looked at in more detail is the potential role of e-learning in supporting student engagement and associated achievement (Seale, 2006). However, there is also considerable evidence that, although disabled students have been entering higher education in greater numbers in recent years, they remain under-represented and their experiences are variable (DIUS, 2009). In addition, research into the experience of disabled students has shown that barriers to learning opportunities do remain, whether in physical access to facilities or in inclusivity of teaching methods (Jacklin, Robinson, O'Meara & Harris, 2005).

Importantly, research on disability is changing in nature, from being 'on' disabled students to 'engaging with' students in the research process and capturing their voices and opinions, as demonstrated in a recent study at a single UK university (Goode, 2007). Goode emphasises that recent UK legislation, operational from December 2006, places a duty on all public authorities, including higher education institutions, to actively promote equality of opportunity for people with disabilities. She recognises that the university under study had a number of initiatives in place to develop good practice in this area, but is clear that questions needed to be asked about 'How do students themselves experience that provision?' Research about people with disabilities has sometimes alienated them by failing to reflect their own perspectives (Goode, 2007, p. 35).

Looking specifically at the engagement of disabled students, the HEA has worked jointly with the Equality Challenge Unit (ECU) to produce a report which focused on developing more effective mechanisms to engage disabled students (May & Felsinger, 2010). Central to this was the development of Disability Equality Schemes (DES) and the Disability Equality Duty (DED), as well as increasing involvement in wider discussions about developing institutional culture with regard to improving disability equality. May and Felsinger state:

> Engaging with disabled students is of particular importance to institutions in shaping their facilities, services, and curriculum and assessment design, not only in meeting the entitlements of disabled students, but those of all students. Through meaningful and sustainable involvement, Higher Education Institutions can achieve a truly inclusive learning environment to the benefit of all students and the institution itself. (Foreword, May & Felsinger, 2010)

They immediately warn, however, that 'Disabled student involvement is not always a straightforward exercise'.

The focus of this chapter is on a Higher Education Academy (HEA) project examining 'Meaningful Student Engagement', which encapsulated in its very title some of the issues outlined above. Through this project, 10 institutions were supported to take forward inclusive activity to focus on the engagement of disabled students. Outlined below is an overview of some of the activity undertaken by these institutions, and detail of emerging themes and trends, aspects of good practice, and recommendations applicable to the sector more widely.

11.3. The Meaningful Student Engagement Project

The Meaningful Student Engagement (MSE) project was funded by the Higher Education Funding Council for England (HEFCE) and the Higher Education Funding Council for Wales (HEFCW) and overseen by the HEA. The 10 participating institutions (listed below) took forward projects and programmes within their institution which focused on disability.

A deliberate attempt was made to ensure that a range of institutions participated, including small and specialist institutions, further education colleges with higher education students, as well as large universities spread over a number of sites: Birmingham City University, Bishop Grosseteste University College Lincoln, University of Central Lancashire, Coventry University, University for the Creative Arts, University of Glamorgan, Newcastle College, Newman University College, Northumbria University, and Wakefield College.

The intended outcomes of the programme for the participating institutions were:

- institutions being better informed as to the nature and implementation of effective strategies to engage disabled students;
- development of institutional strategy and practices;

- embedding of opportunities for dialogue and decision making within the learning process across different discipline areas;
- evaluation of the impact of change.

Each of the participating institutions submitted a case study report of no more than 2000 words, focusing on the four intended outcomes listed above. These reports provided the basis for an analysis of how the approaches of each institution compared. Institutions that deployed similar strategies were then grouped together, with a view to highlighting difference but also ensuring that the distinctiveness of each institution was represented.

Although the focus of the project was to support student engagement of disabled students, many institutions took this as a chance to focus on and improve their student engagement with the wider student body, as a number of principles were the same for all students. The HEA strongly encouraged institutions to take an inclusive approach by mainstreaming their engagement and provision with disabled students rather than generating alternative provision, with 'inclusion' being defined on their website as follow:

> The enabling of full and equitable participation in and progression through higher education for all prospective and existing students. Although it is a relatively new concept in the sector, many institutions are seeking to move towards more inclusive policies and practices and away from remedial interventions. We work closely in partnership with institutions and sector bodies to promote cultural change and evidence-informed practice that will support the enhancement of the learning experience of all students. (HEA, 2013b)

This again is important in relation to a social rather than medical, or remedial, view of how disability should be understood in higher education.

11.4. Defining 'Meaningful Student Engagement'

The analysis highlighted many similarities, as well as some differences in emphasis. When it came to defining 'meaningful student engagement', institutions used very similar language. The participating institutions embraced the importance of students and staff working together, the importance of students engaging with all aspects of their learning and teaching experience, and (from a number of institutions) a firm belief in the importance of students as partners in their learning experience. Examples from the participating institutions are given below, with quotes being taken from the individual case study reports for each institution.

At Bishop Grosseteste University College Lincoln, this was described as 'staff and students working together as partners in all aspects of learning, teaching and assessment provision, delivery, development, monitoring and evaluation'. The

Coventry University case study refers to 'the extent to which our student population is actively empowered to connect and contribute to activities that make up the business of the university'. At the University of Glamorgan it was described as 'working in partnership with students in the development, enhancement and monitoring of their experience as learners and members of the University community through a range of inclusive opportunities. These opportunities will include students acting as change agents at subject, faculty and institutional level.'

Across the institutional case studies, there was consistent reference to 'partnership' across all elements of the learning and teaching experience. In some instances, there was a reference to engagement beyond the wider academic experience and in other there was an explicit reference to 'empowerment' and to 'change agents' and other similar models of engagement activity. At Birmingham City University, they not only referred to involvement and partnership, but stated that it should 'enable students to gain substantial personal development and employability. This aids positive student development and integration that leads to improvement in student achievement.' As well as delivering improvement towards academic achievement, personal development and employability, the Wakefield College case study also referred to 'improved retention of students, increases employability skills, develops self-confidence and adds to the value of the overall student experience'.

As already suggested, the descriptions outlined above, and the other approaches institutions took to defining 'student engagement', generally provided a definition covering engagement with the student body as a whole, rather than simply for disabled students. As encouraged by the HEA, pursuing an inclusive approach was indeed adopted by the participating institutions. This fits with the HEA's own description as to how they intend to take the agenda forward across the sector:

> ... we work with institutions, specialists and sector-wide organisations to promote disability equality and support the development of an inclusive culture within higher education institutions. We aim to enhance disabled students' learning experience in HE and encourage meaningful and ongoing opportunities for disabled students to be actively engaged across all institutional functions. A principal focus of our work is on the design and implementation of learning, teaching and assessment practices that uphold disabled students' entitlement to participate in all aspects of their study programmes and achieve success. (HEA, 2013a)

11.5. The Nature and Implementation of Effective Engagement Strategies

All case study institutions set up a steering group to help manage and oversee their activity. While a number of them were working to either shape or build a broader institution-wide strategy, others had more discrete projects, pursued in order to develop wider activity-building, focused on their definition of 'meaningful student engagement'.

Institutions typically mapped out their current student engagement activity, and used this as a baseline for further improvement. Core engagement activity included staff–student liaison committees, staff employed in student support, and learning and teaching/student experience committees. When examining how best to take forward engagement with disabled students specifically, a number of institutions felt that a forum for disabled students was necessary in order to provide an explicit focus. The approach institutions took varied from informal forums through to more formal committees to address the needs of disabled students. The University of Central Lancashire developed an equality and diversity student committee, a sub-committee of the University's student experience committee, chaired by a student, which will consider learning and teaching issues for students, with a particular emphasis on equality and diversity.

In developing systems and strategies with disabled students, a number of institutions conducted a series of listening exercises and formal consultation to listen to the views of students and to consider how best to move forward in developing engagement with disabled students. Typically, the start point for institutions was to build on structures for student engagement that already existed, usually in the form of staff–student committees, course representation systems and student forums. The engagement of disabled students was usually in addition to student representatives who were already members of decision-making or advisory committees within the institution. When considering engagement with disabled students, or other distinct groups, institutions noted the importance of casting the net slightly further than students sitting formally on committees, not least to help ensure that the voices of disabled students were not lost but also to ensure students felt they had other channels for communication.

A number of institutions set up focus groups to explore this further, including Coventry University and Newcastle College. These focus groups allowed them to drill down into more detail about the particular needs of certain groups of students, but also, crucially, from the perspective of students, to strike up an important dialogue directly with students, who welcomed the chance to air their views. At the University for the Creative Arts, rather than using their current student representation system as the baseline for activity, their intention, working jointly with the students' union, was to use this programme as an opportunity to overhaul the existing system. Steps were taken to formalise and develop transparent aims for the student representation system, as well as a more sophisticated and open process for recruitment and training of representatives. The focus group activity at Wakefield College developed 'a booklet which offers explicit information for disabled students. The students were canvassed for their opinions and suggestions for content and layout. Students were asked for their final approval and suggestions for any improvements, and the final article was produced.' They were also used for 'consultation (and more) with the architectural design team of a new build at the college. Several students with disabilities were involved in offering an insight to this team of designers on the impact of environments for people with a range of disabilities, such as visual impairment, reduced mobility, use of wheelchair and being deaf.'

In the Northumbria University case study, it was interesting to note the following:

> Disabled students did not want to be 'singled' out for the project. Following input from the students' union on the benefits of their 'Go Out and Listen' (GOAL) days, the project team went 'out and listened' to students .... The majority of students highlighted that any engagement should be face to face and not electronic. They did not value communication through flyers, posters or through social media. Some favoured email, others did not, but the overwhelming view was that they preferred we talked to them face to face. The results also indicated that students did not need an incentive to engage with the project but valued activities that they could use for their CVs over financial incentives.

However, as one of the activities at Coventry University (CU), they also developed an online resource that 'focused on identifying all the information currently available about disability support on the University website for students and applicants. A single accessible webpage was then created, linked directly from the CU home page, which provides a two-click access to all this information (see Coventry University, Information for Disabled Students, 2010). Some institutions also outlined specific activity with staff to ensure that development training was being offered to support their engagement with students, as a part of the institutional strategy. At Bishop Grosseteste University College Lincoln, 'every member of staff would attend training related to the Equality Act, or complete an online course in lieu'. At Coventry University, they held 'staff development workshops involving disabled students, to raise awareness of disability issues .... Several disabled students have addressed the University Learning Support Coordinators' meetings and answered questions from attendees about their positive and negative experiences.'

A number of institutions also examined the analysis of student surveys focus groups to help inform institutional thinking as they began to develop their strategy in relation to meaningful student engagement. At the University of Central Lancashire, recognising that

> ... the voices of disabled students can be 'lost' in institutional surveys and feedback structures ... a local survey was developed for School-based students with disabilities which aimed to explore their learning and teaching experiences and engagement activities.

At the University of Glamorgan students, including disabled students, were able to be active partners in the curriculum design process. At Birmingham City University, the student scenarios that condensed 3 hours of filming into a focused 10 minute video (see Birmingham City University, 2010) 'will be part of the University's new rough guide to curriculum design also part of the JISC's

T-SPARC project[1] and will be made available to anyone starting to design a course at the University'. They went on to state, 'we believe the footage will be of interest to staff, students and external organisations and will formally raise the status of disabled students within curriculum design'. This, along with the example from the University of Glamorgan, demonstrated that the institutional case studies were moving beyond simply having students represented on committees to ensuring active power in the hands of students and genuine contributions to curriculum design. The University of Glamorgan developed

> ... a new Curriculum Design Guide[2] which makes explicit the inclu-
> sive curriculum agenda and the importance of the student voice in
> curriculum development. The training explicitly addresses inclusive
> curriculum themes and is provided to all students involved in the
> course validation and review process. This includes disabled students
> who are actively encouraged through the Disabled Students Forum to
> be members of course design project teams and validation panels (see
> University of Glamorgan, n.d.).

A number of institutions also concentrated on assessment as an important element of their evolving strategy to engage with disabled students. Traditional forms of assessment such as examinations and written assignments, which may have gone years without reform, often proved a challenge for ensuring that disabled students were having an improved experience. At Bishop Grosseteste University College Lincoln, a strand of their work looked at developing an inclusive assessment project, as well as an emphasis on improving the liaison with disabled students on their timetabling. The emphasis at Newcastle College in relation to assessment focused on the support for students:

> HE Quality and Standards and Learning Support Services have
> worked together to develop a process to ensure consistent practice in
> the support of assessment arrangements for HE students who have
> disclosed a disability, specific learning difficulty and/or mental health
> disability or specific learning need ... which also established a fair and
> equitable approach to assessment arrangements for HE students.

Northumbria University also developed an inclusive assessment and practice project, as well as a workshop with staff in the School of Computing, Engineering and Information Sciences that 'raised awareness of inclusive learning, teaching and assessment practices with staff and initiated discussions around taking this agenda further including highlighting possible pilot areas for the project'.

---

[1]http://www.jisc.ac.uk/whatwedo/programmes/elearning/curriculumdesign/tsparc.aspx
[2]http://celt.glam.ac.uk/node/128

Because of some of the challenges with engaging with disabled students, the majority of activity within institutions has focused on setting up structures to ensure the involvement of disabled students, as well as mechanisms to listen to their views. For the majority of institutions, this still demonstrates a significant step change and improvement to existing *ad hoc* systems, where it was easy for the views of distinct groups, including disabled students, to fall through the gaps or be overlooked. However, it is noticeable that there is something of an on-going disconnect between the definitions of 'student engagement' that institutions set out, and the practice they have put in place for disabled students. While the mechanisms for listening and meeting with students have certainly been developed across all case studies, there are fewer examples of genuine partnership or empowerment and students as change agents. Given that it was institutions themselves that cited the importance of engagement becoming more than students just being members of committees or being consulted on decision making, it was striking that examples where real decision-making power was granted to disabled students were exceptions rather than the rule.

11.6.   Embedding Opportunities for Dialogue and Decision Making

It was clear that a whole host of activity from institutions has led to activity and dialogue being embedded either within discipline areas or right across an institution. A clear sign of this embedded activity was, for example, where a strategy was being put in place (across a discipline, faculty or institution-wide) or new forums or committees were being established to ensure that the views of disabled and other students were being taken on board, and shaping future decision making. The focus from the institutions has generally been to ensure that their strategies and forums for engagement last beyond the duration of the project, such that they will be sustained into the future, in part, because this chimes with the wider environment where student engagement is being considered more strongly explicitly as a consequence of a number of initiatives highlighted earlier in this chapter. These projects have also ensured that dialogue between the institution and students' union in relation to disabled students specifically has also now been established.

It was clear that these projects have also begun to shift the culture of student engagement in their institutions, particularly with distinct groups such as disabled students. It was also noticeable that due consideration was being given to ensure engagement activity does not drop off the agenda and is properly articulated in institutional strategy. At Wakefield College, an example of activity being continued that would not have done so otherwise includes 'the engagement of students in planning and developing materials for publication as part of the strategic planning for next year'. Where engagement activity has moved beyond a fixed number of discrete actions and is a key or properly embedded across the strategy of an institution, it is a promising signal that a significant number of students are likely to be engaged rather than pockets of students who are usually 'easier to reach'.

Activity at the University for the Creative Arts (UCA) concentrated on the development of the student representation system, and alongside the students' union ensured that this was sustainable and appropriate training, and support was given to the representatives themselves. In addition to the structure that has been devised and implemented, funding from the UCA Strategic Development Fund has been sought to support the appointment of a Student Engagement Co-ordinator, which will ensure that activity continues to be embedded and pursued.

Other references have been made to demonstrate that project activity is not seen as a one-off, and will be embedded within processes and systems at the respective institutions. At Newcastle College, this is helpfully described as a 'process not an event — the activity at Newcastle College will continue to be developed and refined as time progresses. MSE cannot be a one off exercise to satisfy QAA requirements ... the requirements of HE students are catered for in a demonstrable way, providing opportunities for developmental case studies for future institutional audits and MSE funded projects'. Similarly, the University of Glamorgan demonstrated the importance of embedding activity, with the focus on student engagement in the current higher education climate cited as an important issue right now: 'all of the initiatives are seen as crucial to the ongoing engagement between the University and its students. Therefore all of the project outcomes will continue to be part of the ways the University conducts its business.' Further, the five aims pursued at the University of Glamorgan have been 'achieved and are now embedded as normal practice within the University's systems. LTEC will continue to monitor the progress of meaningful student engagement for all learners, including disabled students, as part of the University's agenda for distinctiveness', which is further evidence of activity being embedded beyond the timescale of the project.

A number of projects also developed physical resources, including handbooks for student representation systems, video resources, websites and training guides for staff, which can continue to be used beyond the project, and will now have a place in the annual cycle of academic activity. At Bishop Grosseteste University College Lincoln, they have outlined how their student voice staff development resource will be incorporated in wider staff training: 'in particular we will target new lecturers and visiting tutors, using the resource to raise awareness of the barriers to engagement that students have identified. A commitment to actively ensuring that all staff are aware of their responsibilities under the Equality Act is now embedded within institutional practice.' Also, where areas of institutional policy have been influenced, such as timetabling, the positive impacts will be permanent in the way in which an institution will approach this in future, as outlined by Bishop Grosseteste:

> ... timetabling is now being approached more systematically and the needs of disabled students are now tracked through the timetabling system in order to ensure that their needs are identified and catered for.

There are a number of ways in which the participating institutions embed and sustain activity, but it is worth sounding a note of caution that where student engagement comes in the form of representation on committees, this needs to be judged beyond simple membership.

It is widely accepted that the effectiveness of student members on committees and contributing through forums should not be judged on attendance, but rather through the quality of contributions and the evidence used to inform them, and ultimately the changes effected as a consequence. At this stage, while there are clearly a great number of new forums and places for dialogue that have been established between disabled students, the student body more generally, and the students' union with the institution, it is hard to determine whether these are going to be sustainable and whether quality inputs from students can be supported over a period of time. Often, when a culture of engagement and partnership is struck it still takes on-going effort to ensure that this is maintained. Similarly, where physical resources have been produced like websites, handbooks and training guides, there is an obvious sense in which they have a use beyond the project. However, to ensure that their relevance can be maximised, a small amount of revision and updating will be necessary to help further their appropriateness over time. It is important that institutions note this when considering their future plans and strategies.

11.7. Evaluation of the Impact of Change

There have been a wide range of attempts to evaluate the impact of change. Student engagement has historically been a challenge to measure given that there are a number of variables at play. Impact has of course been largely measured against the intended aims and objectives, but there have also been a number of impacts beyond the intended scope of the project. While a number of key impacts are outlined below, there was a lack of concrete and specific measures put in place across the participating institutions since some of the evaluation had only been considered halfway through the project.

In relation to formal recognition, Wakefield College has been able to cite 'a good practice judgement in the QAA process for the college's work to support disabled students'. In addition, the College has also been able to evidence a significant increase in measurable engagement with disabled students. Noticeably, those in receipt of the Disabled Students' Allowance (DSA) have increased 50 per cent since the start of the project, which is a positive sign of greater engagement of disabled students and the institution.

Greater engagement and dialogue with disabled students can also be reasonably expected to lead to improvement in the retention of students. Not only will this often lead to a more personalised and satisfied experience for students, but improvements in retention also lead to improvement in the finances for an institution due to teaching funding and student tuition fees.

Regarding reforms to specific elements of the learning and teaching experience, a number of institutions had focused on the reform of assessment, as outlined above. In relation to evaluating the impact of these reforms, Newcastle College organised a focus group to hear from disabled students after the changes had been embedded. Some of the positive comments from students included:

> ... helped manage my stress levels.

> ... more structured and focused on my work.

> ... my grades have improved from last year.

> It has made studying better for me and I don't have to constantly worry about having hand in dates after each other knowing I have already made an agreement to have the dates extended.

A significant number of institutions noted that they had set up forums and committees for disabled students and students more generally to feed in their views. Overall, the fact that institutions managed to get students to participate and contribute to on-going decision making, and the formation of institutional strategies to take the engagement agenda forward, is also a sign of the impact of change, beyond simply the setting up of structures.

A number of institutions have also stated that they are looking to measure the impact of changes over a longer period of time. Specifically, reference has been made to tracking changes and improvement to student satisfaction as measured in the NSS, higher levels of retention particularly among disabled students, and the scores in other internal surveys, questionnaires and module evaluation material. Given the relative timescale of the projects it is understandable that some of the metrics for evaluation will not have yet had time to be measured, and although institutions were asked to implement and evaluate change from the inception of projects, this needed to be more robustly reflected in institutional activity.

The evaluation from institutions also touched on the fact that projects often raised questions that had not been previously considered, but in doing so helped to ensure previously neglected areas of decision making were now being addressed. At Bishop Grosseteste, it was outlined that 'our outcome indicator was expected to be limited to a clearer understanding of the barriers in relation to learning and teaching. The data collected identified a much broader spread of potential barriers than we had anticipated, as students were focused upon the whole university experience, not just upon learning and teaching.' On staff training, the College has been able to evidence that 65 per cent of staff have already been through training on the Equality Act, with plans in place to address the remaining staff.

To conclude, there was clear evidence from all the participating institutions that attempts to take an inclusive approach were followed through. A wide range of activity from the diverse range of participants was delivered. For most institutions, the focus was on either setting up or developing more sophisticated systems of student representation. The 2010 HEA/ ECU *Strategic Approaches to Disabled Student Engagement* (May & Felsinger, 2010, p. 32) sets out a pyramid of involvement, and higher education institutions were keen to move up through the proposed levels. In some instances, this was adding a disabled students' forum to widen student listening exercises; in others it was ensuring that the views of disabled students were brought to the fore in staff–student and learning and teaching committees. In the main, these structures and committees have been set up in ways that will last beyond the project, and can therefore be assumed to be sustainable or to have the potential to be sustainable.

However, there was limited evidence of the measurement of the quality of these interventions and engagements, rather a more narrow focus on ensuring that they have been set up. Of course a number of impacts will be slower to show and to be fully measured. For instance, improvements in retention and student satisfaction will most likely only begin to be demonstrated once a full cycle of students have been through an institution. Particularly in the case of student satisfaction as the main measure for this, the NSS is not measured until semester two of the final year of undergraduate study and will inevitably take at least 3 years for the positive impact of changes to reach that point of measurement in the student life cycle. Accepting that many of the most powerful measures of impact will take as long as 3 years to reach fruition, most participating institutions have concentrated on outputs and the delivery of activity rather than tangible measures of impact.

As most institutions pursued a number of projects, there was also a focus on the reform of assessment and the improvement of staff training and induction to ensure an explicit focus on the issues facing disabled students, including a background to the law and the Equality Act specifically. A number of institutions also took the time to develop physical resources such as handbooks, guides, websites and other online materials, which will continue to be useful beyond the project.

Importantly, engaging with students cannot be achieved with a single solution. An appreciation for the diversity of the student population needs to be reflected in a range of approaches for engagement, although the principles for engagement with particularly hard to reach groups can be applied to other groups with a degree of variation. However, crucially, there was a tension between the definition that institutions developed for 'student engagement' and how activity was implemented. The key disconnect centred around the definition referring to 'active partnership' and 'power being in the hands of the students', whereas activity tended to take a more traditional format such as ensuring students were members of committees and that relevant representatives were consulted. While consultation and participation in committees are an important component of meaningful student engagement, it is not quite the active partnership that was referred to in the definitions set out by institutions. According to the definition set out in the HEA/ECU report (May and Felsinger, 2010), the activity of most institutions would more accurately be described as 'consultation', 'involvement' and 'participation' rather than 'engagement', which is described as 'a collaboration (e.g. between a student and an institution), involving joint ownership and decision-making over the process and outcome'.

The challenge of engagement with disabled students is certainly a significant one for the sector, but one that institutions are willing and keen to address. The intention of institutions is certainly that disabled students should be engaged, as any other, in any opportunity that is available, and the non-separation of disabled students from mainstream activity is important. The principles emerging from this project have led to a number of changes for the participating institutions and also to lessons that can be learned for the sector more generally. In particular, the words of Thomas (2004) still need to be heeded:

> ... one might think that considerable advances have been made in the last thirty years .... One must not, however, be fooled by appearances. While the quantity and scope of publications is to be celebrated as indicative of the seriousness with which disability is studied, we need to get beneath this to assess how much our understanding of disability has been enriched. (Thomas, 2004, p. 469)

This chapter shows the potential for enrichment of student engagement for disabled students along with all others. Ultimately though, meaningful student engagement should not limit itself to a process of ensuring appropriate documentation and consulting students about their views, but needs to provide appropriate support to action and empower those students to create change.

References

Birmingham City University. (2010). Retrieved from http://shareville.bcu.ac.uk/index.php?q = resource/disabled-student-perspectives-curriculum-design

BIS. (2011). *Students at the heart of the system*. Higher Education White Paper. Retrieved from http://discuss.bis.gov.uk/hereform/white-paper/

Coventry University, Information for Disabled Students. (2010). Retrieved from http://wwwm.coventry.ac.uk/health/welfare/Pages/InformationforDisabledStudents.aspx

Danforth, S., & Gabel, S. (2006). *Vital questions facing disability studies in education*. Retrieved from http://books.google.co.uk/books?hl = en&lr = &id = ONp3uMZpeMQC&oi = fnd&pg = PR13&dq = disability + in + higher + education:Disability + and + society:+ Emerging + issues + and + insights&ots = YPIpha9BIW&sig = Cy_HE9vxFb2rDrajAW1k1lA5_Sw#v = onepage&q&f = false

DIUS. (2009). *Disabled students and higher education: Higher educational analysis*. Retrieved from www.bis.gov.uk/assets/biscore/corporate/migratedd/publications/d/dius_rr_09_06.pdf

Finkelstein, V. (2001). *The social model repossessed*. The Disability Studies Archive UK, Centre for Disability Studies, University of Leeds. Retrieved from www.leeds.ac.uk/disability-studies/archiveuk/archframe.htm

Gabel, S. L. (Ed.) (2005). *Disability studies in education: Readings in theory and method*. New York, NY: Peter Lang Publishing Inc.

Glamorgan University. (n.d.). *Curriculum design guide*. Retrieved from http://celt.glam.ac.uk/node/128

Goode, J. (2007). 'Managing' disability: Early experiences of university students with disabilities. *Disability & Society, 22*(1), 35−48.

HEA. (2011). *Student engagement research projects*. Retrieved from http://www.heacademy.ac.uk/resources/detail/studentengagement/StudentEngagement_ResearchProjects2011

HEA. (2013a). *Retention and success*. Retrieved from http://www.heacademy.ac.uk/retention-and-success

HEA. (2013b). *Students as partners*. Retrieved from http://www.heacademy.ac.uk/student-engagement

Jacklin, A., Robinson, C., O'Meara, L., & Harris, A. (2005). Improving the experiences of disabled students in higher education. In S. Riddell, T. Tinklin & A. Wilson (Eds.), *Disabled students in higher education — perspectives on widening access and changing policy*. London: Routledge.

May, H., & Felsinger, A. (2010). *Strategic approaches to disabled student engagement*. ECU/HEA. Retrieved from http://www.heacademy.ac.uk/assets/documents/inclusion/disability/Involvement_StrategicApproachesFinal.pdf

QAA. (2009). *Outcomes from institutional audit: Institutions' support for students with disabilities 2002–2006*, Special study. Retrieved from www.qaa.ac.uk/ImprovingHigherEducation/Pages/Published-Outcomes-papers.aspx

QAA. (2011). *UK quality code for higher education — Section 2: Disabled students*. The Quality Assurance Agency for Higher Education.

Reschly, A., & Christenson, S. L. (2006). Prediction of dropout among students with mild disabilities: A case for the inclusion of student engagement variables. *Remedial and Special Education, 27*, 276–292.

Seale, J. (2006). *E-learning and disability in higher education: Accessibility research and practice*. London: Routledge.

Thomas, C. (2004). How is disability understood? An examination of sociological approaches. *Disability & Society, 19*(6), 569–583.

PART 3: STUDENT ENGAGEMENT WITH THE COMMUNITY: THE UNIVERSITY AND BEYOND

Elisabeth Dunne and Derfel Owen

Students have traditionally engaged with their institutions and communities in a multitude of different ways. The 'community' may refer to the University itself, to local, regional or even global communities. As suggested by the University of Adelaide:

> A contemporary university should not stand apart from the community but be an integral part of it. (2013)

In terms of student engagement in the community, the benefit of a formal educational context is that universities often offer systems, structures and explicit means for getting involved with the community, both within an institution or within the wider community, and there is considerable evidence that students engage with these opportunities. Whilst recognising that many students will engage in extracurricular activity in the community, and that this can provide deep learning experiences, the purpose of Part 3 is to look at engagement that is linked in some way to disciplinary study. Such engagement can offer rich experiences that are very different from those available within the usual academic classroom, and they support in particular the development of tangible and transferable skills alongside practical outcomes. Part 3 illustrates a number of initiatives wherein students engage with their institutional community or beyond, including in the workplace. Each chapter reflects enthusiasm for such engagement and the many positive outcomes for students and communities alike, but each also outlines that there are a variety of issues which need to be carefully addressed.

A particular kind of relationship between the university and community occurs when students are within the workplace as a part of their degree study. Chapter 12 focuses on work practice (in this case with 'health and care' graduates who had been studying on a Foundation degree), and highlights how engagement with work becomes of central importance. The chapter extends discussion of the concept of student engagement, and explores feedback from health and care students, relating it to the concept of 'engagement in practice'. It is suggested that 'practice' could be available from numerous activities linked to higher education, such as from any paid work, work experience, community work or work place-ment activity, or university projects, fieldwork, and so on, with 'engagement in practice' becoming a coherent and unifying concept for the many ad hoc activities that contribute to the employability agenda for students. The further chapters in Part 3 illustrate in different ways the concept of engagement in practice, demon-strating its exciting and important potential, but also being realistic about issues and challenges.

The President of Ireland, Michael D. Higgins, stated in 2012 that 'With the privi-lege to pursue knowledge comes the civic responsibility to engage and put that knowledge to work in the service of humanity'. There is a long track-record in volunteering in Ireland and evidence of real potential for connecting students to real world problems, issues and communities, for bringing the higher education institu-tion and the community together, and for developing an ethos of civic engagement and social responsibility. None-the less, as highlighted by Chapter 13, there can be problems with volunteering practices across Ireland: inconsistencies of language and practice are unhelpful; and there is a sense of 'fragility' because, despite the words, community volunteering is not embedded within management structures, or represented in University strategic plans. The multiple examples of engagement in practice in this chapter highlight both the positives and the challenges for anyone wishing to set up community volunteering.

There is evidence in relation to volunteering that those involved in their youth will continue to engage in altruistic activity at later stages of their lives (Brodie et al., 2011). Whiteley (2004) claims that focusing on the needs of others benefits ourselves, and that voluntary activity in the community is associated with better health, lower crime, improved educational performance and greater life satisfaction. It would therefore seem of worth to support students to engage with their commu-nity at this stage of their lives in the expectation that their interest will continue. However, Holdsworth and Quinn (2010) suggest that instrumental rather than altruistic motives are emerging as a dominant discourse, with students becoming increasingly aware of the need to build up their CVs and have experience beyond a degree to offer to employers. This is apparent in Chapter 14 in the context of 'Giving to Sport'; here it is emphasised that community-based initiatives within an assessed programme work best, enabling reflective processes and the making of connections between theory and practice. Further it is recommended that only well-motivated students should be involved, preferably within an optional module, since not all community relationships work to good effect, and not all students engage in acceptable ways. The many challenges of different kinds of community engagement with sport are highlighted throughout the chapter, providing detailed information on a variety of models and their effectiveness.

Chapter 15 highlights a strong sense of engagement in practice by students in 'Creative campus', an initiative at a UK University whereby both undergraduate and postgraduate students have the opportunity to become deeply involved in their community through first researching, and then improving, designing and creating new social spaces on the University's two campuses. Britnell, Andriati, and Wilson (2009) state:

> Campus planners traditionally have guided the planning and building of learning spaces in the university. Historically, they have not invited the stakeholders (users) of the space — teachers and students — to participate in the planning process... Planning typically has been a sequential and "dis-integrated" process involving planners, architects, and lastly teachers and students... To create the conditions for truly engaged students and teachers, we must transform the campus learning-space planning process to include collaboration and participation by stakeholders.

In addition, Graetz (2006) claims:

> ...environments that elicit positive emotional responses may lead not only to enhanced learning but also to a powerful, emotional attachment to that space. It may become a place where students love to learn, a place they seek out when they wish to learn, and a place they remember fondly when they reflect on their learning experiences. (p.8)

The activities described in this chapter capture elements of both: a powerful student contribution, and spaces and places that capture a positive emotional response. For example, a dingy common room was transformed into a flexible, multiple-use space designed by students; and a bookable outside space has been created, with 'mushroom' seats, piles of wooden books and 'newt' and 'frog' benches. Student comments, along with feedback from, for example community artists, reflect the excitement and benefits of being engaged in this activity, both for themselves and for the institution.

References

Britnell, J. C, Andriati, R., & Wilson, L. (2009). Learning Space Design with an Inclusive Planning Process Promotes User Engagement. Educause Review Online. Retrieved from: http://www.educause.edu/ero/article/learning-space-design-inclusive-planning-process-promotes-user-engagement

Brodie, E., Hughes, T., Jochum, V., Miller, C., Ockenden, N., & Warburton, D. (2011). *Pathways through participation: What creates and sustains active citizenship? Summary report*. London: Pathways through Participation.

Graetz, K. A. (2006). The Psychology of Learning Environments. In D. G. Oblinger (Ed.), *Learning spaces*. Washington DC: Educause.

Higgins, M. D. (2012). Remarks at the: Launch of the Irish Centre for Autism and Neurodevelopmental Research. Galway. Retrieved from: http://www.president.ie/speeches/launch-of-the-irish-centre-for-autism-and-neurodevelopmental-research/

Holdsworth, C., & Quinn, J. (2010). Student volunteering in English higher education. *Studies in Higher Education, 35*(1), 113–127.

University of Adelaide. (2013). Community Engagement. Retrieved from: http://www. adelaide.edu.au/community-engagement

Whiteley, P. (2004). Volunteering boosts community happiness. Society Guardian, September.

Chapter 12

Meanings of Engagement to Part-Time, Working Students in Higher Education

Julie Wintrup, Kelly Wakefield and Elizabeth James

Abstract

Research into student engagement has tended to focus on full-time, campus-based students. The relationship between student and university is of great interest in such studies. A criticism of this type of research is that the focus on a two-way relationship excludes the broader networks influencing how students engage. In this chapter we explore research into the experiences of recent graduates who were part of a very particular set of relationships, being sponsored by their employers.

Typically local or commuting, participants were from a broad demographic, often mature, typically female and vocationally educated. For them, education was entered into as a means of improving work skills and progressing careers in health or care services. For employers, a more effective workforce was the intended outcome. Graduates offered insights into higher education designed to fulfil two sets of objectives, at times complementary and at other times contradictory. Practice, understood as the successful performance of work, emerged as a unifying concept.

We propose that academics, higher education professionals and employers who are interested in student engagement would do well to consider it through the lens of engagement with work practice. Such an emphasis legitimises an interest in all the work of students, including placements and casual, paid work. In addition, it offers the possibility of a more enduring framework for the multitude of discrete, ad hoc, *project activities emerging from the 'employability' agenda.*

12.1. Introduction and Background

This chapter is split into four sections: first, an introductory discussion of the implications for the body of work called 'student engagement' given the shifting sands of

The Student Engagement Handbook: Practice in Higher Education
Copyright © 2013 by Emerald Group Publishing Limited
All rights of reproduction in any form reserved
ISBN: 978-1-78190-423-7

higher education (HE); second, the presentation of research involving working health and care students who describe engagement with practice; third, a discussion connecting the two and advocating for a broader view of student engagement, and fourth, a concluding section.

The term 'student engagement' is used abundantly in HE to describe activities ranging from involvement in curriculum development, learning and teaching approaches, pedagogic research, student representation activities and participation in a variety of institutional projects, processes and events (Bryson, 2011). Many of these are extra-curricular, in that they are not part of course requirements, while others are integral to education programmes. The incentive to participate more actively in the broader life of the university or community may be driven by political, social or altruistic aims, or simply by the hope of standing out in an increasingly competitive — and uncertain — global job market (Bryson & Hardy, 2012).

Along with the pressing demand for greater efficiency in HE, such a competitive arena might be seen as reinvigorating the student engagement agenda, given its association with success, achievement and retention (Tinto, 2006). However in this chapter, we contend that such a context also presents a threat to its broader conceptualisation. If the 'contract' between HE and student is defined only in terms of exchange or transaction, however obliquely, 'engagement' is at risk of being defined by the instrumental objectives of both parties. Such a reductionist interpretation is actively resisted by the following constructions of engagement, as a dynamic enacted through agency, community and partnership.

Seminal research into engagement describes a *relationship*, developed over time and through shared activities and interests, between individuals, groups, associations and organisations (Kuh, 2008; Kuh, Kinzie, Buckley, Bridges, & Hayek, 2008). While technological innovations may alter where and how we engage, *that* we do so remains at the heart of student engagement endeavours. Such affiliations take on even greater significance for students, including postgraduates, learning at a distance or online, given the potential for isolation (Mandernach, 2009).

Robinson (2012) offers a comprehensive, historical overview of the international policy and learning/teaching trends attending to student voice and involvement, often in wide range of institutional activities. The concept of 'voice' is challenged by the work of Kay, Dunne, and Hutchinson (2010) as essentially a passive role akin to 'student as customer'. Their influential 'student as change agent' construction is well expedited elsewhere in this volume. A more radical version of agency is manifested in the work of Neary and Winn (2009) and Taylor and Wilding (2009), through the 'student as collaborator and producer' movement. Like Barnett's (1997) description of 'critical beings', such a holistic conception invites a socially and politically aware stance from students and educators.

Debate is lively: researching engagement in the school sector, Fielding (2001, p. 137) concluded that the involvement of students in everyday goings on (such as committees or curriculum development) has the potential to be 'unwitting manipulation'. The more radical 'student as researcher' approach, as espoused by Neary and others, 'insists on a response to fundamental questions', and in doing so, presents a much more radical challenge to staff (Fielding, 2001, p. 137).

No single construction is likely to be meaningful to all students. Adams' (2012, p. 214) research with African Caribbean student societies in the United Kingdom found many black and minority ethnic groups to be 'already segregated' within HE, and in addition to be poorly served by student unions. In our research students — whether international (including domiciled), mature, distance or part-time — described experiencing HE as a somewhat transitional or liminal period. Extensive research into the experiences of vocationally educated students (Hayward & Hoelscher, 2011; Wolf, 2011) and those from working class[1] backgrounds (Crozier, Reay, Clayton, Colliander, & Grinstead, 2008) reinforces the heterogeneous nature of any 'type' of student, and the importance of circumstances. A less well-travelled path (that of the working, sponsored learner) is explored more fully later in this chapter.

12.1.1. Working Students

Worldwide, students work alongside their study; one estimate suggests that among full-time students in the United Kingdom, 47% of men and 68% of women work part-time throughout their education (TUC/NUS, 2006). The number is likely to have risen in the years since. The same report finds the educational achievement of those from the poorest backgrounds to be most affected by part-time work, reflecting similar findings from the United States more recently (ACCT, 2012). In the United Kingdom, conflicting messages are apparent. A minority of universities stipulate that paid work during term-time is not allowed, as study requirements are intensive (Cambridge, 2013). Advice from the University Central Admissions System (UCAS) encourages part-time work, when balanced with study (UCAS, 2012). It is rare, however, to see any reference to the ability students develop *through* paid work, independently or prior to entering HE, as the emphasis is generally placed on 'graduate' skills (see, e.g., CBI/UUK, 2009, p. 6).

Work experience is, however, cited as key to increasing an individual's 'employability'; that is, the right attitudes or mind-set for work, along with the ubiquitous 'transferable skills' (CBI/UUK, 2009, p. 4). Many professional programmes regularly award grades to work placements, which contribute in turn to degree classification. Not surprisingly, considering the importance of entry to a career, many student engagement strategies are infused with the language of employability. Whether role or project based, in the university, local community or another country, work-based learning schemes share the goal of developing skills, understanding and attributes likely to benefit students themselves and others, along with empowering critical, reflective abilities (HEA, 2012).

Work is often described as transformative in terms of personal development (Raelin, 1997) and in terms of future career openings, with its potential for contacts and entry into networks (Rae, 2007). Of course many experiences may well be

---

[1]Using Office for National Statistics Socio-Economic Classification categories, Social Class 3−8.

unaffordable or inaccessible to some even when organised through HE. The organisation and monitoring of such activity is often fraught with problems of access and equity. Placements can be hard to find and often students are obliged to source their own, a task made easier for those with family or friendship connections (IPPR, 2010). Like unpaid internships, such practices are understandably criticised as unfair, reproducing patterns of access to certain types of work and professions (IPPR, 2010). Inequity arises again when placements are unpaid or when high tuition fees are charged alongside the associated placement costs. In the United Kingdom, the Wilson Review criticised high tuition fees for placement years, recommending a much reduced flat fee (Wilson, 2012).[2] The quality of work placement remains the responsibility of the university, requiring quality monitoring and audit (QAA, 2008).

It is clear that work is part of the lexicon of higher learning whether paid or unpaid, voluntary, compulsory, informal or commissioned directly by employers. Meanwhile, the many skills and abilities gained through prolonged, regular work seem in some way invisible or even (albeit by a minority) seen as distracting and detrimental to study. Yet the activities being carried out — say, caring for a disabled child — might equip the student equally well for future work, whether undertaken in a Charity-run mission abroad or a local care agency. While not the focus of this discussion, such an omission in the employability literature is notable.

Later in the chapter we present a case for bringing *all* types of work practice into the student engagement discussion as a central and sustaining element of many students' sense of purpose and direction. In the next section we present findings from research based on a very particular group of recent graduates. While we make no attempt to generalise from their experiences, the intertwined nature of their working practices and formal learning offers a broader view of how they engaged with the totality of their education. In interpreting their words, our intention is to blur the boundary between work inside and outside HE, formally recognised or not, and regardless of status or nature. Our interest is in how the different experiences meaningfully contributed to an engaged stance in the individual, or failed to do so.

12.2.   Work-Based Students' Perspectives

12.2.1.   *Background to Study*

Foundation degrees were introduced in England in 2001 to address a workforce gap in skilled, technical workers and to widen access to HE (HEFCE, 2000). Equivalent to the Diploma or ordinary degree, the Foundation degree became most popular in the public sector where there had previously been few ways of bridging the considerable distance between a vocationally trained support workforce and the degree-

---

[2]The Higher Education Funding Council for England has responded to the Wilson Review by recommending a fee of no more than 25% of a standard tuition fee for a placement or 'sandwich' year out (HEFCE, 2012).

educated professions (Harvey, 2010). A significant amount of work-based learning was required by the 'qualification benchmark' (QAA, 2002), setting it apart from other sub-degree qualifications (Yorke, 2005).

The following research comprised one strand of a longitudinal research project funded through the Higher Education Funding Council for England (HEFCE), as part of a regional Lifelong Learning Network (LLN). Graduates of a Foundation degree, who had been seconded by employers with a view to taking on higher levels of responsibility and/or new job roles, were contacted up to 2 years after completion and asked to reflect upon their experiences during and following their education.

12.2.2.   *Study Design and Methodology*

The study was designed as a brief precursor to a larger, longitudinal study of current students, reported since in Wintrup, James, and Humphris (2012a) and Wintrup, James, Humphris, and Bryson (2012b). Over the course of a year, graduates of a Foundation degree in health and care were contacted and asked to participate in an individual, reflective interview of approximately 1 to 2 hours duration. Its primary purpose was to inform the design and conduct of the larger study, although the opportunity to discover how graduates reflected on their experience and subsequent achievements became of great value in itself.

Interviews were carried out with 30 graduates in total: 18 participated in individual interviews and another 12, from different employers, participated in group interviews in their workplaces. Interviews were recorded and transcribed verbatim, with both forms of data stored and managed in keeping with the Data Protection Act (1998), university regulations and ethical approval conditions.

The theoretical framework of the interview study was informed by the constructionist approach of Holstein and Gubrium (1995), who describe the interview as a social production. This approach was helpful to the interviewer given the high profile and politicised nature of the new, government-driven programme of study. Seeking expert views from experienced and informed individuals enabled a conversational style, with reciprocal discussion and questioning, while allowing the researcher to steer proceedings rather than attempting to 'mine minds' (Holstein & Gubrium, 1995, p. vii). Findings have not been reported in any depth elsewhere, although a parallel strand of the study (with students during study) has been reported by Wintrup et al. (2012a, 2012b).

12.2.3.   *Analysis and Theme Development*

Semi-structured interviews were conducted during 2008/09 at a time when research into the new degree was scarce. Questions were purposefully open and designed with ample scope for supplementary questions, for tangents to be followed, and discussion to ensue. A typical interview schedule comprised the following questions after an introduction: Would you begin by telling me how you came to study the Foundation degree? What are your views on the programme now, on reflection?

What stands out in your memory? What has been happening since you graduated from the programme (at work specifically, in life more generally)? Do you consider the programme to have influenced your job/career in particular ways (if so/if not, how? please elaborate)? Is there anything else you would like to tell me about in relation to the experience or about events since?

The in-depth nature of the interviews provided space for participants to critically reflect on their experiences in light of subsequent events. Meeting graduates for the first time, the interviewer, a Senior Researcher (and third author, EJ), encouraged them to prioritise their own order and importance of reflections and to offer their own interpretation of events with the benefit of hindsight. Interviews were audio-recorded, transcribed and analysed inductively using a grounded approach, developing ideas from data (Atkinson & Delamont, 2005, p. 833). Themes were generated as analysis progressed and subsequently overarching themes were developed to incorporate and integrate subordinate themes.

12.2.4.   *Ethical Considerations and Limitations of the Study*

Following ethical approval from the School of Health Sciences, University of Southampton in 2007, graduates from previous years of study were contacted during 2008/09 and invited to return a slip by post to the researcher for further information. Information packs were sent to those who responded and contact made some 2 weeks later. Of those who subsequently agreed to be interviewed, only a minority were able eventually to participate due to the practicalities of busy working and family lives.

The researcher, who managed all data collection, anonymisation and storage, was not involved at any stage with the graduates' education or subsequent employment. Analysis was shared between the researcher and the first author (JW) on completion of all interviews. A full discussion of the ethical considerations of the larger programme of pedagogic research is available in Wintrup et al. (2012b). A limitation of the research is that the 30 participants represent a small proportion of all graduates (ca. 200 by 2008/09); however, as a qualitative and exploratory study this proved more than adequate for theme generation. Only those who had successfully completed and graduated from the programme were invited to participate, as the primary purpose was to learn from those who had a significant experience of the programme. In hindsight it would have been very useful to have gained approval to contact all who undertook the programme, including early leavers, although this would have been a much larger and different type of inquiry.

12.2.5.   *Themes from Graduate Interviews*

Three overarching themes emerged:

- The importance of the first-line manager
- Becoming a better practitioner by performing and achieving at work
- Realising a different type of confidence

12.2.5.1. Theme 1: The importance of the first-line manager
Interviewees were geographically dispersed and comprised many different health or social care employers. Many discussed the pivotal role performed by an immediate line manager, without whose active encouragement (and occasional subversive manoeuvres) some would not have started the degree. Within this theme were three sub-themes of managers being seen as crucial to the process, providing long-term support and positively intervening when action was required. These managers were seen as essential in changing the lives and careers of the interviewees, by offering complete support and reassurance. In one case this was given even if the student later walked away from the course.

> I can remember when he said to me 'look, you know, I really think you should do this' and I said 'but what happens if I can't do it, what happens if I don't like it?' and he said 'well you just tell me and I'll ring the University and tell them she's not coming back', and once I knew that, if it really was that hard and I couldn't do it, then I'd be able to step out of it I was fine. (FDG6, NHS)[3]

> I didn't know if I was capable, academically, to do it because I'm a more practical person so I was sort of wondering and my team leader and people I work with sort of pushed me and said 'yeah you can do it', you know, and 'you'll be fine' but I was worried. (FDG5, NHS)

The following managers showed a long-term view of staff development.

> The manager I have is really very supportive, (she) was kind of like, 'what way are you going now?' ... so this has opened up for me, all sorts of possibilities, she helped me further my development whereas I might probably just have stayed there actually. (FDG12, NHS)

> They were playing the long game — our manager was with the NHS and she knew that basically within a couple of months of us finishing (the degree) she was going to lose two of her best members of staff, but that health and social care in general would gain two new professionals ... (FDG26, NHS)

Another manager seems to have somewhat heroically thwarted an attempt at sabotage by a more senior manager.

> Our employers, they didn't want us to progress at all ... so he (manager) just filled in the stuff, sent it off, and didn't go to his manager,

---

[3]FDG is shorthand for Foundation degree graduate. Numbering took place as individuals volunteered leading to higher numbers than actually followed through to participate in interviews.

because it was his, the actual area manager, that put a stop to it, but you didn't have to fund anything, so we had to do it over three years and not have a replacement. (FDG16, Social Care)

Many other inequities were recalled around payment of travel, time for study and access to a mentor. These were discovered as students talked to each other, however far away they lived and worked. Despite such active support from immediate line managers, problems occurred elsewhere in the organisation (often at middle management level). The presence of an organisational 'mentor', in one large NHS Trust, ameliorated such difficulties and provided a valued form of continuity and support. Interviews showed that compromises on working hours and funding arrangements were necessary though and were still recalled by interviewees some time later. Whether accurate or not, the perceptions of several were of a work context covertly hostile to the development of support workers.

12.2.5.2. Theme 2: Becoming a better practitioner by performing and achieving at work

Throughout the process of work-based learning the gaining of a recognised qualification and entry to a profession was a hugely motivating factor reported by participants of the longitudinal study. The following quotes are all examples of how becoming a better practitioner was inspired by a sense of purpose, a determination to achieve despite early anxieties and/or changing career paths. Changes in job roles are included in parentheses.

For this person, a sense of purpose drove her from the beginning:

> I kept on, kept on saying 'please let me do it' and then at the end of it I managed to get my Foundation degree and my nursing all seconded. I did it as a stepping-stone to my nursing ... it was a means to an end. (FDG3, NHS Support Worker to Nurse)

Such early determination was less common however than the gradual discovery of a new purpose. Limited goals accompanied anxieties around not achieving, and were only revised over time.

> In the first year I just thought I'd come back and stay in this role and then I had the (homeless team) placement, then I sort of realised, I can't go any further in this job ... so, if I'm going to get this degree I might as well make use of it and that's when it all started ... . From where I am now to where I was two years ago, it's completely different. (FDG5, from NHS to independent sector)

> I'd like to specialise, so since I finished the course I've done adult bereavement, but I want to, I'd really like to work with the siblings of bereaved children .... I will have to do a counselling course, I mean

> this is something I would really, really like to do. (FDG17, after returning to Special Education role)

Some talked of deepening and broadening their practice, often within the same role and place of work:

> I kind of learnt to set up care packages and go through the process of reviewing them, which has been invaluable. It (the degree) gave me time to say 'I want to learn about such and such' whereas I might not have had the time to do that, just in my normal role. It makes you a better practitioner — before I just accepted why we did things — I'm far more proactive now, looking at ways to improve my skill and my work practice. I've got a lot more complex cases ... (FDG12, employed in jointly managed NHS/Social Care team)

> I've been able to use the skills I got through the Foundation degree, because I now receive referrals from GPs, then I phone the patient and triage them on the telephone so I'm able to use the skills I learnt to decide whether it's an appropriate referral, if not I signpost them to another service, decide if there's any urgency, if there is I can get a response .... I really like my job, this job. (FDG50, NHS, community team, remained in same place of work)

The following quotes are from people who had taken radically different directions after graduating, the first realising how poorly suited she had been to her previous role in social care management.

> I always hated being a manager — for 17 years — I couldn't ask people to do something, if they had to go and do really mucky jobs, I'd go and do it with them, I couldn't be what a lot of managers were, and I didn't want to be ... and I sort of got into fostering quite accidentally. You're respected because of your skills, and you're given ones that are very complex, almost like they've gone through your training, all your skills, and they match you up, you are appreciated for what you have done ... (FDG16, Social Care, latterly Foster Carer).

Changing direction was not easy for this graduate who, by the time of the interview, had achieved so well with his new employer he was poised for a significant promotion.

> I wrote about 40 application forms, and I very nearly gave up, I got a few interviews and stuff and every time, every single time it just came down to the 'no professional experience' sort of thing, although I'd had placements with homeless schemes, no one was interested, very demoralising. Then when I got the interview with (Charity) I was on the brink of calling my old boss on the industrial estate to see if I could go back and work for him. (FDG26, NHS to Charitable Sector)

These latter contributions illustrate the broad range of careers available within health and care, not directly through the statutory sectors of the NHS and Social Services. More interestingly, they show the importance to each of performing well at work, through complex and responsible *practice*. Each describes finding a new purpose, which is not necessarily a step 'up' a hierarchical, organisational career ladder but may be a step off in a new direction.

12.2.5.3. Theme 3: A different kind of confidence

Finally, when asked to reflect more generally on the work-based learning experience, numerous discussions of changes in confidence were forthcoming. Such discussions included an increase in personal confidence and how learning at work together with peers raised confidence.

> I've always been quite confident but it's given me a different kind of confidence, I think it's about confidence in your own ability. I'm now very involved in trying to get this glass ceiling removed, so I've picked that up as a new challenge, so it's made me more comfortable and I suppose more secure in your own knowledge and your own abilities. (FDG6, NHS)

> … it's just made such a difference to how I feel about myself in terms of confidence, realising I can achieve more. I've broken the mould in my own mind. (FDG12, NHS)

Learning at work, alongside practitioners, was mentioned over and again as a key feature of this growth in confidence and developing sense of self, typified by the following quote:

> It was through a whole morning, just working alongside this person, and we had coffee together, and she was just so supportive really, and I just came out with this utter clarity that I was in the right place and that I was going the right way and that was good. There have been many times when I've felt the same certainty of purpose … they've all interestingly been (work) placement-based. (FDG2, NHS and latterly private practice)

The quotes within this section are taken from the interesting and enlightening discussions that were held with work-based learners. Such conversations highlight the intrinsic need for supportive and interested management — at all levels — alongside the importance of support to achieve goals as well as a flexible approach to future career options. However, interviewees returned to the topic of confidence both in themselves as well as the confidence work colleagues showed in them, as a practitioner with one foot in the work place and one foot in the university. What we can take from these students' narratives is that as a result of the relatively small proportion of students' time and experience that is intersected by the institution as well as the employer, we can begin to see how each must play a considered role in the meanings of engagement that students take from their work-based learning experience.

12.3. Discussion

12.3.1. *Work-Based Learners' Descriptions of Engagement*

Interviews reinforced enduring themes already discussed, such as the need to belong and be supported in trusting relationships. In addition, themes suggest that for many, their need for engagement was located primarily within their workplace. Those who had been actively supported gave copious details of ways in which others, also from the workplace, had promoted their interests (or in some cases, not). Learning and undertaking new skills, in the workplace, was found to be stimulating and motivating. New opportunities were simultaneously exciting, stressful and unpredictable. Others talked of the sustaining nature of work, as practice, as a community and as a source of new careers. The pivotal role played by line managers — in actively promoting education and accessing resources to support individuals — echoes others' findings (Hales, 2005; Renwick & MacNeil, 2002).

Unlike current students, the problems and frustrations of studying were not uppermost in their minds some 2 years later and when mentioned were seen from a longer view. However highs and lows — managers' active encouragement, barriers and perceived injustices, even those occurring prior to study — were recounted in great detail and with feeling. Equally impressive in terms of both frequency and passion were the accounts of how a new kind of confidence enabled immersion in new work roles and tasks. This combination of self-confidence, born of knowledge and ability, now in supportive environments offering permission to question and to act, is summarised by the graduate who describes herself as '... far more proactive now, looking at ways to improve my skill and work practice'. It is this sense of connectedness with performing at work — in emotional and intellectual ways — which offers a lens through which to reconsider this form of engagement.

12.3.2. *Work as Practice*

Graduates' rich descriptions, like those of current students in our earlier research, place *work practice* squarely in the forefront of their sense of engagement and involvement. Their accounts are of 'the successful performance of work' (Beckett & Hager, 2002, p. 96), which intertwines thinking and doing. One interviewee's description of triaging patients shows not what Schön (1991, p. 30) describes as 'technical rationality' but 'reflection-in-action', as each new referral is explored, weighed, judged, decided and acted upon in its unique context.

Beckett (2010, p. 3) goes further, exploring the reflexivity involved in learning by doing, concluding that such learning is 'social, relational, and perspectival'. The experience of 'just working alongside' a mentor, recounted by an interviewee, describes such an event, as she understands: '... that I was in the right place and that I was going the right way'.

The supportive work environments the interviewees describe correlate with Fuller and Unwin's (2003) expansive settings in which workers are given scope to learn by immersion, experimentation and support. The person who describes 'hating management' has since created an environment for herself in which she feels respected and trusted, rather than being subject to demarcated role divisions.

Finally the work of Colley (2006) reminds us that this highly gendered, low paid section of the caring workforce may well have to 'unlearn' previous expectations of their place in the hierarchy. One interviewee refers to 'the glass ceiling' and another to 'the mould of my own mind'. Such social and political awareness is a reminder of the student as radical agent of change, as producer and as critical being (Barnett, 2007; Fielding, 2001; Neary & Winn, 2009).

The work-based learning network sub-group of UALL[4] promotes work-based learning as a critical pedagogy. Our longitudinal study found students' development as critical thinkers, able to access hallowed professional knowledge, to be foundational to their growing curiosity and confidence (Wintrup et al., 2012b). However it is clear listening to graduates, now largely back in the workplace, that, for most, their critique of the workplace is partial and highly personal, even with the benefit of time. Some continue to feel let down or misled by the enticement of higher grades or new roles. Others give the impression of having 'escaped' into more professionally respected roles, even when their formal status or salary is unchanged. Others left the statutory sector for the independent or private care sectors, finding greater freedom to progress free of the rigid NHS structures (DH, 2004), despite losing other forms of employment protection. However within conversations, a more informed stance is evident: in the awareness of externally imposed limits to achievement, in the sense of 'taking charge' of one's own work and in the rejection of rigid demarcations.

12.3.3.   Domains of Engagement Explored

The complex nature of the meanings of engagement to the work-based learner can be seen through these discussions. From the student perspective, it is complicated if not impossible to unravel the issues which relate *only* to their employment or *only* to their (formal) education, and which are of shared concern to all three parties. Hence disappointment with their education, even a sense of alienation, can result from employer-related problems (as with the reported inequities for pay, study leave, subsequent promotions), and vice versa. In the same way, highs and lows within the workplace are not always connected to their education provision, even

---

[4]The University Association of Lifelong Learning (UALL) has several special interest groups, of which the Work Based Learning Special Interest Group is one, available at http://www.uall.ac.uk/wbl, accessed 21 December 2012.

when a placement or project is arranged and monitored by the higher education institution (HEI). The powerful learning called 'hot action', which Beckett (2010, p. 74) describes as 'intense, dynamic, uncertain and decisional', may be situated forever in the mind of the learner as of the work place, and never revisited or deconstructed within more formal learning despite being a rich source of reflective and reflexive learning. If work practices are to be fully exploited as sites of intellectual and critical development, then greater engagement between academics, students and employers or placement providers is essential.

In the following section, we seek to stretch our definition of the work-based learner to see whether our findings have relevance to broader student engagement activities, such as university-based projects, community work, professional work placements or international field work activities. To test this idea, we will consider 'work-based learning' to be anything taking place outside the classroom, under the aegis of the HEI (for the moment, although we question whether this distinction should remain), which requires immersion in practice. This loose definition might include such diverse activities as the design of a website for a customer, participation in collecting data for a research project, a geography fieldtrip, a work placement or an institutionally sponsored project.

In Figure 12.1, we produce our interpretation of the experience our interviewees described, in which the student provides the only explicit link between the workplace (or project sponsor or community project) and the HEI. Of course there may well be many other links, but they may easily not be visible or explicit to the student. While the student's 'engagement' may be strong, it is likely to be with one or other entity — and in our research, this seems to be strongly with the workplace.

In Figure 12.2, we offer a different way of describing the relationships between all three parties. Visualising the work-based learners' engagement in this way places *practice* at the centre of the Venn diagram, where *all* domains intersect as the shared concern and goal of all parties. In doing so, the multi-faceted nature of student engagement is highlighted in a way that is coherent and has potential to bond rather than to divide.

In caring disciplines the links here are self-evident — for example, the shared concerns of employer and student (worker) are likely to be human resource issues, such as working terms and conditions, and also future career openings, corporate

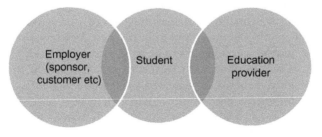

Figure 12.1: Student as link, responsible for engaging with work practices and with the life of the university.

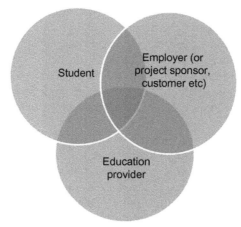

Figure 12.2:   Student as equal partner, in which engagement with practice is a shared concern.

policies and procedures, sensitive or confidential patient/client/organisational knowledge and so on, a domain the HEI or individual educator might be informed of but have no jurisdiction over. Those shared between student and educators ought (in our view) to include such things as academic standards, quality requirements, scheduling processes and personal information such as results of specific learning assessments, assessed work, patterns of attendance and personal health issues. Of course the student may have a responsibility to discuss much of this with an employer, or sponsor, or practice coordinator, but whenever possible such discussions should be entrusted to the student. The penultimate overlapping section is that between the employer (or sponsor and so on) and HEI (or educators) who will necessarily have agreed or arranged the work-based experience.

This is, according to our interviewees, an invisible or covert relationship, the broad scope of which might usefully be made explicit even when details (e.g. commercial transactions) remain confidential. Legitimate shared concerns are likely to include the nature and duration of any contract or financial investment, recruitment processes and where appropriate, disciplinary or complaint processes, commitments made to provide work or experiences (locations, travel costs, expectations of time keeping and so on), mentorship processes and people, the nature and availability of project work (including how agreement is reached on the nature/flexibility of a project), whether and how academic credit is awarded for work, who assesses or grades work and so on. Arrangements for dealing with actual or threatened breakdown of the work activity ought to be agreed and made explicit.

Although only indicative and by no means exhaustive, such a long list might feasibly deter anyone considering learning through work, whether placements, projects or sponsored/paid work. However we found these to be the kinds of issues both current students and graduates reported having to unearth for themselves and then negotiate their way around. First-line managers or mentors were not always positioned to decide the strategic components of this relationship, despite having to communicate and implement them.

Finally, the central overlapping area shared by all three parties — student (worker), employer (or sponsor) and HEI (or educator) — which we consider the *shared concern of practice,* is where we locate the intertwined, inseparable learning, doing and being that is the successful performance of work (as described by Beckett & Hager, 2002). In care work, this domain includes the direct care and treatment of others, as part of a community of practice (as described by Wenger, 1998), with its inherent commitment to maintain and improve standards, its duties to safeguard the vulnerable and minimise risks, to share information appropriately, to act professionally and ethically, to make decisions and to uphold policies and laws (to name a few).

This is indeed where 'hot action' takes place, but where reflection-in and reflection-on action must also occur, drawing on 'types' of knowing intuitively and intellectually, through reasoning. It is the purpose of most classroom or theoretical learning and provides, in turn, new types of knowledge (about self, others, situations, data, information). These shared concerns highlight where student engagement in work practice becomes genuinely dynamic, as part of a community, which includes not only employers and academics, but patients, users of services, carers, families and wider networks. In turn, the institution or individual programme leader might usefully work more closely with both students and employers to better understand the nature of practice(s) and discover ways to connect classroom learning more closely to the concerns of both.

So does our domain model have anything to offer student engagement more broadly, such as student representation roles, advocacy or mentoring projects, community volunteering, work placements or co-design of curricula? Some are easy to adapt being similar to care work in intention (e.g. volunteering on a student helpline) so we will consider something quite different. Let us imagine how the concept of practice might help a full-time politics student contribute to co-designing a new curriculum. First of all we might envisage the curriculum design team as a proxy 'employer' or sponsor, who must make explicit terms and conditions, expectations and so on with both other parties. The HEI or educator might usefully be a personal tutor, supervisor or mentor, able to ensure the educational quality of the plan, its worth in terms of academic credit or personal development and again ensure interests shared with other parties are considered by both. The student has a responsibility to look closely at the opportunity, its comparative benefits and risks, and to raise questions or problems in advance (such as timing of meetings in relation to academic work and so on).

The shared domain of practice might be construed as the active participation in curriculum design and planning, with all its attendant tasks: reading, thinking, reflecting, imagining, planning, meeting, discussing, disagreeing and scheduling (to name a few). All parties share the explicit goal of improving future students' learning, all must wrestle with practical problems or constraints and all must eventually agree and produce a plan to validate the programme. Of course power, vested interests and time limitations will all influence events. Implicit, even covert, goals exist but are more likely to be unearthed and made explicit through discussion of shared goals.

While this approach may only provide a loose fit with internal or unpaid/*ad hoc* types of work project, it offers one way of integrating discrete engagement activities. If we consider work-based learning as a critical pedagogy, then part of the learning is practising within communities and becoming alert to their inherent contradictions, responding to them, reflecting upon them in the moment and experimenting with doing things in new ways (Engeström, 2001).

12.3.4. A Broader View of Student Engagement

In summary, themes from research with recent graduates of a work-based Foundation degree in health and care offered insights into important features of their relationships, with education, employment and practice. All too often, the world of practice appeared to be a parallel one to academia. Interviewees generally described each as discrete arenas of engagement, taking responsibility for bridging the divide, by spending time and energy liaising, translating, and negotiating, reflecting the findings of our longitudinal research. A more coherent and integrated approach is made possible by placing *practice* at the centre of related and shared concerns, and is offered as a potential model for bringing coherence and shared aims to other work-related engagement activities. Such an approach requires a good deal of investment to clarify terms and articulate areas of shared concern. However it has the potential to reinforce *engagement in practice* as a unifying concept and to establish the student as co-researcher and co-producer of work — a far cry from the consumer in a transactional relationship with HE.

12.4. Conclusion

In the introduction we discussed the importance of institutional engagement activities based on employability goals, and considered the logistical and quality challenges posed by a higher uptake of such opportunities. The changing context of work was discussed in light of growing numbers of working students, and the risks of relying too heavily on the exchange concept of education 'purchased' as a route to a career. Constructions of engagement that view students' motives as rationally self-interested were critiqued, as inevitably rewarding an instrumental stance which reinforced the individual good over the social good.

We advocate here for an approach to engagement that values the ordinary lives of all students and takes an interest in their wider experiences. Such a reframing presents an opportunity to engage with students' own agendas, concerns and priorities rather than constructing new types of 'work' open only to the few, in turn reproducing islands of engagement. Graduates' reflections offered a way of broadening our conception of student engagement, to include work practice in its broadest sense.

Acknowledgements

The authors would like to thank the working health and care Foundation degree students who generously gave their time to talk to us. Also, many thanks to peer reviewers, whose observations and comments made this chapter much improved.

References

ACCT. (2012, 21 December). *Association of Community College Trustees and Single Stop USA: Partnership.* 2012 report. Retrieved from http://www.singlestopusa.org/wp-content/uploads/2012/10/ACCT_Report_03.pdf

Adams, N. (2012). Afro-Caribbean societies: The impact on identity, segregation and integration in the university environment. *Journal of Applied Research in Higher Education, 4*(1), 203–216.

Atkinson, P., & Delamont, S. (2005). Analytic perspectives. In N.K. Denzin & Y.S. Lincoln (Eds.), *The Sage handbook of qualitative research* (pp. 821–840). London: Sage.

Barnett, R. (1997). *Higher education: A critical business.* Maidenhead, UK: Open University Press, Society for Research in Higher Education.

Barnett, R. (2007). *A will to learn: Being a student in an age of uncertainty.* Maidenhead, UK: Open University Press.

Beckett, D. (2010). *Reclaiming the tacit: 'Understanding' by doing.* Paper presented at PESA Conference, University of Hawai'i, 3–7 December. Retrieved from http://www2.hawaii.edu/~pesaconf/zpdfs/35becket.pdf

Beckett, D., & Hager, P. (2002). *Life, work and learning: Practice in postmodernity.* London: Routledge.

Bryson, C. (2011). *Clarifying the concept of student of engagement: A fruitful approach to underpin policy and practice.* Paper presented at the HEA Conference, Nottingham University, 5–6 July 2011.

Bryson, C., & Hardy, C. (2012). The nature of student engagement, what the students tell us. In I. Solomonides, A. Reid, & P. Petocz (Eds.), *Engaging with learning in higher education* (pp. 25–46). London: Libri.

Cambridge. (2013). *University of Cambridge advises students against paid work during term time.* Retrieved from http://www.study.cam.ac.uk/undergraduate/finance/costs.html

CBI/UUK. (2009). *Future fit: Preparing graduates for the world of work.* 2009 Report. Retrieved from http://www.cbi.org.uk/media/1121435/cbi_uuk_future_fit.pdf

Colley, H. (2006). Learning to labour with feeling: Class, gender and emotion in childcare education. *Contemporary Issues in Early Childhood, 7*(1), 15–29.

Crozier, G., Reay, D., Clayton, J., Colliander, L., & Grinstead, J. (2008). Different strokes for different folks: Diverse students in diverse institutions-experiences of higher education. *Research Papers in Education-Special Issue, 23*(2), 167–177.

DH (Department of Health). (2004). *Agenda for change.* Retrieved from http://www.dh.gov.uk/en/Publicationsandstatistics/Publications/PublicationsPolicyAndGuidance/DH_4095943

Engeström, Y. (2001). Expansive learning at work: Toward an activity theoretical reconceptualization. *Journal of Education and Work, 14*(1), 133–155.

Fielding, M. (2001). Students as radical agents of change. *Journal of Educational Change, 2*(2), 123–141.

Fuller, A., & Unwin, L. (2003). Learning as apprentices in the contemporary UK workplace: Creating and managing expansive and restrictive participation. *Journal of Education and Work*, *16*(4), 407–426.

Hales, C. (2005). Rooted in supervision, branching into management: Change in the role of the first-line manager. *Journal of Management Studies*, *43*(2), 471–506.

Harvey, L. (2010). *Review of research literature focussed on Foundation degrees*. Retrieved from http://www.heacademy.ac.uk/assets/documents/fdf/Review-of-research-literature-focussed-on-foundation-degrees.pdf

Hayward, G., & Hoelscher, M. (2011). The use of large-scale administrative data sets to monitor progression from vocational education and training into higher education in the UK: Possibilities and methodological challenges. *Research in Comparative and International Education*, *6*(3), 316–329.

HEA. (2012). *Pedagogy for employability*. Retrieved from http://www.heacademy.ac.uk/assets/documents/employability/pedagogy_for_employability_update_2012.pdf

HEFCE. (2000). *Foundation degree prospectus*. Retrieved from http://www.hefce.ac.uk/pubs/hefce/2000/00_27.htm

HEFCE. (2012). *Student number controls and teaching funding in 2013–14 and beyond: Summary of responses and decisions made*. p. 31. Retrieved from http://www.hefce.ac.uk/media/hefce/content/pubs/2012/201219/2012_19.pdf

Holstein, J. A., & Gubrium, J. F. (1995). *The active interview*. London: Sage.

IPPR. (2010). *Why interns need a fair wage*. Retrieved from http://www.ippr.org/images/media/files/publication/2011/05/Why%20interns%20need%20a%20fair%20wage_1788.pdf

Kay, J., Dunne, E. & Hutchinson, J. (2010). *Rethinking the values for higher education – students as change agents?* The Quality Assurance Agency for Higher Education, Bristol. Retrieved from http://www.qaa.ac.uk/Publications/InformationAndGuidance/Documents/StudentsChangeAgents.pdf

Kuh, G. (2008). *High impact practices. What they are, who has access to them and why they matter?* Retrieved from http://www.neasc.org/downloads/aacu_high_impact_2008_final.pdf

Kuh, G. D., Kinzie, J., Buckley, J., Bridges, B., & Hayek, J. C. (2008). *What matters to student success: A review of the literature. ASHE Higher Education Report*. San Francisco, CA: Jossey-Bass.

Mandernach, B. J. (2009). Effect of instructor-personalized multimedia in the online classroom. *The International Review of Research in Open and Distance Learning*, *10*(3), 1–19.

Neary, M., & Winn, J. (2009). The student as producer: Reinventing the student experience in higher education. In L. Bell, H. Stevenson & M. Neary (Eds.), *The future of higher education: Policy, pedagogy and the student experience* (pp. 192–210). London: Continuum.

QAA. (2002). *Foundation degree: Qualification benchmark (final draft)*. Gloucester: Quality Assurance Agency for Higher Education.

QAA. (2008). *Outcome from institutional audit: Work-based learning, and employability, 2nd series, sharing good practice*. Retrieved from http://www.qaa.ac.uk/Partners/Employers/Documents/PlacementLearning.pdf

Rae, D. (2007). Connecting enterprise and graduate employability: Challenges to the higher education culture and curriculum?. *Training and Education*, *49*(8/9), 605–619.

Raelin, J. A. (1997). A model of work-based learning. *Organisational Science*, *8*, 563–578.

Renwick, D., & MacNeil, C. M. (2002). Line management involvement in careers. *Career Development International*, *7*(7), 407–414.

Robinson, C. (2012). Student engagement: What does this mean in the context of higher education institutions?. *Journal of Applied Research in Higher Education*, *4*(1), 94–108.

Schön, D. A. (1991). *The reflective practitioner: How professionals think in action.* London: Ashgate.

Taylor, P., & Wilding, D. (2009). *Rethinking the values of higher education — the student as collaborator and producer? Undergraduate research as a case study.* The Quality Assurance Agency for Higher Education. Gloucester, MA.

Tinto, V. (2006). Research and practice of student retention: What next? *College Student Retention, 8*(1), 1–19.

TUC/NUS. (2006). *All work and no pay.* Retrieved from http://www.tuc.org.uk/extras/allworklowpay.pdf

UCAS. (2012). *UCAS advises part time work will cut down the debt waiting to be paid after graduation.* Retrieved from http://www.ucas.com/students/startinguni/managing_money/balancing_work_and_study

Wenger, E. (1998). *Communities of practice: Learning, meaning and identity.* Cambridge, MA: Cambridge University Press.

Wilson, T. (2012). *A Review of business — university collaboration.* Department for Business, Innovation and Skills. London: HMSO.

Wintrup, J., James, E., & Humphris, D. (2012a). Beyond inequality? A case study of progression, achievements and experiences of health and care workers in higher education, 2005–2011. *Journal of Widening Participation and Lifelong Learning, 14*(3), 172–189.

Wintrup, J., James, E., Humphris, D., & Bryson, C. (2012b). Emotional work: Students realising, negotiating and overcoming barriers. *Journal of Applied Research in Higher Education, 4*(2), 170–185.

Wolf, A. (2011). *Review of vocational education — The Wolf report.* Department for Education. London: HMSO.

Yorke, M. (2005). Firming the foundations: An empirical and theoretical appraisal of the Foundation degree in England. *Journal of Widening Participation and Lifelong Learning, 7*(1), 13–21.

Chapter 13

Student Engagement Through Volunteering

Lorraine McIlrath and Lorraine Tansey

Abstract

The purpose of this chapter is to provide an overview and context, from theoretical and practical dimensions, the purpose and place of student volunteering within higher education drawing from evolving policy and practice within Ireland. While the research literature presented within the chapter is international in orientation, the practical case studies emanate from Ireland where there has been a most recent focus on the role that volunteering can play within the area of student engagement. Typically student volunteering activities have been overlooked from an educational perspective, but in recent years attempts have been made by higher education institutions to recognise and reward volunteering undertaken by students. This chapter casts a light on the variety and diversity of models that exist within the Irish context and are used to interrogate the concept of volunteering as derived from the theory.

13.1. Introduction

Universities are both apart from and a part of society. They are apart in the sense that they provide a critically important space for grasping the world as it is and — importantly — for re-imagining the world as it ought to be. The academic freedom to pursue the truth and let the chips fall where they may isn't a luxury — in fact it is a vital necessity in any society that has the capability for self-renewal. But universities are also a part of our societies. What's the point unless the accumulated knowledge, insight and vision are put at the service of the community? With the privilege to pursue knowledge comes the civic responsibility to engage and put that knowledge to work in the service of humanity. (Higgins, 2012)

The Student Engagement Handbook: Practice in Higher Education
Copyright © 2013 by Emerald Group Publishing Limited
All rights of reproduction in any form reserved
ISBN: 978-1-78190-423-7

As well articulated by the President of Ireland, Michael D. Higgins, universities or higher education institutions (HEIs) form an integral part of society and provide a space for both 'grasping' and 're-imagining' the world. Student volunteering is just one space and manifestation where this can happen. Volunteering when embedded as a core activity within the life of any campus can provide students with interconnections to real-world problems, issues and communities that would otherwise not be part of the normative student experience. Internationally, student-led volunteering has had a long and rich historical tradition through a range of diverse activities; these constitute, to mention just a few, student-led clubs and societies, human and civil rights campaigns, manning of soup kitchens, homework club support and the management of student newspapers and radio stations. Typically student volunteering activities have been overlooked from an educational perspective, but in recent years attempts have been made by HEIs to recognise and reward volunteering undertaken by students.

This chapter will offer a case study of a pioneering student volunteering programme at the National University of Ireland, Galway, now in its tenth year, namely the ALIVE Volunteer Programme. Practical and operational considerations of the programme will be outlined including the structure, practices and development. In addition, an exploration of five other national initiatives to support student volunteering within higher education in Ireland will be presented. A brief literature review will highlight student volunteer motivations, experiences, demographics and impacts. The future of student volunteering in Ireland will be discussed and will offer the challenges in engaging student as volunteers in meaningful opportunities and mechanisms to support volunteer learning that emanates from community experiences.

As Watson (2007) posits, the contemporary university is expected to have many contradictory roles simultaneously — competitive and collegial; traditional and innovative; autonomous and accountable; local and international; and also independent and engaged. But it is the concept of engagement that is dominating the higher education landscape in Ireland since the collapse of the economic boom, coined the Celtic Tiger, and the rise of a severe and hard-hitting recession. The recently published *National Strategy for Higher Education to 2030* places engagement on an equal footing alongside research, teaching and learning. This review (or what it is commonly known as the Hunt Report) seeks to tackle the higher education system and landscape and to transform it to one that is most cost-efficient and effective in terms of delivery and cohesion. The Hunt Report states:

> Engagement by higher education with wider society takes many forms. It includes engagement with business and industry, with the civic life of the community, with public policy and practice, with artistic, cultural and sporting life and with other educational providers in the community and region, and it includes an increasing emphasis on international engagement. (Higher Education Strategy Group, 2011, p. 74)

Engagement as a core priority for higher education is a multifaceted concept and it springs from the responsibility of higher education to contribute to the socioeconomic and cultural well-being of community and society. Engagement is deliberative and intentional and it places higher education firmly within a wider context. It has the potential to formalise a culture of responsibility from social, economic, cultural and political roots within higher education. Internationally and nationally, the experience of engagement within higher education has evidenced transformative benefits to the students, the institution and the wider society. It is here, within this broader concept of engagement, that we situate student volunteering as one crucial and practical component. Student engagement through volunteering has the potential to bring both the HEI and the community closer together; to develop an ethos of civic engagement and social responsibility; and to imbue in the student and graduate populations a lifelong commitment to community, engagement and volunteering.

However, we do know in Ireland that student volunteering as a recognised and supported activity within higher education is fragile. In fact, it is not even mentioned within the Hunt Report as a manifestation of engagement. This represents an oversight, in our shared opinion, especially given the historical tradition of student volunteering in Ireland. A major national survey undertaken in 2010 by the Irish national civic engagement platform, Campus Engage, sought to attain a baseline of civic engagement activities and practice within the context of higher education in Ireland. It represented the 'first time that a survey of this nature has been carried out in Ireland' and it was 'an initial attempt to map the range of civic engagement activities across Irish higher education. It has happened at a time when civic engagement in higher education is in its early stages of development' (2011, p. 6). Civic engagement was defined by this survey as a:

> mutually beneficial knowledge-based collaboration between the higher education institution, its staff and students, with the wider community, through community-campus partnerships and including the activities of Service Learning/Community Based Learning, Community Engaged Research, Volunteering, Community/Economic Regeneration, Capacity-Building and Access/Widening Participation. (Lyons & McIlrath, 2011, p. 6)

The following was gleaned from the survey in terms of student volunteering.

- All participating HEIs in the survey, 24 in total, acknowledged that their institution placed some value on student volunteering from moderate to substantial.
- Just two HEIs, however, reported on the existence of dedicated staff to oversee and organise this activity.
- At other institutions, where posts included a remit for volunteering, 'those responsible are commonly cited as Chaplains, Student Services personnel and Clubs and Societies Officers' (2011, p. 8).

- Seven HEIs reported on the annual hosting of volunteering fairs but all commented that data 'on volunteering is difficult to find and is not usually collected at the individual HEI level' (2011, p. 8), representing a missed opportunity to delve into both the positive and negative ramifications of student volunteering from the HEI perspective.

13.2.   Defining Volunteering and Student Volunteering

While volunteering is a normative word in our daily dialogue, it is rare that we interrogate and define the practice drawing from the literature. Volunteering can be defined as any activity in which time is given freely to benefit another person, group, or cause, outside of one's immediate family (Wilson, 2000). The location in which the activity takes place is distinguished in the literature, with some authors referring to formal volunteering through an organisation being distinct from informal volunteering that organically occurs through human social interaction (Rochester, 2006). For example, formal volunteering takes place within a structured setting like a school, hospital, NGO, charity or community organisation. Informal volunteering includes visiting an elderly neighbour or helping individuals to find their way in a new place, all occurring outside of a formal group. When applying the location distinction within the context of higher education, student volunteering is defined by service to others in either the academic community or service to others outside the campus walls within the local community (Reilly & Odds, 2003). Student volunteering is a niche aspect of voluntary activity and often referred to as community service, extracurricular activity, co-curricular activity or civic engagement.

The inconsistency in language defining volunteering can cloud understanding as each term can have different meanings, depending on the intention regarding its use. Longo & Meyer (2006) call for greater research into the connections and distinctions between political action and community service. Picking up on a close complementary relationship that volunteering and activism share, Rochester (2006) notes civic participation is often distinguished as a separate entity from formal volunteering in the literature. For example, Rochester includes activism, voting and protesting in his definition of volunteering. He goes on to explore the boundaries between volunteering and leisure activity, formulating a tool to navigate definitions of volunteering in the scholarly literature through three elements: remuneration, free choice versus coercion, and formal versus informal volunteering.

Without narrowly defining student volunteering, it is useful to distinguish between volunteering and service learning (or also called community-based learning, as described in detail by Martin and O'Mahony in Chapter 5 of this volume). Service learning can be described as a pedagogy that:

> … promotes student attainment of knowledge, values, skills, and attitudes associated with civic engagement through a structured academic experience within the community. It aims to bring reciprocal benefits

to both the student and the community partner, and the sharing of knowledge across community-university boundaries. (McIlrath, 2012, p. 139)

Importantly it is a:

credit-bearing educational experience in which students participate in an organized service activity that meets identified community needs and reflect on the service activity in such a way as to gain further understanding of the course content, a broader appreciation of the discipline, and an enhanced sense of civic responsibility. (Bringle & Hatcher 1996, p. 222)

As a curricular activity, the time a student spends in the community and the learning acquired in this context is rewarded with academic credit. Winniford, Carpenter, and Grider (1997) note the use of language in the literature as vague and general; for example service learning and volunteering are often used interchangeably.

13.3.   Student Volunteering and the Literature

The literature on student volunteering covers three main aspects including demographics, experiences and impact measurement. Demographic research seeks to measure and quantify how many students engage as volunteers. It also seeks to identify trends in socio-economic backgrounds, ethnicity, gender, geographical location and family history. This research varies from large-scale surveys to smaller institutional comparisons. Holdsworth's (2010) national profile of student volunteering in the United Kingdom, with over 33,000 respondents, correlates the rates of volunteering with demographics, the type of HEI, the subjects studied and whether students worked part-time. The findings revealed students with a caring responsibility were more likely to volunteer, over 22 per cent (22.2 per cent) of students with a disability were actively volunteering, and students studying medicine and dentistry reported the highest volunteering rates.

Demographic research often attempts to predict trends in participation. According to Acheson, Harvey, Kearney, and Williamson (2004), there is a danger that as society becomes more 'atomized, fragmented and individualized,' volunteering will decline (p. 196). A feared decline in student volunteering and a suspected rise in student apathy have driven researchers to gather systematic data (Putnam, 1995). Recent US data is drawn from the Census Current Population Survey and provides analysis of volunteering rates for teenagers and young adults, by state, from 2002 through to 2009 (Kirby, Marcelo, & Kawashima-Ginsberg, 2010). According to this study, the national rate of volunteering for 19- to 24-year-olds increased by one percentage point between 2002 and 2009 to 19 per cent. Overall there are no definitive findings indicating macro trends as there is a lack of consistent data collection at large-scale levels.

The literature on student volunteering provides the context with demographics and then seeks to examine the experiences students' encounter looking at the overall practice of being a volunteer from beginning to end. The beginning is marked by the routes into volunteering travelled by the young person, attitudes to volunteering, their preconceptions, impressions, or images of volunteering, and the barriers they encounter in attempting to volunteer (Ellis, 2004). Gaskin's *Vanishing Volunteers* (1998) investigates whether young people aged 16–24 are losing interest in volunteering and finds a number of benefits of engaging and a number of barriers to involvement, including lack of time, lack of information and lack of 'gatekeepers' as entry points into volunteering. Winniford et al. (1997) called for empirical research on traits and motivations of higher education student volunteers involved in service, while Sergent and Sedlacek (1990) indicate that a better understanding of the characteristics and motivations of higher education students who volunteer can aid efforts to design programmes that will recruit and retain successful volunteers. They argue that programmes are best facilitated when there is a clear understanding of what motivates students to volunteer.

The period of time young people spend volunteering is briefly examined in relation to the organisational structures, retention, incentives and rewards. Descriptions of experiences of student volunteers are not found specifically in the literature. There is a gap in understanding whether a link exists between where a student volunteering programme is situated within the HEI and the student–community relationship and experience. The literature related to student volunteering in particular is difficult to find, with much of the literature coming from the psychological perspective, examining the impact of service on the server (Hodgkinson, 2004). From the United States, Astin and Sax's (1998) study examines the effect of community service participation on undergraduate student development. 3,500 students attending 42 institutions participated in the survey. The results demonstrate that participating in service activities during the undergraduate years substantially enhances a student's academic development, life skill development and sense of civic responsibility.

Astin, Sax and Avalos (1999) found that community service had received relatively little attention in student development research. Their longitudinal study examined whether service participation during the undergraduate years has any lasting effects on students once they leave higher education. The study indicates that undergraduate volunteer participation affects students' educational outcomes, such as attendance at graduate school and the acquisition of higher degrees and the student's perception of how well the undergraduate higher education prepared the student for work. Eley's (2003) longitudinal study of a volunteering programme in the United Kingdom that aimed to increase the citizenship potential of students included an investigation of students' perceptions of volunteering and citizenship. Findings indicated that students see volunteering as both an activity that can be used to their own advantage, but also as a means of displaying concern for others. The respondents appear to have gained an understanding of several qualities associated with citizenship through their volunteer experience.

Through three UK-based case studies, De Souza (2005) examined the role of higher education in developing sports volunteers. The research produced data on the number of volunteers supporting sport in higher education, and an analysis of characteristics and motivations of volunteers. The study analysed the impact of student volunteering on the local community, indicating that student volunteers played important roles in addressing gaps in local sports provision, with students playing a significant role in developing sport in their local communities. Russell (2005) recommends that all HEI should have a volunteering ethos. While Astin et al.'s (1999) study suggests that there may be considerable institutional self-interest in encouraging more students to participate in service-related activities, as it has been shown that undergraduate service participation increased the likelihood that the student will donate money to their alma mater. It is clear that additional research is needed to address the gaps that exist within the literature. A number of research avenues are identified in the literature, most notably the impact of higher education initiatives on community organisations and the sense of civic responsibility in student volunteers.

13.4. National University of Ireland, Galway and the Alive Volunteer Programme

Over a decade ago, the National University of Ireland, Galway established a formal volunteering programme through the Community Knowledge Initiative (CKI). The CKI aims to foster a sense of social responsibility and civic engagement among the student to graduate populations through a range of pathways that connect students to community. The CKI was funded originally by a range of philanthropic bodies in 2001 including a major donation from the Atlantic Philanthropies. The ALIVE programme is the CKI's volunteering pathway and since its creation over 7000 students have successfully undertaken the programme and have been awarded the ALIVE certificate. ALIVE within the context of Ireland was the first formal volunteer programme to be adopted and embedded within an HEI, and it is considered a pioneering programme that has served as a national exemplar to which other institutions have looked to for advice and support in terms of developing other models (Tansey, 2012).

The number of students participating in the ALIVE programme has grown significantly each year from its inception. The growth of the programme can be attributed to the following; including the all-encompassing definition of volunteering adopted by the programme (which includes both on-campus and off-campus volunteering); student vision and partnership in terms of design and delivery; the loose structure and ability to dip in and out of volunteering during the academic year; the university's commitment to developing an ethos and practice of civic engagement makes volunteering normative to the NUI Galway experience, and the natural interest the student population has in getting involved in community volunteering. Volunteering activity has thrived on campus through student-led initiatives and structures, including through domains such as the NUI Galway Students Union, Student Societies, Sports Clubs, student radio (Flirt FM), newspaper (*Sin*) and student mentoring programme. With the advent of ALIVE at NUI Galway, students were provided with a new and innovative opportunity to easily connect and volunteer with the wider community and voluntary sector — through not-for-profit, non-governmental organisations (NGOs), schools, youth clubs and hospital programmes. Over 300 community organisations partner the ALIVE programme and enable the student volunteers to act as bridge-builders between the university and civil society. Student volunteers give as much or as little time as they can, and attend the optional training if they need support. The student experience is of paramount importance to the ALIVE programme. Barriers to engagement are tackled, a clear route to engagement is extensively promoted, and students are rewarded and recognised for their contribution. ALIVE seeks to facilitate a positive student volunteering experience through an integrated programme that includes the following dimensions.

13.4.1. A Volunteer Opportunities Website and Database

The ALIVE programme runs a website that allows community organisations to post volunteer opportunities online and for students to register their interest. The volunteer opportunities on offer span a wide and diverse spectrum and include schools having NUI Galway students act as mentors in local homework clubs; managing promotional events; building websites for health promotion organisations; raising awareness and funds for people with disabilities; and providing friendship to children including refugees, asylum seekers and the new communities of Ireland. Students can search for volunteer opportunities under categories including social justice, disability, older people, and young people or via a calendar of opportunities organised by day and time, or via a map offering geographical breakdown of opportunities, or they can create their own opportunities and bring community activities to the campus. NUI Galway's proximity to Galway City has been an added bonus for the ALIVE programme, as students live throughout the city and can volunteer directly within their neighbourhoods.

13.4.2. A Series of Volunteer Training Workshops

The training is designed to harness students' energy and enthusiasm and provide avenues to, and information on, local, national, and international volunteer opportunities. Workshops cover child protection and safety, volunteer code of behaviour, volunteer skills including first aid, sign language and guidelines for international volunteering. These sessions are important gatherings for peer support and socialisation for volunteers.

13.4.3. Alive Leaders

In the last 2 years students can deepen their volunteering experience and become ALIVE leaders in the community through volunteer management training. ALIVE leaders are usually students who have volunteered extensively and undertake a liaison role to recruit volunteers on behalf of the community organisations, co-facilitate volunteer inductions, support volunteer queries and help recognise their fellow students' volunteer commitment.

13.4.4. *Recognition Through the NUI Galway Alive Certificate*

Students who engage as volunteers throughout the academic year may apply online for the ALIVE certificate, awarded by the President of NUI Galway in recognition of their contribution. This is a certificate of participation, and to receive this award each student volunteer must undertake the completion of a reflection component through an online log and journal that is overseen ad verified by the ALIVE executive committee.

13.5. National Examples

Over the last decade in Ireland, there has been a surge in the growth of volunteering programmes and activities within higher education. Recognition of student volunteers within each programme is a constant with the method varying. Furthermore, student volunteering has evolved to be situated in a variety of spaces within campus structures. Therefore the space student volunteering occupies on each campus is noteworthy for its influence on the development of the programme. For example, the ALIVE volunteer programme is based at the Centre for Excellence in Learning and Teaching (CELT) and as a result has close ties with academic staff and programmes, including an input in the CELT Master of Arts (MA) in Teaching and Learning in Higher Education. The following represents four other student volunteer programmes and a national collaborative initiative that have evolved from Trinity College Dublin, Limerick Institute of Technology, University of Limerick, and University College Dublin and through the existence of Campus Engage. The location of each programme within their respective institution reveals the varying emphasis, including student engagement through student-led societies and student government; widening participation in student engagement with enhancing experience opportunities for students of traditionally marginalised groups; and encouraging engagement within the student experience domain through a student affairs or student services focus.

13.5.1. *Trinity College Dublin (TCD) — Dean of Student's Honour Roll*

Trinity College Dublin (TCD) boasts a long tradition of outreach and community engagement. TCD is connected with society in manifold ways including research and teaching partnerships, staff and student voluntary activity, and dedicated programmes to ensure access to education. This allows members of the College to give back to the community, but it also give students and staff added insight into societal structures, issues and problems. In 2010 TCD established the Dean of Student's Honour Roll to celebrate and recognise student volunteering in clubs, societies and the wider community. To date the programme has recognised the volunteering contribution of over 300 students. The programme is coordinated by the TCD Civic Engagement Officer, student volunteer efforts are celebrated annually through an awards ceremony hosted on campus.

In 2012 the Minister for Children and Youth Affairs, Ms. Frances Fitzgerald T.D., addressed the honourees at the ceremony and stated:

> The level of commitment shown by you over the course of the year in addition to your studies and other commitments is a truly impressive achievement and one of which you should be immensely proud, just as you should be proud of the positive impact that you have had on your communities. The individual decisions that you have made in giving your time and skills are really decisions to participate in the future of your communities and are the essence and foundation of democracy.

Training and support is offered to the students on a range of volunteering dimensions that enable them to prepare for the volunteer activity including international volunteering and working as tutors with children.

There are a number of criteria that students must adhere to for inclusion on the Dean of Students' Roll of Honour including:

- dedication of a minimum of 20 hours to any one form of extra-curricular voluntary activity within the 12 months prior to the application deadline;
- only participation in activities that entail some elements of organisation and/or delivery of the activity in question to be taken into account (e.g. volunteering as a scout leader, student journalist or (sub)committee member of a college club or society);
- verification of the commitment of hours by the club, society or organisation with whom the activity took place;
- completion of the online reflective application form through which students articulate their objectives and expectations of the activity and also any learning derived from the activity.

The Dean of Students' Roll of Honour is based at TCD's Careers Advisory Service exhibiting an emphasis on skill and professional development.[1]

13.5.2.   *Limerick Institute of Technology (LIT) — GIVE (Guided Initiative in Voluntary Engagement)*

The GIVE (Guided Initiative in Voluntary Engagement) programme was developed during the 2007/2008 academic year by the Limerick Institute of Technology's Access Service in association with the President's Office. The GIVE programme

---

[1] For further information on the TCD Dean of Student's Roll of Honour access www.tcd.ie/Community/.

encourages students to engage in voluntary activities under the guidance of the Access Service. In return, the Access Service commits to providing training for volunteers and to assisting them in developing their skills in leadership and communication. Volunteers also learn how to transfer their skills and knowledge in a manner that will benefit the wider community. The GIVE programme benefits both the community and the volunteers by combining a service experience with a learning and development experience. LIT hosts a volunteer fair at the start of each academic year in October/November.

LIT is committed to promoting equitable access to and successful participation in higher education for all members of society. The LIT access agenda flows from a philosophy of integration and social inclusiveness. The aim of the service is to support the Institute's widening access commitment for underrepresented students by delivering targeted strategies to promote and facilitate entry to and successful participation in higher education. These student groups include students who experience socio-economic disadvantage, disability and/or specific learning difficulty, mature students, travellers and ethnic minority students.

The LIT Access Service recognises that students can play a pivotal role in the success of pre-entry and post-entry activities. The GIVE programme is a vital part of this, enabling students to engage with the wider community and participate positively in widening participation from underrepresented groups. GIVE volunteers actively inspire and assist underrepresented groups to experience the benefits of education and lifelong learning. Through contributing to the development of others, GIVE volunteers themselves gain new skills and experiences.

Training is an important dimension of the GIVE programme enabling each volunteer to reach their full potential, as well as gain new skills and experiences. All GIVE volunteers engage in both initial and on-going training and support enhancing knowledge, skills and confidence. Training sessions are run throughout the year and there is also the ability to request additional training in areas which individual volunteers feel would benefit them in their volunteering role.

The President's Commendation is a prestigious, tiered commendation scheme that formally recognises each GIVE volunteer's contribution to the programme based on the number of hours and years each has committed. It has been designed to encourage volunteers to continue to participate in the GIVE programme from year to year and rewards that commitment by escalating the level of the commendation at the end of each year. Bronze Award for 20 hours of activity; Silver Award for 20 + hours and Gold Award can be attained following attainment of the Silver Award and an additional 20 + hours of volunteering.[2]

13.5.3.   University College Dublin (UCD) — Volunteers Overseas

Ten years ago, University College Dublin (UCD) established the Volunteer Overseas (UCDVO) programme that recruits on average 110 student volunteers

---

[2]For further information on the LIT GIVE programme access www.lit.ie/access/give.

each academic year. UCDVO was established in 2003 by the former UCD Chaplain in response to a demand among student body to volunteer abroad. Since its creation UCDVO has extended its activities to work in India (Delhi and Andhra Pradesh), Haiti, Nicaragua and Tanzania and now employs a full-time manager. Seven hundred volunteers have volunteered in a range of activities such as environmental, educational, healthcare, construction and computer training projects in disadvantaged communities. The student volunteers are awarded with certificate of participation by the UCD Vice-President for Students. UCDVO's mission is to provide UCD students, staff and alumni with opportunities to volunteer for the benefit of disadvantaged communities overseas, in response to needs explicitly identified by those communities. The majority of volunteers are undergraduate students, but UCD staff and alumni have also volunteered. While project time overseas is typically for 1 month in June/July, volunteers undertake a pre- and post-placement training programme which spans an 11 month period from volunteer selection in November to debriefing the following September. The training programme covers topics such as the millennium development goals, intercultural learning, ethical volunteering, health and safety, and practical skills training for awareness raising and campaigns. The UCDVO Student Society is an active group of returned volunteers whose role is to engage students in raising awareness of development issues, carry out fundraising activities and promote opportunities for students to volunteer on development projects overseas.

UCD Volunteers Overseas was established by the Chaplaincy campus and is now situated within UCD International with strong student society links.[3]

13.5.4. *University of Limerick (UL) — President's Volunteer Award (PVA)*

Established in 2010 by the University of Limerick (UL), 83 students were the first recipients in October 2011 to attain the PVA and followed by 130 in the second year (2011−2012).

The aim of the PVA programme is to promote and sustain students' commitment to volunteering and deliver on the goals of the UL's strategic plan.

There are three levels of the award including Bronze for 20 + hours commitment to volunteering during an academic year; Silver for 40 + hours; Gold for 60 + hours. For the short-term student, the Plassey Award for 12 + hours commitment to volunteering in a semester has been designed for Erasmus, study abroad and international students. In addition, a special category of Outstanding Award is given to students showing an outstanding commitment to volunteering.

Students are required to submit a signed hourly log of their volunteer hours (log must be signed by volunteer supervisor in the organisation the student volunteers with) and students must also complete a reflective qualitative portfolio. The portfolio is designed to ensure students reflect on their volunteer practice, learning and the

---

[3]For further information on the UCDVO programme access www.ucdvo.org.

impact their work and commitment had on the organisations. The portfolio also directs student to reflect on the organisations, its aims and objectives, the services it offers and the users of their services.

PVA ambassadors (student volunteers) promote volunteering throughout the year. In addition seminars and workshops are delivered throughout the year with a view to explaining volunteering and what's involved, supported and encouraging students to design and create their own volunteering opportunity. Guest speakers from local and national organisations are invited in to UL to speak to students about their volunteering potential and the relationship between employability and volunteering. Each semester a portfolio writing workshop is provided for volunteer students.

The Community Liaison Office (CLO) at the UL coordinates the PVA. The CLO works closely with a range of statutory and non-statutory agencies and organisations across the city. The CLO collaborates with Limerick Volunteering and Paul Partnership in a city and county-wide volunteer fair. In addition the CLO takes part in UL's Annual Careers Fair. The PVA works very closely with Limerick Volunteering and through this relationship Limerick Volunteering has established a student section on their database. Limerick Volunteering database is linked to a national volunteer database and this enables students to apply for volunteering opportunities in their home town.[4]

13.5.5.   'We Volunteer!' 2011 European Union Year of the Volunteer and Campus Engage

The European Commission designated 2011 as the European Union Year of the Volunteer and in 2010 a group of committed higher education staff, community organisation representatives and students came together with support from Campus Engage to develop 'We Volunteer!'

'We Volunteer!' is a physical and virtual photographic exhibition of student volunteering in HEIs across the island of Ireland. Launched in Ireland's National Library in January 2011, the printed photographic exhibition toured HEIs nationwide as well as key conferences, events and in addition a number of European Union locations. The exhibition of student volunteering recognises the extent and diversity of student commitment to communities with diverse organisations ranging from the Christina Noble Foundation in Vietnam to Chrysalis Community Drug Project in Dublin; from the Galway Society for the Prevention of Cruelty to Animals to community enterprise in Belfast; from peer mentoring programmes in Limerick and Cork to Karate coaching in Newry.

The exhibition showcased the work of 20 student volunteers from 20 HEIs across the island of Ireland. In addition an online exhibition enables other student

---

[4]UL's PVA is based within the Student Services. For further information on the UL PVA access www.ulpva.ie.

volunteers to post up their volunteering stories and photos providing a platform to share experiences. Communities, groups and organisations encouraged their student volunteers to add their story and build awareness of the vital work done across Ireland and beyond. Featured online stories include volunteering with the HOPE Foundation, the Bridge Complex, Outreach Moldova, Haven Partnership, St. Vincent de Paul, Operation Smile and Camara, to mention a few.

'We Volunteer!' aimed to celebrate, acknowledge and recognise the contribution of student volunteers; generate a shared connection for student volunteers across Ireland and Europe; and provide an impetus for others to investigate voluntary opportunities and take up the challenge.[5]

13.6.   Conclusion and the Future

Nationally in Ireland, student volunteer programmes will continue to be fragile until deeply embedded within the campus structures, represented in HEI's strategic plans and regarded as central to the engagement agenda. This fragility is borne out by the Campus Engage survey (2011) where 75 per cent of respondents found a moderate or strong acknowledgement of community engagement in their institutions, but far fewer found that it was embedded in terms of management structures and recognition through promotion and other mechanisms. There is considerable unrealised potential for academic community partnerships through volunteering to contribute to the long-term community university engagement.

Those HEIs who have a volunteer programme have chosen to situate these activities in diverse areas including centres for teaching and learning (as is the case with the ALIVE volunteer programme), career development centres (as is the case for Trinity College Dublin), student services, student unions, access offices (e.g. the GIVE programme at Limerick Institute of Technology) and in partnership with local community organisations or volunteer centres. Although this flexibility allows for many advantages, it remains a challenge at the national level to advocate for policy development and to facilitate networking towards the discussion and dissemination of information and issues of importance to student volunteering. With a growth in dedicated staff posts, HEIs will strengthen commitment to civic engagement through student volunteering. In addition, technology is increasingly important for enabling a successful student volunteering programmes and perhaps unexploited in light of working with those who are digitally native, that being the typical or normative undergraduate student. Student volunteers, through an online social platform, will be able to share their volunteering experiences, and organisations will be able to track and mange their volunteers. With greater use of technology measuring student volunteering will be easier, as statistics can be grown at individual HEIs and feature in the national picture of the student experience.

---

[5]For further information and to view the physical and online exhibition access www. wevolunteer.ie.

Irish HEIs are responding to President Higgins' call to service through models of student volunteering as demonstrated through the case studies offered. Indeed, despite the lack of policy support it has begun to emerge as a distinct practical manifestation of university community engagement. Finally as the literature indicates the opportunities for research and measurement of student volunteering are a plentiful and urgent addition to the civic engagement agenda; however there is need for more theoretical and practical work but the terrain is rich and ready.

References

Acheson, N., Harvey, B., Kearney, J., & Williamson, A. (2004). *Two paths, one purpose: Voluntary action in Ireland, North and South.* Dublin: Institute of Public Administration.

Astin, A. W., & Sax, L. J. (1998). How undergraduates are affected by service participation. *Journal of College Student Development, 39*(3), 251–263.

Astin, A. W., Sax, L. J., & Avalos, J. (1999). Long-term effects of volunteerism during the undergraduate years. *The Review of Higher Education, 22*(2), 187–202.

Bringle, R. G., & Hatcher, J. A. (1996). Implementing service learning in higher education. *Journal of Higher Education, 67*(2), 221–239.

De Souza, T. (2005). The role of higher education in the development of sports volunteers. *Voluntary Action, 7*(1), 81–98.

Eley, D. (2003). Perceptions of and reflections on volunteering: The impact of community service on citizenship in students. *Voluntary Action, 5*(3), 27.

Ellis, A. (2004). *Generation V: Young people speak out on volunteering.* Institute for Volunteering Research, London.

Gaskin, K. (1998). Vanishing volunteers: Are young people losing interest in volunteering? *Voluntary Action Journal 1* (1), 33–44.

Higgins, M. D. (2012). *Remarks by President Michael D. Higgins at the launch of the Irish Centre for Autism and Neurodevelopmental Research.* Retrieved from http://www.president. ie/speeches/launch-of-the-irish-centre-for-autism-and-neurodevelopmental-research/

Higher Education Strategy Group. (2011). *National strategy for higher education to 2030.* Dublin: Department of Education and Skills.

Hodgkinson, V. A. (2004). Developing a research agenda on civic service. *Nonprofit and Voluntary Sector Quarterly Supplement, 33*(4), 191.

Holdsworth, C. (2010). *Student volunteers: A national profile.* London: Volunteering England and the Institute for Volunteering Research.

Kirby, E. H., Marcelo, K. B., & Kawashima-Ginsberg, K. (2010). *Volunteering and college experience.* Medford: CIRCLE (The Center for Information and Research on Civic Learning and Engagement). Retrieved from http://www.civicyouth.org

Longo, N. V., & Meyer, R. P. (2006). *College students and politics: A literature review.* Medford: CIRCLE (The Center for Information and Research on Civic Learning and Engagement). Retrieved from http://www.civicyouth.org

Lyons, A., & McIlrath, L. (2011). *Survey of civic engagement activities in higher education in Ireland.* Galway: Campus Engage.

McIlrath, L. (2012). Community perspective on university partnership — prodding the sacred cow. In L. McIlrath, A. Lyons & R. Munck (Eds.), *Higher education and civic engagement — comparative perspectives.* New York, NY: Palgrave Macmillan.

Putnam, R. (1995). *Bowling alone: The collapse and revival of American community*. New York, NY: Simon and Schuster.

Reilly, C., & Odds, J. (2003). *Student volunteering Scotland: A catalyst for change*. Volunteer Scotland: Stirling.

Rochester, C. (2006). *Making sense of volunteering: A literature review*. London: The Commission on the Future of Volunteering. Roehampton University.

Russell, I. M. (2005). *A national framework for youth action and engagement: Report of the Russell Commission*. London: Stationary Office.

Sergent, M. T., & Sedlacek, W. E. (1990). Volunteer motivations across student organizations: A test of person-environment fit theory. *Journal of College Student Development*, *31*, 255.

Tansey, L. (2012). Volunteering within higher education — a literature exploration and case study. In L. McIlrath, A. Lyons & R. Munck (Eds.), *Higher education and civic engagement — Comparative perspectives*. New York, NY: Palgrave Macmillan.

Watson, D. (2007). *Managing civic and community engagement*. Berkshire: Open University Press.

Wilson, J. (2000). Volunteering. *Annual Review of Sociology*, *26*, 215–240.

Winniford, J. C., Carpenter, D. S., & Grider, C. (1997). Motivations of college student volunteers: A review. *NASPA (Student Affairs Administrators in Higher Education) Journal*, *34* (2), 135–147.

Chapter 14

'Giving to Sport': Community Engagement Within and Beyond the Curriculum

Lucy Spowart and Mike Tripp

Abstract

It is generally accepted that student engagement in the community can enhance student learning and increase future employment prospects. Community engagement can also provide an opportunity for students to be educated about their rights and responsibilities for the communities in which they live (Eley & Kirk, 2002), a theme very much at the heart of the UK government agenda. This chapter outlines two community projects that students from the University College Plymouth St Mark and St John (UCP Marjon) engage with. We employ a case study approach, with the aim of capturing the lived experiences of those involved in two community-facing initiatives. We draw on data collected via semi-structured in-depth telephone interviews, semi-structured questionnaires and email correspondence with academics, administrators of the community projects, community providers and students.

Students' motivations to participate were largely personal, and they regarded both community initiatives as vehicles to gain confidence and competence in a range of work-related skills. This throws into question normalised assumptions about the social justice benefits of volunteering promoted by agencies such as the Higher Education Funding Council.

14.1. Introduction

This chapter recounts the story of two community projects undertaken by students at the University College Plymouth St Mark and St John, in the South West of England. Both case studies illustrate an 'authentic' approach to learning that

The Student Engagement Handbook: Practice in Higher Education
Copyright © 2013 by Emerald Group Publishing Limited
All rights of reproduction in any form reserved
ISBN: 978-1-78190-423-7

involves students working on projects that are situated and enacted in 'real world' contexts, and that include student-directed tasks. That said, they also illustrate two contrasting approaches to community engagement through service-learning. For the purposes of this chapter, community engagement is defined as a two-way interaction in which an educational institution, through its staff and students, forms a relationship with a community that has mutual benefits, as well as building community capacity (Holland, 2001).

Drawing on the experiences of those that manage the initiatives, as well as the experiences of students and academics involved, we explore the strengths and weaknesses of the two approaches to community engagement. While our focus is largely on students studying sports-related subjects, we hope that our findings will have relevance to many other disciplines.

The first example, the West Devon Tag Rugby Festival, sits *outside*, but neatly *alongside* the formal curriculum, and offers students an opportunity to volunteer in an activity related to their programme of study. Participation in the organisation of this event is entirely optional, and students must apply to be involved through the institution's formalised application processes. The second example, that of The Special Olympics Plymouth and District, is entirely curriculum-based, and engagement in the placement activity is intrinsically underpinned by the academic work undertaken as part of the students' degree programme. Completion of this placement and associated assessments leads to credits towards the students' final degree classification.

We commence by outlining a brief history of community engagement in higher education, before outlining the development of the two initiatives. We then focus in on some of the experiences of students involved in the projects, and consider their personal reflective accounts. In the final section, we conclude by considering some of the critical factors for a curriculum-based community initiative to be successful.

14.2. History of Community Engagement

Community engagement in higher education is not a new concept. John Dewey (1916) is frequently cited as one of its pioneers, maintaining that experiential learning within the community could extend individuals far beyond the traditional educational boundaries of the classroom (VanWynsberghe & Andruske, 2007). Dewey believed in 'learning by doing', and consequently, he gave experience 'centre-stage' in his theory of learning and development. For Dewey, and other 20th century scholars who share this view (for example Kurt Lewin, Jean Piaget, William James, Paulo Freire and Carl Jung), rather than focusing on outcomes, 'learning is best conceived as a process' (Kolb & Kolb, 2005, p. 193).

According to Dewey, learners assimilate new experiences in relation to their existing knowledge, and subsequently use this information to construct new knowledge. Opportunities for students to engage with the community thus provide many, varied possibilities for students to build upon their existing knowledge base, to reinforce, to challenge or to question what they have learnt within the classroom. The learning that occurs cannot be neatly bounded by the curriculum, since what happens in real-life circumstances cannot always be pre-determined. As long as students have sufficient existing knowledge to cope within the workplace environment, this variation in circumstance helps them to develop their understandings.

As well as advocating experiential learning, Dewey also recognised the potential contributions students could make within their community. According to Dewey (1916, p. 122):

> Social efficiency as an educational purpose should mean cultivation of power to join freely and fully in shared or common activities. This is impossible without culture. One cannot share in intercourse with others without learning — without getting a broader point of view and perceiving things of which one would otherwise be ignorant.

It is easy to envisage how by affording opportunities for students to enter different community contexts, and to work with a variety of community groups, students can extend not only their own understandings of culture, but, in turn, influence the community that they work with. In so doing, there exists the possibility of transforming existing practices and beliefs.

In American universities, in particular, Dewey's emphasis on the promotion of citizenship among student bodies is deeply embedded, and most universities now incorporate community service into their mission statements. 'Campus Compact', an umbrella organisation of more than one thousand institutions, promotes community engagement, and, as a result, the concept of service-learning is commonplace. In America, service learning can be regarded as the formalisation of volunteering opportunities within the curriculum, and is defined as:

> a method under which students or participants learn and develop through active participation in thoughtfully organized service that is conducted in and meets the needs of a community; ... and helps foster civic responsibility ... (The Community Service Act of 1990)

Since 'service-learning' is an American term, there are some definitional difficulties with its use in a UK context. Even in America the term has been used to 'characterise a wide array of experiential endeavours, from volunteer and community service projects to field studies and internship programmes' (Furco, 2011, p. 71). As we have already hinted, the two case studies that we describe in this chapter do not both fit neatly with the concept of volunteering since for one of them, active engagement with the community is a requirement of passing the module. While definitions of volunteering are contested (Cnaan, Handy, & Wadsworth, 1996), common features include the notion of freely choosing to do an activity without compulsion; completing something without payment; and to be motivated by some aspect of altruism. Neither of the case studies include all these features. Nevertheless, as

Furco (2000) points out, any programme that engages with the community with the intention of equally benefiting the provider and the recipient of the service is quite distinct from many other forms of experiential education.

In the UK, the provision of service-learning in higher education (in its broadest sense) is far more fragmented, being 'concentrated in certain departments and with particular staff' (Holdsworth & Quinn, 2010, p. 116). That said, service learning modules have been extended across the curriculum over the past twenty years (Goodlad, 1982, cited in Holdsworth & Quinn, 2010), and there is now a common understanding of the multiple purposes of higher education. These multiple purposes include:

- preparation for the labour market
- preparation for life as active citizens in a democratic society
- personal development
- the development and maintenance of a broad, advanced knowledge base
  (The Bologna Working Group on Qualification Framework, 2005, p. 23).

As a consequence, there are a growing number of examples of community projects, which place curricular concepts in the context of real-life situations (see, e.g., Bednarz et al., 2008; Shah & Treby, 2006). Opportunities for students to volunteer have also increased, supported by funding from the Higher Education Active Community Fund (HEACF), and reflecting 'a wider cross-party political focus on the role of the voluntary sector' (Holdsworth & Quinn, 2010).

In the broad field of sports studies opportunities for students to engage with the wider community are commonplace. This may be attributed to the vocational nature of sports degrees, but is also owing to the sports industry's heavy reliance on volunteers. In the United Kingdom, as in many other countries, volunteers are an essential component of the efficient operation of many sports organisations (Doherty, 1998, 2005, 2006; Eley & Kirk, 2002; Zakus, Skinner, & Engelberg, 2012). This is the case for both non-profit and commercial sports organisations (Warner, Newland, & Green, 2011). Sports degrees thus commonly include modules that consider the significance of volunteers to the sports industry, and the sport degree programmes offered at UCP Marjon are no exception to this.

Offering students the opportunity to work within sports organisations thus gives them an insight into the significance of volunteers as an organisational resource. Understanding the motivations behind sports volunteering, and appreciating the importance of providing appropriate training, recognitions and rewards, is an essential component of sports management and sport development. In turn, this understanding is likely to improve students' employability prospects within the sports industry and beyond. In addition, Eley and Kirk (2002, p. 153) argue that 'early exposure to volunteering and helping activities is vital to creating a sense of citizenship and community in young people'.

While we firmly believe that there are many benefits to be gained by offering students opportunities to study projects that are situated in the community, we do not wish to proceed uncritically. As Holdsworth and Quinn (2012, p. 387) point out in their analysis of student volunteering:

> in England ... student volunteering has been increasingly promoted as a 'win/win' activity that automatically benefits the different communities involved: students, local communities and universities. As such, the student volunteer appears a bland and uncontroversial figure.

In a similar vein, we are conscious that we do not want to present our case studies of community engagement through rose-tinted glasses. In our experiences, as lecturers involved in linking students with community projects, there are also potentially negative consequences for all parties concerned that often remain undisclosed. Despite the normative assumptions about engaging students in 'real world' experiences, we were interested in whether community engagement is in fact good for everyone? Furthermore, does involvement in community-based projects necessarily lead to an increase in students' skills, and/or a sense of community identity? Finally, drawing on the two different approaches to community engagement we hoped to identify some key requisites for a successful community engagement experience.

14.3. Methodology

This chapter discusses data collected via semi-structured in-depth telephone interviews, semi-structured questionnaires and email correspondence with academics (3), administrators of the community projects (2), community providers (3) and students (10) with the aim of capturing the lived experiences and perceptions of those involved in the two community-facing initiatives. The students were given prompts such as 'Why did you choose to volunteer or undertake this module?'; 'How has this module/volunteer experience impacted upon you?' The student data were supplemented with interviews with staff involved in the projects. We also undertook a documentary analysis of the institution's strategic plan, and considered data from the students' module feedback forms as an additional way of knowing (Clegg, 2000).

As is frequently the case in research of this nature, the quality of the data varied considerably as, in some cases, we were reliant upon ex-students completing questionnaires via email. Nevertheless, a thematic analysis of the interview transcripts revealed a number of key themes. The work we are presenting here is a small-scale, exploratory study, nonetheless, the study is of value in considering the similarities and differences between the more bounded learning community (see Wilson, Ludwig-Hardman, Thornam, & Dunlap, 2004) of the second case study, compared to the more flexible approach of the Tag Rugby Festival's use of student volunteers.

It should be noted that the two authors have 'insider' knowledge, in that they were both sports lecturers within the University College Plymouth St Mark and St John, and have had varying degrees of involvement in the two case studies presented. Both authors were involved in data collection and analysis. Like *all* research, we acknowledge that this research is value-laden and culture-bound and as such can only ever be a partial (re)presentation, 'no more outside the power/knowledge nexus than any other human creation' (Lather, 1992, p. 91).

14.4.   Community Engagement at the University College St Mark and St John

The University College Plymouth St Mark and St John welcomes students with a wide range of qualifications and experience. The institution also has a particularly rich history in service-learning opportunities when compared with many higher education institutions in the United Kingdom, perhaps stemming from its origins as a teacher training institution. Training, professional practice, leadership and management are all considered to be strengths of the institution. The strong orientation towards community collaboration is evident from the organisation's mission statement 'to be a high quality higher education institution with a strong community focus serving local, regional, national and international markets and building on the University colleges (distinctive) Christian foundation' (University College Plymouth St. Mark and St. John, 2010, p. 2). The mission statement is further underpinned by seven key aims, including 'working creatively in partnership with people, employers and communities, contributing to their social, cultural and economic development through encouraging participation in University College activities …' (University College Plymouth St. Mark and St. John, 2010, p. 2).

The Faculty of Sport, Media Arts and Management in particular has always maintained good links with the community in which it is located, with staff playing active roles on local and regional sports advisory and coaching networks. In return, local employers have maintained good links with academic staff and welcome opportunities to sit on curriculum advisory panels. The BA Sports Development degree, for example, has a fully functioning Professional Advisory Group which has operated for the past two years. Discussions in this group have led to changes in the way the degree is structured, and an emphasis on employability now underpins the curriculum. Over recent years, there has also been a drive to build on the opportunities for students to volunteer, echoing the national trend (Prime Minister's Strategy Unit, 2007).

14.4.1.   Case Study One: West Devon Tag Rugby Festival

In 1991, the first ever Tag Rugby Festival for primary schools was held on the grounds of what is now known as University College Plymouth St Mark and St John (UCP Marjon) in west Devon and the University College has continued to organise the event; in 2012 the 21st West Devon Tag Rugby Festival took place.

For a number of years, the event held at UCP Marjon regularly involved well over 500 pupils from 72 primary schools, which was believed to be the largest Tag

Rugby festival in the country. The very complex nature of the event has meant that it has required not only very careful planning, but also the support of a large number of individuals in a variety of roles prior to and on the day of the festival. Over the past 21 years, many of these roles have been performed by students at UCP Marjon and, although their involvement has varied over the years, they have typically included such things as refereeing matches; liaising with the local press; sitting on the organising committee; liaising with Devon and Cornwall Police; chaperoning the teams (typically one student per school); acting as marshals; arranging sponsorship; acting as scorers; providing First Aid; and ensuring there are sufficient refreshments.

During the middle and late 1990s students on the BA Sport and Recreation Studies were heavily involved in the organisation and running of the Tag Rugby Festival via a sports event module. Staff who have been involved in overseeing students assisting with the festival regard opportunities such as this, for first-hand experience, as vital to enhancing the student experience, increasing employability prospects and promoting the degree courses to prospective students. As the event grew, the prior planning and organisation was well documented, and there were consequently limited creative planning opportunities for students. Job roles became standardised, and while the event still required volunteers on the day, primary schools involved wanted a set format that was familiar from one year to the next. The increasing numbers also meant that safety was paramount, and the event became increasingly 'professionalised'. Student involvement in the event no longer satisfied all of the learning outcomes of the event management module which requires students to initiate an event and demonstrate all aspects of event organisation.

In recent years, the Tag Rugby event links explicitly to the 'Give to Sport' Programme. 'Give to Sport' was launched in 2009 in order to extend the opportunities for work-related learning to a wider number of students as part of UCP Marjon's commitment to community engagement. The promotion of student volunteering opportunities through the 'Give to Sport' programme is premised on a number of key assumptions that echo HEFCE's position: that participants will actively contribute to community sports groups and will have the opportunity to inspire and transform others' lives; that students benefit by developing skills and improving their employability profile; and that the initiative will lead to an increase in the number of qualified and recognised individuals in sport.

The intention of the scheme is to make sports volunteering as straightforward as possible. Practically, the aims of 'Give to Sport' are achieved by recruiting members who 'sign up' via a website based form. Membership is free, and gives participants access to resources and information. These resources include a weekly e-newsletter alerting members to paid, voluntary and professional development opportunities. There are currently in excess of 600 members who are encouraged to work with a variety of different sports and groups. As one staff member puts it:

> How else can you gain experience of sport event management?
> Students need to experience having to plan sports events, to work to a

deadline, to deliver and to evaluate. No amount of research or class-room discussion really prepares them for the inevitable unforeseen occurrences, and the pressure of having to make decisions. They also benefit from working with a group of people, some of whom are fellow students, and some of whom are members of the community. Whilst this isn't always easy, there is usually a significant amount of learning that takes place.

Perhaps unsurprisingly, the development of student skills is clearly the priority for this academic, with no mention of the potential benefits to the community. It is also evident in this brief extract that despite supporting the principle of community engagement outcomes are not always positive.

Students from a variety of degree programmes have been recruited as volunteers to help with the West Devon Tag Rugby Festival, though, as one would expect, the majority tend to be sports students. Once volunteers have signed up for the festival, they are guided by a small organising committee consisting of UCP Marjon staff and representatives from partner organisations such as the local School Sport Partnership. While the format of the event has gone through several iterations during the past 20 years, we spoke to students from several cohorts about their perceptions of their involvement in the event.

14.4.1.1. Hitting the ground running

Like the staff member above, the students that we spoke to all clearly articulated the personal benefits that they accrued from being involved in the Tag Rugby Festival. John explained it like this:

> I believe that it is essential that we get given opportunities like this throughout our degree. It is no good sitting in a classroom for three years and not practicing the skills that we will need in the workplace. Writing essays isn't really going to help you get a job! Those students that make the most of volunteering opportunities like the Tag Rugby Festival are more likely to be able to 'hit the ground running' when they get to the workplace. In fact, they are probably more likely to secure a job. (John)

The key motivator for John's involvement in the festival was the opportunity to develop employability skills rather than for any altruistic reasons. Of the 10 students we interviewed, all emphasised personal skill development connected to employability as the most important benefit of student volunteering. Our findings match those of Hustinx and Lammertyn (2003) who identified important shifts in motivations for volunteering that pointed to an increasing focus on individualised needs. This shift could be attributed to an increasingly competitive job market, but may also point to the ways that opportunities to volunteer are marketed to students.

14.4.1.2. Opening doors

For many students, engagement in the festival and with the 'Give to Sport' programme more generally provided them with opportunities to connect with the wider community, and to network with a range of people working in the sports industry. This networking opportunity, and the confidence that ensued from it, was regarded by both staff and students as a key benefit to volunteering.

Anecdotal evidence from staff supported the view that those students who put themselves forward as volunteers were better placed when job opportunities did arise. Staff who had worked at UCP Marjon for many years were able to recall students who had made the best of event management opportunities and had later progressed to event management careers, including one ex-student who secured a position as Manager of the Olympic Mountain Bike Event as part of the 2012 Olympic Games. Individual success stories such as this were frequently cited as reasons for student engagement, and perpetuated the dominant discourse that student volunteering is generally a 'good thing'.

14.4.1.3. It's not all plain sailing

Although there were very few negative comments about their experiences from the students that we spoke to, there were some challenges noted by the administrators. One of the administrators in particular was sceptical of releasing too much of the organisation and management over to students. She describes her feelings below.

> For the event in 2010, I was persuaded to release a part of the co-ordination over to a group of students on the Sport Event Management Module and they took over the co-ordination and arrangements for the refereeing part of the festival. It was left to them to negotiate with [one of the organisers] to ensure that appropriate training was provided for student volunteers, and to make sure that sufficient referees were available to cover the day. Unfortunately, this did not go well and although many of our students took the opportunity to do the training course (looks good on the cv), they did not willingly come forward to referee on the day. Contact and coordination of outside bodies previously involved in the refereeing of the festival was poor ... I then stepped in and took over 'control' and managed to pull it around. I had to constantly lead and 'nag' the group of students involved during the whole process and it would have been less time consuming for me if I had done it myself from day one. (Jane, Member of Tag Rugby Planning Committee)

What is apparent from Jane's experiences is that successful community engagement does not just 'happen' by opening up opportunities for students, either as part of the curriculum or as an additional extra-curricular volunteering opportunity. Any successful collaboration requires communication, and a clear commitment to agreed goals and expectations (Cotton & Stanton, 1990). The frustrations articulated above might have been avoided had there been a focused discussion about the needs and concerns of each of the parties involved, and the philosophical and practical nature of the relationship. It appears from the outset that Jane did not 'buy-in' to this collaborative approach and was focused on simply 'getting the job done' rather than creating opportunities for learning to take place through more student-directed tasks. Since Jane fulfils an administrative role at UCP Marjon, this may be expected, nevertheless, it points to the importance of ensuring that all partners in the relationship are carefully considered.

One of the pitfalls of engaging volunteers in community events is the potential for both quality and relationships to be compromised. This is particularly the case when the volunteers' motives are primarily egocentric. Since the Tag Rugby Festival now relies on a pool of volunteers coming through the 'Give to Sport' initiative, the requirement for students to self-reflect upon their voluntary contribution has also been removed. Unfortunately, on this occasion, devolving responsibility to students had not been a success as far as this committee member was concerned, and inevitably, this has tainted her perception of the commitment and capabilities of students. While student volunteering is frequently promoted as a 'win/win' activity,[1] benefiting students, institutions and communities, this supposition is far too simplistic. As Cotton and Stanton (1990, p. 102) argue, 'a frustrating experience with even one student can sour an agency on ever working with students … again.'

While we are not in a position to get the students' perspectives on Jane's comments, this example also highlights the need to acknowledge the limitations of students' time and skills, as well as ensuring that appropriate guidance, training and support are in place for volunteers. This is arguably clearer in the context of a curriculum-based project where students are working towards academic credits (Duignan, 2003), rather than being offered up as a volunteering opportunity. We move now to discuss our second case study which sits within the sports development curriculum, and has been developed with the learner as its primary focus.

14.4.2. Case Study Two: Special Olympics Plymouth and District

In 2009, inspired by their attendance at the 8th Special Olympics National Summer Games held in Leicester, a small committee of interested parents formed the Special Olympics Plymouth and District (SOPD) club aimed at intellectually disabled athletes. The club has grown from just 16 participants in 2009 to 85 in 2012 (Walker, 2012). SOPD is one of 135 clubs from 19 different regions in England, Scotland and Wales that are affiliated to Special Olympics Great Britain (SOGB).[2] SOGB is also

---

[1]See Holdsworth and Quinn (2012) for a fuller discussion of the normalised assumptions around student volunteering.
[2]SOGB is a registered charity formed in 1978 to provide coaching and competition opportunities in 26 individual and team sports for all intellectually disabled people with an IQ of 75 and below.

part of Special Olympics International, which is now regarded as the 'third arm' of Olympic organisations, together with the Olympic and Paralympic Games.

In order to expand its provision and to raise the profile of SOPD, the committee approached UCP Marjon. It was agreed that students enrolled on the 'Sport and Disability' module could provide assistance for SOPD, while at the same time being assessed for their degree. 'Sport and Disability' is an optional third year module that forms part of the BA (Hons) Sports Development degree programme. Unlike the first case study, academic involvement in the design and delivery of this community engagement learning experience is central. The learning that takes place is guided through a process of reflection that forms part of the assessment of the module. This model fits more clearly to commonly held definitions of service-learning as outlined by Boland (2008, p. 20), whereby 'Academic credit is gained on the basis of demonstrated application of discipline-specific theory to practice and for reflection on the experience'.

The taught elements (representing 50% of the module) are delivered through lectures, seminars and guest speakers. Topics covered include the conceptual framework that forms the basis for an understanding of disability; the key principles relating to the process of disability sport classification; the technical developments in prosthesis and mobility aids; the historical background, status and future developments of disability sport; the processes of modification and adaption; the principles underpinning programming from local community-based initiatives through to elite performance development; and the debates relating to segregation and integration.

The remaining 50% of the module is represented by a short placement of 25 hours, which the students are expected to complete in a disability sport environment. Assessment for the module consists of a 3,000 word case study (50% of module grade) based on a critical analysis of the origins, development and classification system of a disability sport or adventurous activity and a presentation of the placement (50% of module grade).

In the academic year 2010−11, seven of the 27 students registered on the module chose to complete their placement with SOPD. In contrast to the experience of students involved in the Tag Rugby Festival, the seven students met with the SOPD committee members on several occasions during the planning phase, and were very well briefed as to the aims and expectations of the committee members, and provided with key information about the participants that they would be leading. They then delivered four 'taster' sessions in a variety of sporting activities for the intellectually disabled participants. The sessions, which emphasised participation and engagement, were not only judged by all the stakeholders as being very successful, especially the commitment and communication shown by the students, but they also attracted coverage by the local newspaper (The Herald, 2011, 11 June).

14.4.2.1. 'Another string to my bow'
In the academic year 2011−12 the number of 'taster' sessions delivered at UCP Marjon increased from 4 to 5 and 12 of the 30 students registered on the module

chose to complete their placement with SOPD. When asked why he had chosen the module one student stated that:

> The module provided a good mix between theory and practical experience. It was also a topic that I had touched upon briefly in my first year of university and I found it quite interesting then. I thought it was a good opportunity to develop my knowledge and understanding of an area that is very prominent in society. (Martyn)

Another student, said simply:

> The module adds another string to my bow so to speak, in terms of wanting to teach P.E. (Debbie)

Once again, both Martyn's and Debbie's motives centred on the development of personal skills and knowledge, rather than building relationships between students and communities, or any other altruistic reasons. This is less surprising in a curriculum-based project, since engagement in some form of placement is a compulsory aspect of this course. Martyn's comments about disability sport being prominent in society are arguably also predictable given that he was interviewed at around the time of the London, 2012 Paralympic Games. Nevertheless, placement opportunities such as this do afford powerful opportunities in which to challenge dominant cultural narratives as we explore in the next section.

14.4.2.2. Shifting perceptions of disabled athletes

A second theme that emerged was the desire for students to experience working with disabled athletes. Many had previously not been exposed to people with learning disabilities; consequently, the placement experience offered new narratives for participants to draw on. While there was still a sense that some students were strategic and regarded these experiences as primarily beneficial in relation to securing jobs, it was also acknowledged that the placement provided an opportunity for them to really 'make a difference' (Rehberg, 2005) in the lives of disabled athletes.

We believe that any opportunities to broaden students' perspectives on social inequalities is a good thing, even if this shift is an unintended consequence. As Richardson (1990, p. 26) puts it:

> At the individual level, people make sense of their lives through the stories that are available to them, and attempt to fit their lives into available stories. People live by stories. If the available narrative is limiting, destructive, or at odds with the actual life, people's lives end up being limited and textually disenfranchised. Collective stories that deviate from standard cultural plots provide new narratives; hearing them legitimates replotting one's own life.

Offering placement experiences where students can engage with disadvantaged groups opens up opportunities for students to reflect and challenge the *status quo*. As one student explained:

> The module gave me a critical understanding of disability sport, provision and disability issues as a whole. Some of the outside speakers who gave presentations gave me great insight into disability provision and some of the contextual issues that [disabled people] face. (Simon)

Even those students who had prior knowledge of working with disabled athletes recognised the benefits of extending their knowledge in this area:

> Prior to my involvement with the module, I had been working for Action for Blind People (Actionnaires) as an Activity Co-ordinator. This job gave me some insight into disability sport provision.

Public awareness of disability sport has improved over recent years, with increasing media coverage of the Paralympic Games 'accelerating the agenda for inclusion' (Gold & Gold, 2007, p. 133). This is particularly the case since the London 2012 Paralympic Games when media coverage was unprecedented. Athletes with intellectual disabilities, however, have a significantly lower profile, with the Special Olympics by comparison receiving very little exposure. Any opportunities to raise awareness and increase public acceptance of people with learning difficulties is regarded as a positive outcome of this community-based initiative.

14.4.2.3. You really have to know your 'stuff'

The activity sessions delivered by the students consisted of adapted versions of badminton, basketball, football, mini games and rounders, with participants experiencing each activity. One of the students involved in the planning and delivery of these sessions commented:

> We aimed to provide the participants with a taster of various sports. Our main objective was to ensure they had fun, with this in mind we used session plans as a template and adapted/modified our session to meet the needs of the participants. A key outcome was to ensure that every participant had a success during the session.

Following the practical sessions, students were tasked with preparing a presentation that gave an overview of their experiences of working with intellectually disabled athletes. In their presentations the students were asked to provide evidence of adaptation and modification of activities, the impact of legislative developments on provision, and how they utilised specialist and non-specialist equipment. They were also required to reflect on their role in the delivery of the sessions. Six SOPD committee members were invited to attend the student presentations, alongside the academic lead for the module.

To be effective, community engagement requires some form of reflective practice. Most commonly, this occurs as an end of task requirement (Cushman, 2002). However, reflection can, and arguably should, also take place during the actual experience (Lodato Wilson, 2005). It was evident in this case that the course structure facilitated a process of on-going reflection. Regular opportunities to meet with SOPD committee members were thought-provoking and encouraged students to adopt a deep, rather than surface approach to learning (Biggs & Tang, 2007).

A deep approach to learning is characterised by students organising information in a more 'holistic way' (Baron, 2002), rather than simply focusing on the assessment requirements of the module. As one student puts it:

> The practical element of the module allowed me to be a lot more engaged in the learning process. (Holly)

The students that we spoke to were actively interested in the subject of disability sport and drew on their prior experiences to 'make sense' of the new challenges presented in the placement activity. It was evident that the authentic experience, and clear module structure, coupled with the students' own curiosity about disability sport lead to a positive learning experience for all those involved. This was supported by feedback from the end of module evaluation questionnaires.

14.5.   Conclusion: Lessons Learnt from Community Engagement

As with all pedagogical approaches, there are strengths and weaknesses to community engagement initiatives, and these need to be carefully considered in relation to the overall curriculum design, the particular needs of the students, and the needs of the communities in which they live. In its current iteration, the Tag Rubgy Festival offers students the opportunity to contribute to a sporting event through the 'Give to Sport' volunteering programme; however, the main focus is on the provision of a service, and on the needs of the participants. Conversely, the student placement activity with intellectually disabled athletes is a curriculum-centred initiative with the needs of the learners at its core.

Regardless of the format, our research found that in both cases, students' motivations were largely personal, and they regarded both initiatives as vehicles to gain confidence and competence in a range of work-related skills. This was particularly the case for the voluntary activity, and throws into question normalised assumptions about the social justice benefits of volunteering promoted by agencies such as the Higher Education Funding Council for England (HEFCE). We believe that the students' focus on developing employability skills can be attributed in part to the ways that both activities are 'sold' to students by academic staff. The dominant discourses of student volunteering among the staff that we spoke to give little attention to communitarian perspectives. For this to shift, staff need to (re)consider the key messages that they give to students.

The 'Give to Sport' initiative supplemented curriculum activity and offered up further opportunities for students to connect with their community; however, without clear negotiation between students, the community group and university staff, there is the potential for negative consequences. Students need a clear understanding of their role, and, if their participation is to be truly 'authentic' (as we understand the term to mean), need to be challenged by open-ended enquiries, rather than simply being given undemanding roles to perform on the day. In many ways, the Tag Rugby Festival is a victim of its own success, and as the event has grown, policies and procedures have been refined such that the once central role played by students has shifted. This has diminished the organisational challenge the event once demanded of students, and as a likely consequence, their overall motivation.

From the evidence gathered, we conclude that for a curriculum-based community initiative to be successful there are a further three critical factors that should be considered. First, our view is that community-based initiatives seem to work better when they are part of the students' programme. Staff are then able to facilitate learning by carefully constructing assessment and building in opportunities for reflection. Students should be encouraged to spend time on self-reflection during and after their involvement in the initiative in order to encourage deep learning. This is more likely to occur when it forms part of the assessment process, although it is important that academic staff demonstrate how reflection should be carried out effectively. In connection with this, there are advantages in the community group being involved in the assessment process, as was the case with the Special Olympics initiative. Both students and the community group are then able to make the connections between theory and practice.

Second, it is clearly advantageous to recruit highly committed and motivated students to the module that is linked to any community-based initiative. This is more likely to be successful when the module is optional. There may be advantages in 'interviewing' students in order to ensure they are suitable for the initiative. This process would also provide a further opportunity for employability skills development.

Finally, any successful collaboration requires effective communication. It is clear that maintaining partnerships with the wider community is demanding, and in seeking sustainability, educational institutions need to broker the relationship between students and community groups very carefully, so that everybody gains. Boland and Mc Ilrath (2005) maintain that this represents one of the most challenging and problematic aspects of community engagement initiatives. Like Holdsworth and Quinn (2012), we also believe that academic staff and members of community groups should jointly engage in a more critical interpretation of the expected outcomes of community projects. There are advantages in having a service level agreement or a memorandum of agreement in order to formalise this process.

While both initiatives have yielded some positive outcomes, institutionally there are some clear challenges in making the Tag Rugby Festival a continued success as far as providing opportunities for students to engage in authentic learning experiences. The role of the Professional Advisory Group in informing curriculum developments at UCP Marjon has been an exciting development over the past few years, and its impact is already being felt in terms of the increased focus on employability and curriculum embedded work placements. Discussions are currently taking place to re-think the organisation of the Tag Rugby Festival, and many academic staff would like to see it return to its original format as a curriculum-based activity.

References

Baron, P. (2002). Deep and surface learning: Can teachers really control student approaches to learning in law? *The Law Teacher, 36*(2), 123–139.

Bednarz, S. W., Chalkley, B., Fletcher, S., Hay, I., Heron, E., Mohan, A., & Trafford, J. (2008). Community engagement for student learning in geography. *Journal of Geography in Higher Education, 32*(1), 87–100.

Biggs, J., & Tang, C. (2007). *Teaching for quality learning at university: What the student does* (3rd ed.), Maidenhead: McGraw-Hill.

Boland, J., & Mc Ilrath, L. (2005). *Developing new learning communities through teaching, research and service — a case study.* All Ireland Society for Higher Education/Staff and Educational Development Association Annual Conference, Belfast.

Boland, J. A. (2008). *Embedding a civic engagement dimension within the higher education curriculum: A study of policy, process and practice in Ireland.* Unpublished doctoral dissertation, University of Edinburgh, UK.

Bologna Working Group on Qualifications Frameworks. (2005). *A framework for qualifications of the European higher education area.* Ministry of Science, Technology and Innovation, Copenhagen.

Clegg, S. (2000). Knowing through reflective practice in higher education. *Educational Action Research, 8*(3), 451–469.

Cnaan, R. A., Handy, F., & Wadsworth, M. (1996). Defining who is a volunteer: Conceptual and empirical considerations. *Nonprofit and Voluntary Sector Quarterly, 25*(3), 364–383.

Cotton, D., & Stanton, T. (1990). Joining campus and community through service learning. *New Directions for Student Services, 50*, 101–110.

Cushman, D. (2002). Sustainable service learning programs. *College Composition and Communication, 56*, 40–65.

Dewey, J. (1916). *Democracy and education: An introduction to the philosophy of education.* New York, NY: The Free Press.

Doherty, A. (1998). Managing our human resources: A review of organisational behaviour in sport. *Sport Management Review, 1*, 1–24.

Doherty, A. (2005). *A profile of community sport volunteers.* London: School of Kinesiology, University of Western Ontario.

Doherty, A. (2006). Sport volunteerism: An introduction to the special issue. *Sport Management Review, 9*, 1–24.

Duignan, J. (2003). Placement and adding value to the academic performance of undergraduates: Reconfiguring the architecture — an empirical investigation. *Journal of Vocational Education & Training, 55*(3), 335–350.

Eley, D., & Kirk, D. (2002). Developing citizenship through sport: The impact of a sport-based volunteer programme on young sport leaders. Sport, Education and Society, 7(2), 151–166.

Furco, A. (2011). Service-Learning: A balanced approach to experiential education. *Education Global Research*, 71–76.

Gold, J. R., & Gold, M. M. (2007). Access for all: the rise of the Paralympic Games. *Perspectives in Public Health, 127*(3), 133–141.

Holdsworth, C., & Quinn, J. (2010). Student volunteering in English higher education. *Studies in Higher Education, 35*(1), 113–127.

Holdsworth, C., & Quinn, J. (2012). The epistemological challenge of higher education student volunteering: 'Reproductive' or 'Deconstructive' volunteering? *Antipode, 44*(2), 386–405.

Holland, B. A. (2001). Exploring the challenge of documenting and measuring civic engagement endeavours of colleges and universities: Purposes, issues, ideas. *Campus Compact*, March 23. Retrieved from http://www.compact.org/advancedtoolkit/pdf/holland_paper.pdf. Accessed on 23 August, 2012.

Hustinx, L., & Lammertyn, F. (2003). Collective and reflexive styles of volunteering: A sociological modernization perspective. *Voluntas: International Journal of Voluntary and NonProfit Organizations, 14*(2), 167–187.

Kolb, A., & Kolb, D. (2005). Learning styles and learning spaces: Enhancing experiential learning in higher education. *Academy of Management Learning & Education, 4*(2), 193–212.

Lather, P. (1992). Critical frames in educational research: Feminist and poststructural perspectives. *Theory into Practice, 31*(2), 87–99.

Lodato Wilson, G. (2005). Attitude change through service learning. *Academic Exchange Quarterly, 9*, 46–49.

Ministry of Science, Technology and Innovation. (2005). *A framework for qualifications of the European higher education area.*

Prime Minister's Strategy Unit. (2007). *Building on progress: Public services.* London: Cabinet Office.

Rehberg, W. (2005). Altruistic individualists: Motivations for international volunteering among young adults in Switzerland. *Voluntas: International Journal of Voluntary and Nonprofit Organizations, 16*(2), 109–122.

Richardson, L. (1990). *Writing strategies: Reaching diverse audiences.* London: Sage.

Shah, A., & Treby, E. (2006). Using a community based project to link teaching and research: The Bourne Stream Partnership. *Journal of Geography in Higher Education, 30*(1), 33–48.

The Herald (2011, 11 June). A desire for inclusion leads sport campaign. *The Herald*. Retrieved from http://www.thisisdevon.co.uk/desire-inclusion-leads-sport-campaign/story-12753153-detail/story.html. Accessed on November 9, 2012.

University College Plymouth St. Mark and St. John. (2010). *5 year strategic plan.* Retrieved from http://www.marjon.ac.uk/about-marjon/institutional-documents/academic-policies-strategies-and-schemes/strategic-plan-2010-15.pdf. Accessed on 28 August 2012.

VanWynsberghe, R., & Andruske, C. (2007). Research in the service of co-learning: Sustainability and community engagement. *Canadian Journal of Education, 30*(1), 349–376.

Walker, B. (2012). Providing a path to Special Olympics. *South Hams Gazette*, October 26, p. 6.

Warner, S., Newland, B., & Green, B. C. (2011). More than motivation: Reconsidering volunteer management tools. *Journal of Sport Management, 25*(2), 391–407.

Wilson, B., Ludwig-Hardman, S., Thornam, C. L., & Dunlap, J. (2004). Bounded community: Designing and facilitating learning communities in formal courses. *The International Review of Research in Open and Distance Learning, 5*(3). Retrieved from http://www.irrodl.org/index.php/irrodl/article/view/204/286. Accessed on 28 August, 2012.

Zakus, D., Skinner, J., & Engelberg, T. (2012). Defining and measuring dimensionality and targets of the commitment of sport volunteers. *Journal of Sport Management, 26*(2), 192–205.

Chapter 15

The Creative Campus: Empowering the University Community to Change Spaces

Ian Bride, Louise Naylor and Carin Tunåker

Abstract

This chapter discusses an innovative process by which students and staff became involved in the improvement, design and creation of social spaces on the University of Kent's Canterbury and Medway campuses. It describes the initial research project that employed students in the framing and implementation of campus-wide surveys, and presents some particularly inspiring activities that were subsequently developed. Most were enabled by 'Creative Campus', a scheme co-ordinated by the Unit for the Enhancement of Learning and Teaching, which supports creative learning opportunities by proving small amounts of funding. As well as pointing out the very positive outcomes of these activities, the chapter also highlights and discusses the general aspects and elements that have tended to help or hinder the support for and materialisation of these sorts of creative ideas when generated from within the University community.

15.1. Introduction

The modern university has been greatly transformed, both in the way it performs its traditional functions and in becoming a more commercial enterprise. For example, it now provides a range of retail outlets and services while trying to meet the varied needs of an increasingly diverse community of staff, students and other users. In 2007 a Finance and Resources Committee meeting at the University of Kent was discussing a number of proposals for improving the quality and balance of the facilities available outside teaching and office spaces, when the then head of the School of Anthropology and Conservation questioned the evidence base for some of the suggestions being tabled. In realising that there were practically no data available concerning the needs and aspirations of members of the University community,

The Student Engagement Handbook: Practice in Higher Education
Copyright © 2013 by Emerald Group Publishing Limited
All rights of reproduction in any form reserved
ISBN: 978-1-78190-423-7

he suggested that the University might usefully commission his School to research this area. As a result, the administration commissioned the Department of Anthropology and Conservation to conduct a study of 'social hubs' on the University's Canterbury Campus.

In accepting to undertake this project, the School of Anthropology and Conservation recognised it as a pioneering enterprise with the potential to show how academic departments can contribute to the understanding and creation of new environments, as well as improving existing ones. It is a truism to state that anthropologists and architects have long been interested in the creation and transformation of space/place, in its use and avoidance, the way buildings/environments reflect, project or impose upon people's needs and identity, and how physical spaces reflect and engage with the theoretical developments in the relevant disciplines. Space has material, conceptual and political dimensions that are of key importance in influencing, and some would say generating, certain aspects of social life.

In undertaking the research, the group of six members of staff formed for the purpose (one from the School of Architecture) decided to pursue the learning and teaching opportunities offered by the project so as to enable some of their best students to gain and employ valuable research skills and experience through participating in a piece of local, real-world research. They handpicked and recruited a core team of 5 postgraduate students and 15 undergraduates from both Schools, who were all employed as paid participants in both the design and execution of the project. Following two initial research design workshops interspaced with walkover and specific site observations, a mixed method participant observation approach was developed that utilised a range of qualitative and quantitative research instruments. Five researcher teams, each managed by a postgraduate student, and in turn line-managed by one of the co-authors (Ian Bride), subsequently observed, interacted with and interviewed occupants of a range of social hubs settings across the campus so as to glean initial field-based information of actual usage, conceptions and needs regarding these spaces. The objectives were to:

- detail the nature of these spaces;
- investigate the patterns of their use (and non-use);
- explore the underlying reasons for these patterns;
- produce an informed critical appraisal, including suggestions for improvements that might be made to these and similar hubs on campus, as well as ideas for new hubs.

The teams, which were allocated specific sections of the campus, next undertook an in-depth survey of one or two busy hub sites and conducted walkover spot surveys of other actual or potential hub sites in their area. For each site, a detailed record of facilities was made and observational, photographic, mapping and diary data were collected, with the research being conducted on Mondays, Tuesdays and Thursdays, when the student presence is greatest. Thereafter, the second stage of the research consisted of the observational study of additional hubs, the conduct of semi-structured interviews of randomly selected occupants at a representative selection of hubs, and a total of 76 targeted interviews of individual members of staff based in several of the main University buildings.

In the event, some 49 individual 'hubs' were identified and evaluated. The resulting data, though gathered in relatively few survey events over just a few weeks, and despite being subject to some degree of variation in the format and detail of their collection, offered some very useful findings and led to some interesting conclusions. The aggregated evidence provided by the study suggested that the University possesses a good range of social spaces, with the nature and quality of many of them being generally appreciated by staff and students alike. Yet it also suggested that there is much that could be done, either to improve particular hubs or to create new and exciting spaces for current and future campus inhabitants. In many cases significant positive changes to existing hubs were identified that could be achieved through the application of relatively simple and inexpensive measures. In others, a clear need for major, or at least significant, innovative investment was highlighted.

As well as a tranche of relatively unsurprising findings revealing the manner in which people access the retail spaces — the use of which was found to vary according to the specific nature of the services on offer; ease of access; value for money; the quality of products and service provided; the presence (or absence) of friends, peers or colleagues; gender; and, the degree of physical and aesthetic comfort and flexibility they provide — the study drew a number of less obvious conclusions. It emphasised the fact that individuals have multiple 'group' memberships, which means that their selection of any particular hub will vary according to which group or groups they are prioritising at any one time; for instance, whether a member of staff may need to meet informally with colleagues either to get to know them better or discuss University business, want to spend time with colleagues and/or postgraduate students talking about academic research, entertain important and/or casual visitors, take a quiet break from a particularly intensive, stressful piece of work, or perhaps simply wish to 'let off steam'. There was clearly no 'one size' of social hub that could fit all, and with the enormous diversity of the community of staff, students and other users of the University Campus, together with their changing and various needs, it was a provision of a portfolio of hubs which are varied and flexible in their use, as well as being widely distributed, that emerged as the overarching requirement.

In addition to highlighting the value of improving existing social spaces, most notably in terms of addressing the issue of the often severe noise 'pollution' in the standard modernist-styled eateries acoustically compromised by the use of hard surfaces throughout, the need to provide social spaces for meeting, talking and generally 'hanging out' that do not require the purchase of consumer items was also strongly emphasised. These were widely identified as being desired both outdoors as well as indoors, with provision made for outdoor spaces in addition to seating and picnic areas. For example, suggestions were made for all-weather furniture and shelters that are accessible from the early Spring through to the Autumn, and for some people (not just smokers), even in winter too! Departmental meeting areas where staff and students can meet informally were also identified as important, with calls to involve the University's School of Architecture in the design of such facilities and for serious thought to be given to providing designated areas for different mixes, e.g. academic staff only, academic staff and postgraduate students, and general staff.

The final report recommended the research and creation of a social hubs master plan, as well as the development of a number of specific sites, with the latter, where possible, being deemed best dovetailed into the activities of the University's Creative Campus project. The idea suggested was to establish an iterative process, which evaluates actions taken, documents changing trends and needs, and links individual overall project outcomes to an enhanced student experience and learning, with particular regard to employability; improved interdisciplinary social contact, communication and creativity; improved staff well-being; and the enhancement of a unique and exemplary profile for the University within the higher education sector. Before describing some of the resulting developments in greater detail, a few explanatory words need to be made about Creative Campus.

15.2.   Creative Campus at the University of Kent

Creative Campus was started in 2008 by the University's Unit for the Enhancement of Learning and Teaching (UELT), involving members of the University staff interested in trying to innovate the formal and informal learning and teaching agenda. The idea was to provide a catalyst for new creative projects on campus that support learning and teaching, the Arts, and the development of the campus environment. Running on a relatively meagre budget and guided by a multi-disciplinary team, it has since provided a steady force for positive cultural and social change by supporting initiatives to improve learning and social spaces, and by promoting well-being, as well as showcasing creative talent. Since it was launched, over 50 projects have been delivered that have engaged more than 1500 staff, students and members of the local community. These have ranged from providing trained intern (part-time, paid students) and other support for the Canterbury Labyrinth (see Labyrinth, 2008), through the sponsorship of exhibitions of students' creative work and ideas — notably a series entitled 'On the Buses' displaying sets of images in advertising space on buses servicing the University, and a competition to design a sculpture for a vacant plinth — to a number of initiatives addressing some of the needs and desires that emerged from the social hubs research.

15.2.1.   Social Hubs Research Outcomes

Following the Hub Final Report in October 2008, a number of specific actions and initiatives were embarked upon. Some took the form of immediate responses by the University Estates Department supported by a social spaces fund that it set up for this purpose; some were pursued via Creative Campus. Notable among the former was the creation of a series of benched enclaves along the front of the library, a zone that had been overwhelmingly identified as the 'centre' and the 'key meeting place' of the Canterbury campus, but which hitherto had had no seating provision. Similarly, sound-absorbing ceiling panels were quickly installed in one of the most popular campus café/restaurants, which had been the brunt of many complaints about the poor acoustic qualities of key indoor gathering places. Another development was the expansion of a library café/informal learning zone, which had been shown to be very popular with students because it allowed them to define many of the parameters of their own environment for study and discussion.

Of those social hubs projects driven via Creative Campus, worthy examples with which the authors have been intimately involved are the CreAte café, the *Quercus genius* outside classroom, the Forensic Science 'incident' area, the University Nature Trail restoration process, and the Iron Gym project at the Medway campus.

15.2.2.   The CreAte café

Following one of the Social Hubs report recommendations, the University authorities agreed a proposal put forward by Creative Campus and the School of Architecture to redevelop a rather dingy and uninspiring common room foyer area in the building shared by the School of Architecture and the School of Anthropology and Conservation. The director of the MA Architecture programme agreed to integrate a design competition into one of the modules and it was agreed that two of the Creative Campus team would role play the client representatives and present a brief to the students, inviting them to participate in a charette competition. The best entries were selected and since each of these had particular elements in their favour the students in question were organised into a team to research and develop a final design. One student in particular, Pier-Luigi del Renzio, emerged as the leading light, becoming deeply involved in and committed to the scheme. The University was sufficiently impressed to decide to institute the project at a cost of some £400,000 in collaboration with MELD, a small, progressive architectural practice with which some of the part-time teaching staff in the School work. MELD employed Pier-Luigi to see the project through to completion during the summer of 2010, and the result has been the creation of a flexible, multi-use space that includes smart screen technology and bench furniture that can quickly be reorganised to form exhibition and display areas.

Despite the steep learning curves and the necessary compromises associated with keeping to the brief and keeping costs down, the project offered a highly stimulating real-world learning and teaching experience to those involved. Although Pier-Luigi was no doubt the student who benefited most from the exercise, his feedback illustrates the actual and potential value of this sort of approach.

> The design 'charette' was extremely engaging for all students involved. The idea of an external body of enthusiastic people supporting creativity in young aspiring designers was a very powerful and reassuring force. Their belief in us raised our hopes that we can design when presented with a specific need … . The collaboration with MELD

architects was brilliant as the project shifted upwards to a professional level with strong leadership. They encouraged me to have full involvement over the entire design, tender and construction process... I'm sure that if in the future a similar scale project was proposed, the opportunity for greater collaboration would be even more of a success — with more students involved with the latter stages of the process... The project also introduced me and the members of my group to the complexities of group working, particularly in 'design' based work. The experience was highly engaging and nourishing as well as supportive of my future as a designer... the resultant space being the true realisation of a student-based project which is now being built before our very eyes. (Pier-Luigi del Renzio, MA architecture, graduated July 2010)

From the point of view of Creative Campus and many of the students involved, the CreAte project was very successful in respect to the learning opportunities it offered. However, this is not to suggest that this initiative was problem-free. The original plan, to allow the architecture students' society (KASA) to use the newly created café kitchen facilities outside service hours, was not honoured after an expensive coffee machine and other equipment were installed, while many of the occupants of the building objected to some brightly coloured, soft 'rubber' settees being installed in the stead of the 'Corbusier' sofas that had been there previously. Thankfully this seating subsequently demonstrated just how furniture can influence people's behaviour, becoming so dirty and damaged as to be removed.

Clearly, the learning benefits to those students directly involved in this project were not shared evenly across the class as a whole, although the group that conducted the site assessment were buoyed by the response of the local planning officer, who described it as the best site assessment she had ever seen. It is also true that a considerable effort had to be made by the Creative Campus team in order to get certain key people in the University to sign up to implementing the scheme. Moreover, despite the many successful aspects of the process and a general recognition of the quality and value of the final product, there has been little enthusiasm and apparently no proactive behaviour on the part of the University to replicate this approach in the context of the subsequent infrastructural developments of a similar nature. This is despite CreAte having been selected for the Royal Institute of British Architects (RIBA) Small Budget-BIG IMPACT Design Exhibition in 2011 (UoK News, 2011). Therefore the possibility of growing and promulgating this approach and integrating it into standard University practice does not seem as likely to be realised as our pedagogical agendas might suggest, wish for, or assume, at least in the near term. It is also true that key persons need to be convinced that this type of project approach can be replicated and the methodology developed so that it can work as least as well as the traditional ways of doing things. This will depend very much upon convincing all the necessary 'powers that be' and involve a significant and concerted effort by Creative Campus and its supporters.

15.2.3.   Quercus Genius

The social hubs research finding that there was a clear and widely held desire for outside seating areas substantiated an idea that one of the authors (Ian Bride) had long held, to create new learning, teaching and leisure spaces in the non-built environment using the material available to hand; the Canterbury campus being blessed in being set within a considerable amount of coppice and mixed deciduous woodland and large areas of grassland, so when a large oak tree fell down near to a site he had previously identified as having good potential for the creation of such a space, the opportunity presented itself in the form of raw materials. With a small amount of funding support from Creative Campus, a local wood sculptor (Peter Leadbeater) was commissioned to collaborate with students in order to produce pieces that could be arranged to form a seating area. Members of the student-run Conservation Society established a dialogue with Peter and Ian and then worked alongside them to design and create carved elements from the oak tree to be assembled and secured on site. Over a week-long period, what became dubbed the *Quercus genius* project resulted in a bookable outside classroom capable of seating 20 students on mushrooms, a large branch, piles of wooden books and 'newt' and 'frog' benches. It now offers an interesting, challenging and unique teaching space, especially when the bluebells are in bloom, as well as a delightfully calm, leisure setting essentially created by, and therefore 'owned' by, the students themselves. Through this project the participating students, who represented several subject areas, developed their communication, team working, practical and, most importantly, their creative skills. For instance, Jules, who became particularly closely involved in the project, made the following observation:

> I think it is important that students feel part of the campus landscape and can leave their mark. When I go back to the benches, I feel like it is partly my work, and that is very satisfying. (Jules, 1st year BSc Wildlife Conservation and Management)

Similarly Grace, the then president of the Conservation Society, offered the following feedback:

> I thought having a new, green-learning space was a wonderful idea! It will be great to encourage especially environmental classes to be taught outside, as well as encouraging a social area for people to congregate and enjoy more the green-ness of campus. We could certainly replicate this elsewhere on campus. I enjoyed the teamwork, and learnt to remove bark with a chisel! Plus a lot of general problem-solving skills, such as collectively moving a really heavy tree branch up a hill. It made me feel happy and proactive! (Grace, 3rd year BSc Wildlife Conservation and Management)

And the artist himself also gained positively from the experience:

> I really enjoyed working with the students and the group process.
> They were enthusiastic, listened well to instructions and to what was
> being explained, and responded quickly with a real sense of purpose.
> We established a creative dialogue through which we were able to
> produce something we can be proud of, and I enjoyed the process of
> setting and allocating responsibilities within clearly defined bound-
> aries. I understand why people become lecturers. If we were to run a
> similar project in future, I would like to spend more time in the design
> process stage, so as to encourage a wider input and thereby involve
> more students. (Peter, wood sculptor)

Of course the creation of spaces of this type also brings forth some degree of
responsibility for caring for and maintaining them. Thankfully, *Quercus genius* is
not very high maintenance, and besides the occasional litter pick and pulling up a
few nettles now and again, the students have been looking after it by themselves, a
fact that tends to reiterate the importance of students feeling a sense of ownership
of the spaces they occupy. At the same time, the University authorities have readily
accepted the value of this project and seem likely to enthusiastically support similar
endeavours in future. So it appears that this sort of creative initiative can be successfully pursued in future and the approach is one that we can recommend to be
employed at other institutions, for even in the absence of green spaces of the type
we at Kent are so blessed with, there will still be opportunities for the student-led
creation of outdoor hubs. Indeed, we have now gained institutional support and
sponsorship funding for a project to use timber from some 20 mature trees felled to
make way for a library extension and create a new social hub between this extension
and an existing building. This project will involve working with artists, the landscape designer, and students mainly from architecture, anthropology and wildlife
conservation to explore the nature of representation and design and make a series
of 'totemic benches' to be arranged in the hub. Students will be learning a range of
research, team-working, design and practical skills, as well as creating an inspiring
legacy for others to enjoy (Totemic Benches, 2013).

15.2.4.   *The Forensic Science Lab/Incident Area*

The idea of creating a forensic field laboratory/incident area in a one eighth hec-
tare block of woodland was brought to Creative Campus by Mark, a lecturer in
Forensic Science. Funds to pay for 150 metres of chestnut fencing and posts were
provided, and the University's Grounds Maintenance was brought in to remove
potentially dangerous branches from existing trees. Thereafter students from
Forensic Science, supported by members of the Conservation Society, trained and
supervised by Mark and Ian, worked as a team to fence off the area. In the process they learnt some important and valuable transferable skills, notably the

proper, safe use of a hammer and saw! These are skills that surprisingly few young people acquire these days as a part of growing up. The organisation of the internal space is currently underway, including a sub-project for the collaborative design and creation of seating in a separate briefing area using materials generated by the coppicing of trees in the vicinity. The field lab will be used to recreate realistic incident and crime scenes, which students will investigate in order to hone scene analysis skills, and conduct studies of specific topics such as infrared soil heat blooms, ultraviolet mapping of disturbed soils, ground penetrating radar and the effects of the environment on a variety of decay mechanisms and their evidential implications – though health and safety concerns will prevent the creation of a body farm. It will provide a nationally unique resource of its kind within the higher education sector (other institutions only having such facilities only in the context of the built environment), greatly improve the student learning experience and turn a previously unused area of woodland in need of management into an invaluable research space that also provides an outside classroom/seating area forming an additional woodland hub that students and staff can use for leisure purposes as well.

In being relatively undemanding of financial resources, once permission had been obtained from the University, the main problem faced by this project was simply that the staff members involved found it difficult to find times at which to gather with students to work on the project. There has tended to be just one or two such slots available per week, which can easily fall victim to other demands or simply the weather. One suggestion currently under consideration, which would go some way to addressing this problem, is the design of a credited module in 'Creative Conservation', in which students are taught the appropriate skills for pro-wildlife habitat maintenance and engage in some weekly tasks as part of the module, of which team-based projects such as developing this Forensic Science outside incident area could be one.

15.2.5.   *The University Nature Trail and a Student-Provided Guided Tour Service*

The University of Kent campus possesses a considerable number of interesting features and resources. Beyond the built environment, which itself boasts significant architectural elements and contains a varied and valuable number of artworks, there is an extensive and attractive estate with impressive views of Canterbury and the Cathedral. The campus bears a range of wildlife habitats (freshwater ponds and streams, mixed deciduous woodland and coppice, lengths of ancient hedgerow, and areas of grassland and wildflower meadow), plus sculptures and archaeological features (including the site of a moated manor house, medieval earthworks, old tile-making kilns, and the world's first passenger railway tunnel). In terms of artefacts, attractiveness and interest, the opportunity for providing a variety of guided tours on campus is therefore clear. Moreover, in terms of the market for guiding visitors, given the large numbers of official 'meet and greet' visitors, prospective students and their parents, conference attendees, and tourist visitors to Canterbury who stay on campus, the possibilities for developing a range of guided campus tours are considerable.

Following a feasibility study for a campus-based guided tour service, which he carried out in 2009 with support by the University's Innovation Fund, Ian designed and set up an undergraduate module in *Guiding and Interpretation*. This module, inspired by the nature trail work and social hubs research findings, is a 'wild' module open to students from across the curriculum (though with preference given to second year students because they will be available as guides for the following year) and for which a themed guided tour comprises the assessment. The hope is that because the module results in the design of a number of different trails each year, the best graduates can provide the campus guiding service originally envisaged, either on a paid or voluntary basis, depending of the client group in question. To this end part of the Innovation Fund award monies were used to employ a student from the Computing Department to produce a web-based booking interface for the business. It is anticipated that the student's campus visitor guiding service will be initiated after the Easter vacation 2013, with students from the 2012/13 *Guiding and Interpretation* cohort being the first to offer tours. The combination of the new module and the guiding initiative will help train and equip students with a valuable set of skills that should not only improve their future job prospects, but also (hopefully) provide a significant supplement to their incomes.

15.2.6.   *The Iron Gym Project at the Medway Campus*

Following on from an idea to use coppiced materials on the Canterbury campus to create an exercise trail, Ian developed the idea of creating something similar on the University's Medway campus. What he envisaged was a series of installations made of industrial artefacts that reference heritage and place, and which would be designed to be exercised on. "Iron Gym", as the project came to be known, then grew through collaboration with three School of Architecture MA students, developing a process and concept ideas, which were supported as part of a *Slipstream Contemporary Arts Showcase* event in autumn of 2010, with the concepts being displayed for public feedback in two further exhibitions.

At the outset, the idea of Iron Gym was to provide one or two exercise installations for the Universities at Medway campus. However, with the MA Architecture students graduating and leaving the University, plus the realisation that given the pressures of study and the demands of assignments it was difficult to involve many students outside of their formal curriculum, the next move was to widen participation. With a small amount of funding support from the University of Kent's Social Spaces and Creative Campus funds, an approach was made to the Centre for Sports Studies and the School of Fine Arts (both based on the University's Medway campus) with the idea of progressing Iron Gym in the context of specific modules. The Director of the Centre for Sports Studies was very receptive to the idea and after discussions with different members of staff, one (David Hooper) took up Iron Gym with the view to integrating it into his module on Sports and Exercise Promotion.

The head of School of Fine Arts was similarly supportive, although here, the integration of the project into the formal curriculum was a rather more difficult goal to achieve — so we settled for promoting the project to the Arts students via email. At this point community artist, Wendy Dawes, and a creative producer, Paivi Seppla, joined the core team and ran a very successful creativity workshop with students on the Sports Management and Sports Science programmes, inspiring them to consider and engage with their own creativity.

The project was also adopted by the South East Higher Education Creative Campus Initiative, as part of what proved to be a successful bid to Arts Council England to support activities leading up to London 2012. This enabled the scope of Iron Gym to extend beyond the physical and conceptual borders offered by the Universities at Medway campus. It also enabled the project to develop a specific research theme, which involved adopting a Participatory Action Research (PAR) methodology. PAR is essentially a methodological approach whereby a project or goal is pursued through an iterative process. In its simplest description PAR consists of a series of actions and reflections, such that each body of reflection directs and informs subsequent actions, while at the same time a record is kept of the overall process. In this context it allowed the project to be adapted and re-directed according to the needs and desires of the participants. With the involvement of students from the Centre for Sports Studies, as well as a particularly encouraging reception from the director of Amherst Fort, an important historic site built to protect the Royal Dockyard against attack, the project shifted its focus to developing sets of exercises and a mapping of the possible routes linking this with a number of other potential installation sites. At this stage too, some Fine Arts students, who had been introduced to the project during a visit to the LV-21 lightship (co-owned by Iron Gym creative producer, Paivi Seppla), became involved, injecting a welcome measure of creative skills and experience.

Following project meetings to discuss and frame the project in more detail, a workshop was held to explore different forms and categories of exercise, which brought a new literacy to the project. It offered participants ways of 'seeing' a range of possibilities for movements and precipitated a step forward in the process, which stimulated the creative 'juices' and the desire to start the design process. 'As everyone has a better understanding of our bodies, I think that this is a good moment to start the actual design process' (Student feedback).

With the link to the fort being developed at the same time there was a tangible feeling that the three key directions of engagement (namely sport, art and heritage) were finally drawing closer together with a common focus. The primary efforts now could be focused on the creation of a first set in a series of maquettes (models) that would act as collaborative research tools, as conceptual referents for the next stages.

In seeking to consider trying to materialise one or more of the maquette concepts at the Fort Amherst site, the project encountered some problems in regards to the resources that might be made available and the controls being requested by the management of the fort. At the same time the LV-21 lightship owners suggested that the project might consider shifting its focus to the ship with a view to creating some installations on board in time for the official Queen's Jubilee celebrations. In keeping with PAR's capacity as a dynamic learning process that can lead in unanti-cipated directions, the team sounded its collective voice in agreement to pursue the path of least resistance and so the creative energies were now directed at this objec-tive. A new round of maquette-making was thereby generated with the donation and purchase of different artefacts and materials, plus help from an experienced seaman (Bob Johnson), who worked for many years in the docks and literally 'knew the ropes'! Bob was delighted to pass on some of his knowledge, and the team was able to construct several installations, which together formed a 'gym' on LV-21 for guests to try out on Jubilee day.[1]

Small exhibitions of the project ideas and materials followed, and after the Olympic and paralympic games had finished, efforts were made to materialise the project in other ways, through looking to bring in significant additional funding and approaching the London Legacy Development Corporation. Although these attempts have so far proven unfruitful, all participants have expressed the opinion that they have learnt a lot from the project. In attempting to be true to the spirit of PAR, we present the positive and negative aspects of the Iron Gym project to date as reported in participant contributions. A useful starting point is a comment from one of the core team students:

> I think the determination to complete the project is founded on the strength of the idea/concept, its presentation to the group and the continued belief that is shown by all members of the group. (Martin, Fine Arts student)

In many ways it was the recognised value of the idea itself that carried the project through to the current stage of fruition. It clearly inspired people in many ways, not simply in terms of pursuing creative outputs, but also in terms of the PAR process itself.

> PAR is a familiar concept that I feel, together with creative documen-tation methods (such as film, audio, visual etc.), forms a very informa-tive tool for developing a variety of different type projects. I will definitely continue to use the method in future projects and feel that the PAR element of the Iron Gym project has expanded my under-standing of it and given me confidence to experiment more with it. (Wendy, community artist)

On a slightly negative note however, other commentators indicated that they felt there have been not enough 'leadership' of the project. So although participants had been told that they were expected to take 'ownership' of it, some thought that at times the project appeared to have no obvious focus or to be 'vague', and that they

---

[1]See the project summary at IronGymProject (2012).

themselves had been insufficiently equipped or supported in the process of 'possessing' it. Moreover, the decision-making process was also identified as not having been properly formalised. These criticisms were levelled both at their respective academic schools and the project team leaders. At the same time, some participants felt that too much time had been spent discussing the project rather than *actually doing it*. Clearly, this picture was partly precipitated by the very nature of the PAR process, a process which seeks to give expressive and decision-making space to stakeholders and to allow leadership to evolve rather than be imposed. It was also no doubt partly due to the specific nature of the project itself, which sought to develop some sort of 'literacy' across a number of very different subject areas where no single individual had mastery of all, and where the overall approach had not been attempted previously in this type of context. The need for more effective management, leadership and support is an important observation that has been acknowledged by the staff team members and is one that will have to be satisfactorily addressed if the project is to be successfully developed to further stages.

Another aspect criticised by some participants was the target-driven nature of the creative process when it came to be set within the realm of the Arts Council England funding via CCI. It was observed that the need to meet specific deadlines tended to rush creativity at a time when participants had formed a body of concepts/maquettes and had begun to consider specific artefacts as part of installations in a properly digested manner.

> The aesthetic value of the work was somewhat forgotten because there was no time left. We could have achieved more in public spaces had we got a strong portfolio of ideas and maquettes together that really showcased what Iron Gym stood for. (Charlotte, Fine Arts student)

Moreover, this stage was considered by some to have been potentially the most creative:

> It was only when we had real life artefacts in our hands that we were able to start to really integrate our experience and ideas with a view to imagining and actually creating something that embodied all the parameters, disciplines and skills we had explored. (Anon student feedback)

Nevertheless, the unanimous view, even of those participants who offered the strongest criticisms (all of them constructive criticisms) of the project, was extremely positive, both in regards to what had been achieved and what had been learnt in the process, and what its future potential might be.

> It is a fantastic project and has a solid concept behind it and I would love to be more involved in the project in the future. (Anon student feedback)

> It has really inspired me. Knowing what we do now, and being where we are now, I feel confident that we can go on to achieve something very special with Iron Gym. (Anon student feedback)

> I think the concept of Iron Gym is excellent and has a long life ahead of it and has the potential to achieve great things. It is a promising idea to combine arts, sports and heritage to create a cultural, interactive installation that enriches the mind and body and working alongside people from various backgrounds has been the highlight of the project for me. (Anon student feedback)

More recently, inquiries have been made as to the possibility of taking the largest piece made for LV-21 and setting it up for use by students on the Medway campus. In the first instance a series of health and safety issues were raised by the University authorities. Although these are quite understandable, many might regard them as somewhat overzealous in terms of trying to minimise risk; there seems to be rather more concern and limits being imposed than would be associated with the equipment provided in a public children's playground. The hope is that these requirements can be satisfactorily addressed and Medway campus-based Iron Gym installations thereby enabled.

By way of a summary, this project has offered excellent opportunities for student learning in and beyond the University, engaging them with an impressive range of key skills that relate to academic progress, creativity and employability, while developing a narrative that cut across disciplinary boundaries. Despite some difficulties in ensuring the feedback and dialogue were regularly maintained, Iron Gym certainly precipitated some valuable contributions and established a spirit of trust that enabled open and honest reflections. It also created a methodological foundation that can be strengthened and built upon, helping the staff most directly involved develop their practical understanding of PAR. Hopefully in the near future our efforts to obtain further funding in order to take the project onto new sites will prove fruitful and we will be able to overcome the barriers and explore and develop the PAR approach in much greater depth.

15.3. Conclusion

These few examples of the University of Kent's Creative Campus projects that were inspired by Social Hubs research findings demonstrate how a range of significant and innovative learning and teaching actions can be instigated with the use of relatively little in the way of financial resources, but given a dose of belief and imagination. The benefits to the students from participating in team-based, real-world, creative activities are manifold. Such activities develop a range of creative, team-working, organisational, communication and practical skills, which not only boost student employability, but also encourage a sense of ownership of place. Furthermore, the value to the staff of working alongside enthusiastic, dynamic, well-focussed students, and doing so in a creative context, cannot be underestimated, not just in terms of the deeper understandings of education that they themselves develop in the process, but also through the positive boost to their attitudes to students and to their own morale, which they carry into other aspects of their work. Put simply, it is a real pleasure to be part of a Creative Campus. Perhaps the last word should be given to one of the students, Laura, one of the postgraduate team leaders for the original social hubs research. Many of those who have followed in her wake would no doubt agree:

> The social hubs research was an invaluable experience for me, and something that I really enjoyed. I already knew that I loved doing interviews from my anthropology coursework, but this was a taste of how to put that love and skill in to the real world. Knowing that the work I conducted would go towards research to benefit students was such a confidence boost, and I am so proud to have been a part of it. Plus it looks great on my C.V. and is a real conversation piece! (Laura, MA Anthropology — graduated 2009)

References

Fort Amherst. (n.d.). Retrieved from http://www.fortamherst.com. Accessed on October 24, 2013.

IronGymProject. (2012). Retrieved from http://www.irongymproject.co.uk. Accessed on October 24, 2013.

Labyrinth. (2008). Retrieved from http://www.kent.ac.uk/counselling/Labyrinth/labyrinth.html

LV-21. (n.d.). Retrieved from http://www.lv21.co.uk. Accessed on October 24, 2013.

Totemic Benches. (2013). Retrieved from https://www.facebook.com/#!/groups/501733699875890/

UoK News. (2011, 3 April). Retrieved from http://www.kent.ac.uk/news/stories/student-staff-collaboration-selectred-for-riba-small-budget-big-impact-design-exhibition/2011

PART 4: STUDENTS TAKING RESPONSIBILITY FOR THEIR LEARNING

Elisabeth Dunne and Derfel Owen

No matter the context, there can be little argument that student involvement in their learning is intrinsically linked, at least in part, to the quality of the teaching provided, the inspiration and motivation offered by teachers and the provision of appropriate and stimulating learning experiences that enable students to make sense of their learning. In short, students are likely to engage when teachers make concerted efforts to engage them. There will myriads of such examples, enough for many books in their own right. However, for this particular part of the Handbook, the interest is not in what the teacher does but in what the student does and in the kinds of provision that support students in taking responsibility for their learning. The examples that are provided highlight areas that are of topical interest in the United Kingdom and beyond, and strongly influence the ways in which students are likely to engage and to make the most of their learning opportunities: through acting as peer mentors, through developing reflective practice, through using assessment as a means for learning, or through learning from difference. These are aspects of education that enable students to become more self-aware (Demetriou, 2000; Demetriou & Kazi, 2006), self-directed and better self-regulated (Zimmerman & Schunk, 2001, 2004) and that promote a sense of self efficacy (Bandura, 1982, 1997; Yorke & Knight, 2006) and being in control of one's learning.

Chapter 16 reviews how students can be supported in taking responsibility for their own learning from the very beginning of a degree, through an orientation process that sets expectations as soon as students arrive at University. This example from Tasmania is set in the context of teacher education, and students therefore have to take on an additional dimension — that of professionalism — alongside learning to be a student in higher education. The model outlined for conceptualising student engagement is powerful in any context, along with the analysis of current-day contextual and personal challenges to students engaging effectively.

One way of helping students to take responsibility for their own development is through peer support; students can be helped to recognise the differences in learning when teachers are not omnipresent — as in school classrooms — and the ways in which degree learning has to be more independent (see Candy, 1991). Peer support is one way by which transitions can be eased and academic and social difficulties resolved, amongst a community of learners where taking responsibility for one's personal growth is the norm. Chapter 17 describes a wide-scale peer support system set up across a single UK university with over 40,000 students. Peer education in various forms is now embedded across almost the entire undergraduate student body, and the chapter gives the detail of a model of peer support, and numerous examples with details of strategy, structures, processes and outcomes. This is a sophisticated system that first began on a small scale in 1995, and the descriptions highlight the depth of thinking that has gone into making the complex raft of activities run smoothly, to the desired effect. Chapter 18 also picks up on the theme of peer education, from a different part of the world (New Zealand), and with a population of postgraduate students. The implementation of peer support is at an early stage, but provides some good pointers and reminders as to why systems need to run over a period of time in order to iron out the issues and challenges. Even with a proportion of students having a Maori background, which is highly dependent on peer learning within the culture and kinship relations, peer progress was not always easy, and the support of enthusiastic champions did not always resolve problems However, overall, students gained a great deal from their experiences, and positive feedback and stories of success will serve to give momentum to future iterations.

Chapter 19 offers a series of practical ideas for engaging students in reflective processes, something that is notoriously hard to do, but which is central to the development of personal autonomy and success in learning. Reflection on experience was seen by Dewey (1933) as underpinning learning and could probably be traced back to the educators of long ago — Aristotle, Plato or Confucius. The key idea of reflection is that it enables access to higher order learning, linking experiences and knowledge so as to promote complex and interrelated mental schema. Hence, reflection is central to learning, and it can be developed through practice and habit, whether through induction and orientation, peer education, assessment, or through working sensitively amongst diverse groups of students. This chapter offers a simple approach to reflection (providing stop-and-think strategies) and outlines theory and a series of activities linked to reviewing, reflecting, recording and action planning, with the intention of supporting students in being able to take responsibility for their learning.

Quality learning also relates to learning from, and alongside, anyone and everyone, benefiting from lively groups and conversations, but also having awareness about those populations of students who might feel alienated for any reason and who may not always engage as readily as others. Alienation has been defined as the absence of a relationship that students might desire or expect to experience (Case, 2007), and the relationship of this to student engagement is clearly very close. Part 4 takes two examples of where alienation might arise and where students might encounter group-specific barriers to success — amongst racial or ethnic minorities in a British classroom, or amongst students with disabilities, in this case deaf students.

Chapter 20 addresses student perceptions of the internationalisation agenda and multicultural group working in a fashion design programme. The (mostly) student authors of the chapter highlight how difficult it is to move from ethnocentric ways of behaving to more ethno-relative thinking — where all are comfortable with many standards and customs. The students highlight perceived tensions in behaviour, attitudes, customs and preferences and offer suggestions for engaging their peers more effectively, for example through projects that focus on diversity, through peer buddying and through greater attention to an internationalised curriculum and assessment that supports diversity. Chapter 21 gives a rich vision of the potential for all of us to learn from disabled students, in this case deaf students. The reader is asked to look more closely at student engagement via a plea to open our minds to how deaf students bring so much to learning situations that other students and educators can benefit from. Deaf students have a whole way of 'seeing' and 'being' that can enhance learning, through the use of sophisticated visual skills, gestural intelligence and community-oriented capacities which support student engagement. As outlined earlier in Chapter 11, we can frame disability as an asset rather than a deficit and we must make sure that we do so. This, in turn, relates to the ability to be reflective, self-aware and better able to take responsibility for one-self.

Chapter 22 again focuses on one of the most important promoters of learning in higher education: assessment. Designing assessment that promotes learning is not an easy task, but ensuring that students view 'assessment for learning' as something worth engaging with is even more difficult. This chapter provides solutions to both, emphasising the importance of a formative ethos that values dialogue, collaboration between students and interaction between teachers and students, along with reflection, peer review and evaluation. Overall, this requires moving away from traditional didactic, transmission models of education to more participative, collaborative and social modes of learning, with formative assessment being a driver for self-regulation (Nicol & Macfarlane-Dick, 2006). It is these approaches that support the metacognitive approach (Flavell, 1979, 1987) that is so important to taking self-responsibility and engaging with the processes of learning that link to understanding and achievement.

References

Bandura, A. (1982). Self-efficacy mechanism in human agency. *American Psychologist, 37,* 122–147.

Bandura, A. (1997). *Self-efficacy: The exercise of control.* New York, NY: Freeman.

Candy, P. (1991). *Self-direction for lifelong learning: a comprehensive guide to theory and practice.* San Francisco, CA: Jossey-Bass.

Case, J. (2007). Alienation and engagement: Exploring students' experiences of studying engineering. *Teaching in Higher Education, 12*(1), 119–133.

Demetriou, A. (2000). Organization and development of self-understanding and self-regulation: Toward a general theory. In M. Boekaerts, P. R. Pintrich, & M. Zeidner (Eds.), *Handbook of self-regulation* (pp. 209–251). New York, NY: Academic Press.

Demetriou, A., & Kazi, S. (2006). Self-awareness in g (with processing efficiency and reasoning). *Intelligence, 34,* 297–317.

Dewey, J. (1933). *How we think: A restatement of the relation of reflective thinking to the educative process.* Boston, MA: D.C. Heath.

Flavell, J. H. (1979). Metacognition and cognitive monitoring: A new area of cognitive-developmental inquiry. *American Psychologist, 34*, 906–911.

Flavell, J. H. (1987). Speculations about the nature and development of metacognition. In F. E. Weinert & R. H. Kluwe (Eds.), *Metacognition, motivation and understanding* (pp. 21–29). Hillside, NJ: Lawrence Erlbaum Associates.

Nicol, D., & Macfarlane-Dick, D. (2006). Formative assessment and self-regulated learning: A model and seven principles of good feedback practice. *Studies in Higher Education, 31*(2), 199–218. Retrieved from http://www.reap.ac.uk/reap/public/papers//DN_SHE_Final.pdf

Yorke, M., & Knight, P. T. (2006). *Embedding employability into the curriculum*. Learning and Employability Series 1 No. 3, Higher Education Academy. Retrieved from http://www.heacademy.ac.uk/assets/York/documents/ourwork/employability/id460_embedding_employability_into_the_curriculum_338.pdf

Zimmerman, B. J., & Schunk, D. H. (2001). *Self-regulated learning and academic achievement: Theoretical perspectives*. Hillsdale, NJ: Lawrence Erlbaum Associates.

Zimmerman, B. J., & Schunk, D. H. (2004). Self-regulating intellectual processes and outcomes: A social cognitive perspective. In D. Y. Dai & R. J. Sternberg (Eds.), *Motivation, emotion and cognition*. Hillsdale, NJ: Lawrence Erlbaum Associates.

Chapter 16

Student Engagement in and Through Orientation

Sharon Pittaway and Timothy Moss

Abstract

The purpose of this chapter is to explore the complexities involved in understanding and planning for student orientation and engagement within the higher education context. Key understandings of what is meant by 'student engagement' are explored through a conceptual framework that draws together five dimensions of engagement: personal, academic, intellectual, social and professional.

Findings: Discussion focuses on the challenges to student engagement in higher education, including contextual/environmental factors as well as personal factors. Examples are provided of ways in which these challenges can be addressed, with a particular focus on students' orientation and transition into the higher education context. The framework articulated in this chapter has wide potential as a foundation for the planning and delivery of activities aimed at enhancing student engagement. The examples in the chapter, drawn from our own practice, illustrate the practical outcomes of using the framework in this way.

Throughout the chapter, the context of teacher education is used as a lens through which to view the broader issues of student engagement, with specific reference to programmes and practices developed within the Australian context. Therefore, the chapter has direct applicability to those involved in teacher education. However, the framework has further value in that it allows for deeper understanding of the demands that engagement makes in terms of a student's academic, personal, social, intellectual, and professional skills, knowledge, aspirations, and dispositions, and to therefore consider how such demands might be addressed for students across a range of backgrounds, within practice and policy.

The Student Engagement Handbook: Practice in Higher Education
Copyright © 2013 by Emerald Group Publishing Limited
All rights of reproduction in any form reserved
ISBN: 978-1-78190-423-7

16.1.   Introduction

There is a growing body of research highlighting the importance of engagement for students' success in their university studies. For instance, Chen, Gonyea and Kuh (2008) claim that 'by being engaged, students develop habits of the mind and heart that promise to stand them in good stead for a lifetime of continuous learning' (p. 2). Krause (2005) highlights the link between engagement and the cognitive aspects of student learning, stating that 'engagement refers to the time, energy and resources students devote to activities designed to enhance learning at university' (p. 3), a point echoed by the Australian Council for Educational Research (ACER) (2011), which defines engagement as 'students' involvement with activities and conditions likely to generate high-quality learning' (p. 3). In much of the established research literature on engagement (e.g. Coates, 2006; Kuh, 2009) there is an emphasis on what the institution can do to improve student engagement, alongside student behaviours that demonstrate engagement. According to Kahu (2011) this 'behavioural perspective' (p. 3) does not adequately acknowledge the emotional aspects of student engagement and therefore 'misses valuable information that would give a much richer understanding of the student experience' (p. 4). If institutional policies seek to mandate what engagement is and how it plays out in practice much may be missed of the students' own experience and understanding of engagement. Similarly, if engagement is understood in too narrow a way, other factors that go beyond student behaviours and institutional actions will not be accounted for when considering how students engage and how to enhance engagement. The whole person, including the context in which that person lives, works and studies, needs to be part of any thinking about engagement if policies and practices are to be successful in enhancing engagement in higher education and in teacher education more specifically. In this chapter we seek to provide a view of engagement that recognises the fundamental importance of 'student-in-context' and to explore how such a view might be enacted within the university context, beginning with students' entry to university.

Although engagement with higher education may begin prior to enrolment, for many students the starting point for their study, and thus their identity as students, is Orientation. This is a key time in establishing expectations and relationships that have ongoing implications for a student's engagement and learning. As with many institutions, at the University of Tasmania the week prior to the formal commencement of classes is designated as Orientation Week. While Orientation is configured differently depending on the School or Faculty, it is recognised across the institution as a key time in students' transition to university. The University of Tasmania, the only university in the island state of Tasmania, has a student population of approximately 25,000, across three major campuses, in Hobart, Launceston, and Burnie, and a growing online student population. The University is a teaching and research institution, divided into six Faculties. Both authors are located within the Faculty of Education, which delivers pre-service, in-service and postgraduate teacher education courses in both face-to-face and fully online modes. Over 50% of students in this Faculty study in the fully online mode, approximately one-third of whom reside outside of Tasmania. While the examples in this chapter are drawn specifically from the context of teacher education, the Framework presented here has applicability across disciplinary contexts, in that it primarily aims to offer a means of understanding and planning for student engagement.

This chapter explores the complexities of understanding and planning for student engagement in higher education from Orientation onwards. In particular, the contextual/environmental factors and personal factors that present challenges to student engagement are outlined, and examples of how these challenges might be addressed through practice are provided. Throughout the chapter, we contend that it is essential for both policy and practice in higher education to recognise the fundamental purpose of engagement: engagement in and for learning.

16.2. Conceptualising Student Engagement

As indicated above, engagement is a complex concept to define, and the term has been used variously in the literature to date. Pittaway (2012) developed an Engagement Framework as a way of unifying our understandings of engagement, identifying and presenting five inter-related dimensions of engagement that break apart the broader construct of 'engagement' as defined by Kuh (2009), ACER (2011), Krause (2005) and others. This Engagement Framework identifies five distinctive, non-hierarchical dimensions of engagement that are fundamental to students' success at university. These dimensions are personal, academic, intellectual, social, and professional. In what follows, we provide an initial discussion of the environment in which the Framework is situated, and then present a brief overview of each of the five dimensions of the Framework, supported by relevant literature.

16.2.1. Key Principles

Underpinning the Engagement Framework are four key principles that seek to establish the optimum environment for engagement. These principles are drawn from a range of literature encompassing the scholarship of teaching and learning, student engagement, and university teaching policy (see, e.g., ACER, 2011; Allen & Allodi, 2010; Clarke, 2007; Dunn & Rakes, 2011; Krause, 2005; Middlecamp, 2005; University of Melbourne, 2007).

1. Staff engagement is a prerequisite for student engagement.
2. Respectful and supportive relationships are essential for learning and teaching.
3. Students must be given, and actively take, responsibility for their own learning.
4. Scaffolding, communicating expectations and setting high standards lead to the continued development of knowledge, understanding, skills and capacities

These environmental principles play a significant role in shaping the dimensions of the Framework, and are significant in unit design, teaching and support practices. The intersecting nature of the dimensions of the Framework and the non-hierarchical structure mean that one dimension (such as social) might be particularly significant for students at a specific point in time, while at other times, personal or intellectual engagement may play a more significant role. This is consistent with the notion that engagement 'plays out in different ways at different points of the educational cycle' (ACER, 2011, p. 1). This Framework can be applied in a variety of ways, with regard to both staff and students. For example, unit developers may use the Framework when designing the learning outcomes, tasks and assessment of a unit. Students, on the other hand, may use the Framework in taking responsibility for their own learning and making decisions about what, when, and how they will engage in their studies. This flexibility in the application of the Framework is intentional, and allows for individual preferences and/or needs of those involved in teaching, learning and support.

16.2.2.   Personal Engagement

Personal engagement is the necessary first dimension of the Engagement Framework. It encompasses ideas such as aspiration (Appadurai, 2004) and the personal belief that university is valuable and worthwhile, requiring an active decision to enrol in a university course, and the development of an identity as a student (Moss & Pittaway, 2012). Personal engagement, which therefore begins before the student enrols, also requires students to hold a belief that they can succeed at this level, and can continue to learn and develop (Dweck, 2006). It also requires a degree of conative capacity — that is, a will to learn (Riggs & Gholar, 2009). Other attributes of this dimension include self-efficacy, goal-setting, awareness of intention, resilience and persistence. This dimension is primarily about awareness: of intentions, expectations, assumptions, level of skill and the responsibilities associated with the choice to enrol at university (Walker et al., 2009). Staff too must be personally engaged (see Key Principle 1) in their work with students and be aware of how their engagement plays out in their teaching and support of student learning and development.

16.2.3.   Academic Engagement

Academic engagement includes identifying and managing student and staff expectations, both within the formal learning environment and outside of it. Success in the university context requires students to draw upon knowledge and skills that go beyond disciplinary boundaries (Lea & Street, 2006). This dimension encompasses the capacity for students to take 'active control ... by planning, monitoring and evaluating their learning' (Scevak & Cantwell, 2007, p. 37), which might include monitoring their development of such attributes as personal, computer and information literacy, academic writing, referencing, note-taking and time management (Brick, 2006). Opportunities for such development must be provided over the course of a degree programme, with more or less support depending on the context of the unit (e.g. stage within the degree), and these opportunities should also take account of the specific disciplinary context (Lea, 2004). Without these skills and capacities, students are unlikely to be able to engage intellectually, although academic engagement is not necessarily a prerequisite for intellectual engagement.

16.2.4. *Intellectual Engagement*

This dimension of the Framework centres on disciplinary contexts. Specifically, intellectual engagement refers to students' engagement with the ideas and concepts of their discipline, and the social, political and ethical issues that are part of that context (Bowen, 2005). Intellectual engagement is demonstrated through critical thinking, and through students taking an interest in current debates about their discipline, wide reading, discussion with others (peers and academic staff) and an awareness of their own beliefs, values and attitudes in relation to the disciplines to which they are exposed. For academic staff, this dimension of the Framework can be taken into account when designing unit learning outcomes, weekly tasks and assessment. Through the design of such tasks within a supportive environment, students are more likely to develop confidence when their ideas are challenged, be prepared to ask questions, recognise the strengths and weaknesses of their own thinking, and be open-minded to the views of others (Judge, Jones & McCreery, 2009), thus leading to enhanced engagement and learning.

16.2.5. *Social Engagement*

Social engagement is primarily about relationships, allowing students to confront other ways of seeing the world, and can deepen and extend their own views, beliefs and perspectives (Beachboard, Beachboard, Li & Adkison, 2011; Reason, Terenzini & Domingo, 2006). Krause (2005) argues that the social aspects of engagement are 'equally as important as intellectual pursuits' (p. 9). This dimension is just as relevant for students studying in the fully online mode. Edwards, Perry and Janzen (2011) claim that effective online teaching promotes social interaction between students, and between students and teaching staff. Leong (2011) cites Shea, Fredericksen and Pickett (2000), who 'determined that the level of students' interaction with the instructor and classmates was significantly correlated with the level of satisfaction and perceived learning in online learning courses' (p. 6). Students can also demonstrate social engagement outside of the formal learning environment, through organising student-led societies, which provide opportunities for networking and professional engagement.

16.2.6. *Professional Engagement*

The fifth dimension of the framework is professional engagement. This is particularly important for those courses preparing students for specific professions (such as teaching or nursing), but has implications across all degrees. This dimension of the framework relates to the nexus between theory and practice, allowing for theoretical constructs to be tested in professional contexts such as work-integrated learning programmes. Through engaging professionally in a regular and sustained manner while studying, university students have the opportunity to apply, consolidate and challenge their knowledge, beliefs and skills as learners and as developing professionals (Bowen, 2005). Examples of such engagement may include students attending professional learning opportunities outside of the university context, and joining professional associations. Again, academic staff have a role to play in assisting students to identify and manage their involvement in such activities, through the design of learning tasks and/or assessment within units and the ways they value and promote these activities. Although this dimension could be seen as a sub-section of social engagement, the key difference is one of emphasis, in that professional engagement looks forward to the contexts in which students will operate as graduates, and beyond their immediate cohorts and contexts. Through professional engagement, students can also form ongoing communities of practice by networking and creating opportunities for lifelong learning.

Across all five dimensions of engagement, the Framework assumes that the fundamental purpose of students' engagement in their studies is engagement in and for *learning*. The framework attempts to highlight those dimensions that facilitate effective learning, towards both disciplinary and generic outcomes. This focus on learning takes into account the context in which the student studies and seeks to ensure that the whole person is engaged in higher education. It is our contention that focusing our conversation on engagement in and for learning allows us to identify a number of fundamental challenges to engagement, which have the potential to impact upon students' attainment of their (and our) intended outcomes of university study.

16.3. Challenges to Student Engagement

In order to engage successfully in the context of the contemporary university, there are many challenges that students must address. Some of these challenges might be considered contextual or environmental, in the sense that they relate primarily to the university environment regardless of the individual. Others may be described as more learner-centred or personal challenges, in that they centre on the individual student, and his/her motivations, skills, prior experiences and intended goals of studying. In this section, we consider both types of challenges, with a particular focus on the widening participation agenda operating within the contextual challenges, and mapping the personal challenges against the dimensions of the Engagement Framework described above.

16.3.1. *Contextual Factors*

Government policy in Australia and internationally has recently given much attention to the concept of 'widening participation' in higher education. Within Australia, for example, in 2009 the Australian government announced its '20/40 targets' (Gale, 2010), which set out two related aims for student participation in higher education, namely that 'by 2020, 20% of all undergraduate students in higher education will come from low socioeconomic status (SES) backgrounds; and, by 2025, 40% of all 25–34 year olds will hold a Bachelor's degree' (Gale, 2010, p. 2). A similar focus on widening participation can be seen in UK policy (e.g. Hockings, Cooke & Bowl, 2007) and in other international contexts. According to Hockings et al. (2007) non-traditional students (e.g. adult students, and those from low SES backgrounds) may experience 'a number of unexpected challenges to their sense of identity, belonging and self-esteem' (p. 722), and these may arise due to cultural factors, and/or pedagogical factors. In terms of cultural factors, students from non-traditional backgrounds may feel alienated and excluded by the experience of university: alienated from the largely middle-class culture of the institution, and excluded by their university peers and their home communities (Hockings et al., 2007). Further, agendas that aim to widen participation can lead to pedagogical challenges for institutions as well: as student numbers increase, class sizes increase (Gale, 2010), and university lecturers may begin to rely on teacher-focused strategies such as lectures (Hockings et al., 2007). As the 'gap' between teacher and student increases, there is less space and time in which to adapt the curriculum to the needs of the full range of learners present. In this pedagogical environment, engagement becomes the sole responsibility of the student.

In addition to the challenges raised by moves towards widening participation in higher education, there are other contextual factors that may impact on students' capacity to engage in their studies. Students who balance study commitments with paid employment, for example, can find it difficult to leave sufficient time for independent study, and can experience tension as a result (Pittaway & Moss, 2006). In the Australian context, the number of students engaged in paid employment has increased steadily over time (Pittaway & Moss, 2006), a situation that is similar internationally (Hockings et al., 2007), despite research highlighting the potential difficulties that such work can cause for students' academic performance (Watts, 2002).

The contextual factors discussed above suggest many challenges that students and institutions must take account of, in considering how to most effectively engage students for learning.

16.3.2. *Personal Challenges*

Analysing the student experience through the Engagement Framework presented earlier highlights a second 'set' of challenges that must also be addressed: personal challenges. These involve challenges related to engaging academically, intellectually, personally, socially and professionally in the university context. It is important to note that these challenges overlap and intersect with the contextual and environmental factors noted above; students coming to university from non-traditional backgrounds may experience academic, social, personal or professional challenges differently than those students from more traditional backgrounds.

In order to engage successfully in university study, it is essential that students have the requisite academic skills that will enable them to participate and communicate effectively (Brick, 2006). Of particular note in this regard are the increasingly diverse levels of academic preparation that students bring to their tertiary studies. Students can face challenges ranging from a need for focused assistance with assignments (Peel, 1998) through to more substantial concerns in terms of literacy, numeracy and computer literacy, and substantial variation within a cohort is likely. Perhaps more concerning is the fact that many students do not even view themselves as sufficiently prepared with the skills and knowledge required to engage at university (Clerehan & Walker, 2004), which raises issues related to overcoming self-efficacy concerns.

In addition to potential challenges to engagement that arise from students' academic skills and capacities, the university context also draws upon particular approaches to knowledge and ways of knowing that may exclude some students (Hockings et al., 2007), or at least present challenges to their intellectual engagement. Lecturers who adopt a teacher-focused approach (due perhaps to the contextual factors noted earlier) may not appear to demonstrate an interest in their students' existing ways of knowing or their questions and ideas about an area of study, which can 'reinforce a sense of exclusion and alienation … in which students are largely dependent on the lecturer as authority' (Hockings et al., 2007, p. 723). When dealing with the complexity and ambiguity of knowledge (Mann, 2000) in the higher education context (particularly in disciplines such as teaching, where there are few, if any, 'correct' answers to be found), such an approach has the potential to severely limit students' capacity to engage intellectually with the kind of critical thinking and questioning required of them.

One of the most significant predictors of students' success in making the transition to university is their social engagement (Huon & Sankey, 2002), and with this in mind, it is important to consider challenges students face in engaging socially. Research in the Australian context shows that at least a quarter of all students who responded to a survey on their university experience indicated that they had not made close friends at university, and generally kept to themselves (McInnis, James & Hartley, 2000). Jones (2008) claims that 'strong positive relationships are critical to the education process' (p. 6) although we know from experience that social engagement is even more complex for students who do not study face-to-face, and who must therefore find opportunities to establish meaningful connections with their peers and teaching staff in the somewhat impersonal online environment (Moss & Pittaway, 2012). Students may also face other barriers to social engagement, such as long-distance travel to attend university, paid employment, and family, sporting and/or community commitments.

Related to both the social and personal dimensions of engagement are challenges associated with forming and maintaining a student identity. Forming a strong sense of identity as a student is important as a precursor to other dimensions of engagement: if students do not commit to the role of university student, it is extremely difficult to engage academically (McInnis, James, & McNaught, 1995). This situation is further complicated when students study off-campus; many students' anecdotal reports suggest that the only time they feel like 'real' university students is when they physically attend a campus for (non-compulsory) residential schools (see, for instance, Moss & Pittaway, 2012). In Hillman's (2005) report of an Australian survey of students who withdrew from their studies in their first year, the main reason given by students for their withdrawal was that the course was 'not what they wanted' (p. 34). In this sense, students may enter university with a view of their studies as the passport to a desired profession, rather than as a learning experience in its own right, and this may impact on their developing student and professional identity and thus their personal engagement more broadly.

We have written elsewhere of the complexities involved in taking on an identity as a university student with regard to the professional dimension of student engagement (Pittaway & Moss, 2006). For students in teacher education, this is particularly problematic, as they must balance multiple roles, including university student, student teacher and eventually practising teacher (Moss & Pittaway, 2012), often simultaneously. They must learn to exist at multiple points along a 'novice to expert' continuum, becoming experts in the role of university student while also being seen as novices while on professional experience placements. This differentiation can lead to disorientation and disengagement, either from particular roles (Pittaway & Moss, 2006) or from particular dimensions of engagement. The challenge for students, staff and institutions, then, is to find ways to enable students to understand these diverse roles, and fit them to the overall goals of their course of study.

As the above discussion illustrates, student engagement is not only complex to understand, but also potentially challenging for students to achieve and maintain. Considering the challenges across all five dimensions of the Engagement Framework highlights several important themes, such as the need to attend to students' ways of knowing and their levels of academic preparedness. Further, issues of student belonging and identity, and their aspirations for their study, must be accounted for in practices and policies that seek to enhance student engagement. In short, it is important to take account of the whole person in seeking to address student engagement.

16.4.   Addressing the Challenges in Orientation (and Beyond)

In this section, we offer examples from practices at our institution as a way forward in understanding and addressing the challenges to student engagement in orientation and beyond. In terms of Orientation, the University of Tasmania does not mandate a particular approach to activities in the week prior to semester, allowing Faculties to develop their own approaches; however, central services do offer a range of sessions across the week, which Faculties are able to connect with as part of their own schedules. Within the Faculty of Education, Orientation has developed over time, from origins in a one-day, on-campus introduction to central support services through to a whole-week on-campus series of sessions and workshops (Pittaway & Moss, 2006). In recent times, the programme has broadened to include a focus on the context and needs of students studying online, has expanded to be offered across three Australian states (Tasmania, Victoria and South Australia) and has been redefined as a Faculty-led, one- or two-day focused series of presentations, workshops and activities. Orientation is offered both face-to-face and in fully online mode. In redesigning the programme to take account of the wider range of students and modes of study now operating within the Faculty, the Engagement Framework was used as a starting point to address challenges to student engagement, and all five dimensions of the Framework were incorporated in the revised programme.

16.4.1. Academic Engagement

Diverse levels of academic preparation are a key challenge for students in engaging in their studies, due in part to agendas and policies that aim to widen participation (and thus draw in students who initially may not have imagined a future that involved university studies). Academic engagement is addressed within the face-to-face Orientation programme through sessions that give students hands-on opportunities to explore the university's Learning Management System, and also incorporate discussion from academic staff of the kinds of skills and knowledge that students require in order to achieve success in their studies. Beyond Orientation, ongoing instruction and resources with regard to key academic literacy skills (such as finding and using information, and writing in an academic context) are embedded within specific unit curricula. Assessment tasks throughout students' first year of study are structured so that ongoing literacy (and numeracy) development is assessed, and additional units of study are offered (that carry course credit) for those students who require more focused development in these areas. Students' literacy, numeracy and Information and Communication Technology (ICT) proficiency are also assessed through a programme of competency-based 'hurdle tests', where students are given detailed information about their current level of proficiency against levels that are deemed to be required to be an effective teacher. Where their own proficiency does not yet match these standards, students are advised of suitable support mechanisms, and can retake these hurdle tests as many times as necessary throughout their studies. In this way, we acknowledge the importance of academic literacy development in order to enable students to engage more fully in their studies, recognising the importance of academic skills as a foundation for other forms of engagement. This approach therefore recognises that developing academic literacy is more than just acquiring a set of skills; rather, the processes involved in becoming engaged academically are 'complex, dynamic, nuanced, situated and involving both epistemological issues and social processes' (Lea & Street, 2006, p. 369). Perhaps just as importantly, this continual feedback to students on their levels of academic proficiency is also intended to enable them to develop the self-efficacy required for success (Clerehan & Walker, 2004).

16.4.2. Intellectual Engagement

Intellectual engagement is a significant focus within our Orientation programme, in assisting students to understand the particular ways of knowing that are privileged within the university context, and also to assist students in understanding the ambiguity of knowledge that characterises university learning and thinking. Students are introduced to intellectual engagement in university study through the presentation of a range of 'problems' related to education, and academic staff guide them through a process of critiquing, analysing and developing a position on these problems. Following this practical exercise, general principles about engaging with the ideas presented at university are highlighted and explored with students. Expectations of students, in terms of how they might show that they are intellectually engaged (particularly while studying online), are also covered in this session. Beyond Orientation, students are able to enrol in the unit *Thinking and Writing at University*, offered by our Faculty, which explores in more detail the processes and products of critical thinking.

16.4.3. *Social Engagement*

Social engagement (assisting students to overcome challenges related to feeling as though they 'belong' in the university environment) is a key focus of the face-to-face and online Orientation programmes. For students attending Orientation face-to-face, social engagement is a focus across both days of the programme, beginning with a session facilitated by Course Coordinators to introduce the details of the particular degree in which students are enrolled, and also incorporating a 'panel' of current students, discussing their own experiences of studying. We ensure that this panel is representative of the wide range of students who enrol in the Faculty, including students from non-traditional backgrounds who have achieved significant levels of success in their studies (including mature-aged students, those who have entered university without high levels of self-efficacy in relation to academic skills and those who study fully online), in the aim of challenging traditional stereotypes of what a 'university student' is or looks like. Campus tours are also incorporated in this session, led by current students and staff from the Faculty. This focus on social engagement continues on the second day of Orientation, with a session called 'The Great Race', where students undertake team challenges that require them to revisit key sites from the campus tour, and work in teams to complete problem-solving challenges. This session provides an 'authentic' reason for students to actually engage with each other (to achieve particular goals), rather than the somewhat aimless 'get to know you' sessions that characterised earlier versions of our Orientation activities. In terms of the online Orientation programme, social engagement remains a significant area of focus: each Course Coordinator presents a short video introduction to themselves and the degree programme (which helps to provide a 'face to a name' for the new students), and students work through a series of tasks in a 'sample online unit' which explicitly calls for them to introduce themselves in an online discussion board and make connections with other new students. Students are also introduced to the Engagement Framework in this online site, and the importance of making connections to other students is emphasised. Beyond Orientation, first-year units maintain a focus on social engagement through tutorials (and online activities) that explicitly require students to work together, to provide feedback, solve problems and complete tasks. Online students' engagement in such tasks is monitored by tutors, and those students who do not appear to be participating in collaborative tasks are contacted (either by email or telephone) to remind them of the importance of this aspect of their studies and to offer support if required.

16.4.4. Personal Engagement

Addressing students' personal engagement in their studies, and particularly the issues associated with identity formation (e.g. taking on multiple roles), is a key aim of our Orientation activities. Personal engagement is addressed in part through a session exploring the services available to students within the university (such as counselling services), and is also addressed through the student panel discussed above. In terms of students' personal engagement beyond the Orientation programme, this area remains a key focus within their core first-year units. One such unit, *Foundations of Teaching*, requires students to complete a 'self-assessment' quiz before they are able to access any of their study materials for the unit, which requires them to reflect on their own preparedness to engage in their studies, and their motivations for entering teaching. Such meta-analysis of motives and engagement is reinforced throughout this unit, to assist students in both understanding and shaping their sense of identity as a student, and as a future teacher.

16.4.5. Professional Engagement

Identity issues are further addressed in sessions aimed at exploring the profession of teaching. One of the first sessions of the face-to-face Orientation programme involves a range of invited speakers from the professional context, who speak to students about issues such as what it means to be a teacher, the challenges and joys of teaching, and the role the university plays in preparing students for this context. This final topic is particularly significant, given the issues that students can face in balancing the multiple roles of university student, and student teacher. Engagement with the profession remains an area of significant focus beyond the Orientation programme, and indeed, students undertake a unit in their final year of study named *Preparing for the Profession*, which aims to enable a smooth transition for students upon graduation. Professional engagement is an important foundation for fully online students, many of whom are currently employed in support roles in education contexts. Many units incorporate tasks such as observation exercises which must be completed within the professional setting, and such activities help to 'bridge the gap' between the university and the school contexts that could otherwise be problematic for students studying in this mode.

16.4.6. *Sustaining Engagement*

Orientation, of course, is only one step in the students' journey. Ongoing connections are maintained through a series of Engagement Days, available to those students studying fully online, which seek to address the additional challenges or barriers to engagement that this mode may present. These days are offered at least once a semester, on each main campus of the University and also in a number of interstate capital cities. The focus of these Engagement Days is not on the specific content of particular units of work, rather each addresses specific dimensions of the Engagement Framework (such as academic engagement, where the focus may be on creating an argument, or information literacy). There is one 'constant' element, which is addressed in every Engagement Day: social engagement. This reflects both the importance of building networks for student success, and the difficulties associated with establishing such networks in the context of fully online study. To determine which other dimensions will also be incorporated into an Engagement Day, students are consulted as to their current needs, and where they are experiencing difficulties. The language of the Engagement Framework is used explicitly within the sessions to reinforce to students the importance of monitoring their engagement, and to provide them with a language and a structure to achieve this.

It is also important to note that the Faculty is addressing the challenges to student engagement *within* the curriculum, as well as the measures discussed above (which largely take place outside of the context of specific units). For example, our first-year undergraduate units now explicitly link learning outcomes to the dimensions of the Framework, indicating to students where the content might be expected to contribute to their engagement in an academic, professional or intellectual sense. Tasks are also designed around the dimensions of the Framework, both for assessment purposes, and as part of regular weekly tutorials and online activities. Student surveys and feedback on their experience of our units also incorporate reference to the dimensions of the Engagement Framework (e.g. Baker & Pittaway, 2012) to further embed this model of engagement within students' experience. In addition to being endorsed by Faculty Executive, the Engagement Framework has also been presented to staff in other Schools within the University, and a University-funded Community of Practice is now in place to develop and sustain conversations around ways of enhancing practice using the Framework.

Through the processes and practices we have described in this section, we have come to believe that the Engagement Framework provides two benefits: first, it provides a common language to discuss student engagement that goes beyond 'engagement with the University' in a generic sense, instead allowing us to move the debate on to how we might best engage students *in learning and teaching* specifically. Second, the Framework provides a lens through which we can begin to understand, and potentially overcome, the variety of challenges that can stand between our students (and particularly those who do not fit within the stereotypical 'white middle class school leaver' image of the university student) and the

achievement of the personal, social, intellectual, academic and professional outcomes that they and we would consider to be the fundamental purpose of coming
to university. The Framework allows us to consider how these challenges might
manifest in students' first steps into the university context (and therefore the role
of Orientation programmes in making an effective transition), and also how
student engagement might continue to be relevant throughout students' time at
university. That is, if we want our students to be engaged, we must seek to engage
the whole student: their minds, bodies, beliefs, attitudes, dispositions and aspirations, while taking into consideration their domestic and other environmental/con-
textual factors.

16.5. Conclusions

It is clear from the literature and institutional discussions that student engagement
is complex; defining what we might mean when we refer to engagement is difficult
enough, let alone considering how best to engage students throughout their studies.
At our own institution, this lack of clarity regarding student engagement has the
potential to lead to a lack of direction and common purpose: it is difficult to determine how to engage students if we do not fully understand what such engagement
might look like, and why it might be important. With this in mind, we contend that
the Engagement Framework has much to offer as a foundation for the planning
and delivery of Orientation activities, and also for our ongoing efforts to engage students in their learning. This Framework allows us to consider the whole student
in their context (whether this be at home online, or in a lecture theatre on campus)
and, perhaps more importantly, allows us to move the focus of engagement to
student learning, considering directly how academics and students might best work
together to understand the dimensions that make up the student experience. The
examples above, drawn from our own practice, illustrate the outcomes of such
a focus.

We feel that there is much potential here for policymakers as well. Within the
context of widening participation, it is reasonable to state that certain dimensions of
the Framework will have greater prominence than may have been the case in the
past. It is no longer possible (if, indeed, it ever was) to imagine that we are dealing
with one kind of student, and that this student is middle-class, well-versed in the discourses of academia, coming to university directly from schooling that would serve
as preparation for this environment, studying full-time, and attending classes on
campus. The Framework allows us to understand more fully the demands that
engagement makes in terms of a student's academic, personal, social, intellectual
and professional skills, knowledge, aspirations and dispositions, and to therefore
consider how such demands might be addressed for students across a range of backgrounds. Perhaps most importantly, the Framework offers a potential way for policymakers to recognise the centrality of student learning as the intended outcome of
any engagement initiatives and activities.

References

ACER. (2011). Dropout DNA, and the genetics of effective support. *Research Briefing, Australasian Survey of Student Engagement, 11*, 1–18. Retrieved from http://www.acer.edu.au

Allen, J., & Clarke, K. (2007). Nurturing supportive learning environments in higher education through the teaching of study skills: To embed or not to embed? *International Journal of Teaching and Learning in Higher Education, 19*, 64–76. Retrieved from http://www.isetl.org/ijtlhe/articleView.cfm?id = 164

Allodi, M. (2010). The meaning of social climate in learning environments: Some reasons why we do not care enough about it. *Learning Environments Research, 13*, 89–104.

Appadurai, A. (2004). The capacity to aspire: Culture and the terms of recognition. In V. Rao & M. Walton (Eds.), *Culture and public action* (pp. 59–84). Palo Alto, CA: Stanford University Press.

Baker, W. J., & Pittaway, S. (2012). The application of a student engagement framework to the teaching of music education in an e-learning context in one Australian University. *Proceedings of the 4th Paris international conference on education, economy and society* (pp. 27–38).

Beachboard, M., Beachboard, J., Li, W., & Adkison, S. (2011). Cohorts and relatedness: Self-determination theory as an explanation of how learning communities affect educational outcomes. *Research in Higher Education, 52*, 853–874.

Bowen, S. (2005). Engaged learning: Are we all on the same page? *Peer Review, 7*(2), 4–7.

Brick, J. (2006). *Academic culture: A student's guide to studying at university*. Sydney: Macquarie University.

Chen, P., Gonyea, R., & Kuh, G. (2008). Learning at a distance: Engaged or not? *Innovate, 4*(3). Retrieved from http://www.innovateonline.info

Clerehan, R., & Walker, I. (2004). Student perceptions of preparedness for first-year university assignment writing: The discipline of marketing. *Language and Academic Skills in Higher Education, 6*, 37–46.

Coates, H. (2006). *Student engagement in campus-based and online education*. London: Routledge.

Dunn, K., & Rakes, G. (2011). Teaching teachers: An investigation of beliefs in teacher education students. *Learning Environments Research, 14*, 39–58.

Dweck, C. (2006). *Mindset: The new psychology of success*. New York, NY: Random House.

Edwards, M., Perry, B., & Janzen, K. (2011). The making of an exemplary online educator. *Distance Education, 32*(1), 101–118.

Gale, T. (2010, July). *Rethinking higher education: Implications of the Australian government's expansion and equity agenda*. Paper presented at the Teaching & Learning Annual Symposium, University of South Australia.

Hillman, K. (2005). *The first year experience: The transition from secondary school to university and TAFE in Australia*. Camberwell: Australian Council for Educational Research.

Hockings, C., Cooke, S., & Bowl, M. (2007). Academic engagement within a widening participation context — a 3D analysis. *Teaching in Higher Education, 12*(5–6), 721–733.

Huon, G., & Sankey, M. (2002, July). *The transition to university: Understanding differences in success*. Paper presented at the 6th Pacific Rim Conference on First Year in Higher Education, Christchurch NZ.

Jones, R. (2008). *Strengthening student engagement*. International Center of Leadership in Education. Rexford, NY. Retrieved from http://www.svsd410.org/departments/curriculum/instructional5framework/Resources/Engagement/strengthening%20student%20engagement.pdf

Judge, B., Jones, P., & McCreery, E. (2009). *Critical thinking skills for education students.* Exeter, UK: Learning Matters.

Kahu, E. (2011). Framing student engagement in higher education. *Studies in Higher Education*, 1−16.

Krause, K. (2005). *Understanding and promoting student engagement in university learning communities.* Centre for the Study of Higher Education. Retrieved from http://www.cshe. unimelb.edu.au/resources_teach/teaching_in_practice

Kuh, G. D. (2009). The national survey of student engagement: Conceptual and empirical foundations. *New Directions for Institutional Research, 141*, 5−20.

Lea, M. (2004). Academic literacies: A pedagogy for course design. *Studies in Higher Education, 29*(6), 739−756.

Lea, M., & Street, B. (2006). The academic literacies model: Theory and applications. *Theory Into Practice, 45*(4), 368−377.

Leong, P. (2011). Role of social presence and cognitive absorption in online learning environments. *Distance Education, 32*(1), 5−28.

Mann, S. (2000). Alternative perspectives on the student experience: Alienation and engagement. *Studies in Higher Education, 26*(1), 7−19.

McInnis, C., James, R., & Hartley, R. (2000). *Trends in the first year experience in Australian universities.* Canberra: Department of Education, Training and Youth Affairs.

McInnis, C., James, R., & McNaught, C. (1995). *First year on campus: Diversity in the initial experiences of Australian undergraduates.* Canberra: Australian Government Publishing Service.

Middlecamp, C. (2005). The art of engagement. *Peer Review, 7*, 17−20.

Moss, T., & Pittaway, S. (2012). Student identity construction in online teacher education: A narrative life history approach. *International Journal of Qualitative Studies in Education, iFirst article*, 1−15.

Peel, M. (1998). *The transition from year twelve to university.* Melbourne: Monash University.

Pittaway, S. (2012). Student and staff engagement: Developing an engagement framework in a Faculty of Education. *Australian Journal of Teacher Education, 37*(4), 37−45.

Pittaway, S., & Moss, T. (2006, July). *Contextualising student engagement: Orientation and beyond in teacher education.* Paper presented at the 9th Pacific Rim First Year in Higher Education Conference, Gold Coast, Queensland.

Reason, R., Terenzini, P., & Domingo, R. (2006). First things first: Developing academic competence in the first year of college. *Research in Higher Education, 47*(2), 149−175.

Riggs, E., & Gholar, C. (2009). *Strategies that promote student engagement: Unleashing the desire to learn* (2nd ed.), Thousand Oaks, CA: Corwin Press.

Scevak, J., & Cantwell, R. (2007). Stepping stones: A guide for mature-aged students at university, Camberwell: ACER Press.

University of Melbourne. (2007). *Nine principles guiding teaching and learning: The framework for a first-class university teaching and learning environment.* Retrieved from http://www. unimelb.com.au

Walker, S., Brownlee, J., Lennox, S., Exley, B., Howells, K., & Cocker, F. (2009). Understanding first year university students: Personal epistemology and learning. *Teaching Education, 20*(3), 243−256.

Watts, C. (2002). The effects of term-time employment on academic performance. *Education and Training, 44*(2), 95−108.

Chapter 17

Peer Education

Marcia Ody and William Carey

Abstract

While the use of peers supporting others has been in existence for some time there have been boom periods. As the current culture of higher education is focusing on personalised student experiences, engagement and partnership, along with the recognition that the higher education maze is challenging to navigate, it is perhaps not surprising that more Peer Education is evolving. The use of peers in higher education is not a new concept; indeed there are more than 40 years of literature supporting benefits of peers impacting positively on the learning experience of others. This impact is found in students' transition to college, social and emotional development, leadership and career skills development, satisfaction with college, learning and academic performance and persistence and retention. However, both practitioners and to some degree the literature are ambiguous in definition and there are often interchanges in descriptive language and terminology used. This chapter will discuss practice and nomenclature, propose definitions, provide a range of case studies, suggest an evolving model and consider strategic, operational and logistical factors. It is hoped that the experience of The University of Manchester in the field of Peer Education since 1995 will support the reader in creating an understanding of Peer Education that can be used to inform future practice.

17.1. What Is Peer Education?

The concept of peer-to-peer education is not new. It could be traced back as far as Aristotle in ancient Greece, or to the 'Madras' system in India in the early 1800s — a utilitarian and cost-effective response to a dire lack of teachers, with older boys supervised in teaching younger children (Bell, 1808). This became more commonly

The Student Engagement Handbook: Practice in Higher Education

Copyright © 2013 by Emerald Group Publishing Limited

All rights of reproduction in any form reserved

ISBN: 978-1-78190-423-7

known as the Lancastrian system and was widely adopted by schools both in the United Kingdom and around the world (Lancaster, 1805). Peer Education became particularly popular in the early 1960s in the context of young persons' health and lifestyle issues. In the context of higher education, it has been documented in the literature over a period of more than 40 years, with increasing evidence of peers impacting positively on the learning experience of others (see, e.g., Astin, 1999; Chickering, 1993; Pascarella & Terenzini, 1991; Topping, 2001). This impact is found in a variety of areas:

- students' transition to college (Brissette, Scheier & Carver, 2002; Crissman Ishler & Schrieber, 2002);
- social and emotional development (Harmon, 2006);
- leadership and career skills development (Donelan & Kay, 1998);
- satisfaction with college (Coffman & Gilligan, 2002);
- learning and academic performance (Astin, 1993);
- persistence and retention (Potts, Schultz & Foust, 2003–2004).

The extent of impact is exemplified by quotes from just two of the above authors. Pascarella and Terenzini (1991) state: 'Students' interactions with their peers … have a strong influence on many aspects of change during college, [including] intellectual development and orientation; political, social, and religious values, academic and social self-concept; intellectual orientation; interpersonal skills; moral development; general maturity and personal development' (pp. 620, 621). This is further supported by Astin (1993) who claims, 'The student's peer group is the single most potent source of influence on growth and development during the undergraduate years' (p. 398).

As the current culture of higher education in the United Kingdom is focusing increasingly on personalised student experiences in a mass market, as well as on student engagement and partnership, and since the higher education 'maze' is challenging to navigate for students, it is perhaps not surprising that Peer Education is becoming formalised in a number of ways. However, this arena is also becoming complex, with many different practices, ambiguous definitions, and often with interchanges in descriptive language and terminology (Cuseo, 2010). This chapter provides a review and discussion of the variety of nomenclature and definitions, suggests an evolving model, and outlines a range of case studies of practice at The University of Manchester (a leader in the field of Peer Support that considers strategic, operational and logistical factors). The purpose is to clarify and provide enhanced understanding of the topic and the many forms of peer education, specifically to support those who wish to engage with this kind of activity.

The complexity can be seen immediately in the variety of names given to peer educators, with Newton and Ender (2010) noting that '… many terms seem synonymous, examples include: Peer Counselor, Ambassador, Student Coach, Peer Mentor, Student Assistant, Class Recitation Facilitator, Tutor, Resident Assistant, and Orientation Leader' (p. 6). If these are then set in the context of the variety of names given to the many models of peer education — such as Peer Tutoring, Peer Mentoring, Supplemental Instruction, Peer Assisted Study, Peer Assisted Learning, Learning Communities or Transition Mentoring — it is immediately obvious that there will be room for confusion. In addition, the variety of models may be very different in purpose and therefore designed with varied characteristics, including whether they are based on one-to-one or group activity, whether they are dependent on tutoring or facilitation; whether the focus is curricular, co-curricular or extra-curricular; whether activity is compulsory or non-compulsory for students; or whether there is a specific or a generic focus. Further aspects include the length of any formalised peer relationship, whether these are for remedial or non-remedial activities and whether they are paid or voluntary. Further, a variety of theoretical perspectives are used as foundations, giving models a strong grounding and credibility, but with different foci.

There is yet another important distinction to be made. To date, Peer Education has been reported in the context of formalised intentional interactions. However, we consider Peer Education as being inclusive of a greater number of peer learning opportunities, in particular informal, opportunistic, spontaneous and student-led interactions that are equally valuable in terms of a student developing towards their educational goals — for example, independent self-selecting study groups with no institutional structured leadership, training or support, or opportunistic peer interactions within halls of residence, student common rooms, and so on.

As outlined above, there are numerous terms for peer educators, but there is also a clear distinction between those who offer peer leadership and those who offer peer support. Having extended the definition of Peer Education, we are defining Peer Leadership as 'students who have been selected, trained and designated by a campus authority to offer educational services to their peers'. These services are intentionally designed to assist peers towards attainment of educational goals (Newton & Ender, 2010), and therefore include all of the aforementioned models of Peer Education practice, with some leaders taking on a 'paraprofessional' role within the curriculum and others being outside of this. Those who offer 'peer support' have a slightly different role, focused on the facilitation and enhancement of a learner's experience, but not in a tutoring or teaching role.

17.2. Peer Support

The characteristics of Peer Support are that it is dependent on small groups, is open to all, is non-compulsory, takes place in a safe environment with no potential assessors, is fun and is dependent on the engagement of immediate or near peers with shared experiences. Importantly, it must be supplementary to necessary staff interaction, needs to be structured and purposeful and should have appropriate training and support. There are many peer support schemes that have been developed in higher education and that formalise and embed the characteristics outlined. Several of these will be outlined below.

17.2.1.   A Model of Peer Support

Before outlining some examples of practice, we propose a model which brings together (1) the learning approach and (2) the intended objectives or purposes, and acknowledges (3) the individual learner stage (Figure 17.1).

1. Our proposed model suggests that a 'Learning and Enabling' process should be at the centre (the branch) of any peer support model or scheme. This process supports any particular scheme's aims (the leaves).
2. Any scheme may have differing intended objectives or purposes, albeit with an overarching aim of enhancing, supporting and personalising the student experience. We propose six categories: Orientation, Community Development, Social Interaction, Academic Content, Learning Strategies and Pastoral. However, we also recognise from experience that, despite any scheme's aims, each individual's journey is different and may result in different and unintended outcomes.
3. We acknowledge that learners have different experiences and different goals, and will be at different stages of learning, but the near peer will advance the learning process through objectivity, shared experiences, and structured intentional interaction.

The creation of a cooperative and collaborative learning environment advances and equips students as independent learners. Peer Support focuses on what they achieve through their interactions rather than what they attain. The journey through Peer Support focuses on growth in which an individual is still advancing and deepening their own learning through peer interaction, as the growth of the tree continues. It is also important to ask: is the nomenclature really important or is it

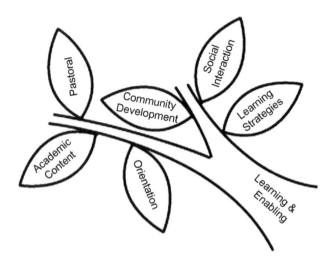

Figure 17.1:   Our model of Peer Support.

about getting the aims and characteristics right for the particular cohort of students in the context of their own institution's culture?

Importantly, this is a constantly evolving model, with continued questioning on whether the titles are right, whether there should be additional categories or change over time, what should be measured and how, and whether it works for different definitions of peer support and different contexts.

17.3.   An Institutional Approach to Peer Support

The University of Manchester first implemented recognised Peer Support structures in 1995. Significant growth has taken place since this time and the programme of activity is now well established and embedded across the institution with central coordination housed in the Teaching and Learning Support Office (TLSO) based in the Directorate of the Student Experience. The Institutional Aims and Objectives are currently (i) to enhance the quality, quantity and diversity of student learning within a discipline; (ii) to involve students as partners in their learning experience; (iii) to provide further opportunity for the development of intellectual and professional competencies; and (iv) to provide students with a supportive environment to assist the transition into and within higher education.[1] Strategically, the institution recognises Peer Support as one mechanism of co-curricular support that can personalise and improve the student experience through enhanced interaction with peers (within and outside any year cohort), and that can forge the development of communities and relationships at various levels. The University's approach of 'centrally coordinated, discipline owned and student led' ensures consistency across the institution, but also allows for multiple Peer Support schemes to develop with localised objectives, agreed in consultation with staff and students, and thereby providing well-tailored activity to any target cohort of students.

17.3.1.   Structures

The University Peer Support structures facilitate partnerships to support the schemes at all levels, between central services and the discipline, between academic and professional support staff, between students and staff, and between students in different year groups (Figure 17.2).

The *Strategic Central Coordination Team* has responsibility for strategic oversight and quality assurance. The team manages and coordinates operational activity and numerous formal processes relating to establishing aims and objectives for local schemes, identifying areas where peer support could be introduced, supporting

---

[1]http://www.tlso.manchester.ac.uk/students-as-partners/peersupport/

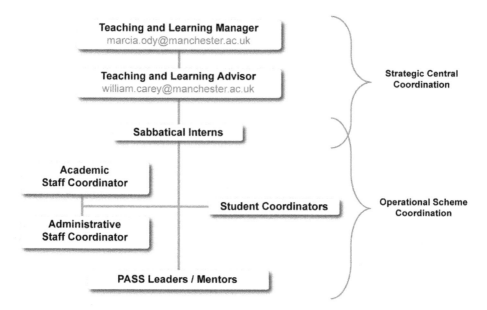

Figure 17.2:   Structures of Peer Support at The University of Manchester.

implementation through offering consultation and sharing of expertise, and linking with other institutional services such as Careers or Students Support, and external programme sponsors (PricewaterhouseCoopers). They are also responsible for recruitment and training, identifying good practice, dissemination, evaluation and institutional recognition and reward.

The team comprises a *Teaching and Learning Manager* who has strategic over-sight, and development and management responsibility for institutionally recognised Peer Support activity. The *Teaching and Learning Adviser* coordinates operational activity including training, production of resources and supervision of Sabbatical Interns and managing the staff and student coordinator networks. *Sabbatical Interns* work in partnership with *Staff and Student Coordinators* to maintain, develop and implement new ideas and ensure the strong continuation and promo-tion of the schemes throughout the academic year. They meet regularly with all par-ties involved, acting as the main communication channel, ensuring sustained enthusiasm and motivation. Located centrally in the TLSO, they operate as part of the central coordination team but have a defined set of schemes for which they are responsible.

A successful Scheme Coordination Team, within any discipline, typically com-prises an allocated Sabbatical Intern, an Academic Coordinator, an Administrative Coordinator (Professional Support Staff) and a Student Coordinator (experienced Mentor or Leader). The way in which activity takes place may vary and functions are allocated thorough discussion between all Coordinators, and monitored regu-larly. The Scheme Coordination Team work in partnership to ensure the scheme addresses the needs of the discipline or cohort. This team has specific responsibility for a number of tasks:

- communicating effectively with all relevant parties including staff and students in the discipline, other central services and, the Peer Support central coordination team;
- recruiting and motivating students who will lead the scheme;
- promoting scheme activity to target group of students;
- assigning groups;
- organising logistics including timetabling, room booking, provision of appropriate resources (e.g. funding);
- organising the scheme activity including production of materials, events, sessions/workshops;
- monitoring and engagement;
- providing academic guidance and support;
- recognising and implementing development areas;
- quality assurance at a local level;
- evaluation and feedback.

Operational activity is carried out by *Mentors and Leaders* — student volunteers who interact with lower year students within the scheme. They are usually level 2 or 3 students (who have had a similar experience, almost always having already completed at least 1 year within the same programme or discipline) who support students with their transition into University. All Mentors and Leaders go through appropriate training to equip them with the skills to fulfil their roles, and are provided with ongoing support. They have regular interaction with the scheme's student target group in line with the objectives and are supported by both the scheme and central coordination teams.

17.3.2.   *Resourcing*

Central resources include:

- staffing as outlined in structures (Figure 17.2) including the appointment of the Sabbatical Interns;
- staff time from other central services;
- central budget for training (resources, catering and payment for student trainers), and recognition and reward (Annual Celebration evening);
- space for training, meetings and events.

Scheme resources include:

- staff time;
- space for activity;
- scheme budget for subsidised activity, resources and local recognition and reward.

The above considerations are now highlighted in the context of specific examples of Peer Mentoring and Peer Assisted Study Sessions (PASS).

17.4.   Case Studies of Peer Support

Six brief case studies of Peer Support in The University of Manchester are outlined below, each exemplifying different ways of working and having different purposes and outcomes, but all demonstrating the powerful ways in which students can support each other. The University of Manchester has the largest student community in the United Kingdom with 39,953 students (27,996 Undergraduate; 8346 Postgraduate Taught; 3611 Postgraduate Research) of which more than 9000 are overseas students from more than 150 countries. The core goals of the research intensive institution are World Class Research, Outstanding Learning and Student Experience, and Social Responsibility. The University is currently ranked 40th in the World, 7th in Europe and 5th in the United Kingdom by Shanghai Jiao Tong World ranking. It also has a long and successful international track record in peer education in 2009 becoming the UK National Centre for Peer Assisted Study Sessions (PASS) and Supplemental Instruction. The PASS programme (see case study 2) was also recognised as the UK national benchmark in 2003.

The first two studies presented below focus on cross-institutional initiatives with differing purposes: (1) 'Peer Mentoring' and the social and pastoral aspects of student life, and (2) 'Peer Assisted Study Sessions (PASS)' with primarily an academic focus. A variety of other Peer Support schemes have evolved from the well-established Mentoring and PASS practice and four further case studies highlight tailored support: (3) Peer-led discussion groups beyond the first year in the Faculty of Life Sciences; (4) 'Special Topics' mentoring in the School of Physics and Astronomy. Case study (5) reports on Peer Engagement within international foundation programmes and (6) considers learning communities in student halls of residence.

17.4.1.   Case Study 1: Peer Mentoring

Peer Mentoring currently operates in almost all disciplines at The University of Manchester, with approximately 1000 Peer Mentors. Its primary focus is to assist transitions and to provide student-led social and pastoral support structures for incoming first year students (Figure 17.3). The specific aims include preparing students for arrival, assisting with realistic expectation setting, supporting the orientation to campus and city, familiarisation with processes and support structures, providing ongoing support at key critical transition points throughout the academic year and fostering a sense of belonging within a discipline or school community. Peer Mentors provide an informal point of contact, supplementing support from staff, taking every opportunity to share their experience and knowledge by providing top tips, signposting services and being available to answer practical questions. Schemes use a variety of ways to communicate between staff, Mentors and mentees

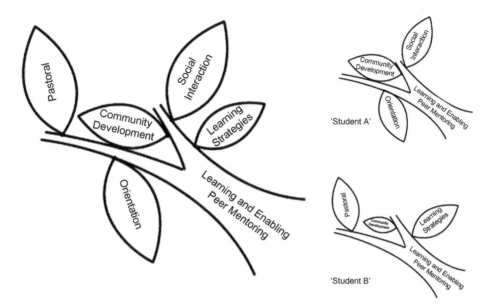

Figure 17.3: Model of Peer Mentoring activity and potential outcomes for different students.

including newsletters and social media. All first year students are assigned Peer Mentors from the same discipline area.

The *Operational Coordination Team* works with Peer Mentors to shape a programme of activity relating specifically to Semester 1. However, mentors are encouraged to continue activity throughout the year, supporting the many transitions and developing a sense of community. Activities can be in place to support the transition of an entire year, for example first year mentoring running over both semesters, but can equally support a specific transition point or stage or targeted group of students, for example study overseas preparation or dissertation support. New students are informed about Peer Mentoring before arriving on campus, through Pre-arrival Guides (Moran, Birch, Carey, & Ody, 2013). Students then meet their Mentors in allocated groups during Welcome Week and typically will have a tailored campus tour and some social activity. Throughout the year Peer Mentors will organise various other events, such as coffee 'mornings', book sales, cultural activities, social activities (often linked to societies), careers talks or skills workshops (e.g. essay writing).

The University's Framework for Peer Mentoring sets out minimum requirement for scheme operation and aspirational activity, and defines the roles and functions for coordination. Peer Mentors receive reflective, interactive, generic training delivered in mixed discipline groups, touching on the role of the mentor, boundaries, referrals and confidentiality, and the student life cycle and transitions. A supplementary 'Planning Ahead' session is delivered within the discipline, encouraging ownership and supporting mentors to creatively develop their scheme and plan activity.

All Peer Mentor training is co-delivered between staff and experienced Peer Mentors. The central coordination team provides additional training and ongoing support, and the *Academic Staff Coordinator* supports the quality assurance of the local scheme by checking all material and supporting the delivery of activity (any academic activity is delivered in partnership).

Numerous benefits of Peer Education were highlighted earlier. Specifically in relation to Peer Mentoring, Andrews and Clark (2012) identify a framework of best practice and report widespread gains. Similarly at The University of Manchester, evaluation gives evidence of the benefits of supporting the transition, socialisation and academic integration of first year students. For example, 88 per cent of Speech and Language Therapy first year students found meeting their mentor in Welcome Week helped them settle into life on their course, and 84 per cent of first year medical students commented that the scheme is beneficial to their University experience in Semester 1. Mentees recognise the confidence it gives them, support in making friends, understanding expectations and maximising time:

> It has created a friendly place where I can voice what I don't understand and learn from peers. It has encouraged me to think outside of the box in terms of problem solving and benefited me in terms of time management and organisational skills.

Peer Mentors also acknowledge benefits for peers:

> I think the students have gained a sense of community as we have introduced them to second year students and also by putting together socials they have a chance to get to know each other outside of the course. I think the students who have asked for help and guidance feel a sense of security knowing that someone is always there.

In addition, Peer Mentors recognise the benefits for themselves:

> Peer Mentoring has helped me to improve my organisational and communication skills. In addition it has helped me reinforce my own knowledge of the subject … it has also enhanced my CV and developed my leadership qualities' and communication skills and enabled me to consolidate my own knowledge to the course I feel happy to the university programme as I feel I belong to a group.

17.4.2.   Case Study 2: Peer-Assisted Study Sessions

PASS was introduced in the United Kingdom in the 1990s as an adaptation (Rust & Wallace, 1994) of the international Supplemental Instruction (SI) model. The international model of Supplemental Instruction provides a good example of a model grounded in theory with continuous research and evaluation demonstrating continued benefits (Arendale, 1993; Hurley, Jacobs & Gilbert, 2006, Jacobs, Hurley & Unite, 2008). It was initially piloted in Chemistry in 1995 at The University of Manchester, with the aim to increase academic performance and retention. Wider benefits were recognised and subsequently aims have focused on enhancement and development of the student experience. The primary aim of PASS is to provide supplementary academic support. Currently PASS operates in 29 disciplines with approximately 750 Leaders, and provides an opportunity to (Figure 17.4):

- discuss learning strategies in small groups through collaborative and active learning;
- encourage a student-centred approach to learning;
- deepen the understanding of fundamental academic principles and develop intellectual and professional competences within an informal social environment;
- increase individual confidence in learning rather than superficial strategic learning to pass exams;
- promote the concept of academic and social communities;
- provide an additional mechanism for communication and feedback between teaching staff and students.

In addition, there is an opportunity to enhance the learning experience and personal development of PASS Leaders. All students are assigned to two volunteer PASS Leaders from the same discipline and are allocated to groups of approximately 15 students based on the programme. In addition to the *Academic Staff Coordinator,*

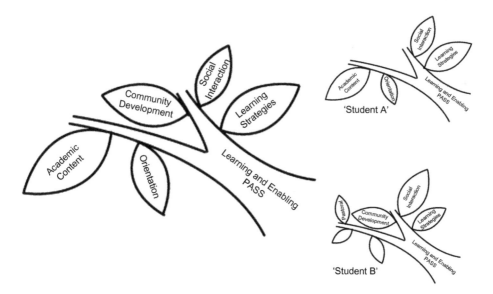

Figure 17.4: Model of PASS activity and potential outcomes for different students.

the Sabbatical Intern promotes PASS, observes weekly sessions, organises and co-facilitates leader debriefs, and designs and deliver ongoing training which supplements the compulsory 2 days generic leader training (delivered by trained SI Supervisors) (Figure 17.4).

The majority of schemes focus on first year students, but with a growing number of schemes beyond that. Specifically noted by Ody and Carey (2009), 'PASS is attached to a challenging unit within a degree course and provides a safe environment for students to discuss ideas, share problems and resolve questions in a setting that supplements the core curriculum. [In sessions] students compare notes, clarify what they read and hear, analyse, criticise, question and seek verification of ideas'. Initial meetings take place in Welcome Week when activity is focused on group development including Campus Tours, or city treasure hunts. Beyond Week 1, sessions focus mainly on academic issues on particularly challenging areas of the course identified by the attendees to set the agenda of each session. Students are encouraged to attend sessions regardless of their academic ability; those choosing not to attend are electing to 'opt out'. PASS Leaders create a friendly learning environment, developing the confidence of their students to ask 'stupid' questions. Leaders take their role seriously and do not teach or deliver new academic material; they work hard to design fun learning activities, share their experiences and model good study skills.

Evaluation consistently supports the benefits to a variety of stakeholders. There is a strong correlation between students regularly attending PASS and an increase in academic performance (approximately 10 per cent), lowering of the failure rate and an increase in high achievement (a threefold increase of those obtaining >70 per cent) (Fostier & Carey, 2007). Other benefits from Peer Support and guidance include increased academic confidence and benchmarking of ability against other students, 'demystifying' of the higher years of study and building the attendees' confidence to progress through University (Ody & Carey, 2009), the potential for deeper learning and community development. Attendees recognise the diverse benefits:

> PASS is all about getting used to University life and meeting new people on your course, so that in lectures you recognise friendly faces and feel more at ease .... PASS introduces important study skills as well as balancing academic work with social time ... it is a place where students can meet others, ask questions and help each other. Everybody gets different things out of PASS ...

> [We] realise that we are not the only ones facing a problem. The problems shared are also fed back to the lecturers and they can help as soon as possible.

Leaders recognise a variety of benefits to themselves including revision of core materials, understanding of learning theory in practice, academic development, increased engagement with academic staff, academic and employability skills development and increased confidence.

> Since getting involved in PASS, I've felt more like an integral member of the University (rather than a student 'customer') … it feels like I am contributing to the teaching and learning experience within the School. I feel more valued as a consequence.

> I didn't know whether I had the confidence to be a Leader. But after only a few sessions it became second nature to me.

Academic staff have reported changes in the level of student engagement recognising the programme's positive impact on community and collegiality. PASS forges links between year groups and creates student partnerships between academic and administrative staff. The development of academic and employability skills of Leaders has also been recognised by employers and professional accreditation bodies; the Institute of Chemical Engineers reported positively on the use of PASS in the School of Chemical Engineering and Analytical Sciences and notably on its impact on the development of graduate skills.

17.4.3.   *Case Study 3: Higher Year Discussion Groups*

The third case study is of an initiative in the Faculty of Life Sciences which has an intake of approximately 600 students and operates a well-embedded and successful PASS scheme for all first year students. This experience led to student demand for further structured collaborative learning opportunities. Students acknowledged that as they progressed into higher years, their friendship groups were no longer their study groups given the breadth of module choice. A different approach to PASS was required to enable the formation of new peer study groups to discuss course material and extra reading outside lectures. The opportunity is promoted to all second and final year students but, given they are self-selecting, the number of groups and participants varies each year. Group sizes are kept to a maximum of 15, with an immediate peer to act as group coordinator.

Groups focus on a specific module identified annually, dependent on student interest. As a student led initiative for a group to form there has to be a volunteer coordinator:

> My role is to initially bring about these groups and book rooms for the sessions to take place. Most importantly, all these sessions are all student-led, so there will be no lecturers present. I think this would be a great way to also learn and understand the lecture notes and since we all come from different degree programs, it will give us a chance to broaden our perspectives. (Group Coordinator to participants)

One of the Sabbatical Interns will brief Group Coordinators and provide a structure and logistical support to set up the first meeting. Within the study groups, students work collaboratively to deepen understanding of lecture content, and to share independent reading and relevant research in an informal encouraging environment.

Students set their own agenda to cover the course material. Group Coordinators are provided with a briefing and resource packs for supporting a group (Ody and Carey 2011) and they provide feedback to lecturers about content discussed. Online surveys with attendees highlighted that discussion groups helped them to manage their own learning and contextualise knowledge by pulling together the central concepts of the module and drawing links between lectures/similar modules:

> Attending discussion groups definitely gives you a better understanding of the subject and allows you to go through past papers and see other peoples' points of view on a topic. This means you can pick up things you wouldn't always think of!

> I didn't even know what it was that I didn't understand until other people question the incorrect assumptions I had made about concepts.

In addition to developing a deeper understanding of the academic material, many students attributed a direct link to supporting their own revision and exam performance:

> If anything, they prepare your mindset for exams and revision, giving you a basis to start from and realise what you need to work on … everyone has their strengths and weaknesses and methods of revising which may be new to you!

17.4.4. Case Study 4: 'Special Topics' Mentoring

The fourth case study outlines an initiative in the School of Physics and Astronomy, which has a student intake of approximately 300 first year students. The School recognised that first year interaction with immediate peers was limited, and had concerns about students feeling isolated, not forming natural study groups and not developing the necessary interpersonal skills for effective study. Hence a module ('Special Topics') was introduced to develop communication skills, introduce group learning, encourage first year interaction, introduce research skills and enable students to cope with transitions. Peer Support using higher year students as Mentors and Facilitators was implemented, with an additional scheme aim of facilitating effective group working to manage an assessed project. The 'Special Topics' module initially (Weeks 1−6) consists of a series of specialist lectures focusing on a different area of modern day physics research. In Weeks 7−11, students work in their pre-allocated groups on an assessed group project. This scheme is unique at The University of Manchester and draws from the good practice of Peer Mentoring to provide pastoral support and PASS to provide facilitation to the group project. Higher year students are allocated to groups to support relationship development prior to the group project, initially acting as Peer Mentors and then as Facilitators from Week 7. Higher year students receive standard Peer Mentor Training and bespoke facilitation training.

Outcomes are similar to those reported in the Peer Mentor case study, but arguably benefits are maximised as the module requires all students to meet with their Facilitator.

> Somebody nearer to my age and yet experienced to share the initial anxieties with. It gave us a chance to meet other physicists from other years. It helps to know that they experienced the same difficulties and yet settled in fine.

Students report that they find the module assessment challenging as many of them are apprehensive and out of their comfort zone working in groups. Continued evaluation of this scheme since 2007 has reported that mentees consistently identify Mentors helped them ensure everyone left the meetings with clearly defined tasks, with one mentee commenting:

> It was helpful to have someone to talk to about the course or just about general university related issues who had already been through 1st year. Starting the course was quite scary and the Mentor made things seem less overwhelming.

17.4.5. *Case Study 5: INTO Peer Engagement*

The INTO Manchester International Foundation programme provides guaranteed progression on to a University of Manchester undergraduate degree in a range of subjects including all fields of engineering, management and business, social sciences, architecture, pharmacy and psychology, provided the necessary grades are achieved. The programme provides preparation designed specifically for study at the University, combining academic study, intensive English language preparation, study skills and cultural orientation. As the programme is delivered by the University's partner, INTO, in an external location, the Peer Engagement scheme provides links between University students and the INTO student cohort. The primary objective is to create a relationship that presents the University as a chosen place to study, with the Peer Engagement scheme providing exposure to the dynamic student environment. Peer Mentors are drawn from University students — from second and third years or from students who have been through the INTO programme, and from existing Peer Mentors and PASS Leaders. They partner with previous INTO students to facilitate and lead discussion. Staff from INTO and University Link Tutors are present at all events and agree the discussion topics/activities in advance.

Students on the programme benefit by being able to use the University's library and sports facilities, having support in making an application to the University, and being invited to take part in a number of visits throughout the year to participate in inspirational lectures, to meet with academic staff and to become familiar with the

University environment. Peer activity is built around these events to maximise attendance. The scheme enables existing University students to share their experiences and excite INTO students about life at the University. Activity has typically been structured around 'speed networking' and focused discussion groups relating to topics and activities such as 'Sports at University', 'Getting involved in societies', 'Making the most of your free time', 'Independent Study', 'Campus Orientation Tours' or 'Scavenger Hunts'. Attendance at events has been high, enabling all INTO students to meet current University students and to hear a variety of student experiences.

> This evening was a great opportunity to learn about the student life and University in general from a student's perspective.

The informal environment with structured discussions creates opportunities for INTO students to ask questions, deepen their knowledge of the University, form relationships and aspire to study at Manchester.

> I found this meeting very useful as I had a chance to speak to students, ask several questions and gain some experience ... you guys are just awesome!

17.4.6.   *Case Study 6: Learning Communities in Halls*

The University of Manchester offers more than 9200 places in 32 Halls of Residence, which are all unique in character and design. Student choice is varied, with options including catered or non-catered, en-suite or shared facilities, flat or corridor configurations and different social spaces. The Residential Services Division is committed to ensuring that their services and facilities enhance the student experience. Pastoral support is provided through Hall Wardens, residential hall tutors and non-residential advisors. The 'Learning Communities in Halls' scheme supports the Division's strategic goals and in particular the following operational priority: 'to develop and successfully implement new social activities for residents to increase engagement in Hall communities and ensure these activities add positively to the wider learning agenda'. One key action to support this priority is as follows: 'working with Directorate for the Student Experience and University colleagues, introduce a residential lecture series running through the academic year covering topics such as careers, volunteering and social responsibility'. The establishment of learning communities aims to change the perception of hall culture by encouraging students to study in their living environment — thus bridging the gap between their academic sphere (primarily when 'in' University) and their social sphere (primarily their living environment).

A pilot initiative is operating in one of the University's catered halls, which has a mix of new and returning students. In this case study the strategic coordination and operation coordination teams are slightly larger and include a general manager for Pastoral Care, the Warden of the pilot Hall of Residence, and non-residential advisers, residential tutors, University service staff (e.g. Careers) and discussion facilitators (drawn from existing PASS Leaders), all of whom are residents in the pilot Hall. This scheme's activity is divided into two strands.

1. The discipline strand: facilitating students from the same discipline to study together in small groups. The opportunity to partake in this stand was publicised to all students who were invited to express their interest. Pastoral staff coordinated meetings by bringing together interested students from the same or similar disciplines. Introductions of discussion facilitators and participants were initiated over dinner with the aims being explained and participants identifying discussion areas. Once established, these groups are self-regulated, with the frequency of meetings being agreed by group members.
2. The skills strand: a programme of structured workshops has been developed in conjunction with University services. Non-residential advisers, in consultation with residential tutors, have identified potential seminar sessions/workshops. These are delivered by University colleagues with a mixture of after dinner and weekend sessions. Activity in this pilot has included 'Making a positive impact when job hunting' (Careers), 'Managing your time effectively' (Learning Commons), and 'Presentation Skills' (Teaching and Learning Support Office). Sessions are open to all students from any discipline or year group and are promoted online and through residential tutors.

As this is a pilot initiative, the impact has not yet been fully evaluated, but there is an expectation for additional friendships and study groups, greater awareness of University services, increased use of Hall study space, a changing culture — encouraging more 'studious' students to engage in wider Hall social life and assisting the 'socially energetic' to have an appropriate academic focus, and creating discipline communities. Anecdotal evidence also supports a broader peer support aim of students taking responsibility for their learning, with one student noting:

> I would like to talk about the possibility of opening up the library to all Hall residents — we could take full responsibly for how it is kept and taken care of. I think this will really help everyone in Hall.

17.5. Learning from The University of Manchester's Journey

Peer Support at The University of Manchester dates back to the mid-1990s and for more than a decade grew organically (arguably haphazardly albeit with central support), based on where enthusiasm existed. Today, Peer Support is recognised as a beacon of good practice nationally and is being established elsewhere; for example:

> You are leading something of a revolution through PASS by initiating (and helping others to initiate) increasing opportunities for explicit

'learning about learning' and hands-on group work development for students. These are fundamental for success both in HE and employment and what's more, students who participate overwhelmingly enjoy it too, it's win-win-win! ... Our 'principles of PALS' have been heavily informed by ones you designed and have helped us establish clear parameters for our leader roles and our sessions ... there's a sense of collegiality and growing scholarship in the field, and a rich relationship developing with the wider field of learning development ... (John Hilsdon, Head of Learning Support and Wellbeing, Plymouth University)

Such a growth has not continued haphazardly, but has been built into institutional structures. Funding was for some time reliant on small grants from a variety of internal sources before becoming embedded with an allocated budget. Peer Support was embedded into University Teaching and Learning Strategy and the Widening Participation Strategy in 2003–2004. In 2007 the Institutional Undergraduate Review of Education recognised the benefits and placed emphasis on strategic growth both horizontally and into higher years of study, and in 2008 the University's 'Personalised Learning Policy' stated: 'All students should have access to some form of Peer Support during their studies'. Hence, Peer Support in its many forms is thoroughly embedded into the practice and strategy of the University for all students, and the Institution now has a Peer Support Strategy Group.

The planned growth and journey have resulted in steady expansion of staffing structures enabling effective central scheme management. In 1995, the initial schemes were run by discipline and central enthusiasts; in 2001 a full-time central member of staff was introduced to support the development of Peer Support (along with other student engagement activity); in 2003 the role of scheme based Student Coordinators were introduced; in 2004 two Sabbatical Interns were piloted to work with schemes within a Faculty; the successful pilot of Sabbatical Interns has seen growing expansion to the current number of six. The University frameworks set minimum requirements for establishing and running a successful, quality assured scheme including academic and administrative staff engagement. In 2001 internal evaluation identified that target students who were not attending PASS or engaging with their Peer Mentors wanted to, but chose not to, opt in for fear of labelling themselves as struggling or not knowing what questions they would ask. In 2002 the emphasis shifted and schemes were switched from an 'opt in' to an 'opt out' approach (all target students being allocated a Mentor or PASS group). Other significant changes which have resulted in enhanced benefits have included the following:

- Regular developments to training and support, including the involvement of experienced Peer Leaders in delivery
- Enhanced observations and feedback
- Production of pre-arrival materials written by higher year students (Moran et al., 2013)
- Introduction of Staff and Student Coordinator networks

- Development of communication channels (including student written newsletters, email bulletins and the use of social media)
- Fostering of links with employers, including a sustained relationship with PricewaterhouseCoopers, which provides a range of activity including a bespoke personal development course available to students engaged in peer support.

The recognition of two institutional widespread schemes gave a high profile to the benefits of Peer Support and resulted in strong partnerships with a variety of stakeholders across the institution. Other divisions within the University have recognised opportunity for collaboration in using already engaged students to assist with activities including open days, university wide widening participation and welcome activity. Peer Support as a model of student engagement has encouraged colleagues to consider different ways of working with students and they have sought advice and assistance to develop partnered activity in areas including employability awareness, pre-university mentoring and study abroad. In addition, locally within a discipline, School or Faculty, staff and students have seen the flexibility of Peer Support and have worked with central colleagues to develop bespoke schemes. It has been recognised that, at every level of activity, it is essential to recognise and reward the committed students (and staff) without whom no activity would function as effectively. This happens through an Institutional Presentation Evening, 'Outstanding Contribution to Peer Support' Awards, Volunteering hours accredited through the 'Manchester Leadership Programme', acknowledgement of activity on the UK Higher Education Achievement Report, and School-level funding to provide meals or events for Peer Leaders. Critical to the success of The University of Manchester's activity has been profiling activity to colleagues at all levels. The programme reports to the University's Teaching and Learning Group and the Sabbatical Interns meet regularly with senior Faculty staff to ensure the activity is aligned to Faculty's student engagement agenda(s). The programme is given a strong position in which to highlight activity, showcase achievements (and challenges) and engage key decision makers in development.

All the factors considered above have been essential drivers of Peer Education at The University of Manchester, from the naming of roles to the embedding of strategies. As at The University of Manchester, Peer Support can start small and grow from the grassroots level but equally can be implemented on a large scale across an institution. Some initial questions might include:

- Is it a local desire or an institutional strategic project? Will it be organic growth or strategic development?
- Why is this important? What is the mission? What will be the goals, objectives and intended outcomes? (What will be your tree branches?)
- Are the aims tied to strategy? (How does your tree relate to your institutional woodland?)
- Are there any existing practices that can be built upon?

- Is the nomenclature really important, or is it about getting the aims and therefore the characteristics right for the cohort of students existing in the context of their own institution's culture?

It is also important to know how success or impact will be measured. Success will be reliant on appropriate management structures and staff/student engagement, and the following will need to be planned for:

- Who will own responsibility?
- How will any scheme be funded and resourced?
- What functions need to be fulfilled and who will undertake them?
- Is it possible to partner with internal service providers?
- How will staff and students be engaged, motivated and recognised?
- Who will be the appropriate student target group?
- How will the scheme be quality assured?

There are also a number of logistical practicalities in establishing Peer Support schemes, including:

- approval, awareness and value from a course teaching team;
- identification of academic and administrative support;
- timetabling and room booking;
- recruitment and selection of Leaders/Mentors;
- training (students and staff) and ongoing support;
- observation and monitoring;
- marketing the scheme to target students;
- recognition and reward;
- evaluation.

Above all, the experience at The University of Manchester demonstrates that Peer Support empowers, motivates and engages students. Throughout the entire process in preparation for implementation and in initiating practice, consulting with staff and students at every level and stage is essential to ensure that it is tailored to meet needs and that there is local ownership and leadership. Most importantly, Peer Support has, at its heart, a continually growing cohort of altruistic and energetic students. The students energy and enthusiasm is infections and in turn motivates their peers and their staff. Driving development and fostering the community of students as partners. Peer Education is something that all universities should seriously address.

References

Andrews, J., & Clark, R. (2012). *Peer mentoring works! How peer mentoring enhances student success in higher education.* Birmingham: Aston University.

Arendale, D. (1993). Foundation and theoretical framework for supplemental instruction. In D.C. Martin & D. Arendale (Eds.), *Supplemental instruction: Improving first year student success in high risk courses* (2nd ed., pp. 19−26, Monograph Series Number 7). Columbia, SC: National Resource Center for the First Year Experience and Students in Transition.

Astin, A. (1993). *What matters in college?: Four critical years revisited.* San Franscico, CA: Jossey-Bass.

Astin, A. W. (1999). Student involvement: A development theory for higher education. *Journal of College Student Development, 54,* 208−225.

Bell, A. (1808). *The Madras School comprising the analysis of an experiment in education.* London. Retrieved from http://books.google.co.uk/books?id = 9ppDAAAAIAAJ&printsec = frontcover&dq = bell + experiment + madras&source = bl&ots = lHsTBqzPs&sig = Cpu DKD0FPHSEzIRXWGR4YAsXV4&hl = en&ei = H4QJTKTNLIH20wToObBu&sa = X& oi = book_result&ct = result&resnum = 5&ved = 0CCQQ6AEwBA#v = onepage&q&f = false

Brissette, I., Scheier, M. F., & Carver, C. S. (2002). The role of optimism in social network development, coping, and psychological adjustment during a life transition. *Journal of Personality and Social Psychology, 82,* 102−111.

Chickering, A. (1993). *Education and identity* (2nd ed.), San Francisco, CA: Jossey-Bass.

Coffman, D. L., & Gilligan, T. D. (2002). Social support, stress, and self-efficacy: Effects on students' satisfaction. *College Student Retention, 4,* 53−66.

Crissman Ishler, J. L., & Schreiber, S. (2002). First-year female students: Their perceptions of friendship during the first-year experience. *Journal of the Freshman Year Experience and Students in Transition, 14,* 89−104.

Cuseo, J. (2010). Peer leadership: Definition, description and classification. *E-Source National Resource Center, 7*(5), 3.

Donelan, M., & Kay, P. (1998). Supplemental instruction: Students helping students' learning at University College London (UCL) and University of Central Lancashire (UCLAN), *The Law Teacher, 32*(3), 287−299.

Fostier, M., & Carey, W. (2007). *Exploration, experience and evaluation: Peer Assisted Study Scheme (PASS), sharing the experience of the University of Manchester: 480 1st year bioscience students.* Paper presented at the Science, Learning and Teaching Conference, Keele University, UK.

Harmon, B. V. (2006). A qualitative study of the learning processes and outcomes associated with students who serve as peer mentors. *Journal of the First-Year Experience and Students in Transition, 18*(2), 53−82.

Hurley, M., Jacobs, G., & Gilbert, M. (2006). The basic SI model. *New Directions for Teaching and Learning, 2006,* 11−22. doi: 10.1002/tl.229.

Jacobs, G., , Hurley, M., & Unite, C. (2008). How learning theory creates a foundation for SI leader training. *Journal of Peer Learning, 1*(1), 6−12. Available at: http://ro.uow.edu.au/ajpl/vol1/iss1/3

Lancaster, J. (1805). *Improvements in Education, as it respects the industrial classes of the community* (3rd ed.). London: Longman and Co.

Moran, L., Birch, L., Carey, W., & Ody, M. (2013). Academic and social survival guides: Student produced pre-induction/pre-arrival material. In J. Andrews, R. Clark & L. Thomas (Eds.), *2nd Compendium of effective practice in higher education retention and success*: Aston University and Higher Education Academy.

Newton, F. B., & Ender, S. C. (2010). *Students helping students: A guide for peer educators on college campuses* (2nd ed.), San Francisco, CA: Jossey-Bass.

Ody, M. & Carey, W. (2009). *Demystifying Peer Assisted Study Sessions (PASS): What ...? How ...? Who ...? Why ...?* Paper presented at the 6th Annual ALDinHE Conference, Bournemouth, UK.

Ody, M., & Carey, W. (2011). Academic peer support beyond the first year — a trio of examples. In M. Morgan (Ed.), *Improving the student experience*. London: Routledge.

Pascarella, E. T., & Terenzini, P. T. (1991). *How college affects students: Findings and insights from twenty years of research*, San Francisco, CA: Jossey-Bass.

Potts, G., Schultz, B., & Foust, J. (2003–2004). The effect of freshmen cohort groups on academic performance and retention. *Journal of College Student Retention: Research, Theory and Practice*, 5(4), 385–395.

Rust, C. & Wallace, J. (1994). Conceptualising SI. In C. Rust & J. Wallace (Eds.), *Helping Students to Learn from Each Other: Supplemental Instruction*. Birmingham, UK: Staff and Educational Development Association.

Topping, K. J. (2001). *Peer assisted learning: A practical guide for teachers*. Cambridge, MA: Brookline Books.

Chapter 18

'We Need Support Too': Providing Postgraduate Peer Support

Jacques van der Meer, Lucy Spowart and Simon Hart

Abstract

While there are numerous support systems and structures in place at undergraduate level, postgraduate students are frequently left floundering in relative isolation. Many students struggle to integrate with their peers to find the support that they need above and beyond that offered by their supervisors. This chapter reflects on an initiative that set about 'manufacturing' postgraduate peer support at a University in Aotearoa/New Zealand in 2009. Drawing on concepts related to student engagement, peer-learning, indigenous (Māori) pedagogical concepts and Lave and Wenger's concept of 'communities of practice', the project aimed to increase students' sense of belonging to a postgraduate community, and their efficacy as research students.

Successful postgraduate communities had a clear vision, strong leadership, varied membership, and support from their department. Participants experienced the initiative as beneficial, both in terms of supporting their studies and enhancing their overall postgraduate student experiences. The organisers learned that sustaining the initiative at both the institutional and departmental level needs renewed and ongoing attention.

Research has highlighted the many difficulties students experience along their postgraduate research journeys. Few studies, however, have focused on the possible role of peer learning as a means to enhancing students' experience of postgraduate studies. This study contributes to the understanding of the benefits of this particular approach.

The Student Engagement Handbook: Practice in Higher Education
Copyright © 2013 by Emerald Group Publishing Limited
All rights of reproduction in any form reserved
ISBN: 978-1-78190-423-7

18.1. Introduction

Research has highlighted the many difficulties students experience along their post-graduate research journeys (Conrad, 2006; Nettles & Millet, 2006). While there are numerous support systems and structures in place at undergraduate level, postgrad-uate students are frequently left floundering in relative isolation. Many students struggle to integrate with their peers to find the support that they need above and beyond that offered by their supervisor(s) (Conrad, 2003). There is also increasing pressure on postgraduate students to complete their studies in a timely manner, and this often induces high levels of stress (Boud & Lee, 2005). This chapter recounts the story of the development of a postgraduate peer support initiative at one univer-sity in New Zealand.

The context of doctoral study is a particularly intriguing subject to investigate since, historically, research in this area has tended to focus on supervisory relation-ships (Delamont, Atkinson, & Parry, 2000), while the importance of other social interactions, including those with peers has been rather underplayed. In our research we attempt to redress this imbalance. Our aims are twofold: first to highlight the practical steps involved in establishing the peer mentoring initiative, paying particu-lar attention to how we engaged with mentor training and support. Our second aim is to (re)examine the notion of peer mentoring through the lens of Lave and Wenger's situated learning theory, discussing the potential benefits of adopting a more collaborative approach to postgraduate research.

At the undergraduate level, peer mentoring, whereby an experienced student gives direction and support to a more inexperienced student, has received a signifi-cant amount of attention as a way to improve students' educational experiences and retention rates (Johnson, 2002; McLean, 2004; Pagan & Edwards-Wilson, 2002; Terrion, Philion, & Leonard, 2007). At the postgraduate level, peer mentoring initiatives have not received anywhere near as much consideration (Conrad & Phillips, 1995). That said, there is an increasing recognition that research students benefit greatly from developmental discussions between peers (Fenge, 2012; Hadjielia-Drotarova, 2011; Wisker, Robinson, Trafford, Warnes, & Creighton, 2003). In particular, the positive effects of peer interaction have been highlighted in relation to improving research skills (Cooper & Juniper, 2002), reducing isolation (Conrad & Phillips, 1995; Fenge, 2012; Johnston & McCormack, 1997) and in providing a 'safe space' for reflection and the sharing of ideas (Fenge, 2012).

This chapter is written as a 'jointly told tale' (Van Maanen, 1988, p. 136). Two of the authors are University staff who were involved in conceptualising and establish-ing the peer mentoring initiative in 2009. At the time, one of the authors was the Learning Services Librarian in the Library, one was the Head of the Student Learning Centre, and one was a doctoral student, entering her final year. Together, we aim to provide a rich authentic voice to a project that has at its heart relation-ship building and development, hence, we employ a case study approach, in part using an auto-ethnographic narrative structure (Anderson, 2006). We commence by sketching the birth of the ideas that lead to the peer mentoring initiative, and outlin-ing our theoretical approach. We then provide our account of the project launch, monitoring and evaluation, including some of the challenges we faced in convincing key personnel that peer mentoring was not only beneficial, but cost-effective. In the final section, we conclude by reflecting on some of the critical factors for an initiative such as this to be successful.

18.2. Background to the Project

The university where the peer mentoring programme was piloted is one of the largest and most research intensive institutions in Aotearoa/New Zealand.[1] That said, the results of a 2007 survey of recent graduates indicated that less than half of the PhD students surveyed felt that they had clear instructions into research skills: only 48% agreed with the statement that 'My home department provided a good induction into postgraduate research'. Although there were some training initiatives taking place at the departmental level, this was not universally the case. The extent literature is clear that postgraduate students need support in developing research skills (Cooper & Juniper, 2002; Delamont, Atkinson, & Parry, 1997; Mullen, 2001). Consequently, there was a clear need to address this particular issue.

Centrally, the University's Student Learning Centre runs a number of workshops on topics such as how to compose a literature review, 'Preparing a Research Proposal', and 'Thesis Writing'. These workshops are typically over-subscribed, from which could be inferred that they are meeting a need. These workshops are of a generic nature, in order to provide for students from all disciplines. However, the needs of postgraduate students are diverse and complex (Lee, 2012). Research skill development is but one small part of the jigsaw. The Library also offers postgraduate students workshops on using reference management software and provides one-to-one consultations for more in-depth inquiries. Ongoing scaffolding and development is also extremely valuable, including both academic and social support, as well as extensive support for particular student concerns, such as preparation for conference presentations and future employability.

Despite proffering an extensive and established suite of academic workshops and one-to-one student consultations, results of the student survey demonstrated a clear need to consider alternative support structures for postgraduate research students. It was evident that the developmental support provided by research supervisors was not always regarded as sufficient by students. One explanation for this could be attributed to the fact that supervisors are, by necessity, in a more hierarchical relationship to students. For this reason, we felt that at times 'advice and guidance from a peer [could be] ... more meaningful' (Muldoon, 2008).

While peer-learning programmes had been operating successfully in this university at the undergraduate level, the question that arose was: *could a peer learning*

---

[1]Based on the Performance Based Research Funding exercise, a range of quantitative and quality indicators set by the New Zealand government's Tertiary Education Commission.

programme also be a feasible and desirable option for postgraduate research students? In exploring this idea, the Head of the Student Learning Centre discussed this with the Library's Learning Services Librarian. In promoting lifelong learning, the Library has set a strategic directive to specifically target support services to students engaged in research. However, with the increasing numbers of research students, sustainable options needed to be considered to meet the increasing needs within the existing resources.

Reflecting on the clear need to provide for the support of postgraduate research students, the Student Learning Centre together with the Library started to consider various ideas around the broad idea of peer support, rather than support by academic or general staff.

18.3.   Theoretical Framework and Local Context

There is an increasing recognition among educationalists of the importance and value of students learning from each other through working together. This is the case for Aotearoa/New Zealand (Brown & Thomson, 2000; Leach & Knight, 2003; van der Meer & Scott, 2008) and overseas (Brookfield & Preskill, 1999; Fowler, Gudmundsson, & Whicker, 2006; Johnson & Johnson, 1999; Johnson, Johnson, & Smith, 1998; Kagan, 1994; Ladyshewsky, 2001, 2006; Nelson, Kift, Creagh, & Quinn, 2007; Sharan, 1994; Topping, 1996). The concept of students working together towards achieving particular academic goals is referred to by different names (Topping, 1996, 2005), the more common names being cooperative and collaborative learning. Cooperative/collaborative learning can broadly be described as active engagement of students in small groups for the purpose of completing tasks. We consider peer learning to be conceptually belonging to collaborative or cooperative learning strategies. The key aspect is that learning development is facilitated through interaction and collaboration between students. Peer learning as a beneficial academic activity is also incorporated in the broader concept of 'student engagement' as formulated, for example, by Kuh (2001) and Coates (2010). Both in the North American version of the student engagement survey instrument (Kuh, 2001), and the Australasian version (Coates, 2010), the activity of working together with students outside of the class environment for academic-related tasks is considered to benefit students' experience of engagement. The survey instruments relate to undergraduate students. However, postgraduate may similarly benefit.

Although cooperative/collaborative learning is considered beneficial in many educational contexts, in Aotearoa/New Zealand this approach has particular historical and cultural significance, being strongly reflective of the values and language of the indigenous Māori population. Educational developments in Aotearoa/New Zealand over the last few decades, from pre-school to tertiary education, increasingly reflect the values of Māori learning and learning relationships (van der Meer, 2011). In Māori pedagogy, the concept of peer learning is well recognised. *Tuakana Teina* (elder/younger, senior/junior) is central to Māori kinship, and refers to a relationship whereby someone (traditionally a sibling) who is slightly more advanced (in knowledge and/or age) is involved in mentoring a more junior person (Greenwood & Te Aika, 2009; Rata, 2002).

The Māori concepts of *Ako*, reciprocal learning, and *Whakawhanaungatanga*, relationship building are also key aspects to successful peer mentoring, and were afforded special attention in setting up the mentoring scheme in this university. In practical terms this meant that we took our time in building and maintaining meaningful relationships with a wide range of staff across the campus, and with students. In our workshops with students, we readily and frequently acknowledged our own role as learners in this process, and often specifically referenced and acknowledged some of the key pedagogical values underpinning the design of the project. Many workshops included food and refreshments, observing the values embodied in the concept of *Manakitanga*, caring for/extending hospitality.

There is strong theoretical support for peer learning as an academically beneficial activity (Boud & Lee, 2005; Hadjielia-Drotarova, 2011; Ladyshewsky & Gardner, 2008). One example is the 'situated learning theory', which stems from the work of Lave and Wenger (1991). They maintain that learning occurs in a social context, as individuals participate in communities of practice, and that 'far from being trivially true, this fact is a central aspect of learning' (Wenger, 1998, p.4). A community of practice is defined as

> an activity system about which participants share understandings concerning what they are doing and what that means in their lives and for their community. Thus, they are united in both action and in the meaning that the action has, both for themselves, and for the larger collective. (Lave & Wenger, 1991, p. 98)

This approach offers a challenge to cognitivist learning theories that focus on the mental processes. We share Lave and Wenger's socio-cultural perspective, which comfortably sits alongside the Māori learning-related concepts as outlined above and provides a useful lens through which to interrogate a peer mentoring initiative.

In explaining their notion of community of practice, Lave and Wenger employ the term 'legitimate peripheral participation' 'as a way to speak about the relations between newcomers and old-timers, and about activities, identities, artefacts, and communities of knowledge and practice' (Lave & Wenger, 1991, p. 29). In order to move from the position of 'newcomer' to the centre of a community, learners need to engage in group practices and share a common language, and a common goal. Legitimate peripheral participation provides us with a way of understanding learning, and may be particularly useful when looking at peer mentoring activities since 'learning through legitimate peripheral participation takes place no matter what educational form provides a context for learning, or whether there is any intentional form at all' (Lave & Wenger, 1991, p. 40).

We move now to discussing the practicalities involved in establishing the peer mentoring 'communities' at the particular university in which this project was implemented.

18.4.   Setting Up of the Mentoring Project

In developing the proposal for a university-wide postgraduate peer mentoring initiative, discussions were held with a range of university staff, including library staff, heads of departments and programme coordinators, as well as other staff members with an interest in services for graduate research students. Throughout the development phase of the pilot project notes were kept. As the researchers were members of the social world under study (Anderson, 2006), it felt appropriate to use an auto-ethnographic approach to draw and reflect on these notes. This will provide an authentic voice to the account of the setting up of the project and its challenges. Also, we anticipate that readers working in similar environments might resonate with these accounts, and may find our reflections helpful in considering similar interventions.

18.4.1.   The Idea

The initial idea, in a nutshell, entailed a blend of both academic and social support in a peer-learning context, organised around disciplinary-specific small groups. Student Learning Centre learning advisors as well as the Library's Learning Services Librarian would prepare and support advanced PhD students from different departments (or divisions) to facilitate small group discussions between postgraduate researchers. These peer leaders would also act as 'conduit' or liaison between their groups and the Library and Student Learning Centre to access particular resources or support where and when needed. We anticipated that students who were more advanced in their research 'journey' would be able to act as both guide and mentor, and also benefit themselves from the peer interactions, as well as from the resources and support they accessed for and on behalf of their groups.

However, we did not want to predetermine everything, or set the initiative up as completely stand-alone and disconnected from other support initiatives that might already be in place. We were keen for ideas to arise from participants and not set ourselves as the font of all knowledge as to what participants might need. We considered this to be congruent with the Māori philosophy of *Ako*, being also learners in this process. We were also mindful that in some areas of the university, support structures were working very successfully for some students. Therefore, we were open to, and keen for, the development of groups to take any course that was deemed beneficial for the students' particular needs. We were also careful to emphasise to everyone concerned that the proposed initiative we sought to develop did not seek to invalidate, or make redundant, any successful programmes operating within departments. Instead, it sought to supplement those existing postgraduate support provisions.

18.4.2.   Development of the Proposal

At the start of the project, we realised that success would depend on the support from some key people. We approached the then director of the office in the university who provides support for research students. A joint application was made for central funding intended for quality enhancement—related projects. The financial support we sought was mainly to pay the students involved a modest recompense for time spent on the project, as well as some money for training expenses. However, it was clear from the outset that some of the students involved were not interested in participation for financial reasons, and subsequently did not claim their hours. From our interaction with these students it was clear that some considered their involvement in the project sufficient recompense; they wanted to be part of the project to be 'part of something', to contribute, to give back to the institution. In one particular department where some postgraduate students had already assumed leadership in setting up support structures, it was felt that accepting payment by the student in our particular initiative would have been divisive.

Early in the project, one of the authors shared the tentative ideas with colleagues in the Library. Initially, the scheme was met with some suspicion and resistance:

> Peer leadership pilot has nothing to do with the Library! It is just something you are doing to help the Student Learning Centre because they are under-resourced. (Library staff member, as recorded in Learning Services Librarians research notes)

This type of response was probably not entirely surprising: harnessing support for cross-institutional initiatives is a common challenge (Cook, Eaker, Ghering, & Sells, 2007). Reflecting on this comment in his research journal, the Learning Services Librarian responded:

> I wonder whether they had they forgotten that this project was one of a number of initiatives that the Library had identified to align its support for information skill development within wider learning support? (Research notes from Learning Services Librarian)

It was pointed out to the staff member that peer support was a successful sustainable model, and seemingly a successful mode of learning, at undergraduate level at the university. After some persuasion, the library staff member's initial position shifted:

> Well, I suppose that if students could help one another out, then we may get fewer reference questions.

In his research journal, the Learning Services Librarian acknowledged the importance of treading carefully and adopting the 'softly, softly' approach:

> Perhaps I have to be gentle with them. The concept of the project was challenging for some. It did not easily fit into their view of their role of Librarians. Perhaps I should also remind myself that the Library team were moving from a model of Reference Support in the Library

to a model of Liaison and outreach to the community. A bit of patience and understanding may be warranted, after all, we are talking about a major paradigm shift here! (Research notes from Learning Services Librarian)

The Library was indeed in the process of a major rethink of its role. Senior management had started to consider ways of building sustainable support structures that targeted preferred modes of learning within a wider learning support framework. This rethinking reflected similar developments elsewhere (e.g. Bell, 2000; Dewey, 2005; Tenofsky, 2005). It was no longer 'just' about the Library as a place-based service offering bibliographic instruction; librarians are increasingly encouraged to reach out to embed themselves within communities, partner with other learning support groups on campus to foster seamless learning and to place information skill development in the broader context of students' learning (Peacock, 2006; Roberts & Stewart, 2008).

It was not just some staff members in the Library, however, who were cautious and not always overly enthusiastic. Academic staff too did not always fully appreciate the ideas behind a postgraduate peer support initiative. This came through in particular as the Learning Services Librarian started the process of connecting with staff and students to set up the pilot groups. A senior academic commented:

You need to understand that these are our students, they work for us, they work 6 days a week, we expect them to be in the labs all hours, it's a bit like a factory, we can't have them getting distracted off-task. (Research notes from Learning Services Librarian)

Comments such as this reflect the pressure on supervisors to ensure that their doctoral students complete their study in a timely manner. While this pressure is not new, this 'completion mindset' (Green & Bowden, 2012) can impact upon the relationship between student and supervisor. When the major goal is successful completion, it is perhaps unsurprising that supervisors do not want students 'distracted', and wish to instill a strong work ethic. Nonetheless, the discourse of ownership that arises here gave us some cause for concern. It was also interesting that this particular academic clearly did not consider that peer mentoring might actually assist and support students to reach their goal of completion, despite research to the contrary.

Another senior academic stated:

I have seen it all before. It's the blind leading the blind. This will take up too much of the students' time, it is the role of the supervisor to support student and this idea can't possibly be financially sustainable. (Research notes from one of the authors)

Again, we see a concern over time-management arising. There is also an assumption that supervisors are best placed to offer guidance, and that students themselves are incapable of assuming any useful mentoring role. While supervisors undoubtedly play a critical role in the doctoral experience, including achieving timely completion (Halse, 2011; Lee, 2008), we found this thinking quite surprising.

In spite of some tentative and more overt opposition, we did find support through carefully approaching academic staff who we thought would act as champions for the scheme. One senior administrator was clearly enthusiastic when she stated:

> We have seen this work with our Undergrads. This is exactly what we need for postgraduates. We have a real need to build a community, in particular with so many students coming from out of town, and out of New Zealand. Can we organise a meeting of all the students to explain the idea to them. We will fund any extra groups that emerge. (Research notes from Learning Services Librarian)

In the department where one of the authors was studying, one student responded:

> This is a really great idea, it would help to connect the science and social science groups in the department from the bottom up.

In this case, the department in question consisted of two distinct groups of researchers and teachers. Addressing the gulf between these two groups was a challenge identified by leadership. The development of the postgraduate peer support group was one strategy that contributed to addressing this.

In summary, although we had mixed responses in the beginning, enough of a critical mass of support was garnered from staff to enable us to start the process of student recruitment. In the next section we describe the process of selecting, training and supporting peer leaders. We certainly do not consider that we got everything 'right', but we hope that the lessons we learnt along the way will have some practical use to others involved in similar projects.

18.4.3. *Training and Support*

For the pilot, it was agreed that students would be 'shoulder-tapped', that is to say, we would invite students who had been identified by staff as suitable candidates; we referred to these students as 'peer leaders'. The recruitment evolved reasonably smoothly, and 12 peer leaders were found from across the four major academic areas within the university. These peer leaders in turn ended up facilitating small groups between 3 and 12 postgraduate students depending on levels of participation over time.

The student peer leaders initially participated in a half-day training programme followed by subsequent workshops organised by the Head of the Student Learning Centre and the Learning Services Librarian. The workshops were designed to include and/or point to resources for the following aspects:

- General issues for postgraduate research students
- Information literacy skills (including referencing software and RSS feeds)

- Document management approaches (including using styles, document maps)
- Generic thesis writing skills (including research proposal, literature review, thesis writing styles, thesis structures)
- Translating generic thesis writing skills into specific disciplinary thesis writing skills
- Facilitation of groups and ethics (including group contracts)
- Group organisational issues (logistics and communication; e.g. Blackboard and iGoogle)

These workshops were held over a period of a few months. The workshop format was a mix between planned material and formats, and flexibility to allow for student needs to emerge and be responded to. In reality, the content of the workshops shifted considerably as one of the authors noted in their journal:

> Ok, we threw out our workshop outline. The peer leaders took over. As they started to share their experiences, they were really keen to learn from one another and at the same time get some affirmation that they were on the right track. It became apparent that they were all at different stages with very different groups. There was no right or wrong way, it was a matter of working with what came up. After all this was always intended 'for students, by students'.

18.4.4. Social Context

What was clear from the start was that the peer leaders considered the social context to be just as important, if not more important than the espoused academic nature of the project. The project funding allowed for some modest expenses for refreshments. This we felt was reflective of the ethos of *manakitanga*, the Māori concept that expresses a sense of hospitality, looking after, and caring. To our surprise, the social needs were less about a night in the pub, and more about time to have a coffee, share food, and be together.

> You would think that the peer leaders would use the available funds to pay for drinks at the Staff Club or the Postgraduate Lounge? We were wrong! 'Can we use the money to rent a van so that tour families can travel out of town for a day trip?' In explanation the student said that many of the students have young families, and a day trip would help them to connect outside of the study context, where they were more neutral, in the context of people with lives outside of University. Asked why they would not use the money for a round of drinks, he said that they were kind of over that, 'been there done that in under-graduate years'. They had 'real' lives, busy juggling time: study, work and family.

The importance of the social aspect of the project was confirmed in the interviews of the 12 peer leaders when they were interviewed at the end of the pilot (Buissink-Smith, Hart, & van der Meer, 2013). For example, peer leaders frequently reiterated the importance of connecting through face-to-face interactions.

18.4.5. *Development of Groups*

In the months that followed, the various groups started their lives as peer support groups. There was no one single format, but many different group formats, each with a slightly different emphasis. Some groups focused more on the social aspect, others more on academic aspects. Although most peer leaders attended all support and training sessions, not all did. Some group leaders were grateful for us starting the initiative, but were happy to take it from there without a need for attending any support sessions. For example, this was the case for a group consisting of mainly Māori students. We speculated that the particular focus on relationships, peer support and reciprocal learning may have resonated well as reflective of *Ako* and *whanaungatanga*. We did not specifically inquire into this. This may well be a focus for a future initiative/research project.

One particular group stood out as excelling in developing a comprehensive social and academic programme, and in doing so energising the whole department. The success of this group was in part due to the timing of our initiative and the willingness of the leadership of the particular department and its staff to support it. In this particular case, postgraduate students had already taken it upon themselves to elect a social secretary, and convene regular departmental 'get-togethers', usually held at local restaurants. The newly appointed peer leader worked closely with the student social secretary to extend the opportunities for postgraduates to mingle. Monthly meetings were arranged in an on-campus venue with hot drinks offered as an enticement. These additional networking opportunities opened up informal lines of communication, and although they were initially met with some scepticism by students, it soon became apparent that students were sharing information and resources more readily than they had previously. Students cited many examples where they had been given a 'helping hand' by their peers. While several of the examples cited were relatively minor, such as assisting with referencing software and funding applications, some students received quite substantive support in helping to understand threshold concepts.

Threshold concepts are core concepts in a particular discipline, which once understood, operate as a transformative gateway (Meyer & Land, 2005). Conversely, if students do not understand these concepts, then progress can be severely limited. Some students felt that they were more able to discuss difficult concepts with their peers in a 'safe' environment, rather than revealing their lack of understanding to their supervisors. The postgraduate journey was thus undertaken as a joint enterprise, and the accumulated knowledges and experiences contained within this particular community of practice were shared on an ongoing basis. The presence of an organised scheme seemed to legitimate seeking advice and support and, for some, this meant barriers were removed.

The academic initiatives of this particular peer group culminated in a student-organised symposium. All postgraduate students in the department were invited to present at the symposium. A student organising committee acted as editors and also offered more inexperienced students the opportunity to rehearse their presentations and gain valuable feedback. While some students felt pressurised into submitting abstracts and presenting, in the main the symposium was regarded, by both students and staff, as a successful event that provided students with the opportunity to develop a range of skills associated with a career in academia. Importantly, the symposium also facilitated the beginnings of many cross-disciplinary discussions between students and also among staff.

18.5. Evaluation

As part of the application for financial support, we were asked to evaluate the project for its effectiveness. We undertook research into the effectiveness of the programme in a number of ways. We surveyed participants of the group at the end of their first year to ascertain the usefulness and effectiveness of the programme. Peer leaders were asked to maintain a simple semi-structured journal that would assist the programme coordinators to assess effectiveness from their point of view as well as identify training foci and needs for the further development of the programme. The interviews yielded a wealth of data (Buissink-Smith et al., 2013). Using a general inductive approach (Thomas, 2006), some key aspects for a successful peer group were identified. The overall conclusion that could be drawn was that peer leaders considered the initiative to be of worth.

To make the evaluation and research also useful for a wider audience, we summarised our findings in an informational brochure entitled 'Postgraduate research peer support: factors that contribute to successful research communities and peer groups'. These findings were also shared in a university forum with both staff and students. The following summary is a condensed version of the findings as incorporated in the brochure (University of Otago, n.d.).

1. Connections. Successful communities and groups created connections. A positive research community or peer support group helped to connect students to each other, to staff, to their department, and to the University as a whole …
2. Focus. Successful communities and groups had a clear idea of what they wanted. One of the major differences between our successful postgraduate research communities, especially peer support groups, was their focus. For example, some focused on academic matters (e.g. how to cope with all those references), some on social aspects (sometimes actively discouraging talk of 'work'), or some on a mixture of the two …

3. Leadership. Successful communities and groups demonstrated strong leadership. While the sort of skills a peer leader might need depends on the type of group they lead, our fantastic leaders shared some characteristics — open mindedness; the ability to draw on their own strengths and on the skills of others; friendliness; patience; good organisation; and the ability to talk to staff members and to ask for help when necessary. The opportunity for group leaders to meet with each other was considered to be extremely valuable ...

4. Structure. Successful communities and groups were open to different structures. There is no one 'right' formula for establishing a successful postgraduate research community or peer support group. Many leaders found it helpful to survey their peers, formally or informally, to help them discover the particular needs of their group. To establish a successful postgraduate research community regular 'peer support' meetings were not always necessary.

5. Open membership. Successful communities and groups were open to a varied membership. Groups were formed along different lines. For example some were formed on the basis of shared methodologies, others across broad subject areas (e.g. health). Some groups were departmental-wide while others were within a specific course ...

6. Departmental support. Successful communities and groups experienced some support from their department. While some groups existed in difficult departmental situations with little or no encouragement, our most successful groups did have some form of support from their department. Some peer leaders were empowered simply by the knowledge that the staff had 'faith' in them, and others were encouraged by words of support from their supervisors and administrative staff ...

7. Safe environment. Successful communities and groups created a safe and comfortable environment for everybody. It was important for successful postgraduate communities or peer support groups to appear to provide a safe and comfortable environment that was welcoming to all students. Meeting in an alcohol-free, day-time situation proved to be the most popular setting ...

8. Face-to-face interaction. Successful communities and groups created opportunities for face-to-face interaction. Student leaders reported the benefits of the groups meeting in a face-to-face situation. While some groups used a social networking site to organise their meetings there was no support amongst our leaders for any form of online support ...

9. Optimal numbers. Successful communities and groups had an optimal number. Leaders reported needing a 'critical mass' of at least six to eight students to enable them to enjoy good discussion

and vitality. Having quite relaxed entry criteria enabled groups to easily replace departing students with new ones. This often happened through word-of-mouth connections with existing members.

10. Successful communities and groups celebrated milestones. Many successful groups enjoyed celebrating the academic and social milestones of their members. Over the long course of postgraduate study it was very beneficial for students to have a place they could share and celebrate their milestones — however, big or small! — finishing a chapter; completing data collection; writing a paper; handing in a draft; getting a good mark ... (University of Otago, n.d.)

18.6. Future Considerations

Many of the findings suggesting that the initiative may have been successful were encapsulated in the brochure as summarised above. There were also other concerns that we believe needed further consideration.

The most pressing of the issues we considered was the sustainability and 'embeddedness' of the initiative. Although the peer leaders and other stakeholders believed it was successful, we recognised that this success was dependent to a large extent on the involvement of a few key people. Although there are some ongoing and newly formed peer-mentoring groups, the career progression of some staff within the organisation has meant that the momentum on this particular project has slowed down. The challenge for this institution, and other institutions considering similar ideas, is to ensure that new initiatives such as these are embedded organisationally. This would mean, for example, that the 'manufacturing' of peer support groups becomes part of the strategic direction of the organisational units concerned. In our case, this would mean the central unit charged with postgraduate services in general, and the unit charged with learning support services. With a strategic direction comes implementation and resourcing directives that would ensure its continuance, independent of individual champions.

A second consideration is how this support initiative can be made to work for particular groups of students to ensure equity. The obvious question is how this could meet the needs of students enrolled at a distance. A considerable proportion of the postgraduate students at this institution are distance students. This might mean some adaptation to accommodate the specific limitations and affordances of distant/online courses. To date, this adaptation has not taken place.

While taking into account issues of equity, we also need to ask questions about the provision for Māori and Pacific Island students. This is a particular focus of the Aotearoa/New Zealand government since both of these groups are currently underrepresented at both undergraduate and postgraduate levels (Bishop et al., 2009; Scott, 2005). We wondered whether this initiative would work for these two groups of students. Although one of the peer support groups was established in an area of study with a strong representation of both Māori and Pacific Island students, no systematic evaluation was done as to the effectiveness of the initiative for this group. It is hoped that, in close collaboration with Māori and Pacific Island support structures and within the context of culturally appropriate research protocols, this could be done in the future.

Another consideration that may be of worth is how the impact of this initiative could be measured after students' completion of their research degree. Currently, one of the authors is carrying out a qualitative study among the members of the particular peer support group she belonged to. Of interest are, for example, benefits such as seeking collaborative writing opportunities, networking, and the sharing of information and resources. We are also interested in the perceived value of peer mentoring in supporting postgraduate students and early career researchers in shifting their identities to 'become' academics.

18.7. Conclusion and Epilogue

The groups in this pilot project can be said to have provided a good example of 'student engagement', that is students' involvement in academically meaningful activities that enriched their studies (Kuh, 2001). The choice to enhance student engagement for postgraduate research students through a peer learning initiative that included a distinctive leadership role for slightly more advanced students was a successful one. It confirmed that this was not just an approach that worked at undergraduate level. Feedback from the mentors also corroborated with some of the existing literature on the topic that suggests that research students have much to gain from engaging in conversations with their peers (e.g. Fenge, 2012; Hadjielia-Drotarova, 2011).

While the peer support initiative was considered to be of worth by peer leaders and their groups, institutionally there are some clear challenges in making this a continuing, sustainable and viable programme. At the time of writing, there are no intentionally organised initiatives that seek to build on this successful pilot. However, some of the authors anticipate that impending organisational changes, mainly in the area of staffing, may offer new opportunities to reignite a second iteration of this project. At the risk of stating the obvious, a clear learning outcome for us is the realisation that to be sustainable, any new initiative cannot rely on the drive and input of a few champions. There needs to be a commitment to a planned and deliberate phase of 'embedding' in the structures and strategic planning of the most appropriate organisational unit or units. To achieve this it is important that initiatives such as these become operationalised as 'business as usual'. This would include defining processes, the allocation of resources, and formalising task responsibilities within position descriptions. Following this, detailed performance measures would be set and continuous process improvement enabled. This would reflect the development of this new initiative towards the stage of 'capability maturity' (Kerzner, 2005).

References

Anderson, L. (2006). Analytic autoethnography. *Journal of contemporary ethnography*, *35*(4), 373–395.

Bell, S. (2000). Creating learning libraries in support of seamless learning cultures. *College & Undergraduate Libraries*, *6*(2), 45–58.

Bishop, R., Berryman, M., Cavanagh, T., & Teddy, L. (2009). Te Kotahitanga: Addressing educational disparities facing Māori students in New Zealand. *Teaching and Teacher Education*, *25*(5), 734–742.

Boud, D., & Lee, A. (2005). Peer learning as pedagogic discourse for research education 1. *Studies in Higher Education*, *30*(5), 501–516.

Brookfield, S., & Preskill, S. (1999). *Discussion as a way of teaching: Tolls and techniques for university teachers*. Buckingham: SRHE.

Brown, D., & Thomson, C. (2000). *Cooperative learning in New Zealand schools*. Palmerston North: Dunmore.

Buissink-Smith, N., Hart, S., & van der Meer, J. (2013). 'There are other people out there!': Successful postgraduate peer groups and research communities at a New Zealand university. *Higher Education Research & Development*, *32*(5), 695–705.

Coates, H. (2010). Development of the Australasian Survey of Student Engagement (AUSSE). *Higher Education*, *60*(1), 1–17.

Conrad, L. (2003). *Five ways of enhancing the postgraduate community: Student perceptions of effective supervision and support*. Paper presented at the Learning for an Unknown Future: 26th Annual HERDSA Conference, Christchurch, New Zealand.

Conrad, L. (2006). Countering isolation: Joining the research community. In C. Denholm & T. Evans (Eds.), *Doctorates downunder: Keys to successful doctoral study in Australia and New Zealand*, (pp. 34–40). Camberwell: ACER Press.

Conrad, L., & Phillips, E. (1995). From isolation to collaboration: A positive change for postgraduate women? *Higher Education*, *30*(3), 313–322.

Cook, J. H., Eaker, R. E., Ghering, A. M., & Sells, D. K. (2007). Collaboration: Definitions and barriers. In J. H. Cook & C. A. Lewis (Eds.), *The divine comity: Student and academic affairs collaboration*. Washington, DC: NASPA. Retrieved from http://www.naspa.org/publications/books/student-and-academic-affairs-collaboration-the-divine-comity

Cooper, G., & Juniper, S. (2002). *A postgraduate research training programme in generic skills and strategies: Description and evaluation*. Paper presented at the HERDSA 25th Annual International Conference.

Delamont, S., Atkinson, P., & Parry, H. (2000). *The doctoral experience: Success and failure in graduate school*. London: Falmer Press.

Delamont, S., Atkinson, P., & Parry, O. (1997). Critical mass and doctoral research: Reflections on the Harris report. *Studies in Higher Education*, *22*(3), 319–331.

Dewey, B. I. (2005). The embedded librarian. *Resource Sharing & Information Networks*, *17*(1–2), 5–17.

Fenge, L. (2012). Enhancing the doctoral journey: The role of group supervision in supporting collaborative learning and creativity. *Studies in Higher Education*, *37*(4), 401–414.

Fowler, J., Gudmundsson, A., & Whicker, L. (2006). *Groups work: A guide for working in groups*. Bowen Hills: Australian Academic Press.

Green, P., & Bowden, J. (2012). Completion mindsets and contexts in doctoral supervision. *Quality Assurance in Education*, *20*(1), 66–80.

Greenwood, J., & Te Aika, L. (2009). *Hei Tauira: Teaching and learning for success for Maori in tertiary settings.* Retrieved from http://akoaotearoa.ac.nz/download/ng/file/group-3846/n3866-hei-tauira—full-report.pdf

Hadjielia-Drotarova, M. (2011). *Peer reflection within the doctoral student process: A community of practice perspective.* Paper presented at the British Educational Research Association Annual Conference, Institute of Education, University of London. Retrieved from http://www.leeds.ac.uk/educol/documents/204460.pdf

Halse, C. (2011). Becoming a supervisor: The impact of doctoral supervision on suprevisors' learning. *Studies in Higher Education, 36*(5), 557–570.

Johnson, D., & Johnson, R. (1999). Making cooperative learning work. *Theory into Practice, 38*(2), 67–73.

Johnson, D., Johnson, R., & Smith, K. (1998). Cooperative learning returns to college: What evidence is there that it works? *Change,* July/August, pp. 27–35.

Johnson, W. B. (2002). The intentional mentor: Strategies and guidelines for the practice of mentoring. *Professional Psychology: Research and Practice, 33*(1), 88–96.

Johnston, S., & McCormack, C. (1997). Developing research potential through a structured mentoring program: Issues arising. *Higher Education Research & Development, 33*, 251–264.

Kagan, S. (1994). *Cooperative learning.* San Clemente, CA: Kagan Cooperative Learning.

Kerzner, H. (2005). *Using the project management maturity model: Strategic planning for project management* (2nd ed.), Hoboken, NJ: Wiley.

Kuh, G. (2001). *The national survey of student engagement: Conceptual framework and overview of psychometric properties.* Bloomington, IN: Indiana University Center for Postsecondary Research & Planning.

Ladyshewsky, R. (2001). *Reciprocal peer coaching: A strategy for training and development in professional disciplines.* Jamison: Higher Education Research and Development Society of Australasia.

Ladyshewsky, R. (2006). Peer coaching: A constructivist methodology for enhancing critical thinking in postgraduate business education. *Higher Education Research & Development, 25*(1), 67–84.

Ladyshewsky, R., & Gardner, P. (2008). Peer assisted learning and blogging: A strategy to promote reflective practice during clinical fieldwork. *Australasian Journal of Educational Technology, 24*(3), 241–257.

Lave, J., & Wenger, E. (1991). *Situated learning: Legitimate peripheral participation.* Cambridge, MA: Cambridge University Press.

Leach, L., & Knight, M. (2003). Collaboration for learning and teaching. In N. Zepke, D. Nugent & L. Leach (Eds.), *Reflection to transformation: A self-help book for teachers,* (pp. 139–154). Palmerston North: Dunmore.

Lee, A. (2008). How are doctoral students supervised? Concepts of doctoral research supervision. *Studies in Higher Education, 33*(3), 267–281.

Lee, A. (2012). *Successful research supervision: Advising students doing research.* Oxon: Routledge.

Lennox Terrion, J., Philion, R., & Leonard, D. (2007). An evaluation of a university peer-mentoring training program. *International Journal of Evidence Based Coaching and Mentoring, 5*(1), 42–57.

McLean, M. (2004). Does the curriculum matter in peer mentoring? From mentee to mentor in problem-based learning: A unique case study. *Mentoring and Tutoring, 12,* 173–186.

Meyer, J., & Land, R. (2005). Threshold concepts and troublesome knowledge: Linkages to ways of thinking and practising within the disciplines. In C. Rust (Ed.), *Improving student learning: Improving student learning theory and practice — ten years on.* Oxford: Oxford Centre for Staff and Learning Development.

Muldoon, R. (2008). Recognising and rewarding the contribution and personal development of peer supporters at university. *Journal of Further and Higher Education, 32*(3), 207–219.

Mullen, C. (2001). The need for a curricular writing model for graduate students. *Journal of Further and Higher Education, 25*(1), 117–126.

Nelson, K., Kift, S., Creagh, T., & Quinn, C. (2007). *Enhancing transition at QUT: Teamwork protocol.* Brisbane: QUT.

Nettles, M. T., & Millet, C. M. (2006). *Three magic letters: Getting to PhD.* Baltimore, MD: Johns Hopkins University Press.

Pagan, R., & Edwards-Wilson, R. (2002). A Mentoring program for remedial students. *Journal of College Student Retention, 4,* 207–26.

Peacock, J. (2006). *THINK systemically, ACT strategically: Sustainable development of information literacy in the broader context of students' learning.* Paper presented at the Proceedings of IATUL 2006: Embedding Libraries in Learning and Research, Faculdade de Engenharia Universidade do Porto, Portugal.

Rata, E. (2002). The transformation of indigeneity. *Review (Fernand Braudel Center), 25*(2), 173–195.

Roberts, S., & Stewart, J. (2008). Towards the holistic university: Working collaboratively for student learning. In M. Weaver (Ed.), *Transformative learning support models in higher education: Educating the whole student* (pp. 19–31). London: Facet.

Scott, D. (2005). Retention, completion and progression in tertiary education in New Zealand. *Journal of Higher Education Policy and Management, 27*(1), 3–17.

Sharan, S. (1994). *Handbook of cooperative learning methods.* Westport, CT: Greenwood.

Tenofsky, D. (2005). Teaching to the whole student: Building best practices for collaboration between libraries and student services. *Research Strategies, 20*(4), 284–299.

Thomas, D. R. (2006). A general inductive approach for analyzing qualitative evaluation data. *American Journal of Evaluation, 27*(2), 237–246.

Topping, K. J. (1996). The effectiveness of peer tutoring in further and higher education: A typology and review of the literature. *Higher Education, 32*(3), 321–345.

Topping, K. J. (2005). Trends in peer learning. *Educational Psychology, 25*(6), 631–645.

University of Otago. (n.d.). *Postgraduate research peer support: Factors that contribute to successful research communities and peer groups.* Retrieved from http://media.otago.ac.nz/ GJttbUHVUu/9NVNeCr2/Peer_Support_Brochure_2010.pdf. Accessed on 4 September 2012.

van der Meer, J. (2011). Māori and Pasifika students' academic engagement: What can institutions learn from the AUSSE data? In A. Radloff (Ed.), *Student engagement in New Zealand universities.* Melbourne: Australian Council of Educational Research.

van der Meer, J., & Scott, C. (2008). Shifting the balance: From teacher instruction to peer-learning primacy. *The Australasian Journal of Peer-Learning, 1*(1), 70–79.

Van Maanen, J. (1988). *Tales of the field: On writing ethnography.* Chicago, IL: University of Chicago Press.

Wenger, E. (1998). *Communities of practice: Learning, meaning and identity.* Cambridge, MA: Cambridge University Press.

Wisker, G., Robinson, G., Trafford, V., Warnes, M., & Creighton, E. (2003). From supervisory dialogues to successful PhDs: Strategies supporting and enabling the learning conversations of staff and students at postgraduate level. *Teaching in Higher Education, 8*(3), 383–397.

Chapter 19

Reflection as a Strategy to Enhance Students' Engagement in their Learning

Janet Strivens and Rob Ward

Abstract

This chapter is about the educational benefits of a set of processes: reviewing, reflecting, recording and action planning. Our focus is on activities which aim to create a space in which the learner pauses to 'take stock' of her learning. We have labelled these 'stop-and-think' activities: they are broadly strategies which, so to speak, interrupt the flow of the performance of a task, giving the learner the opportunity to analyse, evaluate and perhaps reconsider her performance, reframe the task she is engaged in or change direction to pursue a different course. Such approaches, sometimes referred to as metacognitive strategies, have the potential, when appropriately and consistently supported, to enable learners not only to engage more fully with the subject matter, but also to develop their sense of self as a learner.

'Stop-and-think' strategies are first divided loosely into a matrix according to whether the focus of attention is the past, the present or the future. Within these divisions an overview of theory is presented, and also some illustrations of successful practice which could be seen to derive from theoretical principles.

While the limitations of current evidence are acknowledged, the combination of theory and practice presented strongly supports the value of such metacognitive strategies for student engagement in learning. There is a particular emphasis on using such strategies within a peer group, both in terms of increasing motivation and for added value in learning.

The chapter takes a new perspective on the familiar topic of reflection, with a consistent focus on the practicality of theoretically informed strategies (their immediate usefulness to practitioners). Evidence is drawn from a considerable range of disciplines and perspectives, the connections between which could help to enhance the credibility of the suggestions made for practice.

The Student Engagement Handbook: Practice in Higher Education
Copyright © 2013 by Emerald Group Publishing Limited
All rights of reproduction in any form reserved
ISBN: 978-1-78190-423-7

19.1.   Introduction

This chapter is about the educational benefits of a set of associated 'learning activities': reviewing, reflecting, recording and action planning. Collectively in UK higher education they have often come to be known as 'personal development planning' (PDP) (Gough, Kiwan, Sutcliffe, Simpson, & Houghton, 2003; QAA, 2009). However they are clearly not the prerogative of this sector: together or separately and under differing terminology they are used and valued in school education, vocational education, professional development and employment across the world. While this widespread usage lends weight to the notion that these are somehow useful activities, it comes at the cost of a certain conceptual 'muddiness'.

It could for example be argued that 'reflection' is the overarching concept which encompasses all these activities.[1] But reflection, like student engagement, is an oft-defined term which still ends up meaning different things to different people. Therefore the discussion which follows is grounded in activities — the tasks which students do, often because they have been set by tutors, designed to increase their learning, to improve their execution of a skill or to heighten their awareness of themselves and their environment. We could have referred to these as personal development planning activities, but PDP too is a much-debated term and its use could also serve to restrict the context of the discussion. Instead we have chosen the more directly descriptive name of 'stop-and-think' activities.

Although the focus throughout the chapter is on such activities, we want to avoid resorting to a completely atheoretical account of 'what works', which would in our view inhibit the ability to generalise from the specific examples of practice offered. Neither do we think it sensible simply to avoid the use of the term 'reflection'. Our response to the 'conceptual muddiness' around reflection is to maintain a focus on the activities themselves and to keep two key questions about them in mind: what is the evidence that these activities promote student learning and, if they are seen to be effective, how can this be explained? We will aim to steer a course between the kind of theoretical over-simplification which leads to conceptual confusion and an over-complex model of reflection which, given the focus of this Handbook, serves little useful purpose.

19.2.   'You Have to Stop and Think — It's Hard!'

For the purposes of this discussion, the origin of the term 'stop and think' comes from the work of the Israeli psychologist Reuven Feuerstein. Feuerstein is

---

[1]The EPPI systematic review of the effectiveness of personal development planning saw PDP as 'proxy for a number of constructs that attempt to connect and draw benefit from reflection, recording, action-planning and actually doing things that are aligned to the action plan' (Gough et al., 2003, p. 1). The review question which guided the inclusion criteria was: What evidence is there that processes that connect reflection, recording, planning and action improve student learning?

associated with a range of interventions all based in the belief that the right teaching strategies can develop basic cognitive functioning — that what we call intelligence can actually be learned.[2] The comment quoted above, 'You have to stop and think — it's hard!' was allegedly made by a child on his Instrumental Enrichment programme many years ago: for us it captures the essence of a truth many teachers have come to accept. There are learning strategies which have the effect of shifting the learner's focus of attention, refocusing on the 'how' of learning rather than the 'what'. They are often experienced by the learner as effortful — needing a greater degree of concentration, a sharper focus of attention. They are however powerful in their effects, enabling the learner to generalise from immediate experience; to make new connections and see new insights within information already acquired; or to access different strategies to attack problems.

Higher education in the twenty-first century is well used to the idea that its graduates are facing a world of ill-defined problems and uncertain knowledge. More explicitly than ever before, higher education institutions seek to give their students the tools and dispositions to take well-calculated risks, work with partial information and always remain open to new knowledge and new interpretations of old knowledge. It is quite clearly not enough to teach students information — even brand-new information — and how to do things (although this is where we must start). Graduates will have to be able to seek out and evaluate new knowledge and constantly develop better ways to do different things. We will be arguing here that an essential component of these skills and attributes is the ability to detach attention from the immediacy of an experience, so as to be able to think *about* that experience and what it means; to detach oneself from the awareness of a looming problem so as to be able to analyse that problem and consider ways of solving it; and to detach oneself from the *wanting* of something so as to plan the steps of how to get it.

We propose to refer to these strategies collectively as 'stop-and-think' strategies. Using this term makes an implicit claim that there is a commonality across different areas of literature and practice. Academic research may well refer to these as 'meta-cognitive strategies', often within a model of self-regulated or self-directed learning (Brookfield, 1985; Zimmerman, 2000). Those in the professions are more likely to talk generally of the value of reflection for professional development and the importance for the professional of developing self-judgement. In UK higher education, such strategies are easily recognised as a key aspect of what are known as personal development planning activities. In making the claim for a strong family resemblance between the activities described in these different ways, we (the authors) are striving for a simple and clear conceptual model which makes sense to practitioners. However, the concomitant risk is over-generalisation. We hope to avoid this through presenting examples of the strategies used successfully in different contexts and carefully articulating what we take to be key features contributing to their

---

[2]For a good general introduction to Feuerstein's work see Sharron and Coulter (1987).

success. The aim is to invite dialogue and constructive critique of the model so that it aligns more closely to practitioners' experience.

It is characteristic of 'stop-and-think' strategies that they are distinguishable from the task or learning experience itself. Tynjälä (1997) calls this 'explicitation of learning strategies' — maybe a clumsy term but it captures the idea that both learner and teacher are aware of using a strategy and can pay it separate attention. This suggests that such strategies are in some sense disruptive, they may well be experienced as interrupting the flow of a task. If, in addition to this disruption, utilising a 'stop-and-think' strategy is experienced as effortful — entailing greater concentration or more focused attention — it seems clear that both learners and their teachers will need to be thoroughly convinced of their value, in order to practise using them until their use becomes habitual.

Is there an evidence base for the value of 'stop-and-think' strategies? As noted above, different bodies of literature refer to such strategies in different ways and this makes robust evaluation difficult. Nevertheless, despite the confusion of multiple terminologies and perspectives, there is a growing body of evidence from meta-evaluations of different teaching and learning interventions that the direct teaching of such strategies and their subsequent internalisation by learners can be highly effective in improving learner performance (Hattie, Biggs, & Purdie, 1996; Gough et al., 2003; Moseley et al., 2004). It is valuable to have such evidence and a necessary step towards understanding better exactly what kind of strategies work best for which learners in which situations. However, it is often the case that practitioners are already more convinced by their own experience (Clegg, 2005; Moseley et al., 2004) and have incorporated such strategies into their daily practice and their avowed understanding of best teaching and learning practice within their disciplines.

19.3.   Are there Different Levels of Reflection?

So far we have been linking and claiming some kind of common identity for a range of teaching and learning strategies normally found and discussed in different arenas. Nevertheless some categorisation may be useful to practitioners trying to choose appropriate activities and probably necessary if they wish to take the further step of assessing or grading the outcomes.

Several influential writers (Bell, 2001; Hatton & Smith, 1995) have approached the categorisation of reflection (or 'reflective practice') in terms of a gradual deepening of the reflective process. The model developed by Jenny Moon (2004) which moves through four levels from description to transformation has had a particularly strong influence on current thinking and practice in UK higher education. This is in part due to her particular concern with reflective writing and how to assess it within an assessment culture which expects to grade performance. She recognises that the use of structured questions and models for reflective analysis of experiences may be initially helpful 'but they should be seen as props to be dispensed with as soon as possible' (Moon, 2007, p. 194). This is because they do not necessarily help learners to move from a 'superficial and descriptive' level of reflection to deeper, 'better quality' reflection.

It is undoubtedly the case that tutors looking to discover what their students have learned from, say, a clinical placement will want the record made by the students to go beyond an account of what happened: they will be looking for students to demonstrate a sense-making process, seeking interpretations and imagining alternative scenarios with better outcomes. Nevertheless there are some problems here. The first and most frequently recognised is that individuals differ in the way they use the writing process. There are those who genuinely discover insights through the process of writing: as Donaldson (1978) noted, writing acts as a 'signalling system' beyond verbal language itself to capture and hold an idea in such a way as to facilitate further examination of it. In this way writing is almost indispensable as an aid to analytic and abstract thought. Nevertheless, some people find the writing process sufficiently effortful in itself to be a distraction to the process of thought while others seem to have developed sufficiently powerful mental abilities to sort, connect and process ideas without the same need for representation. Both of these may be more likely to treat a reflective writing exercise performatively, focusing on what they think the tutor wants rather than finding value in the task itself.

It would also be unfortunate if the use of a levelled model of reflection caused tutors to undervalue the huge importance of the initial step: *noticing*. It is difficult to see how a learner can become engaged in making sense of something that has initially not even been noticed. Noticing something is another way of saying that a learner has brought a different kind of attention to bear on it: it has somehow been recognised as having significance. A key purpose of 'stop-and-think' activities seems to be to help or even induce learners to notice something of which they were previously unaware.

19.4. A Matrix of 'Stop-and-Think' Activities

Rather than a categorisation by the level or depth of the outward evidence of reflection, we find it useful to focus on the 'stop-and-think' activities themselves described along two dimensions. One is chronological: do the activities primarily involve the learner in looking backwards, in thinking about the present or in looking towards the future? We will make use of these differences in the focus of the learner's attention to sort and discuss the different strategies, while recognising that a particular activity will often involve the learner in moving between time frames. The other key dimension we find important is the learning context: whether the activities are carried out by the individual in isolation or collaboratively within a peer group, and also the extent to which a tutor or significant other (which could be a work-based mentor or supervisor as well as an academic) plays an important role in motivating or engaging the learners.

In relation to motivation, it is worth stressing again the point made earlier, that 'stop-and-think' strategies take effort on the part of the learner. This Handbook is about student engagement: what motivates students to continue to engage in learning. Yet the 'stop-and-think' approach seems to be deliberately making learning more difficult. So, what are the pay-offs for the learner, whether immediate or more long-term, and how much of the effectiveness of these strategies is dependent on helping the learner see and feel these pay-offs? For example, does it help students to maintain their motivation if they are given a clear and explicit rationale for an activity we are asking them to engage in?

Keeping in mind this issue of student motivation and in particular the boost to motivation that comes from being part of an engaged peer group or from the timely intervention of an enthusiastic tutor, we will turn now to a discussion of specific strategies and examples of their use. The examples have been selected from the authors' own experience of practices which other practitioners have found both attractive and feasible to transfer or adapt to their own contexts. The categorisation of examples will be roughly chronological, that is, starting with those which focus on the analysis of past experience.

19.5.   Activities with a Focus on Analysing Past Experiences

One of the authors usually introduces workshops on reflection with an exercise which asks participants to label in their own terminology some brief scenarios describing forms of thinking (see Table 19.1). The main point of this is to demonstrate the diversity in how different people think of reflection and define it themselves. While lack of consensus over what constitutes reflection is typical, the greatest degree of agreement is usually around scenarios involving the learner (or thinker) in recalling a past experience and analysing it in some way. The experience could have been already 'captured', for example in an exercise asking the learner to describe a 'critical incident'. Such an exercise is commonly used in clinical or other work placements to help the learner make sense of this less structured learning environment. The analysis may be facilitated by a series of *structured questions* — probably the most common form of support for reflection (see Figure 19.1 for an example of these). A more explicit variant which is still aimed at taking the learner through a structured analytic process is the use of a *model of reflection* (see, e.g., Gibbs 1988; Johns 1994).

Recording and analysis of critical incidents is often made an assessment requirement. There are two sorts of justifications for this practice. One is simply to induce the learners to take more careful notice of what is going around them in the first place (see above). The other is of course to allow the tutor access to the learner's thinking, to check what connections are being made and what conclusions drawn. In some circumstances tutors can feel uncomfortable with using assessment as a lever to induce students to reveal their thoughts and perhaps their private emotions about their own experiences. This dilemma gives rise to less formal strategies: thus,

Table 19.1: Scenarios to identify individuals' perceptions of reflection.

Would you call this reflection? If not, what would you call it?

You listen to a teacher/lecturer explaining a concept or theory (perhaps explaining the behaviour of people — or particles?) As you listen you are making connections with what you already know about the subject and/or applying the theory to observations you have made in the past. New questions are forming in your mind.

In a discussion someone offers a piece of new information which doesn't fit with what you think you know already, or draws a different conclusion, which seems quite logical, from a set of facts you know you both share and agree on. You are aware that there is a problem with accepting both the new and the old information as 'true' and/or you can recognise and accept the rationale for the alternative interpretation but realise that this is incompatible with your previous interpretation/conclusion.

You are faced with a problem to solve. You try to recall what you know about problems that seem similar (or an example comes immediately to mind). You compare the situations, identifying points of similarity and difference; imagine some possible solutions or at least some strategies; imagine possible consequences or work them out.

At a personal transition point (leaving university, applying for a job) you need to decide on the next step and/or present yourself for acceptance into the next step. You try to identify your feelings and emotions about possible future steps, by imagining yourself doing them or identifying the positive/negative feelings associated with them. You may also identify skills you have to offer by recalling past successful experiences and/or feelings of confidence associated with the names of skills.

An event comes to mind which you have recently experienced. You are aware of something associated with it which is nagging — a puzzle? Something not understood? Something which left you feeling uncomfortable? You review the event in your mind, trying to pinpoint the source of discomfort/trying out different explanations/solutions.

---

the learner could be asked to keep a learning journal or online blog with a suggested frequency of entries. In the case of a written journal, perhaps the learner will not be required to share entries or in the case of a blog, she or he will retain control over viewing permissions, have some say over what content is shared or create a separate commentary for sharing.

When reflection on past experiences is such an individual and private activity, it is nearly impossible to evaluate as a means of engaging students in their own learning. When it is individual but not private, that is, when it is in some way an assessment requirement, it remains difficult to gauge the effect on engagement (Boud & Walker, 1998; Crème, 2005; Ross, 2012).

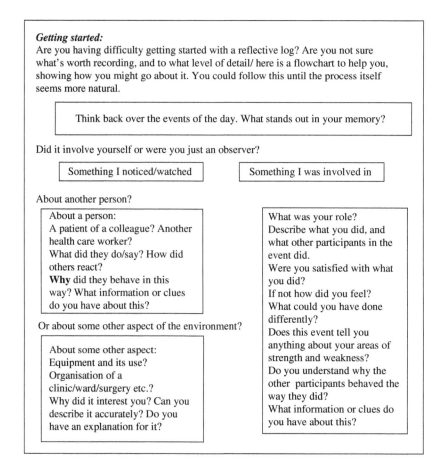

Getting started:
Are you having difficulty getting started with a reflective log? Are you not sure what's worth recording, and to what level of detail/ here is a flowchart to help you, showing how you might go about it. You could follow this until the process itself seems more natural.

Think back over the events of the day. What stands out in your memory?

Did it involve yourself or were you just an observer?

Something I noticed/watched

Something I was involved in

About another person?

About a person:
A patient of a colleague? Another health care worker?
What did they do/say? How did others react?
Why did they behave in this way? What information or clues do you have about this?

Or about some other aspect of the environment?

About some other aspect:
Equipment and its use?
Organisation of a clinic/ward/surgery etc.?
Why did it interest you? Can you describe it accurately? Do you have an explanation for it?

What was your role?
Describe what you did, and what other participants in the event did.
Were you satisfied with what you did?
If not how did you feel?
What could you have done differently?
Does this event tell you anything about your areas of strength and weakness?
Do you understand why the other participants behaved the way they did?
What information or clues do you have about this?

Figure 19.1:   Structured questions for clinical placements: An example.

In contrast, as a peer-group activity, reflection on past experiences — especially critical incidents — has the capacity to generate deep engagement. Students will be attentive and willing to contribute, partly because they know that they could very likely face something similar themselves: analysing an incident faced by one student yesterday could mean them handling their own problem more effectively tomorrow. Students may be reluctant to reveal what they regard as personal failures to a tutor in charge of assessing performance, but if one takes the plunge with a sympathetic group of peers, this provides the tutor with the opportunity to model constructive feedback, encouraging the more reticent members of the group to open up. Initially the tutor may be modelling the questions which help the students make connections, see alternatives and find solutions, but as the group becomes accustomed to sharing and analysing experiences as an important aspect of professional development, the tutor can withdraw to a facilitating role.

19.5.1.   *Example 1 — Student Teachers Share their Classroom Experiences Online*

This engagement was very clear on a Foundation course for Teaching Assistants. Students on this programme had the benefit of being linked by an online tool which offered a range of functions including individual blogs: these were typically shared by the students with their peers and the course tutor. Students wrote about their work-based experience to an audience keen to offer sympathy when needed but also to learn from each other. The enthusiastic course tutor modelled responses which were quick, supportive and pushed the group to further learning. The result was a vibrant learning community willing to spend the time after a hard day's work in school writing about their experiences and responding to their peers' accounts.

19.5.2.   *Example 2 — Sharing Learning about the Research Process*

Another example comes from a large Humanities course, where all final year Combined Honours students participated in a module called 'Individual Academic Development'. This was framed around a final dissertation and supported by a group tutorial process in which students met on a weekly basis to review and report their progress. Previously all the weekly meetings took the form of seminars where every student took turns to present papers which were critiqued by fellow students and the tutor. This was changed to set aside half the available time to consider and reflect upon the process of researching for the dissertation. Students now recounted their progress and shared the obstacles and problems they were encountering. The sharing and solving of problems in small group settings with peer feedback was found to encourage planning and give rise to the explicit consideration of a research and writing process characterised by a greater emphasis upon independent study and 'project management' than that encountered elsewhere in the degree. Thus, 'stopping and thinking' was explicitly built into these meetings and became a wider expectation of the approach adopted.

19.6.   Activities with a Focus on Recognising and Articulating Current Achievements

Another group of 'stop-and-think' activities focus around helping learners to become more aware of what they have already achieved, what skills and attributes they already possess. These activities are often thought of as the realm of careers staff, helping students with the necessary skills of writing applications and curriculum vitae which will present themselves positively but fairly to future employers. While the need to find a job may be highly motivating, students can find this process of self-analysis difficult. If it is regularly repeated it may also become tedious, leading to superficial engagement, the reuse of stock phrases and examples which carry little conviction.

19.6.1.   Example 3 — Recognising Skills Developed Through the Workplace

Graduate Opportunities Wales have developed a process incorporating 'stop-and-think' activities to support work placements, leading to a City and Guilds Professional Development Award. This is a staged scheme characterised by flexibility of approach: it supports both part-time and full-time placements and student and graduate opportunities. Common elements within it are:

- a structured and supported self-audit, which enables individuals to frame their placement opportunity in terms of personal and professional objectives;
- goal-setting, which helps with refining the framing, and also encourages the recognition of achievement;
- the review of progress on an on-going basis, which is shared with a tutor periodically for comment and formative feedback, allowing revision of original objectives where it is felt that these have been achieved or where changes in the working context make achievement very unlikely. This 'periodic log' is also likely to include independent evidence of skills and knowledge gained (e.g. in the form of employer/supervisor comment, or photographic evidence of artefacts produced), and;
- a final report (of approximately 2000–3000 words)) following completion of the work placement or activity. This reviews their experience as a whole and charts and evidences progress in terms of original and subsequent personal and professional objectives. In the report, candidates are asked to describe clearly outcomes from the experience, to evaluate their personal and professional development and to analyse the extent to which goals have been met, including any changes in personal expectations, problems that arose and how they were overcome. They are also expected to identify the implications of the experience for further development and progression.

Within this context, given the number of external reference points, 'stopping and thinking' occurs throughout — within the audit process, throughout the review process, when seeking external support and evidence, and in constructing the final report. At each stage the framing of the task supports them in analysis of and reflection on their learning.

It is not only in the realm of general and employability skills that 'stop-and-think' activities aimed at taking stock of current achievements are relevant and useful. Many educationalists have recognised that requiring students to re-read and assess their own work, trying to see it through the eyes of their tutors, is a highly effective 'stop-and-think' activity to improve academic performance. The literature on effective formative feedback stresses the value of students being routinely expected to carry out a self-assessment of their assignments prior to submission, using the same criteria that tutors will use (see, e.g., Nicol & MacFarlane-Dick, 2006; Yancey, 1998). While this could be a straightforward individual activity, there are some powerful examples of a combination of self-assessment and peer-assessment tasks being built into the design of modules to foster greater student engagement, particularly with large cohorts (Baxter, 2007). A group of peers reading and comparing each other's different responses to the same task brief can help each other to develop the skills of critical analysis, to correct errors, to refine their judgement and to recognise superior ways of expressing ideas.

Practice in applying the assessment criteria increases their understanding of the criteria themselves, helping to support their future performance (Rust, O'Donovan, & Price, 2005). Here again there is the characteristic separation of the initial learning task from the metacognitive act of evaluation. Student evaluations of such modules indicate a greater degree of engagement and satisfaction and tutors have noted an overall improvement in performance.

19.6.2. *Example 4 — The 'Patchwork Text' as an Assessment Format*

A slightly more formal curriculum design incorporating the same principles of reflection on personal learning achieved throughout a module can be seen in the Patchwork Text model of curriculum design and assessment (Trevelyan & Wilson, 2012; Winter, 2003). Working in small groups, students are set a task each week to complete and bring to the following session. The task is short enough for everyone in the group to share their response with everyone else, compare and discuss the differences in response within the contact session. Variety in the tasks will play into the diversity of the group and the different strengths of its members. It may also help to sensitise the group to differences in genres — for example, the difference between a short reflection on personal experience and an article review. The discussion in the group and comparison of the members' responses to the tasks set help each individual understand the task better, appreciate different perspectives and evaluate his or her own response more accurately. Weekly tasks increase the opportunities to practise skills and the students are continuously engaged in the process of developing, sharing and reviewing their knowledge.

At the end of the learning period, students are required to review their overall learning through a synoptic reflective assignment in which they evaluate their learning, typically against the stated learning outcomes, using a selection of the weekly tasks or 'patches' as evidence of the insights they offer.

The Patchwork Text model is far from being rigid and different elements of it have been adapted by tutors to their own purposes. As outlined, the design has several 'stop-and-think' elements which can be disaggregated but which also work powerfully together.

19.7. Activities with a Focus on Identifying Goals/Setting Targets and Planning to Achieve Them

As can be seen from some of the examples above, the process of self-audit may naturally include target-setting. This may particularly be the case within a professional programme where performance standards have been set by a professional body. In learning to use feedback to evaluate one's performance, a large body of literature stresses the importance of well-defined standards or descriptions, whether of acceptable or outstanding performance, which give the learner clear targets (Ericsson, 2008; Nicol & MacFarlane-Dick, 2006).

If we follow the paradigm learning environment suggested in Ericsson's work, self-motivated and reflective learners require the availability of expert judgement on their performance[3] and the willingness to practise, paying focused attention to precisely those aspects of performance which the expert judge has identified as in need of improvement. Elite coaching in sport or music seems to fit this paradigm best, so how might this expensive resource-intensive model apply more generally in higher education?

Whether the performance is writing an academic essay or using a clinical skill, learners who want to improve need to be sensitised to those aspects of their performance which require attention. The processes of peer-assessment and self-assessment used together, while they may lack the expert judgement of the tutor, can help students in the initial recognition of salient aspects of performance through comparison of their different responses to the same task. Including this 'stop-and-think' stage of comparison and assessment into the design of a learning activity can greatly increase the value of the tutor's subsequent feedback.

19.7.1.   Example 5 — Dental Students Learn Practical Skills

As an example, a workshop on making crowns for third-year dental students was disliked by both tutor and students: the students seemed motivated mainly by the desire to get out as quickly as possible, putting an undue amount of energy into (individually) trying to persuade the tutor to pass their efforts as satisfactory. The tutor redesigned the workshop into three stages. Working in a small group, the students would each create their crowns as before. But in the second stage, the group then had to judge their efforts, rank-order them using a set of criteria and decide at what point the products fell below an acceptable standard. At the third stage when they had reached agreement, the tutor came to give his judgement on the decision they had made, pointing out the reasons for his own assessments. This was actually less work for the tutor but student evaluations of the workshop went up and their engagement in the task and their performance also improved.

There is an obvious sense in which striving to achieve a performance target is future- orientated — and such striving may also be associated with the achievement of a long-term personal goal. Or it may not: a learner who motivates herself effectively by short-term challenges may not hold a clear view of what sort of life she

---

[3]There may also be categories of skilled performances where the nature of the performance contains sufficient feedback for the learner to self-correct, particularly those involving complex motor skills or auditory feedback.

wants to lead, what kind of work would bring her personal satisfaction. Individuals vary a great deal in the extent to which they are aware of personal goals and ambitions (Stevenson & Clegg, 2011). A few will be very clear about their chosen path,[4] more will have vague hopes with varying degrees of realism and some appear to be drifting through life eschewing any hint of personal agency. The activities needed here could be more to do with 'stop and feel' than 'stop and think'. There is some evidence (Mainwaring & Hallam, 2010; Stevenson, 2012) that holding realistic personal goals is partly dependent on the individual's being able to imagine themselves in a future role and to feel that this is consonant with their current sense of personal identity.

19.7.2. Example 6 — Encouraging Able Students to 'Raise their Sights'

Although developing a personal goal may seem to be a highly individual task, the peer group could have a critical role in validating the imagined future self as an appropriate and realistic choice. In designing a programme of activities for 'high-flyer' students, one university careers service wanted to ensure that its many students from state schools were not limiting their ambitions through their inability to imagine themselves as captains of industry or the like. Students were asked to think both forwards and backwards — what could life be like for graduates like them in 50 years time but also, what would it have been like 50 years previously? The exercise in imagination, shared with peers, helped them to see how rapidly lifestyles, expectations and opportunities had changed and could change again in the future.

Equally, of course, the peer group could act to limit imagination and ambition and encourage stereotyped images of a possible future self. In practice there appears to be a key role here for carefully selected 'significant others', individuals with whom a learner can identify who themselves embody wider possibilities.

Identifying a desired goal presents one kind of problem: achieving it is a separate problem. Evidence summarised by Wiseman (2009) suggests the efficacy of some 'stop-and-think' strategies in achieving goals, and the complete inefficacy of others. By itself, visualising a desired goal (otherwise known as day-dreaming or fantasising) has no, or possibly a negative, effect on one's likelihood of achieving it (Oettingen & Mayer, 2002; Oettingen & Wadden, 1991; Pham & Taylor, 1999). Wiseman's own study tracked over 5000 people for 6 months or 1 year as they attempted to achieve a range of aims and ambitions. Participants were asked to describe the techniques that they had employed and their level of success. Only around 10% of participants had achieved their aims at the end of the study. By

---

[4]Although in the current climate this might be interpreted as 'inappropriately fixated', where 'flexible planfulness' is to be commended.

comparing the techniques used by successful and unsuccessful participants, Wiseman identified five effective strategies:

- make a plan, one which breaks the overall goal into a series of steps: focus on creating sub-goals that are concrete, measurable, and time-based;
- reward yourself as you achieve each sub-goal;
- tell others about your goals: this seems to increase both the fear of failure and the sense of being supported;
- write down your plans and keep a record of your progress;
- regularly remind yourself of the benefits associated with achieving your goals. (Wiseman, 2009)[5]

Practitioners might well wonder how best to combine the insights from 'future selves' researchers with the experimental findings cited by Wiseman. Fortunately Wiseman has a practical suggestion, also based on Oettingen's research on self-regulation (Oettingen & Gollwitzer, 2002; Oettingen, Pak, & Schnetter, 2001). It seems that a two-step process is highly effective: first, visualising the desired goal and then thinking about the barriers and problems one is likely to encounter in achieving it. This linking of motivation with realistic planning to overcome obstacles appears to lead to the most successful outcomes (Wiseman 2009, p. 100).

19.8.   'Stop-and-Think' Activities as a Refocusing of Attention

We began our discussion by suggesting that 'stop-and-think' activities have in common the aim of detaching attention from the immediacy of experience. But 'attention' is a complex phenomenon, far from being fully understood. Broadly we can distinguish two aspects, one internal and the other external: attention as concentrated thought, sifting and organising already-held information, and attention as alertness, responding to a change in the environment or new information with a heightened level of consciousness.[6]

When the ideas of student engagement and reflective learning are linked, it is likely that we have in mind the internal aspect of attention, the kind of deep, focused concentration that Csikszentmihalyi (1992) referred to evocatively as 'flow'. The question inevitably arises in our enthusiasm for 'stop-and-think' strategies:

---

[5]To these five strategies identified in his own studies, Wiseman adds a sixth with particular relevance to chronic procrastinators: make yourself start an activity and you are more likely to continue (Fritzsche, Young, & Hickson, 2003).

[6]The findings of neuroscience suggest that each of these two aspects of attention is a function of one hemisphere of the brain (the right hemisphere having the capacity to register new information, the left working with the already known and familiar). This functional differentiation is found not only in human beings but in all vertebrates (McGilchrist, 2009).

might they have the effect of distracting the learner and interrupting the flow of effort or perhaps the opposite effect of prolonging a student's willingness to stick at the task?

This may be in part an issue of when they are used. Many 'stop-and-think' strategies can be seen as a means of creating significance in a phenomenon by bringing attention to bear on it. As Moon suggests, structured questions and models are best seen as a way to 'kick-start' this process of seeing significance and focusing attention — arguably a critical aspect for student engagement in the process. However, when immersed in a problem or a process of trying to make sense of something, the importance of metacognitive strategies is likely to be at the point where we have a sense of being stuck. Rather than yield to demotivating frustration, the learner can shift focus through employing a conscious strategy which could mean finding a way to break through.

Certainly in the accounts one reads of thinkers who have made truly creative leaps, they often appear to have a capacity for deep absorption indifferent to external distractions − the ultimate model of engagement! But these are experts in their field with a deep well of information and understanding already at their disposal. 'Stop-and-think' strategies may be of greater immediate use to more novice thinkers, helping them to find ways of engaging, finding personal significance and overcoming barriers which drain their motivation.

19.9.   Summary

In this chapter we have presented a range of activities with examples of how they have been used explicitly and strategically to improve understanding, learning and performance. There is considerable — though scattered — evidence of their effectiveness. The reader must judge whether our claim for the relatedness of the various activities is sufficiently convincing to warrant regarding the disparate evidence as cumulative. As to *why* they are effective, this is less clear. Some seem designed to help the learner focus attention more narrowly, others to make that attention broader and more receptive to noticing whatever is new, unexpected or unexplained in the wider environment. This may turn out to be an important distinction when more is understood about how the brain processes information. Our current lack of knowledge in this area should caution us against both an over-generalised concept of reflection and an uncritical assumption that asking students to 'do' it is always valuable.

In relation to student engagement, we have drawn attention to the 'effortfulness' associated with 'stop-and-think' activities. This suggests that if we think them worth using we need to consider carefully what might motivate students to engage with them. It may well be that they become their own reward to the learner for whom they have become habitual and who has discovered their value. This might be in terms of a fuller engagement with the subject matter, awareness of developing skills or a more general sense of empowerment as a learner.

However, for the novice learner, the initial motivation may need to be more external. Certainly learners should be told why they are being asked to engage in 'stop-and-think' activities although this rarely has great power to motivate on its own. The tutor's role is sometimes important, particularly when individualised feedback is needed to improve a skill. However, the peer group appears in many of our examples as a prime motivator, sharing the effort of focusing attention and offering both encouragement and feedback. In the literature on reflection, it often appears to be quite a solitary process, confined to the mind of the individual until written down for the benefit of a tutor. Perhaps we need to explore more the ways in which reflection can be a shared activity, using the power of collaboration to support and engage the learner until control over the focusing, shifting or broadening of attention as most appropriate to the task becomes a matter of habit.

Acknowledgements

Many colleagues have shared ideas, references and examples of practice during the writing of this chapter. We would particularly like to thank Julie Hughes and Paul Redmond for permission to describe their practice.

References

Baxter, J. (2007). A case study of online collaborative work in a large first year psychology class. *REAP international online conference on assessment design for learner responsibility*, 29–31 May, 2007.

Bell, M. (2001). Supported reflective practice: A programme of peer observation and feedback for academic teaching development. *International Journal for Academic Development, 6*(1), 29–39.

Brookfield, S. (1985). *Self-directed learning: From theory to practice. New directions for continuing education.* San Francisco, CA: Jossey-Bass.

Boud, D., & Walker, D. (1998). Promoting reflection in professional courses: The challenge of context. *Studies in Higher Education, 23*(2), 191–205.

Clegg, S. (2005). Evidence-based practice in educational research: A critical realist critique of systematic review. *British Journal of Sociology of Education, 26*(3), 415–428.

Creme, P. (2005). Should student learning journals be assessed? *Assessment & Evaluation in Higher Education, 30*(3), 287–296.

Csikszentmihalyi, M. (1992). *Flow: The psychology of happiness.* London: Rider.

Donaldson, M. (1978). *Children's minds.* London: Croom Helm.

Gough, D. A., Kiwan, D., Sutcliffe, K., Simpson, D., & Houghton, N. (2003). *A systematic map and synthesis review of the effectiveness of personal development planning for improving student learning.* London: EPPI-Centre Social Science Research Unit. Retrieved from http://eppi.ioe.ac.uk/EPPIWebContent/reel/review_groups/EPPI/LTSN/LTSN_June03.pdf. Accessed in June 2013.

Ericsson, K. A. (2008). Deliberate practice and acquisition of expert performance: A general overview. *Academic Emergency Medicine, 15*(11), 988–994.

Fritzsche, B. A., Young, B. R., & Hickson, K. C. (2003). Individual differences in academic procrastination tendency and writing success. *Personality and Individual Differences, 35*(7), 256−268.

Gibbs, G. (1988). *Learning by doing: A guide to teaching and learning methods.* Birmingham: SCED.

Johns, C. (1994). Nuances of reflection. *Journal of Clinical Nursing, 3,* 71−75.

Hattie, J., Biggs, J., & Purdie, N. (1996). Effects of learning skills interventions on student learning: a meta-analysis. *Review of Educational Research, 66,* 99−136.

Hatton, N., & Smith, D. (1995). Reflection in teacher education − towards definition and implementation. *Teaching and Teacher Education, 11*(1), 33−49.

Mainwaring, D., & Hallam, S. (2010). 'Possible selves' of young people in a mainstream secondary school and a pupil referral unit: A comparison. *Emotional and Behavioural Difficulties, 15*(2), 153−169.

McGilchrist, I. (2009). *The master and his emissary: The divided brain and the making of the Western world.* New Haven, CT: Yale University Press.

Moon, J. (2004). *The handbook of reflective and experiential learning.* London: Routledge.

Moon, J. (2007). Getting the measure of reflection: Considering matters of definition and depth. *Journal of Radiotherapy in Practice, 6,* 191−200.

Moseley, D., Baumfield, V., Higgins, S., Lin, M., Miller, J., Newton, D., ..., Gregson, M. (2004). *Thinking skill frameworks for post-16 learners: An evaluation.* Trowbridge: Learning and Skills Research Centre.

Nicol, D., & MacFarlane-Dick, D. (2006). Formative assessment and self-regulated learning: A model and seven principles of good feedback practice. *Studies in Higher Education, 31*(2), 199−218.

Oettingen, G., & Gollwitzer, P. M. (2002). Self-regulation of goal pursuit: Turning hope thoughts into behaviour. *Psychological Inquiry, 13,* 304−307.

Oettingen, G., & Mayer, D. (2002). The motivating function of thinking about the future: Expectations versus fantasies. *Journal of Personality and Social Psychology, 83,* 1198−1212.

Oettingen, G., Pak, H., & Schnetter, K. (2001). Self-regulation of goal setting: Turning free fantasies about the future into binding goals. *Journal of Personality and Social Psychology, 80,* 736−753.

Oettingen, G., & Wadden, T. A. (1991). Expectation, fantasy and weight loss: Is the impact of positive thinking always positive? *Cognitive Therapy and Research, 15,* 167−175.

Pham, L. B., & Taylor, S. E. (1999). From thought to action: Effects of process- versus outcome-based mental simulations on performance. *Personality and Social Psychology Bulletin, 25,* 250−260.

QAA. (2009). *Personal development planning: Guidance for institutional policy and practice in higher education.* Retrieved from http://www.qaa.ac.uk/Publications/InformationAnd Guidance/Documents/PDPguide.pdf. Accessed on 5 February 2013.

Ross, J. (2012). Performing the reflective self: Audience awareness in high-stakes reflection. *Studies in Higher Education iFirst.* Retrieved from http://www.tandfonline.com/action/ showCitFormats?doi = 10.1080%2F03075079.2011.651450. Accessed on 25January 2013.

Rust, C., O'Donovan, B., & Price, M. (2005). A social constructivist assessment process model: How the research literature shows us this could be best practice. *Assessment & Evaluation in Higher Education, 30*(3), 231−240.

Sharron, H., & Coulter, M. (1987). *Changing children's minds: Feuerstein's revolution in the teaching of intelligence.* London: Souvenir Press.

Stevenson, J. (2012). An exploration of the link between minority ethnic and white students' degree attainment and views of their future 'possible selves'. *Higher Education Studies*, *2*(4), 103–113.

Stevenson, J., & Clegg, S. (2011). Possible selves: Students orientating themselves towards the future through extracurricular activity. *British Educational Research Journal*, *37*(2), 231–246.

Trevelyan, R., & Wilson, A. (2012). Using patchwork texts in assessment: Clarifying and categorising choices in their use. *Assessment and Evaluation in Higher Education*, *37*(4), 487–498.

Tynjälä, P. (1997). Developing education students' conceptions of the learning process in different environments. *Learning and Instruction*, *7*(3), 277–292.

Winter, R. (2003). Contextualising the patchwork text: Addressing problems of coursework assessment in HE. *Innovations in Education and Teaching International*, *40*(2), 112–122.

Wiseman, R. (2009). *59 seconds: Think a little, change a lot*. London: Macmillan.

Yancey, K. B. (1998). *Reflection in the writing classroom*. Logan, UT: Utah State University Press.

Zimmerman, B. J. (2000). Self-regulatory cycles of learning. In G. A. Straka (Ed.), *Conceptions of self-directed learning, theoretical and conceptual considerations* (pp. 221–234). New York, NY: Waxman.

Chapter 20

Breaking Down the Walls: Engaging Students with the Development of their Intercultural Competencies

Christine Hardy, Sean Prince, Viola Borsos, Christopher Demirjian, Ji Kim, Nga Mok and Oliver Roman-Worsley

Abstract

This chapter will describe and discuss initial findings from a project, funded by the Higher Education Academy, which explores student engagement with the internationalisation agenda, focusing on Fashion Design student experiences of the international classroom and multicultural group working. Findings from 10 focus groups, comprising home and international students, revealed that the development of intercultural competencies was felt to be important by all students due to the international nature of the fashion industry. One way of gaining these competencies was working with students from a culturally diverse background, but it transpired that this proved difficult for both home and international students as students preferred to study in monocultural educational settings. This is due to the language barrier and cultural differences and the perceived threat by home students of the reduction in marks when working multiculturally. These difficulties substantially weakened the relationships between home and international students and the development of intercultural competencies for all students. From the findings from primary and secondary research, this chapter concludes that multicultural relationships do not arise naturally and so an intervention must be made by the tutors on the course. This could include multicultural workshops and cultural days, the development of a 'buddy system', investigation of the composition of multicultural groups, development of materials for staff and students for improving the effectiveness of multicultural group working, and the development of projects that utilise intercultural competencies.

The Student Engagement Handbook: Practice in Higher Education
Copyright © 2013 by Emerald Group Publishing Limited
All rights of reproduction in any form reserved
ISBN: 978-1-78190-423-7

20.1.   Introduction

Over the last 3 years, the BA (Hons) Fashion Design course at Nottingham Trent University, School of Art and Design, has seen an increase in international students to over 20 per cent of the cohort (approximately 100 students in total), which has brought many challenges to both staff and students in creating inclusive learning environments, particularly in the international classroom (teaching settings when home and international students are accommodated in the same classroom and do not share a common native language) and multicultural group working (consisting of home and international students who work on a specific project and do not share a common language). Fashion Design is a 'practice based' course, with students gaining practical skills in a studio setting with the contextualisation of the subject being taught in a lecture/tutorial setting, and students are expected to work together informally and formally, with peer support and feedback being an important part of learning.

The fashion industry is a global industry and entry into it is very competitive, and for graduates to be successful they are expected to have developed an under-standing of the international context in which they will be working; to gain a competitive advantage they need to have experience of working in this international context. To this end students are encouraged to enter national and international competitions and participate in industry projects, both individually and as a member of a group while studying in the United Kingdom. Students are also offered opportunities to work for international companies outside of the United Kingdom (internships) or periods of study abroad (under the Erasmus scheme). It is in these settings, both at home and abroad, that students are expected to develop the intercultural and international competencies that will give them an advantage in applying for jobs in the industry. However, many students cannot take advantage of international opportunities abroad, due to factors such as working or having a family, not being able to travel abroad due to cultural or religious reasons (Beelen, 2007), lack of language proficiency (Beelen, 2011) and perception of it not being related to the course or financial implications (NUS/HSBC, 2010/11, p. 56). This has led to an increasing focus on internationalisation at home, which is 'any internationally related activity with the exception of outbound student and staff mobility' (Wachter, 2000, p. 6), including participation in the international classroom and multicultural group working.

As previously stated, encouraging successful engagement in these settings is challenging for both staff and students, where there is often a lack of integration between home and international students, both academic and social. Academic integration relates to academic performance, self-perceptions, academic progress and belief that lecturing staff are personally committed to teaching and supporting students. Social integration embraces self-esteem and the quality of relationships established with teaching staff and peers (Tinto & Goodsell-Love, 1993). However, Tinto (1997, p. 618) argues that 'the social, is, for many students, a developmental precondition for addressing the need for intellectual engagement', and Astin (1993, p. 398) claims that peers are 'the single most potent source of influence' in the lives of college students; therefore establishing 'trust' relationships between students and staff and students and peers is essential in fostering student engagement (Bryson & Hand, 2007), both generally and with the international agenda.

To understand more fully the difficulties in establishing effective multicultural relationships for working and studying, funding was gained from the Higher Education Academy (HEA) in 2011 to examine student and staff perspectives of multicultural working; their expectations and experiences through examination of the curriculum itself and relationships between staff/students and students/students with the expected outputs of students generating their own ideas for creating inclusive learning environments and gaining intercultural and international competencies.

Intercultural and international competencies, although linked, are different. Intercultural competence is 'the development, respect and empathy for people with different national, cultural social, religious and ethnic origins', whereas international competence is 'the knowledge about the ability in international relations (e.g. foreign language skills and knowledge about the political, social and economic development of countries/regions)' (Beelen, 2007, p. 2). The former is demonstrated by behaviour but underpinned by beliefs and attitudes, whereas the latter is an increase in knowledge, which is often very specialist. Both are necessary to some extent when working in a diverse environment and with people from diverse backgrounds, such as in Fashion.

In this chapter we are focusing on internationalisation at home, particularly intercultural learning, which facilitates the development of intercultural competencies, through the formation of the international classroom and multicultural group working. It is possible to achieve intercultural learning and hence intercultural competencies through these types of encounters, which could

> ... create personal sensitivity for one's *own* cultural background and values. Furthermore it can initiate the development of positive attitudes towards other cultures, and behavioural skills to act efficiently and adequately in an intercultural context. (Otten, 2000, p. 18)

This type of learning is a process of personal growth with cognitive, affective and behavioural dimensions, and according to Otten (2000, p. 18) is 'without doubt the most involving form of learning'. This process, therefore, is a 'personal journey of deconstruction and reconstruction' (Sanderson, 2004 in Hyland, Trahar, Anderson, & Dickens, 2008), a 'lived experience' and this, as explored by Hyland et al. (2008), includes staff difficulties in meeting the needs of culturally diverse groups, and encouraging some students to break out of their familiar cultural groups to socialise or work cross-culturally.

> On the surface, most academics value intercultural cooperation of their students. However, a degree of teachers' tolerance to otherness and different styles can dwindle quickly when teaching and learning demand more time, energy and patience. Moreover, the acceptance of other approaches and different views in the classroom can decline

when this endangers the achievement of what is supposed to be the 'standard' of academic excellence. (Otten, 2003, p. 14)

Multicultural work groups do not generally arise naturally (Peacock & Harrison, 2009) as home and international students prefer to study in monocultural educational settings (De Vita, 2002), finding it difficult to get to know each other (UNITE, 2006). There are many reasons for this, according to Peacock and Harrison (2009), including the degree of comfort that the UK student feels in the presence of international students and their desire to interact; barriers include language, misunderstanding of academic norms, fear of causing offence and the lack of common cultural artefacts (particularly humour and comedy). One of the main areas of difficulty in encouraging multicultural groups is the perceived threat that an international student could bring the marks of the group down through their lack of language ability, knowledge of the United Kingdom or understanding of British pedagogy (De Vita, 2002; Kimmel & Volet, 2012; Peacock & Harrison, 2009). In addition, the performance advantages of culturally diverse teams do not manifest themselves until after 17 weeks of collaboration (Watson, Kumar, & Michaelsen, 1993) and many student projects are of a shorter duration. However, student perceptions are often not borne out by the data, with cultural diversity often being linked to enhanced group performance (Summers & Volet, 2008, De Vita, 2002), personal skills development and higher order learning (Sweeney, Weaven, & Herington, 2008). The majority of international and home students perceive that international contact is a valuable part of the student experience (UNITE, 2006), but for benefits to accrue to students, enabling them to gain intercultural competencies, tutors have an important role in designing and monitoring learning activities ensuring that they contain interdependent task features incorporating cultural dimensions and that students are supported with structured help, coaching and debriefing (Kimmel & Volet, 2012; Sweeney et al., 2008).

20.2. Methodology

With an emphasis on examining student and staff perspectives of internationalisation at home and their expectations and experiences, the HEA-funded project offered bursaries to recruit five undergraduate students from the School of Art & Design at Nottingham Trent University to work with two academic members of staff. With a focus on Fashion Design, the positions were advertised and promoted to all first year students. Selection was through an interview process and the strength of applicants enabled the recruitment of a truly multi-cultural team with students from South Korea, China, Hungary, Cyprus and the United Kingdom.

The initial stage of the project composed of three full days of development activity where all members of the research group were involved in team building exercises, research methods and writing the research questions. It was decided to use a qualitative approach to secure rich descriptions in terms of the meanings student and staff bring to their relationships and experiences of multicultural working and to '… seek answers to questions that stress how social experience is created and given meaning' (Denzin & Lincoln, 1994, p. 4) as 'from a constructivist perspective, mere exposure to difference is not enough, rather it is how one perceives and conceptualises those events that determine developmental cultural competence' (Pedersen, 2010, pp. 72, 73). This enabled the group to 'mine the terrain' (McCracken, 1988, p. 17), recognising that 'there are no universal truths to be discovered, and that all knowledge is grounded in human society, situated, partial, local, temporal and historically specific' (Coffey, 1999, p. 11). The methods chosen were student focus groups and staff interviews, and appropriate materials were developed including a student focus group guide, an interview guide for staff, consent forms and information for participants. Ethical approval was gained from the University Inter-college Ethics Committee.

To date 10 focus groups have been undertaken (spanning two academic years) with an average of six undergraduate participants per group. The groups comprised home students, international and home students and international students from each year group. This enabled additional examination of participation, engagement, integration and intercultural competencies. Each focus group lasted between 45 and 90 minutes depending on the strength of the discussion, and the participants were self-selecting volunteers, recruited by the students in the research team. Each focus group was conducted by two research students and a rota was developed to give them the opportunity to work with each other. The interim results from the focus groups with Fashion Design students will be presented in this chapter, concentrating on the student experience and the support they feel that they need to develop intercultural competencies. The focus group areas for discussion were:

- Student experiences of internationalisation of the course they are studying
- Student feelings about intercultural competencies, if they are important and why
- Any challenges students face in gaining intercultural competencies
- An exploration of the relationships, both current and possible, with students from diverse backgrounds
- Student relationships with the staff on their course
- Support they feel they need for developing intercultural competencies.

All focus groups were transcribed and a paradigmatic analysis carried out to '… locate common themes or conceptual manifestations among the … data' (Polkinghorne, 1995, p. 13), which were inductively derived.

20.3.   Initial Findings

20.3.1.   *Intercultural Competencies*

All students considered gaining intercultural competencies important due to the international nature of the fashion industry.

> ... because [of] globalization. ... I'm from Taiwan ... maybe in the
> future I will work for a British company, and I think these skills are
> really important. So people from different countries can work
> together in the future, they are more ... competent, confident. (3rd
> year female international student)

> ... and also it makes you more open minded ... we live in the times of
> globalization, it's really essential. (1st year female home student)

When asked about how these competencies are gained on the course, students
felt that the course was mostly Eurocentric with the exception of the presence of
international students. Both international and home students recognised the benefits
of working within a diverse student body, but particularly the home students, when
talking about the international students:

> They'll bring something to the table that we don't know and we bring
> things — you're only going to get better and stronger by sharing
> these. (1st year female home student)

> ... international students ... they can bring information and ideas
> that you are not exposed to beforehand, so they can give you an
> insight into techniques, or, I suppose their culture , which can influ-
> ence the way you work as well — your ethic as well as design work —
> so very beneficial and bring lots to the group. (1st year male home
> student)

20.3.2.   *The International Classroom*

Both home and international students acknowledged that there are difficulties in
working together, in tutorials, workshops and lectures. These difficulties were
mainly language and cultural issues which present problems in terms of communication and mutual learning.

The methods of teaching and learning in the United Kingdom are not familiar to
the majority of international students, particularly independent learning, as one
Persian student put so succinctly:

> ... [in my home country] they explain it two or three times to make
> sure that you understand it, but here they just say to go and do it by
> yourself. So that is the other problem that I have here, because I
> don't know how they study here ... (1st year female international
> student)

The focus of the educational process in fashion is also different from what many
international students are used to, where the focus is on 'doing'. Students on design
courses in the United Kingdom are expected to produce portfolios and sketchbooks,

where they present the development of their ideas and also contextualise their work through the research they have undertaken.

> I think the concepts of fashions are very different from our country — maybe our country we focus on pattern cutting. (3rd year female international student)

> ... I think Chinese people are focused on results and British people quite enjoy the whole process. I think that [is] good, I think that's a big difference .... (3rd year female international student)

> ... in the lectures the tutors give a lot of research to do, about research I learnt quite a lot ... because British people's mind is quite open and they know how to do research, but international student ... maybe the culture is different and the thinking way is different ... maybe we don't know how to do it ... (3rd year female international student)

The tutorials are an arena where students present and discuss their ideas with the tutor and fellow students, and these present particular difficulties for the international students, in terms of the different learning styles with the added complication of the language barrier. All students, home and international, recognised language to be an issue which affected the ability of international students to express themselves or discuss their work, which makes them 'just feel confused and uncomfortable ...' (1st year female international student).

> We have different cultural background, like British students, they're very positive, they like discuss with people the works and their ideas, sometimes in the group, but I think maybe international students they are not that good at talking ... (3rd year female international student)

> UK students, they sometimes, they only have one or two pages of sketch book and they have a lot to talk [about], but even we have more than ten pages, but we can't talk. (1st year female international student)

Tutors often don't recognise these problems and find it easier to involve those students who appear to be more engaged, which quite often are those who speak the same language.

> During pattern cutting and toiling ... the tutors would speak to English speaking students, obviously not intentionally, but of course, they would address us, because we would be the ones who replied — in a way that's quite bad, but I probably didn't notice it at the time... because we are always in a pressurized environment, because of the course we're on, I think sometimes tutors don't always think about taking some extra time to get their point across to feel comfortable in a situation ... [the international students] feel panicked and don't always say what they want to. (3rd year female home student)

The problems of discussing work in tutorial settings impacts on the international students, in that they believe that tutors think they are not studying as much as the home students:

> '... you know the UK student, looking for idea, talk a lot — teachers think international students don't work — it's not fair'. (1st year female international student)

This can impact on their engagement, and some international students stop going to tutorials.

International students (and some home students) also have problems with the technical vocabulary used by tutors and find that tutors often talk too fast for them and make reference to British culture that they do not understand, '... we don't know what is famous and we can't talk about work and daily life and things like that ...' (1st year female international student). Often the international students would seek clarification from the home students:

> ... the international student I was working with was asking 'what did she say?', 'what does she mean?'. We'd be repeating what she was saying earlier, for the internationals to catch up with the English, which is obviously just — I don't mind. (3rd year female home student)

Not all home students would not help the international student to understand 'they just don't care, just talk by themselves ...' (1st year female international student).

Even when a written brief is available for the student, or slides are available on the virtual learning portal, international students often do not understand what is required of them '... all international students were put in one group, and when they actually presented, they really didn't understand the brief' (1st year female home student).

It would be beneficial to all students if they worked together effectively, learning from each other, but in scheduled sessions and the studio environment those from the same backgrounds tend to stick together and all students find difficulties in penetrating these groups, even though they know it would be advantageous to do so, '... breaking the boundary between the two, it's almost like two different sides of the studio' (1st year female home student). Students suggested that the main reason for this is staying in comfort zones and a lack of mutual understanding.

> Just the same thing, much easy to talk with international student because actually we can find here a lot of Chinese, and they've got the same opinion and we just feel more comfortable, thinking or working together. Actually we want to make friends with British but we just find it quite difficult, it's about the language, but also about the different culture, maybe some British guys think that just so boring and not interesting. (1st year female international student)

Just as the international students want to work with home students, home students want to work with the international students, but find it difficult to approach them when they are in a group.

> ... yes the language barrier, I hate to say this, but they stick together quite a bit, it's quite intimidating to barge in and start talking to them, break into groups. (1st year female home student)

> ... but sometimes I find it difficult because I'm not, I don't know about their culture, I don't want to ask things that would be rude, so say the wrong thing. (1st year female home student)

One home student commented on the behaviour of the international students when they work together in the studio, particularly how they worked together, compared to when they worked with home students:

> We worked in a room with a lot of international students, when they are together they're really loud and they are all throwing ideas at each other, I don't know it's just completely different to how they are with us. (3rd year female home student)

20.3.3. *Multicultural Group Working*

The problem of integration and working together is recognised by the staff on the course, so they mix home and international students for group working on specific projects, but this can be a mixed experience for all involved, and issues can be exacerbated by communication problems and differences in learning styles.

> ... every group had a different experience. My experience was positive, there were 4 UK students and one international — what was negative [is that] she felt very isolated and we tried so hard to integrate her, we went out for lunch together and do things together and stuff, but she didn't really speak up, in group tutorials to making group decisions about designs, it was very much like a dialogue between UK students, rather than — I just felt that while we all got on very well as friends, I just felt — even though we asked her, a confidence issue, she felt outnumbered. (3rd year female home student)

Other international students are not so fortunate within their group, with the British students tending to work together and ignoring the international student, who consequently feels isolated.

The difficulty in making decisions is a common experience for all students involved, quite often the home students making design decisions or decisions about what is included in a presentation without involving the international student. This impacts on the social integration of the international students, particularly the quality of the relationships.

> I just feel not happy and sometimes if they show something to me I can't understand ... sometimes there are two design ideas, they don't ask me about this, we design and you just do it, [I] am not happy because they do not listen to my opinion ... (1st year female international student)

> In my group I had two international students, but I don't feel like ... they don't want to speak up. If you've all got to make decisions, they didn't really like it ... they didn't want to speak up, so it was hard, to know ... what they wanted to do, or what they are about, or what kind of stuff they like. (3rd year female home student)

In other cases, the home students did all the work, not involving the international students at all.

> They don't really trust me. They think maybe I don't understand or I talk too good, so they just do it more. When I answer other things I can help with, they say 'it's OK, we've already done it'. (3rd year female international student)

There are many possible reasons for this. One is the question of being marked as a group: '... when you are being marked as a group it's quite hard ... to do the same amount of work and have them participating in the presentation as much as you are' (3rd year female home student). Home students also thought that working in a group with international students meant more work for them, particularly in correcting the work due to lack of understanding: 'they try to do it, but it would always be wrong because they didn't understand' (3rd year female home student); 'she would do it but then you would need to correct it as she didn't understand the question' (3rd year female home student).

However, some groups recognised the specialist skills of the international students and made use of them.

> She went on to do her own thing, but when we put the portfolio together, we would all sit together and she was a fantastic illustrator. That kind of helped ... the language barriers are a struggle, but if they are willing to learn ... you do kind of battle through it. (3rd year female home student)

Again, one of the issues for group working was the different ways of working and learning styles.

> But I think they do a lot more than us, some of them work differently to us, they like to keep themselves and their work to themselves, that has happened a lot. (3rd year female home student)

> I think British always want to work at the very end of the project, end of the week, we want to do the whole thing. (1st year female international student)

Group work is, therefore, taxing for all those involved, with international students feeling that they are not fully involved and the British students taking the lead. This can lead to perceptions by the international students that they are not being given credit for the amount of work they have done.

> One of my friends is doing group work. [For] the presentation she did a lot of things, powerpoint slides, some of the UK students [did not do] anything. During the presentation, because her English is not that good, she didn't speak a lot, but the one who didn't do anything, they just can speak when they see the slide, they just speak. So she said that the tutor misunderstand[s] — maybe that she didn't do any work. (1st year female international student)

20.3.4. *Student Suggestions for Engaging Students in Intercultural Learning*

Students had many suggestions for improving engagement with intercultural learning. Due to the real issue of language being a barrier to communication, this was an area that many students focused on. Some students suggested that English language classes should be made compulsory for international students or that extra help should be provided, with an allocated tutor (preferably multilingual) and extra drop in sessions with the aim of clarifying issues previously dealt with:

> If [we] got one tutor only for international students ... if we've got some problem, we can just go there and talk to them ... it would be more helpful to us. (1st year female international student)

> Almost need that extra bit of help from the tutors ... I think it should be a tutor that speaks their language. (3rd year female home student)

> I think the university should put some extra, maybe not classes, but sessions for international students, eg sewing or pattern cutting, because we have just — you don't remember if it's just one class. If there was any extra class ... I would pay. (1st year female international student)

In addition some international students felt that more lectures on fashion history and art as well as artists would be welcome so they could have a better understanding of European fashion and art. Other suggestions for improving intercultural competencies included more student exchanges, more trips abroad, more international competitions, more culturally driven projects and visiting international lecturers.

Most students focused on how international and home students could work together more effectively, feeling that it was important to have integration from the start of the course.

> I think ... international students need more encouragement to mingle, and equally all of us, home students need that encouragement as well. As much as it should just happen — we should be all wonderful, welcoming — but we are not ... people struggle with it, there is a negative association with it. (1st year female home student)

Ways of facilitating this integration were suggested, including workshops and mini projects that celebrate cultural diversity that were organised from the start:

> I would definitely say workshops would work ... the way people do things it's different ... it's different in different countries ... different things from different countries ... to get you in the spirit of it ... (1st year female home student)

> Maybe have days, culture days, culture cooking classes, dance — I think it'd be brilliant if we had international days (all in agreement) — fun events. (1st year male home student)

The students believed that these events would not only encourage students to mingle from the start, but would provide them with knowledge and understanding of different cultures and learning styles, thereby facilitating mutual respect.

One very specific suggestion was to have a 'buddy system' which one student experienced on her foundation course:

> ... we were all actually paired up. My foundation was almost more international than home students, and got paired up. [We] had little sketchbooks and portfolio reviews and bits and pieces every so often ... you'd have a specific lesson where everyone went to their partner and you really got to know that person and actually fed back on each other's work — 'this is what I've done this week' ... 'you're missing this element or you could do this' ... I got to know my friend by the end of it ... and my friends that I was really close to ... got together ... and by the end of the year our class was a really strong group — it really worked. (1st year female home student)

Regarding group work, students felt that mixed groups with both international and home students are very beneficial; however, views on the ideal number of international students varied. Some thought that half home, half international would be ideal, but most students felt that the definitive number is two international students per group.

> I think though from what I've seen ... because she's the only one, she is quite shy, but when they are put together, when there is more than

one, they seem to talk a lot more. But when there is only one they get so shy … (1st year female home student)

I just feel safe, [in the DCC] group we have two international students … we have the same language … I don't feel so scared to speak with them [British students]. (1st year female international student)

In addition to the mix of students within the groups, some students felt that they needed guidance on how to work in groups, particularly when they are multicultural.

Team guiding — good team work — being able to build confidence to maybe approach people and work with people from different backgrounds would definitely give me more confidence and even make [me] more approachable. (1st year female home student)

20.4.   Discussion

The students in our study see the value of gaining intercultural competencies to compete within a 'globalised' working environment, but feel that the curriculum is mainly Eurocentric. Although academics are still to be interviewed, the reasons for lack of internationalisation of the curriculum are well documented, and include insufficient financial resources (for funding of travel, scholarships, research partnerships and development of new services) and, in the opinion of higher education institutions, limited faculty interest, limited experience and expertise of staff and/or lack of foreign language proficiency (Beelen, 2011, p. 260). These issues will be investigated with the development of the project, but as can be seen from some student comments, there appears to be an issue with some staff preferring to work with home students, as also identified by Otten (2003).

Although students did not feel that the curriculum was internationalised, home students did recognise that the presence of international students could aid the development of intercultural competencies through mutual working, and international students concurred. There was recognition of the barriers to working together that were mainly focused around language and culture which created negative affective effects for the international students, such as isolation, lack of confidence and a feeling of unfairness in tutor assessments. In the international classroom, there was a lack of interaction between international and home students, and sometimes with the home lecturer, so that valuable opportunities to engage in meaningful intercultural and peer learning were missed. International students did not participate in these sessions as effectively as home students and although some international students sought support from the home students, this support was variable and depended on the individual student's willingness to cooperate. Home students recognised these problems but did very little to alleviate them within the sessions due to the amount of work and learning that had to be undertaken in a 'very pressurised' environment. Home and international students tended to work in monocultural groups which they found comfortable, and all students found difficulties in penetrating these groups, finding them 'intimidating'.

Multicultural group working proved to have mixed outcomes, depending on the individuals within the group and their willingness to work together in an authentic way. Group working is a problem across the sector, whether the group is monocultural or multicultural, due to varying levels of student contribution and differing ways of working (Bryson & Hardy, 2009), but when the group is multicultural these problems are amplified. International students can feel isolated, with the home students making all the decisions and taking the lead in the presentation of the work, whether written or oral. One reason for this could be that group work is often assessed, contributing to academic outcomes and there is a 'lack of trust' of the contribution from international students by home students. Some groups, however, recognised the skills of the international students and 'gave' them appropriate work to do but the students were not fully involved in the decision making regarding the development or outcomes of the project.

Successful academic and social integration is important for improved academic outcomes (Hardy & Bryson, 2010), and this is achieved through relationships between students and students and students and staff, but from this study it is clear that relationships between home and international students and international students and staff is weak. This could impact on international student outcomes, as indicated when examining the data on degree qualifications by domicile from the UK Higher Education Statistics Agency for 2010/2011 (HESA, 2013, online) where it does appear that UK students perform better than non-UK students. Strong relationships are important for supporting students through their studies, promoting self-esteem, reducing stress and enabling students to understand study requirements (Hardy & Bryson, 2010), but do not arise naturally in a multicultural setting (Peacock & Harrison, 2009). Therefore it is incumbent on the university to engender these relationships.

Students in this study identified many solutions to the issue. One was multicultural workshops and cultural days where students from diverse cultural backgrounds would learn about each other. These 'cultural awareness activities', according to Bennett (1986), encourage students to examine their frame of reference and move from being 'ethnocentric' whereby they use their own set of standards and customs to judge all people (often unconsciously) to 'ethno-relative' where they are comfortable with many standards and customs and have an ability to adapt behaviour and judgements to a variety of interpersonal settings, thereby gaining intercultural competence.

One student had a positive experience of a 'buddy system' where students were paired up and this would be a way of encouraging social and academic integration and intercultural learning in a non-threatening environment; it could also be a way of providing authentic additional informal language support which is focused within the discipline, rather than being an 'add on'.

As previously stated, group work is difficult for all students and often students are expected to work in groups without any previous experience and/or advice/training in how to develop the group and work effectively; materials on multicultural group working for staff and students would help alleviate this situation. However, the work that groups are set must be reassessed, as 'unless you design projects and tasks where cross-cultural skills are an asset, or use intercultural competence as a learning outcome, mixed groups will often function less effectively than mono-cultural ones' (Carroll, 2002, p. 3). The composition of the group should also be considered; students in this study suggested that there should be two international students per group so that they could support each other and this has been undertaken in the second term on the Fashion Design course with positive results.

Internationalisation of the curriculum is another area for exploration, and could include such things as more international case studies and projects, more international lecturers and increased international visits.

20.5. Conclusion

It has to be recognised that this project is a 'work in progress' and so the discussion is based only on the student focus groups, concentrating on the experience of students in the international classroom and working in multicultural groups. We need to reflect on this preliminary analysis, undertake further research and explore the literature much more to compare our findings with others.

However, from the initial findings, it is clear that the relationships between home and international students and international students and tutors are weak, which could impact on academic outcomes and the development of intercultural competencies for all students. We have made the following suggestions to improve the situation:

- Multicultural workshops and cultural days
- Development of a 'buddy system'
- Consideration of the composition of multicultural groups
- Development of materials for staff and students for improving the effectiveness of multicultural group working
- Development of projects that utilise intercultural competencies.

These could be used to support student engagement in any setting where there is a mix of home and international students.

References

Astin, A. (1993). *What matters in college? Four critical years revisited.* San Francisco, CA: Jossey-Bass.

Beelen, J. (Ed.). (2007). *Implementing internationalisation at home* [ebook]. European Association for International Education (EAIE). Available via: EAIE library [19 December 2012].

Beelen, J. (2011). Internationalisation at home in a global perspective: A Critical Survey of the 3rd Global Survey Report of IAU. In *Globalisation and internationalisation of higher education* [online monograph]. Revista de Universidad y Sociedad del Conocimiento (RUSC). Vol. 8, No 2, pp. 249−264. UOC. Retrieved from http://rusc.uoc.edu/ojs/index.php/rusc/article/view/v8n2-beelen/v8n2-beelen-eng. Accessed on 10 October 2011.

Bennett, M. J. (1986). A developmental approach to training for intercultural sensitivity. *International Journal of Intercultural Relations, 10*, 179−196.

Bryson, C., & Hand, L. (2007). The role of engagement in inspiring teaching and learning. *Innovations in Teaching and Education International, 44*(4), 349−362.

Bryson, C., & Hardy, C. (2009). An investigation of students' engagement throughout their first year in university. *UK national transition conference: Research and good practice in promoting student engagement in the first year*. University College London, London, 24 April 2009.

Carroll, J. (2002). *Suggestions for teaching international students more effectively* (online). Oxford Centre for Staff and Learning Development: Learning and Teaching Briefing Papers Series. Retrieved from http://www.brookes.ac.uk/services/ocsld/resources/briefing_papers/international_students.pdfHA. Accessed on 18 January 2013.

Coffey, A. (1999). *The ethnographic self: Fieldwork and the representation of identity*. London: Sage.

Denzin, N. K., & Lincoln, Y. S. (1994). Introduction. In N. K. Denzin, & Y. S. Lincoln (Eds.), *Handbook of qualitative research* (pp. 1−17). Thousand Oaks, CA: Sage.

De Vita, G. (2002). Does assessed multicultural group work really pull UK students' average down? *Assessment and Evaluation in Higher Education, 27*(2), 153−161.

Hardy, C., & Bryson, C. (2010). The social life of students: Support mechanisms at university. *Society for Research into Higher Education annual research conference 2010: 'Where is the wisdom we have lost in knowledge?': Exploring meaning, identities and transformation in higher education*, Wales, 14−16 December 2010.

Higher Education Statistics Agency. (2013). Students in higher education institutions 2010/11 — comprehensive data on students and qualifications obtained: Introduction [online]. Retrieved from http://www.hesa.ac.uk/index.php?option = com_content&task = view&id = 2411&Itemid = 278. Accessed on 18 January 2013.

Hyland, F., Trahar, S., Anderson, J., & Dickens, A. (2008). *A changing world: The internationalisation experiences of staff and students (home and international) in UK higher education*. York: Higher Education Academy.

Kimmel, K., & Volet, S. (2012). University students' perceptions of and attitudes towards culturally diverse group work: Does context matter? *Journal of Studies in International Education, 16*(2), 157−181.

McCracken, G. (1988). *The long interview. Qualitative Research Methods Series 13*. Newbury Park, CA: Sage.

NUS/HSBC. (2010/11). *Student experience full report* (online). National Union of Students, London. Retrieved from http://www.nus.org.uk/PageFiles/12238/NUS-HSBC-Experience-report-web.pdf. Accessed on 11 January 2013.

Otten, M. (2000). Impacts of cultural diversity at home. In P. Crowther, M. Joris, M. Otten, B. Nilsson, H. Teekens, & B. Wachter (Eds.), *Internationalisation at home: A position paper* (pp. 15−20). Amsterdam: European Association for International Education (EAIE).

Otten, M. (2003). Intercultural learning and diversity in higher education. *Journal of Studies in International Education, 7*(12), 12−26.

Peacock, N., & Harrison, N. (2009). 'It's so much easier to go with what's easy': 'Mindfulness' and the discourse between home and international students in the United Kingdom. *Journal of Studies in International Education, 13*(4), 487–508.

Pedersen, P. (2010). Assessing intercultural effectiveness outcomes in a year-long study abroad program. *International Journal of Intercultural Relations, 34*(1), 70–80.

Polkinghorne, D. E. (1995). Narrative configuration in qualitative analysis. In J. A. Hatch, & R. Wisniewski (Eds.), *Life History and Narrative* (pp. 5–23). London: The Falmer Press.

Sanderson, G. (2004). Existentialism, globalisation and the cultural other. *International Education Journal, 4*(4), 1–20.

Summers, M., & Volet, S. (2008). Students' attitudes towards culturally mixed groups on international campuses: Impact of participation in diverse and non-diverse groups, *Studies in Higher Education, 33*(4), 357–370.

Sweeney, A., Weaven, S., & Herington, C. (2008). Multicultural influences on group learning: A qualitative higher education study. *Assessment and Evaluation in Higher Education, 33*(2), 119–132.

Tinto, V. (1997). Classrooms as communities: Exploring the educational character of student persistence. *The Journal of Higher Education, 68*(6), 599–623.

Tinto, V., & Goodsell-Love, A. (1993). Building community. *Liberal Education, 79*(4), 16–22.

UNITE. (2006). *The international student experience report*. Bristol, UK: UNITE.

Wachter, B. (2000). Internationalisation at home: The context. In P. Crowther, M. Joris, M. Otten, B. Nilsson, H. Teekens, & B. Wachter (Eds.), *Internationalisation at home: A position paper* (pp. 5–13). Amsterdam: European Association for International Education (EAIE).

Watson, W. E., Kumar, K., & Michaelsen, L. K. (1993). Cultural diversity's impact on inrtaction process and performance: Comparing homogeneous and diverse task groups. *The Academy of Management Journal, 36*(3), 590–602.

Chapter 21

Reframing Diversity and Student Engagement: Lessons from Deaf-Gain

Peter Felten and H-Dirksen L. Bauman

Abstract

Both the student engagement framework and popular attitudes toward disabilities contribute to many practices in higher education that, however unintentionally, highlight the perceived deficits that "disabled students" bring to university campuses. In this chapter, we explore the possibility of reframing disability and student engagement through the lens of deaf-gain. Building on emerging scholarship about neuroplasticity and diversity, deaf-gain calls attention to the ways in which the visual, spatial, and kinesthetic structures of deaf epistemologies may provide insights into ways of knowing that are advantageous for both deaf and hearing people. We focus on the visual skills, gestural intelligence, and community-oriented capacities that, when approached from a deaf-gain perspective, present new possibilities for engagement and learning for all students.

21.1. Introduction[1]

Student engagement is a powerful heuristic for higher education. By emphasizing the importance of both students and institutions as actors, student engagement provides a useful framework for planning and research (Kuh, 2009). Put most simply, students must engage to learn, and high-quality institutions support frequent, deep engaged activities by students to promote learning.

No matter how research-based and practical, however, heuristics are not value-free. Shulman (2002) emphasizes the utility of frameworks like student engagement:

---

[1]Portions of this chapter are adapted from H-Dirksen L. Bauman (no date). "Reframing the future of deaf education: From hearing loss to deaf-gain." The Canadian Hearing Society.

The Student Engagement Handbook: Practice in Higher Education
Copyright © 2013 by Emerald Group Publishing Limited
All rights of reproduction in any form reserved
ISBN: 978-1-78190-423-7

"They help us think more clearly about what we're doing, and they afford us a language through which we can exchange ideas and dilemmas." But then he warns: "They are powerful in these ways as long as we don't take them too seriously." Heuristics act as cognitive lenses, simultaneously bringing into focus certain aspects of the world while obscuring things that are outside of our line of sight (Lakoff & Johnson, 1980).

The student engagement heuristic does just that. While highlighting the utility of student engagement, Trowler (2010) argues that this framework also "often has a normative agenda" (p. 5), washing away diverse identities to focus on the generic "student." Indeed, research on engagement has been so influential in part because of this norming. Kuh (2003), for instance, demonstrates that student learning and success are linked more closely to what students do at university than to what they bring to higher education. That is a powerful claim that institutions can use to shape academic programs.

While this research has resulted in positive outcomes for many institutions and students, including historically disadvantaged students (Kuh, 2008), the norming inherent to the engagement framework can lead to practices that alienate certain students. Perhaps most often, this is seen in well-intended efforts to listen to the "unheard voices" of students who are not fully engaged on campus (Harper & Quaye, 2009). Institutions reach out to those on the margins in a variety of ways, aiming to bring them into the norm (Cook-Sather, 2007; McLeod, 2011). At its worst, as Trowler (2010) notes, this can produce "a reductionist approach, such as suggesting that students with disabilities or ethnic minority students share their opinions about architecture or artwork for the walls of buildings" (p. 9).

By minimizing the complexity of student identity, engagement's normalizing agenda also contributes, however unintentionally, to a presumption that students who do not fit the norm are somehow lacking. Institutions, for example, prepare for students who are "very foreign" to the culture and goals of the academy (Krause, 2005, quoted in Trowler, 2010). Compared to "normal" undergraduates, these students present a serious challenge because they have characteristics that make them difficult to engage. Bensimon (2005) refers to this as a "deficit cognitive frame" that shapes the expectations individuals have and the strategies institutions employ to enhance student engagement. For instance, Harper's research (2009) demonstrates how a focus in the United States on Black male undergraduate deficits leads institutions to a particular "*orientation* (focus on stereotypical characteristics associated with the culture of disadvantage and poverty), *discourse* (lack of preparation, motivation, study skills, blaming students and/or their backgrounds), and *strategies* (compensatory educational programs, remedial courses, special programs, all focused on fixing the student)" (p. 148, emphasis in original). Harper shows how these can cause institutions and individuals both to act in counterproductive ways, treating all Black males the same, and also to ignore what could be learned from the experiences of high achieving Black male undergraduates.

Race and ethnicity are hardly the only aspects of student identity that are normed. The frame of "disability" as a deficit and disadvantage remains largely unquestioned within and beyond higher education (Solomon, 2012). It is particularly difficult to imagine disability as anything other than negative when the word itself articulates the frame: dis-ability. That understanding only makes sense, however, within the larger construct of normalcy, which reinforces the view that disabilities are inherently a problem, they are something to be remediated, accommodated or repaired.

Yet not all persons with a disability desire to be fixed or normalized. For instance, there is a powerful movement within the autistic community that reframes that "condition" from a problem to a resource. This emerging concept, sometimes referred to as neurodiversity, posits a view that there is no single norm for the properly functioning mind, and the diverse ways of perceiving and knowing the world provide distinct insights and new capabilities (Blume, 1998; Solomon, 2012). By calling attention to normalcy and neurodiversity, we must be careful not to romanticize disability. People's lives can be profoundly affected in many ways that are not positive, often including physical pain, unemployment, limited access to education, transportation, and other basics for quality of life. However, disability affects different people in different contexts and at different points in their lives in different ways. As Solomon (2012) notes: "Being gay was a disability in the nineteenth century in a way that it isn't now; and it is now a disability in some locations in a way that it isn't in others; and it was a disability for me when I was young and it isn't one for me today" (p. 33). While disability can be experienced as a profoundly negative, even tragic condition, there are a host of ways that disability reveals hidden capabilities and unearths new perspectives on human potential. These experiences should not be overlooked as we work to enhance student engagement; indeed, insights from "disabled" students can and should be mined for insights into how to optimize educational experiences and engagement for all students.

When we approach disability from an assets-oriented frame, we may notice stunning human capacities for resilience and adaptation. For instance, for centuries common wisdom held that the ability to develop a natural human language required the input of speech sounds. However, linguistic research now has demonstrated that the human mind is just as hard-wired to develop a signed as a spoken language. Thanks to "neuroplasticity," the brain is designed to produce language, regardless of modality (Petitto et al., 2000). While language typically takes the form of speech, it does not have to: "the human brain does not discriminate between the hands and the tongue … people do" (Petitto, 2009). As this example demonstrates, attention to assets rather than deficits, to signing rather than hearing loss, helps us see and understand the world in fundamentally new ways. Scientists made this breakthrough because of deafness, not despite it. What might we understand about engagement if we take a similar approach?

21.2. Defining Deaf-Gain

When seen through the frame of normalcy, deafness can only be imagined as a loss. As a result, deaf people can only be seen as being incapable of normal human communication, unless they are rehabilitated or cured. Institutions of medicine and education have long sought to fix the conditions of hearing loss through pedagogies and procedures of normalization — from speech and hearing rehabilitation to surgical procedures, and even more recently, to genetic testing that provides parents with the options of avoiding the birth of deaf children altogether (Bauman & Murray, 2010). The common-sense notion that deafness is a condition that must be fixed, however, is often at odds with the life experiences of those closest to deafness, deaf people themselves (Lane, Hoffmeister, & Bahan, 1996).

Instead of being defined by hearing loss, deaf people often experience the fullness of their lives through their perceptual, linguistic, and social ways of being in the world. When seen through the frame of diversity rather than normalcy, deafness is not defined as loss, but as an expression of human variation that results in bringing to the fore specific cognitive, creative, and cultural gains that have been overlooked within a hearing-centered orientation. In this new frame, hearing loss gives way to "deaf-gain" (Bauman & Murray, 2010).

Deaf-gain calls attention to the ways in which the visual, spatial, and kinesthetic structures of deaf epistemologies (i.e., ways of knowing) may provide insights into ways of knowing that are advantageous for all humans, regardless of hearing capacity. As such, deaf-gain aligns with the increasing recognition of "multiple intelligences." Originally described by Gardner (1983), the theory of multiple intelligences is predicated on the notion that intelligence, as it has been measured by IQ tests, is based on too narrow an understanding of human knowing. "The problem," Gardner writes, "lies less in the technology of testing, than in the ways in which we customarily think about the intellect and in our ingrained views of intelligence. Only if we expand and reformulate our view of what counts as human intellect will we be able to devise more appropriate ways of assessing it and more effective ways of educating it" (1983, p. 4). In order to expand the notion of human intelligence, Gardner identifies distinct frames of mind which lead toward different intellectual types: (1) Linguistic Intelligence; (2) Logical-Mathematical Intelligence; (3) Visual-Spatial Intelligence; (4) Bodily-Kinesthetic Intelligence; (5) Musical Intelligence; (6) Interpersonal Intelligence; and (7) Intrapersonal Intelligence.

Since deaf-gain may be most apparent in relation to Visual-Spatial Intelligence, we will begin there. We also will explore gestural intelligence and eye to eye culture as additional areas where deaf-gain might inform how students engage and how institutions could more effectively structure learning experiences.

21.3.   Deaf-Gain in a Visual World

Visual-Spatial Intelligence "involves sensitivity to color, line, shape, form, space, and the relationships that exist between these elements. It includes the capacity to visualize, to graphically represent visual or spatial ideas, and to orient oneself appropriately in a spatial matrix" (Armstrong, 1993, p. 2). If this were the sole measure of intelligence, deaf people would be likely to fill all the seats in honors programs at universities. Deaf people do not see any better than anyone else, of course. What they do with what they see, however, often demonstrates capacities far beyond what non-deaf people can do visually. The link between enhanced visuospatial abilities and use of sign languages has been documented in studies of speed in generating mental images (Emmorey & Kosslyn, 1996; Emmorey, Kosslyn, & Bellugi, 1993), mental rotation skills (Emmorey, Klima, & Hickok, 1998), increased facial recognition skills (Bettger, Emmorey, McCullough, & Bellugi, 1997), increased peripheral recognition skills (Bavelier et al., 2000), and increased spatial cognition (Bellugi et al., 1989). These scientific studies are a small sampling of the preponderance of research into the plasticity of the mind and its perceptual abilities brought to the fore by the visual aptitudes of deaf signers. Indeed, Bahan (1989) has suggested that deaf people shift from referring to themselves as deaf, and instead call themselves "seeing people." Viewed from this perspective, deaf students often bring essential and unusual capacities with them to the university.

Understanding and cultivating visual intelligence is becoming a more important goal for higher education (Little, Felten, & Berry, 2010). Over the last century, revolutions in imaging and network technologies have made visuals perhaps the primary means of global communication — in print, on screens, and online. Many of these same tools not only prompt us to view the images that surround us, but also allow ordinary people as never before to create, manipulate, and share visuals (Sturken & Cartwright, 2001). Mitchell (1994, p. 2) has dubbed this a "pictorial turn" in global history, an inflection point where images re-emerge alongside texts as the primary sources of knowledge and meaning in the world, after several centuries in the West dominated by knowledge almost exclusively coming from the printed word. As Little et al. conclude: "To best prepare students for life in the twenty-first century, we must more deliberately consider how we help them learn to make meaning of and with images" (Little et al., 2010, p. 49).

Within this evolving context, the visual capacities that many deaf students have developed should be seen as a model for all other university students. Researchers should study how deaf students' build and use these capacities so that higher education institutions can develop high-impact curricula and practices that would help non-deaf students better cultivate the skills and knowledge necessary to thrive in our highly visual world. If universities need to develop "visuals across the curriculum" to prepare students for life after graduation, as Elkins (2007) contends, then deaf students may be a vital resource for all higher education institutions.

21.4. Learning Through Gestural Intelligence

Gardner's framework of multiple intelligences distinguishes between linguistic and bodily kinesthetic capacities. For people who use sign language, however, a strong relationship exists between these two, creating something that may be referred to as "gestural intelligence" — the capacity to use and interpret diverse bodily actions that convey meaning (Bauman & Murray, 2010).

Research on deaf and non-deaf students demonstrates the power of gesture in developing conceptual understanding. Drawing on a complex series of experiments, Cook, Mitchell, and Goldin-Meadow (2008) conclude, "Gesturing can thus play a causal role in learning, perhaps by giving learners an alternative, embodied way of representing new ideas." Educators often have not intentionally used the power of gesture, perhaps because the common assumption that all language is spoken constrains our understanding of what is possible. In everyday life, non-signing people routinely use gestures to convey messages, including everything from waving or smiling to reaching out to comfort or crossing fingers for luck. Looking across time and culture, Wilson (1998) makes a compelling case for seeing the hand as a central actor in human communication: "I would argue that any theory of human intelligence which ignores the interdependence of hand and brain function, the historic origins of that relationship, or the impact of that history on developmental dynamics in modern humans, is grossly misleading and sterile" (p. 7).

Recognizing the potential of gestural intelligence, then, suggests that people who use sign language to communicate bring essential capacities to higher education that could be used to help all students engage and learn. For instance, American Sign Language's rich classifier system provides distinctly different ways than spoken English to describe important biological processes such as mitosis. Students fortunate enough to have a professor with sophisticated gestural intelligence could be taught with a fully linguistic three-dimensional map in motion of this physical process — in words, images, and gestures. And if students had developed their gestural intelligence, they might be able to ask better questions and demonstrate more completely their emerging understandings. With gestural intelligence's outer display of inner thought, teachers can spy directly into the organization of ideas in students' thinking. Conversely, students may be more privy to mental representations from a professor's disciplinary expertise. Since making thinking visible like this is an essential component of effective teaching and learning (Ambrose, Bridges, DiPietro, Lovett, & Norman, 2010), a deaf-gain perspective on gestural intelligence points to a powerful asset for deepening student learning and engagement in higher education.

21.5. Engaging Eye to Eye

Sociologists have documented a diminishing sense of community and civic engagement over the past several decades in the United States (McPherson, Smith-Lovin, & Brashears, 2006; Putnam, 2000). Complex factors including suburban living patterns, media use, and work and family structures have contributed to this decline. When students come to university without strong social connections, they often struggle to find a place where they feel they belong. This difficulty may be magnified by the increasing diversity of students attending higher education institutions (Antonio, 2001). The less students feel welcome and at home on campus, the more difficulty they have in engaging in ways that yield positive academic outcomes

(Cole, 2007). Helping all students to develop a solid sense of belonging to a college community is a fundamental goal for institutions aiming to enhance student engagement (Trowler, 2010).

By approaching this problem from the vantage point of deaf-gain, new possibilities for developing community and engaging students might be seen. Scholarship of deaf communities demonstrates that while deaf people often are perceived to be socially isolated, deaf individuals commonly describe themselves as being part of strong and vital communities. The physical engagement that is required by sign language, literally communicating eye to eye, is a foundation for that feeling of connection and belonging (Bauman & Murray, 2010). This is not unique to deaf people; research has demonstrated that sustained eye contact is an important element in building strong, intimate relationships (Reid & Striano, 2005).

Attention to this eye to eye culture has produced a new movement focused on "Deafspace," the study and design of living environments that are optimal for deaf and signing individuals. Going beyond notions of accessibility usually found in Universal Design principles, Deafspace attends to the visual and tactile dimensions of built environments, aiming to create welcoming and functional spaces for everyone, regardless of audiological status. At a basic level, Deafspace favors gathering spaces that allow everyone present to engage eye to eye with everyone else; a group of students sitting in a circle, for example, follows this principle while students seated at a rectangular seminar table do not. The social dynamic of sitting in a circle versus a rectangle has far reaching implications for teaching, learning, and engagement. In a circle, everyone is invited into a communal conversation if they so wish (Brookfield & Preskill, 2005). Everyone easily can make eye contact with each person at the table, something that can be a challenge in more angular spaces.

The focus on eye to eye connection not only shapes how we might design campus spaces for engagement, but also shapes how individuals move through space. Robert Sirvage's research, for example, examines the nature of the "deaf walk" as opposed to the "hearing walk" (Shier, 2012; Sirvage, 2009). Hearing individuals may walk and talk in many different configurations, as long as they can hear each other speak. Hikers, for instance, may walk single file and still communicate. The same is not true, however, for signing walkers. They must be within the range of vision in order to communicate. Carrying on a visual conversation while navigating through the environment requires that each signer watch out for the other's well-being, in case there are objects (people, street signs, trees, and so on) that may be in the way. This seemingly minor activity leads to a deaf cultural norm for each person to entrust the other with his or her well-being (Bauman & Murray, 2010). The deaf cultural practice of visual reciprocity while walking together is a far cry from the social isolation that many students experience on college campuses. And this is a learned skill, something that universities could cultivate to complement existing programs aimed to develop civic-minded citizens (Colby, Ehrlich, Beaumont, & Stephens, 2003).

Even if the eye to eye culture that undergirds sign language cannot be fully integrated into university life, lessons from deaf-gain could be used to influence the design of classrooms, dormitories, and other spaces on campus as well as to create opportunities for (perhaps even norms of) direct, meaningful contact between people within our institutions.

21.6.   Conclusion

In this chapter, we have separately discussed deaf-gain insights about the visual, gestural, and community-oriented capacities linked to student engagement. In reality, however, deaf students and academic staff typically possess these not as discrete entities but as a unified whole. A new project at Gallaudet University is beginning to study the implications for deaf-gain on campus. Gallaudet, in Washington, DC, is the world's only university designed for deaf and hard of hearing students. Unlike at many universities, classroom layout at Gallaudet has been the subject of careful study. Seats always are arranged in a semi or full circle, and the quality of lighting is of paramount importance to ensure that everyone in the room can clearly see all others. Within these deaf-friendly (and, indeed, hearing-friendly) spaces, class sessions often begin with a simple ritual of establishing visual connection before teaching begins. As students enter, the professor will establish eye contact with each, and students are encouraged to greet one another in a similar way. Bags, cups of coffee, and other visual distractions are removed, opening up the visual field to encourage direct connection. Then, throughout the class, eye contact is maintained as much as possible, facilitated by the design of the space and thoughtful choice of pedagogy. The student (and faculty) experience in such a classroom, sometimes called a "Sensory Commons" at Gallaudet, can feel dramatically different from what happens daily at other universities, as students may drift anonymously through classrooms and across campus.

While a deaf-gain perspective is not a panacea for student engagement, we believe that it offers great potential to help us creatively tackle persistent problems in higher education. However, considering student engagement from the vantage point of deaf-gain requires reframing conventional understandings and assumptions about disability, learning, and education. Rather than focusing on the particular deficits of certain students, deaf-gain draws attention to the distinct assets that some students bring to higher education, including capacities linked to visual sophistication, gestural intelligence, and interpersonal connection. While this orientation might seem unfamiliar to some, it reflects not only an appealing view of human capability but also a scientific appreciation for the value of diversity. In a biological environment, a more diverse environment often is the most adaptive and resilient — the most likely to thrive in changing conditions. Might the same be true for human communities?

Learning and applying lessons from deaf-gain, however, will not necessarily be simple and easy. Indeed, deaf-gain might represent a threshold concept for many in higher education. As Meyer and Land (2006) explain, a threshold concept "is akin to a portal, opening up a new and previously inaccessible way of thinking about something" (p. 3). Crossing such a threshold often involves wrestling with what

Perkins (1999) refers to as troublesome knowledge — knowledge that may seem counter-intuitive or odd when first encountered. Such troublesome knowledge also may call into question issues of personal and social identity; as one of the co-authors of this chapter recalls, until he began working with deaf students, he never consciously understood himself to be a hearing person. That realization, like other thresholds, cannot be forgotten. Once crossed, a threshold is transformative and integrative, fundamentally and permanently changing the way a concept or even the world is understood. We contend that recognizing the existence of deaf-gain, and taking similar approaches with other categories of students who might be marginalized on our campuses, will transform how we view our work and the academy as a whole.

Having recognized the potential for new insights from deaf-gain, we need to be careful not to jump naively into action. The literature on student voice serves as a helpful guide as we work to listen more closely to deaf students and communities. Scholars have begun to identify the benefits of engaging students actively in shaping their learning and campuses (Kay, Dunne, & Hutchinson, 2010; Werder & Otis, 2010). Emerging evidence suggests that approaching students as partners in higher education enhances motivation and self-efficacy for both students and academic staff (Bovill, Cook-Sather, & Felten, 2011; Cook-Sather, 2011; Mihans, Long, & Felten, 2008). Yet naive or simplistic approaches to listening to "student voices" can lead to ironic outcomes, homogenizing perspectives and further marginalizing some students (Sabri, 2011). Engaging students as partners is so complex because it requires attending to the intersectionalities within student identities (McLeod, 2011). A particular student, for example, might not only be deaf but also female and from a minority religious community. In different contexts, different aspects of that student's identity will be more or less salient. Therefore, as we strive to act on deaf-gain, or other unrecognized capacities that students bring to our campuses, we must avoid envisioning students as members of simplified, singular, and stable categories (Cook-Sather, 2007).

Despite the complexity of this work, the potential benefits from reframing diversity are vast. We believe that an educational system that optimizes deaf-gain would lead to deeper engagement for all students.

References

Ambrose, S. A., Bridges, M. W., DiPietro, M., Lovett, M. C., & Norman, M. K. (2010). *How learning works: 7 research-based principles for smart teaching.* San Francisco, CA: Jossey-Bass.

Antonio, A. L. (2001). Diversity and the influence of friendship groups in college. *The Review of Higher Education, 25*(1), 63−89.

Armstrong, T. (1993). *Multiple intelligences in the classroom.* Alexandria, VA: Association for Supervision and Curriculum Development.

Bahan, B. (1989). Seeing people. In S. Wilcox (Ed.), *American deaf culture: An anthology.* Burtonsville, MD: Linstok Press.

Bauman, H.-D. L., & Murray, J. J. (2010). Deaf studies in the 21st century: Deaf-gain and the future of human diversity. In M. Maschark & P. E. Spencer (Eds.), *Oxford handbook of deaf studies, language, and education* (*Vol. 2*), New York, Ny: Oxford University Press.

Bavelier, D., Tomann, A., Hutton, C., Mitchell, T. V., Corina, D. P., Liu, G., & Neville, H. J. (2000). Visual attention to the periphery is enhanced in congenitally deaf individuals. *Journal of Neuroscience, 20,* 1−6.

Bellugi, U., O'Grady, L., Lillio-Martin, D., O'Grady Hynes, M., Van Hoek, K., & Corina, D. (1989). Enhancement of spatial cognition in deaf children. In V. Volterra & C. Erting (Eds.), *Gesture to language in hearing children.* New York, NY: Springer Verlag.

Bensimon, E. M. (2005). Closing the achievement gap in higher education: An organizational learning perspective. In A. J. Kezar (Ed.), *Organizational learning in higher education: New directions for higher education* (Vol. 131, pp. 99−111). San Francisco, CA: Jossey-Bass.

Bettger, J. G., Emmorey, K., McCullough, S. H., & Bellugi, U. (1997). Enhanced facial discrimination: Effects of experience with American Sign Language. *Journal of Deaf Studies and Deaf Education, 2,* 223−233.

Blume, H. (1998). Neurodiversity. *The Atlantic.* September 30.

Bovill, C., Cook-Sather, A., & Felten, P. (2011). Students as co-creators of teaching approaches, course design, and curricula: Implications for academic developers. *International Journal for Academic Development, 16,* 133−145.

Brookfield, S. D., & Preskill, S. (2005). *Discussion as a way of teaching: Tools and techniques for democratic classrooms* (2nd ed.). San Francisco, CA: Jossey-Bass.

Colby, A., Ehrlich, T., Beaumont, E., & Stephens, J. (2003). *Educating citizens: Preparing America's undergraduates for lives of moral and civic responsibility.* San Francisco, CA: Jossey-Bass.

Cole, D. (2007). Do interracial interactions matter? An examination of student-faculty contact and intellectual self-concept. *The Journal of Higher Education, 78*(3), 249−281.

Cook, S. W., Mitchell, Z., & Goldin-Meadow, S. (2008). Gesture makes learning last. *Cognition, 106,* 1047−1058.

Cook-Sather, A. (2007). Resisting the impositional potential of student voice work: Lessons for liberatory educational research from poststructuralist feminist critiques of critical pedagogy. *Discourse: Studies in the Cultural Politics of Education, 28,* 389−403.

Cook-Sather, A. (2011). Layered learning: Student consultants deepening classroom and life lessons. *Educational Action Research, 19,* 41−57.

Elkins, J. (Ed.) (2007). *Visual literacy.* New York, NY: Routledge.

Emmorey, K., Klima, S. L., & Kickok, G. (1998). Mental rotation within linguistic and non-linguistic domains in users of American Sign Language. *Cognition, 68,* 2221−226.

Emmorey, K., & Kosslyn, S. (1996). Enhanced image generation abilities in deaf signers: A right hemisphere effect. *Brain and Cognition, 32,* 28−44.

Emmorey, K., Kosslyn, S., & Bellugi, U. (1993). Visual imagery and visual-spatial language: Enhanced visual imagery abilities in deaf and hearing ASL signers. *Cognition, 46,* 139−181.

Gardner, H. (1983). *Frames of mind: The theory of multiple intelligences.* New York, NY: Basic Books.

Harper, S. R. (2009). Institutional seriousness concerning black male student engagement: Necessary conditions and collaborative partnerships. In S. R. Harper & S. J. Quaye (Eds.), *Student engagement in higher education: Theoretical perspectives and practical approaches for diverse populations* (pp. 137−156). New York, NY: Routledge.

Harper, S. R., & Quaye, S. J. (2009). *Student engagement in higher education: Theoretical perspectives and practical approaches for diverse populations.* New York, NY: Routledge.

Kay, J., Dunne, E., & Hutchinson, J. (2010). *Rethinking the values of higher education — students as change agents?* QAA, Gloucester, UK. Retrieved from www.qaa.ac.uk/students/studentengagement/undergradaute.pdf

Kuh, G. D. (2003). What we're learning about student engagement from NSSE. *Change, 35*(2), 24–32.

Kuh, G. D. (2008). *High-impact practices: What they are, who has access to them, and why they matter.* Washington, DC: Association of American Colleges and Universities.

Kuh, G. D. (2009). What student affairs professionals need to know about student engagement. *Journal of College Student Development, 50*(6), 683–706.

Lakoff, G., & Johnson, M. (1980). *Metaphors we live by.* Chicago, IL: University of Chicago Press.

Lane, H., Hoffmeister, R., & Bahan, B. (1996). *Journey into the deaf-world.* San Diego, CA: Dawn Sign Press.

Little, D., Felten, P., & Berry, C. (2010). Liberal education in a visual world. *Liberal Education,* (Spring), 44–49.

McLeod, J. (2011). Student voice and the politics of listening in higher education. *Critical Studies in Education, 52,* 179–189.

McPherson, M., Smith-Lovin, L., & Brashears, M. (2006). Social isolation in America: Changes in core discussion networks over two decades. *American Sociological Review, 71*(3), 353–375.

Meyer, J. H. F., & Land, R. (2006). *Overcoming barriers to student understanding: Threshold concepts and troublesome knowledge.* New York, NY: Routledge.

Mihans, R., Long, D., & Felten, P. (2008). Power and expertise: Student-faculty collaboration in course design and the scholarship of teaching and learning. *International Journal for the Scholarship of Teaching and Learning, 2,* 1–9.

Mitchell, W. J. T. (1994). *Picture theory: Essays on verbal and visual representation.* Chicago, IL: University of Chicago Press.

Perkins, D. (1999). The many faces of constructivism. *Educational Leadership, 57,* 3.

Petitto, L. A. (2009). Scientific research on the positive effect of signed language in the human brain. *Effect of language delay on mental health conference.* October 16. Toronto, Canada.

Petitto, L. A., Zatorre, R., Gauna, K., Nikelski, E. J., Dostie, D., & Evans, A. (2000). Speech-like cerebral activity in profoundly deaf people while processing signed languages: Implications for the neural basis of human language. *Proceedings of the National Academy of Sciences, 97*(25), 13961–13966.

Putnam, R. (2000). *Bowling alone: The collapse and revival of American community.* New York, NY: Simon & Schuster.

Reid, V. M., & Striano, T. (2005). Adult gaze influences infant attention and object processing: Implications for cognitive neuroscience. *European Journal of Neuroscience, 21*(6), 1763–1766.

Sabri, D. (2011). What's wrong with the 'student experience'? *Discourse: Studies in the Cultural Politics of Education, 32*(5), 657–667.

Shier, R. (2012). Seeing eye to eye: Examining how deaf people move through the world. *WAMU 88.5: American University Radio* (October 19). Retrieved from http://wamu.org/programs/metro_connection/12/10/19/seeing_eye_to_eye_gallaudet_research_shows_how_deaf_people_navigate_space

Shulman, L. (2002). Making differences: A table of learning. *Change, 34*(6), 36–44.

Sirvage, R. (2009). *Walking signers: An investigation on proxemics.* Unpublished master's thesis. Gallaudet University, Washington, DC.

Solomon, A. (2012). *Far from the tree: Parents, children, and the search for identity.* New York, NY: Scribner.

Sturken, M., & Cartwright, L. (2001). *Practices of looking: An introduction to visual culture.* New York, NY: Oxford University Press.

Trowler, V. (2010). *Student engagement literature review.* The Higher Education Academy, UK.

Werder, C., & Otis, M., (Eds.). (2010). *Engaging student voices in the study of teaching and learning.* Sterling, VA: Stylus.

Wilson, F. (1998). *The hand: How its use shapes the brain, language, and human culture.* New York, NY: Pantheon.

Chapter 22

Engaging Students Through Assessment

Kay Sambell

Abstract

There is little doubt that student engagement is receiving a considerable amount of attention in research, policy and educational development. A wide array of engagement initiatives have recently flourished in the United Kingdom and elsewhere, often with a view to helping students adjust and adapt to university culture so that they are enabled and encouraged to engage in university life on a number of levels. This chapter focuses on the ways in which assessment can play an important part in helping or hindering students' levels of engagement with academic study. First, drawing on recent scholarship in the field of assessment, which asserts the need for widespread shifts in the ways in which assessment is conceptualised: it highlights the ways in which assessment offers a fruitful and potent arena in which faculty can make concerted efforts to engage students with their studies and the experience of being and belonging at university. It goes on to warn, however, about some of the problems that emerge if the underpinning principles of the new paradigm are poorly understood or applied in restrictive ways, because these act as barriers to engagement. Next, it focuses down on the links between assessment and engagement, which are then related to holistic models of assessment for learning (AfL). Finally, the chapter offers some concrete examples of the ways in which assessment can be designed to promote engagement and improve the student experience of learning. Illustrations of students' views of the benefits are offered, drawn from empirical studies conducted as part of a large-scale initiative to implement AfL in a UK university (Sambell, McDowell, & Montgomery, 2012). Broadly speaking, these link strongly to themes of engagement.

Overall, the chapter argues that, because the new paradigm involves establishing and sharing a set of assumptions, concepts and values, designing assessment to promote learning is more complex and profound than is sometimes assumed (Boud & Molloy, 2012). However, a sustained focus on issues of engagement in

The Student Engagement Handbook: Practice in Higher Education
Copyright © 2013 by Emerald Group Publishing Limited
All rights of reproduction in any form reserved
ISBN: 978-1-78190-423-7

AfL research and practice development offers a particularly valuable lens through which to view and gauge our assessment practices and alerts us to important ways forward when designing assessment for the benefit of student learning.

22.1. Introduction: The Emergence of the Assessment for Learning Agenda in Theory and Practice

The rethinking of assessment at a theoretical level focused on its capacity to improve and foster, as well as measure learning, aiming for this to become recognised by staff and students alike. This has been an international endeavour. Havnes (2012) has called this the short history of assessment for learning (AfL), saying it denotes important theoretical shifts in conceptualisations of assessment in higher education over the past 20 years. He argues this meant recognising assessment's role in defining what students need to learn and its capacity to drive educational practice, becoming part of quality teaching. Assessment became viewed as a prerequisite for learning, rather than simply a measure of it. Havnes asserts this entailed an expansion of focus from

- outcomes to process;
- control of learning to support of learning;
- students being assessed to students also taking part in assessment;
- assessment as a distinct practice to assessment as embedded in learning.

According to Birenbaum (1996) this called for a new assessment culture and AfL started to be used as a specialist term embodying a call to improve educational practice.

Early exponents built on the outcomes of prior research into student perspectives on assessment, which demonstrated that while summative assessment tasks might be viewed as purely a way of measuring learning and progress, they could also have a significant impact on learning and teaching. For example, the work of Miller and Parlett (1974) in universities showed that what and how students went about learning could be strongly influenced by the ways in which they were assessed and marks were awarded. This was later termed the backwash effect, and it was not always positive. Attempts were made to try and reduce negative assessment backwash and promote high-quality learning by diversifying assessment tasks to make them more authentic and engaging (Brown & Knight, 1994; Bryan & Clegg, 2006). Our own early research into the impact of assessment on students' approaches to learning supported this shift (Sambell, McDowell, & Brown, 1997). Further, the idea of constructive alignment (Biggs & Tang, 2007), where assessment as part of an integrated learning-teaching-assessment system is designed to issue messages that foster students' active engagement in deep, lasting learning, also became particularly prominent. New terms began to emerge, such as 'learning-oriented assessment' (Carless, 2007) to highlight these aspects of AfL.

Another key shift in view of assessment was an increasing recognition of the active role of students. Earl (2003) used the term assessment as learning to include the students' engagement in self-assessment and their active participation in directing their own learning. This view recognises that the student response to assessment is not just determined by assessment task design. Students act on the basis of their individual and collective perceptions of assessment requirements, interpreted in the context of their own standpoint as a student. A common practical reaction was to place more emphasis on providing guidance and information to help students to understand the requirements of assessment. In the 1990s a growing tide of opinion in universities assumed that simply providing information to students about learning outcomes, grade criteria, assignment briefs and marking rubrics would help students develop (Price, Rust, O'Donovan, & Handley, 2012). Providing feedback as a means of informing students about the quality of their current achievements was also frequently emphasised. This trend continues, especially in recent years, as universities seek to address the poor scores students often award to feedback in national satisfaction surveys.

Giving students information like this are aspects of formative assessment and may justifiably be considered as an element of AfL. However, limited conceptions present some problems. For instance, if feedback is framed exclusively as a product which is given to students (Boud & Molloy, 2012), or if tactics to advise students about assessment requirements are simply written down or basically 'dropped in' to existing courses, with no account of the sense students make of them, they do not sit easily with the underpinning philosophy of the AfL agenda. Indeed, empirical research has subsequently led to the recognition that simply giving students feedback or information on assessment requirements has limited effectiveness in supporting learning (O'Donovan, Price, & Rust, 2004). Even worse, this kind of restricted approach to AfL can undermine the principles of learner empowerment and engagement that the new assessment culture aimed to promote. Torrance (2007) warns, for instance, that sometimes approaches to formative feedback methods that have been designed to 'help' students can actually displace learning. Instead of promoting shared understanding and participation, some enhancement practices designed, ostensibly, to engage students with assessment or feedback simply become a matter of 'teaching to the test' or controlling student behaviour. Here students and teachers are seen to focus on completing assessment tasks and attaining good marks to the detriment of real engagement with learning (Ecclestone, 2002). In practice, then, restricted conceptions of formative assessment and one-way feedback practices can worryingly result in conformity, poor quality learning and procedural compliance: all alienated experiences that Mann (2001) urges us to counteract if we are serious about creating environments that enable, rather than hinder, student engagement.

Sadler (1989) established that feedback could actually only have an effect if a student was able to develop an understanding of the standards and qualities required in their subject, relate their own performance and the feedback on it to those standards and take action towards producing higher quality work. This clearly requires active engagement of students in the assessment process and, in a broad sense, self-assessment. The ASKe Centre for Excellence in Teaching and Learning (CETL)

(Price et al., 2012, p. 25) has recently documented a change in their own practical approaches over time in line with this. They have gradually moved from simply giving students criteria and rubrics (which the Centre calls 'passive engagement' with criteria and standards), towards methods more in line with 'active engagement' to assist students' understanding of the qualities and standards of good work in their discipline, such as active use of assessment criteria in workshop discussions and use of exemplars. More recently there has also been a focus on the acquisition of tacit understandings through participation in disciplinary communities (O'Donovan, Price, & Rust, 2008). The need for dialogue, discussion and student participation in assessment and feedback (Osney Grange Group, 2009) has emerged from a range of different research perspectives, for example the work by Laurillard (2002) on a conversational model of teaching which, in contrast to one-way transmission, enables understanding to be checked and clarified between students and teachers.

22.2.   Assessment for Learning and Engagement

In general terms, then, shifts like this can be seen as attempts to ensure that assessment practices change in sympathy with constructivist views of learning and teaching, which have come to epitomise the hallmark of university education (Barkley, 2009; Biggs & Tang, 2007). Once it is accepted that, in order to learn and participate in the complex and situated epistemological practices which characterise higher education, learners need opportunities to make meaning and build their own mental constructs, rather than passively receive information and didactic instruction, then it follows that similar opportunities and roles for students should also be embodied within our assessment practices. Price et al. (2012) have recently argued that, to bring this about and foster active engagement, staff and students need high levels of assessment literacy. This entails being similarly conversant with assessment's relationship to learning, sharing an appreciation of appropriate standards and criteria, seeing the importance of and developing the skills for self-evaluation and developing the skills to choose and apply appropriate approaches to assessed tasks.

Many arguments about the need to explicitly develop students' assessment literacy, rather than leave it to chance, are firmly rooted in two dimensions of engagement as outlined by Trowler and Trowler (2010) in their substantial review of student engagement. The first dimension is individual engagement with learning activities and subject matter, where informal formative tasks and discussions embedded in the specific context of the subject domain promote a kind of learning by doing. Engaging like this helps students begin to recognise the tacit assumptions of the discipline, which are crucial to assessment literacy because they underpin the *real* (but often tacit) requirements of the assessment tasks that students are asked to undertake (Bloxham & West, 2007; Sambell, 2011). This dimension also relates strongly to the assertion that students must be actively supported to develop understandings of assessment which position them as active participants in the learning process, so that they can monitor and control their own learning

(Boud & Associates, 2010). This involves enabling students to learn to *do* assessment and proactively make judgements for themselves, rather than simply receiving and responding to the instructions of others.

Further, a second relevant dimension is engagement through participation and development of identity. This is a sort of learning via participation and relates strongly to a student's developing sense of the deep-level principles and rules of engagement in the subject community, which manifest themselves, again tacitly, in the ways of thinking and practising (Meyer & Land, 2005) of the discipline. Again, a main way of developing this appreciation is via active and social learning experiences, where students learn, gradually, to absorb the ways of thinking and practising of the subject domain by being collectively immersed in a constant flow of disciplinary discourse (Northedge, 2003) which they work on with peers and 'old timers' in a process of epistemic apprenticeship (Claxton, 2011). In another sense, this is also about stakeholders explicitly recognising the relational, dialogic dynamic in learning and assessment. It relates strongly to the growing awareness that students come to a fuller appreciation of the tacit assumptions of academic practice, with its emphasis on learner responsibility and autonomy, by participating actively with more experienced learners and peers in social interactions and discussions focused around concrete assessment practices within and beyond the formal classroom (Orsmond, Merry, & Callaghan, 2012). Barnett and Coates (2005) have argued that curriculum reinvention is necessary to ensure that students are triply engaged: in knowing, acting and being.

Some perspectives on engagement and assessment foreground important aspects of identity in other ways. Academic literacies research as pioneered by Lea and Street (1998) highlights the importance of student participation and the development of new ways of seeing the world and themselves with regard to students' academic writing practices, thus bringing issues of identity to the fore in relation to assessment. From a socio-cultural perspective, Mann (2001) has argued that the ways in which assessment practices, experienced by students as a site of power and disciplinary control, need to be reconfigured to reduce alienation and promote engagement in a much broader sense. From this viewpoint, issues surrounding engagement and assessment are social and political, rather than purely to do with cognitive processes and accurate measurement. It is worth recognising that, for some exponents, the main issues are overtly ideological, political and ethical. Bryan and Clegg (2006, p. 225), for instance, urge their readers to 'take the moral high ground' by implementing new approaches to assessment. Progressive educational principles, antithetical to oppressive regimes of authority and discipline, underpin the philosophical thrust of many pedagogically focused engagement initiatives around assessment practices (see, for instance, McArthur & Huxham, 2013; Clughen & Hardy, 2012).

22.3.   Towards an Holistic Approach to Assessment for Learning

As suggested earlier, a number of AfL models have developed a more holistic conception located in what is commonly regarded as teaching and learning (see, for instance, Boud & Associates, 2010; Carless, Joughin, & Mok, 2006). They propose ways of radically rethinking assessment in overall terms so that it becomes learning-oriented, rather than focusing on quick technical fixes or partial adjustments. One of these was the work of the national Centre for Excellence in Teaching and Learning (CETL)[1] in AfL at Northumbria University, which had the principles of individual and social engagement at its heart.

Our model of AfL (Sambell, McDowell, & Montgomery, 2012) is characterised by a feedback-rich learning environment that has formative assessment at its core with the intention of enabling all students to enhance their achievements. The notion of feedback is expanded to include not only the 'normal' tutor feedback on student work but also tutor–student dialogic feedback, which is part of interactive teaching and learning and peer feedback from a range of formal and informal collaborative learning activities. This interaction enables students to identify the strengths and weaknesses of their own work, rather than simply expecting tutors to perform that role for them.

By engaging students as active participants in learning activities and feedback, we seek to induct them into the requirements of their discipline or professional area of study enabling them to understand and subsequently interrogate and challenge the standards, outcomes and criteria used for the evaluation of high-quality work. Social learning, collaborative inquiry and group discussion are valued and promoted with students increasingly taking control of their own learning and its evaluation. These capabilities include students directing their own learning, evaluating their own progress and attainments, and supporting the learning of others, which are at the heart of autonomous learning and of the graduate qualities valued by employers and in professional practice.

AfL provides for verification of student attainment without allowing this summative function to dominate learning and teaching. There will be 'summative-free zones' where learning (and teaching) can take place without some of the direct, negative backwash effects of assessment for grading. Students are offered opportunities to practice and rehearse skills and knowledge to make mistakes and to learn collaboratively in a low stakes context (Knight & Yorke, 2003). AfL challenges the assumption that unless marks are attached students will not do something and enables productive learning to happen without the direct reward of marks or grades. It tackles the downward spiral where marks and grades are used to control student behaviour and, as a response, students deploy effort only when this will be directly rewarded by marks. Here our model seeks to ensure that high-stakes summative assessment is used rigorously but sparingly, so that formative assessment can drive the learning, offering students extensive opportunities to engage in the kinds of tasks that develop and demonstrate their learning, thus building their confidence and capabilities before they are summatively assessed.

---

[1]CETL AfL was one of 74 centres of excellence established by the Higher Education Funding Council for England in 2005

Both summative and formative assessment must be well-constructed and designed and there may in fact be considerable crossover between the two within the learning environment. The assessment strategy must employ a diversity of methods to assess genuine and valued learning. Views of assessment as measurement of capability have left us with a legacy of assessment methods which may effectively serve the purpose of producing numerical marks and differentiating between students. These methods are normally of much less value in developing and evaluating authentic and worthwhile performances of understanding, application, creativity and commitment. AfL requires appropriate assessment tasks — methods which stimulate and evaluate worthwhile learning through the assessment process and foster the capabilities and dispositions for learning in professional and personal life beyond graduation.

This implies, of course, that AfL is much more than a set of simple tactics which can be adopted by teachers, and inflects more towards our view of AfL as a philosophy, which frames learning, and the associated staff–student and student–student relationships, in particular ways. Our model was developed as a means of trying to ensure that participating teachers developed sophisticated levels of assessment literacy which they could then use as a basis from which to critically interrogate and inform their practice. To this end it was based on six conditions which act as interlinking pedagogic principles which could be used to guide the development of effective AfL practice and harness the power of assessment to support learning. The six conditions are, briefly, about trying to create an overall assessment environment which:

1. is rich in formal feedback (via, e.g., tutor comment; self-assessment systems; peer review);
2. is rich in informal feedback (through, for instance, dialogic teaching, peer interaction and carefully designed classroom assessment which provide students with a continuous flow of feedback on 'how they are doing');
3. provides opportunities for students to try out and practise knowledge, skills and understanding before they are summatively assessed;
4. contains assessment tasks which are authentic or relevant and meaningful in some ways, beyond 'just acquiring marks';
5. assists students to develop independence and autonomy;
6. strikes an appropriate balance between formative and summative assessment.

22.4. Putting AfL into Practice

During the course of the CETL funding period, six experienced academics in different subject areas became CETL Fellows who led the redesign of over 30 modules using the AfL conditions as guiding principles. This was a significant undertaking, as, in practice, it often meant redesigning the whole module's mode of delivery to bring learners' experiences and engagement, rather than content, to the fore.

Sixty-seven teaching staff and 1500 students were involved in this strand of the CETL's enhancement activity and a research programme was established to investigate the outcomes.

This section briefly illustrates the student response to nine of these redesigned AfL modules, based on data gathered as part of the overall research programme. First, the broad outcomes of survey work will be presented. Here a questionnaire was used to capture the responses of the whole student population on seven of the enhanced modules. Next, practical examples of the different ways in which staff put aspects of AfL into operation on three modules in the subject area of childhood and community studies will be discussed. It is important to bear in mind that, while for the sake of illustration and clarity the examples are being presented separately, in reality each 'type' of AfL practice was actually part of an integrated overall approach within the respective module. All three modules became case studies in the research programme, in which observation studies and interviews were used to build detailed sightings of students' views and lived experiences of AfL. The students' voices that accompany each example have been included to give readers a feel for some of the challenges and issues involved in developing students' assessment literacy, as well as indicating their levels of engagement.

22.4.1. *Students' Overall Responses*

As part of the overall CETL research programme a student questionnaire — the AfLQ — was developed as a quantitative instrument that would give a broad picture of the ways in which students experience the AfL environments that were designed and implemented (for details, see McDowell, Wakelin, Montgomery, & King, 2011). This allowed us to study the general student experience ($n = 353$) of seven AfL modules. On an important level, the survey demonstrated that students noticed a discernible difference between modules which had been redesigned using the conditions, and those that had not. Results indicated that the overall student experience was more positive in modules where AfL approaches were used and students were more likely to take a deep approach to learning. It also demonstrated that the student experience of AfL became centred on staff support and module design, feedback, active engagement and peer learning. These, of course, are all aspects of engagement as defined in the literature (Kuh, Kinzie, Schuh, & Whitt, 2010).

22.4.2. *Illustrative Examples*

We also had a well-established framework and tools for research and evaluation using qualitative approaches. For instance, a series of detailed case studies were undertaken and three of these are drawn upon below. In each case, an independent researcher conducted semi-structured interviews with student volunteers at selected points in each module. In the following three sections, quotes are taken from these interviews to illuminate students' viewpoints, with pseudonyms being used to designate individual students' voices.

22.4.2.1. Engaging students in pre-assessment tasks
This first example focuses upon a first year module, where, in the ninth week of study, students were invited to work collaboratively on exemplars. The lecturers hoped that enabling students to see and discuss concrete illustrations of actual student writing might help learners to become clearer about the standards and criteria against which work would be judged. They felt this would enable students to evaluate and calibrate their own achievements, in time, if necessary, to adjust their approaches before their work 'counted' in terms of marks. As such, Sadler's (1989) seminal formulation, mentioned earlier in the chapter, inspired the activity, as did Nicol's (2009) injunction to encourage students to generate, rather than simply receive, feedback. Additionally, Carless's (2007) ideas were influential, especially his discussion of pre-emptive formative assessment. Here lecturers use their experience to identify common misconceptions that learners often make at a particular stage in the course and draw these to students' attention, so that students have time to become aware of the pitfalls and adjust their approaches before any marks are at stake.

The activities were set up as follows. A two-hour teaching session, with over 90 students working in a tiered lecture theatre with two members of staff, was dedicated to workshop activities based on exemplars. Before the two-hour session, students were asked to prepare a short piece of writing explaining a key concept in the disciplinary area being studied. This was not to exceed 500 words, and students were advised to try and practice using academic writing conventions. Students were asked to bring their writing to the session, where they were given four exemplars. The exemplars were based on previous students' attempts to explain the concept. The teachers selected them to epitomise a range of responses from 'good' to 'inadequate', with one completely misunderstanding the concept in question, muddling it with a different concept entirely.

First, the session started by involving students in a criteria-setting activity in which, together with staff, they generated some statements which could be used to judge the exemplars. Students were then asked to work in small groups, trying to use the criteria to place the four exemplars in rank order. They were also asked to draft some feedback which would improve each exemplar. This all took about an hour. Next, tutors revealed and discussed the rankings they would award, and talked about the thinking behind their decisions. Students had the opportunity to ask any questions. Finally, students were asked to revisit the draft feedback they had prepared, augmenting or amending it, if necessary, based on the discussions so far. Again, they were encouraged to ask any questions. Students were also advised to reflect on how they would improve their own piece of writing, in the light of the session.

Student Perspective.   On one level all seven students who were interviewed afterwards about the activities claimed to find them extremely useful. They seemed prompted to develop their assessment literacy in a range of ways. First, they felt the session offered them chance to develop their views of criteria in a concrete, rather than abstract way. For instance, one student explained:

> I think seeing it just makes you understand it more. Like, someone can stand there and say, 'You shouldn't do this and that' but until you've actually seen it then you don't know what that looks like. I think it's harder if you just get a list of rules and have to figure out for yourself how to apply it. (Jill)

Some felt they had learned to improve their own work as a result. It was extremely common for students to realise they were required to undertake considerably more reading than they anticipated, as in the following instance:

> I suddenly learned that reading is so vital, as it builds up your knowledge and helps you gain a better understanding. That was the light bulb moment of the whole semester! (June)

Some also began to pay closer attention to the nuances of definition and terminology within the subject area, which prompted them to engage more deeply with the ideas:

> When we discussed the task in class I realised that what I had written didn't focus on the question! It was this that made me read around the subject more. (Stacey)

Many said, too, that they felt clearer about their teachers' expectations when it came to writing assignments. For instance, the following student realised the tutors did not want to see students reproducing their secondary reading verbatim but preferred them to summarise it, putting it into their own words to develop an argument:

> I was surprised with what they expected. They didn't want so many long quotes and all the information and detailed knowledge from my reading. (Jill)

Four groups of students were also observed by the research team throughout the workshop. This revealed the extent of the 'gap' between staff and students' assumptions about the nature and standards of quality work, which, in most instances, was sizeable, yet, from the lecturers' perspectives, invisible. Despite repeated encouragement for students during the workshop to ask questions and clarify uncertainties, few did. Most of their apparent revelations took place backstage, as it were, in discussions among the student groups.

The insights gained by the participant researchers were particularly illuminating, as they revealed the immense difficulty that students were having in adjusting to the epistemological premises of university-level work and associated study, writing and assessment practices. For instance, it is especially noteworthy that in their initial group discussions of the merits of each exemplar, all the students who were observed only noticed and discussed technical aspects, such as spelling or referencing, rather than the arguably more important features, such as analysis and argument. Even more importantly, before any form of dialogue was opened up with tutors and despite access to the assessment criteria, students almost exclusively ignored issues pertaining to the nature of knowledge in the subject domain, even though this was the implied focus of the 'question', and despite 'understanding' being a superordinate criterion for staff.

Classroom observation further revealed that very few groups of students actually placed the exemplars in accordance with the rank order the tutors allocated. Many students found, often to their surprise or consternation, 'What we thought was best or worst was different to what they thought!'(Laura, Group 3).

While some groups simply muddled the two 'best' exemplars, several believed the exemplar which had misunderstood the key concept was actually the best piece of work, and the most effective response was often considered 'worst'. In short, most students seemed unable to discern the exemplars at the extremes. Once they heard the teachers talk about the rankings they would award, all the observed groups were anxious to look again at the exemplars. Although they had been asked to amend their draft feedback for each exemplar, in practice, nearly all their discussion focused on the exemplar which the tutors felt to be a fail. In one sense, students were attempting to see afresh from the teachers' point of view, but this was by far from an easy, rapid or straightforward process. In their discussions students repeatedly looped back to apply technical advice about 'good essay-writing' they had received at secondary school and via university study skills sessions, which continued to distract them from looking for meaning and a deeper-level engagement with the texts.

This example serves as a salutary reminder, then, of the difficulties of helping students to make the adjustment to university academic culture so that they come to understand the real rules of the game and are enabled to engage by developing their assessment literacy. On one level this is unsurprising. Research (e.g. Kember, 2001) draws attention to the huge conceptual shifts students need to make with regard to their views of the nature of knowledge, teaching and learning when moving from school or college to university. This is a gradual, developmental process, which is likely to take time, rather than happen suddenly. This is all the more reason, arguably, to ensure that, as far as possible, the overall student experience of assessment aligns with and fosters the espoused goals and attributes of higher education. While pre-assessment activities such as those described above may be useful catalysts to engagement, they should not be seen as a solution or end in their own right, but rather as part of a longer term process, as the following two examples imply.

22.4.2.2. Putting informal feedback into practice

Boud and Associates (2010, p. 2) argue that, in AfL environments, 'everyday learning activities as well as special tasks and tests provide opportunities for the provision of feedback'. This example focuses on instances in which feedback occurred extremely informally, as part of the normal flow of teaching and learning, almost as a by-product. Classroom activities, tasks and associated directed study were designed to maximise the formative potential of the university classroom. Here the teachers' role was to create effective conditions for learning by placing student involvement, effort and activity at the heart of the learning and teaching environment. By carefully structuring progressively challenging classroom activities, staff sought to ensure that students were provided with a continual flow of feedback which enabled them to see how they were doing.

This kind of feedback could not be planned in detail, but relied on designing a climate that encouraged dialogue, collaboration among students and interaction about subject-related tasks between teachers and students. To this end tutors worked hard to structure the formative tasks and activities they asked their students to become involved in, moving strongly away from didactic, transmission models of teaching towards interactive, participative classroom experiences which were designed to foster student activity, application, discussion and social interaction around subject material. Arguably, informal interactions with peers are massively important ways of developing assessment literacy in universities, because this places emphasis on a process of reflection, peer review and evaluation (Black & McCormick, 2010).

As part of the 2 hour weekly teaching sessions on the module, 70 final-year students worked in groups to build posters over a period of three consecutive weeks. The posters were informal, graffiti-like displays, rather than polished performances. The tutors emphasised that they were intended to act as tools for learning, so presentation issues did not matter, other than the material should be accessible to other students and teachers in the class when groups circulated to explore and discuss the findings of other groups' posters. The lecturers set a series of academic tasks for their students each week. To prepare for each session, individuals were asked to research material, which they brought along to contribute to the development of their group's poster. Over a 3 week period, students worked on their posters to develop different sightings of a key concept which the tutors believed underpinned high-order thinking and mastery in their particular domain. In the first week learners were required to discuss their personal interpretations of primary source material, then in subsequent weeks they incorporated different perspectives from a range of specified sources, which offered fresh perspectives that they layered on to their developing posters. This helped them link new ideas to their existing concepts, so that new ways of thinking were generated.

The students were supported to work collaboratively as groups. Ground rules were negotiated, with students agreeing among themselves that everyone must participate, that consensus should be achieved before anything went on the poster and that assertions anyone put forward should be supported by evidence and a convincing rationale. This was important because discussion was the main means by which learners were to engage with the new material each week. As learners endeavoured to understand the ideas within their own personal frames of reference they interacted with peers and their teachers, who circulated around the groups, listening in to informally appraise students' understandings of the material, interjecting to ask questions to clarify students' understandings of key concepts, or push the thinking further.

Student Perspective.   Later, in interviews with the research team, six students talked about the value of negotiating common meaning with their fellow students. They felt this gave them insight into the extent to which they were grasping the relevant ideas:

> You make sure that it makes sense and then, er, to see if you can actually have an, er, a debate about it and have, have enough knowledge to back your arguments through when they go 'Well, hang on a minute, what about this, what about that?' (Briony)

Within this perspective, students seemed to feel that the lecturers' role was to keep students on track in relation to the subject.

> They went around the groups, saying: OK, good point. Maybe work a bit more on such and such. So you knew if you went terribly wrong, someone would say! (Fiona)

Black and McCormick (2010) observe that oral discussion, involving interactive dialogue where the teacher can explore and steer by sensitive challenge should be one of the main ways through which the learner is apprenticed into the world of academic discourse by being inducted into its practice. In the poster work students framed the lecturers as authorities who could help students 'see' the nature of the subject specialism, and its particular ways of viewing material, by means of asking specific questions:

> It's knowing what questions to ask, which somebody who knows their subject knows. I didn't know the questions [how to approach the material]. That's something that clicks through time rather than clicking because you're told it. (Lesley)

Here the student notes how it takes time, lots of active engagement with the subject and on-going participation with knowledgeable others to develop a feel for what a subject is *really* all about. Without this insight, however, it is difficult for students to form a genuine sense of academic standards and requirements.

22.4.2.3. Authentic assessment tasks

This final example briefly highlights the importance of the backwash of the summative task, and the idea of constructive alignment. In a second year option about educational assessment, instead of writing an essay, students were required to produce guides to assessment which would be suitable for using with first year undergraduates. The guides took shape gradually, and as the module progressed, teaching sessions were given over to their design and development, with ample opportunity for student–student and staff–student dialogue. This approach helped students to see how the knowledge they were developing, and the way they were building towards the assignment, had direct relevance and importance in the real world, even though the students did not necessarily envisage going on to undertake a professional teaching qualification. It also helped them to think of themselves as authors, encouraging them to argue a case. Learners were highly motivated and creative in their approaches. They chose a variety of formats, including booklets, catalogues, DVDs, games and leaflets to put their points across. Interestingly, given the choice, most students elected to develop their materials in small self-selecting groups or pairs rather than working alone.

Student Perspective.   Seven interviewees said this offered them a more 'natural' way of working in which ideas were shared and co-produced in a constructive process of dialogue, negotiation and peer review:

> Working on the same thing together is kind of helpful with this. Because we both have a working knowledge of the topic, we could actually say, No, I don't think that's right. Does this mean this? Should we put it this way? [Becky]

Hounsell (2007) argues that collaborative assignments like this can help foster connoisseurship and a fuller appreciation of academic standards among students, because participants can learn from co-generation and co-writing as they work together on subject material.

Further, students claimed to approach this task in markedly different ways from other summative assessments. For instance, they found themselves investing personally in learning, rather than, as the following quotes suggest, finding themselves overly preoccupied with performance goals and the alienating effects that the sense of being marked can entail (Mann, 2001):

> Normally I don't write it for me. I don't think I write my academic assignments for myself, I'm writing them for the person who is reading them. (Sally)

> Normally, I have my 2:1 in mind, I need a 60% for my postgrad course, and that's what I am writing for. (Helen)

By contrast, Sally claimed:

> I used it to think through the things with assessment that had happened to me. It was about me, which my assignments aren't normally. I just normally check what they're asking and put bits in on each criteria [*sic*].

Moreover, Helen talked of experiencing a sense of authorship which she associated with addressing an audience, rather than her assessor:

> The sense that someone would read this — I think that helped us create it, especially after seeing the guides that they handed out as

examples and they had said it might [be displayed]. People might pick it up, have a look through it.

Elander, Pittam, Lusher, Fox, and Payne (2010) argue that the concept of authorial identity can be useful in mainstream attempts to understand and improve student writing practices in university courses. AfL approaches and authentic tasks have an important part to play in this regard, helping students to genuinely engage with the real rules of the game in academic writing. Importantly, for instance, Sally found that her experiences of authorship on this module had a knock-on effect to the way she approached other assignments:

> I saw what they wanted- like a light bulb went off in my head. I started to rethink the whole way I did things on every assignment and suddenly I started to do better- across the board!

22.5. Conclusion

This chapter has argued that assessment is a significant influence on students' experience of university study and all that they gain from it. Because assessment powerfully frames how students learn and what students achieve, it is useful to focus explicitly on improving assessment practice to improve the quality of teaching, learning and the student experience. It is crucial that students develop a broad understanding of assessment, are assured of its role in their learning and aware of their role in the process.

However, as Price et al. (2012, p. 14) point out, there are clearly some significant challenges to be faced in developing assessment literacy among staff as well as students. If widespread transformations to assessment are to become a reality in higher education assessment experts assert that a planned and sustained staff development strategy is needed (see, e.g., HEA, 2012, p. 15). It is important, for instance, to recognise the extent to which our CETL offered a whole range of staff development activities and opportunities for its associates, helping them to rethink assessment. This included, for example, one-to-one support, master-classes, reading groups, practice exchanges, mentoring, collaborative research and development projects, all led by international experts in the field of assessment in higher education. This represented a significant resource allocation, which was supported by the originating team's successful bid into a competitively allocated central funding stream to support learning and teaching innovation. The current economic climate places increasing pressure on the resourcing of pioneering pedagogic initiatives.

Nevertheless, carefully developed AfL approaches offer some practical and feasible ways forward, even in resource-constrained circumstances. To develop the work further we need to know more about the ways in which students develop and use assessment literacy, especially over time and beyond the academy in the longer term. However, it seems clear that, as part of students' overall experience of being at university, assessment has an impact on their broader experience of engagement. By the same token, the nature of student engagement has an influence on the ways in which they view and respond to assessment. Well-developed AfL practice provides an important key to engaging students via quality teaching and learning.

References

Barkley, E. (2009). *Student engagement techniques: A handbook for college faculty*. New York, NY: Jossey-Bass.

Barnett, R., & Coates, K. (2005). *Engaging the curriculum in higher education*. Maidenhead, UK: SRHE/Open University Press.

Biggs, J., & Tang, C. (2007). *Teaching for quality learning at university* (3rd ed.). Maidenhead, UK: Open University Press.

Birenbaum, M. (1996). Assessment 2000: Towards a pluralistic approach to assessment. In M. Birenbaum & F. J. R. C. Dochy (Eds.), *Alternatives in assessment of achievements, learning processes and prior knowledge* (pp. 3–29). Boston, MA: Kluwer.

Black, P., & McCormick, R. (2010). Reflections and new directions. *Assessment and Evaluation in Higher Education, 35*(5), 493–499.

Bloxham, S., & West, A. (2007). Learning to write in higher education: Students' perceptions of an intervention in developing understanding of assessment criteria. *Teaching in Higher Education, 12*(1), 77–89.

Boud, D., & Associates. (2010). *Assessment 2020: Seven propositions for assessment reform in higher education*. Sydney: Australian Learning and Teaching Council.

Boud, D., & Molloy, E. (2012). Rethinking models of feedback for learning: The challenge of design. *Assessment and Evaluation in Higher Education*. iFirst Article, 1–15.

Brown, S., & Knight, P. (1994). *Assessing learners in higher education*. London: Kogan Page.

Bryan, C., & Clegg, K. (2006). *Innovative assessment in higher education*. London: Routledge.

Carless, D. (2007). Conceptualizing pre-emptive formative assessment. *Assessment in Education: Principles, Policy and Practice, 14*(2), 171–184.

Carless, D., Joughin, G., & Mok, M. (2006). Learning-oriented assessment: Principles and practice. *Assessment and Evaluation in Higher Education, 31*(4), 395–398.

Claxton, G. (2011). *Higher Education as epistemic apprenticeship*. Keynote speech to the NAIRTL/CELT Annual Conference, Galway, June 2011.

Clughen, L., & Hardy, C. (2012). *Writing in the disciplines*. Bingley: Emerald.

Earl, A. M. (2003). *Assessment as learning: Using classroom assessment to maximize student learning*. Thousand Oaks, CA: Corwin Press.

Ecclestone, K. (2002). *Learning autonomy in post-compulsory education: The politics and practice of formative assessment*. London: Routledge.

Elander, J., Pittam, G., Lusher, J., Fox, P., & Payne, N. (2010). Evaluation of an intervention to help students avoid unintentional plagiarism by improving their authorial identity. *Assessment & Evaluation in Higher Education, 35*(2), 157–171.

Havnes, A. (2012). *Assessment in higher education: A CHAT perspective*. Paper delivered at the EARLI SIG Conference: Linking Multiple Perspectives on Assessment, Brussels, 28–31 August.

HEA. (2012). *A marked improvement: Transforming assessment practice in higher education.* New York, NY: HEA.

Hounsell, D. (2007). Towards more sustainable feedback to students. In D. Boud & N. Falchikov (Eds.), *Rethinking assessment in higher education. Learning for the longer term* (pp. 101−113). London: Routledge.

Kember, D. (2001). Beliefs about knowledge and the process of teaching and learning as a factor in adjusting to study in higher education. *Studies in Higher Education, 26*(2), 205−221.

Knight, P. T., & Yorke, M. (2003). *Assessment, learning and employability.* Maidenhead, UK: Open University Press.

Kuh, G., Kinzie, J., Schuh, J., & Whitt, E. (2010). *Student success in college: Creating conditions that matter* (2nd ed.). San Francisco, CA: Jossey-Bass.

Laurillard, D. (2002). *Rethinking university teaching: A conversational framework for the effective use of learning technologies* (2nd ed.). London: Routledge Falmer.

Lea, M. R., & Street, B. V. (1998). Student writing in higher education: An academic literacies approach. *Studies in Higher Education, 23*(2), 157−172.

Mann, S. J. (2001). Alternative perspectives on the student experience: Alienation and engagement. *Studies in Higher Education, 26*(1), 7−19.

McArthur, J., & Huxham, M. (2013). Feedback unbound: From master to usher. In S. Merry, M. Price, D. Carless, & M. Taras (Eds.), *Reconceptualising feedback in higher education* (pp. 92−102). London: Routledge.

McDowell, L., Wakelin, D., Montgomery, C., & King, S. (2011). Does assessment for learning make a difference? The development of a questionnaire to explore the student response. *Assessment and Evaluation in Higher Education, 36*(7), 749−765.

Meyer, J. H. F., & Land, R. (2005). Threshold concepts and troublesome knowledge: Epistemological considerations and a conceptual framework for teaching and learning. *Higher Education, 49*(3), 373−388.

Miller, C. M. L., & Parlett, M. (1974). *Up to the mark: A study of the examination game.* London: SRH.

Nicol, D. (2009). *Transforming assessment and feedback: Enhancing integration and empowerment in the first year.* Mansfield: QAA.

Northedge, A. (2003). Enabling participation in academic discourse. *Teaching in Higher Education, 8*(2), 169−180.

O'Donovan, B., Price, M., & Rust, C. (2004). Know what I mean? Enhancing student understanding of assessment standards and criteria. *Teaching in Higher Education, 9,* 325−335.

O'Donovan, B., Price, M., & Rust, C. (2008). Developing student understanding of assessment standards: A nested hierarchy of approaches. *Teaching in Higher Education, 13*(2), 205−216.

Orsmond, P., Merry, S., & Callaghan, A. (2012). Communities of practice and ways to learning: Charting the progress of biology undergraduates. *Studies in Higher Education.* iFirst, 1−17.

Osney Grange Group. (2009). *Feedback: An agenda for change.* Retrieved from www.brookes. ac.uk/aske/documents/OGG%20agenda%20for%20change.pdf. Accessed on 28 September 2012.

Price, M., Rust, C., O'Donovan, B., & Handley, K. (2012). *Assessment literacy: The foundation for improving student learning.* Oxford: OCSLD.

Sadler, D. (1989). Formative assessment and the design of instructional systems. *Instructional Science, 18,* 119−144.

Sambell, K. (2011). *Rethinking feedback in higher education: An assessment for learning perspective*. Bristol: ESCalate.

Sambell, K., McDowell, L., & Brown, S. (1997). "But is it fair?" an exploratory study of student perceptions of the consequential validity of assessment. *Studies in Educational Evaluation, 23*(4), 349–371.

Sambell, K., McDowell, L., & Montgomery, C. (2012). *Assessment for learning in higher education*. London: Routledge.

Torrance, H. (2007). Assessment as learning? How the use of explicit learning objectives, assessment criteria and feedback in post-secondary education and training can come to dominate learning. *Assessment in Education: Principles, Policy and Practice, 14*(3), 281–294.

Trowler, V., & Trowler, P. (2010). *Student engagement evidence summary*. York: Higher Education Academy.

PART 5: STUDENT ENGAGEMENT IN CURRICULUM DESIGN AND DELIVERY

Elisabeth Dunne and Derfel Owen

> Those who have tried it give a clear message: don't be afraid to take risks, change can have powerful benefits both for academics and students. (Cooper, 2011)

Previous parts of this book have taken time to explore student engagement in structures, decision-making and activities associated with the curriculum. It is noticeable, however, that there is a clear trend towards involving students more actively and directly in shaping their own curriculum (Owen & Stubbs, 2010). Part 5 highlights a set of innovative and effective ways in which staff and students have worked in collaboration to develop and deliver the curriculum. This is not always a straightforward experience, the UK National Union of Students (NUS, 2011) recognised this:

> Like any change to a traditional way of working, student involvement in curriculum design can be a threatening process for participants. Academics might naturally fear the loss of control over modules which they have developed over several years, whilst students may be nervous about voicing their opinions, or risking their educational experience by making changes to trusted formats. (2011)

The sense of authority that academics derive from the fact that they have years of experience and scholarly activity to inform their curriculum is particularly powerful and it is understandable that this sense of authority and status can be seriously undermined and challenged by the notion that students, the academic apprentices, may have something serious to contribute to curriculum design and innovation.

Five examples in this part from very different institutions demonstrate how students can take responsibility for change, from developing resources, to contributing to the professional development of staff, and how they can shape their own educational experiences.

An extreme interpretation of this agenda to involve students in curriculum design and delivery would put students in a position where they are in complete control of what and how they learn and academics are there to act as hosts, supporting their efforts. Chapter 23 describes the experience of a senior academic at a UK university where circumstance made this the only viable way in which she could deliver a particular course. She describes her experience as one that fundamentally challenged her and her students' perception of their respective roles and how empowering students to take control of their curriculum in a structured and well-supported way can be challenging and highly reward for all involved.

Chapter 24 describes a similar journey, but at a very different university and from different beginnings. Here we hear a story of a university listening to feedback from its students and not just responding to that feedback but engaging those students in the process of improvement and then challenging them to play a part in delivering the solutions. While listening to and responding to feedback is not particularly innovative, the way in which the students and academic staff here collaborated and worked in partnership to reshape and co-deliver the curriculum provides a useful model for other universities seeking engage student in curriculum design and delivery.

Engaging, for example with students as collaborators and change agents in the context of technology is particularly powerful, since the students of today are well-informed, understand the potential of the technologies they use, and are creative in the ways that they work and often have greater expertise that their teachers. In chapter 25, Ryan co-authors a chapter with staff and students from three UK universities that have been exploring students involvement in the curriculum, and curriculum change and development, through technology. Case studies from the three institutions highlight very different practices, each with their benefits, issues and challenges. The first considers students engaging as 'e-champions' with students new to university; they reflect on their experiences of using Facebook and consider the impact of their role on peers and staff as well as on their own social and digital identities. The second considers the impact of student-led projects in evaluating and innovating technology provision in a Business School, with many positive benefits but also lessons to be learned. The third examines a recruitment process for a student-led interdisciplinary research group and proposes some key recommendations. This chapter is of interest for its exploration of aspects of technology through the eyes of students who are engaging with change and are recognised by their respective institutions as being at the heart of change processes.

The examples captured in this part are only a snapshot of the range of interest and activity to engage students in curriculum design and delivery. In chapter 26 Catherine Bovill explores some of her own experience of engaging students and sets this in a much wider context with a review of literature and examples of practice to analyse whether students and staff co-creating curricula can be considered as good practice. In particular, the chapters gives an overview of some of the rationales given by staff to explain why they are interested in providing opportunities for students to co-create curricula and the benefits resulting from their experiences.

Finally, in chapter 27 Brand et. al. tell the story of their experience of reshaping a university's entire approach to curriculum design and innovation by actively supporting partnership between students and staff. Here we see how a university began to explore opportunities to involve students more directly in curriculum design and by methodically reviewing the benefits and impact of this were able to align the activity with the university's strategic priorities and gain support from senior strategic managers and academic staff simultaneously so that the initiative could grow. The outcome is an approach to partnership working that has revolutionised the relationship between students and staff at the university and is national and internationally recognised as a model of good practice.

The experience described in each of these chapters show instances where students and staff have faced concerns, of their own and from others, but have concluded that it was worth taking the risk to try to make things better. The experiences of the authors show that there are significant benefits to working in partnership with students to design and co-deliver the curriculum, but that this is not an easy process, it is challenging for the students and staff involved.

References

Cooper G. (2011). Case study: Independent study module. *Student engagement: Students as active partners in shaping their learning experience*. Retrieved from http://www.heacademy. ac.uk/assets/documents/studentengagement/Case_study_Newcastle_University_Independent_ study_module.pdf

NUS. (2011). *Student involvement in curriculum design*. Retrieved from http://www.nusconnect. org.uk/resourcehandler/9e2f03b5-1474-4a57-9b7a-54753f0975c3/

Owen, D., & Stubbs, W. (2010). *Shaping and quality assuring the curriculum: The employer and the student voice*. Paper to the 32nd annual EAIR Conference. Retrieved from http:// www.eair.nl/forum/valencia/pdf/723.pdf

Chapter 23

Active Participation in Learning: Students Creating their Educational Experience

Joan Walton

Abstract

This chapter gives an account of teaching a second year undergraduate module entitled 'Active Participation in Learning'. It is argued that a positivist paradigm which separates the world into 'subjects' and 'objects' is not helpful when considering how to encourage the full participation of students in all aspects of their university education. Rather, a participative paradigm (Heron, 1996) provides a theoretical framework which dissolves the subjective–objective divide, and establishes an ethos of equality and mutuality which is, arguably, integral to achieving the full engagement of students in enhancing their own learning experiences. This case study is a first person account of a lecturer who explains and analyses the process and outcomes of taking an action research approach to the teaching of a two-semester module. A major aim is to evaluate the usefulness of teaching and learning being guided by a participative world view. The study includes an account of the experiences and responses of the students, from their initial surprise at being given the opportunity to be involved in the creating of the module curriculum to their final conclusions which includes not only a passionate commitment to student engagement but also ideas about how this can be encouraged in practice.

23.1. Introduction

The aim of this chapter is to give an account of teaching a group of second year undergraduate students, who were encouraged to create their own educational experience in a module entitled 'Active Participation in Learning'. The student group was registered for an honours degree in Education Studies at a university in the north-west of England.

The Student Engagement Handbook: Practice in Higher Education
Copyright © 2013 by Emerald Group Publishing Limited
All rights of reproduction in any form reserved
ISBN: 978-1-78190-423-7

The account begins with an explanation of my approach to teaching, and the educational influences that have inspired my thinking and actions. These influences include Dewey's (1916) ideas of experiential learning, a participative reality (Biggs, 1996; Heron, 1996) notion of constructive alignment, Schön's (1995) new epistemology for a new scholarship, and improving practice through values-based action research (Reason & Bradbury, 2001; Whitehead & McNiff, 2006).

This is followed by the 'story' of the module, which shows the interweaving relationship between my teaching philosophy and the students' responses as they engage with what is for them a new experience of teaching and learning. They were encouraged to actively participate in creating and delivering the curriculum, determine forms of assessment and continuously learn from and evaluate their experience through a series of action reflection cycles.

The chapter is written from a first person perspective, reflecting a living theory approach to action research (Whitehead & McNiff, 2006) which was guiding my research-informed teaching. The chapter ends with a brief reflection on the significance of this methodology as one means of enhancing student engagement.

23.2.   Theoretical Framework

My approach to learning and teaching is informed by an ontological view of the world which has been greatly influenced by John Heron's views of a 'participative reality'(1996). This world view challenges the 'subject−object' divide which forms the basis of positivist perceptions of the world. Within a participatory worldview, the world is not seen as existing independently of any observer, just waiting to be known through a process of observation and analysis. Rather, it views human beings as equal participants in the world, who co-create a reality which is shaped by the nature and quality of our subjective−objective relationships.

A participative reality (Bateson, 1979; Merleau-Ponty, 1962; Reason & Rowan, 1981; Skolimowski,1994) sees the world as subjective−objective, where there is an 'intermarriage between the creative construing of the human mind and what is cosmically given. ... This ontology calls for a new view about truth and ways of knowing ...' (Heron, 1996, p. 162).

The underlying assumption is that, in meeting people, there is the possibility of reciprocal participative knowing. Unless his process is truly mutual, we are not able to properly know the other. Buber (1937) with his notion of 'I-Thou' suggests that the reality of the other is found in the fullness of our relationships, where we 'each engage in mutual participation' (Heron, 1996, p. 11).

A participative view of reality has major implications for the way we view ourselves, and others in relation to ourselves. It challenges the power disparities that exist in social structures, where people are valued according to their perceived objective status in a hierarchically structured universe. From this ontology emerges an epistemology that emphasises a participative relationship between the knower and known, and between knower and knower. There is no separation in these interactive relationships.

A participative paradigm supports a view of human interaction which sees all people of equal importance and value in continually evolving, co-created view of reality, where 'human flourishing' is perceived as a valuable end in itself.

> What is valuable as a means to this end is participative decision-making, which enables people to be involved in the making of decisions, in every social context, which affect their flourishing in any way. (Heron, 1996, p. 11)

Entering a classroom to work with groups of students in ways that reflect a participative paradigm is clearly a challenge when in a professional context which traditionally emphasises the 'subject–object' divide. Much of the theory on teaching and learning focuses on the 'separation' between teacher and learner, rather than on the development of a mutually informing relationship. For example, Biggs and Tang (2007) differentiate between three levels of thinking about the effectiveness of teaching. The first level suggests that the teacher is the 'expert', and transmits knowledge, normally by lecturing. Generally, students are assessed through being given 'marks' according to how accurately they can reproduce the knowledge received, and if they get a low mark, this is because they have been a poor student. When a teacher evaluates their sessions, they are in effect evaluating the ability or motivation of the students rather than the competency of their own teaching.

In level 2, the emphasis is still on the transmission of knowledge; but the teacher takes greater responsibility for developing a range of teaching methods that are likely to better communicate that knowledge. In evaluating their sessions, the teacher will evaluate the effectiveness of their teaching methodologies, and how they might adjust these for better outcomes.

In level 3, the focus returns to the student, but centres on what the student learns, and whether that learning achieves identified outcomes. Within this context, Biggs has developed the well-recognised process of 'constructive alignment', an approach to curriculum design which aims to optimise the conditions for quality learning (Biggs, 1996; Biggs & Tang, 2007).

In a number of ways, constructive alignment addresses my belief that effective learning emerges from the relationship between teacher and learner. In constructive alignment, it is recognised that the quality of the learning of the student is influenced by the nature of the learning activities. The learning is not transmitted from teacher to student, but is something the students have to create for themselves. Teaching in this way is seen as a catalyst for learning. The teacher's responsibility, then, is to establish a learning environment which ensures that the activities undertaken by the students are likely to achieve the learning outcomes. Consequently, it is important to 'align' planned outcomes, learning activities, teaching methods and assessment tasks.

Much of the recent pedagogical literature focuses on models of learning which closely reflect or are directly based on Biggs and Tang's 'third level' to form appropriate theoretical frameworks that guide curriculum planning and implementation (Hoddinott, 2000; Savin-Baden, 2004; Treleaven, 2008; Walsh, 2007).

Traditional learning, with the teacher spouting facts and figures, and with participants regurgitating the information without deeper involvement, is a very ineffective form of learning. A much more effective and long-lasting form of learning is to involve the learner by creating a meaningful learning experience. (Beard & Wilson, 2006, p. 1)

There is also a growing emphasis on the value of reflective practice as a means of enhancing the learning of both teachers and students (Brockbank & McGill, 2007; Cowan, 2006).

However, there is still a separation between lecturer and student in that most of the literature assumes that the teacher will determine the curriculum without involving the student. This assumption is being challenged by the idea of promoting 'student voice' and 'student engagement' which, though originating in the school environment, is also relevant for university students (Taylor & Robinson, 2009; Cook-Sather, 2006).

Although the terminology changes, the idea is not new. As far back as the early 20th century, Dewey (1916) was advocating that students should be actively involved in their own learning. In an educational setting, 'each subject is not only a body of facts but a form of living personal experience' (Tanner, 1991, p. 103).

Heron (1999, p. 131) suggests:

... a fully educated person is, among other things, an awarely self-determining person, in the sense of being able to set objectives, to formulate standards of excellence for the work that realises those objectives, to assess work done in the light of those standards, and to be able to modify the objectives, the standards or the work programme in the light of experience and action; and all this in discussion and consultation with other relevant persons ....

Unfortunately, the educational process in most of our major institutions does not prepare students to acquire this kind of self-determining ability. For the staff in these institutions unilaterally decide student objectives, work programmes and assessment criteria, and unilaterally do the assessment of student work. This goes on until graduation, so that fledgling professionals are undereducated so far as the *process* of education is concerned; they have had no experience in setting objectives, planning a work programme, devising assessment criteria, or in self-assessment; nor have they acquired any skills in doing any of these things co-operatively with others.

Taylor (2007, p. 41) accepts the desirability of students being centrally involved in all aspects of the learning process, and has developed the concept of 'whole person learning' which has integrated within it the following principles:

1. The more involved the learner is required to become in their own learning, the more the conditions of that learning need to reflect the nature of an adult to adult relationship.

Table 23.1: Taylor's distinction between traditional learning and whole person learning.

Traditional learning expects:	Whole person learning encourages:
Acceptance of external decisions	Participant involvement in planning
Respect for those in authority	Participants developing a questioning attitude
Acceptance of predetermined objectives	Participants identifying their own learning objectives
Adherence to aims based on content	Objectives based on participants' needs
Formal procedures and relationships	Individual focus on personal objectives
Focus upon content and presentation	Process: learning how to learn

2. 'Communities of practice' are successfully able to evolve without hierarchical authorities.
3. Individuals can be involved not only in what they are learning, but in what they are going to learn, in how they are going to do that learning, and also in assessing how successfully they have accomplished their learning.

Taylor (2007, p. 132) differentiates between what traditional learning expects, and what whole person learning encourages (see Table 23.1).

There is a growing demand for whole person learning and student engagement, supported by a recognition of its educational benefits (evidenced in the handbook which contains this chapter). However, there is little literature which identifies methods that have been successfully used to promote the active participation of students in all aspects of their own learning. Given that I had an ideological commitment to student engagement, but did not have a ready-made 'procedure' for ensuring it happened; I chose an action research approach to establishing and improving my practice of enabling students' active participation in all stages of their own learning process.

23.3. An Action Research Approach to Teaching and Learning

Boyer (1990), when challenging traditional notions of scholarship in higher education, proposed that scholarly activity in universities should not just focus on research, but should include teaching, and the application of learning to practice. He claimed that teaching means 'not only transmitting knowledge, but transforming and extending it as well' in a way that stimulates 'active, not passive learning and encourages students to be critical, creative thinkers, with the capacity to go on learning' (1990, pp. 23, 24).

Schön (1995) argued that this would require a new epistemology of practice, which he suggested would take the form of action research. Action research is described by Reason and Bradbury as 'an orientation to research that is aimed at improving participants' lives' (2001, p. xxi). They further contend:

> By bringing scholarship and praxis back together ... our immodest aim is to change the relationship between knowledge and practice ... as the academy seeks additions and alternatives to its heretofore 'ivory tower' positivist model of science, research and practice .... Action research is therefore an inherently value laden activity, usually practised by scholar-practitioners who care deeply about making a positive change in the world. (2001, p. xxxiv)

Whitehead (1989) and Whitehead & McNiff (2006) also promote values-based practice in their development of a living theory approach to action research. Living theory is a form of research which has 'I' at the centre, where the values of the researcher are fully acknowledged, and where the researcher is accountable for the ways in which she or he lives their values in their practice. A living theory inquiry centres on a series of action–reflection cycles in a process where the aim is to improve a situation of interest and concern to the researcher.

Kemmis makes a distinctive claim when he states that he considers the first concern of action researchers should be '*the contribution of their action to history, not so much to theory*' (2010, p. 425, italics in original). He suggests that action researchers are not only, or even necessarily, contributing to a theoretical body of knowledge, but rather are generating transformational actions, which lead to a 'disposition to act wisely in uncertain practical situations' (p. 422), with the aim of benefiting 'the good of each person and the good of humankind' (p. 425). Action research should be concerned with the flourishing of humanity rather than analysing, conceptualising and philosophising about it. The latter have their place, but in action research these serve the former.

In working with students in educational contexts, my aim is to create a learning environment where they feel inspired and empowered to gain knowledge in ways which they experience as transformative. Ideally, I want students to feel personally changed as a result of their engagement with the course I am teaching. So, in taking a values-based action research approach to improving my ability to achieve this aim, the values I am explicitly seeking to live in my practice are those of participation, mutual empowerment and respect. Encouraging students' participation is essential if they are to be fully engaged in their learning. However, as students often defer to the traditional authority of the teacher, it is important to enable all students to feel empowered to fully contribute, and to encourage others in the group to do the same. Creating an ethos of respect for each other and the experience that each brings to the education process is, I consider, a prerequisite to creating a transformational learning environment. The values of participation, mutual empowerment and respect are interconnected; facilitating a process that supports mutual empowerment can only authentically be achieved through respecting those with whom I am working, in an environment where everyone has equal right and opportunity to participate in the decision-making.

The theory is that if I live this values-based action research approach in teaching situations, the students will have a transformative learning experience. The next part of the chapter offers my account of what emerged in one educational context when I committed myself to this approach.

23.4.   Students Creating their Educational Experience: A Case Study

23.4.1.   *Introduction*

This section tracks the development of a second year, two-semester module entitled 'Active Participation in Learning'. This was an optional module for students who were hoping to gain employment post-university in an educational setting, generally but not exclusively in schools or youth services. A formal objective was that they learn how to encourage the active participation in learning of children and young people in any future professional work context.

The module had run the previous year, led by a lecturer who had now left the university. I was informed that the module had received a poor evaluation from students, and that I was free to develop it in any way I wished. The course specification was relatively generalised, so gave me considerable scope for development.

This account of the module is written from my perspective, with myself as sole author. Ideally this would be a co-authored account, with all the students as equal contributors. However they have now gone their individual ways with their time prioritised on their chosen professional and personal activities. Nevertheless, I wanted to stay as true as possible to the principle of the students actively participating in all stages of the process. With this principle in mind, I have chosen to write the case study such that the students' voices are integrated into the narrative, in the form of extracts taken from their reflective accounts written during and at the end of the module. It is hoped that by taking this approach, the truly participatory nature of the development of the module will be communicated, including the wide range of emotions, uncertainties and sense of achievement that were experienced at different stages of the process.

23.4.2.   *The First Session*

From the beginning, it was obvious that the students did not have much awareness of what they were signing up to.

> When choosing the 'Active Participation in Learning' module, I was unsure what to expect. I had no prior knowledge of the concept of active participation. I struggled to find a definition. The dictionary defines it as 'the involvement, either by an individual or a group of

individuals, in their own governance or other activities, with the purpose of exerting influence'. I was intrigued ... (Student 1)

When explaining the purpose and benefits of participation, I introduced the United Nations Convention on the Rights of the Child (UNCRC), where the child's right to participation is identified as a fundamental right in all situations where adults are making decisions that affect them (1989, Article 12). Article 42 specifically spells out the responsibility governments have in ensuring that every child and adult is informed about the Convention.

However the students in the class did not have any knowledge or understanding of the UNCRC. Although the United Kingdom ratified the Convention in 1991, no legislation has been passed which requires schools to teach it, nor requires teachers to implement it. Consequently, it is common for school leavers to enter university with little knowledge, experience or confidence in actively participating in decisions concerning the content and process of their educational experience. The students registered for this module were all in this position.

A major challenge, then, was how to introduce the idea that I wanted the students to engage in the process of planning the curriculum for the whole module, with me facilitating the process but not determining it. This created a strong response from the outset.

> I was surprised and a little worried by the approach to the first lecture. To be asked what we might like to learn and to be presented with a number of options was so alien to my previous experiences of academic education .... My primary concerns were ones of responsibility. If I were to agree how I would like to learn and how I would like to be assessed, all excuses for failure and non-engagement would be removed and I would truly be responsible for my own learning and outcomes. This did raise some concerns in me as it is harder for me, and others, to undertake a deep approach to learning when nervous or anxious (Entwhistle, 1996). (Student 2)

There was an immediate fear that it would have adverse consequences for their assessment.

> On learning that there was no set course outline for this module, I was rather taken aback, ... At first I was a bit worried about how we were all going to be assessed throughout the course, if we didn't yet know what we were going to be doing ... I might find myself not fully engaging in the course, and that this would lead to me not achieving my best. As a result, I would not achieve a good grade at the end of the year. I also felt the course would not really go anywhere if there was no direction to follow on from each lesson. (Student 3)

The first session was as demanding for me as it was for the students. I was aware of their uncertainty, and had to resist the pressure to take control of the decision-making. Instead I tried to communicate to them what I was hoping to achieve. I stated that in working with them, I would be researching my own practice, and would be encouraging them to do the same. I introduced the values of respect, participation and mutual empowerment that underpinned my educational work with students, and proposed that, although I would support them as much as they required, I would like them to accept the challenge of creating their own curriculum.

In terms of a knowledge base, and in addition to exploring the meaning and legislative background to active participation, I briefly introduced experiential learning theory (Kolb, 1984), and the idea of reflective practice (Bolton, 2005; Moon, 1999).

By the end of the first session, it felt as though the students, though rather bemused, were willing to experiment in creating their own educational experience.

> The first session with the tutor was a revelation, the most startling part was her honesty .... This was an exciting yet daunting prospect. In my educational career it has been the norm to be told what we are to learn and how we are to learn it, rather than create a course ourselves. However the thought also filled me with apprehension; would I, left to my own devices, push myself academically as hard as I would have to work on a proscribed course? (Student 4)

23.4.3. *Planning the Curriculum*

During the next two sessions the students, in consultation with myself, discussed their aim and objectives, and established them as listed in Table 23.2.

The aim was a formal wording of what I was proposing they do, and which they accepted. When considering learning objectives, the students felt that these may differ for each of them, so each should take responsibility for identifying their own, then be accountable to the others in the group for how they were met.

> Despite my initial concerns, I thought it was a really good idea when it was decided that we would create our own module and decide what we each wanted to learn, rather than just being told what we had to learn. I felt that it would be a really good way of engaging everyone in the lessons if they were learning about something they were interested in. I was rather excited about this ... (Student 3)

Having been given an introduction to the purpose and process of reflection, they decided that one form of assessment should be a reflective account of their experience of the module, to be submitted at the end of the year, and in the meantime, they should keep a reflective diary that charted their experience of the course, and of their placement.

As the module title was 'Active Participation in Learning', it was agreed that at all stages of the module, we should ensure the principle of active participation was encouraged. There was extended discussion as to how to achieve this in a way that

Table 23.2: Aim and objectives for active learning module agreed between students and lecturer

---

Active Participation in Learning

Aim

For students to participate in the planning, implementation and evaluation of their own learning, in their second year module 'Active Participation in Learning'

Objectives

In collaboration/consultation with their tutor and other members of the group, each student to:

1. Identify their own learning objectives.
2. Identify and arrange a placement which will enable them to meet their learning objectives.
3. Write a reflective diary which will enable them to record their experience on the module and explore what helps and hinders them achieving their learning objectives.
4. Research articles and books that help them understand more about active participation in learning, both in relation to themselves as learners and to the engagement of others within a professional context.
5. Agree with the group appropriate forms of assessment.

---

shared the responsibility for enabling it to happen, rather than it being seen as my responsibility.

Finally one of the group members proposed that each student could take turns in planning and running a teaching session. Rather than be given a subject to teach, they would identify this for themselves. I suggested that they could be imaginative in their thinking about what the focus might be. They could take the opportunity to research a subject that was of educational interest to them, then plan a session where they would 'communicate' (i.e. teach) what they had learned to the others in the group. This 'communicating' was to be done with the active participation of the learners, in the same way that I was encouraging their active participation.

Again, this resulted in a mixture of emotions.

> It was decided amongst the group that we would each come up with a plan of our lesson, based on something that we are interested in and present it to the rest of the class. I was excited by this as I thought it was an excellent idea and the perfect opportunity for all of us to engage and take control of our own learning. However the only issue I had about choosing to run my own session, was I felt there was a greater pressure to deliver an interesting and successful lesson about something I was interested in, and that I had no-one else to blame but myself if it didn't turn out as I first planned. (Student 5)

Active Participation in Learning   411

As these sessions would form a central element of the module, it was agreed that the second form of assessment would consist of an evaluation of how they were planned and run. The criteria by which students would be assessed provoked considerable discussion, and resulted in them determining the following criteria:

- Quality of session plan
- Level of active participation in session
- Extent to which identified aims of session were achieved
- Extent to which the individualised learning outcomes of the student (leading the session) were achieved
- General comments with a grade.

They also expressed a wish to contribute to the assessment process. One way of doing this was to give each other feedback as the module progressed, through discussions on Moodle (the virtual learning environment used by the university). The students were used to using Moodle as a means of gaining course information and reading lists and various other supportive learning materials from their subject tutors. However using it as a forum for dialogue and for peer formative assessment was new to them.

> I decided to research formative assessment through active participation in order to get an idea of the processes ahead of us and what I could gain from this type of course. I felt this approach had the benefit of creating a feeling of ownership within the group, motivating us to make the module succeed. (Student 4)

The course specification did not allow for summative peer assessment. However it was agreed that the students would each complete an assessment sheet after each student's session and submit it to me; I would take their comments and grades into consideration when compiling my own.

During these early sessions I was also continuing to provide knowledge on experiential learning and reflective practice, in order to provide a theoretical basis for the work they were committing themselves to, and to give them options for writing and structuring their reflective diary. The students used this to reflect on their own practice.

> Whilst planning the curriculum and applying for placements, we were also having lectures on reflective learning. The most enlightening session for me was the lecture on Kolb's learning cycle. The model proposes the idea that we can engage in a continual learning process that adapts to the situations we find ourselves in. Kolb suggests that we must move through four stages in order to learn from our experiences:
>
> - Concrete experience — doing/having the experience
> - Reflective observation — reviewing/reflecting on the experience

- Abstract conceptualisation — concluding/learning from that experience
- Active experimentation — planning/trying out what you have learnt (Kolb, 1984)

> I was surprised to find that I was repeatedly only achieving stages one and two of the cycle, having the experience and looking back at it. I have always been an analytical person but it seemed that there was room to improve my thinking by researching areas both in my studies and wider personal experiences and testing the new knowledge in practice. I decided whilst on the course I would not only reflect on what I had found challenging but research theories and models of education which would allow me to overcome those challenges. (Student 4)

Although initially a number of students were not sure how to write a reflective journal, their confidence in this grew as the module progressed.

> A key part of the knowledge that our tutor shared with us was reflective practice, as this was seen to be an important part of understanding the learning process we were to actively engage in. Moon's description of the reflective learning process is 'a set of abilities and skills, to indicate the taking of a critical stance, an orientation to problem solving or state of mind' (Moon, 1999, p. 63). Moon feels that a large part of the overall learning process takes place when the learner begins to organise and clarify what they feel they have learned (Moon, 1999, p. 15). The learning journal that we each completed following every session was a successful way of helping us clarify and understand what knowledge, skills or new concepts we had learned during each session.

23.4.4. *Student-led Sessions*

The range and creativity of the sessions planned and run by the students were impressive. Although after the initial apprehension and uncertainty, they seemed happy to commit themselves to planning a session, I had no idea what would emerge. I had to work hard to 'trust the process'; to trust that if I stayed true to the values of respect, participation and mutual empowerment, and responded to the students' requests for help as and when they arose, the outcome would be worthwhile. My own reflective journaling shows that there was at times a strong temptation to take control, but as I wrote, I realised that the temptation was more about creating security for myself, rather than responding to what the students were now needing. They were flourishing with the freedom. The challenge for me was to provide a structure sufficiently stable for them to feel supported and able to ask for help and information as they required, but sufficiently flexible to encourage them to develop their ideas as creatively and imaginatively as they were able.

The outcome was a series of interactive sessions which were diverse in nature, where the students learned a considerable amount, developed good relationships with each other and engaged the active participation of everyone in the group, including myself as an equal group member.

Their own reflections communicated their aims, and what the experience had meant to them, the following being just one example:

> To demonstrate to the group how children learn through creative play and the benefits this has for their learning, I decided to ask the group to engage in a creative activity using play dough and other art materials, as well as creative writing which encouraged them to use their own imaginative skills. I also wanted to give them ideas about how the curriculum can be incorporated within creative play. Duffy (1998) believes that 'creativity and imagination are part of the process of learning across all curriculum areas' and that 'creative play contributes to children's development in all areas of learning'.
>
> I was eager to see how well my session would go and if the group members could relate it to their own education and tell us if creative play and development had helped with their learning. They firstly had to work on their own with the playdough, or use the paints, to create a model or picture. They then had to work together in pairs, and come up with a short play, poem or story that would explain what the playdough models or artwork meant for them, and to present it to the rest of the group.
>
> Creative play is cross-curricular and can link subjects together, as my activity demonstrated. For examples I was combining artistic creativity with English. A good example of this was how C and H combined C's creative skills in English which she used to write a rhyming poem, with H's playdough model-making. Together they enacted a play using his playdough models as 'puppets', and her poem for the script. H was particularly pleased with the outcome, as he had been unaware he even had these skills, as he had not been encouraged to do anything creative at school. (Student 3)

The task encouraged the class to work together and develop their team and social skills. At the end of the session I asked the class if creative play had impacted on their own learning and education, and if they thought it had been beneficial. This allowed the class to reflect upon their own learning, and to think about how their creativity and participation at school could have been improved.

The students seemed to take on a different persona when stepping into the role of presenter. The impact could be transformative both for the presenter himself/herself, as well as for the other group members. One young man had been very quiet at the beginning of the module, and contributed rather less than the others at the initial planning stage. However, he introduced his session by bringing out a guitar, and singing some very energetic heavy metal rock music, which he had composed himself. His session was an exploration of the role that music plays in a wide range of social and cultural settings — such as dolphin music used by pregnant women for relaxation, and gospel music as a means of expressing religious passion and inspiration. He grounded his choice of subject in his own story:

> I suffer from bipolar disorder, and as a result have had a lot of trouble in the past controlling my moods. Because of this, my life is made difficult as people who do not understand my disorder make assumptions about me and assume that I am being simply antisocial .... I wanted to show the class that bipolar disorder is something that does not mean I cannot have normal social interactions, and with understanding, is not something that needs to have such a large impact on my life. I also wanted to show how the genre of heavy metal has helped me with channelling my moods into something productive. As a result I based my presentation on what has helped me, as the music itself is a release and how creating it myself has given me something to channel my energy into. In reflecting on this experience, I think it worked well because it perhaps gave the class a different perspective on me, and showed them a side of me that they had not seen before. I think it also worked well, because it allowed them to see how much music can help individuals, and because I used examples of other people and other situations where music is used for specific purposes, I think the point came across well. (Student 6)

Participating in sessions such as these had several outcomes.

> I think one of the main benefits in us each having our choice of what we wanted to learn and communicate to others, was that it really opened my eyes to issues I might not otherwise have become aware of .... It has helped me see things from other people's perspectives, and increase my knowledge and interest in other areas of education. Hutchings (2009, p.142) states that 'learning is an intensely personal activity ... it seldom happens in isolation and is influenced by whom we learn with and the place where we learn'. (Student 8)

The feelings, thoughts, experiences and reflections that the students had throughout the year were collated in their reflective accounts presented for final assessment.

23.4.5.   *Final Reflections*

In their evaluation of the module, the students provided considerable evidence that creating their own educational experience, and reflecting on it, had personally changed them. It had given them knowledge about themselves.

The Active Participation in Learning module has been a different learning experience from those I am used to. I found the emphasis on taking responsibility for my learning both worrying and liberating. The initial concern at the lack of excuses available to me should I fail was soon replaced by a feeling of enthusiasm about learning about myself and how I can best apply myself in order to achieve as highly as possible. I found that this module challenged me to take responsibility for my learning in a manner which the other more traditional subjects have not allowed. I was initially dismissive of the learning journal, but as I tried to write more and explored the theory behind it I have found it a successful learning tool. The experience of keeping a journal has allowed me, for the first time, to be honest with myself in regard to how my behaviour affects other people. This self-honesty, and also the reinforced feeling of personal responsibility has transferred positively to the rest of my studies, and I feel that this module has enhanced my skills and increased the chance of me achieving a good degree. (Student 2)

It had also developed their confidence.

From my own experiences of this module, I would definitely say that actively participating in your own learning raises self-esteem, self-motivation and confidence as the learner sets challenges for themselves and overcomes them. (Student 7)

They appreciated the value of the relationships that developed in the process of working together.

I feel that the success of the course was due to the engagement in all sessions by all students and the tutor. I felt that this led to the development of trust within the group as we evolved into a 'community of practice' (Wenger, 2006), and that good relationships developed as a result of the learning we experienced through our mutual involvement in these activities. (Student 8)

They came to understand the purpose and value of reflective practice.

I found that reflecting on how well my lesson went after I had presented it to the rest of the group was extremely helpful for my learning. I thought about how I wanted my session to go and compared this to how I felt the session actually went. This boosted my confidence as I felt I had been successful in being able to plan and deliver my own session and that I had taken charge over my own learning and achieved my goals. The course has also taught me how to reflect on my own learning, and how important reflection is, rather than just talking about how to reflect. Teaching reflection is just as important as talking about reflection on our education. 'Teach people how to reflect, through the assignments given, and then demonstrate how the assignments had developed skills of reflective practice' (Russell, 2005, p. 201). (Student 5)

Finally, the students' views on what they felt should happen in other modules were influenced by their experience on this one, sometimes expressed strongly.

During discussions throughout the year, the notion that active partici-pation should be central to higher education was often raised. Many students shared their discontent about their other modules on their course, and said that many students did not participate in lectures. They often reported that this was disheartening and made the learning process rather dull. This was my experience of university. I believe that contributing in lectures and teaching sessions should be built into the assessment process, rather than just be a side line to it. This then would enable a balance to be struck between hearing about theory and learning what it means in practice.

The following comment summarised the conclusion reached by the whole group:

A benefit of creating our own course curriculum was that we were able to influence what we wanted to learn, and at a pace that was suitable for all our needs. From my experience of this module, I think that if universities want to encourage students to get involved in their own education, they need to input their ideas as to what they want out of the course and what they want to learn. I think that if this were allowed to happen, students will find their learning more relevant, and it will help strengthen the role they play as stakeholders. (Student 3)

23.5.   Concluding Comments

I had begun the module with the wish that 'students feel personally changed as a result of their engagement with the course I am teaching'. The actions and reflec-tions of the students provide evidence that this happened. At the end of the year they presented their experience of the module at a conference, *Students as Stakeholders,* organised by the Higher Education Academy. Their presentation received considerable acclaim, including a letter being sent from the organisers to the Vice-Chancellor of their university, praising the quality of their presentation.
  This delighted the students:

We were extremely pleased with the positive comments we received from other students and professionals about our presentation and its content. We were asked many questions, including how other students in other places could implement this 'active participation' approach in different subject areas, and we were able to say how we thought they should have more of a say in both the content and the assessment of whatever subject they were doing. (Student 5)

Undertaking this study has provided evidence that a participatory paradigm, with its underpinning principles of relationship and mutuality, offers a useful view of the world when considering how to encourage student engagement. Through staying true to these principles, and engaging in the values-based action–reflection cycles of a living theory methodology, my decisions were founded not on academic theories about what constitutes 'good teaching' but on what emerged out of the moment-by-moment process of the students, in dialogue with myself, agreeing how they could create their own educational experience in ways that were of maximum benefit to themselves.

In challenging the mind-set that leads to the 'subject–object' divide of conventional teaching in higher education, I was role-modelling a method of working with students that I suggest would merit further exploration. I was able to do so in this context, because the course specification was general enough to allow me considerable leeway. If this approach were to be adopted more widely, then courses would need to be planned and submitted for validation in a form that would give lecturers substantial scope to engage students in all aspects of curriculum development and implementation.

The feedback from the students in this case study suggests that such moves could be very worthwhile. There was general agreement that having an active role in the choice of their assessable work not only motivated them to work harder than they would normally have done but also gave them a sense of responsibility for achieving good results as they could not blame anyone else if they did not do well. Writing a reflective journal became a meaningful activity, not only because it gave them a new skill, but also because they had direct experience of how it enabled them to clarify and understand what they were learning.

Despite the evident success of the module for the students themselves, and the knowledge that has been gained about the value of approaching teaching and learning from a participatory world view, there are limitations in this case study. Most significantly, it does not explicitly address the socio-cultural context of the university in which the module took place. It would need a much larger study, and a commitment from staff and managers at all levels, to investigate whether a participatory paradigm could effectively inform processes that would lead to enhanced student involvement in creating their own educational experiences. Consequently this study omits an important dimension when considering what needs to happen to integrate student engagement into university practice when using this approach. The socio-cultural perspective 'highlights the need for institutions to consider not just the student support structures but also the institutions' culture, and the wider political and social debates impacting on student engagement' (Kahu, 2011, p. 7).

I acknowledge fully that for student engagement to be incorporated at an institutional level, these wider issues would need to be recognised and addressed. However, no matter how supportive the institutional environment, each individual teacher and lecturer will always have the challenge of working out how she or he can better relate to students in ways that encourage their active participation. This chapter is intended to provide evidence to support the theory that educators will be better equipped to achieve student engagement through committing themselves to a values-based action research approach to improving their practice, grounded in a participatory world view.

References

Bateson, G. (1979 *Mind and nature: A necessary unity*. New York, NY: Dutton.

Beard, C., & Wilson, J. (2006). *Experiential learning* (2nd ed.). London: Kogan Page.

Biggs, J. (1996). Enhancing teaching through constructive alignment. *Higher Education, 12*, 73–86.

Biggs, J., & Tang, C. (2007). *Teaching for quality learning at university*. Maidenhead, UK: Open University Press.

Bolton, G. (2005). *Reflective practice* (2nd ed.). London: Sage.

Boyer, E. L. (1990). *Scholarship reconsidered: Priorities of the professoriate*. Princeton, NJ: Princeton University Press.

Brockbank, A., & McGill, I. (2007). *Facilitating reflective learning in higher education*. Maidenhead, UK: Open University Press.

Buber, M. (1937). *I and thou*. Edinburgh: Clark.

Cook-Sather, A. (2006). Sound, presence, and power: Exploring 'student voice' in educational research and reform. *Curriculum Inquiry, 36*(4), 359–390.

Cowan, J. (2006). *On becoming an innovative university teacher* (2nd ed.). Maidenhead, UK: Open University Press.

Dewey, J. (1916). *Democracy and education*: New York: Macmillan.

Duffy, B. (1998). *Supporting creativity and imagination in the early years* (2nd ed.). London: YHT.

Entwhistle, N. (1996). Recent research on student learning and learning environment. In J. Tait & P. Knight (Eds.), *The management of the learning environment*. London: SEDA/Kogan Page.

Heron, J. (1996). *Co-operative inquiry*. London: Sage.

Heron, J. (1999). *The complete facilitators handbook*. London: Kogan Page.

Hoddinott, J. (2000). Biggs' constructive alignment: Evaluation of a pedagogical model applied to a web course. In J. Bourdeau & R. Heller (Eds.), *Proceedings of world conference on educational multimedia, hypermedia and telecommunications 2000* (pp. 1666–1667). AACE, Chesapeake, VA.

Hutchings, M. (2009). The ecology of learning. In J. Sharp, S. Ward & L. Hankin (Eds.), *Education studies: An issues-based approach* (2nd ed.). Exeter: Learning Matters.

Kahu, E. (2011). Framing student engagement in higher education. *Studies in Higher Education, 38*(5), 758–773.

Kemmis, S. (2010). What is to be done? The place of action research. *Educational Action Research, 18*(4), 417–27.

Kolb, D. (1984). *Experiential learning, experience as the source of learning and development.* NJ: Prentice-Hall.

Merleau-Ponty, M. (1962). *Phenomenology of perception.* London: Routledge & Kegan Paul.

Moon, J. (1999). *Reflection in learning and professional development.* London: Kogan Page.

Reason, P., & Bradbury, H. (Eds.). (2001). *Handbook of action research: Participative inquiry and practice.* London: Sage.

Reason, P., & Rowan, J. (1981). *Human inquiry: A sourcebook of new paradigm research.* Chichester: Wiley.

Russell, T. (2005). Can reflective practice be taught? *Reflective Practice, 6*(12), 199–204.

Savin-Baden, M. (2004). Understanding the impact of assessment on students in problem-based learning. *Innovations in Education and Teaching International, 41*(2), 221–233.

Schön, D. (1995). Knowing-in-action: The new scholarship requires a new epistemology. *Change,* (November/December), 27–34.

Skolimowski, H. (1994). *The participatory mind.* London: Arkana.

Tanner, L. N. (1991). The meaning of curriculum in Dewey's Laboratory School (1896–1904). *Journal of Curriculum Studies, 23*(2), 101–117.

Taylor, B. (2007). *Learning for tomorrow: Whole person learning.* Boston Spa: Oasis Press.

Taylor, C., & Robinson, C. (2009). Student voice: Theorising power and participation. *Pedagogy, Culture & Society, 17*(2), 161–175.

Treleaven, L. (2008). Integrating the development of graduate attributes through constructive alignment. *Journal of Marketing Education, 30*(2), 160–173.

Walsh, A. (2007). An exploration of Biggs' constructive alignment in the context of work-based learning. *Assessment & Evaluation in Higher Education, 32*(1), 79–87.

Wenger, E. (2006). *Communities of practice. A brief introduction.* Retrieved from http://www.ewenger.com/theory/. Accessed on 20 March 2013.

Chapter 24

Engaging Students for Professional Practice in Global Health

Manisha Nair and Emma Plugge

Abstract

This chapter examines an initiative at the University of Oxford to use near-peers (doctoral students) to develop a programme of teaching for MSc students. Near-peer teachers have a number of benefits for the teachers, the students and the learning environment. The doctoral students developing the curriculum in this initiative had graduated from the MSc Global Health Science and identified a 'gap' in the teaching of practical skills in this programme — skills important for their future careers as researchers or policy-makers.

The doctoral students were more than partners in this initiative: they led on the curriculum development and delivery. They defined what additional skills would enhance student employability in the field of global health and, drawing on their experience of the MSc, they determined that writing, oral presentation, advocacy and debating skills should be the core of a 'Practical Skills Training Programme' for MSc students. They themselves, as doctoral students, needed to develop teaching skills. Initial evaluation has suggested that all participating students valued the initiative and that the programme had achieved its goals of enhancing specific professional skills of doctoral and MSc students alike. It also produced several unintended benefits perceived to be important assets by employers, such as enhancing time-management skills. Doctoral students developed skills not only in teaching but also in organisation and leadership. The MSc students felt that despite the intensity and pressure, it was a worthwhile use of their time, enabling them to develop skills that they believed would be useful for their future careers.

The Student Engagement Handbook: Practice in Higher Education
Copyright © 2013 by Emerald Group Publishing Limited
All rights of reproduction in any form reserved
ISBN: 978-1-78190-423-7

24.1.   Introduction

> Embedding employability into the core of higher education will
> continue to be a key priority of Government, universities and colleges,
> and employers. This will bring both significant private and public
> benefit, demonstrating higher education's broader role in contributing
> to economic growth as well as its vital role in social and cultural
> development. (HEFCE, 2011)

The University of Oxford is a well-known institution, consistently ranked in the top
10 of universities worldwide (University of Oxford, 2013). The mission of the
University of Oxford is to achieve and sustain excellence in every area of its teaching
and research and although a research-driven university, it is also renowned for its
teaching excellence. There are over 22,000 students, 93% of whom are satisfied with
their course quality (University of Oxford, 2013). Within the Department of Public
Health in the University's Medical Sciences Division, the MSc in Global Health
Science is a 1-year, full-time course, which also achieves high levels of student satisfaction and has a reputation for high-quality teaching. The MSc aims to promote in-
depth understanding of global health issues by study of a range of disciplines in bio-
medical and social sciences. It provides a broad curriculum covering essential foundation material for those wanting to pursue a career in global health but also
offering students the opportunity to study across the spectrum of global health —
from lab-focused disciplines such as Vaccinology to the clinical content of Tropical
Medicine to the policy orientation of International Development.

Within the MSc, class sizes are small, with only about 25 students being admitted
each year. However there is considerable diversity within this small group; these students come from a variety of cultural, academic and professional backgrounds.
Evidence to date suggests that this is beneficial to the learning experience (Plugge &
Cole, 2011) and on graduation, many students secure jobs in research or professional practice in the field of global health. About 40% of students go on to study
at doctoral level and many secure places within the University of Oxford. This is
seen as a positive development by a course that seeks to nurture and prepare
researchers, many of whom will assume academic leadership positions in the future.

As part of the MSc's quality assurance mechanisms, feedback is sought from
both current and former students in a variety of ways. Current students are asked
to complete weekly online surveys throughout each term to identify both the positive elements of the course and also areas for improvement. Since the MSc's inception in 2005, a consistent theme of the course evaluation surveys has been students'
concerns about the apparent 'gap' in the teaching of practical skills in this MSc programme — skills important for their future careers as researchers or policy-makers.
This has been reinforced by feedback from the MSc alumni which has been sought
through email contact and telephone or Skype interviews. A key suggestion has
been to provide more opportunities for 'professional development'. The alumni felt
that while the MSc Global Health Science provided the required theoretical understanding of global health it did not engage in transition of 'knowledge to practice'.

This is unlikely to be an issue unique to this MSc, as other existing MSc programmes in the discipline of Public Health do not often provide the students with the flavour of practical applicability of the knowledge that they acquire through the existing curriculum. However, as a consistent feedback theme, it undoubtedly merited further consideration by those involved in developing the MSc.

While the Oxford MSc students wanted 'hands-on' experience in public health practice, the doctoral students in the Department of Public Health were voicing the need for teaching opportunities to enhance their teaching and learning experience for an academic career. It is not mandatory for the doctoral students to engage in teaching at the University of Oxford, so interested students have to pursue teaching opportunities for themselves. Doctoral students' desire for teaching experience is not confined to the Department of Public Health; in the graduate students' meetings held University-wide, the doctoral students have expressed a need for more teaching opportunities and this has been articulated in reports circulated by the Oxford University Students' Union (OUSU) (OUSU, 2011). This need is being addressed within the Medical Sciences Division by the provision of a teaching skills development programme but also at a 'local level', within individual departments.

24.2.   Genesis of the Initiative

Early in 2012, the Higher Education Academy of the United Kingdom released a call for applications to join the 'Students as Partners' Change Programme. The aim of this programme was to help higher education institutions to

> develop their capacity to involve students in institutional change more rigorously, across areas including curriculum design; quality assurance and enhancement; student participation in institutional decision making; student transition, progression and achievement'. (HEA, 2012)

One of the course directors saw this call and forwarded this to her co-director and two doctoral students who were involved in delivering occasional teaching sessions to MSc students. She suggested they meet to discuss the possibility of responding to the call. The initial meeting was very productive. Although facilitated by a member of staff, the students were the main contributors and by the end of the meeting, the group had reached agreement on the content of a draft proposal and this document reflected the ideas and thoughts of the students rather than the staff. Furthermore they formed a 'curriculum development group', co-opting a further doctoral student with an interest in teaching onto the committee. The group wanted to submit a proposal in response to the HEA call; they saw participation in this change programme as an effective way of supporting and enhancing change within the department as well as addressing the expressed needs of the students.

The final successful submission outlined how the 'Practical Skills Training Programme' would be developed and delivered by doctoral students within the

Department of Public Health in order to enhance their own learning. The objective of the initiative was to improve both MSc and doctoral students' prospect of future employment by enhancing their professional skills through three key aspects of student learning experience:

- essential practical public health skills for the MSc students
- problem-based learning and critical thinking for the MSc students
- developing and enhancing teaching skills of the doctoral students.

The three doctoral students involved in the curriculum development group had all recently undertaken the MSc and therefore were ideally placed to develop and deliver the curriculum of the 'Practical Skills Training Programme'; they were familiar with the existing curriculum and were able to identify skills that had not been developed at MSc level although were necessary for their doctoral studies and future careers. The students led the discussion moderated by the course directors. Several ideas were discussed by the students based on their needs as well as the needs of other students documented in the evaluation surveys. Although the contents of the curriculum were decided during the initial planning meeting, these were developed over a period of 6 months and there were several follow-up meetings. Students led the process of developing the three strands of the curriculum, based on their expertise and interest. The follow-up meetings enabled the students to discuss the hurdles faced and the concerns that they had, and helped to enlist support from all members to address them. The factors that resulted in successful development of the curriculum in 6 months was dedication of time and effort from all members as well as a level playing field for the students. There was a lot of freedom to express ideas, to build them and also to criticise them constructively. The students identified mutual respect, freedom and encouragement as important in keeping up the momentum of the process of developing and implementing the 'Practical Skills Training Programme'.

24.3.   Skills Training Programmes for Graduate Students

As described above, the group involved in curriculum development considered two skills training programmes that have been successful in providing opportunities for postgraduate student professional development. The first was the 'Public Health in Practice' (PHIP) initiative developed and coordinated by an MSc Global Health Science alumna (McHardy, Ariana, & Plugge, 2011) and the second was the 'Leadership Programme' for Oxford University scholars of the Weidenfeld Scholarships and Leadership Programme (Institute for Strategic Dialogue). PHIP was introduced into the MSc Global Health Science in 2009–10 and was the idea of a doctoral student who had studied on the MSc. PHIP requires students to develop and implement a small public health initiative locally within a limited budget. The evaluation results in the first year of its implementation demonstrated that 82% of the MSc students agreed that PHIP provided them with relevant 'hands-on' expei ence for public health (McHardy et al., 2011). The curriculum development groi decided to build on the success of PHIP which would become part of the broad 'Practical Skills Training Programme'. This skills training programme would al include other complementary activities. The curriculum development group look at another successful on-going skills training programme for Oxford scholars, t Weidenfeld Scholarships and Leadership Programme of the Institute for Strate; Dialogue, London, the United Kingdom (Institute for Strategic Dialogue, 2013), further inform the inclusion of appropriate content.

The Weidenfeld Scholarship and Leadership Programme aims to 'cultivate i leaders of tomorrow' by providing fully funded scholarships to students fri the transition and emerging economies (Institute for Strategic Dialogue, 2013). 1 leadership programme is available to all Weidenfeld scholars at the University Oxford and comprises short courses for scholars to develop specific practical sk such as conflict management, negotiation, communication, presentation, debati advocacy, writing, policy analysis, organisation and management. It is seen an integral component of the scholarship programme. The Weidenfeld scho over the years have benefitted considerably from these activities in develop their leadership potential. One of doctoral students participating in the curricul development group was a Weidenfeld doctoral scholar and she was able to in duce the ideas to the curriculum development group for consideration. The curr lum development group selected and adapted four activities from the Weiden programme — presentation, debating, advocacy and writing — all perceived tc relevant to the development of the students 'employability' in the field of gl health.

24.4.   The Concept of 'Employability'

Employability is more than a set of skills. Yorke and Knight (2004) defined it set of achievements — skills, understandings and personal attributes — that r graduates more likely to gain employment and be successful in their chosen occ tions, which benefits themselves, the workforce, the community and the econc It is therefore important to note that the curriculum development group dic see this programme as the only means to enhance students' employability; it simply one innovative and creative way of doing so and would comple other areas of their learning at post-graduate level. Furthermore, it has been i that there is considerable value in 'empowering' future researchers to take cc of their professional development; this is something that will help them as become 'lifelong learners' and independent, autonomous professionals (Metca Gray, 2005).

The doctoral students and MSc alumni themselves defined the employa skills that were lacking in the MSc. Many students who enrol in the MSc gramme have prior work-experience, often in testing settings such as healt delivery in low or middle income countries. They are thus aware of the work place challenges and the skills needed to overcome them. Through the MSc course the students aim to develop their knowledge in global health–related issues and enhance their employability skills to complement their work experiences. While much was achieved in terms of gaining knowledge, the doctoral students/alumni felt that there were not many opportunities to develop important practical skills. They felt that adding a 'skills training' component to the curriculum would better fulfil their expectations and increase the impact of the MSc programme. The MSc alumni were well placed to assess their needs and identify the skills that they thought would be most valuable. The skills that they identified were broadly in line with those identified for the wider workplace (UKCES, 2009). There is a broad consensus about the attributes that employers expect to find in graduate recruits and these include working in a team, good oral communication, communication in writing for varied purposes/audiences and planning, coordinating and organising ability (Pedagogy for Employability Group, 2006). In addition, the doctoral students wanted to develop teaching skills which they perceived to be valuable for their future employment and beyond. Their perceived development needs echoed the findings of the *Roberts' Report* (2002). Over 10 years ago, in his influential report on the supply of people with science, technology, engineering and mathematic skills, Sir Gareth Roberts (2002) highlighted the importance of strengthening training in transferable skills and noted that while doctoral study prepared students for research, it often did not prepare students for other aspects of academic professional life, such as teaching.

Thus, the 'Practical Skills Training Programme' was developed by students in partnership with academic staff in response to perceived student needs. It was supported by a national initiative run by the Higher Education Academy and informed by the literature on both employability and student engagement.

24.5. Delivery of the Skills Training Programme

The goal of this initiative was to provide opportunities to both the MSc and the doctoral students for the development of skills relevant to their future careers. As already noted, many doctoral students had recently graduated from the MSc and were ideally placed to develop the curriculum of the 'Practical Skills Training Programme' as they were familiar with the existing curriculum and were able to identify skills 'gaps'. They themselves wanted to gain teaching skills. Considering that educational research supports the use of 'near-peers', the curriculum development group decided to pursue peer-tutoring as an effective and efficient means for delivering the 'Practical Skills Training Programme'. The three doctoral students in the curriculum development group took the lead for each of the three strands of the initiative. They were responsible for working with the MSc and other doctoral students to ensure the effective delivery of their strand. They were accountable to the group and provided progress reports at monthly meetings.

Peer-tutoring is defined as 'people from similar social groupings who are not professional teachers, helping each other to learn and learning themselves by teaching' (Topping, 1996). It is suggested that while 'peer-tutoring' has advantages for the tutee in terms of participatory learning, open discussions and lower anxiety, it provides an opportunity to the 'peer-tutors' to gauge their existing knowledge and skills and enhance their cognitive processes of organisation, management and delivery of the curriculum (Topping, 1996). Thus, developing and delivering the 'Practical Skills Training Programme' by 'peer-tutors', in this case the near-peers of the MSc students, that is, the doctoral students, would potentially result in gains for both the tutors and the tutees. The evidence suggested that while delivering the initiative to enhance the practical skills of the MSc students, the doctoral students would themselves have the opportunity to improve their teaching skills and to learn new skills in the process.

As previously noted, the curriculum development group examined the existing PHIP sessions (McHardy et al., 2011) more closely to understand the feasibility and benefits of 'peer-tutoring'. The success of this session in three cohorts since 2009–10 clearly demonstrated the benefits to the MSc students in terms of developing practical skills, the feasibility of delivery by peer-tutors and teaching opportunities for the doctoral students (the peer-tutors). It also suggested that curriculum delivery through doctoral students is sustainable considering that the coordination of PHIP was smoothly handed-over to a first year doctoral student (also an MSc alumni) by the out-going doctoral student. This provided some ground level evidence that doctoral student tutors would be suitable to deliver the 'Practical Skills Training programme' to the MSc Global Health Science students while enhancing their own teaching skills. Therefore, the implementation of the initiative was opened to all doctoral students who were the peer-tutors in the programme. However, we stipulated that all interested doctoral students must have completed two basic teaching skills training courses run by the Medical Sciences Division of the University, totalling three days of training.

24.6.   Alignment with the Existing Curriculum

Having decided on the key components of the 'Practical Skills Training Programme' and its delivery, it was important to align the planned activities with the existing MSc Global Health Science curriculum. This was again based on experience of the doctoral students who were leading on curriculum design and who had experienced the intensity of the MSc programme. The doctoral students knew that 'work-load' could be a potential hurdle to implementing the 'Practical Skills Training Programme' — they understood the pressures the MSc students were under. Although the skills programme was designed to cater for important educational needs of the MSc and the doctoral students, the MSc students would need to spend considerable time away from their normal course work. The MSc alumni (doctoral students) realised that this could be a disincentive, especially considering that the performance in the skills training programme would not add to the final exam results of the MSc. The question was whether the MSc students would be willing to trade-off time spent on reading and preparing for exams with developing 'practical skills'. What would convince them? The answers came from the doctoral students themselves (the MSc alumni).

Given that all activities would increase the workload of the students without being summatively assessed, the students involved in developing the curriculum suggested that it would be important to align the programme with the existing curriculum to motivate the MSc students to participate. This would help the students to see how the 'Practical Skills Training Programme' was relevant not just to their future but also to their immediate performance during the MSc course. The curriculum development group considered the modules taught in the course and the feedback from the external examiners. A general concern of the external examiners of this course has been lack of critical and analytical thinking among majority of the students. It was decided that all MSc students would participate in either an academic presentation seminar or a debate which would help them to gain these important professional skills by leading them through a process of critical and analytical thinking. The presentation, debating and advocacy skills training were intended to build the confidence of the MSc students on general public speaking and team-working, specific understanding of global health topics, critical thinking, constructing arguments and delivering them, and global health advocacy.

In addition to the presentation, debating and advocacy skills development, two activities were planned for the writing skills component — essay writing for the exams and academic writing for publication in scientific journals. The MSc students are a diverse group of students from across the world and they are not often familiar with the Oxford style of essay writing which can be daunting for many. This had been an issue raised by alumni at the MSc's 5 year review by the Medical Sciences Division. The course exams require students to write unseen essays in 45 minutes and to write a 10,000 word dissertation. A session on essay writing for the exams by MSc alumni who are also doctoral students would give them a chance to clarify their concerns, develop their skills and boost their confidence. The writing of the dissertation is well supported by senior academics within the department but students are usually 'left alone' to subsequently develop this into a paper for scientific publication. The academic writing session was planned to address this but it was also intended to confer one of the most essential academic skills to the MSc and the doctoral students.

As noted earlier, the MSc students would not be formally assessed on what they had gained from the skills training programme, but they were formatively assessed in a number of ways that were appropriate to the skills being developed. So, for example, those students developing their debating skills took part in a formal debate at the Oxford Union, one of the world's most prestigious debating societies (The Oxford Union Society, 2013). Students subsequently received individual feedback on their performance.

24.7. The Benefits of the Initiative

Having successfully developed and implemented the 'Practical Skills Training Programme', we concentrated on evaluating the initiative. During evaluation we focused particularly on the student experience: what had doctoral and MSc students gained from their involvement? Did the initiative achieve its stated outcomes? Were there additional, unanticipated benefits or challenges? In the course of the evaluation, we spoke to all doctoral students involved and a convenience sample of MSc students. Preliminary evaluation suggests that students not only gained those skills identified as key learning outcomes for the skills training programme but also developed other unanticipated skills such as flexibility, independent working, ability to work under pressure, and planning, coordination and organising abilities. Research suggests that these are all skills that employers expect to find in graduate recruits (Pedagogy for Employability Group, 2006). Indeed, students felt that they developed attributes beyond skills, identifying that the programme had had a positive impact on their confidence and self-esteem. It has been suggested that developing such qualities may be even more important for employability than specific skills (Pedagogy for Employability Group, 2006). One student articulated succinctly what he had gained:

> A big thank you to you all, [because] even the opportunity to stand in the Oxford Union was great. You are able to believe in yourself, able to feel more than just a little MSc student. It was difficult to argue on a topic that you don't agree with, but you have to stand for it, and at the end when you come up with evidence, you learn how to critically analyse and push the agenda to others. This is a skill in public health that you need. (MSc student)

As already noted, for the MSc students, this new initiative had not replaced anything within the existing curriculum but had simply been added in to an already busy schedule. Despite initial resistance, the MSc students were emphatic that their time had been well spent on the activities. They were able to identify some of the key skills and other benefits they gained. Students recognised that there were 'trade-offs' to be made; with limited time, they had to refocus their energies on preparing for the tasks demanded of the skills training programme. On balance, however, they felt that this was worthwhile.

> Yes, it was definitely worth it. Each student went through the grip, but at the end you feel really happy that you did the presentation. (MSc student)

It was important that the material they were engaging with in preparing for presentations or debates related to the core curriculum in order for them to see the short-term, exam-related benefits.

> The PHIP created opportunity to work in a team, also during the holidays. It brings you close to your classmates and the course curriculum, but at times there was stress within the team. (MSc student)

Indeed, the MSc students identified time management and team-working as key skills they developed. These skills might be regarded as key employability skills although time management is often not always seen as an important skill by students (Pedagogy for Employability Group, 2006) but will undoubtedly be an issue for these individuals entering a highly competitive workplace throughout their lives. Students were able to see the importance of team-working in their future careers. Team working skills were particularly relevant to employability as students were assigned to teams rather than being able to self-allocate to groups with their friends. This mirrored the workplace situation; as another student noted:

> Team working was a great experience. I learnt things about myself and about the frustrations of working with different people which you can sometimes have. (MSc student)

Furthermore, the students noted the longer term benefits, suggesting that what they had to do was, in some ways, similar to 'real-life' professional situations:

> Pressure of presenting in public made us devote more time [to the task], and yes, it definitely took time away from reading, but I learnt a lot from it. I learnt a whole topic from scratch within a limited time. It was worth it. What if my boss asks me to present in two days? We will have to do it. (MSc student)

The benefits did not solely accrue to the MSc students. The doctoral students also identified a number of skills which they had developed.

> It was a great experience for me to work with the MSc students. I was moved to see the efforts and the dedication they were putting towards making the most from the activities of the practical skills training programme. In the process of facilitating and tutoring the MSc students I enhanced my organisation and management skills. All doctoral students should have this opportunity. (Peer tutor)

> I participated at debating workshops and developed my skills on public speaking. I had the opportunity to talk about this initiative at the departmental graduate studies committee meeting with the course director and explain it to other senior members. At the beginning, most of the MSc students felt debating was a difficult skill to develop but we organised two successful debates within a short period of time and this helped to increased our confidence to take new challenges. (Peer tutor)

One doctoral student explained how she felt that her participation had had a very important impact on how 'employable' prospective employers would view her:

> I hope to pursue a career in academia ... in the US, and one of the major requirements for a successful job application is teaching experience. Traditionally, teaching experience has not been part of the DPhil at Oxford, and I had considered reading for a second PhD back in the US partly because of this limitation. However, the initiative provided a unique hands-on experience ... In talking to several US academics, this is akin to a US teaching assistant position, and it is one more reason that I may not need that second PhD after all.

The MSc students appreciated the input of their near-peers; they readily identified the benefits of peer-tutoring. The doctoral students were friendly and approachable and had a good understanding of their learning needs. This is in line with other research which has described the value of such 'cognitive congruence' (Lockspeiser, O'Sullivan, Teherani, & Muller, 2008). As one MSc student noted, 'Students felt that the doctoral student tutors were friendly, available and approachable.' Another student remarked:

> It was helpful to learn from people who have gone through this before. They [doctoral student tutors] were able to make the students see what you do and don't need to do.

24.8.   The Importance of Formative Assessment

From the outset, the curriculum development group acknowledged the risk of introducing a new component to the course that would be formatively not summatively assessed. We were concerned that the MSc students would be too exam focused and not engage fully in the programme if they knew that their performance would not contribute to their final marks. However, the group identified effective ways to tackle this. First, the programme used near-peers to convince the students of the value of the programme. These near-peers were particularly credible because of their status as alumni; they had personal experience of the course workload. Second, by linking the tasks, such as presentations, to the core curriculum, the students were simultaneously learning about the core content, although they were required to 'package' it in a different way. They were of course engaging with core material and this was likely to enhance their understanding of the material. It was also important to highlight to the MSc students that skills such as critical analysis would be necessary for their final exams and the skills training programme was likely to develop these further.

Formative assessment was undoubtedly the most appropriate way to assess the students. Not only would the assessment provide the students with useful feedback but the tasks set would be appropriate to the skills under development — the assessment was aligned with the stated learning outcomes (Biggs, 1999). The formative assessment used tasks that presented real, messy, 'in-the-wild' problems — 'authentic' tasks — which are of more relevance to future employment (Pedagogy for Employability Group, 2006). Thus, students developing their presentation skills were required to present and those working on their debating skills participated in a debate. As Yamnill and McLean (2001) asserted, 'training is useless if it cannot be translated into performance'. Furthermore such learning was 'active', engaging the students and not seeing them as 'passive recipients of curriculum material' (Pedagogy for Employability Group, 2006). On the existing evidence, the concerns of Knight and Yorke (2003), that formative assessment has a 'great potential for promoting attitudes required to develop employability that is often unfulfilled', were not realised here. The formative assessments proved to be useful, authentic tasks and were widely acknowledged by the students to have been helpful.

24.9.   Developing Employability Skills: An Issue in this Context?

The majority, 94%, of leavers from the University of Oxford are employed 6 months after graduating (University of Oxford, 2013). Therefore graduates are not likely to find it difficult to become employed. However, the concept of 'employability' is not simply about the ability to find employment; it relates more to personal skills and attributes that are lifelong, that enable the individual to pursue a successful and rewarding career. The doctoral students involved in this initiative were not concerned with the one-off event of finding a job but rather feeling adequately prepared to perform well in the workplace. In other words, they identified skills they felt important to develop for *employability* rather than *employment*. Moreover, while the skills they identified might be classed as 'transferable', they were not, as Bridges (1993) has suggested, seen as antithetical to knowledge and understanding, but as complementary and were integrated into the curriculum in a way that reflected this.

The initiative did not seek to undertake a thorough examination of what employability skills and attributes graduates in global health should develop and then develop a complete raft of skills training. Rather it was student-led: the students identified and defined what employability meant to them, identified the key skills for further development, constructed the curriculum to deliver these and then delivered them. They were fully engaged in the process from its genesis to its delivery and evaluation. This is in contrast to many 'student engagement' initiatives: as Trowler and Trowler (2010) note, 'Students are typically presented as the customers of engagement, rather than co-authors. Where students are involved in shaping the design and delivery of curriculum, it tends mostly to be indirectly through feedback surveys.' The level of engagement within the 'Practical Skills Training Programme' proved to be invaluable in developing the doctoral students' skills and ensuring the efficient and effective delivery of the programme. The doctoral students formed a true partnership with the academic staff. From the outset, the students led on key aspects of the initiative: they decided on the key learning outcomes for the MSc students and how these would most appropriately be delivered. They took responsibility for specific elements of the training programme and demonstrated leadership in their delivery. The two academic staff in the curriculum development group took a 'backseat' role, facilitating the initiative and monitoring its progress. Of course they would have had to be more active if the doctoral students had not delivered. However, the doctoral students 'owned' the initiative; they had been there at its inception, they had decided what was to be delivered and how, and they ensured this was carried through. Their genuine sense of ownership engendered a strong commitment to the training programme.

While there are many and varied potential positive outcomes from student engagement, it is particularly important for 'non-traditional' students, who might experience university culture as 'foreign, alienating or hostile' (Trowler, 2010). International students are considered to be non-traditional and therefore more likely to experience negative feelings about the institution (Anderson, Carmichael, Harper, & Huang, 2009). All doctoral students involved in this initiative were international, as were 21 out of the 22 MSc students. Thus the initiative may have provided additional value by engaging those who might be at risk of becoming alienated and disengaged. The University has recently published a report on the experience of International Students (International Students Teaching and Support Project Forum, 2012). It identifies a number of areas for development across the University. At a departmental level, public health does well in meeting the needs of its postgraduate international students and already delivers on many areas of good practice identified in the document. However, the report notes that international students at the University of Oxford can feel isolated and it will be worth exploring in more depth whether this initiative, with its emphasis on teamwork and working in partnership with staff, contributes to students' sense of 'belonging' at the University.

24.10. Have We Developed Employability?

The development of employability is multi-factorial and should be an on-going process. A simple initiative such as this will not of course have ensured the students involved have all the requisite skills and attributes. We acknowledge that any evaluation in the short-term will be limited (UKCES, 2009); we have been unable to demonstrate that students have actually become more employable. Atkins (1999) contested the notion that 'We Know How These Skills and Attributes Develop and Therefore Designing Them into the Learning Experience of Students Is Unproblematic' and we agree that it is not unproblematic. However, we believe that it is possible to tease out a number of positive aspects of this initiative, features suggestive of developing students' employability skills. These should be built on in the future and evaluations conducted in the longer term too, so that alumni can reflect on whether the skills developed have been of value in the workplace.

As noted previously, many students involved were international students. This has implications for the potential benefits, and also for the more immediate programme development. The evaluation identified a number of positive but unanticipated learning outcomes, for example time management skills, and it will be important that these are clearly stated in the future. 'Making the tacit explicit' (Pegg, Waldock, Hendy-Isaac, & Lawton, 2012) is even more important in a class where over 80% are from overseas where 'differently situated knowledge gives rise to exclusion rather than inclusion' (Trahar, 2010).

Fullan (2001) suggested, 'Educational change is technically simple and socially complex'. This small scale innovation within an existing course, developed and delivered by students, suggests that positive change need not be difficult. It is likely that student engagement has been one of the important features in ensuring this is so. Although the idea of responding to an HEA call was initiated by a member of staff, it was the doctoral students who identified what was needed in the MSc curriculum, how it might be delivered and were instrumental in its delivery. From the start, they took responsibility for clearly designated aspects of the delivery and, feeling a clear sense of ownership for the programme, ensured that it was indeed delivered effectively. Furthermore, as near-peers and course alumni, they had the necessary credibility to identify essential skills training and convince the MSc students of the programme's value. They were able to assuage the MSc students' fears about pressure of time; they had, after all, recent experience of the MSc themselves and were aware of the pressures. The MSc students saw the doctoral students as 'people who have gone through this before'. As outstanding students who were familiar to course staff, the doctoral students had little convincing to do in terms of the validity of their ideas or whether their ideas might be achieved. That there would be a small additional burden on staff seemed a small price to pay for an innovative and exciting new component to an MSc with a reputation for teaching excellence.

In his report, Professor Sir Gareth Roberts (2002) stated, 'The aim is to make postgraduate study attractive to able graduates and prepare them for creative and leadership roles in industry, academe and the public sector.' While the majority of the University of Oxford graduates do not struggle to find employment, this initiative has provided a small number of MSc and doctoral students with the opportunity to enhance their skills in leadership and beyond. Engaging students in the programme has undoubtedly made their experience of postgraduate study more attractive as well as more fruitful.

References

Anderson, G., Carmichael, K. Y., Harper, T. J., & Huang, T. (2009). International students at four-year institutions: Developmental needs, issues and strategies. In S. R. Harper & S. J. Quaye (Eds.), *Student engagement in higher education: Theoretical perspectives and practical approaches for diverse populations* (pp. 17–37). New York, NY: Routledge.

Atkins, M. J. (1999). Oven-ready and self-basting: Taking stock of employability skills. *Teaching in Higher Education, 4*(2), 267–280.

Biggs, J. (1999). *Teaching for quality learning at university*. Buckingham: SRHE and Open University Press.

Bridges, D. (1993). Transferable skills: A philosophical perspective. *Studies in Higher Education, 18*(1), 43–51.

Fullan, M. (2001). *The new meaning of educational change* (3rd ed.). London: Cassell.

Higher Education Academy. (2012). *Students as partners change programme*. Retrieved from http://www.heacademy.ac.uk/resources/detail/change/SAP_CP

Higher Education Funding Council for England. (2011). *Opportunity, choice and excellence in higher education*. Bristol: HEFCE. Retrieved from http://www.hefce.ac.uk/news/hefce/2011/strategy.htm

Institute for Strategic Dialogue. (2013). *The weidenfeld scholarships and leadership programme*. London: Institute for Strategic Dialogue. Retrieved from http://www.strategicdialogue.org/programmes/cultural-exchange/scholarships-and-leadership

International Students Teaching and Support Project Forum. (2012). *International students' teaching and support project report*. University of Oxford.

Knight, P., & Yorke, M. (2003). *Assessment, learning and employability*. London: Society for Research into Higher Education and Open University Press.

Lockspeiser, T., O'Sullivan, P., Teherani, A., & Muller, J. (2008). Understanding the experience of being taught by peers: The value of social and cognitive congruence. *Advances in Health Science Education, 13*, 361–372.

McHardy, K., Ariana, P., & Plugge, E. (2011). Public health in practice: Translating theory into action. *Medical Education, 45*, 1142–1142.

Metcalfe, J., & Gray, A. (2005). *Employability and doctoral research postgraduates*. Learning and Employability Series Two. New York, NY: ESECT and HEA.

Oxford University Student Union. (2011). *Survey of graduate student satisfaction 2010–11*. OUSU, University of Oxford.

Pedagogy for Employability Group. (2006). *Pedagogy for employability*. Learning and Employability Series One. New York, NY: ESECT and HEA.

Pegg, A., Waldock, J., Hendy-Isaac, S., & Lawton, R. (2012). *Pedagogy for employability — update document*. New York, NY: Higher Education Academy. Retrieved from http://www.heacademy.ac.uk/assets/documents/employability/pedagogy_for_employability_update_2012.pdf

Plugge, E., & Cole, D. (2011). Oxford graduates' perceptions of a global health master's degree: A case study. *Human Resources for Health, 21*(9), 26.

Roberts, G. (2002). *SET for success: The report of Sir Gareth Roberts' Review. The supply of people with science, technology, engineering and mathematical skills*. London: HM Treasury.

The Oxford Union Society. (2013). *The Oxford Union*. Retrieved from http://www.oxford-union.org/

Topping, K. J. (1996). The effectiveness of peer tutoring in further and higher education: A typology and review of the literature. *Higher Education, 32*, 321–345.

Trahar, S. M. (2010). Has everybody seen a swan? Stories from the internationalised classroom. In E. Jones (Ed.), *Internationalisation: The student experience* (pp. 143–154). London: Routledge.

Trowler, V. (2010). *Student engagement literature review*. Department of Educational Research, Lancaster University.

Trowler, V., & Trowler, P. (2010). *Student engagement evidence summary*. Department of Educational Research, University of Lancaster.

UK Commission for Employment and Skills. (2009). *The employability challenge*. UKCES. Retrieved from http://webarchive.nationalarchives.gov.uk/+/http://www.ukces.org.uk/pdf/8080-UKCES-Employability%20ChallengeFinal.pdf

University of Oxford. (2013). *Facts and figures*. Retrieved from http://www.ox.ac.uk/about_the_university/facts_and_figures/index.html#aoxford_international

Yamnill, S., & McLean, G. N. (2001). Theories supporting transfer of training. *Human Resource Development Quarterly, 12*(2), 195–208.

Yorke, M., & Knight, P. T. (2004). *Embedding employability into the curriculum*. Learning and Employability Series One. New York, NY: ESECT and HEA.

Chapter 25

Students as Digital Change Agents

Malcolm Ryan, Emma Franklin, Tanbir Galsinh, Dale Potter,
Jenny Wren, Mark Kerrigan, Antony Coombs and Simon Walker

Abstract

This chapter traces the embryology of students as change agents in relation to digital practices, including their experiences of operating in different disciplines and contexts. It outlines benefits, issues and challenges of employing students as digital change agents and proposes a model for implementing cultural change. Mini case studies include first-year students operating as 'e-champions' within a university module, the second considers the impact of student-led projects in evaluating and innovating technology provision in a business school and the third examines recruitment to a student-led interdisciplinary research group. The 'e-champions' reflect on their experiences of using Facebook at Wolverhampton and consider the impact of their role on peers and staff and on their own social and digital identities. Lessons learnt at Exeter reveal that institutions who embrace the passion, creativity and energy of their most talented students gain positive, tangible and lasting benefits. Reflecting on a novel recruitment process at Greenwich, the student research group were found to be enterprising and dynamic and the mini case study proposes a series of recommendations. Throughout this chapter the experiences and 'voice' of the students provide unique insights alongside practical guidance to those wishing to employ the concept of student digital change agents within their institution.

25.1. Introduction

The student experience and changing relationships between students, their institutions and their learning are at the heart of future thinking about the direction of higher education. The National Union of Students (NUS) (HEFCE, 2010)

The Student Engagement Handbook: Practice in Higher Education
Copyright © 2013 by Emerald Group Publishing Limited
All rights of reproduction in any form reserved
ISBN: 978-1-78190-423-7

recommends that 'All institutions should have an ICT[1] strategy ... and students should be actively engaged in the process of developing that strategy.'

Research into the student experience of learning with technology has resulted in a growing number of reports extolling the virtues of listening carefully to our learners and responding appropriately to what we 'hear' (Creanor, Trinder, Gowan, & Howells, 2006; HEFCE, 2010; JISC, 2008; Ryan, 2008; Sharpe, Benfield, Lessner, & DeCicco, 2005). It has become almost fashionable for academics and researchers to speak about the 'student voice' and how important it is to provide opportunities for students to tell us what they think about a whole range of topics related to their studies in higher education.

What we have witnessed in a very short space of time is an embryonic development from first listening, and hearing, that technology should be used to enhance learning (Creanor et al., 2006), to discovering that technology, in all its forms, is central to a student's life (Ryan, 2008). Evolving into an understanding that student-driven ICT is not just beneficial but often more likely to succeed than tutor-driven technology initiatives (JISC, 2008). This listening and responding has developed further into engaging with students as change agents. Within a digital age, this can be a powerful driver because the students of today are well-informed, understand the potential of the technologies they use and are creative in the ways that they think and work (QAA, 2010).

The following institutional case studies clearly illustrate and are a testament to the energy, enthusiasm and creativity that students bring to enhancing learning and teaching within an institution. They also illustrate a partnership approach, with authors of the chapter including both staff and students.

The first case study is of two first-year students at the University of Wolverhampton acting as digital change agents within a course module. They write from their own unique perspective of the experience and express what they feel they have gained and learnt from engagement with this project.

25.2. Case Study 1: E-Champions at Wolverhampton

We were approached as a class by our tutor, who asked whether anyone would be interested in taking on an 'e-champions' role for a term. (As it happened, we were the only two volunteers, but had more students shown an interest, there would have been a selection process.) As part of our role as e-champions, we would be responsible for creating and maintaining an online space for one of our modules and we were told that we would each be given a £100 Amazon voucher at the end of the project. The monetary incentive was certainly a factor in our decision to take on the work, but our main reasons for taking part were simply that we were keen to gain

---

[1]Information and Communication Technology.

the experience and we felt that this could really benefit a module such as ours, which at that time had rather poor communication between students and staff.

After our introductory meeting with the project leader, we decided to build our online space on social networking site Facebook, and there were several reasons for doing this. First, the majority of the students were already on Facebook and we felt that the university system (the virtual learning environment (VLE), the intranet) would not be quite as popular as it was not such a private space. Facebook is a free service and so we felt that it was a convenient platform (although roughly a quarter of the class did not use Facebook and chose not to create an account for the purposes of the group). We also found that because Facebook is quite a familiar setting for a lot of students, it was seen as a place where they could be open and honest. We made sure that we set up a closed group on Facebook (this means that members must be invited in order to view or add to the content) and we let the class know about it via the University e-mail system.

25.2.1. How We Started

We began by setting ground rules within the Facebook group. Our reasons for this were to provide a sense of structure and to minimise any unfair criticisms. It was also important to respect confidentiality, which we stressed to the members of the group, assuring them that no tutors or members of staff would be able to view their comments. After making our initial posts, we encouraged our peers to continue the conversations.

The group was mainly used to answer any queries from our classmates, such as assignment due dates, how to go about re-sitting, if necessary, and other administrative issues. We continuously maintained the online space, which proved fairly easy for us as Facebook is a platform which we use on a daily basis. Once the issues were raised, we then liaised with the tutors, giving only general information, and returned their comments to the students. This meant that problems could be resolved without the students' identities being known to the tutors, which was important in situations where the student might feel embarrassed about approaching them. One such example was a student who had missed many of the classes and wanted to know how to go about resuming the module, without potentially being reprimanded by the tutor. As fellow students, we could gently encourage this student to simply return to class, while offering our support.

25.2.2. The Benefits

We found that the online forum facilitated instant responses to queries and issues. Another benefit was that students became more involved in the module content. Although a lot of the forum was general chat, there were also a significant number of topical posts and links to websites which directly related to the module. We found that some students were a lot more forthcoming with their ideas and personal findings within the online space than they were in the classroom. This online discussion helped with formative assessment, as students were able to contribute ideas and debate the topics that would need to be discussed as part of the final assignment.

Not only did the group facilitate mediation between students and staff which enabled rich discussion outside of class, but it also, perhaps as a result, appeared to boost morale among our fellow students. Whether it was a result of the project we cannot be sure, but there was a marked increase in the overall attendance rate. Another valuable outcome of the project was the quality of feedback we managed to collect from students, who perhaps felt that they could speak more openly and honestly within an online, anonymous space — and may have felt more relaxed due to the setting of Facebook.

The benefits of the project were evident not only to the class as a whole but also to us as individuals. Due to our heavy involvement in the module, we were more motivated and felt that we did better than perhaps we would have, had we not been involved as e-champions. It also meant that we were invited to later present our experiences at a conference, where we were able to network with students and staff from other universities. This experience was hugely valuable to us, as we gained an insight into academic conferences, which is not common for first-year university students. We could not help but feel privileged to be in such a position and wondered whether there would have been more volunteers for the project, had these benefits been made clearer at the beginning.

25.2.3. *Unanticipated Outcomes*

There were many advantages to our taking part, but also outcomes that we had not expected. As part of the conference presentation, we were asked for our consent to be filmed for the purposes of the conference proceedings. We did not realise until months later that all of these videos would be uploaded to a popular, search-engine-based media-hosting website and were therefore easily accessible and could be found by searching for the speakers' names. While to our tutors this did not raise any concern, we felt, as first-year students, that for our names to be searchable and a video of our first academic presentations to be found alongside our personal social networking profiles, our digital identities were profoundly affected. For those whose careers have spanned from before the use of such media-hosting websites, a video of a polished conference presentation is no cause for alarm, but as young and inexperienced students we were not keen on our first attempts at public, academic speaking to be viewable by all of our friends, co-workers and potential future employers. Of course, we are not at all regretful of our participation in the conference, but perhaps this has shown us that to combine academia with social networking does not always have the desired effects.

Another unexpected outcome of the project was the range of attitudes towards the use of Facebook as a platform for academic discussion. Although it was well received by most in the class, there were a few who felt that this was not a suitable environment and openly disapproved of the project. Whether this was because they did not use Facebook at all, or because they had strict ideas about the purpose of social networking sites, was unclear, but our choice of platform certainly had mixed reviews and some students did not participate at all. We found that, in general, we received more positive responses from the younger students in our class, while our older peers did not seem so comfortable with the idea. Perhaps it was the proximity to their personal online spaces that caused them to hold back, despite our stressing that the group was 'closed' and therefore a safe place for discussion, without the need to be 'friends' on the site or see each other's personal Facebook profiles. Whatever the reasons, Facebook did not seem a natural choice for some students.

25.2.4. *Statistically Speaking*

At the time the project was conducted, Facebook had over 500 million active users worldwide, with the 18−24 demographic growing the fastest at the rate of 74 per cent in 1 year (Online Schools, 2011). Although, at that time, the 35+ demographic represented roughly 30 per cent of the user base, it was still clear that Facebook was a site for the younger generation, which was reflected in the wall posts of our group. Out of the nine pages of discussion in which our project had culminated, around eight of these pages were made up of the posts by the younger (18−24) students, with only a couple of the mature students taking part. With mature students making up between 15 and 20 per cent of our class, yet only contributing one-ninth of the posts, it is clear that the older (25+) generation was somewhat underrepresented within the group (Figure 25.1). Whether this was because they did not use Facebook already (as the statistics would suggest, with the majority of the user base aged 24 or below), or because they were not heavy internet users, we do not know,

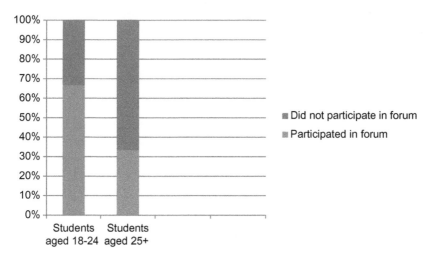

Figure 25.1:   The proportion of students from each age group who participated in the forum.

but it might be that to use a site such as Facebook for academic purposes is not particularly inclusive.

25.2.5. *Evaluation*

With all of these points in mind, we feel that the project was successful, but not without its drawbacks. It clearly facilitated useful discussion and encouraged students to be more active within the module outside of the classroom and created a support network for those who needed help and advice. Using the forum, we were able to collect high-quality feedback and, as a result, improve the communication between students and staff by acting as intermediaries. Our module enjoyed better attendance rates and a boost in class morale, which, we believe, had a direct effect on the work produced. It was hosted by a website that is free and simple to join — although some people chose not to join at all — and based in a setting that is familiar for many students. Although there was some objection to the use of Facebook, we still feel that it was a popular platform with most students. We also feel that the project was more successful than it might have been, had we chosen to use the university's internal systems, where all posts would have been viewable by members of staff with the students having had to make a conscious decision to visit, unlike Facebook, which is already being used by most for social networking purposes.

Overall, we would not hesitate to participate in such a project again in the future if the opportunity were to arise. We would highly recommend this experience to any student at any point in their university career; we realise now, looking back at the project, just how much we have gained from it. If we could offer any advice to those embarking on a similar project, it would be to ensure that if it is to be hosted on a social networking website, it would need to be kept separate from the social side of the site and it might be worth asking the students first which platform they would most like to use. We might also warn the students that, if their project is to culminate in a conference presentation, they may be filmed and their performance may well be shared with more people than they realise. We have only now come to see the long-term effects of using social networking sites for academic purposes, with our digital identities (and digital footprints) linked, for the foreseeable future, to our involvement in this academic project.

With all of that said, the benefits have gone far beyond the £100 voucher and we would gladly do the same again without the need for any monetary incentive. We hope that this practice will continue within our university and we would urge other universities to enable their students to have this experience too.

25.3. Case Study 2: Student as Change Agents at the University of Exeter

This second set of mini case studies from the University of Exeter provides examples of students as active drivers, co-creators and partners in intra-curricular activities.

They overview how student engagement is emerging, and is being encouraged for both individuals and within large groups. In particular, they highlight its impact on learning (the students' perspective), teaching (the academic perspective) and the university (the institutional perspective). Since 2008, more than 100 'Students as Change Agents' projects have occurred across the institution, involving over 2000 individuals. Research generated from student-led projects has provided students with evidence to support and, at times, challenge institutional practice, and overall engagement is very high.

There appears to be something special about student engagement at Exeter with around 80 per cent of students active in student-organised extra-curricular academic, sports and social activities. Student demand for leadership and committee positions is higher than the opportunities that exist (Owen, 2011).

From the top of the organisation, through academic colleges and central professional services teams, there is a real institutional commitment to create 'management engagement with students that is real and meaningful' (*ibid.*). Two models encapsulate what we mean by student engagement at Exeter, an adaptation of a community engagement model by Owen (2011), and Dunne and Zandstra's (2009) model of integrating students into educational change. First, the community model maps levels of engagement in the extra-curricular student experience. The framework presents five categories of involvement, from students as bystanders to students as change agents (Figure 25.2).

Second, the Dunne and Zandstra (2009) model categorises the drivers of change, and differentiates between student voice and student action (Figure 25.3), which characterises the change agents' approach.

25.3.1. Students as Drivers of Technology Investment

The case studies presented here focus on three innovative uses of educational technologies at the module level in the business school. Students who enjoyed engaging

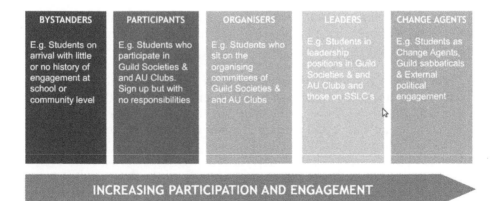

Figure 25.2:   Future of community model.

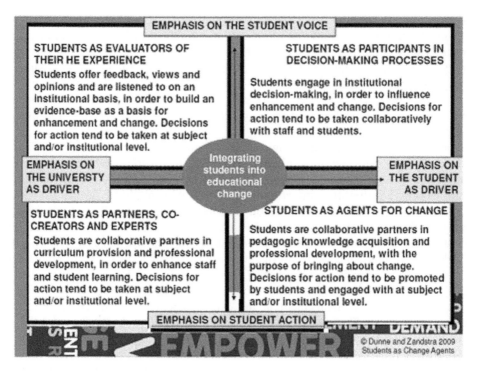

Figure 25.3:   Model of integrating students into educational change.

with audience response systems, podcasting and handheld video recorders wanted to be more involved in their use in the educational process. Two students on the Business School Committee that brings together student programme representatives, professional services and academic staff designed research that helped focus technology investment decisions. Sam Vaughan (third-year Business Economics and committee chairperson 2008–9) and Tim Lowe (first-year Economics & Finance) gathered 207 student views on pilot uses of educational technologies. This included video capture of lectures, use of handheld video cameras in tutorials and implementation of audience response handsets in large module lectures. University staff responses to the research included:

> The student had clearly thought through the issues, asked useful, searching questions — some of which I would never have thought of myself. The research was useful, in helping us to take forward the project, disseminating it and persuading other staff to think about using the technologies. (Juliette Stephenson, Senior Lecturer)

Key findings from the report show that students used video-recorded lectures to look over material that had troubled them in the lecture to revise, to help with writing up notes and to support the completion of assignments. The majority of students did not feel the availability of video-recorded lectures affected their attendance, and most wanted to see all lectures video-streamed across all subject areas. Staff and students both found the audience response system very useful. Students felt this voting system enhanced focus in lectures and appreciated the interactivity it allowed. Most students wanted to use the system in further lectures (Vaughan, Zandstra, & Dunne, 2009). As a consequence of this student-led research, decisions were taken by senior managers in the business school to expand the use of these technologies. Most notably, 3000 audience response handsets were purchased and distributed to students the following year, and this investment has continued with new intakes each year since.

Previously, students had felt that their input to this committee was somewhat limited. However, here it was clear that students played a key part in preparing information that influenced investment decision-making. This genuine partnership process significantly enhanced the understanding and appreciation of the issues and benefits of using technology from both student and university perspectives.

25.3.2. *Challenges in Student-Led Proposals for Podcasting Systems*

This second case describes how the realities and complexities of change management within a large university can sometimes be frustrating to students. Here, a proposal to introduce a system for podcasting lectures stalled in the face of difficulties at a variety of organisational levels. Henry Morris (second-year Economics) had worked within an entrepreneurial small business prior to university. Upon recommencing his studies, he had permission to record his lectures as a dyslexic student. Fellow students attending lectures alongside him became curious about these recordings and, sensing their value, asked for copies. Students could see that it was easily possible to share recordings.

A student-designed proposal was developed to initiate an audio recording system authorised by the institution. It was calculated that provision for 20 modules would require 48 GB of server space and investment in audio recorders of £600. Compared to the video recordings captured using an existing system, the proposed idea could deliver 80 per cent of that value at a significantly reduced cost. One student per module would be equipped with a handheld audio recorder. By arrangement with their lecturer, student 'technology champions' would record the lecture and upload the resulting sound file to accompany standard PowerPoint files on the University of Exeter's Virtual Learning Environment.

Unfortunately, the students involved, who were developing this idea to enhance their personal learning, had not considered the legal implications for the institution, or the personal backlash that would follow. Despite some staff appreciation of the positive learning and cost-benefit that this proposal could offer, there were many difficulties in bringing all university stakeholders together. Teaching staff were divided about whether they thought this was a good idea for students. In some cases, they were sensitive about intellectual property infringement and had concerns about the impact on student attendance. Business school and central Information

Technology (IT) services were challenged, it seemed, by the whole question of a potential explosion in digital data capture and how and where to deal with the issues raised.

From the student perspective, there was clear frustration that these relatively simple technologies could not be formally made available. It seemed this technically adept student was able to recognise and respond to demand within his immediate peer group and establish a small scale solution quickly and easily. The digital nature of this type of content and its ease of capture and sharing means that material like this is being shared among diligent students anyway, with or without staff permission.

This project highlighted that students with wide-reaching proposals require dedicated support at different levels of the university to navigate the challenging organisational and interdepartmental dynamics. Additionally, staff who champion such projects would benefit from clear routes to senior managers to ensure those with greatest potential to enhance student learning are suitably placed to support challenges.

25.3.3.   *Re-personalising Learning with Handheld Video Cameras*

This third case applies Owen's model to a large first-year module where skills acceleration is encouraged alongside traditional delivery methods and students act as organisers, leaders and change agents within this process. Owen's model had been presented at the University of Exeter's annual internal teaching and learning conference and had prompted a range of discussions about its intra-curricular application.

'Theory and Practice of Management' is a one semester, 15 credit module, with around 200 students per cohort. This is a core module for all first-year students taking management programmes and it is also open to students across the university as an optional choice.

Traditionally, it featured a blend of weekly lectures and tutorials based on assessed group work. Students' grades were heavily weighted towards a final individual examination. With student participation and attendance levels initially around 25 per cent, the student engagement model offered new ways to think about how a variety of Wright's roles could be embedded alongside a greater focus on academic skill development. One of these opportunities came with the introduction of handheld video cameras. Within each tutorial group, student 'video champions' became involved in the weekly organisation of the module in capturing and uploading group presentations. Listening to these student voices and engaging with them as co-creators is an illustration of the second model (Dunne & Zandstra, 2009; see Figure 25.3) of student engagement adopted at the University of Exeter. The discussions with these students to evaluate and develop the technical processes resulted in leaders and change agents emerging alongside further innovative teaching practices and uses of the technology.

Also, and more surprisingly, in terms of the student engagement model, the video champions' involvement quickly changed the majority of students from bystanders to active participants and tutorial attendance quickly rose to around 95 per cent. Many students (around 25 per cent) have now become active organisers within their subgroups, volunteering as 'video champions', transferring recordings and draft reports between groups. Others want to be more involved and have become learning champions, coaching other group members in aspects such as library skills, research and referencing skills, and international integration. This has resulted in lively and engaging tutorials that students want to attend — even though all tutorials are videoed and made available for students.

The students who become involved in the weekly organisation of tutorials attend briefing and review meetings with programme staff. They are also invited to meetings with staff from the university's education enhancement, and innovation and implementation, teams to evaluate this and other new learning technologies.

This increased student involvement has resulted in curriculum changes. Five additional tutorials have been added to the module covering speed building relationships, research and referencing skills, as well as a formative assessment and peer learning process.

25.3.4. *Conclusions and Recommendations*

Student engagement is clearly a big theme across the University of Exeter, with a strong desire to further embed the positive outputs achieved so far. Within the business school, these case studies demonstrate the quality of input students can bring, but also the need for strong project support. To achieve the greatest results, the value of roles which cross over and connect traditional job families and departments is also emphasised. This way, staff champions can act as bridges between students, academic departments and central services. Applying models to the intra- and extra-curricular learning processes have shown how skills development and enthusiasm for learning can be accelerated within core taught modules. It also generates its own momentum where skills continue to be developed within students' peer networks, as well as in later years of study and career pathways.

Case study students Tim and Henry comment that it offers unique and interesting experiences to bring to interviews and skills to build on in their professional lives. It is becoming clear that these skills are attractive to leading employers. Two students currently involved as change agents have just secured consultancy internships.

Most immediately and surprisingly, the impact on student engagement is profound. Anecdotally, engagement, levels of interaction and achievement continue to improve as reported by teaching and professional services colleagues as well as evidence of students maintaining contact through the 'change agents' process. With the right support, change agents initiatives offer benefits on multiple levels. For students, involvement develops individual skills in leadership, innovation and change management. For institutions, student action offers fresh approaches to problems and can become a strong driver of institutional responsiveness in an increasingly consumer style higher education environment. The 'intrapreneurial' skills emerging from this 'intra-curricular' development process seem to have great potential. These graduates are developing the skills to generate, incubate and gather support for new approaches and products, contributing to driving innovation within many large organisations.

25.4. Case Study 3: University of Greenwich

The final institutional case study explores the concept of a student-led interdisciplinary research group (IRG) at the University of Greenwich and the importance of matching the recruitment process to the intended outcomes and overall purpose of such an approach.

25.4.1. Background

Digital Literacies in Transition in Higher Education (DLinHE) is a 2-year project, one of 11 national projects funded by JISC[2] during 2011–13. At the heart of this project is a student-led IRG. The IRG comprises students (>10) across academic years from all campuses of the university. They are funded by studentships worth £1500 per academic year and supported by a student intern, who draws from his own experience and currency as a recent graduate. For this group to be successful it needed to comprise enterprising, dynamic and enthusiastic students. Therefore a novel recruitment process was created and deployed. In this case study, the rationale behind the IRG is described, along with the recruitment process and the students' experience of the recruitment process, followed with a series of recommendations should others wish to adapt it for their own purpose.

Since 2005 there has been a strong drive to incorporate the student voice into numerous educational processes (Creanor et al., 2006). Sixteen nationally funded projects, between 2005 and 2009, examined ways in which learners were using digital technologies and interacting with institutional infrastructure and resources. Quality Assurance processes supporting the involvement of learners were enshrined within the government's White Paper on 'Students at the Heart of the System' (BIS, 2011), with the University of Exeter's change agents initiative being used as an example of good practice. Many universities developed approaches to involve students to inform policy, champion change and communicate actions to the student cohorts, with a particular but not exclusive focus on digital technologies. Good examples include the universities of Westminster, Leeds Metropolitan and Edinburgh Napier, whose work on the student voice was highly effective, resulting in an increase in student satisfaction. In DLinHE the concern is not just with amplifying the student voice, nor simply with the student potential as change agents, but reconceptualising their role into change entrepreneurs within the overall context of helping the

---

[2]Joint Information Systems Committee.

Table 25.1: Categories of students within a project.

Student voice	Students as change agents	Students as change entrepreneurs
Students' opinion and ideas sought	Students engage and work closely on a particular project following guidance	Students actively engage in research around a problem within a particular project
Student incorporated into QA/QE processes	Students support staff and student development	Students develop and create evidence-informed resources to solve a particular problem
Students communicate actions to peers	Students publish their work both internally and externally	Student feed into and foster both internal and external networks
Students involved in external communication and dissemination	Students may be funded for their work	Students work across multiple disciplines, schools and institutions

institution to develop and enhance its digital practices. For the purpose of this project, this embryology is summarised in Table 25.1.[3]

Students were required to engage across the entire university, develop their own strategies for working and respond to a brief based on what they were given, as well as what they identified as necessary. This research-centric activity required students who were able to act entrepreneurially to engage with multiple stakeholders as well as deliver discrete outcomes.

25.4.2. Recruitment Process

For students to be successful as change entrepreneurs they need to have a diverse skill set as well as a high degree of intrinsic motivation, the ability to work autonomously and communicate not only with each other but also with unfamiliar external audiences as well as working as a dynamic member of a research team. Furthermore, to meet the demands of the project, the students needed to be able to work across disciplines and academic years. A novel recruitment process was developed and adopted that permitted students to exhibit their strengths while still

---

[3]Note that at the University of Exeter, for example, the change agents approach is more like the entrepreneurs approach described in this model — with student-led research and solution of problems being fundamental.

meeting the requirements of the role. It has previously been noted that traditional application/selection processes can influence the quality of the applicant as well as provide a limited view of their ability. Our process was designed to address these issues. Recruitment followed a three-staged process (Figure 25.4) whereby students were able to demonstrate their own strengths through a procedure that aligned their core knowledge and skills with their academic subject.

Each step of the process was designed to assess a different set of skills and attributes as shown in Table 25.2. To score each candidate and aid in the selection process, step one was worth 10 per cent of the final score, steps two and three were worth 45 per cent each. Finally, all aspects of the grading took place after step three to ensure that the assessors had no prior knowledge of the applicants or the work they produced.

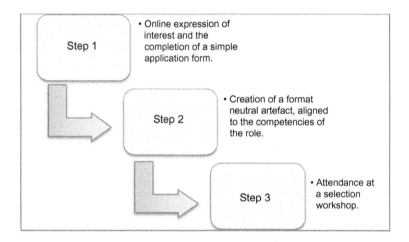

Figure 25.4:   Three steps of the IRG recruitment process.

Table 25.2: Alignment of attributes with the recruitment process.

Online application form	Format neutral artefact	Face-to-face workshop
Motivation to work on the project	Understanding of the project background	Work within a diverse team
Evidence of working within a group	Research new ideas and present in a stimulating and clear way	Ability to show initiative and different team-working skills
Understanding of working in a group	Contextualise the project in the higher education sector	Ability to work in a range of situations
Ability to meet deadlines	Ability to use digital tools	Creativity aligned to the project brief

25.4.2.1. Step one
Studentships of £1500, to be paid in blocks of £500 on the production of deliverables, were advertised using numerous internal professional and staff/student networks to encourage as many applications as possible. A quote from one of the students describing when they heard about the project:

> ... (our course leader) came into our classroom and told the whole class about this once in a life time opportunity. He told us about the project in small detail and said that it would be a scholarship that will be funded to us. Great on the CV and also money helps towards our degree shows.

Through the university's student 'Job Shop', advertisements were created and disseminated across undergraduate and postgraduate lists. It was important to ensure compliance with university employment regulations concerning the hiring of students and using this process of engagement ensured that we followed institutional policy. This step was delivered using an online form (Google) via a website advertising the scholarships and offering more information. Students were given up to 4 weeks to complete this activity.

25.4.2.2. Step two
Following the submission of step one, the students were asked to complete the second stage of the application. This activity involved the creation of an artefact, aligned to digital literacies, that could comprise any combination of text, sound and imagery, in response to a given brief. Example formats included (but were in no way limited to) posters, narrated presentations, videos, sound recordings, text documents, storyboards and comic strips. Importantly, the chosen format was not part of the selection criteria, so applications in any format were treated equally. When creating the brief for applicants, it was recognised that there was a difficult balance to be struck. On the one hand, offering too much guidance risked over-determining what applicants produced — it was important not to limit the imaginative nature of their responses or prejudice which format(s) they might choose, by conveying any messages that might imply a method or format that might provide a more successful outcome. On the other hand, providing too little guidance risked leaving applicants unsure of what was required from them. Here the concern was that applicants may have been encouraged to play safe and select more traditional formats and content. It is recognised within design communities that imaginative responses feed on the constraints of a situation as much as its freedoms. The artefact needed to address the following brief:

- Requires between 4 and 6 minutes to consume (read, view, listen, etc.)
- Demonstrates the ability to present ideas effectively and appropriately
- Exhibits research and independent thought aligned to the brief
- Equal to up to 6 hours of researching, planning and creating.

The applicants were also asked to note the following:

- Ideas are more import than technical expertise with media.
- If the format requires a physical presentation, they must contact the person in charge of applications.

25.4.2.3. Step three

In this final stage all students were asked to attend a selection workshop in which they engaged in a series of group tasks aligned to the core competencies described in

Table 25.3: Tasks used in the face-to-face workshop.

Task	Instructions
1. The Picture: 'Identify one word that is essential for digital literacies, related to people who are just about to start at university'	Lay the task out to the students Give each student a piece of paper for planning Ask students to compose a 30 second video about one aspect on DL that relates to their stakeholder. They can use props, move around the university and be creative Each student is to record their video clip using a FLIP camera or their smartphone, provided they can upload from this to the facilitator's computer All the videos should be transferred to the workstation computer. If time, they can be stitched together, else this will be completed by the project team Summary by the facilitator at the end of the workshop
2. The Video: 'produce a 30 second video clip exploring one issue for academic staff in relation to digital literacies'	Lay the task out to the students Give each student a piece of A4 paper Ask students to choose one word each that is essential for DL and linked to pre-university/ prospective students Each individual is to write this word on the paper and can illustrate or embellish it as they wish Each student is to compose a short paragraph on why that word is important Each student should have their photograph taken holding their paper All the photographs should be uploaded to the album and the short paragraph pasted into the description Summary by the facilitator at the end of the workshop

step two. Upon arrival students were given a badge and then asked to take a seat in the presentation area of the room. The students were given an introduction to the session and a description of the tasks that they were required to perform, as it was important the process is as transparent as possible to promote engagement as well as support participation. The students were subsequently divided into groups of approximately seven (alphabetically) and set two tasks. Each task required 40 minutes to complete, during which a facilitator took notes on the students. The prescribed tasks are described in Table 25.3.

Following the completion of the tasks, individual groups assembled and provided a summary. It was important to bring the session to a close and address any final questions, as well as to provide a timeframe for letting the applicants know the outcome. Importantly, the material produced by the students had value to the project and therefore all participants were asked to sign a permission slip permitting use of their material within the project. Using the information from all three steps, the assessors were then able to grade all of the applicants across all three steps and the successful students were informed. Interestingly, the majority of successful applicants cited their tutors as the route by which they heard about the roles, although this was unknown at the time of grading.

25.4.3. Student Feedback

Feedback from the students about the recruitment process was generally positive because it facilitated an open approach that recognised the diversity of ideas and cultural practices and allowed all participants to show their creativity irrespective of their background. Importantly, while students were able to apply using any chosen format, the underlying message had to be clear, which was essential for the role. Students were asked for their feedback in writing and some of their responses are shown in Table 25.4.

The students also commented on why they applied (Table 25.5).

Table 25.4: Student comments on the application process.

Aspect	Student feedback
Online application form	'... Having browsed through the project material online, my initial understanding of it was that it was going to investigate the level of digital literacies in students. I filled out the form with this view. It was while I was preparing the artefact that I got a wider view. I understood that there were more stake holders than students, i.e. employers and staff. I had also never thought about the concept of us living in a digital age and the need for people to have these literacies.' 'Compared to any other job or a new day at a work place, my experience and application to the IRG was quite different.'

Table 25.4: (*Continued*)

Aspect	Student feedback
Format neutral artefact	'… . In making the artefact [sic] I knew I had to communicate what I understood the project was and what I would bring to the group if I was chosen.' 'First thoughts were … "I think they want someone who is digitally literate and knows some programming" so I set out to impress.' 'I found the IRG recruitment process fairly reasonable and straightforward to an extent. However, it did take me a while to eventually find the format neutral artefact [sic] which described what was required.' '… I then received an email with written I had to produce a format-neutral artefact [sic] (my first reaction was … what the hell is that???).' '… I realised I could do basically everything I wanted, at first I was really happy with that because I like spending time thinking about new ideas and creative stuff, also that was giving me an escape from my not-perfect English ….'
Face-to-face workshop	'I found the workshops interesting. I have no problem working in groups so I was comfortable. As for the tasks, I remember the first one was about us filming (can't remember what the topics were). I enjoyed this task.' 'In the second task we had to draw and write one word that had something to do with digital literacy! I was feeling a little inadequate about the task. I am more creative with the mouse than with pen and paper.' 'The interesting bit was the discussions we had on the table.' '… This is where we got to know each other and showed how we worked in a team.' 'Finally, the day of the workshop arrived and I remembered being? [Q]uite nervous because I was not really sure of what we were going to do.' 'We split ourselves in 2 groups and we had to do two tasks: produce some videos and drawings, I found it challenging and interesting because the tutors were observing us on our teamwork skills but at the same time we were aware they were going to choose only some of us.' '… and I can just advise [sic] everyone to apply for next year (and if it will be possible I will apply again myself).'

Table 25.5: Comments on why students applied to the IRG.

Aspect	Student feedback
Reasons for applying	'Overall this process was quite fun because we interacted with everyone within the group and also it showed us that this project is fun and exciting. I know there is money at the end of this project but overall you get to help one another in gaining new experiences and skills. This is rewarding outcome and it shows great prospect.'
	'What motivated me to look into applying at the time was due to how convenient the skills and experiences I could gain from it and the fact that it related to my many different career paths that I have in consideration.'
	'... the magic words that made me stop were "a 1500 pound scholarship." That's the reason that made me click on the link and read more but it's definitely not the reason that made me apply.'

25.4.4. Recommendations

The process of recruiting students to the IRG using this process has been highly beneficial and the outputs produced by the group have been very useful, in that having a group of students with diverse skills, interests and experiences has significantly shaped the project as well as provided links and networks into both schools and the wider student population. The process can be intensive to manage, requiring constant communication but the investment is worth it when one considers all of the benefits.[4] There are some core messages for those who wish to use this technique.

1. Tap into as many networks as possible to advertise the studentships and do not underestimate personal recommendations from tutors.
2. Be clear and transparent on the grading and selection process and have defined criteria for staff.
3. Provide structured instructions for the format-neutral artefact, remembering that offering too much guidance risks over determining what applicants may produce and offering too little guidance risks leaving applicants unsure of what is required of them.
4. Design the outputs from each step carefully as they can be recycled and used as part of the bigger project.

---

[4]The IRG works as part of the Developing Digital Literacies Programme funded by JISC within the University of Greenwich. All resources can be accessed at http://www.DLinHE.com.

5. Students who are not selected should still be engaged with the project as they have completed a series of tasks and may have a lot to offer as change agents working in a different capacity.

In this way, it is possible to achieve an equitable and fair approach to selection, with the outcome of an effective group with members who are skilled, who understand their role and the necessary commitment, and who will be engaged with the research processes they will be undertaking. While the students in this group worked within the context of the development of digital literacies and practices at the university, it is proposed that the processes outlined above could be used for the recruitment and selection of students to any change agents initiative.

25.5. Implementing Cultural Change

When reflecting upon these case studies, one is immediately struck by the similarities and differences in approach adopted by these three universities and the diverse range of benefits to students, the curriculum and the institutions overall. In each case, the primary motivation for the adoption of any kind of 'student as change agents' initiative seems to be the belief that students are really at the heart of learning and teaching and rather than adopting a passive role as consumers, they need to be actively and dynamically engaged as co-creators and leaders. Institutions that encourage and promote creativity and innovative thinking among students, that challenge previously held notions of more traditional relationships between the teacher and the taught and that shift the locus of control from the former to the latter are seen to be hugely rewarding and mutually beneficial.

Summarising these benefits, one is aware of improved communication, engagement, attendance, retention and performance. Students feel more valued, they enhance their life skills, including digital literacies, and believe themselves to be more employable. Each of the contexts described in these cases provides opportunities for enhanced peer support and many of the ideas generated by student-led research have resulted in new and exciting ways of learning and teaching, culminating in curriculum review and renewal.

Lessons to be learnt include advising students to consider keeping their academic and personal virtual personas separate. It is important to note that once students appreciate the 'value' associated with being a change agent, they are often more than willing to undertake a wide range of tasks without financial remuneration. There are many ways of rewarding students, including accreditation of additional skills and recognition of achievements, both internally and through external bodies. However, change agents initiatives need to be supported strategically and scaffolded to ensure that students are not overwhelmed by the task, nor by the bureaucracy of the institution.

A number of models have been presented in the case studies that have been used to frame the operation of the initiative or seen as a lens through which to view

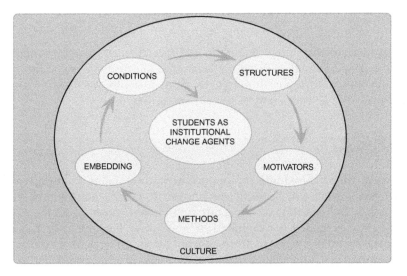

Figure 25.5:   A model for implementing cultural change.

the results of such engagement. Each has its merits, and institutions seeking to replicate the experiences presented here may wish to utilise or revise them to suit their own particular circumstances and reasons for implementing a change agents initiative.

The model in Figure 25.5 delineates recurring features of change agents and similar projects, as illustrated both by the above institutional case studies and a number of related projects operating across the United Kingdom between 2010 and 2013. Of particular note is that, despite the great variation in initiatives, the same factors are relevant, no matter the context or the activity that the students are undertaking. Although the model draws upon the specific contexts of students as change agents primarily with reference to technology enhanced learning, it may also be more broadly applicable to other transformational or cultural change initiatives.

If each of the five factors (conditions, structures, motivators, methods, embedding) are addressed — in any sequence — in the planning and execution of a student focused digital change agent project, then the proposed change is likely to be successful and sustainable.

25.5.1.   Conditions

The kinds of conditions that students discuss relate to a prevailing culture in which there has already been recognition of the existence of the 'student voice', a willingness to listen to what is being said and a desire to act upon what has been heard. To enable students to act as change agents, the institution must be willing to acknowledge them as partners and ensure that they are empowered to act, to take decisions and to make a difference.

25.5.2. *Structures*

In addition to a healthy culture willing to embrace change, structures need to be in place that will operationalise the ideas generated and provide ways and means to explore possibilities, to report findings, to input formally into institutional structures and give voice and meaning to student endeavour.

25.5.3. *Motivators*

In many cases simply providing the opportunity for students to engage in institutional problem-solving will be sufficient reward. It would, however, be misguided not to consider the possibility of incentivising change agent activities so that the time and energy expended is recognised in some way. This might be financial but could also be in other forms such as course credits for service to the university, enhanced supporting statements on exiting the university or goods and services in kind such as printer credits or discounts and vouchers for the bookshop.

25.5.4. *Methods*

Ways of engaging students as change agents will depend on current priorities and initiatives within an institution and may be driven, for example, by quality enhancement, graduate skills or student evaluation agendas. They may be at course, programme, department or institutional levels and include student representatives on policy and decision-making committees, mentors to managers or programme directors, leading student forums, undertaking action research or organising events.

25.5.5. *Embedding*

Institutional change should be a continuous process and student-driven initiatives will be one contributing aspect. The impact of engaging students as change agents needs to be evidenced and made visible to the whole organisation. The embedding of processes that enhance the institution's ability to engage students as agents of change is not an end in itself. It is a necessary pre-cursor to further sustainable changes and challenges that will need to be addressed.

25.5.5.1. Finally …
Whatever your reasons for wanting to consider employing a 'students as change agents' initiative at your institution, the authors of this chapter hope that you will have found some inspiration in the experiences they have recounted. However you decide to proceed, we hope you acknowledge from the outset that students are remarkable, can often surprise and will work with integrity, enthusiasm and ingenuity.

References

BIS. (2011). *Higher education: Students at the heart of the system.* Retrieved from https://www. gov.uk/government/uploads/system/uploads/attachment_data/file/32409/11-944-higher-education-students-at-heart-of-system.pdf

Creanor, L., Trinder, K., Gowan, D., & Howells, C. (2006). *LEX: The learner experience of e-learning.* JISC. Retrieved from http://www.jisc.ac.uk/uploaded_documents/LEX% 20Final%20Report_August06.pdf

Dunne E., & Zandstra R. (2009). *Students as agents of change.* Bristol: HEA/ESCALATE. Retrieved from http://extra.shu.ac.uk/irconference2009/docs/presentations/Roos_Zandstra_&_ Liz_Dunne.pdf

HEFCE. (2010). *Student perspectives on technology — demand, perceptions and training needs.* Retrieved from http://www.hefce.ac.uk/pubs/rdreports/2010/rd18_10/

JISC. (2008). *Great expectations of ICT: How higher education institutions are measuring up.* Retrieved from http://www.jisc.ac.uk/publications/publications/greatexpectations.aspx

Online Schools. (2011) *Are we obsessed with Facebook?* Retrieved from http://www.online schools.org/blog/facebook-obsession

Owen, D. (2011). *The University of Exeter student participation and engagement strategy.* Retrieved from http://as.exeter.ac.uk/media/level1/academicserviceswebsite/studentand staffdevelopment/educationenhancement/sacadigitalage/lt/B6_Opportunities_for_enhancing_ student_engagement_.pdf

QAA. (2010). *Rethinking the values of higher education — students as change agents?* Retrieved from http://www.qaa.ac.uk/students/studentengagement/studentschangeagents.pdf

Ryan, M. (2008). *The Student Experience of E-learning Laboratory (SEEL): Pathfinder project journey.* University of Greenwich, London. Retrieved from http://www.heacademy.ac. uk/assets/documents/learningandtech/completed/pathfinder/Journey_Reports/Greenwich. pdf

Sharpe, R., Benfield, G., Lessner, E., & DeCicco, E. (2005). *Scoping study for the pedagogy strand of the JISC e-learning programme.* JISC. Retrieved from http://www.jisc.ac.uk/ uploaded_documents/scoping per cent20study per cent20final per cent20report per cent20v4.1.doc

Vaughan, S., Zandstra, R., & Dunne, E. (2009). The University of Exeter Business School: Student engagement in lectures. Retrieved from http://escalate.ac.uk/downloads/8186.pdf

Chapter 26

Students and Staff Co-creating Curricula: An Example of Good Practice in Higher Education?

Catherine Bovill

Abstract

Over the last decade, there has been a resurgence of interest within the higher education sector in students becoming producers, partners and co-creators of their own learning (Bovill, Cook-Sather, & Felten, 2011; Little, 2011; Neary & Winn, 2009; Werder & Otis, 2010). Individual academic staff and some institutions are creating exciting ways of engaging students more meaningfully in curriculum design. This chapter explores the literature and examples of practice and analyses whether students and staff co-creating curricula can be considered as good practice.

I present background literature and an overview of some of the rationales given by staff to explain why they are interested in providing opportunities for students to co-create curricula. I also briefly outline some of the benefits resulting from the processes and outcomes of co-created curricula. I then summarise a range of examples to illustrate ways in which students and staff are working together to co-create curricula. Finally, using Chickering and Gamson's (1987) seven principles of good practice in undergraduate education, I analyse whether students and staff co-creating curricula demonstrates any of these seven principles of good practice.

26.1. Introduction

The last five years has witnessed a surge of interest in examining the ways in which students can take more responsibility for their own learning. The earlier chapters in this book refer to a rich range of examples covering different forms of student engagement, from students' active engagement in university quality assurance and enhancement systems, to students collaborating as co-researchers in authentic

The Student Engagement Handbook: Practice in Higher Education
Copyright © 2013 by Emerald Group Publishing Limited
All rights of reproduction in any form reserved
ISBN: 978-1-78190-423-7

research and development projects. This range of practice is increasingly supported by recognition from policymakers that student partnership is a key priority within the current higher education context.

However, the suggestion that students should become more involved in their own learning experiences is not new. John Dewey, in the early 20th Century was one of the first modern educational philosophers to argue for new approaches to education that he described as 'progressive' (Dewey, 1938), and which placed students more centrally within decision making and discussions about their own education. Dewey's ideas were built upon by others, and a growing dissatisfaction with formal schooling reached its height in the 1960s and 1970s with questions about the potential damage formal schooling was having on children (Illich, 1970; Rogers & Freiberg, 1969; Willis, 1977). This era also witnessed the birth of critical pedagogy — an approach that argued for adopting a critical stance towards education and challenging the accepted purposes and practices of teaching and learning. Critical pedagogy led to further questioning of the existing dynamics between teachers and students, arguing for more collaborative and negotiated forms of education that would lead to co-creation of new experiences and knowledge that challenge existing views of the world (Darder, Baltodano, & Torres, 2003; Giroux, 1981).

Influenced by debates within the schools sector, authors in higher education began to propose and debate the value of negotiated curricula (Boomer, 1992; Breen & Littlejohn, 2000). Boomer argued:

> If teachers set out to teach according to a planned curriculum, without engaging the interests of the students, the quality of learning will suffer ... negotiating the curriculum means deliberately planning to invite students to contribute to, and to modify, the educational program, so that they will have a real investment both in the learning journey and in the outcomes. Negotiation also means making explicit, and then confronting, the constraints of the learning context and the non-negotiable requirements that apply. (Boomer, 1992, p. 14)

Other authors recognised the value of university students contributing to decisions about assessment; recognising the key role of assessment as a potential driver of learning within curricula (Falchicov, 1986; Stefani, 1998).

In this chapter, I explore what is possible in co-creating curricula, presenting some examples of current practice, before moving on to examine whether co-creating curricula demonstrates principles of good practice in higher education.

26.2.   Defining Co-Creation of Curricula

In using the term 'co-creation of curricula', there is an implied sharing of the design process, which may not be equal (as perhaps implied by the term partnership), but which involves academic staff and students. Co-creation suggests a collaborative approach to the design and creation of learning and teaching experiences. This contrasts with some of the capitalist market conceptualisations of learning and teaching currently predominant in higher education policy circles where students are considered to be consumers of education. It also moves away from some of the manufacturing metaphors that talk about students as co-producers (McCulloch, 2009). Co-creation implies a mutual process that is imaginative, inventive and resourceful. It draws on ideas from staff and from students.

The term curriculum can be slightly problematic because it can be defined in a range of ways, particularly across different international contexts. However, the contestability of definitions enables us to explore the possibilities of what exactly staff and students might consider co-creating. In this chapter, the term curriculum is intended to encompass more than the programme or course subject content and the intended learning outcomes. Although content and intended learning outcomes are important, curriculum can also be considered to include the teaching and learning structure, processes of design and implementation, and the context of learning, as well as a consideration of broader graduate skills development and connections to the workplace (see, for example, Barnett & Coate, 2005; Kelly, 1999). It can also include consideration of how to support students' development of 'ways of thinking and practising in the subject (McCune & Hounsell, 2005). In broadening the definition, the intention is to include both the specific aspects of curriculum design, such as co-creation of assessments or teaching resources, as well as the more over-arching co-creation of content or students becoming members of curricula course or programme design committees.

Fraser and Bosanquet (2006) outline four key conceptualisations of curriculum held by staff: 'a: the structure and content of a unit (subject); b: the structure and content of a programme of study; c: the students' experience of learning; d: a dynamic and interactive process of teaching and learning' (Fraser & Bosanquet, 2006, p. 272). The first two definitions are perhaps more familiar to many readers, where curriculum is often thought of as study 'units', with a distinction between module/course and programme/degree level curricula. The second two definitions imply more of a sense of co-created curricula, with the authors expanding upon the fourth definition of the curriculum to describe it as '… a dynamic, emergent and collaborative process of learning for both student and teacher' (Fraser & Bosanquet, 2006, p. 272), and a view of the 'teacher and student acting as co-constructors of knowledge' (Fraser & Bosanquet, 2006, p. 275).

Combining some of Fraser and Bosanquet's definitions could be helpful, leading to curriculum being viewed as the design of the content, structure and processes of courses and programmes through a dynamic interaction between staff and students, both informed by and being influenced by the learning experience of the student. This definition encompasses the centrality of the student in the curriculum, reflecting the views of some academic staff that the curriculum cannot exist without students (Bovill, 2013).

Fundamentally, co-creation of curricula implies a shift in the conceptualisation of the teacher—student relationship towards a more reciprocal model where students and staff have a role, a voice and agency to influence and meaningfully participate in teaching and learning processes. Students and academic staff have different expertise to bring to the process, and there will be times when staff may appropriately have more voice, and other times when students may appropriately have more voice. Co-creation is not about giving students complete control, nor is it about staff maintaining complete control over curriculum design decisions. The relative levels of control over decision making and appropriate levels of partnership are likely to depend upon the context, the level of study, the relative experience levels of the students and the staff, the attitudes of students and staff, what is being discussed, and the level of influence of professional bodies over the curriculum (Bovill & Bulley, 2011). Crucially, co-creation of the curriculum is likely to imply a change to the power dynamics in most real or virtual classrooms.

Mann (2008) argues that students are often passive within university curricular processes. Indeed, it is common for academic staff to act as gatekeepers to curriculum design (Bourner, 2004; Bovill, 2013). In other words, where there are examples of staff and students co-creating curricula, these have involved in most cases, a conscious decision by staff to create opportunities for students to be involved in curricula design processes. This often requires a change to accepted and institutionalised curriculum design practices as well as to the relationship between the teacher and students. As Mann points out, 'whilst power may reside in an individual by virtue of their position as teacher; the particular dynamics of any one interaction may involve a shift and flux in the flow of power within the group, between teacher and students, and students and students' (Mann, 2008, p. 66). However, this potential for flux in the flow of power within a group of teachers and students may feel unfamiliar or uncomfortable to both staff and students where the predominant model of behaviour is premised upon the teacher being in control.

My own interest in, and rationale for, exploring and enacting co-created curricula is motivated by a desire to change the dynamics between staff and students to one where students are enabled to contribute meaningfully to designing their own learning experiences. This is underpinned by my own critical theoretical perspective and desire for more democratic forms of higher education teaching and learning. Not all staff will be interested in, or motivated to pursue, initiatives involving students in co-creation of curricula. However, staff engaging in collaborative partnerships with their students describe different motivations. These motivations include a desire for: a more democratic approach to education often underpinned by principles from critical pedagogy or ethical citizenship; enhanced student engagement in learning; enhanced student engagement in the university as a whole; enhanced learning; improved quality of teaching and learning in a currently problematic or 'broken' course or programme; and constructing knowledge with students rather than simply handing over fully constructed knowledge (Cook-Sather, Bovill, & Felten, 2014). These are just some of the motivations that staff describe. There is mounting evidence of the beneficial outcomes of co-created curricula and co-created learning and teaching approaches (see, for example, Bovill, Cook-Sather, & Felten, 2011; Sambell & Graham, 2011), and this evidence is likely to provide another motivating factor for some staff.

There are overlaps between the motivating factors presented above and those found within the schools based literature. However an interesting difference is that there appears to be a more political emphasis on student rights that is not so apparent in the higher education literature. In schools, discussion of student rights is often linked to the United Nations Convention of the Rights of the Child, emphasising pupils' rights to be involved in and consulted about any decisions that affect them, and in this case, that affect their education (Huddleston, 2007; Lundy, 2007; United Nations General Assembly, 1989).

Essentially, staff create opportunities for students to co-construct curricula for many different reasons. Both the range of curricular definitions as well as the range of motivations for co-creating curricula open up a substantial range of what is possible and desirable in terms of student participation in curriculum design in different contexts (Bovill & Bulley, 2011). There is a continuum of different forms of partnership and participation that are possible in different circumstances.

26.3.   Examples of Practice

Setting out to co-create curricula with students may be nerve-wracking for some staff (Bovill et al., 2011). So it can be worth considering starting with smaller scale initiatives or partnerships that seem lower risk in the first instance. For example, co-creation might seem safer with a smaller group of students or with students at a higher level of study. It is also possible to start with co-creating smaller elements of the curriculum rather than designing the whole curriculum.

Some staff provide students with choice over the content of part of a course, such as a choice of different topics for study. Other staff might provide a choice of readings for the subject of study. Enhancing choice can improve student engagement with a course and a subject, often by emphasising personal relevance to students. This is perhaps demonstrated most commonly through the high level of investment many students demonstrate in their research projects and dissertations. These projects frequently involve a student studying a topic/problem that is of particular interest, and requires them to develop a deep approach to learning and investigation of their chosen topic.

Many staff already ask students to give them feedback on course content, processes, teaching approaches and on whether they are learning key concepts. Evaluation processes are another area of the curriculum where students can help to co-create or redesign courses. Staff can meet with students to discuss the feedback they have provided, and ask for more information about their suggested changes and how these changes might be made. This approach can include students more meaningfully in redesign of existing courses than if we deem students' participation to finish once they have responded to our questionnaires. In an initiative several years ago, I asked course participants if they would be interested in evaluating their own course. Participants designed evaluation exercises, gathered feedback and collated and analysed this feedback. One participant commented:

> 'I was much more engaged in the process and thought about the way the module was running throughout, rather than just at the end'.

Another participant reported that

> 'the approach with this module engaged my interest and ... I probably thought more deeply about what I wanted to say and how my learning/knowledge was developing'.

Participants described the experience as more fun and engaging and some of this was perceived to have been due to the changing nature of the relationship between the course participants and me in my role as the tutor. The following comments illustrate this: '... we were treated as equals from day one', the approach '... engaged the entire class, giving individuals ownership and equity with the course leader ...' (Bovill et al., 2010, pp. 148–149).

One of the other authors in this volume, Alison Cook-Sather, has been undertaking exciting work at Bryn Mawr College in Pennsylvania, USA. She co-ordinates a programme where students act as 'consultants' in learning and teaching and offer constructive feedback to staff on their teaching. They have regular dialogue about approaches to teaching and learning that have been transformative for both staff and students. One student participant commented: 'It makes me a much more conscious student. I look at my classes through the perspective of both students and teachers'. Another student stated:

> Now I am constantly aware of how pedagogy works or fails, and I find myself constantly studying the teachers I admire — perhaps more than I study the material they teach. I think this sense of elevated consciousness alone will shape my thinking far into the future; now that I have been so exposed to this level of awareness, I really don't think it would be possible for me to enter a classroom WITHOUT thinking about the way class is being taught (as opposed to simply what is being taught). (Cook-Sather, 2011, pp. 45–47)

There are examples where, staff include students' work within the curriculum or as a springboard to discussion. For example, Mary Gilmartin at the National University of Ireland, Maynouth asked her geography students to take photographs of what contemporary social and cultural geography in the 21st Century meant to them. Mary then used these student photographs to stimulate class discussion and even used one of the photos within the end of course exam as the basis of a discussion question. Many staff try to use relevant real world examples. Indeed, Scandrett (2007) argues that real world problems can be used as the basis for collaboratively discussing and planning different practical strategies for political action in a programme on about environmental justice.

Students may create resources that can be used for learning and teaching purposes. One example of this comes from the University of Loughborough, where some senior mathematics students have produced worksheets and resources to help first year students understand mathematical concepts (Duah & Croft, 2011). Not only did this initiative seem to achieve its aim of enhancing first year students' understanding but one of the senior students commented, 'it's good to be able to comfortably talk to lecturers about interesting points in mathematics, it's also interesting to hear what they do as mathematicians …' (Duah & Croft, 2011, p. 9). At University College Dublin, staff in geography employed some third year students to design the virtual learning environment for first year students (Bovill, 2013).

Yet another form of co-creation involves staff and students collaborating to co-design the marking criteria for a course assessment. This not only involves students in co-defining what a good piece of work should comprise, but also helps students to understand assessment expectations (Hounsell et al., 2007). Collaboration can also focus upon the assessment itself. One lecturer at the University of Reading provides students with a list of key words that are pertinent to the content of his Classics course. He then asks students to create their own essay title using these key words (Kruschwitz, 2012).

In the literature, there are fewer examples of students working in partnership with staff on curriculum design committees. At Elon University in North Carolina, staff in the education department included students from previous years, as well as first year students about to undertake the programme, as partners within the curriculum design committee. One of the first decisions they made was to choose the course text from a selection of 25 course texts used in similar courses across the United States. The genuine level of participation that was encouraged by staff in this book review process was considered critical in students becoming convinced they were being taken seriously by staff (Mihans, Long, & Felten, 2008).

Having seen a range of different examples of co-created curricula, we turn to consider whether these examples and the broader aims of co-created curricula might be considered to be 'good practice'.

26.4.   Do Co-Created Curricula Processes Constitute Good Practice?

Beneficial outcomes from co-created curricula initiatives are being increasingly documented and include benefits for students, for academic staff, and for institutions. Both staff and students have reported gaining a deeper understanding of learning and teaching processes through co-creating curricula. There are also reports of staff and students changing the ways in which they relate to one another (Bovill et al., 2011). Hounsell and colleagues critiqued a range of literature focusing on student involvement in assessment and while they raise some concerns about the quality of some of the published studies that they examined, there were a range of claimed benefits including: students developing personal and lifelong learning skills;

enhanced learning; helping students overcome unrealistic expectations; and development of shared understanding (Hounsell et al., 2007).

Manor, Bloch-Schulman, Flannery, and Felten (2010) describe staff becoming more thoughtful about teaching and learning and reconsidering the ways they think about classroom collaboration in more democratic ways as a result of working in partnership with students. Other staff describe the benefits of gaining a student perspective on academic practice that can enable new approaches to student engagement to emerge (Sorenson, 2001; Werder & Otis, 2010). Meanwhile, students often grow in confidence through taking more responsibility for designing their own learning experience and there are many reports of enhanced student motivation, enjoyment, and enthusiasm (Little, 2011; Sambell & Graham, 2011).

Co-created curricula approaches are connected to a range of beneficial processes and outcomes, but when approached from another angle, to what extent can they be viewed as representing 'good practice'? In the United States, Chickering and Gamson published a set of seven principles of good practice in undergraduate education in 1987. These principles were the result of discussion and debate among a range of expert researchers who had been investigating factors impacting upon student learning (Chickering & Gamson, 1987, 1999). Since their first publication, these principles have been widely used and adopted internationally and remain relevant to discussions about higher education learning and teaching.

According to Chickering and Gamson, good practice in undergraduate education:

1. Encourages student–faculty contact.
2. Encourages cooperation among students.
3. Encourages active learning.
4. Gives prompt feedback.
5. Emphasizes time on task.
6. Communicates high expectations.
7. Respects diverse talents and ways of learning (Chickering & Gamson, 1987, p. 2).

Chickering and Gamson's principles of good practice provide us with an alternative way of considering the benefits of co-created curricula.

1. *Encourages student–faculty contact*
   The processes of co-creating curricula are based upon the first principle of encouraging student–faculty contact. Co-creation initiatives do not just encourage contact, but they tend to either unintentionally lead to, or more actively promote, changes to the student–teacher relationship, characterised by dialogue, negotiation and shared responsibility for the teaching and learning process. The type of contact and relationship in any co-creation activity will vary a great deal between initiatives where students are making a simple choice between two or three possible case studies that illustrate a key learning concept, through to initiatives where students are part of a curriculum design committee. Chickering and Gamson (1987) emphasised the importance of student–faculty contact inside as well as outside the classroom in order to enhance student motivation.

Many studies of co-created curricula have demonstrated enhanced student motivation, with students often getting involved much more deeply in curriculum design, but also in the life of the university more broadly (Bovill, 2013; Dunne & Zandstra, 2011).

2. *Encourages cooperation among students*
   The second principle is also broadly consistent with a co-created curricular approach. Not only does the student—teacher relationship change, but students often feel an enhanced sense of responsibility towards one another in the planning of learning and teaching. As Chris Manor and colleagues report from their work at Elon University in North Carolina: 'the value of group discussion and collaborative learning is lost when the power/responsibility to educate is seen as resting solely in the hands of the teacher. Years of conditioning have taught students to accept the information bestowed on them by the professor and to dismiss as irrelevant the perspectives of their peers' (Manor et al., 2010, p. 11). Co-creating curricula provides opportunities to ensure that students and their peers recognise their mutual responsibility for, and ability to make meaningful contributions to, their shared learning experiences. In addition, the co-operative nature of the process adds to the potential for developing deeper understanding: 'the knowledge constructed in a classroom, because it evolves through a collective process — through the texts, through the classroom discourse and the social practices of the group — is greater than any single individual could create, including the teacher' (Breen & Littlejohn, 2000, p. 22).

3. *Encourages active learning*
   Co-creating curricula encourages students to actively participate in the design process. There are some compelling reports of enhanced meta-cognitive understanding of learning and teaching processes in a range of papers (see, for example, Cook-Sather, 2011). Evidence suggests that students co-creating curricula are not just actively learning, but also transforming their views about learning. Indeed, 'learning is not a spectator sport' (Chickering & Gamson, 1987, p. 1), and students tend to learn more and learn more deeply where they are more engaged and active in the process. Active learning is a central assumption within co-created curricula. Where staff provide opportunities for students to participate in decision making about learning and teaching, this can result in students being able to choose content, structures, processes and experiences that are more likely to be relevant and motivate students to adopt deeper and more active approaches to learning.

4. *Gives prompt feedback*
   The fourth principle focuses on giving students prompt feedback and suggestions for ways to improve their performance. If we start by considering this principle from the angle of feedback linked to students performing assessment tasks, co-created curricular processes might be considered to have weaker links with this principle unless co-creation is focused specifically on designing assessment and feedback practices and marking criteria. Where students are meaningfully

involved in design of assessment and feedback practices, students can develop a much better awareness of what is required of them in the assessment process and consequently any feedback received is ultimately likely to be more meaningful, with the student perhaps more able to act upon the feedback given (Falchivov, 2005; Hounsell et al., 2007; Sambell & Graham, 2011).

Many of the current concerns about the importance of prompt feedback are emphasised by students providing evaluation of the programmes and courses we teach. In the United Kingdom, the National Student Survey (NSS), and equivalent national level surveys in other countries, frequently report that students wish to see improvements in the promptness of feedback. Although it should be noted that Mendes, Thomas, and Cleaver (2011) suggest that the questions within the NSS relating to promptness of feedback may be flawed and we may need to pay closer attention to 'managing' student perceptions and expectations. I would prefer to suggest we discuss perceptions and expectations with students rather than 'manage' their perceptions and expectations, however, it is useful to be reminded of the need to be wary of taking some of the NSS results at face value.

If we consider this fourth principle from another angle (and one I suspect not intended by Chickering and Gamson), the process of co-creating elements of teaching and learning can involve meaningful conversations about the curriculum that frequently involve immediate feedback on a students' performance/contributions to joint design processes. Indeed, feedback is often two-way and in this sense; staff also receive feedback on their teaching practices.

5. *Emphasises time on task*
Chickering and Gamson's fifth principle is emphasising time on task. They believed that using time well is crucial to effective learning. The time spent discussing and planning an entire course or programme curriculum or elements of a curriculum within co-created curricula approaches has been shown to enhance students' motivation, engagement and meta-cognitive understanding of the teaching and learning process (Bovill et al., 2011; Cook-Sather, 2011). However, whether this increase in motivation and engagement is related to students spending more time studying those courses where they co-create the curriculum is unclear. It is also unclear whether co-creating curricula contributes to substantial improvements in students' subject knowledge in the discipline. Therefore, the connection between co-creation of the curriculum and this fifth principle is relatively weaker than for other principles. However, examining the impact of student involvement in co-creating curricula upon the time they spend studying and their developing knowledge of the subject could be a useful area for future research.

6. *Communicates high expectations*
The sixth principle refers to communicating high expectations to students. Chickering and Gamson recognised that having high expectations tends to be a self-fulfilling prophecy. Several studies of students and staff co-creating curricula have demonstrated students' delight that staff considered that their opinions mattered and that they have the ability to contribute to curriculum design.

However, even where staff have high expectations of students, many staff still express surprise that students exceed these expectations, perhaps suggesting their high expectations are still set slightly too low (Bovill, 2013). Nevertheless, the very act of inviting students into curriculum discussions that are usually considered to be the domain of staff, communicates to students a higher value and expectation that staff place on students' experiences, perspectives and contributions.

7. *Respects diverse talents and ways of learning*
Finally, initiatives where students and staff co-create curricula seem to align well with the seventh principle of respecting diverse talents and ways of learning. The principles of co-creation are based upon the added value of bringing together the diverse and often unique talents, skills and knowledge of different students and staff. The aims of co-created curricular processes assume that there are many different ways to learn and to teach. The particular students and staff involved in any co-creative approach will bring their own views, experiences, skills, and knowledge to their own initiative. There will always be many ways in which curriculum design can be approached, but co-created curriculum is coherent with this principle of good practice in not just respecting diverse talents and ways of learning, but actively seeking to surface these talents and perspectives and using them to inform enhancements to learning and teaching for shared benefit.

26.5.   Discussion

Overall, when considered against Chickering and Gamson's seven principles of good practice in undergraduate education, students and staff co-creating curricula appears broadly to be highly consistent with principles one, two, three, six and seven. In contrast, there were somewhat more nuanced, weaker links with the fourth and fifth principles. However, there are several other points to consider. First of all, Chickering and Gamson's principles were written with undergraduates in mind. It is clear that receiving prompt feedback is particularly important in the first year undergraduate setting, as well as in the rest of the undergraduate years of study. However, many of the principles would still be useful and relevant in a postgraduate setting, although their particular emphasis might differ and some supplementary principles might be added. Indeed, there are some very valuable co-created curricula examples that have been carried out in the postgraduate setting and many of Chickering and Gamson's principles would still be relevant to frame this work.

Another consideration in exploring the principles is that any initiative involving students and staff working together is highly dependent upon the motivations of the individuals involved. It is possible to talk in radical ways about student participation, engagement and transformation, while continuing to maintain traditional patterns of power distribution and conservative views (Kane, 2005). Indeed we need to be careful of making claims for student participation and involvement that are not genuine as we are likely to cause longer term disengagement through insincere and disingenuous opportunities for participation. Therefore when we consider the extent to which any co-created curricula initiative is consistent with Chickering and Gamson's principles, this will always be highly dependent upon the outlook of the staff and students involved. Staff attitudes are particularly powerful as it is only where they consider co-creation to be a possible and legitimate way of working that students will have the opportunity to be involved. Taking the first principle as an example, staff will have individual views about the level of partnership and collaboration with students that they consider appropriate and comfortable, so the nature of any co-created curricula initiative will vary greatly.

It is also important to recognise that within every institution there are constraints to academic staff and students practising with the freedom they might wish to have. Cooke and Kothari (2001) argue that, '... participatory ideals are often operationally constrained by institutional contexts that require formal and informal bureaucratic goals to be met' (Cooke & Kothari, 2001, p. 8). This might require additional creativity to work within these constraints. In addition, it might require the political will to try to challenge and overcome constraints where they appear to prevent co-created curricula initiatives that demonstrate many principles of good practice.

There is no guarantee that any particular co-created curricular initiative will meet all of Chickering and Gamson's seven principles of good practice, but the fundamental aims of students and staff co-creating curricula are certainly broadly consistent with these principles of good practice. Chickering and Gamson's principles are of course not the only lens with which we can interrogate co-created curricular initiatives. One alternative example is Bain's (2004) work outlining 'what the best college teachers do', which emphasised: actively fostering student participation, intellectual stimulus, and building meaningful rapport between staff and students, as key factors for student engagement and success. There is clear overlap between Bain's factors and Chickering and Gamson's principles, and unsurprisingly there is also some coherence again between Bain's factors and the aims, processes and outcomes of co-created curricula.

26.6. Conclusions and Recommendations

Although there is clearly room for further research into co-created curricula — particularly longitudinal impact studies and well evaluated contextualised examples of co-creation in action — in this chapter I have outlined how co-created curricular initiatives demonstrate the majority of Chickering and Gamson's (1987) principles of good practice in undergraduate education.

Based on the existing literature about co-creating curricula, the following recommendations are intended to support those wishing to co-create curricula with students:

Remember that participation and co-creation can take many forms and involve partnership on many levels. *Explore different possibilities*, start small if it feels risky, consider new areas for co-creation if you are more experienced.

Start co-creation early. Many people think first years are not in a position to contribute to curricula design. Certainly, they may not be able to contribute meaningfully to curricula content on day one, but even small increases of choice in early stages of university learning experiences can communicate the message that student involvement in teaching and learning is welcome. Starting co-creation early can help students to develop sophisticated skills in negotiation and meta-cognitive understanding of the learning process by the end of their degree.

What is possible will be highly contextual. Professional bodies, your institution, your department and your own opinions will all influence what you can achieve. *Acknowledge constraints and work within them or try to reduce them*, but try not to see constraints as preventing co-creation. There is often a great deal of flexibility within set parameters, for example professional bodies may set key competency outcomes but often leave a great deal of flexibility of choice in teaching and learning approaches.

Talk to your students. Discuss learning and teaching ideas and dilemmas with them. They often have alternative and useful perspectives. Students also often value being given insights into what academics do. The growing evidence for the benefits of co-created curricula suggests that meaningful conversations between students and staff focused on learning and teaching are ultimately extremely rewarding and valuable for both students and staff.

For many academic staff and university policymakers, the idea of students and staff co-creating curricula is radical. Even those who choose to undertake co-creation of curricula with their students find that the process can feel risky. We need more research evidence, greater articulation of the benefits of co-created curricula, and support for co-created curricula from senior university staff, to enhance individual and collective confidence to pursue co-created learning and teaching processes. This chapter contributes to this need by establishing that co-created curricular processes and outcomes are consistent with well-researched principles of good educational practice. Students and staff have varied motivations, ideas and practices, but it is this variety that can both positively influence, and be captured through, collaborative curricular decision making and that has the potential to offer new and exciting forms of student learning and teaching.

References

Bain, K. (2004). *What the best college teachers do*. Cambridge, MA: Harvard University Press.

Barnett, R., & Coate, K. (2005). *Engaging the curriculum in higher education*. Maidenhead: Open University Press/Society for Research into Higher Education.

Boomer, G. (1992). Negotiating the curriculum. In G. Boomer, N. Lester, C. Onore & J. Cook (Eds.), *Negotiating the curriculum: Educating for the 21st Century* (pp. 4–14). London: Falmer Press.

Bourner, T. (2004). The broadening of the higher education curriculum, 1970–2002: An ipsative enquiry. *Higher Education Review, 36*(2), 39–52.

Bovill, C. (2013). *An investigation of co-created curricula within higher education in the UK, Ireland and the USA. Innovations in Education and Teaching International*. Retrieved from http://www.tandfonline.com/doi/abs/10.1080/14703297.2013.770264

Bovill, C., Aitken, G., Hutchison, J., Morrison, F., Roseweir, K., Scott, A., & Sotannde, S. (2010). Experiences of learning through collaborative evaluation from a Postgraduate Certificate in Professional Education. *International Journal for Academic Development*, *15*(2), 143–154.

Bovill, C., & Bulley, C. J. (2011). A model of active student participation in curriculum design: exploring desirability and possibility. In C. Rust (Ed.), *Improving student learning (18) global theories and local practices: Institutional, disciplinary and cultural variations* (pp. 176–188). Oxford: The Oxford Centre for Staff and Educational Development.

Bovill, C., Cook-Sather, A., & Felten, P. (2011). Changing participants in pedagogical planning: Students as co-creators of teaching approaches. Course design and curricula. *International Journal for Academic Development*, *16*(2), 197–209.

Breen, M. P., & Littlejohn, A. (2000). The Significance of negotiation. In M. P. Breen & A. Littlejohn (Eds.), *Classroom decision-making: Negotiation and process syllabuses in practice.* Cambridge: Cambridge University Press.

Chickering, P., & Gamson, Z. (1987). Seven principles for good practice in undergraduate education. *The Wingspread Journal*, *9*(2), 1–10. Retrieved from http://www.uis.edu/liberal studies/students/documents/sevenprinciples.pdf

Chickering, P., & Gamson, Z. (1999). Development and adaptations of the seven principles for good practice in undergraduate education. *New Directions for Teaching and Learning*, *80*, 75–81.

Cook-Sather, A. (2011). Layered learning: Student consultants deepening classroom and life lessons. *Educational Action Research*, *19*(1), 41–57.

Cook-Sather, A., Bovill, C., & Felten, P. (2014). *Student faculty partnerships in higher education: a practical guide to pedagogical and curricular collaboration.* San Francisco, CA: Jossey Bass.

Cooke, B., & Kothari, U. (2001). The case for participation as Tyranny. In B. Cooke & U. Kothari (Eds.), *Participation the New Tyranny?* London: Zed.

Darder, A., Baltodano, M. & Torres, R. D. (2003). Critical pedagogy: An introduction. In A. Darder, M. Baltodano & R. D. Torres (Eds.), *The critical pedagogy reader.* New York, NY: RoutledgeFalmer.

Dewey, J. (1938). *Experience and education.* Indianapolis, IN: Kappa Delta Pi.

Duah, F. K., & Croft, T. (2011). Students as partners in mathematics course design. An ethnographic case study. *CULMS Newsletter*, *4*(Nov), 4–11. Retrieved from http://www.math.auckland.ac.nz/CULMS/wp-content/uploads/2010/08/CULMS-No4.pdf

Dunne, E., & Zandstra, R. (2011). *Students as change agents. New ways of engaging with learning and teaching in higher education.* Bristol: ESCalate Higher Education Academy Subject Centre for Education/University of Exeter.

Falchicov, N. (1986). Product comparisons and process benefits of collaborative peer group and self assessments. *Assessment and Evaluation in Higher Education*, *11*(2), 146–165.

Falchivov, N. (2005). *Improving assessment through student involvement: Practical solutions for aiding learning in higher and further education.* London: RoutledgeFalmer.

Fraser, S., & Bosanquet, A. (2006). The curriculum? That's just a unit outline, isn't it? *Studies in Higher Education*, *31*, 269–284.

Giroux, H. A. (1981). Hegemony, resistance and the paradox of educational reform. In H. A. Giroux, A. N. Penna & W. F. Pinar (Eds.), *Curriculum and instruction alternatives in education.* Berkeley: McCutchen Publishing.

Hounsell, D. Falchikov, N., Hounsell, J., Klampfleitner, M., Huxham, M., Thomson, K., & Blair, S. (2007). *Innovative assessment across the disciplines: An analytical review of the literature*. Final Report, Higher Education Academy. Retrieved from http://www-new2. heacademy.ac.uk/assets/documents/research/Innovative_assessment_LR.pdf

Huddleston, T. (2007). *From student voice to shared responsibility, effective practice in demo-cratic school governance in European schools*. Strasbourg: Citizenship Foundation/Council of Europe. Retrieved from http://www.citizenshipfoundation.org.uk/lib_res_pdf/0629.pdf

Illich, I. (1970). *Deschooling society* (Reprint, 2004). London: Marion Boyers.

Kane, L. (2005). Ideology matters. In J. Crowther, V. Galloway, & I. Martin (Eds.), *Popular education: Engaging the academy. International perspectives*. Leicester: Niace.

Kelly, A. V. (1999). *The curriculum: Theory and practice* (4th ed.). London: Sage.

Kruschwitz, P. (2012). *Of red tape and green rookies: Student involvement in the Classics curriculum planning*. Presentation at Student Engagement Symposium, 2nd May, University of Reading.

Little, S. (Ed.). (2011). *Staff-student partnerships in higher education*. London: Continuum.

Lundy, L. (2007). 'Voice' is not enough: conceptualising Article 12 of the United Nations Convention on the Rights of the Child. *British Educational Research Journal*, *33*(6), 927–942.

Mann, S. (2008). *Study, power and the university*. Society for Research into Higher Education. Maidenhead: Open University Press.

Manor, C., Bloch-Schulman, S., Flannery, K., & Felten, P. (2010). Foundations of student–faculty partnerships in the scholarship of teaching and learning. In C. Werder & M. M. Otis (Eds.), *Engaging student voices in the study of teaching and learning* (pp. 3–15). Sterling, VA: Stylus.

McCulloch, A. (2009). The student as co-producer: Learning from public administration about the student-university relationship. *Studies in Higher Education*, *34*(2), 171–183.

McCune, V., & Hounsell, D. (2005). The development of students' ways of thinking and practising in three final year biology courses. *Higher Education*, *49*, 255–289.

Mendes, P., Thomas, C., & Cleaver, E. (2011). The meaning of prompt feedback and other student perceptions of feedback: Should National Student Survey scores be taken at face value? *Engineering Education: Journal of The Higher Education Academy Engineering Subject Centre*, *6*(1). Retrieved from http://84.22.166.132/journal/index.php/ee/article/viewArticle/172/247.html

Mihans, R., Long, D., & Felten, P. (2008). Power and expertise: Student-faculty collaboration in course design and the scholarship of teaching and learning. *International Journal for the Scholarship of Teaching and Learning*, *2*(2), 1–9.

Neary, M., & Winn, J. (2009). The student as producer: Reinventing the student experience in higher education. In L. Bell, H. Stevenson & M. Neary (Eds.), *The future of higher education: Policy, pedagogy and the student experience* (pp. 192–210). London: Continuum.

Rogers, C., & Freiberg, H. J. (1969). *Freedom to learn* (3rd ed.). New York, NY: Macmillan Publishing.

Sambell, K., & Graham, L. (2011). Towards and assessment partnership model? Students experiences of bring engaged as partners in assessment for learning (AfL) enhancement activity. In S. Little (Ed.), *Staff-student partnerships in higher education*. London: Continuum.

Scandrett, E. (2007). Environmental justice in Scotland: Policy, pedagogy and praxis. *Environmental Research Letters*, *2*, 1–7. Retrieved from http://iopscience.iop.org/1748-9326/2/4/045002/

Sorenson, D. L. (2001). College teachers and student consultants: Collaborating about teaching and learning. In J. E. Miller, J. E. Groccia & M. S. Miller (Eds.), *Student-assisted teaching: A guide to faculty-student teamwork* (pp. 179–183). Bolton, MA: Anker.

Stefani, L. A. J. (1998). Assessment in partnership with learners. *Assessment and Evaluation in Higher Education, 23*(4), 339–350.

United Nations General Assembly. (1989). *Convention on the rights of the child.* Geneva: United Nations. Retrieved from http://www.un.org/documents/ga/res/44/a44r025.htm

Werder, C., & Otis, M. (Eds.). (2010). *Engaging student voices in the study of teaching and learning.* Sterling, Virginia: Stylus.

Willis, P. (1977). *Learning to Labour: How working class kids get working class jobs.* Aldershot: Ashgate publishing.

Chapter 27

Students as Partners: A Three-Layered Approach for Enhancement

Stuart Brand, Luke Millard, Paul Bartholomew and Paul Chapman

Abstract

This chapter describes a three-layered approach to engagement of students as academic partners in curriculum design and delivery. The first focus is on partnership work at individual or small group level manifested through Student Academic Partner development projects, delivered in three academic years since 2009, and a range of mentoring initiatives. The chapter discusses the significance of process of partnership as well as emergent product; data is also presented relating to participating students, uptake of opportunities and resources required. The second level relates to the redefinition of programme teams to incorporate comparable numbers of academic staff and students working together in curriculum design and enhancement activities as part of a university-wide redesign project. Here consideration is given to the expectation of participants as well as the lived experience of collaboration. The final layer concerns institution level partnerships to underpin culture change, notably partnership between a university and its students' union, with consideration of the impact on both. Examples are provided for each of the levels together with lessons drawn from experience of implementation and possibilities for further development to meet the challenge of seeking both wider and deeper impact.

27.1. Introduction

In this chapter we will describe a three-layered strategy at Birmingham City University to our work on student engagement through a partnership approach. The levels considered are:

1. Project work as a vehicle for partnership between individual or small groups of students with academic staff;

The Student Engagement Handbook: Practice in Higher Education
Copyright © 2013 by Emerald Group Publishing Limited
All rights of reproduction in any form reserved
ISBN: 978-1-78190-423-7

2. Student engagement in curriculum design through a process of programme team redefinition;
3. Institutional arrangements to underpin partnership between staff and students.

The purpose of this work focuses around initially creating, and now enhancing, an academic learning community in which students feel they wish to belong and participate. The cultural change this imposes upon the institution will be discussed as the initiative continues to seek to bring student engagement alive and embed it as a 'state of mind' for students and staff across the university and its various campuses.

It is our belief that student engagement is a broad church that encompasses a wide range of activities from curriculum enhancement and student support to student employment. The definition of student engagement by Trowler (2010, p. 3) is one which resonates well with our approach as it signifies the inherent effort that both the university and students need to make if the student engagement partnership is going to be a success for both parties.

Student engagement is concerned with the interaction between the time, effort and other relevant resources invested by both students and their institutions intended to optimise the student experience and enhance the learning outcomes and development of students and the performance, and reputation of the institution.

27.1.1. Background

The drive at Birmingham City University to develop effective partnerships between staff and students has its origin in a previous project that really illuminated a future path for us and changed our thinking. Between 2002 and 2005 a number of staff and students from the university were engaged in this project jointly led by the then University of Central England, later to be renamed as Birmingham City University, and the Generic Centre of the Learning and Teaching Support Network, later part of the Higher Education Academy.[1] This project, Managing Effective Student Assessment (MESA) involved nine universities and had, as an early part of its operation, parallel working groups of academic staff and students. However, a key lesson, which transformed the delivery of the project, was that much greater

---

[1]The Higher Education Academy (HEA) champions excellent learning and teaching in higher education. It is a national and independent organisation, funded by the four United Kingdom Higher Education funding bodies and by subscriptions and grants.

progress was made whenever these parallel groups were merged and staff and students from the various universities and different disciplines worked in partnership. This was because shared understanding of key issues was achieved: an understanding that was different in kind to that produced by either staff or students working alone.

Later, between 2005 and 2010, the university hosted a Higher Education Funding Council for England Centre for Excellence in Teaching and Learning (CETL),[2] the Centre for Stakeholder Learning Partnerships. This CETL was initially focused on partnership with employers in the National Health Service as a key stakeholder group for the work of a health faculty. However, in the latter part of the funding period, from 2008, a productive focus on students was achieved. It is that focus which initially underpinned the work described in this chapter.

27.1.2. Institutional Approach

In 2005, a signal had been provided by the Quality Assurance Agency[3] at an institutional audit that a greater institutional focus on quality enhancement would be desirable. In consequence, a further key trigger for these developments was a need identified in 2007–2008 to review and repurpose the university's Learning and Teaching Strategy. This was achieved through a widespread consultative process and led to renewed focus on the need to engage students in active learning. A departure from previous practice was the recognition of a need to develop 'an active partnership with the Students' Union[4] to ensure that together we meet students' wider educational, social, cultural, sporting, welfare and personal development needs'.

Our focus from 2008 onwards was then on creating a greater sense of learning community. The university could perhaps at this time still be described as a place to which students commuted and in which they saw their role as solely related to the acquisition of academic credit through successful completion of modules. There was only a limited sense of being part of an academic learning community. Indeed, we recognised that, in order to achieve a higher level of student success it would be necessary to engender much more active participation in, rather than passive

---

[2]The Centres for Excellence in Teaching and Learning (CETL) initiative represented the Higher Education Funding Council for England's largest ever single funding initiative in teaching and learning. The initiative had two main aims: to reward excellent teaching practice, and to further invest in that practice so that CETLs funding delivered substantial benefits to students, teachers and institutions. £315 million was invested between 2005 and 2010 in 74 CETLs.

[3]The Quality Assurance Agency for Higher Education (QAA) exists to safeguard quality and standards in UK universities and colleges, so that students have the best possible learning experience.

[4]Students' union is a student-led organisation present in many colleges and universities. In higher education, the students' union is often accorded its own building on the campus, dedicated to representation, social, organisational activities, and academic support of the membership.

consumption of, educational provision. In this context, the work of Kuh (2009) now seems very pertinent. He defined student engagement as 'the time and effort students devote to activities that are empirically linked to desired outcomes of college and what institutions do to induce students to participate in these activities.' For us at Birmingham City University, the desire was to develop a wider range of such activities, to engage students in them and to break down significant barriers between students and staff. In this way it was hoped that progression and retention of students on programmes would improve and that student satisfaction would be enhanced, with better outcomes in the National Student Survey. These major measures of success were however for us secondary. We chose partnership rather than consumerism for the reason that we passionately believed this would make our university a better place to be for staff and students alike.

Interestingly, this raised interesting presentational and practical issues: clearly senior management level support for an attempt to develop a real sense of learning community was only likely to be achieved if the proponents could assert those potential effects on key indicators of performance such as student progression and retention. However, senior management level support was critical only as a signal of permission. It was always the case that top-down instruction would be a relatively ineffective vehicle for such change. D'Andrea and Gosling (2005) draw interesting comparisons between whole institution approaches and the perhaps relatively isolated position of individual change agents. In the work we describe here we will show that a more substantial population of such change agents may have the capacity to exert whole institution effects. The same authors identify the significance of students' relationship with not only their programme of study but also their department and the wider institution. This view has recently been strongly reinforced in a major study of issues influencing student retention and success in higher education (Thomas, 2012). The principal finding of the work of Thomas was that 'belonging' was the key factor in determining students' ability to participate in and make the most of their opportunities in higher education.

27.2.   Partnership with the Students' Union

As already identified, a new University Learning and Teaching Strategy had suggested a move towards partnership working with the Birmingham City Students' Union. This departure was a significant one, as relations had been previously couched mainly in terms of the union reacting to the performance of the university and thus perhaps rather adversarial. Chapman, Blatchford, and Hughes (2013) describe traditional methods of securing the student voice: 'debates between unions and universities can result in a reaffirming of the traditional 'them and us' position (Grattan & Meakin, 2012), defended by structures and memorandums which can often lead to stalemate and political toing and froing (Bell, Greatrix, & Horton, 2006). The emergence of a collaborative approach, adopted by BCSU and BCU, is now becoming more common and seen in much more of a positive light (Greatrix,

2012). Despite this approach gradually being perceived as good practice, the debate continues within the student union (SU) movement itself looking at the implications of partnership and collaboration. 'What does an SU put at risk by working more closely with their institution, what does the SU potentially gain by doing so and which argument carries more weight?'

This quote reveals the key concern at the early stage of partnership development, namely that any students' union might be taking a risk by pursuit of partnership; the risk would be a diminution of the ability, through conventional representation mechanisms, of the SU to hold the university to account. Another way of presenting this dilemma might be to recognise it as the challenge implicit in moving from reactive to proactive approaches. Indeed it could be suggested that this manifestation of partnership at institutional level furthers the move away from notions of students as consumers and towards roles as active partners, as discussed by Ramsden (2008).

Doors gradually began to open following investment from the CETL (2005–2008) in a research post in the SU. A new set of sabbatical officers in 2008–2009 was amenable to discussions about collaboration for enhancement. Subsequently, the appointment of a Membership Engagement Manager (MEM) to the staff of the SU provided important continuity for emergent partnership working. Such continuity is always likely to be a critical issue, given the short periods of office for which union officers serve. However the appointment was the first full-time post named in this way in the United Kingdom and has provided real catalysis for a wide range of initiatives, to the extent that an agreement was reached during 2010 that the university would second the MEM to work in the university's Centre for Enhancement of Learning and Teaching (CELT) for a proportion (currently 40 per cent) of his time. It is important to reflect here that the principal lever for change in the SU-university relationship was the vision of officers and this MEM for a different, more developmental future in which the benefits of proactive work rather than the limited scope of reactive response were realised. In this way developmental process in academic work was now able to become a real vehicle for progress rather than the after the event evaluation that had previously dominated.

27.3. Project Work as a Vehicle for Developing the Learning Community

The first of the three layers under consideration relates to work involving individual students or small groups becoming engaged in partnership project work. Student satisfaction surveys and other internal measures had indicated that the university's locally based students, which formed a majority, did not see the university as a place in which they belonged or wished to remain beyond their need to study. CELT decided to respond to this view through the creation of a new initiative that sought to generate aspects of that sense of learning community. The flagship project within this area was one that sought to bring students and staff together in real partnership to work on educational development projects. Thus, the Student Academic Partner (SAP) initiative was born with this overarching aim of creating a greater sense of learning community at Birmingham City University. The SAP development group decided that students would be paid[5] to work alongside academic staff to create innovative new approaches to learning and teaching that would improve the learning experience, not only of those students employed, but also of the wider population of students studying the programmes being enhanced. The decision to pay students was based on practice observed elsewhere, in such places as Copenhagen Business School. They had identified that many students needed to have paid employment and thus in order to make such opportunities available to all, rather than only to those who could afford to work on a voluntary basis, payment was necessary.

Through the partnership with the students' union, students were encouraged to apply for SAP projects, while CELT targeted academic and support staff. The partnerships approach to recruitment of participants symbolised the collaborative approach to project generation. Our philosophy here was to, through the reduction of a 'them versus us' attitude, deliver a new approach to localised educational development initiatives. Students who work on these projects had, normally, just experienced the aspect of their course in which they saw the potential for improvement. This offered the university the opportunity to create impactful student led enhancement of its curriculum.

The SAP scheme is now entering its fourth iteration and has seen over 300 learning and teaching projects proposed over that time. Of these just over 200 have been funded for employment of students. The projects fall into three broad categories:

- Curriculum focused — development of new content, learning resources or assessment approaches
- Learning Community building focused — consultation, survey, networking projects
- Professional practice focused — employability, employment, professional practice and placement experience

A key aspect of the scheme is the layers of benefits that it offers. At a programme level, it improves the learning experience for all those students studying in future years. It also assists the student partner involved in the project as not only do they receive financial reward, but also they develop a suite of employability skills such as project management, leadership and presentation skills. For the academic staff member it offers them an opportunity, through partnership, to pursue a development which may have been previously hindered through lack of time. However, there is a further invaluable benefit: that of contemporary relevance obtained through the fresh insight and different perspectives of one or more current students. These claims are supported by the quotes presented below:

---

[5]The initial rate of pay in the SAP scheme in 2009/10 was £10 per hour.

The project was extraordinarily engaging and exciting and through it
I have acquired many skills that I am confident will benefit me greatly
in the future. (Student comment)
Seeing the students' enthusiasm for the project and the archives
reignited my own enthusiasm and has inspired me. (Staff comment)

The Student Academic Partners scheme is now widely recognised and has been
influential in design of initiatives by a number of other universities across the sector.
It has also led, at the time of writing, to the Student as Partners Change Programme,
collaboration between the Higher Education Academy and Birmingham City
University. This Change Programme has been designed to support higher education
institutions as they develop and implement institutional change initiatives through
partnership between students and staff. Ten universities are participating in
2012–2013.

The key question for us at BCU concerns the extent to which the SAP initiative
has influenced the organisation. We will return to this later but we do believe that
we have changed thinking to the extent that working in partnership with students is
now seen as not only optimal in securing internal discretionary funding, but also as
the best way to secure enhancement of provision. Three years on, the SAP scheme
remains in great health and has also now started to spawn other student engagement
approaches. Learning from the scheme has shown the great strength to be drawn
from peer to peer based activities. We have chosen, for example, to invest in peer
mentoring to build on the academic partnership projects and in direct response to
demand from faculties. The resultant Student Academic Mentoring programme in
its first pilot phase saw the employment of over 60 mentors across the university
supporting a range of activities including teaching assistant roles, tutorials, resit preparation sessions and skills workshops. A further call for 2012–2013 has led to 23
programme or faculty based initiatives being supported and we expect further
expansion. An interesting feature of this work has been that much of the supporting
material and induction work has been developed and delivered by students
themselves.

In addition, the SAP scheme has shown the value of the sharing of ideas across
programmes and disciplines; crucially the desire to create the learning community
means that students should be engaging with more than just a programme based
experience. Feedback from SAP projects where this took place has been very
encouraging and therefore the university is now committed to the expansion of the
SAP scheme into a new internally funded stream which will encourage larger, cross-
disciplinary projects and break down barriers between different parts of the university. We believe that these projects, while developing excellent products, will be as
valuable for the processes and the relationships they develop. If through the creation
of these new broader relationships we can enthuse academic staff and students with a
wider vision and understanding of the university experience, then the progress to the
creation of the learning community will take a major leap forward.

The move towards developing the learning community has not been without its
challenges. There was a suspicion within the university that these student

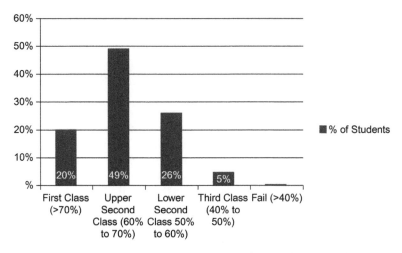

Figure 27.1:   Performance of BCU students during their time of employment as Student Academic Partners.

engagement activities would only attract a particular elite selection of student enthusiasts, sometimes referred to as the 'usual suspects'. Some staff questioned whether we could reach out beyond the first class student who was known to the tutor and was always at the forefront of developments. A further question was whether participating students would see their involvement as related to a wider community development or simply focus narrowly on their individual funded project. Research into the first three cohorts of SAP participants provided some interesting insights into these issues. Evidence from the 395 student participants showed that it was not merely those usual high flying suspects who participated in the SAP scheme. Analysis of student assessment results revealed that the majority of participating students did demonstrate strong academic attainment. However, detailed analysis showed that the largest proportion of students, 49 per cent, achieved upper second class grades, with 26 per cent gaining a lower second class mark and 20 per cent achieving a first class grade Figure 27.1.

The question around student attitudes and participation in the learning community was also explored. A survey of the same set of students, during their time as Student Academic Partners, revealed that 67 per cent strongly felt part of the learning community within the university and this was supported by figures that showed 67.5 per cent strongly believed that they had equality of partnership within their relationship with the staff working on their project Figure 27.2.

27.4.   Student Engagement in Curriculum Design — Programme Level

Students' contributions to curriculum design activity allow for a very important set of experiences and perspectives to be considered as part of the design process; yet

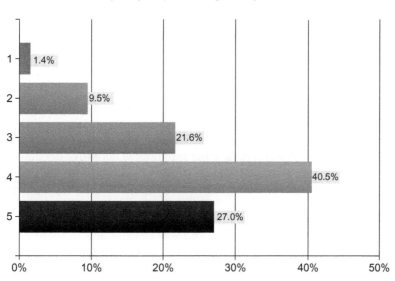

BCU is seeking to develop a learning community of student and staff partners working collaboratively to improve learning experiences On a scale 1 to 5 (1 being not at all and 5 being fully engaged) How much do you feel you are part of a learning community at BCU?

Figure 27.2: Perceptions of Student Academic Partners about learning community development at BCU.

such engagement does not necessarily occur as a matter of course. To create a situation where students become engaged in a meaningful manner in curriculum design, we have found the need to build mechanisms and processes that have, as the default position, an expectation for student engagement not only to occur — but also to be evidenced.

Our approach of designing such mechanisms emerged from a pan-university curriculum redesign project we begun in 2008. Our original project, known as RoLEx (Redesign of the Learning Experience), was the vehicle through which we sought to use a Senate-mandated restructuring of the entire undergraduate portfolio (from a 12-credit module structure to a 15-credit module structure) to enhance the student learning experience through, for example, elimination of unnecessary complexity and redesign of assessment (Bartholomew, Brand, & Cassidy, 2010).

During the first iteration of the RoLEx project, we learnt a great deal about how students engage (or do not engage) in curriculum design activity. We learnt that student aspirations for involvement in the redesign of their programmes were generally not well developed. Furthermore, programme teams tended to engage with students, and other stakeholders, mostly in a tokenistic way. We also came to realise that the curriculum design and approval process itself offered little by way of a mechanism to collect evidence of engagement with stakeholders. In short, our processes allowed for secure scrutiny of the end *product* of curriculum design (as represented by the definitive documentation) but little scrutiny of the design *process* itself.

As a consequence of our findings, BCU set about revolutionising its design and approval processes. Bolstered by significant funding from the Joint Information Systems Committee's (JISC), Institutional Approaches to Curriculum Design programme, we ran a four-year project to embed stakeholder (including student) engagement into curriculum design. Much, but not all, of the focus of our work was in the exploitation of technology to support the collection and representation of the student voice in the curriculum design process. Our primary method of so doing was the movement of our curriculum design and approval processes into an approval-panel-free virtual (Microsoft SharePoint-based) system that allowed for:

• Stakeholders to contribute to forum-based discussions during the design process.
• Stakeholders to input into and review the programme definitive documentation.
• Authentic accounts of vested interests, as captured in audio and video artefacts, to be appended to the discussions and to be viewable by those conferring approval.

Through this new process, programme approval is conferred when definitive documentation is verified as being in order, and when evidence is in place demonstrating that the design process has been sufficiently responsive to the articulated needs of all stakeholders (including students). This evidence is in the form of appended video and audio files; forum contributions; images of events; minutes of meetings; or any other artefacts that have been accrued as a consequence of engagement activity.

Of course, just 'capturing' and sharing student perception is insufficient; programme teams are required to demonstrate how they have responded to the student perspectives (or not — with a rationale, as appropriate). This new scrutiny of process, in parallel with scrutiny of product, has established a mechanism through which student engagement is built into the curriculum design process. At the time of writing, these processes have been piloted with nine programme teams and Stage 2 pilots are about to commence.

Software-supported solutions can only go so far though and we have recognised that we need to do more to encourage academics and students work together on curriculum design. By the time we got to the third iteration of the RoLEx initiative in 2011, we had developed strategies to encourage and reward such co-working. We hosted and ran curriculum design events in which programme teams were asked to attend with comparable numbers of students. This idea of insisting on student inclusion in the design teams was met with trepidation by some academics at first; but by the end of each of the days, we were hearing testimony from previously reluctant academics as to how useful the student perspective had been. For their part, students spoke of how positive they felt as a consequence of having been included. They felt a sense of empowerment in how their ideas were being taken on board and actioned.

Action cascading from discussion was not accidental or fortuitous; rather it came about as a consequence of central intervention. In order to support action, relatively small amounts of money (£1000) were made available to each of the staff/students teams so that their collaborative responses to curriculum challenges could be brought to fruition. We have cascaded this model to other areas of staff development provision (outside of the RoLEx project) and prefer to run all our bespoke development workshops on this basis — with programme teams only being able to access support where they include students as part of the team.

This insistence, on the inclusion of students in developmental activities, has cascaded into our Stage 2 pilots for our new approaches to curriculum design. At the beginning of each programme design or redesign process, the programme team will be required to attend a Design Initiation Event. Here, they receive briefings on the new curriculum design and approval processes, and begin to develop the philosophy and aims of their programme. The inclusion of students in these events is now a requirement and this will persist through to the mainstreaming of these new approaches at the beginning of next academic year. We hope, by requiring engagement of students at the inception point of new programmes, that their early input will be encouraged and their ongoing contributions sustained.

27.5. Institutional Impact and Next Steps

It has been the intention throughout this development period that cultural change would ensue; change that was no longer dependent on those usual enthusiastic suspects but was firmly embedded in mainstream process. There are, we believe, a number of manifestations which suggest that we are part way on that important journey.

A key tenet from the outset was the nature of the relationship between the SU and university. In our view this is now significantly recast. Within the last year the SU has produced an academic manifesto, the first seen in BCU, which makes a major contribution to the quality enhancement work of the institution. In particular, the SU is now emerging as a significant driver in our work to promote development of employability attributes and focus on development of students as individuals. The MEM and Union President (2012–2013) are also leading one of the HEA Students as Partners Change Programmes: their team, with strong university staff and student involvement, is working on an initiative entitled 'New Student Conversations: from QA to QE'.[6] This work seeks to revitalise old and invent new mechanisms for capturing student opinion. The team aim for a much wider range of student conversations within the whole quality enhancement agenda. Interestingly, there is great enthusiasm for this work from the university itself, with many believing that extant mechanisms such as Boards of Studies are tired and unproductive.

A further manifestation of the culture change we seek has been the growth in demand for student partnership working. In the table below we set out the variety of approaches now established Table 27.1.

---

[6]In other words, from retrospective assurance of quality towards prospective enhancement of quality.

Table 27.1: Range of student engagement initiatives at BCU.

Partnership activity	Student participants	Funding	Notes
Student Academic Partnership Scheme (SAP)	Individuals or small groups working in partnership with staff	Students employed by SU (project funding to SU from university). Typical employment for a student is 70–100 hours in academic year	In first four iterations 216 projects funded across all faculties and some central services
Student Academic Mentoring Programme (StAMP)	Individuals or small groups working in partnership with staff to provide peer mentoring	Students employed by BCU as part of OpportUNIty initiative	60 students employed in 2011–2012 pilots. 21 initiatives funded across the university in 2012–2013
OpportUNIty — Collaborative projects	Groups of students and staff from more than one discipline collaborating in live projects with multiple beneficiaries	Students employed by BCU as part of OpportUNIty initiative	Initial call yielded 31 bids of which 21 have been funded in 2012–2013
HEA/BCU Students as Partners Change Programme (2012/13)	SU team with university staff members	Expenses only	Aim for major reform of student representation
Redesign of Learning Experience (RoLEx) development workshops	Programme teams defined as requiring comparable representation of staff and students	£1000 made available to each participating team for short-term follow up	43 programme teams participated in 2010–2011, each with full student participation
OpportUNIty Student Jobs on Campus	BCU team participated in HEA Change Academy 2011–2012	Expenses only	Aim to develop 1000 student jobs on campus by 2015

These approaches have all grown from the initial development of the SAP scheme in 2009. Although they were developed by small steering groups in each case, they should be seen as response to emergent demand rather than merely attempts to impose such engagement activities on an unwilling population! One indicator of the extent of progress thus far is that the StAMP work and Collaborative Projects developments both were directly driven by students employed in CELT. These then are not developments for imposition, with students cast as passive recipients, but rather student-led partnership initiatives which have attracted management approval and faculty staff enthusiasm, evidenced by the quantity and quality of bids received. All parts of the university are engaged in the initiatives presented in the Table 27.1 and there is a contagious impact; whereas originally the staff who enthused about SAP developments in 2009 were a select group already known to be well disposed towards such work, others have now been infected. Often, the infection spreads just by colleagues perceiving the benefits accrued from such partnership work: this applies to staff and students alike.

It thus came as a natural sequel in 2011 for the university to apply for a Change Academy initiative with the HEA. This reflected the desire of the university's staff and students to extend the student employment opportunities pioneered in the SAP scheme to a variety of further functions and services. The initiative has been successful with a number of generic job descriptions for student employment developed and opportunities emerging in many locations. There are, of course, barriers to be removed, but there is real momentum and great demand from students themselves.

Interestingly, in an optional question in the National Student Survey, asking about the extent to which 'I feel part of an academic community in my college or university', the positive response rate has risen from 65 per cent in 2009 steadily to 76 per cent in 2012. We would suggest that this provides consistent evidence, over this four year period, that we are succeeding in our original aim of building a greater sense of academic learning community.

Finally, we would claim that student-staff partnerships are now seen as a key feature of the university's operation. In 2011/12, BCU reviewed its Corporate Plan and now includes an Objective 'to be an exemplar for student engagement, working in partnership with students to create and deliver high levels of student satisfaction and graduate employment'. The inclusion of such an objective five years earlier may well have looked premature; now it appears, to most, as a natural next step arising from the partnership development work that has already occurred. We conclude with a quote from a senior member of academic staff in one of our faculties, the Birmingham Institute of Art and Design. A participant herself on the SAP scheme and witness to the impact the student engagement initiatives are having within her School, she concludes:

> ...this SAPs thing has already started to infect ideas that are going on in the faculty about how we do define our relations with students .... Because we are stuck with this absolutely horrendous thing of customers which I think is so wrong. I think it could have a significance way beyond the SAPs project itself in that we are entering uncharted

waters about how students view themselves and how staff operate in academia and it is really up for grabs.

This seems to us a very reasonable summary of exactly what we are about.

27.6.   Conclusion

We have presented a review of the three-layered approach that we have adopted at Birmingham City University as we seek to develop a real learning community. We have throughout this period espoused a partnership approach. However, the term partnership is much used and perhaps merits some clarification in our context. When considering the work of the university 'in partnership with' the 'Students' Union', helpful context is obtained from the work of Boddy, Macbeth, & Wagner (2000, p. 1004) who suggested that partnership or collaboration, here used interchangeably, is defined as:

> a situation in which there is an attempt to build close, long-term links between organisations ... that remain distinct, but which choose to work closely together.

The operation of any such partnership, we would suggest, crucially depends upon the maintenance of that distinction and on the need to recognise that, as Wenstone indicates (NUS, 2012):

> The word 'partnership' is an attractive one, and hard to disagree with, but in order to make a meaningful choice we need to examine and reject the alternatives.

The decision to reject the notion that students are only consumers is at the centre of our work but we will do well, as we seek to increase impact across our institution to keep in mind this need to keep under review the aims and aspirations of our partnership working.

References

Bartholomew, P., Brand, S., & Cassidy, D. (2010). Distributed approaches to promote stakeholder ownership of postgraduate programme design. In C. Nygaard, L. Frick & N. Courtney (Eds.), *Learning and teaching in higher education: Postgraduate education — form and function.* Faringdon: Libri Publishing.

Bell, T., Greatrix, P., & Horton, C. (2006). *Universities and their unions: The future relationship between universities and Students' Unions.* The University of Warwick.

Boddy, D., Macbeth, D., & Wagner, B. (2000). Implementing collaboration between organisations: An empirical study of supply chain partnering. *Journal of Management Studies*, *37*(7), 1003–1017.

Chapman, P., Blatchford, S., & Hughes, E. (2013). Student engagement creating our learning community. Lightening up the dark side: A partnership approach between a students' union and the university. In C. Nygaard, S. Brand, P. Bartholomew & L. Millard (Eds.), *Student engagement: Identity, motivation and community*. Faringdon: Libri Publishing.

D'Andrea, V., & Gosling, D. (2005). *Improving teaching and learning in higher education: A whole institution approach*. Milton Keynes: SRHE/Open University Press.

Grattan, J., & Meakin, B. (2012). *University view 11th October 2012*. Retrieved from http://www.walesonline.co.uk/news/education-news/2012/10/11/as-much-as-a-good-library-is-at-the-core-of-a-university-a-vibrant-students-union-is-at-the-heart-of-an-excellent-student-experience-91466-32008378/. Accessed on 25 October 2012.

Greatrix, P. (2012). *Working with, not against*. Times Higher Education 15th March. Retrieved from http://www.timeshighereducation.co.uk/story.asp?storycode=419348. Accessed on 3 September 2012.

Kuh, G. D. (2009). What student affairs professionals need to know about student engagement. *Journal of College Student Development*, *50*(6), 683–706.

NUS. (2012) *A manifesto for partnership, National Union of Students*. Retrieved from http://www.nusconnect.org.uk/news/article/highereducation/Rachel-Wenstone-launches-a-Manifesto-for-Partnership/. Accessed on 1 April 2013.

Ramsden, P. (2008). *The future of higher education: Teaching and the student experience*. Retrieved from http://www.nus.org.uk/PageFiles/350/The%20Future%20of%20Higher%20Education%20(Teaching%20and%20the%20student%20experience).pdf Accessed on 20 February 2013.

Thomas, L. (2012). *Building student engagement and belonging in higher education at a time of change: Final report from the what works? Student retention & success programme*. New York, NY: The Higher Education Academy.

Trowler, V., & Trowler, P. (2010). *Student engagement evidence summary*. New York: The Higher Education Academy.

PART 6: STUDENT ENGAGEMENT IN DISCIPLINE AND PEDAGOGIC RESEARCH

Elisabeth Dunne and Derfel Owen

There is currently an interest in the balancing of teaching and learning with research so as to give students the best education, and there is little doubt that there is a tension between the two areas. The European Union's (EU) High Level Group[1] on the Modernisation of Higher Education (2013) has recently highlighted the issue of research taking precedence over teaching; the group are adamant that not enough emphasis is placed on teaching in many of Europe's top universities, and that this balance must be redressed. Further to this, research is not always viewed in a positive light within the learning and teaching environment:

> Our view is that university research often detracts from the quality of teaching. We regret the continuing elevation of research and the systematic neglect of the quality of instruction. (Pocklington & Tupper, 2002)

This view from Canada is one that is oft-voiced, by students as well as by researchers, from across the world, and especially from within research-intensive universities. Whatever the truth of such a statement, Ellis (2006)[2] proposed a very different view: that universities should provide an opportunity for all undergraduates to conduct research — to create knowledge.

The former view reflects a conceptualisation of research that is almost entirely removed from teaching and that is distant from the student; from this stance, students may at the very best be the inspired recipients of research-led knowledge and understanding, and at worst may find that the institutional emphasis on research leaves little time for the development of high quality teaching. From the latter perspective, instead of students and teaching taking second place to research,

---

[1]The group, headed by the former president of Ireland Mary McAleese, is composed of distinguished European academics plus the chair of Microsoft Corporation in Europe, Jan Muehlfeit.
[2]Director of the National Science Foundation's chemistry division.

there is potential for shared endeavour that is of value to both parties. In 1810, the German educator and philosopher Wilhelm von Humboldt famously wrote, in his outline of the future university of Berlin, that 'universities should treat learning as not yet wholly solved problems and hence always in research mode'. This seems a healthy way to consider the relation between teaching and research and, as suggested above by Ellis and demonstrated by Healey and Jenkins (2009) in their collection of cases from around the world, students can engage in this constant and continuing research mode. In the words of Jenkins and Healey:

> Humboldt's vision for higher education ... needs to be translated into the needs of a mass higher education system. We argue that the task now is to reinvent or reinvigorate the curriculum to ensure that all institutions should experience learning through and about research and inquiry. The key strategy for us is to facilitate the integration of undergraduate research and inquiry into the curriculum. (Healey & Jenkins, 2009, p. 6)

When students act as researchers, relationships between students and staff, and the nature of student engagement and expertise, are immediately challenged: students can become active knowledge-makers, collaborators, partners or co-creators of their learning experiences; they are active stakeholders instead of comparatively passive receivers of research wisdom. This requires a fundamental shift in thinking, in the conceptualisation of the role of students, and in how students should engage with the curriculum.

Each of the chapters in Part 6 illustrates how, when enabled to do so, students can take responsibility for researching within their discipline, within the community, or within the arena of pedagogy, and how they can work at the level of partners and experts. Further, they demonstrate how they can be empowered and, as an outcome of research, how they can have a real impact, including on bringing about change on both the small and the large scale.

Chapter 28 starts with a clear vision of the future: 'We believe that true curriculum renewal will, in the future, rest equally in the hands of students and staff'. The chapter then addresses the rationale for this statement along with a model for students as change agents, and outlines some first steps towards curriculum renewal and institutional change. The whole is premised on the concept of 'deliberative democracy' (Bessette, 1980, 1994), with its principles of inclusion, influence and authentic deliberation as central to decision-making, and with the intention that it should be free from distortions of power and open to multiple perspectives. This is important as a concept as in many ways it underpins so much of the thinking and approaches outlined in the handbook, especially in Parts 5 and 6. The translation of deliberative democracy into a World Café session with 560 Business students, as described in this chapter, highlights the power of engaging in conversational approaches with students, how it is possible to learn more deeply from student's module feedback, and how students agreeing on priorities for change can have a strong impact. Although in its infancy, the approach taken in this Australian context has clear and well-delineated strategies for engaging students and staff together, in order to learn from each other and to bring about change in deliberate, focused and determined ways.

Chapter 29 explores the practice of students as researchers, in this case of their own digital media practices. The intention was to create a collaborative community of inquiry, with students acting as research partners or co-researchers, having equal status in the planning and execution of research and responding to outcomes. Case studies give evidence of students engaged in researching their own practices, and in producing new knowledge, with the suggestion that this creates a context of 'epistemic engagement' for students. As with so many of the practice-oriented chapter in this Handbook, there were — and are — challenges to be addressed; the lack of prior expertise in research, students not all engaging as expected, goals not always being shared by a group, research aims being introduced by researchers not students, which had a ongoing impact on ownership and power relations, with genuine empowerment through control and decision-making needing to be in hands of students. difficult how to sustain and nurture to become embedded in systemic change in research activity. Not quick fixes rec/reward.

Chapter 30 focuses specifically on students as change agents, an initiative that has been running for five years and that is developing and changing in shape from year to year. It is founded on the key idea that the student voice has been well heeded over the past decade, but that institutions have not given students the opportunity to respond to issues, to recommend solutions or to bring about the required changes in the learning and teaching environment. Further, the concept of 'listening to the student voice' — implicitly if not deliberately — supports the perspective of student as 'consumer', whereas 'students as change agents' explicitly supports a view of the student as 'active collaborator' and 'co-producer'. An additional key point is that students are required to research their area of concern, so that change is founded on evidence rather than whim. This chapter reviews some practical models of student engagement that have both arisen from, and supported development of the change agents' initiative. Issues of recognition and reward are discussed and related to case studies of practice that focus on different ways in which students are bringing about evidence-led change.

The focus on pedagogy is continued in Chapter 31, with a portrayal of a program in the United States wherein academics work with undergraduates as pedagogical consultants over a semester-long partnership, thereby enabling a deeper understanding of the complexity of teaching and learning and shifting from passivity of the student to agency. This close attention to issues and questions surrounding practice is more akin to action research. Differently to the change agent initiative above, staff who engage in this process are given course release or a stipend, student volunteers apply for a consultant role and are paid, and they also work outside their own area of disciplinary study. This chapter highlights in particular the dialogic nature of the relationship between academic and student, looking at both academic and student viewpoints. For example, staff may initially feel vulnerable; students may find it difficult to feel legitimate in their consultant role, because of the usual power dynamics inherent in more usual staff-student; but the developing relationship also creates space for self-awareness, personal agency and empowerment, and transformational change.

As in the examples above, chapter 32 reviews a context in which students take their role more seriously than they otherwise might, in this case because they are required to take responsibility for useful outcomes in a community organisation. It is also a context where relationships and collaborative dialogues are all important, with a potential for change through students and university staff bringing new ideas and perspectives to community partners in the workplace. The chapter describes both Community-based learning and community-based research initiatives, the two approaches existing along a continuum of experiential learning and participatory research activities. In particular, the Community Partners scheme enables students to undertake research projects that allow them to apply academic knowledge to a real context, to engage with peers, academic staff and community partners in a meaningful way around an issue of common concern, and to become aware of the local, social impact of research. A key tenet is that community engagement work should be of mutual benefit for all partners through co-creation of knowledge which reflects the shared interests of students and the communities with which they engage

The final chapter of the handbook outlines an initiative wherein research and research-like teaching are being embedded in all courses at all levels across the university, with students being involved in the design and development of their own educational programmes. Student as producer provides 'intelligent resistance' to the notion of student as consumer and, through a process of debate and consultation, there is a high level of ownership of the initiative. The university is committed to empowering students as producers of their own learning and through this strategy, as producers of their university, making university life richer and more rewarding for all. Importantly, this endeavour includes postgraduates with an emphasis on students engaging with each other across their disciplines. The interest of this initiative lies in part in its sense of vision, its 'dynamic narrative', and also because student engagement policy requires in practice that students should work together with staff in developing and implementing solutions, because they are the experts in the student experience; all parts of the university are expected to embrace and benefit from student engagement. Ultimately, student as producer could provide a model of co-operative education, with students involved in the management and leadership of the whole institution.

References

Bessette, J. (1980). Deliberative democracy: The majority principle in Republican government. In D. L. Schaefer (Ed.), *How democratic is the constitution? Democratic decision-making: Historical and contemporary perspectives* (pp. 102–116). Washington, DC: AEI Press.

Bessette, J. (1994). *The mild voice of reason: Deliberative democracy & American national government*. Chicago, IL: University of Chicago Press.

Ellis, A. B. (2006). Creating a culture for innovation. *The Chronicle in Higher Education*, *52*(32), B20 (April 14).

European Union (EU). (2013). High Level Group on the Modernisation of Higher Education. Report to the European Commission on Improving the Quality of Teaching and Learning in Europe's Higher Education Institutions.

Healey, M., & Jenkins, A. (2009). *Developing undergraduate research and inquiry*. New York, NY: Higher Education Academy. Retrieved from http://www.heacademy.ac.uk/assets/York/documents/resources/
publications/DevelopingUndergraduate_Final.pdf

Pocklington, T., & Tupper, A. (2002). *No place to learn: Why universities aren't working*. Vancouver, BC: University of British Columbia Press.

Chapter 28

Deliberative Democracy for Curriculum Renewal

Amani Bell, Lyn Carson and Leanne Piggott

Abstract

When students and academics co-design curricula, benefits include deeper student engagement in learning, increased staff enthusiasm for teaching, and curricula that meet students' needs. However, there are few examples of active student involvement in curriculum design processes in Australia. Our literature review shows that (1) students need a voice in higher education that goes beyond course feedback surveys, (2) the 'students as change agents' approach is well-established internationally and (3) deliberative processes can equitably and effectively involve students in curriculum renewal processes. In this chapter we discuss a case study where staff and students worked in partnership for curriculum renewal. A process, based on deliberative democracy principles and techniques, was used to facilitate student and staff deliberation on how to improve a unit of study. Staff and students then co-designed the next iteration of the unit. This pilot trial, in which 560 students participated, led to three immediate changes to the curriculum. We conclude by exploring opportunities for further expansion, such as devising an online version of the process; participation of employers and other stakeholders; and implementing the process at the programme level.

28.1. Introduction

We believe that true curriculum renewal will, in the future, rest equally in the hands of students and staff. Current approaches that rely on student feedback surveys pay only lip service to the democratic ideals espoused in university policies. The significant change in approach that we trialled created a more meaningful partnership between students and staff. It is important to note that while the change we propose

The Student Engagement Handbook: Practice in Higher Education
Copyright © 2013 by Emerald Group Publishing Limited
All rights of reproduction in any form reserved
ISBN: 978-1-78190-423-7

will usher in a new paradigm of curriculum development, it is a change that is simple to make.

We trialled a curriculum renewal process based on the principles of deliberative democracy. The trial provides an evidence base for proposing the wider adoption of a 'students as change agents' approach. The trial also enables refinement of the process and the creation of resources to support its universal adoption.

28.2.   Literature Review

28.2.1.   *The Student Voice in Higher Education*

Ramsden and others have drawn attention to both the need to consider higher education from the student perspective and the benefits for student outcomes in doing so (e.g. Biggs & Tang, 2007; Ramsden, 1992). Ramsden asserts that we 'will not be able to take the student experience forward unless we see it as a joint venture between students and those who provide higher education' (2008, p.1).

Students are key stakeholders in the curriculum design process, yet 'are consulted less often than employers and other stakeholders' (Bovill, Bulley, & Morss, 2011a, p. 203). In Australia, the main way that students have input into curriculum design is feedback via surveys. While surveys of student experiences of university can provide valuable data, there is evidence that students see surveys as 'merely a ritual' and that they do not always think that their feedback is acted upon (Freeman & Dobbins, 2013, p. 142). Thus students become 'survey-fatigued' and feel disengaged from the feedback process (Porter, Whitcomb, & Weitzer, 2004). In addition 'evaluation tools rarely allow space for open dialogue between educators and students' (Freeman & Dobbins, 2013, p. 145).

Therefore, there is room for students to play a more active role in decision-making for curriculum renewal.

28.2.2.   *Students as Change Agents*

In the tertiary context, 'students as change agents' generally means students and staff working in partnership to enhance university education. The model is well-established internationally, particularly in the United Kingdom and the United States. The University of Exeter's project was instrumental in bringing the term 'students as change agents' to global attention. In the Exeter initiative, students carry out research projects on their learning and teaching experiences and present their recommendations at an annual conference (Dunne & Zandstra, 2011).

There are benefits to the 'students as change agents' approach for students, staff and universities. Students become more engaged in their learning (Werder, Ware, Thomas, & Skogsberg, 2010), feel valued (Delpish et al., 2010), develop graduate attributes (Dunne & Zandstra, 2011) and are able to articulate their learning in new ways (Delpish et al., 2010). Teaching staff feel more enthused about their teaching

(Werder et al., 2010) and learn to value student expertise (Delpish et al., 2010). For universities, the 'student as change agents' approach has contributed to enhancements in policy and practice (Dunne & Zandstra, 2011), including curriculum renewal (Delpish et al., 2010).

Healey (2013) has collated over 50 examples of initiatives where tertiary students are engaged as change agents. The majority of the initiatives are occurring in the United Kingdom and the United States, with the following emerging work taking place in Australia:

- the ULTRIS programme at the University of Western Australia involves students as Scholarship of Teaching and Learning practitioners (Sandover, Partridge, Dunne, & Burkill, 2012a), with the associated Matariki Undergraduate Research Network connecting student Scholarship of Teaching and Learning practitioners across four countries (Sandover, Partridge, Spronken-Smith, Remenda, & Burd, 2012b);
- student-led learning programmes at the University of Ballarat (University of Ballarat, 2013);
- a student−faculty retreat to improve the Law School curriculum held at the Australian National University (O'Brien, 2012);
- students pitching ideas to improve the student experience to senior staff at the Australian National University (Australian National University, 2013).

Projects where students act as change agents have been used for various purposes. Our focus here is on students as co-designers of courses. There are several examples of students successfully being engaged in this role (e.g. Healey, Bradford, Roberts, & Knight, 2013, and see Healey, 2013 for summaries of 20 projects), yet most of these initiatives either involve only small numbers of students (e.g. Bovill, Cook-Sather, & Felten, 2011b) and/or are very costly in terms of time (e.g. Kerns, Miller, & Kerns, 2004).

Where only small numbers of students are able to participate in such projects, it is possible that these students are the 'usual suspects' — the high-achieving students who are already very engaged in their studies. We propose a time-efficient approach based on the ideals of deliberative democracy (Carson & Hartz-Karp, 2005), where students are randomly selected to represent their cohort in a discussion-based curriculum renewal process or where all students participate as per our pilot project.

28.2.3. Deliberative Democracy

Deliberative democracy is a form of community or stakeholder engagement in which deliberation is used for decision-making (Gastil & Levine, 2005; Leighninger, 2006). Deliberative democracy

> seeks to address barriers and build the capacity and confidence of
> people to participate in, and negotiate and partner with, institutions

that affect their lives, in particular those previously excluded or disenfranchised. (International Conference on Engaging Communities,
2005)

We see deliberative democracy (its principles and practices) as an ideal method of
engaging students in the curriculum renewal process. The principles of deliberative
democracy are (Carson, 2011a):

1. inclusion or representativeness: the latter is best achieved through random selection;
2. deliberation: there must be opportunities for participants to wrestle with complexity dialogically, including weighing up strengths and weaknesses of various
   options; and
3. influence: participants' recommendations should be seriously considered by decision-makers.

Deliberative democracy involves an understanding of beliefs and priorities, analysis of factual information, acknowledging the value of multiple perspectives and
consideration of the various and sometimes competing concerns of all stakeholders
(Doherty, 2008). Participants meet to discuss issues, and, ideally, to effect changes.
If change is the desired outcome of a deliberative democracy event, then the actions
proposed by participants must link into decision-making processes.

There are various methods of facilitating deliberative democracy processes,
including World Café (Carson, 2011b), which we used in our project trial. Though
World Café is typically a creative, divergent approach, it was adapted here in order
to achieve convergence, which is more consistent with deliberative democracy
principles.

The deliberative democracy approach is well suited to the development of 'the
whole student' — graduate attributes that go beyond knowledge and skills to encompass dimensions such as morality and emotion (Quinlan, 2011). In higher education,
the benefits of deliberative practices include students developing graduate attributes
such as leadership and communication skills, a stronger sense of having a voice on
campus and in their communities, and an appreciation for diverse views (Doherty,
2008; Harriger & McMillan, 2008). Other academics have also pointed to deliberative democracy as a way of changing higher education, seeing it 'as part of a broad
civic renewal movement' (Grattan, Dedrick, & Dienstfrey, 2008, p. 5). At a more
practical level, deliberative democracy is a tool for active critical thinking through
collective student engagement, and in turn improved class discussion. Further, participants in deliberative democracy processes often experience changed attitudes and
take action to bring about change (Harriger & McMillan, 2008).

As an example of where deliberative practices led to change: Wake Forest
University made changes to its first-year orientation programme and developed
a new social meeting space due to a student-led, campus-wide deliberation on 'building community at Wake Forest' (Harriger & McMillan, 2008). Another example
is where 58 students studying physiotherapy were involved in a half-day 'participatory research and action' session; they identified curriculum-based issues and

came to a group consensus on four key solutions to put into action (O'Neill & McMahon, 2012). Students appreciated the opportunity for group dialogue and felt empowered.

28.3.   Case Study

28.3.1.   *Our Context*

The University of Sydney is a research-intensive university founded in 1850, with 50,206 students and 3474 academic staff (University of Sydney, 2013). In our descriptions below, we use the term 'unit of study' to describe an individual subject/ class. We use the term 'staff' to describe the teaching staff. At our university, 'tutor' is used, rather than casual academic, sessional staff, hourly paid staff, graduate teaching assistant or adjunct faculty.

28.3.2.   *Background*

In 2012, Professor Carson and Dr Piggott taught a postgraduate unit of study called *Critical Thinking in Business* with around 560 students enrolled. About 70 per cent of the students were from non-English speaking backgrounds; they were intelligent but were grappling with the language and with the concept of critical thinking. This was evident in student responses to the mid-semester (Week 6) feedback conducted both online and in tutorials. Professor Carson drew on her background in deliberative democracy to create an opportunity for the students to give feedback on the unit, and to model a different way to collectively decide in large groups. Additionally, students would eventually be able to utilise the decision-making method in the workplace, thereby giving additional power to this way of working.

28.3.3.   *Process*

At the end of a preceding lecture, Professor Carson explained what was going to happen in the tutorial: that building on a summary of the online and tutorial feedback, a World Café would be conducted (Carson, 2011b), i.e. an iterative conversation to see what students wanted to change about the unit of study, both in the current semester and the next one. Each of the tutors was given information about the World Café process, and charged with this information, and a process, the tutors each convened their tutorial groups, usually of about 20 students.

In preparation, students were given 5 minutes to silently read the summary of the mid-semester feedback given by students during the previous week. There were then four World Café rounds, each of about 10 minutes. At the end of each round all but the host scattered and found a different table. In the first and second rounds, the groups were asked to discuss 'What would we like to change about this unit of study — for this semester and next?' Students were provided with the following prompts:

- Consider both the summary of the data plus your own opinion.
- Remember to interrogate any suggestions for change.
- What has been your best experience of a unit of study?
- What evidence is there that this suggestion would work?
- Would this suggested change benefit everyone?
- How would that suggestion lead to better graduates?

These prompts ensured that the World Café was more than a conversation. Instead, deliberation was experienced as students wrestled together with both the challenges and possible solutions.

In the third round, students were asked to discuss their most effective suggestions and to begin to make a group decision. They were reminded to ensure that the suggested changes were workable. In the final round, the groups were asked to reach agreement about the two most effective suggestions: one for this semester, one for the next semester. The students then used the 'Dotmocracy' voting technique (Diceman, 2010) to vote on their preferred option. Each small group wrote the suggestions on two Dotmocracy templates (one for the current semester, the other for future semesters). The sheets were then affixed to the wall or laid out on tables. The students then voted on each idea using a six-point Likert scale (Strong Agreement, Agreement, Neutral, Disagreement, Strong Disagreement, Confusion), with space to comment if they wished.

> It was clear that it was an unfamiliar experience for most students when I gave them the instructions ... for example ... you stress that it's terribly important that if you are usually very verbose that you must hold back and that if you are quite timid that you step into the space a bit more, and the combination of those two things should mean that you are having equal time and making an equal contribution. Perhaps, that kind of instruction is not typically given to students in tutorials because I could see that it was already having an impact. (Professor Carson, extract from reflective journal)

28.3.4. Outcomes

A representative from each tutorial group attended a meeting where Professor Carson summarised the outcomes from the Dotmocracy sheets and the group helped to create the final list of suggested changes. After an hour, the unit coordinator came into the meeting, with the guarantee that she would implement whatever changes the group proposed (with the proviso that the changes needed to be consistent with the university's policies). The unit coordinator heard what the students wanted, asked a few questions and they offered additional comments. The agreed changes were:

- to reduce the 400 word weekly reflective journal entry to 150 words;
- to provide specific assessment feedback comments, starting with the words: 'In order for you to improve you should …'; and
- for the teaching team to explicitly highlight the connections between the lectures, tutorials, reading material and assessments.

These changes were reported back to all students in tutorials and in the lecture.

> I think there was general sense that the students were being taken seriously by someone and it was clear that the unit coordinator wanted to take them seriously. It was a very respectful handover of recommendations to the decision maker, which is ideal. The unit coordinator certainly was not threatened by it or feeling that her role was being usurped. It was just a different way of getting feedback from students, of which she was very supportive. (Professor Carson, extract from reflective journal)

Another benefit of the process was that students experienced a way in which a very large organisation could make decisions for the benefit of all, without involving the entire organisation — or, if they did, to do so with ease and efficiency. All students were asked, in their reflective journals, to

> Describe what it was like for you to participate in the deliberation activity in tutorials this week (Week 7) and hypothesize why it had such an impact on you. For students who did not attend this week's tutorials, answer the same question by thinking about a past scenario where you had to vote for a cause.

The students commented about how the World Café helped them to appreciate multiple perspectives (the theme for the Week 7 lecture). They explained that they had no idea that other people, in the same situation as them, could think so differently about the same issue (e.g. what type of feedback students would prefer). The activity seemed to facilitate a realisation that diverse opinions exist among members of the same group, even in a group whose interests are supposedly the same. Some suggestions about future relevance included that, in the future in the business world, they would discuss matters as a team, with all team members and customers, instead of making decisions without their input. Tutors also commented that the World Café was one of the highlights of the semester.

28.4. Next Steps

We propose further trials of the 'students as change agents' model detailed above. It would be useful to trial the model in units of study of different sizes and in different disciplines. In our case study, the World Café process was directly linked to the unit of study topic (critical thinking); we have some suggestions as to how the idea might be 'sold' to those teaching disciplines where the process does not link with the subject material. For example, the model could be proposed as a different way of facilitating a tutorial, where one week the process is used to collect student feedback, and the next week it is used to discuss a particular discipline-based topic. Alternatively, we suggest random selection of students, plus incentives for participating, outside of class time. Food could be provided — when a World Café is conducted with the general public, it's important to provide sustenance — it draws on the history and ambience of cafés as places for both socialising and learning, i.e. 'pleasurable learning' (McWilliam, 2011, p. 266). Student representatives in each faculty might facilitate the Cafés. Our work has many other opportunities for further expansion, such as:

- exploring an online version of the process (including an online phase that enables students to develop the options for change prior to face-to-face deliberations), to cater for students studying across multiple campuses or at a distance;
- participation of employers and other stakeholders (including alumni);
- implementing the process at the degree rather than unit of study level;
- providing practical application of critical thinking through democratic deliberation in student—staff curriculum design; and
- a longitudinal study to explore the experiences and perceptions of staff and students over time.

28.5.   Conclusion

End-of-semester surveys often resemble the superficial responses derived from opinion polls or focus groups in the political landscape and this is why those in deliberative democracy circles distinguish between 'public opinion' and 'public judgement' (see, e.g., Yankelovich & Friedman, 2010). The comments tell us little and give us no clear direction for change. Using the World Café process, we were able to make some immediate changes to a unit of study, based on the active engagement of students and staff. Deliberative democrats are interested in informed discussion through genuine dialogue, where options are weighed and top-of-the-head opinions are converted to opinion based on evidence. World Cafés, involving students in curriculum design, are a way to harness collective intelligence, through deliberation, to reach a collective judgement.

Acknowledgements

We thank the original proposal team for their enthusiasm and ideas: Phoebe Drake, Luong Thi Hong Gam, Professor Martin Hayden, Nivek Thompson and Donherra

Walmsley. Thank you to Mick Healey for generously sharing his fantastic 'students as change agents' resources. Head tutor Cecile de Vries provided invaluable support in conducting the pilot project.

References

Australian National University. (2013). Leadership and Influence in a Complex World. Retrieved from http://studyat.anu.edu.au/courses/VCUG2002;details.html

Biggs, J., & Tang, C. (2007). *Teaching for quality learning at university* (3rd ed.). Buckingham UK: SRHE & Open University Press.

Bovill, C., Bulley, C. J., & Morss, K. (2011a). Engaging and empowering first-year students through curriculum design: Perspectives from the literature. *Teaching in Higher Education*, *16*(2), 197–209.

Bovill, C., Cook-Sather, A., & Felten, P. (2011b). Students as co-creators of teaching approaches, course design, and curricula: Implications for academic developers. *International Journal for Academic Development*, *16*(2), 133–145.

Carson, L. (2011a). Dilemmas, disasters and deliberative democracy. *Griffith Review*, *32*, 25–32.

Carson, L. (2011b). Designing a public conversation using the World Café method. *Social Alternatives*, *30*(1), 10–14.

Carson, L., & Hartz-Karp, J. (2005). Adapting and combining deliberative designs: Juries, Polls, and Forums. In J. Gastil & P. Levine (Eds.), *The deliberative democracy handbook: Strategies for effective civic engagement in the twenty-first century* (pp. 120–138). San Francisco, CA: Jossey-Bass.

Delpish, A., Darby, A., Holmes, A., Knight-McKenna, M., Mihans, R., King, C., & Felten, P. (2010). Student–faculty partnerships in course design. In C. Werder & M. M. Otis (Eds.), *Engaging student voices in the study of teaching and learning* (pp. 96–114). Sterling, Virginia: Stylus.

Diceman, J. (2010). *Dotmocracy handbook*. Retrieved from www.dotmocracy.org

Doherty, J. (2008). Individual and community: Deliberative practices in a first-year seminar. In J. R. Dedrick, L. Grattan, & H. Dienstfrey (Eds.), *Deliberation and the work of higher education* (pp. 59–87). Dayton, Ohio: Kettering Foundation Press.

Dunne, E., & Zandstra, R. (2011). *Students as change agents – new ways of engaging with learning and teaching in higher education*. Bristol: A joint University of Exeter/ESCalate/ Higher Education Academy Publication. Retrieved from http://escalate.ac.uk/8064

Freeman, R., & Dobbins, K. (2013). Are we serious about enhancing courses? Using the principles of assessment for learning to enhance course evaluation. *Assessment & Evaluation in Higher Education*, *38*(2), 142–151.

Gastil, J., & Levine, P. C. (2005). *The deliberative democracy handbook*. San Francisco, CA: Jossey-Bass.

Grattan, L., Dedrick, J. R., & Dienstfrey, H. (2008). Introduction: Creating new spaces for deliberation in higher education. In J. R. Dedrick, L. Grattan, & H. Dienstfrey (Eds.), *Deliberation and the work of higher education* (pp. 5–16). Dayton, Ohio: Kettering Foundation Press.

Harriger, K. J., & McMillan, J. J. (2008). Contexts for deliberation: Experimenting with democracy in the classroom, on campus, and in the community. In J. R. Dedrick,

L. Grattan, & H. Dienstfrey (Eds.), *Deliberation and the work of higher education* (pp. 235–265). Dayton, Ohio: Kettering Foundation Press.

Healey, M. (2013). *Students as change agents.* Retrieved from http://www.mickhealey.co.uk/resources

Healey, M., Bradford, M., Roberts, C., & Knight, Y. (2013). Collaborative discipline-based curriculum change: Applying change academy processes at department level. *International Journal for Academic Development, 18*(1), 31–44.

Kerns, S. E., Miller, R. K., & Kerns, D. V. (2004). Designing from a blank slate: The development of the initial Olin College Curriculum. In Committee on the Engineer of 2020, Phase II & Committee on Engineering Education, National Academy of Engineering, *Educating the Engineer of 2020: Adapting engineering education to the new century.* Washington, DC: The National Academies Press.

International Conference on Engaging Communities. (2005). *Brisbane declaration.* Retrieved from http://www.darzin.com/webdarzin/wp-content/uploads/2010/09/brisbane_declaration.pdf

Leighninger, M. (2006). *The next form of democracy.* Nashville, TN: Vanderbilt University Press.

McWilliam, E. (2011). From school to café and back again: Responding to the learning demands of the twenty-first century. *International Journal of Leadership in Education, Theory and Practice, 14*(3), 257–268.

O'Brien, M. T. (2012). Walking the walk: Using student-faculty dialogue to change an adversarial curriculum. *Journal of the Australasian Law Teachers Association, 4*(1/2), 129–135.

O'Neill, G., & McMahon, S. (2012). Giving student groups a stronger voice: Using participatory research and action (PRA) to initiate change to a curriculum. *Innovations in Education and Teaching International, 49*(2), 161–171.

Porter, S. R., Whitcomb, M. E., & Weitzer, W. H. (2004). Multiple surveys of students and survey fatigue. In S. R. Porter (Ed.), *Overcoming survey research problems* (pp. 63–73). San Francisco, CA: Jossey-Bass.

Quinlan, K. M. (2011). *Developing the whole student: Leading higher education initiatives that integrate mind and heart.* London: Leadership Foundation for Higher Education.

Ramsden, P. (1992). *Learning to teach in higher education.* London: Routledge.

Ramsden, P. (2008). *The future of higher education teaching and the student experience.* Retrieved from http://www.heacademy.ac.uk/assets/York/documents/ourwork/policy/paulramsden_teaching_and_student_experience.doc

Sandover, S., Partridge, L., Dunne, E., & Burkill, S. (2012a). Undergraduate researchers change learning and teaching: A case study of two universities in Australia and the UK. *CUR Quarterly, 33*(1), 33–39.

Sandover, S., Partridge, L., Spronken-Smith, R., Remenda, V., & Burd, E. (2012b). *The matariki undergraduate research network (MURN): The challenges of a global classroom.* Paper presented at International Society for the Scholarship of Teaching and Learning, Oct 24-27, Hamilton, Canada.

University of Ballarat. (2013). Student Futures Program. Retrieved from http://www.ballarat.edu.au/staff/learning-and-teaching@ub/clipp/succeed@ub

University of Sydney. (2013). Facts and Figures. Retrieved from http://sydney.edu.au/about/profile/facts-figures.shtml

Werder, C., Ware, L., Thomas, C., & Skogsberg, E. (2010). Students in parlour talk on teaching and learning. In C. Werder & M. M. Otis (Eds.), *Engaging student voices in the study of teaching and learning* (pp. 16–31). Sterling, Virginia: Stylus.

Yankelovich, D., & Friedman, W. (2010). *Toward wiser judgment.* Nashville, TN: Vanderbilt University Press.

Chapter 29

Students as Co-Researchers: A Collaborative, Community-Based Approach to the Research and Practice of Technology-Enhanced Learning

Sue Timmis and Jane Williams

Abstract

This chapter explores community-based approaches to student engagement in researching their own practices, in particular, when this involves the use of digital media in their learning. Student engagement has been described as active involvement in one's own learning, emphasising individual agency (Trowler, 2010). We argue for a relational view of agency (Edwards, 2005) involving dynamic realignment of thoughts and actions between different actors in response to problems and challenges. This has led to the development of a collaborative model of inquiry, with students and staff working on authentic research and knowledge production projects within disciplinary communities. This methodology involves students acting as co-researchers in researching their own digital media practices. Digital practices often cross formal and informal boundaries, making authentic accounts difficult to obtain. Involving students as partners increases validity and shared purposes. Students can engage in meaningful research and reflect back on their own practice. Three co-inquiry projects are presented, reporting on aims, methodologies and practical implications and challenges, including incentives, rewards, assessment constraints and equality of involvement. The findings demonstrate the need for continual re-negotiation of roles, rebalancing power relations and motivation within co-inquiry models. Addressing these more explicitly would ensure a more negotiated set of outcomes. We conclude that co-inquiry models are not quick fixes to student engagement but part of a longer term relational shift which takes time and mutual commitment to the process. Despite these challenges, this model offers potential as a more inclusive approach to scholarship and more authentic forms of student inquiry.

The Student Engagement Handbook: Practice in Higher Education
Copyright © 2013 by Emerald Group Publishing Limited
All rights of reproduction in any form reserved
ISBN: 978-1-78190-423-7

29.1.   Introduction

This chapter aims to explore the possibilities and challenges for students to engage in researching their own practices, in particular, when this involves the use of digital media in their learning. There are many possible benefits to this, for the students themselves, for researchers in developing new lines of research inquiry, teaching staff in ensuring greater student engagement in learning and for universities whose concerns over enhancing the student experience are well documented (see Trowler, 2010).

The desirability for including research and inquiry-based activities in the undergraduate curriculum has been well rehearsed in the literature (see Healey & Jenkins, 2009; Spronken-Smith & Walker, 2010; Zimbardi & Myatt, 2012). The renewed focus on 'the student experience' in higher education suggests that students need to 'be active partners in shaping their learning experiences' (HEA, 2011).

Yet, others are calling for a more radical positioning of students as members of a community of scholars. Brew (2006, 2007) has argued that research is typically restricted to particular categories of people within universities, and influenced by the hierarchical relationships between academics, students and support staff which suffer from a kind of 'academic apartheid' 'where some people (students and also support staff) are denied access to certain kinds of power and resources' (Brew, 2007, p. 6.). Students need to be engaged in a search for authenticity in learning where being critical and enquiring are key elements and where 'such criticality is achieved in the spirit of research' (Barnett, 2007, p. 126). Indeed, 'inclusive knowledge-building communities' should be fostered, in which we reconsider who the scholars are and how different groups might work in partnership (Brew, 2007).

The recent 'student as producer' movement (Neary & Winn, 2009) also argues for a radical realignment of roles and a rethinking of what constitutes 'the student experience'. Reconceptualising students as producers involves: 'undergraduate students working in collaboration with academics to create work of social importance that is full of academic content and value, while at the same time reinvigorating the university beyond the logic of market economics' (Neary & Winn, 2009, p. 193). These ideas suggest that designing curricular to include research or inquiry-based activities might only be a starting point.

The challenges associated with researching students' digital media practices in both practical and meaningful ways were also influential in the development of our approach. Obtaining authentic data and sustained accounts of how students engage with digital media has become very challenging because this involves continual boundary crossing between personal and private, formal and informal, institutional and personal spaces (Timmis, 2012). This means that traditional research methods such as interviewing or capturing data from institutional environments, such as virtual learning environments (or learner management systems) will not always adequately address research questions that explore the lived experience of students using digital media (*ibid*). There are also many ethical concerns associated with capturing digital data that is created outside of institutional 'walls'. Therefore more participatory forms of research and inquiry also offer opportunities for collecting more authentic and situated data as well as providing a more radical positioning of students as co-producers of research and new knowledge.

This chapter discusses issues raised above in relation to our work in developing community-based models of research inquiry. We begin by exploring the concepts of student engagement and agency in relation to communities of inquiry. This is followed by an outline of the methodology we have developed before three illustrative case studies are then presented. Finally limitations and challenges are discussed before we offer our conclusions on the potential of this approach to scholarship and researching digital media practices.

29.2. Student Engagement and Agency

In this section, we discuss our understanding of 'student engagement' and its relationship to the concept of agency, both of which are key aspects of our approach but can be understood in different ways.

Student engagement is high on the policy agenda internationally but it is often unclear what is meant by this term and how and in what circumstances students are to become engaged? On the one hand, this may mean students' involvement in community or institutional projects (Kuh et al., 2007) or it can equally refer to students' motivation and involvement in their studies or university life. The concept of 'engagement' suggests not just involvement in activities but 'requires feelings and sense making as well as activity' (Harper & Quaye, 2009, p. 5.) so that to be engaged involves both commitment and attachment. Yet, many of the definitions of student engagement also imply normative 'requirements' where behavioural, emotional and cognitive engagement is seen as the means to improve individual attitudes and learning (see Trowler, 2010). Hu & Kuh (2002) suggest that engagement is 'the quality of effort students themselves devote to educationally purposeful activities that contribute directly to *desired* outcomes' (p. 555, emphasis added). This seems problematic because it raises questions of ownership and authority: what kinds of desired outcomes are valued and by whom? We need to be careful of viewing engagement as an expectation and adherence to prescribed activities.

Closer to our own thinking is the idea of *epistemic engagement* (Larreamendy-Joerns & Leinhardt, 2006; Shea & Bidjerano, 2009). This concept was developed in relation to engagement in online and distance educational environments; knowledge and learning are viewed as practices within the structure of a domain and a disciplinary community. Larreamendy-Joerns and Leinhardt (2006) suggest this kind of engagement involves initiating and participating in epistemic or knowledge building practices typical of disciplinary communities through a wide range of opportunities for intellectual engagement and interaction. Related to this, is Ludvigsen's (2012) idea that a core aim of education is to foster participation in specialised discourses. Participation in specialised discourses always involves understanding and embracing the culture and practices associated with disciplinary communities. This suggests a more communitarian view of engagement, where students are seen as partners in the educational project rather than the objects of it. It is this view of engagement that has informed us in developing the model of co-inquiry outlined in this chapter.

In addition to this more egalitarian understanding of engagement, a different perspective on agency underpins our model. Agency is frequently individually conceived, relating to self and the 'powers of ongoing reflexive monitoring of both self and society' (Archer, 2002, p. 19). However, this individualised view of agency has been challenged by a number of people, working in different areas. Jones and Healing (2010) argue that in considering how learners engage with digital media, our understanding needs to be expanded towards a collective form of agency, active at all levels of an activity system, in order to avoid technological determinism and reducing agency to one individual. Edwards (2005) has also argued that we need a more relational understanding of agency and introduced the concept of 'relational agency' that is shared and distributed. This involves 'a capacity to align one's thought and actions with those of others in order to interpret problems of practice and to respond to those interpretations' (Edwards, 2005, p. 169) enabling a dynamic realignment of thought and action between different actors in response to particular problems and challenges.

To summarise, we consider engagement and agency as underpinning our approach but from a community-based, authentic and relational perspective where students are valued as members of a community of scholars engaged in joint actions as part of the educational project. In our case, this has focused in particular on developing approaches to researching digital media practices amongst the students through co-researcher models.

29.3.   Collaborative, Community-Based Approaches to Research into Digital Media Practices

This section discusses the methodological approach that underpins the co-inquiry work that we have been undertaking. Broad methodological influences are summarised before the different elements of our approach are outlined.

As mentioned already, Brew's (2007) work on inclusive knowledge building communities has influenced our thinking on how students are positioned within research into teaching and learning in higher education. Co-operative inquiry, research undertaken '*with* people not *on* them or about *them*' (Heron, 1996, p. 19) has also influenced the design of this research. Co-operative inquiry operates on two levels of participation, full and partial. In the full form:

> … all those involved in the research are both co-researchers, who generate ideas about its focus, design and manage it, and draw conclusions from it; and also co-subjects, participating with awareness in the activity that is being researched. (Reason, 1994, pp. 41–42)

The intention in our research was to aim for this full form, with students acting as research partners, working alongside researchers and others, on a range of research activities. In some cases, this has also involved tutors and others providing institutional, subject or professional expertise. The aim was to develop a collaborative working environment where students and researchers work together on the planning, execution and outcomes of the research. Despite our aims that students would have equal status as co-researchers in a community of inquiry, it is important to acknowledge that achieving this was challenging. Students do not necessarily come into the community with pre-existing research expertise and therefore require support as they acquire the skills and experiences that will enable them to engage meaningfully as researchers and become full members of the community (Wenger, 1998). Additionally, the initial research aims were introduced by the researchers and not the students. Although these were adapted and students gradually began to take initiative and demonstrate growing confidence, it was found that this ownership of the 'project' had a continuing effect on power relations. This is discussed further in the section below on 'The challenges of adopting more inclusive approaches to research'.

Our focus has been on students' *own* digital media practices in different contexts and on knowledge creation activities that they initiate and sustain. Students' use of digital media frequently crosses boundaries between the institutional and the personal through the multiplicity of tools that are used both together and separately across different time and space configurations (Timmis, 2012; Wenger, White, & Smith, 2009). Obtaining authentic accounts of such practices using traditional data collection methods therefore becomes difficult because of the personal nature of some of the data and the potential for intrusion. This is particularly the case if the research requires investigation of 'naturally occurring data' (Silverman, 2006), such as communications rather than relying solely on accounts of practice, for example in interviews. This is also problematic in terms of recording personal experiences such as collaborations or studying practices which might take place in a variety of different settings and in particular may occur outside of institutional walls. Zamorski (2002) conducted a study into the relationship between research and teaching, where students were recruited as a parallel group to academic staff and asked to undertake an active role in the research. This allowed privileged access to data from key participants, namely students, and provided a distinctive learning experience for those taking part (Zamorski, 2002). Zamorksi's study demonstrates how involving students themselves in research can be helpful in accessing authentic accounts of student experiences and of giving them a voice and influence over the research design where they play a critical in obtaining such accounts.

In summary, this approach to working with students as co-researchers can be characterised as participative and collaborative. We have not sought simply to involve students but to work together on developing shared goals, where everyone is involved in shaping the project and its outcomes have relevance for students own work and development. The approach is also longitudinal rather than focusing on short term 'snapshots' and seeks to influence and change practice over time. Finally, we aim to conduct research involving students own digital media practices 'in the wild' across and beyond institutional boundaries. This means that outcomes are more open ended and include students' own views and understandings of the research agenda in how digital media can influence and benefit higher education.

29.4.   Putting the Approach into Practice: Three Case Studies

We now introduce three different cases and provide a detailed account of how these projects were conducted. In all cases the importance of introductory support, induction and familiarisation with key methods and approaches are emphasised as well as the fostering of students own ideas and understandings of the nature of the research problem. Planning and designing the research as a collaborative process were also critical to the success of the projects. Each project will now be outlined in turn, followed by a wider discussion of the challenges of adopting this kind of approach to researching digital media practices.

29.4.1.   Case Study 1: Investigating Undergraduate Online Communication and Collaborative Practices

The first case centres on how existing studies can be expanded and reconfigured to involve students in research activities, particularly where this includes their own practices. In this first study, third year undergraduates who were based at a large, teaching-focused UK university,[1] were invited to take part in a project aimed at investigating collaborative work using digital media. The students were studying one of two optional 10-credit modules in Information Systems. The teaching and learning activities on both modules included fortnightly lectures and a collaborative group project conducted in online special interest groups (called Sigs). The project involved between three and six students working together to form a group and identify a topic of common interest from within an overall set of themes. Groups were tasked with researching this topic collaboratively, communicating online (and off line if they so chose) using any digital tools or online spaces that met their needs. At their first lecture, students were invited to take part in an educational research study investigating how students engaged in the co-creation of artefacts and shared knowledge building practices and how the digital tools and online spaces mediated such practices.

As discussed above, investigating how students engage in study-related activities in online spaces is best undertaken in partnership with the students themselves, encouraging reflexive inquiry into how these practices influence learning. In addition, without access to authentic conversations and online contributions, there are risks that the research might not be able to investigate collaborative practices *in situ* and in sufficient depth, which is a common problem of e-learning research (Shih, Feng, & Tsai, 2008). Additionally, collecting data on personal conversations that

---

[1]This university is not named as they wished to remain anonymous, all names used are pseudonyms.

take place across the institutional and personal boundaries could be intrusive and fraught with ethical and practical challenges. A participative approach aims to be both empowering and practical. Ethics procedures were conducted following university guidelines and informed consent was obtained from all students.

All students were initially invited to become part of a study group that would investigate their own practices over the course of the 12 weeks in which they would be involved in the collaborative projects. Work in the study group was in addition to the work they were doing within their modules. Around 10 from each group volunteered and these students were then invited to an initial meeting where plans and ideas for the research were discussed and students were encouraged to ask questions. Students were invited to collect and archive their personal communications data that related in any way to the work of the collaborative projects and using any digital media and how this might be conducted was discussed and agreed amongst the group. Timings, activities and methods of communication for data collection were agreed. Data was collected at key points over the course of the 12 weeks and in addition, students took part in group interviews. One of the students was appointed as chair and although an interview guide was provided, students were encouraged to explore any areas that they felt were important, drawing on the research questions. In addition, students were given a series of questions in advance to work through and reflect on, in order to support their thinking. Group interviews allow for a more negotiated set of outcomes and can produce rich, elaborated data which develops over time (Fontana & Frey, 2000). One frequently cited potential pitfall concerns the emergence of 'groupthink' — where individual voices and ideas converge and alternative positions are constrained. However, this suggests that interviews of any kind can uncover an independent reality. However, if they are understood as interventions which will always influence outcomes, they become 'negotiated accomplishments of both interviewers and respondents that are shaped by the contexts and situations in which they take place' (Fontana & Frey, 2000, p. 663).

Students responded very enthusiastically to these challenges and appreciated the consultation over timing of activities and experience of research it gave them. They kept in contact and were very reliable at turning up to meetings and reported that the research was helpful in helping them to reflect more on their own practices with digital media.

> Doing a research project like this has ... helped understand that people do communicate in many different ways .... It has allowed me to assess the various technologies ... and solutions ... which might prove to be useful one day. (Lawrence)

In some cases, it helped students to make connections with other parts of their course and other disciplines:

> It's an enjoyable experience and it's nice ... 'cause I do Psychology as well so I have to study a lot of research projects so its nice to actually take part in one as well. (Phil)

Some of the students were, however, more motivated by extrinsic goals. As participation was voluntary and tasks were conducted in addition to coursework, they were offered an academic reference should they ever need one, refreshments at all meetings and a high capacity memory stick as a small thank you gift. Several students commented on extrinsic motivators as contributors to their commitment, as shown by this conversation:

> *It's just something to put on my CV and also I could put Bristol University rather than BigCity University* (...) (Alex)

> *So it is the putting it on your CV and the fact that I said I'd write references for you is that all?* ... (Researcher)

> *... and the free food yeah.* (Alex)

Clearly, the reasons for participation in extracurricular research projects, such as this cannot be assumed to be divorced from the wider context of student life and the heavy emphasis on assessment and employability goals.

There were also some ethical challenges in this study, in part because this focused on communications. Students in the study group collected their own communications but because these were always two-way conversations, it was necessary to obtain consent to use the data from the whole cohort. Some students did not give permission for their data to be used and therefore some conversations had to be removed from the data set. Because of the intermingling of personal and study related dialogue, it was also necessary to stress to study group members to review their own data and only archive material they were happy to share publicly. In addition to this, in one case some further discussion took place about a particular conversation, because of the highly personal nature of what had been archived.

Nevertheless, the study could be considered to be successful in engaging students in research that was not part of their assessed or formal work and that they found to be worthwhile and helpful towards future careers. It was also successful in investigating communications at the boundary between formal and informal practices which is usually an unknown territory.

29.4.2. *Case Study 2: Medical Students' E-Learning Development Projects*

This second case concerns the digital media practices of undergraduate medical students at the University of Bristol when developing technology-enhanced learning (TEL) materials as part of an inquiry-based e-learning[2] development initiative (Williams et al., 2011). Students take the opportunity to develop innovative online

---

[2]Technology enhanced learning or TEL has now replaced the term e-learning but it is included here for historical purposes as this is what the initiative was first called and is referred as such in student quotations.

learning resources on a clinical topic of their choice during set periods of independent study, as required by the General Medical Council (GMC, 2009). Bristol undergraduate medical students spend years 3−5 studying and learning the practice of medicine in a number of NHS-based Clinical Academies. Students rotate through the Academies receiving all their clinical teaching and experience, pastoral care and taking part in assessments. TEL through a range of interactive, digital learning resources, is an integral part of providing a consistent student learning experience across the academies where learning opportunities may vary. Students identify a clinical topic and area of need based on their own personal learning experiences and through researching those of their peers. They investigate and experiment to combine different media and interactive elements with a variety of software tools to achieve their objectives. The aim is to develop materials that will be used by their peers and embedded within the medical education curriculum for future use.

This inquiry-based learning initiative has been running for over 10 years beginning with one student developing an online learning package for their project and encouraging others to do similar work the following year. Projects are student-led with support from an academic supervisor and staff in the TEL development team in the Centre for Medical Education on an ad hoc basis. Over time, more comprehensive support and quality assurance frameworks have evolved, refined by student feedback and in response to changes in technology; so too has the sophistication of the resources as the students learn from their predecessors, further developing the practice model. Support offered includes preparatory workshops, drop in sessions to obtain advice and technical support, an online support course with a series of FAQs, how to guides with top tips for success and links to examples of best practice. Many students engaged regularly with the support opportunities available. Students are also asked what would be helpful to them during the development of their projects and some years, 'show and tell' sessions mid-way through their project periods have been requested to share ideas and progress and to gain feedback from each other on their designs. After the formal project timeframe, students continue to work with TEL staff, supervisors and other subject experts to refine their learning resources so that they can be integrated into the medical education curriculum and offered to other students.

In addition to their learning resources, students are assessed on a written reflective account offering insights into the process of developing their resource. Using Glaser's (2001) grounded theory approach, analysis[3] of a sample of 25 of these accounts together with reflective accounts from former students and TEL staff revealed how through the process of producing learning materials, students were researching their own digital media practices developing a range of skills; literature searching, technical/IT, media capture and manipulation, time and resource management and negotiation (e.g. consent and licencing). Students also articulated their rationale for their chosen topic and for developing educational materials. This was

---

[3]Previously this activity has been classed as teaching innovation. However, this designation is now changing and ethical approval will need to be sought in future.

frequently based on their own personal experiences of online learning tutorials and those of their peers, identifying gaps in their knowledge. Students were developing a personal inquiry, creative problem-solving skills and an understanding of educational theory and learning design setting learning objectives and evaluating these through user needs analyses, questionnaires and focus groups and researching the content.

> The process of the researching, learning, designing and creating my own tutorial has provided me with a wealth of experience which I have used in my foundation years as a doctor. I have confidently taught medical students on several occasions, and often use the skills I learnt from researching for my tutorial to produce interesting and interactive slides for teaching sessions. (Student 1)

The same analysis also provided a rich picture of how students perceive interactive online learning materials, what they believe they contribute to their learning, how it compares to other forms of learning and how this kind of material is best designed and structured. As part of the partnership, TEL development staff have reported that, students bring new and fresh ideas and combine media elements and software tools in creative ways adding to the combined knowledge and digital media practices of both students and TEL staff. New models of TEL development have emerged whereby rather than 'just being on the receiving end', through researching their own digital media practices including researching the content, students are active participants in the development of their learning and meaning construction.

> They take ideas and materials from a variety of sources and produce something that is very different, and very much their own. For us this represents the creative process working at its best. Our students have provided us with a variety of inspirational and professional products and have incorporated many of their ideas into our own online learning material development. (TEL staff member)

The above quote also begins to illustrate the multiple collaborations and partnerships that have emerged through the reflective accounts. The quotes below illustrate the empowerment and relational agency that the students report as part of these activities:

> I felt a strong sense of partnership with my supervisor, who as a consultant radiologist could offer the expertise and core knowledge, knowing that I was bringing an idea of what kind of information and learning experience we needed as students. Through creating learning content for the first time, becoming an active contributor rather than just a passive user, I felt a new partnership with the faculty which had previously been a distant, didactic presence in the course at Bristol. The following year many students in the year below asked me for

advice on creating an e-tutorial and so I became involved in a partnership with them, sharing ideas and offering advice. The faculty offered technical support with the basics of using software, and an opportunity for others creating e-learning tools to meet and share problems and ideas. This created a healthy sense of community and helped prevent isolation. (Student 2)

I think the whole process of creating my e-tutorial for my eSSC was a partnership between various different people. (Student 3)

However, not all students reflect on the collaborative aspects of developing online educational materials, and for some the project is simply a means to an end. This is discussed again in the section below on Challenges.

Brew (2006) in investigating the relationships between teaching and research and the implications for inquiry-based teaching and learning in higher education argues for academic communities of practice in which relationships between teachers and students are renegotiated. In this research and development, we argue that students and staff are mutually engaged in the production of knowledge and inquiry.

29.4.3. Case Study 3: Understanding Students' Uses of Digital Tools When Working on Placements

This case study also focuses on undergraduates medical students at the University of Bristol. In this example, students were in their third year, when they become fully immersed in clinical practice. Medical students have to learn to operate across multiple learning environments involving informal, formal and hidden curricular (Monrouxe, Rees, & Hu, 2011) and learning will vary according to local specialisms and different clinical and workplace contexts (Wenger, 1998). As mentioned before, the medical programme at Bristol has adopted a Clinical Academies model, which means that teaching takes place in geographically dispersed academies, attached to hospitals across the South West of England, making differences and variations in educational experiences more likely. Work they carry out on clinical placements, the teaching that they experience and their own studying practices are all likely to involve multiple engagements with digital media but we argue that these practices and how students manage them and how digital media may help or constrain learning and studying are poorly understood and often part of the hidden curriculum because they take place in different space and time configurations. This study aimed to understand how, when and why medical students used ICT to support their studies both formally and informally across different settings during clinical placements. Following on from our experiences in the two previous case studies discussed above, we planned to build a community of inquiry (Brew, 2006), where we would work in partnership with a group of students and involve them, as far as possible in all aspects of the research design, planning, collection and analysis and writing up results and subsequent papers. The student co-researchers would be able to explore their experiences firsthand, investigating their use of ICT in everyday situations, choices and decisions.

Students were invited to participate through an email introducing the study. Six students from three academies, following different specialisms, took part. Data collected was longitudinal and in-depth, collected over six months and represented experience of all four teaching units in the year three programme. Ethics procedures were conducted following University of Bristol guidelines. Consent forms were distributed and signed and an initial research plan was discussed, adapted and agreed at our first meeting. In a second meeting, we discussed qualitative research methods, research design and general principles of action research in order to help the students become more familiar with educational research methods which were very different to the research methods they had experienced previously as medical students. We agreed that keeping video diaries would enable students to record what they were doing and how they were using digital tools in their work and studies over time.

In order to make diary keeping easy to manage and to capture richer data, we obtained low-cost, handheld video cameras and each student maintained a video diary from February to July 2010, recording entries approximately weekly. To show our appreciation of the extracurricular efforts made, we agreed that students could keep these 'flip' cameras for personal use. Students recorded over 100 entries, totalling over 500 minutes. Diaries included observations, demonstrations (of resources), contextual information and reflections on data. They described and demonstrated (on camera) how they used digital tools and resources including problems and resolutions. The longitudinal, video-based design enabled comparisons across time and contexts and it also facilitated collaborative analysis (Büscher, 2005). Video data was reviewed by the whole group but independently transcribed to obtain verbatim transcripts that were then checked for accuracy. The analysis was jointly conducted by the whole group, staff and students working together through regular group analysis sessions, following a five-step thematic framework (Ritchie & Spencer, 1994, 2004) Summaries of key findings were then prepared by the students and again discussed collaboratively. Following this, students and staff have worked together on two conference presentations, posters and a journal article that is currently under submission to disseminate the findings from the study and our approach. As we met on a fairly regular basis, usually during evenings as this was easiest for the students involved, we gradually became more familiar with each other, with our ways of working and individual strengths and weaknesses. Students contributed more and more ideas and took ownership of the project and its outcomes.

The co-inquiry group has worked together for three years and now that the students have graduated, we have plans for further work with them as they move into becoming doctors and then doctors that teach. The original group of six students was joined by two others in the second year of this work and while there were benefits to this, it also resulted in some challenges in terms of group dynamics and inclusivity. This is discussed more fully in the section on challenges below. Nevertheless the longevity of involvement and continuing commitment of the individuals, now graduates, to this project has been outstanding and has made this a very rewarding experience for all concerned. It has also resulted in research with detailed insights into how students engage with digital media across multiple boundaries and settings, the challenges this involves and the ways in which students adapt to such challenges.

29.5. Summary of the Three Case Studies: Authenticity and Agency

Authenticity is revealed in different ways in these case studies. Case studies 1 and 3 show how students researched their own practices with opportunities to shape research about the use of digital media in higher education. In case study 2, the focus was on working with professionals and disciplinary experts to produce new knowledge that has equal status with other teaching resources. Students engage in research as part of the ongoing process of knowledge production that their projects involve. Despite contrasting aims, in all three studies, students were engaged in researching their own practices, harnessing research skills and expertise and producing new knowledge as part of an epistemic community. These case studies illustrate how co-inquiry projects embody *relational* agency which necessitates that you work with others to interpret problems of practice and take appropriate action (Edwards, 2005).

29.6. The Challenges of Adopting More Inclusive Approaches to Research

While many positive aspects of the studies outlined above have been highlighted, there have been challenges in adopting more inclusive or student-led approaches to research and knowledge creation initiatives.

This handbook is about engagement so it is important to note that not all students were fully engaged and the reasons for engagement were diverse. In the case of the student e-learning development initiative, not all students fully engaged with the support offered throughout their project periods, some of these are self-starters and go on to develop outstanding educational materials. Others appear to see the project simply as a means to an end and it is evident from their learning resources and reflective accounts that closer relationships with the TEL staff would have been beneficial. Equally, in the first case study with Information Systems students, the numbers involved in the study groups reduced over the course of the work from around 12 people starting off to eight continuing through to the end. With self-selected, extra-curricular activities such as these, there is, of course, no compulsion and therefore some level of attrition can be expected. Also, as discussed earlier, of those who took part throughout, some of their reported motivations were more extrinsic, driven by the rewards and credit that involvement offered, rather than the pursuit of new knowledge and insights. In the student e-learning development projects, further support is often provided through encouraging students to evaluate their learning resource further and submit conference papers and journal papers which are more tangible outcomes. There has been some success with this, where students have won awards at major international medical education conferences. Therefore, it needs to be recognised that students will not all respond in the same way when engaging in projects or initiatives to those that were envisaged and a collaborative approach requires that we understand and address this, while still working towards broader aims.

In the third case study, the group was again self-selecting. In this case, we found that tension was generated through the inclusion of additional recruits rather than a lack of engagement. This occurred when two further students approached the academic staff involved and asked if they could join. Seeing this as a positive outcome and a mark of success, we readily agreed. In doing so, we made an assumption that newcomers would be welcomed by the existing group. However, as we had all worked together for over six months at this stage, existing student researchers were unhappy and did not want others to be involved at this later stage. They felt the group had become a strong and trusting community and did not want this disrupted. This was a key learning point for us because we realised that through these actions, we had unintentionally disempowered the existing group and resumed our 'leader' roles. We sought ways to negotiate this amongst the group and to ensure that existing members were able to take back some control and decision making. This has made us reflect on how challenging it is to work collaboratively with students on research projects when the balance of power is so often still in the hands of the initiators. Rebalancing power relations, or at least attempting to do so, requires continuous attention as part of the ongoing, dynamic realignment of relationships that a relational agency perspective embodies (Edwards, 2005).

There are also issues in giving credit to students for the work that they undertake in such partnerships. If the work is extra-curricular as in case studies 1 and 3, then how can student effort be acknowledged and rewarded? In these studies it was felt that we should provide some tangible rewards, offer help with travel and other expenses, provide refreshments and small thank you gifts. Some might argue that asking students to devote extra time without payment for their services is exploitative but without external funding this may not be feasible and may also conflict with university policies. Furthermore, university rules and assessment systems which are almost completely geared towards giving credit on an individual basis can conflict with the aims of collaborative projects and initiatives such as we have outlined. There have also been problems in our third case with authorship for students on papers and posters because the Medical Training Application Service (MTAS) application, a points-based system which new medical graduates apply to for their first post, will only award a point for the first author on a conference presentation or paper. For some involved in the research, this was a strong motivation for participating and so there were real difficulties in ensuring an equitable distribution of dissemination activities and outputs. Universities and professional bodies may therefore need to think more carefully about rewards and incentives if they are serious about student engagement in research and other scholarly activities.

Finally, it should be noted that the activities included in these case studies have established partnerships and collaborations which have themselves generated further collaborations with others, which we have worked hard to foster and because of this, there has been no real end point to these activities. While ongoing partnerships are obviously welcome, it will be important to consider how such collaborations are sustained and nurtured over time and how they can become part of a wider, more systemic change in the research and practice activities in universities.

29.7. Conclusions

The three case studies have outlined different approaches to fostering student partnership and community involvement in research. Each of these was conducted over a different time period and variable lengths of time. They had different aims and the way that students were involved in these studies was distinct and tailored to particular groups and research interests. The approach outlined previously, builds on the work of others involved in the development of undergraduate research, inquiry-based and empowerment models (Brew, 2006; Healey & Jenkins, 2009; Neary & Winn, 2009). However, our emphasis is on students working in collaborative partnerships with each other and with staff with varying roles across the university and beyond where the focus is on researching their own digital media practices. Students reported on their desire to develop something unique, taking pride in their achievements bringing a sense of ownership and empowerment. This authenticity is, we believe, a powerful aspect of the work we have done. In constructing their own meanings through investigating their own practices and creating new knowledge, students have been able to become more fully engaged in the practices of an epistemic community (Larreamendy-Joerns & Leinhardt, 2006; Shea & Bidjerano, 2009).

There are, however, particular challenges in the negotiation of roles and addressing power relations within co-inquiry models and we found that tensions can emerge where staff or students retain existing positons, sometimes unconsciously. Furthermore, it cannot be assumed that everyone necessarily shares the same goals and finding ways to address this more explicitly could ensure a more negotiated set of outcomes. As Edwards (2005) argues, relational agency requires the ongoing and dynamic realignment of roles. We also maintain that time to develop these new relationships is essential so that multiple roles and postions can be accommodated and adapted. We conclude that co-inquiry models are not quick fixes to student engagement but part of a longer term relational shift which takes time and mutual commitment to reflection on the process. Nevertheless, we argue that, with due to attention to the issues raised, this approach to engagement can lead to the development of new relationships, knowledge and research expertise, where the roles of educator and educated are repositioned, and the opportunities for authenticity are increased.

Acknowledgements

The authors would like to thank all the students who took part in the case studies discussed in this chapter for their feedback on the community of inquiry models and invaluable contributions to the work outlined above.

References

Archer, M. (2002). Realism and the problem of agency. *Journal of Critical Realism, 5*, 11–20.

Barnett, R. (2007). *A will to learn: Being a student in an age of uncertainty.* Maidenhead: Open University Press/Society for Research into Higher Education.

Brew, A. (2006). *Research and teaching: Beyond the divide.* Basingstoke: Palgrave Macmillan.

Brew, A. (2007). Research and teaching from the students' perspective. International policies and practices for academy enquiry. *An International Colloquium on Research and Teaching.* Winchester, UK. Retrieved from http://portallive.solent.ac.uk/university/rtconference/2007/resources/angela_brew.pdf

Büscher, M. (2005). Social life under the microscope? *Sociological Research Online.* Retrieved from http://www.socresonline.org.uk/10/1/buscher.html

Edwards, A. (2005). Relational agency: Learning to be a resourceful practitioner. *International Journal of Educational Research, 43*(3), 168–182. doi:10.1016/j.ijer.2006.06.010

Fontana, A., & Frey, J. H. (2000). The interview: From structured questions to negotiated text. In N. K. Denzin & Y. S. Lincoln (Eds.), *Handbook of qualitative research* (2nd ed., pp. 645–672). Thousand Oaks, CA: Sage.

General Medical Council. (2009). *Tomorrow's doctors: Outcomes and standards for undergraduate medical education.* Retrieved from www.gmc-uk.org/TomorrowsDoctors_2009.pdf_27494211.pdf

Glaser, B. (2001). *The grounded theory perspective: Conceptualisaion contrasted with perception.* Mill Valley, CA: Sociology Press.

Harper, S. R., & Quaye, S. J. (2009). Beyond sameness, with engagement and outcomes for all: An introduction. In S. R. Harper & S. J. Quaye (Eds.), *Student engagement in higher education theoretical perspectives and practical approaches for diverse populations* (pp. 1–15). New York: Routledge.

HEA. (2011). *Student engagement: The higher education academy.* Retrieved from http://www.heacademy.ac.uk/ourwork/universitiesandcolleges/studentengagement

Healey, M., & Jenkins, A. (2009). *Developing undergraduate research and inquiry* (p. 156). York. Retrieved from http://www.heacademy.ac.uk/assets/documents/research/DevelopingUndergraduateResearchandInquiry.pdf

Heron, J. (1996). *Co-operative inquiry: Research into the human condition.* London: Sage.

Hu, S., & Kuh, G. D. (2002). Being (dis)engaged in educationally purposeful activities: The influences of student and institutional characteristics. *Research in Higher Education, 43*(5), 555–575.

Jones, C., & Healing, G. (2010). Net generation students: Agency and choice and the new technologies. *Journal of Computer Assisted Learning, 26*(5), 344–356.

Kuh, G. D., Kinzie, J., Buckley, J. A., Bridges, B. K., & Hayek, J. C. (2007). Piecing together the student success puzzle: Research, propositions, and recommendations. *ASHE Education Report, San Francisco: Jossey-Bass, 32*(5), 1–181.

Larreamendy-Joerns, J. J., & Leinhardt, G. (2006). Going the distance with online education. *Review of Educational Research, 76*(4), 567−605.

Ludvigsen, S. R. (2012). What counts as knowledge: Learning to use categories in computer environments. *Learning, Media and Technology, 37*(1), 40−52. doi:10.1080/17439884. 2011.573149

Monrouxe, L. V., Rees, C. E., & Hu, W. (2011). Differences in medical students' explicit discourses of professionalism: Acting, representing, becoming. *Medical Education, 45*(6), 585−602.

Neary, M., & Winn, J. (2009). The student as producer: Reinventing the student experience in higher education. In L. Bell, H. Stevenson & M. Neary (Eds.), *The future of higher education: policy, pedagogy and the student experience* (pp. 192−210). London: Continuum.

Reason, P. (1994). Human inquiry as discipline and practice. In P. Reason (Ed.), *Participation in human inquiry* (pp. 40−56). London: Sage.

Ritchie, J., & Spencer, L. (1994). Qualitative data analysis for applied policy research. In R. Burgess (Ed.), *Analyzing qualitative data* (pp. 173−194). London: Sage.

Ritchie, J., & Spencer, L. (2004). Qualitative data analysis: The call for transparency. *Building Research Capacity Journal, February* (7), 2−4. Retrieved from http://www.tlrp. org/rcbn/capacity/Journal/issue7.pdf

Shea, P., & Bidjerano, T. (2009). Community of inquiry as a theoretical framework to foster 'epistemic engagement' and 'cognitive presence' in online education. *Computers & Education, 52*(3), 543−553. doi:10.1016/j.compedu.2008.10.007

Shih, M., Feng, J., & Tsai, C. (2008). Research and trends in the field of e-learning from 2001 to 2005: A content analysis of cognitive studies in selected journals. *Computers & Education, 51*, 955−967.

Silverman, D. (2006). *Interpreting qualitative data: Methods for analyzing talk, text and interaction* (3rd ed.). London: Sage.

Spronken-Smith, R., & Walker, R. (2010). Can inquiry-based learning strengthen the links between teaching and disciplinary research? *Studies in Higher Education, 35*(6), 723−740. Retrieved from http://www.tandfonline.com/doi/pdf/10.1080/03075070903315502

Timmis, S. (2012). Constant companions: Instant messaging conversations as sustainable supportive study structures amongst undergraduate peers. *Computers & Education, 59*(1), 3−18. Retrieved from http://dx.doi.org/10.1016/j.compedu.2011.09.026

Trowler, V. (2010). *Student engagement literature review* (p. 74). York, UK. Retrieved from http://www-new2.heacademy.ac.uk/assets/documents/studentengagement/StudentEngagement LiteratureReview.pdf

Wenger, E. (1998). Communities of practice: Learning, meaning and identity. In J. S. Brown (Ed.), *Learning in doing: Social, cognitive and computational perspectives*. Cambridge: Cambridge University Press.

Wenger, E., White, N., & Smith, J. D. (2009). *Digital habitats: Stewarding technology for communities*. Portland, OR: CPsquare.

Williams, J., Alder, D., Cook, J., Whinney, M., Connell, O., Duffin, W., & King, P. (2011). Students and staff as educational partners in the development of quality-assured online resources for medical education. In S. Little (Ed.), *Beyond consultation: Developing staff-student partnerships in learning and teaching development and research*. London: Continuum.

Zamorski, B. (2002). Research-led teaching and learning in higher education: A case. *Teaching in Higher Education, 7*(4), 411−427.

Zimbardi, K., & Myatt, P. (2012). Embedding undergraduate research experiences within the curriculum: A cross-disciplinary study of the key characteristics guiding implementation. *Studies in Higher Education.* Retrieved from http://www.tandfonline.com/doi/pdf/10.1080/ 03075079.2011.651448

Chapter 30

Students Engaging with Change

Elisabeth Dunne, Jackie Bagnall and Barrie Cooper

Abstract

The 'Students as Change Agents' initiative at the University of Exeter in the United Kingdom is an innovative student-led action research project which brings students and staff together as partners in improving their higher education experiences and in implementing change. In this chapter, a series of background models on approaches to student engagement is addressed, followed by four case studies that consider different ways in which the theme of change agents has been translated into practice at the university. They include descriptions of single modules as well as institution-wide activity. The first gives a general overview of change agent projects; the further three case studies outline how the concept of students engaging with change has been developed in different ways: for undergraduate modular credit within the mathematical sciences, with students improving the quality of teaching resources for use by their peers; within the business school, where students consider change in relation to societal and environmental issues; and amongst postgraduate research students who address the development of digital literacies across their many disciplines, for a small amount of remuneration. Each case study describes the context of the activity, what students do, and what they gain from their engagement, including aspects of reward and recognition. Overall, student engagement in change has huge benefits for the university, for the students involved in projects, and for future students who will gain from the changes made.

30.1. Introduction

There is a subtle, but extremely important, difference between an institution that 'listens' to students and responds accordingly, and an institution that gives students the opportunity to explore areas that they believe to be significant, to recommend solutions and to bring

The Student Engagement Handbook: Practice in Higher Education
Copyright © 2013 by Emerald Group Publishing Limited
All rights of reproduction in any form reserved
ISBN: 978-1-78190-423-7

about the required changes. The concept of 'listening to the student voice' — implicitly if not deliberately — supports the perspective of student as 'consumer', whereas 'students as change agents' explicitly supports a view of the student as 'active collaborator' and 'co-producer', with the potential for transformation. (Dunne in the Foreword to Dunne & Zandstra, 2011, p. 4)

As is illustrated by this Student Engagement Handbook, there is currently considerable discussion worldwide on the role of students in higher education, and on the nature of their engagement with their learning environment. Recent arguments have suggested that we should be considering a move away from current trends for students to be considered as customers, to practices where students take on the role of 'engaged collaborators' (Ramsden, 2008), and the vocabulary of 'partnership' is now ubiquitous across UK higher education.

This chapter describes activities from a cross-institutional initiative — 'Students as Change Agents' — that calls on students from across the University of Exeter to participate fully in their learning environment and to engage in the processes of enhancement and change. The university is a medium-sized institution (17,000 students), with three campuses set in the countryside of the southwest of England. It recruits high calibre students, is research-led and ambitious to maintain or increase its high ranking for student satisfaction, as well as its world ranking. Importantly in relationship to student engagement, there are excellent links between the university and the students' guild (union). This contributes in part to Exeter's national reputation in terms of student engagement, as well as to the current success of the Students as Change Agents process. In this context, asking students to engage in change could be seen as a deliberate response to the potential negativity of a customer relationship (see Kay, Hutchinson, & Dunne, 2010, and many authors in this Handbook), but it also relates strongly to what quality learning and engagement should look like whatever the surrounding national or global context.

30.2.   Models of Student Engagement

Before considering the detail of various change-agent activities, a set of models of engagement practices are outlined since they give a good indication of the thinking behind the initiative. The design of models has been important in the 'change agents' journey; they have been developed in an iterative way, first as a means of capturing practice and then as a tool for gaining feedback from those who engage with them, within the university and beyond. They provide a means of providing an 'at a glance' message which, even if not entirely accurate, has enabled the development of practice further.

The Higher Education Academy has provided a model of the dimensions of student engagement (see HEA, 2013). These include individual learning, curriculum design and delivery, discipline, school and department, institutional and national policy. Whilst this is appropriate for considering the context of institutional structures in which student engagement might occur, it is limited in its approach and does not address what it actually means for students to engage. There are now numerous models of student engagement, one by Bryson and Hardy (2011) being the most comprehensive, but also the most complex and difficult to follow. Several further models are presented in this book (see, e.g. Solomonides in Chapter 3, or Ratcliffe and Dimmock in Chapter 4), each premised on a different lens, from the more psychological to the behavioural, but each taking into account what engagement actually means for a student.

Figure 30.1 outlines a model that focuses on the way that a student behaves — or is enabled to behave through institutional organization and structures — setting out four tiers of student engagement that have been emerging in institutional approaches to the support of enhancement (see Kay, Owen, & Dunne, 2012; Stubbs & Owen, 2010), moving from 'least actively' (1) to 'most actively' (4) engaged.

Although a hierarchy of engagement is intended, it is important to recognize that each of these tiers may be of value in its own right, and there may be positive overlap between them. The 'Evaluator' shows evidence of engaging with the learning environment and contributing to quality processes, but this form of engagement is comparatively passive. 'Observers' will engage in meetings where decisions are made, but institutions remain in control. These two levels of engagement are common and assumed to be regular practice in many parts of the world (see Quality Assurance Agency, QAA, 2009, for the United Kingdom); not engaging students in these ways would be considered unusual. The 'Expert' may be trained and inducted into institutional culture and share control and responsibility for meetings and decisions. However, institutions still remain in control of the implementation of change. With 'Partners', characteristics from level 3 will be found, but students will act as collaborators, taking a lead, or shared leadership, in implementing changes to the learning and teaching environment.

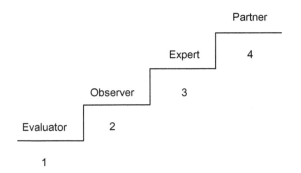

Figure 30.1: Tiers of student engagement in relation to quality enhancement (Kay et al., 2012, p. 366).

This model is important for characterising differences in behaviour. Building on this conceptualisation, Dunne and Zandstra (2011) present a very similar idea, but with a clearer focus on the difference between students having a voice or engaging in change processes, and clarifying in any context whether it is the institution that is responsible for, and drives, change, or whether students can take a role as active partners in shaping their learning experiences. The model presented in Figure 30.2 summarises these characteristics and highlights the different roles that students can play.

Students' involvement in educational change in most universities has largely been at the level of evaluating their experience (lower left quadrant) or being involved in the decision-making processes of committees. It should be emphasised that both these kinds of activity are highly important. There are also accumulating examples of students working as partners, co-creators and experts, but where the motivational lead has been the staff in the department or university. What the university of Exeter is aiming for is to have at least a proportion of students who take a leadership role in bringing about change, as in the top right of the quadrant. It should be emphasised that these quadrants are indicative only, that there will always be a complex and fluid relationship between them, and student engagement may cut across all of them in particular circumstances.

A further model (see Figure 30.3) takes into consideration a different and often hotly debated factor, that of reward and recognition for students who engage with

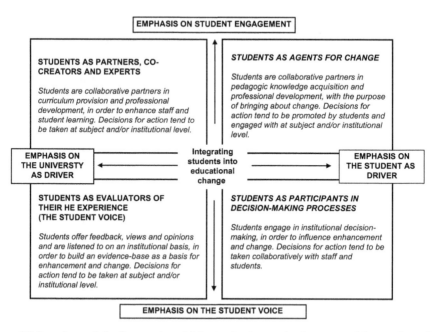

Figure 30.2:   A model of ways in which students can be integrated into educational change (adapted from Dunne & Zandstra, 2011, p. 17).

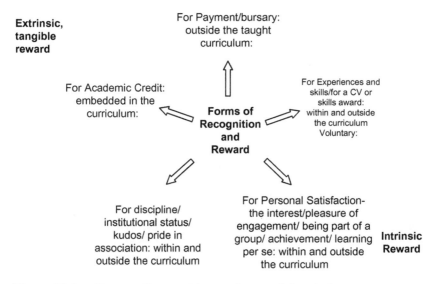

Figure 30.3:   Forms of recognition and reward for student engagement.

extra-curricular activity. Five key forms are proposed as relevant to students engaging with change; that is engagement for

1. the extrinsic reward and recognition of academic credit (embedded in the curriculum);
2. the extrinsic reward of receiving payment or a bursary (outside the taught curriculum);
3. the extrinsic reward of skills and experiences suitable for a CV or for a non-credit bearing award (e.g. The Exeter Award) (within and outside the curriculum);
4. the extrinsic reward of gaining status or kudos for being seen to engage with an initiative (e.g. as a student technology champion or a change agent), with an intrinsic element of pride; and
5. the intrinsic reward of personal satisfaction in learning and achieving outcomes or being part of a group (within and outside the curriculum).

These forms may not always be clear cut and may overlap on occasion, especially as all such experiences, whether paid or unpaid, curriculum embedded or not, are likely to lead to skills and experiences that will enhance a student's CV, and most may hold intrinsic motivation.

Four case studies of students engaging with change at the University of Exeter will highlight aspects of each of the models above, with a particular focus on students working as experts and partners (Figure 30.1) and on driving improvements through acting as change agents (Figure 30.2). Each will also illustrate different forms of reward and recognition as the potential drivers for student engagement (Figure 30.3).

30.3.   Case Studies of Students as Change Agents

The four case studies address different ways in which the theme of change agents has been translated into university practice. They range from descriptions of single modules wherein thinking about and enacting change is a particular focus, to institution-wide activity. The first case study gives a general overview of the 'Students as Change Agents' initiative at Exeter, which was founded on the principles outlined in Figures 30.1 and 30.2 above, is dependent on voluntary engagement by students, and is set in the context of pedagogic research. The three other case studies outline how the concept of students engaging with change has been developed in different ways: for undergraduate modular credit within the mathematical sciences, with students improving the quality of teaching resources for use by their peers; within the business school, where students consider change in relation to societal and environmental issues; and amongst postgraduate research students (PGRs) who address the development of digital literacies across their many disciplines, for a small amount of remuneration. Each case study describes the context of the activity, what students do, and what they gain from their engagement.

30.3.1.   *Voluntary Engagement with Pedagogic Development: Students as Change Agents*

30.3.1.1. Setting the scene
The University of Exeter has developed an innovative student-led action research project which brings students and staff together as partners in improving experiences of higher education. Students from across the institution have been given the opportunity to engage as change agents, collaborating to bring about improvements in learning and teaching within their subject areas. In relation to the models above, there is a firm emphasis on the student as the driver of change. There is no payment for any involvement, and the only extrinsic reward is that students are offered certificates, signed by the deputy vice chancellor and listing the skills they have been developing. Students from 10 subject areas across the university engaged as a pilot study (2008–2009) in a variety of learning and teaching activities; this was highly successful and the initiative has continued to grow year on year.

30.3.1.2. What do students do?
Students select aspects of teaching and learning that are of concern within their student–staff liaison committees, develop a research question, and plan their own methods of data collection. Any student, or group of students, can engage with the initiative, so long as they have a well thought-through proposal and can outline potential benefits. Research methodologies have included focus groups, informal interviews and questionnaire surveys.

There have now been at least 100 projects over five years, involving undergraduate and postgraduate students in almost all discipline areas from across the university's three campuses, and investigating topics such as assessment and feedback, seminar provision, technology, inter-campus teaching, employability, personal and peer-tutoring, digital literacy, sustainability and academic writing. Outcomes have included research reports as well as students organising a buddy system and peer tutoring, and running sessions on writing skills and careers; students have also produced study guides in a variety of areas and have engaged in large-scale cross-discipline projects on aspects such as the development of learning spaces. More recently, there have been projects in areas such as student representation, student volunteering in the community and environmental sustainability (a case study on this theme is outlined below). Overall, many hundreds of students will have participated in the various studies and many thousands will be gaining from the outcomes.

There have also been parallel initiatives that support the change-agent philosophy. For example, 10 recent graduates converted the virtual learning environment (VLE) to a new platform and have supported staff with resource development. In addition, a Reciprocal Shadowing project[1] has been running for three years, with senior university managers shadowing students for a day, and vice versa, with the potential of highlighting areas for change and development. The concept of students acting as change agents has also been built into modular provision, and a group of PGRs has been working to change attitudes and practices in digital literacy (see case studies below). Overall, it has meant that changes in practice are led by student-gained research evidence rather than hearsay; this is especially important at a time of diminishing resource, ensuring that most effort is put into areas that really matter to students and that are demonstrably in need of attention.

The initiative seems to be timely; it contributed in small part to the judgement of 'commended' practice in the recent QAA Institutional Review, and outcomes of projects have been presented at six student-led conferences at Exeter, either local or national in orientation, with 650 delegates in all and 130 student speakers. The ideas have also gained national acclaim.[2] Hence, the change-agents initiative has developed from being a small-scale pilot to an activity that pervades a considerable part of institutional life. Importantly, it has developed from a project run by enthusiasts at the centre to an initiative that is devolved to each of the five colleges and is largely funded and supported by them. To some extent, it is embedded into the philosophy and practice of the university as a whole. Most importantly, it has attracted a wide range of student participants: those with a strong desire to be leaders of the future, those who wish to express themselves in original ways, those who are disabled and have specific messages for the institution; those who have a commitment

---

[1]Supported by the Leadership Foundation: http://www.lfhe.ac.uk/en/research-resources/small-development-projects/sdp2011/exeter-po.cfm.
[2]A case study in a government publication a 'think-piece' with the university's deputy vice chancellor published by the QAA (Kay *et al.* 2010); a case study and resources for the National Union of Students; a publication for the UK Higher Education Academy's Subject Centre for Education (Dunne & Zandstra, 2011); and many invitations to seminars and conferences across the United Kingdom.

to their community, their environment, their university and/or their college or discipline. Overall, it allows students to engage in their university life in new and imaginative ways, empowering them to take real responsibility for change.

Descriptions of projects have been offered elsewhere (Dunne & Zandstra, 2011; Kay et al., 2012); however, one example gives an indication of the creative way in which students can act as change agents. Many projects relate to curriculum-based, academic work. 'The Peacock' is a different kind of project prompted by the newly built forum, a multi-million pound 'heart' to the University of Exeter. This was built over a two-year period and includes library, teaching and social facilities in a stunning, award-winning environment. Based on the theme of sustainability, the peacock sculpture is formed from materials discarded from the construction of the forum and specifically aims to promote recycling. It is a large metal sculpture designed by members of the University of Exeter's Art Society and built in collaboration with a local Devon artist. It now sits centrally in the university grounds, with an appropriate background of trees and shrubbery, and has an important message about change. The group of three students (from three different disciplines) who contributed most to the piece say:

> The increasing pressure to reduce waste is essential to sustaining today's lifestyle. Through this sculptural piece, we aim to highlight the issues surrounding sustainability and hope that the audience reflects on their own commitments to recycling and reusing materials...

> ...As well as an animal of beauty, the process of replenishment in the peacock's feathers mirrors the construction of The Forum project, converting old to new. This is fundamentally what the sculpture is; we have used the old hoardings to create something new and beautiful...

The Devon artist who advised on construction states:

> I think they have done an absolutely brilliant job. This should be added to the sculpture trail so it can have legacy and people can understand where it has come from.

The Peacock is a highly visible reminder of what Students as Change Agents can achieve as an initiative, and what students can bring to the university if given the opportunity. It is also a constant reminder of what student engagement can mean — dedication to a cause, commitment to bringing about change, complex practical problem solving; hard work and effort, a legacy for the future, and a real sense of pride in achievement.

30.3.1.3. What do students gain?
Students are often astonished at the impact they can have and what they achieve:

> It was so exciting when we handed out the booklets we'd written and all the students seemed really pleased with them. I can't really believe what we've managed to do. (First year Biosciences undergraduate)

> I think the most exciting part of this project has been that it is possible to make a change even at such a large institution. Before this project I did not expect it to be possible to make a change, but this has shown me that with a little work and dedication you can make things happen. (First year Business undergraduate)

Comments illustrate enthusiasm: 'a fantastic and innovative opportunity' and, in particular, indicate recognition of the power of evidence in bringing about change: 'Conducting real research into what students actually think and being able to present this information to senior staff in full knowledge that what you're saying is backed up by proof'; or 'Making recommendations to the School with research support and the hope that this can make the Uni a better place for students'. They highlight the skills they gain for a CV, and for some students their experiences are transforming: 'Completely changed how I think'; 'I have learnt that I really enjoy the process of carrying out projects/research and this is influencing my choice in career path'.

Overall, however, it seems highly likely that the success and impact of the 'Students as Change Agents' initiative comes largely from the fact that projects are conceived and designed by students according to their needs and interests, with support and guidance from academic and central services staff to achieve their aims. This in itself provides motivation. After an initial sense of astonishment on being asked: 'Well, what are you going to do about it?' students give continuing evidence that they can take responsibility and rise to the challenge, giving them a sense of leadership, ownership and empowerment.

30.3.2. Engagement with Curriculum Change for Academic Credit: Mathematics

30.3.2.1. Setting the scene

As all students, mathematics students are busy people with many demands on their time: academic studies; work to fund their university education; relaxing and socialising; more experience from industrial and commercial placements. Extra engagement with activities such as course evaluations, student–staff liaison committees or curriculum development projects represents a decision to invest precious time and energy in one activity at the expense of another. In many ways, it is a small miracle that *any* of our students choose to engage with such activities. Whom exactly does it serve to fill out a course evaluation questionnaire when this is conducted after the course has been delivered? What precisely can you get from sitting on a student–staff liaison committee that you could not get from a debating society, or working part-time? Assuming that the opportunity to engage with curriculum development projects is an investment decision in which the student invests their time as capital, two natural questions arise:

1. What is the expected return on the investment?
2. To what extent are the outputs of value to the student?

The single most successful student engagement stories in the mathematical sciences at Exeter have focused on the creation of learning resources by students for themselves and their peers. Since this activity is embedded within the curriculum for credit, there is a clear return on investment if students are successful, and the outputs are of value both to themselves and to their fellow students. It also highlights two further key elements to creating an environment in which students will readily engage with curriculum design. The first is that, to bring such a project to a successful conclusion, tells both staff and employers a lot about their potential to work effectively in the graduate workplace. Hence, it seems sensible to bring such opportunities within the auspices of the curriculum itself, ensuring that students can obtain accreditation of key graduate attributes within their degree programmes. Second, if we truly believe in the participative, socially mediated models for learning that form the founding principles of co-creation (Wenger, 1998; Wenger, McDermott, & Snyder, 2002), then we need to move towards an assessment model in which the outputs are of value to the wider community of practice, rather than having a life expectancy restricted to the present assessment cycle and for the eyes of one or two individual experts only.

30.3.2.2. What do students do?

A student-led audit of employability in the curriculum (a change agents project) identified areas for curriculum improvement, particularly in the third year when students need examples of skills and activities for CVs and interviews. A key outcome from the audit was the design of a third year assessed group project. These projects have been offered for the last two years and are compulsory for all final year students on the BSc mathematics programme. Students complete an extended project over three months in a group of six to eight, with a subject specialist as an adviser. Typically this will be a project in their research area, but academic staffs have also offered curriculum development projects. The student groups devise their own project title, aims, objectives, methodology, time-line and evaluation strategy and submit these within one month of the project starting as an assessed piece of work There are common assessment criteria for all projects, which must contain elements of data gathering and analysis, a discussion of the aims and methodology pursued in the project, a comparison of the findings of the project with the published literature, and execution of an evaluation strategy to determine the success of the project in relation to its original aims.

In two years, 153 students have been offered 21 projects. Six projects have focused on curriculum development or design, with a total of 72 students. The demand for curriculum projects has outstripped the number of projects on offer and, in both years, additional advisers had to be recruited to cater for this. Topics covered have concentrated on technology-enhanced learning (TEL), research-led education in mathematics, e-assessment, feedback in mathematics and designing resources to challenge misconceptions in the theory of relativity.

An example highlights what students have been doing. Several groups decided to work on TEL, with the broad aim to explore how technology could be used to enhance the student experience in the mathematics curriculum. To this end, students chose one module (or in the case of one group, two modules to do a comparative study between the potential for TEL in different types of module), for which they would design resources and measure student engagement and satisfaction with them. The student groups requested and were given their own pages on the university VLE (Moodle) and worked with lecturers and e-learning specialists to develop their resources. Two groups chose to concentrate on developing resources for a module they were currently studying, whilst another focused on a module that was a critical foundation for the more advanced material they were studying in their final year. The pages were truly innovative, pushed the technology close to its limits, and are being used as exemplars of best practice around the university. All staff involved directed students to the new resources with a subsequent impact on the learning experience of approximately 300 students. One particular highlight was that students came to challenge the notion that 'interactive' can be used synonymously with 'multi-media', finding that to produce truly engaging and interactive pages, they had to do more than embed videos and other media clips. There has been a wider impact on academic practice both within and outside mathematics at Exeter, with internships to produce student-designed resources having been offered in mathematics, physics and medical imaging, as a result of the successes of these projects.

30.3.2.3. What do students gain?
Student feedback from focus group interviews gives a rich picture of what they thought of the module. Although they were proud of their outputs, it was involvement in the processes that engaged them the most. Despite being little practised in managing a project, these third year students particularly appreciated being allowed to organise their activities: 'We had to do that ourselves, it is much more grown up'. This feeling was repeated over and again.

> From the beginning we had to just pick a topic but it was quite an open ended topic so then we had to decide what direction we wanted the project to go in... what level of workload we wanted, what deadlines we wanted, and we just managed the project ourselves.

> It is the first project that I have done where you have not had a set of bullet points... and get a paint-by-numbers project at the end of it, all groups will have their own one and they will all be different.

There was a recognition not only that they had to be successful as a group but also that there was a broader community who would be worth collaborating with, and this was perceived as a very different ethos to the competitive world of their degree:

> We all had to learn to take responsibility for the group as a whole rather than just our own sections.

> I am surprised that the groups that weren't even doing the same topic as us we were able to collaborate with as well.

A genuine sense of motivation, involvement and enjoyment was also apparent:

> In this, you have got the freedom to actually enjoy what you're looking at ... as opposed to essentially doing a 'wikipedia presentation'.

> Because you are so involved in it ... you want to tell people about it so you want to write the report, you want to do the presentation so people can see how your group is doing and because you are so involved in it, you know what you want to write and what you want to say.

> Especially in maths, we are always working towards, how can we do this coursework right? How can we do well in the exam? Whereas this project was, how can we show what we have done?

The work seemed more 'real', both in terms of maths and in relation to employability:

> With the tutor not holding your hand, that was a bit like how it would be with a client... you would get given this brief outline and you would be told to sort the project out yourselves and that is like what we had to do.

Of interest also was the importance they gave to having opportunities to develop as people, not just to study mathematics: 'In the 1000 word evaluation, it was good to be able to actually talk about yourself'; 'It did help the whole class... develop us as people'. The comparison between knowledge and whole person development is marked:

> ...would definitely say it has been one of the ones [modules] that has helped me develop more than other ones where it is just about gaining knowledge, increasing your knowledge...this one was something different and actually developing you as a person.

The difference in style of this module clearly captured the students' interest and commitment. It allowed them to develop as people, leading to the comment: 'I would say if you only take one module, make it be this one'.

30.3.3.   *Engagement with Societal Change for Academic Credit: The University of Exeter Business School*

30.3.3.1. Setting the scene

The third case study, from the University of Exeter Business School, describes a second year undergraduate module which has now run twice, and in which around 100 students have been supported in leading the design of a social or environmental change project. It is centred on experiential learning, with students being immersed in the process of enquiry, bringing theory to life through real-life issues. The module is delivered in partnership by an academic lead with experience in industry, and an industry partner with experience in active citizenship and community engagement. The industry expert acts as lead tutor and works with students in the active learning and outreach stages of the module to develop their collective leadership capabilities and to locate enterprises in the community. This allows students to tap in to a ready-made network of community-based leaders and project groups, and introductions by this tutor ensure a positive reception to student requests. The tutor's skills of working in 'real life' community projects are transferred to the student groupings, ensuring that collaboration is encouraged and challenges resolved quickly to move groups towards action.

Rather than avoiding the inevitable issues of group-work in large cohorts, students engage with the idea that multiple perspectives are an essential part of working with others to lead change. As emphasized by the Johnson's several decades of research in the United States (see Johnson & Johnson, 2003), group-work is not an easy option, but it can be highly effective. Culturally heterogeneous groups, as in this module, tend to provide benefits over homogeneous groups, including greater numbers of ideas, improved creativity and flexibility (Kirchmeyer, 1993), provided students have the skills and time to manage the group process (Watson, Kumar, & Michaelsen, 1993). Students learn that if they want to move through society, shaping and influencing, then they must take the time to listen and to understand the perspective of others. That *world view* is an important part of effective communication; drawing upon one of Covey's effective habits, they are told 'seek first to understand and then to be understood' (Covey, 1989). From week 1, they are asked to 'switch on their curiosity' and to start noticing and asking questions about the things they see and hear around them, sharing opinions, ideas and questions. This process supports the group to have a sense of agency, and to identify the change that they would like to see, justify the need for that change and move forward to research and design the project plan. Any difficulties that the students face are highlighted as learning opportunities, supporting them to engage with an unfamiliar and sometimes threatening learning environment. The fear centres inevitably on attainment and uncertainty about assignments and how to do well on the module; many were only used to content which they learnt in order to repeat back.

30.3.3.2. What do students do?

Part 1 requires students to *engage in active learning*, where students are placed in random enquiry groups of six and through a series of exercises begin to form a united group, getting to know each other and establishing the group rules for effective team work. The first three weeks focus on the group learning process, individual differences and multiple perspectives. The in-class exercises are designed to unite the students, aligning personal values and creating a cohesive in-group identity (Haslam, 2004). It is by spending time carefully creating this identity that commitment to the process and the module as a whole is developed. The support invested at the start of the module is essential and seeks to strengthen group identity and underpin the creative process. By the end of this phase, students have begun to shape the social or environmental change projects that they want to pursue. They have an understanding of group values and can see how leadership works as collective experiences. Students are also reminded of the higher order thinking skills required at this stage of their degree programme and how, in developing academic ability, they are also developing skills which transfer to other aspects of their lives. Engagement with the academic literature surrounding leadership and leading change is essential, but students are invited to move beyond theory and consider how ideas and concepts can highlight ways to shape and improve practice.

For Part 2, they *engage in enquiry*, practising their questioning techniques and being coached in the use of enquiry to open up their thinking and challenge their assumptions. They spend time thinking about their change proposal; now is the time to shape their ideas, to use their exposure to others from the wider community to ask questions and to test their project plans. Over two weeks, external practitioners come in to the class; leaders of community projects share their stories and make themselves available for questions. Throughout the enquiry stage, students identify external projects or organisations that interest them. As the students work together to agree upon and then design their change project, they are required to justify the need for their change. This requires engagement with empirical evidence. For some, this will be the first time they have spent time researching a contemporary issue and getting to grips with the validity and reliability issues of data. Students are expected to undertake an external visit to a local charitable or social enterprise to conduct their research. This is often a turning point in their understanding of what it takes to lead change. Through interviewing those that lead change, managers and community workers, students come to appreciate the challenges faced: for example limited or reduced funding, staff turnover, motivating volunteers, preserving the dignity of those in receipt of aid or the need for resilience in pursuit of a strong belief. These challenges may be covered in much of the literature, but the literature does not engage the students in the same way as the impact of their own research.

In Part 3, they draw the experience together by *engaging in reflection*, both as a group when compiling their group project and as an individual when writing their reflective essay. The final student presentations showcase what they have designed, how they have worked together and what change they feel is needed and why. They are asked to share with the audience their values as a group and the leadership approach which they feel best reflects them, to celebrate their unique identity as change agents. This group process comes to an end with the submission of the project assignment, after which they work individually on a reflective essay ('What does it take to lead change?'), critically reflect on the whole process, use the literature to reflect upon their own experience and use their experience to reflect upon the literature (Brookfield, 1998).

30.3.3.3. What do students gain?

The students' reflective essays highlight that, for many, there was an uneasy start, especially for some of the international students:

> This module is different. It involves using your knowledge and what
> you learned during module into practices and it inevitably requires

teamwork, which I do not want to be involved in. When I got what the module is completely about, I immediately decided to change module after the induction. But during the induction, being told the purpose of the course, how it will affect your skill and your life, I was inspired by the passion of the founder of the course who wants to make society, the world better.

Students later highlight many gains, especially in relation to the processes of working together and what learning really means. There is a sense of 'journey':

I realised it took more than what meets the eye at first glance. Working with different people from all around the world, each possessing different cultures and an array of ideologies was no mean feat.

Made me understand that I shouldn't just assume, but I should wonder and challenge.

I realised how little I knew — the quest to understand what it actually took to lead change successfully opened up with anticipation and eagerness.

The developing sense of empowerment is widespread, influencing their futures:

This has enabled me to step outside the box and engage in active learning; I didn't stop when the lecture finished — I was only just getting started.

We learn best when in a relationship with others who share a common practice. I therefore hope to increasingly become part of, and create, 'communities of practice' where skills and knowledge can be exchanged between people (Wheatley, 2002, p. 6).

Enquiry has allowed me to be actively involved in a project, rather than people involved in a linear learning process and having a wrong or right answer which you can investigate no further. Therefore I have become inspired in creating a change initiative.

I decided to take challenges and have a sense of curiosity to learn techniques to change my life, my society.

Many comments, similarly to the mathematics students, focus on their self-awareness and identity, as a person, a learner and a change agent:

Reflecting back on those experiences and feedbacks has helped me understand myself better.

...has changed my thinking from now and forever.

...has taught me many lessons that help to build a better me.

I have become a change agent.

30.3.4. Paid Engagement Outside the Curriculum: Digital Literacies

30.3.4.1. Setting the scene

This case study describes some of the outcomes from an externally funded project[3] (Cascade), with the overarching aim to design and implement a range of innovative strategies and curriculum activities to help students and staff develop their digital capabilities. The focus was on supporting PGRs to become change agents in promoting and developing digital scholarship, with a particular interest in the challenges associated with becoming digitally literate in a research context. Many PGRs are drawn to Exeter as a result of its reputation for providing high-quality education and an excellent student experience in a research-rich environment. Seventeen postgraduate students were recruited to the project to work as interns over a period of six months. This was different from the initial expectation of recruiting one intern per college, that is, five in all; such a large number of students wrote outstanding applications and interviewed so well that it was decided to broaden into having a disciplinary spread and to see how the university might best gain from the wide array of interests. Most of these students were involved in teaching undergraduates, which was important in terms of 'cascading' digital skills; several talked very clearly about their desire to engage with change; all were familiar with a variety of technologies, from social networking tools to specialist technologies that were pertinent to their disciplinary study.

Although, as outlined above, most change agent activity is unpaid at Exeter, a small amount of funding was specifically available for students in this instance, through the external body. This was of importance since postgraduate students — many of whom have complex lives to juggle — were clear that they would not have engaged without payment:

> I wish to be clear that the reason the Cascade project was successful (and indeed, possible) was that the internship was a paid opportunity. As a mature student and a mum with young children who lives remotely, I am usually unable to take up voluntary opportunities... I would like to think that this investment in students can ensure a higher quality of student take up and engagement with such projects. Such work should be paid, and the resulting outcomes for the university should more than balance out the offset. (Student 1)

However, despite the wish for payment, many of this group put in far more time than paid for and the engagement with their activities was intense.

---

[3]The Exeter Cascade project was supported through JISC — the Joint Information Systems Committee — within their e-Learning programme: developing digital literacies strand http://www.jisc.ac.uk/whatwedo/programmes/elearning/developingdigitalliteracies/Cascade.aspx

30.3.4.2. What students do

The interns became a cross-disciplinary group, spending small amounts of time together, helping to design their own programme for sharing ideas,[4] focusing on their personal digital growth and that of the group in relation to the scholarly use of digital tools and media. Baseline research for the project indicated that many digital habits are acquired from peers; in addition, postgraduates take great pleasure in talking about their work and are highly effective communicators, and these factors were built into the ways of working with the interns group. They also received mentoring through the project to support them in undertaking a small-scale development project, building opportunities for other students to enhance their digital capabilities. Each student then wrote a case study[5] of their work, accompanied by a 'learning journey'. It was participation in the activities and submission of the case study that led to the small financial payment for their time.

The intern's case studies are extremely diverse, mostly highly practical and describing activities and resources to support their peers at both postgraduate and undergraduate levels. They range from a study of international students in transition to the Exeter digital study environment; data sets for developing skills in statistical analysis; a pilot project to establish a blog and online forum where PGRs can share research techniques and other information related to their studies; a video resource exploring the impact of digital media on the elusive processes that occur in the drama studio and classroom; the development of re-usable online and video-based resources on digital research skills for psychology students to building robots for exploring patterns in data in engineering and mathematics.

These change projects, and the associated resources, have been supportive in their particular disciplines, and also in impacting on institutional discussion of the term 'digital literacy': 'I know it put it on the agenda' (Student 2). Indeed this project, and the support of the interns, has meant that words which were previously barely heard at this institution are now widely prevalent. Further, the careful analysis of the term by the interns led to a deeper understanding of what the words might mean. Comments such as the following make an important distinction between technical proficiency and what it means to be digitally literate.

> My definition of digital literacies changed during the course of the Cascade project. At the start of the project, I associated the concept with a set of finite and practical technical skills... the specific ability to use software, the tech-savvy to know how to scan a QR code, etc. During the project, this definition evolved, and now I see digital literacies as a complex and reflective openness to the ways in which digital mediums enhance our ability to engage with the world and communicate more effectively with each other. This means not just learning

---

[4]Conceived and run by Helen Beetham, co-manager of the project and a nationally recognised consultant on digital literacy.
[5]See http://exeter.ac.uk/cascade.

new skills (although that may well be a necessary part of it), but
encountering new technologies with a critical reflectiveness. (Student 1)

The interns have many reasons for using technology: 'To improve my daily
work, communication and share my research ... and allow you to perform tasks
that were impossible few years ago' (Student 2). They are also clear about reticence
of use of new technologies unless there is an immediate and obvious 'benefit from
investing precious time and effort in learning them' (Student 3).

There are clear messages to the university from all these interns about the need
for digital literacy for all students, and why they believe this to be so necessary:
'digital literacy gives users freedom of choice and empowerment' (Student 4).

> It is important to follow up consumption of digital technologies for
> entertainment and other purposes and slowly move towards other
> applications that would benefit users and encourage the creation of a
> 'thinking society' that generates new ideas, rather than a society that
> reduces itself to a number in a marketing pitch for a new consumer
> product. (Student 6)

> More and more resources and tools are available through digital
> devices and the internet which have the capability to save time and
> money. It has perhaps got to the stage that those who aren't digitally
> literate are being left behind! It is critical therefore that people and
> particularly researchers are digitally literate in order to excel in their
> chosen field. (Student 7)

> On a more practical level, digital literacy is an essential part of the
> skill set sought by employers. (Student 2)

Through the project, these postgraduates also come to recognise the tensions of a
university world, and the difficulty of 'Creating a space for reflection and thought
about notions of digital literacy within an increasingly impact-driven institutional
culture'. They also discuss the need for criticality in technology use:

> I believe digital literacy consists of the ability, awareness and imagina-
> tion to find out about possible digital tools, to learn how to use them,
> and use an appropriate solution for an appropriate job... the appro-
> priate use of technology is key — digital literacy does not necessarily
> mean adopting the latest and greatest technology simply because it is
> there, particularly if a low-tech solution is already sufficient. It does
> mean being able to adopt such things where they offer an advantage.
> (Student 3)

The interns are highly aware of the difficulties of working with technology and
the frustrations it can cause. They also appreciate how hard it can be to get staff or
students to engage at all, and offer strategies:

> The university should be integrating digital literacy development into
> the curriculum, because the opportunity of being 'trained' in these

skills and ideals outside of the context of a discipline will not be taken up by students. (Student 7)

My two recommendations would be to embed digital literacy in the staff personal development review so they are supported in enhancing their awareness and technical proficiency, and to deliver sustained and tailored support to staff and students.

They also perceive the cross-disciplinary aspect of the project as something the university has to pursue:

More sharing of knowledge. There must be people and students who have knowledge in all areas of digital tools and skills and more effort needs to be made to share this. This particularly needs doing across the discipline and even college boundaries. (Student 5)

30.3.4.2. What students gain

Although working to support other students and the university in developing digital literacy, the project was repeatedly described as having 'enormous' and 'important' impact: 'It resulted in a significant shift in my own studio/research practice (Student 1); 'I had a great time at the sessions and realised that I have been missing doing computer programming and video editing... I have started doing much more programming and other cool digital stuff' (Student 4); 'I got precious contacts with interesting people around the campus' (Student 2). They report being more aware of why they need to use technology, and realising there is so much to learn, as well as recognising that they need to make more effort when they teach to ensure that undergraduates 'get the message'. Some also report that the experiences are life-changing, and one of them reports that, as an outcome of Cascade, she (Student 5) gained a job as an education consultant 'focused on implementing strategic change in universities with respect to technology-enhanced learning'.

30.4.   Discussion

It cannot be dismissed that students may perceive themselves as customers, with a powerful voice; they may decline the opportunity to actively engage with change processes; they may disagree with the concept of change agents. In the words of one academic: 'why should students be asked to make improvements — aren't they paying for us to do that?' What is important is that those students who wish to engage with change can do so in numerous different ways, and it is clear that many of them do want to have this opportunity to act as 'engaged collaborators', both in developing their own learning and attributes, and in focusing on bringing about change. Their reasons for this are manifold: for the excitement and passion of being involved in change; for entirely altruistic motives and wanting to improve the education of students to come; because they are committed to their discipline or the university and genuinely want to see improvements for the future; because they are motivated by the 'edge' that engagement gives them on a CV and in interview processes; they may be attracted by financial payments. In addition, feedback over a five-year period highlights that so many of them take pleasure in learning about the pedagogy of their discipline and the processes of change. They create understandings through interaction with peers, academic and professional staff, and others beyond the immediate university, testing out knowledge and opinions in a social context, and building on the perspectives and views of others. This shared context enables students to make new meaning together and grow in confidence and autonomy as a member of a community of practice.

For the institution too, there is a range of potential benefits; interest in the initiative may help to attract the best tariff students, or those who wish to engage fully with the university; hence, it can be used as a selling point and raise its profile in the sector as an institution that embraces change and innovation. That students gain a range of employability-related attributes and skills and have experiences to talk about at interview is also important to the institution, since graduate employment is a key success factor. The continual improvement of the student experience in areas that are selected by and meaningful to students may impact on student satisfaction scores. Less tangible is the impact on the ethos and culture of the university through promoting a sense of collaborative partnership, but this remains an important aim.

It is not now easy to separate out what might specifically be seen as change agent activity amongst the hundreds of projects and activities that engage students within and beyond the curriculum. Student engagement, and change agents within this, is part of the everyday conversation and expectation of the university. This may suggest that change agents is a 'mature' process, fully embedded within the rich variety of engagement opportunities that students are surrounded with, part of the fabric of the institution, how the university perceives itself and wishes to be known. Nonetheless, there is always room for development and improvement. From the case studies above, a key recommendation would be to embed the promotion of change into the curriculum far more widely, for academic credit. In addition, there is certainly room for re-considering the needs and interests of postgraduate students, moving away from an isolationist approach with individual researchers as experts only in their narrow discipline, to one where they are perceived as having multiple forms of expertise that they can share and develop together, with digital literacy being one such arena. The Cascade digital literacy approach will also be developed further across multi-disciplinary groups including both postgraduates and undergraduates. The majority of change agent activity at Exeter will almost certainly remain outside the curriculum, with students engaging for many different reasons. Having observed and worked alongside the many students who have engaged with such initiatives, not only is it evident that engagement in change gives them confidence and belief in their abilities but it also gives them faith in learning and their development as people, whatever the initial motivation to engage. In the words of a Chinese student: 'I will know better the difficulties and have wisdom to solve them. I am excited and looking forward for the future!' This is surely what student engagement is about, indeed what a university education is about, and we must work to be sure that every student leaves the university with this sense of agency and empowerment. If a focus on change can help to achieve this, then we must ensure as a university that 'Students as Change Agents' continues to flourish.

References

Brookfield, S. (1998). Critically reflective practice. *The Journal of Continuing Education in the Health Professions*, *18*, 197–205.

Bryson, C., & Hardy, C. (2011). Clarifying the concept of student of engagement: A fruitful approach to underpin policy and practice. Paper presented at the HEA Conference, Nottingham.

Covey, S. (1989). *Seven habits of highly effective people*. Free Press.

Dunne, E., & Zandstra, R. (2011). *Students as change agents*. Bristol: HEA/ESCalate. Retrieved from http://escalate.ac.uk/8242

Haslam, S. A. (2004). *Psychology in organizations: The social identity approach* (2nd ed.). Thousand Oaks, CA: Sage Publications.

HEA (Higher Education Academy). (2013). Dimensions of student engagement. Retrieved from http://www.heacademy.ac.uk/resources/detail/studentengagement/Dimensions_student_engagement

Johnson, D. W., & Johnson, F. P. (2003). *Joining together: Group theory and group skills* (8th ed.). Boston, MA: Allyn and Bacon.

Kay, J., Hutchinson, J., & Dunne, E. (2010). *Rethinking the values of higher education — Students as change agents?* Gloucester: QAA.

Kay, J., Owen, D., & Dunne, E. (2012). Students as change agents: Student engagement with quality enhancement of learning and teaching. In I. Solomonides, A. Reid & P. Petocz (Eds.), *Engaging with learning in higher education*. Oxfordshire: Libri Publishers.

Kirchmeyer, C. (1993). Multicultural task groups. *Small Group Research*, *24*(1), 127–148.

QAA (Quality Assurance Agency for Higher Education). (2009). *Outcomes from institutional audit — student representation and feedback arrangements*. Gloucester: QAA. Retrieved from http://qaa.ac.uk/reviews/institutionalAudit/outcomes/series2/students09.pdf. Accessed on 6 June, 2013.

Ramsden, P. (2008). *The future of higher education teaching and the student experience*. Retrieved from www.dius.gov.uk/higher_education/shape_and_structure/he_debate/~/media/publications/T/teaching_and_student_experience_131008. Accessed on 6 June, 2013.

Stubbs, W., & Owen, D. (2010). Shaping and quality assuring the curriculum: The employer and the student voice. Paper presented at EAIR 32nd Annual Forum, Valencia, Spain.

Watson, W. E., Kumar, K., & Michaelsen, L. K. (1993). Cultural diversity's impact on group process and performance: Comparing culturally homogeneous and culturally diverse task groups. *The Academy of Management Journal*, *36*(3), 590–602.

Wenger, E. (1998). *Communities of practice: Learning, meaning, and identity*. New York, NY: Cambridge University Press.

Wenger, E., McDermott, R., & Snyder, W. M. (2002). *Cultivating communities of practice: A guide to managing knowledge*. Boston, MA: Harvard Business School Press.

Wheatley, M. (2002). Supporting Pioneering Leaders as Communities of Practice: How to Rapidly Develop New Leaders in Great Numbers. Educational Leaders. New Zealand Ministry of Education. Retrieved from http://www.educationalleaders.govt.nz/Pedagogy-and-assessment/Leading-learning-communities/Developing-New-Leaders.

Chapter 31

Catalysing Multiple Forms of Engagement: Student–Staff Partnerships Exploring Teaching and Learning

Alison Cook-Sather

Abstract

The purpose of this chapter is to analyse the multiple forms of engagement that academic staff and undergraduate students experience and facilitate through the Students as Learners and Teachers (SaLT) program at Bryn Mawr College in the United States. The SaLT program provides structures and processes through which academic staff work with undergraduate students positioned as pedagogical consultants and partners in exploring classroom teaching and learning. This discussion draws on data from an on-going action research study; data sources include audiotaped conversations of weekly meetings of student consultants and selected meetings with academic staff participants, mid- and end-of-semester feedback from those students and academic staff and follow-up interviews. Findings indicate that through their participation in this program, both academic staff and students experience multiple forms of engagement that are at once reciprocal — affecting in similar but not identical ways the participants involved — and inclusive of those beyond the partners in reciprocity. Such engagement facilitates more nuanced understandings of the complexities of teaching and learning, inspires empathy and appreciation, and deepens a sense of responsibility for the educational process. These findings should be of interest to all who pursue and support engaged teaching and learning and wish to position students as change agents in higher education. More research into the experiences of academic staff and students in pedagogical partnership across higher education contexts could further illuminate the potential of this approach.

The Student Engagement Handbook: Practice in Higher Education
Copyright © 2013 by Emerald Group Publishing Limited
All rights of reproduction in any form reserved
ISBN: 978-1-78190-423-7

31.1.   Introduction

Most discussions of engagement focus on students as active agents (Wolf-Wendel, Ward, & Kinzie, 2009) in relation to the acquisition, integration and, in some cases, co-construction of knowledge (Davis & Sumara, 2002; McCulloch, 2009). The purpose of this chapter is to analyse the multiple forms of engagement that both students and academic staff experience and facilitate when they partner through the Students as Learners and Teachers (SaLT) program at Bryn Mawr College in the United States. This program provides structures and processes through which academic staff work with undergraduate students positioned as pedagogical consultants in exploring, affirming and revising classroom teaching and learning.

I evoke the various meanings of 'catalyse' — to modify, especially to increase, the rate of a reaction; to bring about or initiate; to produce fundamental change in; to transform — to describe the deepened and more complex involvement in and excitement about teaching and learning experienced by students and academic staff. These include (1) multiplied forms of academic staff–student engagement — (a) between academic staff and student consultants; (b) between academic staff and other students; (c) between student consultants and their academic staff partners; and (d) between student consultants and other academic staff — and (2) multiplied forms of student engagement — (a) for student consultants themselves and (b) between student consultants and other students.

31.2.   Context and Programmatic Approach

The SaLT program is based at Bryn Mawr College, a selective liberal arts college for women in the north-eastern United States. A total of 1300 undergraduate women and 400 graduate students from 61 countries around the world choose to attend Bryn Mawr to study with leading scholars and conduct advanced research. With a student:academic staff ratio of 8:1; 36 major areas of study and 38 minors to choose from; and close collaboration with nearby Haverford College, Swarthmore College and the University of Pennsylvania, students benefit from a small-college environment with expansive resources. Academic staff are committed both to research and to teaching, and the college strives to 'foster the development of women who embrace an intense intellectual commitment, a purposeful vision of their lives, and a desire to make a meaningful contribution to the world' (http://www.brynmawr.edu/about/).

SaLT is part of the Teaching and Learning Institute at Bryn Mawr College, supported by a grant from The Andrew W. Mellon Foundation and by the Provosts' offices at Bryn Mawr and Haverford Colleges. The program invites undergraduate students to take up the paid position of pedagogical consultant to academic staff who choose to participate in the program; they work in pairs in semester-long partnerships to analyse, affirm and revise the staff member's pedagogical approaches in a course as s/he teaches it. Participation in SaLT is entirely voluntary, and staff choose to participate for a wide variety of reasons. Incoming tenure-track staff are given a course release by Bryn Mawr and Haverford College provosts if they choose to participate, and full-time, continuing staff members earn stipends for their participation through the Mellon grant. Academic staff participants span ranks and divisions and range from new to the colleges to those with 45 years of teaching experience.

Student consultants are second-year through fourth-year enrolled as undergraduates at Bryn Mawr or Haverford College. They major in different fields, claim different identities and bring varying degrees of formal preparation in educational studies (from those with no coursework in education to those pursuing certification to teach at the secondary level). The application process to become a consultant includes writing a statement regarding their qualifications and securing two letters of recommendation, one from an academic staff member and one from a student. These students are not enrolled in the courses for which they serve as consultants; some have experience in the discipline of the course for which they consult, others do not. On average, student consultants spend seven hours per week and, paid by the hour, can earn up to $900 through the Mellon grant for their participation in a semester-long partnership with an academic staff member.

Each student consultant has the following responsibilities:

(1) Attend an orientation that I facilitate in my role as coordinator of the SaLT program and review a set of guidelines for developing partnerships. The orientation and guidelines help prepare students for the challenges and possibilities of partnering with academic staff but do not prescribe or control the way the partnerships unfold.

(2) Visit one class session of his or her staff partner's course each week and take detailed observation notes on the pedagogical challenge(s) the staff member identifies. These notes take the form of clinical observations, with a column for time on the left, a column for observations in the centre and a comment for reflections on the right. After each visit, the consultant types up these notes and presents them, along with a short summary of main points for discussion, to his or her staff partner.

(3) Meet weekly for 30−60 minutes with the staff member to discuss observation notes and other feedback and implications. These meetings provide a forum for both the staff member and student consultant to exchange their perspectives and insights and to discuss what is working well in the staff member's class and what might be revised to promote deeper engagement.

(4) Participate in weekly meetings with other consultants and with me in my role as coordinator of the program to discuss how best to partner with academic staff in the work of developing productively challenging, engaging, and inclusive classrooms.

I form the staff−student partnerships largely based on participants' schedules and, where possible, taking into consideration personality and disciplinary experience. Between 2007 and 2013, 180 academic staff and 104 student consultants have participated in over 250 partnerships.

31.3.   Theoretical Framework and Methodology

Engagement is a complex phenomenon, encompassing student involvement, excitement and persistence (Ahlfeldt, Mehta, & Sellinow, 2005), layered and meaningful participation in and commitment to learning (Kuh, Kinzie, Schuh, & Whitt, 2010), and emotional as well as intellectual investment. It is the opposite, as Mann (2001) so strikingly put it, of alienation. Always situated and often relational (Webber, 2004), student engagement may vary across contexts in higher education — within a classroom or in relation to a particular task or assignment, within and across the course or program of study, and so on (Bryson & Hand, 2007).

Theories of student engagement, student voice and collaborative models of postsecondary staff development that include students as partners all situate students as active participants — as actors with significant roles — in learning itself, in conversations about learning and the teaching that supports or hinders it, and in collaborative efforts to affirm and improve teaching and learning. They all take as a premise or as an explicit focus of analysis students' active involvement in and commitment to enriching the educational process.

When students take such active responsibility for the educational process, often facilitated by choice (hooks, 1994; Rogers & Freiberg, 1969), there is not only a shift from passivity to agency but also from merely doing to developing a meta-cognitive awareness about what is being done. Such a shift changes 'not just what the learner knows…but also who the learner is' (Dreier, 2003, in Wortham, 2004, p. 716; see also Cook-Sather, 2006). Bryson and Hand (2007) have argued that, in order for students to feel genuinely engaged, there need to be three levels of engagement present simultaneously: between academic staff and students (discourse); between academic staff and subject (enthusiasm); between academic staff and the teaching process (professionalism) (p. 360).

Student voice takes engagement beyond the realm of students' own individual learning and into larger conversations about and revisions of educational practice. Developed largely in the context of K-12 schools in Australia (Holdsworth, 2000), Canada (Levin, 2000) and the United Kingdom (Fielding, 2004, 2006; Rudduck, 2007), student voice embraces a students' rights perspective in relation to student engagement in school and in analyses and reform of education. The basic premises of this work are that young people have unique perspectives on learning and teaching; that their insights warrant not only the attention but also the responses of adults; and that they should be afforded opportunities to actively shape their education (Cook-Sather, 2006, 2009a, 2012). 'Voice' signals sound, presence and power (Cook-Sather, 2006) — the actual practice of each student speaking as and for herself and the valuing of what is said collectively by students as a group as an essential contribution to dialogue that informs action. Thus, voice refers both to what is literally spoken by individual students and to a cumulative, collective chorus — not a monolithic voice but rather the presence of, active participation in, and influence of students within conversations about and reform of educational practice.

Collaborative models of professional development that include students as partners in post-secondary academic staff development programs (Bovill, Cook-Sather, & Felten, 2011; Cook-Sather, Bovill, & Felten, in press) bring the fact and spirit of student voice work to higher education. Such models position students as pedagogical consultants (Cook-Sather, 2008, 2009b, 2010; Cook-Sather & Alter, 2011; Cox & Sorenson, 2000; Sorenson, 2001) and members of teams with academic and support staff who design or redesign course curricula (Bovill, 2013; Delpish et al., 2010). Through these and other programs, students are not only partners but also change agents, a term that 'explicitly supports a view of the student as "active collaborator" and "co-producer", with the potential for transformation' (Dunne in Foreword to Dunne & Zandstra, 2011, p. 4; see also Neary, 2010). Recent work in the Scholarship of Teaching and Learning (SoTL) has similarly begun to recognize students 'not as objects of inquiry…but as co-inquirers, helping to shape key questions, gather and analyse data, and then push for change where it is needed' (Hutchings, Huber, & Ciccone, 2011, p. 79; see also Werder & Otis, 2010). As in the student voice literature, students within some SoTL projects are positioned as actively engaged in inquiry; their perspectives inform the questions that are asked; their interpretations inform understandings; their participation is part of the action that unfolds — they are partners in dialogue and in action with academic staff.

Situated within the theoretical frameworks offered above, this discussion draws on data from an on-going action research study guided by these basic questions: What happens when academic staff and students engage in structured dialogue with one another about teaching and learning outside of the regular spaces within which they interact? and how can such dialogic engagement become a part of both students and teachers' practice? Integrating action and research to challenge the routines of the *status quo* (Somekh & Zeichner, 2009), I have practiced collective, collaborative, self-reflective, critical inquiry (McCutcheon & Jung, 1990) with participants in the SaLT program. Respectively and together, we move repeatedly through the 'spiral of self-reflective cycles' of planning a change, acting and observing the consequences of the change, reflecting on these processes and consequences, and then re-planning (Kemmis & Wilkinson, 1998, p. 21). (See Cook-Sather, 2011a, 2011b, for other discussions of the ways in which this program scaffolds the action research cycle for participants.)

Data sources include audiotaped conversations of weekly meetings of student consultants and selected meetings with staff participants, mid- and end-of-semester feedback from those students and staff and follow-up interviews. All participants understood these forms of feedback to be for purposes of reflecting for themselves and for documenting and disseminating the work of the SaLT program. These data sources have been transcribed and coded using constant comparison/grounded theory (Creswell, 2006; Strauss, 1987) in order to determine themes and trends in the experiences and perspectives of participants.

31.4.   Findings: Catalysing Multiple Forms of Engagement

In other discussions of the SaLT program, I have described the ways in which student consultants experience their identities and perspectives as legitimate and important, develop their voices within the forums of the SaLT program, build confidence in their capacities as students and consultants, and feel empowered within and beyond their partnerships with staff in the program (see Cook-Sather, 2010, 2011a, 2012). I have also described how academic staff with whom these student consultants work experience the power of gaining insight into the student perspective through listening to the student voices, become more reflective practitioners as a result of partnering with students and come to see all their students more as colleagues (Cook-Sather, 2008, 2009b, 2011b). In the present discussion, I build on those previous findings to explore how participation in the SaLT program catalyses — both initiates and constitutes transformation of — engagement in teaching and learning.

A central feature of these multiple forms of engagement is that they are at once reciprocal — affecting in similar but not identical ways the participants involved — and inclusive of those beyond the partners in reciprocity. Thus, they have implications for impact and scalability — for spreading these forms of engagement beyond those directly involved in the SaLT program or programs like it.

31.4.1.   *Catalysing Multiple Forms of Engagement between Academic Staff and Students*

SaLT catalyses multiple forms of staff–student engagement. Various facets of the same relationship (i.e. staff–student), each of these forms embodies a somewhat differently manifested fundamental change in the engagement between the two partners in this relationship.

31.4.2.   *Academic Staff Catalysing Multiple Forms of Engagement with Student Consultants*

The SaLT program structures opportunities and provides support for academic staff to work in partnership with students outside of the standard staff–student dynamic. This basic structure and support invite staff to initiate or to accelerate a multiplication of forms of engagement they might experience with their student consultants. Not required to convey a body of knowledge or evaluate the student, the staff member can engage with student consultants around different dimensions of the educational experience. One staff member captured succinctly what creates the space for this new form of engagement:

> What makes this relationship so amazing is that [the student consultant is] not responsible for the content and...free of the grading.

That's why we can be more honest. And because we have confidentiality I can [talk about] what I am struggling with in ways that I would NEVER talk to a student. Because we are outside of the normal relationship.

Because they are 'outside of the normal relationship', staff can share their thinking about teaching, unpack their pedagogical rationales, reveal their questions and uncertainties, and ask student consultants for their perspectives as students and also as collaborators in exploring how to translate pedagogical goals into effective classroom practices. As one staff member explained:

My Student Consultant provided truly insightful feedback on both the day-to-day details of my teaching style and on larger scale class dynamics and tone. Working with the Student Consultant encouraged me to continually reflect on which aspects of my teaching I wanted to observe and improve upon: she asked me each week what I would like her to pay attention to, forcing me to constantly ask myself what I was working on in my teaching practice − and forcing me to pay attention to it myself.

This new form of engagement is at once exhilarating and difficult for staff: Becoming a partner with a student in explorations of pedagogical practice is both vulnerable making and empowering. As one staff member put it.

This was such a powerful experience—wonderful and also scary at times to let someone else so deeply into my classroom and also, in certain ways, into my psyche, since I think teaching is so often private (strange, given that those 25 or so students are also there!)

When academic staff work in such deeply collaborative ways with student consultants, engaged as true partners, they can develop a stronger sense of where deeper engagement might unfold with their students more generally. In other words, this deep form of engagement between staff and student consultant catalyses staff members' desire to multiply forms of engagement with their own students. As another staff member explained:

[The student consultant] did a good job of reconnecting me to the students. She was a bridge back to me being an advocate for the students and serving them well. She reminded me of how much I care and made me refocus my attention on helping students as opposed to simply setting up challenges and obstacles that I expect them to meet. At the end of the year I evaluated myself, I really repositioned myself as their advocate because of this program. Because I believe collaborative learning is an effective way to engage students, I told my students that next semester we're going to do more to get them working together.

This staff member's final comment both highlights a danger of this work — that staff can focus so much on initiating productive change that they forget that the students with whom they gained that insight might not benefit from it since they are moving on — and links this example of expanded engagement between staff members and student consultants with the positive side of this work, the second form of engagement under this category, discussed in the next section.

31.4.3.   *Academic Staff Catalysing Multiple Forms of Engagement with Other Students*

After experiencing the kind of engagement that can come through partnering with a student consultant to explore teaching and learning within a particular course, many academic staff apply this transformed notion of engagement to other collaborative ventures with students: gathering feedback on and planning courses, interacting with students more as partners in that planning.

When student consultants gather mid-semester feedback on their staff partners' courses, they generate with staff members a set of questions, gather student responses to those and analyse them with their staff partners, and then staff share the responses with students in the class, engaging in a conversation about what can be changed and why and what needs to remain as is and why (see Cook-Sather, 2009b, for a discussion of this process). Engaged as colleagues, as one student consultant put it, 'who [are] working toward the same goal but from different sides of the problem', this approach prompts staff to feel 'like there is more of a sense that we all own the class a little more'. Student consultants confirm this sense. About the change in engagement between staff and students in the class after the staff member conducted mid-semester feedback, one consultant wrote: 'Students are working with [academic staff] to build courses, to build their learning experience'. Inviting students of offer assessment feedback is receiving growing attention as a way not only of engaging students but also of increasing their success (Clouder, Broughan, Jewell, & Steventon, 2012).

When conducted as a communicative and collaborative process, such exchanges around assessment can catalyse other forms of engagement between staff and students in their courses. About planning future courses, one staff member explained:

> [My student consultant and I] agreed to invite the teaching assistant for the course and several other students who had taken multiple courses with me to a meeting. I put on the table the idea that I wanted them to imagine a course that would be conducted along lines that would maximize their learning.

This staff member's effort to consult students about what would 'maximize their learning' embodies a fundamental change in the way most academic staff and students engage with a course they are planning to teach and take, respectively.

Not only in planning but also simply in conducting the course as it unfolds, staff who have partnered with student consultants talk about how they have transformed their thinking. A new staff member described a change in attitude and practice that he experienced:

> One unexpected side effect of working with the Student Consultant was a subtle change in attitude that I experienced. I have always strived to adjust course content and process to match student interests and needs, but I had always seen that as a process of *me* adjusting things for *them*. Mid-way through the semester of working with my Student Consultant, I realized that I was thinking about my class in a more collaborative way than I had before: I was thinking about building the course *with* the students, as partners. I first noticed this when a student came to talk to me about a concept she was struggling to grasp. We ended up talking about not just the concept, but how one could best teach the concept to others, and we designed and re-designed a new set of activities, re-teaching the concept for the rest of the class. We then implemented it for everyone, and got great feedback (and great test results!) from the new method. I felt this throughout the class: that the students and I were engaged in building this class together. I believe this change arose directly from my experience collaborating with my Student Consultant, and I think it's taken my teaching to an amazing new level — both for my students, and for me personally.

Experienced staff members have used similar language to describe how they have transformed their forms of engagement with students in their courses, clarifying that taking up this more collaborative approach 'doesn't mean that you are giving over control of the course. But there are elements of the classroom that we are co-responsible for, that we are travelling through together'. Or, as another experienced staff member put it:

> I work with students more as colleagues, more as people engaged in similar struggles to learn and grow. I have become even more convinced that students are experts in learning and essential partners in the task of creating and developing new courses and refining existing ones.

Catalysed by these multiple, new forms of engagement with student consultants and their own students, academic staff also transform their modes of engagement with colleagues, working more deeply and collaboratively in planning, teaching and assessing their courses. This has been the case particularly in relation to the new 360-degree course clusters recently developed at Bryn Mawr College, many of which have evolved with support from student consultants (see http://teachingandlearning together.blogs.brynmawr.edu/archived-issues/seventh-issue-fall-2012).

31.4.4.   *Student Consultants Catalysing Multiple Forms of Engagement with Academic Staff Partners*

The flip side of academic staff catalysing new forms of engagement with student consultants and with other students is student consultants initiating such changes with their staff partners and with other academic staff. Just as the SaLT program structures opportunities and provides support for staff members to work in relationship with students outside of the standard staff–student dynamic, creating space and opportunity to engage with students on different terms, the program creates spaces and opportunities for students to engage with staff in a different way. Because of the power dynamics inherent in standard staff–student relationships, it is important to legitimate student authority and perspectives, as the formal role of student consultant and the on-going support that student consultants have while in the role do.

It often takes a little time before student consultants feel legitimate within the role. As one student consultant explained:

> At first I was kind of sceptical because you are a student and these profs have been doing this for quite some time they have advanced degrees, you're a kid with some college. And you are trying to come in and say, 'Do this better, do that'. You could easily be dismissed, and I didn't want to have that experience. I am honored that things I say have any value. It was so good that people wanted to hear and took into the perspective that I was bringing. It was so nice to think I had a perspective [my staff partner] hadn't thought about.

While the level of confidence and capacity student consultants feel varies across partnership and depending on how much consulting experience those students have, there is, overall, a steady growth over the course of individual partnerships and over multiple semesters as student consultants move through different partnerships. As student consultants experience new and multiple forms of engagement, they increasingly value and seek them out:

> This semester my partner is incredibly open to new ideas and has been thinking about education and teaching for a long time. I think my favorite part is that we feel comfortable bouncing ideas off of each other. He does not mind disagreeing with me and I feel comfortable voicing half-formed thoughts, which is great...I can just say, 'I was wondering about...' and that will start a conversation that ends up being immensely helpful for both of us.

From a legitimate programmatic position (consultant), with on-going support, and through building a relationship of mutual respect, student consultants multiply forms of engagement with their staff partners. The SaLT program supports the fundamental change, the transformation, participants effect in how they engage with one another. As one consultant argued:

> The [SaLT program's] goal of creating new spaces in which [academic staff] and students can interact as colleagues is exactly what occurs within these partnerships, especially in the one-on-one meetings with professors. These meetings allow us to jointly construct a unique space, for a limited time period, where we can safely challenge existing ideas about pedagogy, campus structures, or discipline-based ideas and also just connect, as people.

31.4.5. *Student Consultants Catalysing Multiple Forms of Engagement with Other Academic Staff*

Once they learn that academic staff will take them seriously and listen to their perspectives, students pursue forms of engagement that connect them more deeply to their staff/partners but also prompt them to think more broadly about the nature of teaching and learning and strive for such engagement with other staff. One consultant explained:

> Working as a student consultant has allowed me to observe the dynamic nature of the teaching and learning process. This is constantly evolving and my work has shown me that the process of teaching and learning is fostered by both the teacher and the learner in the classroom. Constant input is required from both participants to shape what happens within and even outside the classroom. This insight is important for me because it is empowering for me as a student to know that my input is relevant for my learning in any sphere. Teaching and learning is not a passive process where I can lie back but it requires an in-depth engagement. My respect for professors is deepened and enriched by my work and these insights prepare me to pursue a positive discourse between professors and students.

Student engagement extends to include a kind of empathy and advocacy for academic staff — a feeling of solidarity born of the deeper understanding consultants gain of what it takes to teach:

> I feel like I am more of a professor advocate. Sometimes when I hear things about professors, it just makes me so angry. I just think a lot of students don't reflect on themselves, they don't look at what they are doing that limits or takes away from their learning experience, and I just want to be like, 'What are YOU doing? Think about what you are doing in that class — Are you not paying attention? Are you not participating?'

Another student consultant summed up the change in her way of engaging in her studies and with other students born of her experience of engaging differently with academic staff through the SaLT program. Every semester virtually every consultant offers some version of this statement:

> This program has really made me more aware of my responsibility as a student – in my own classes, how and when I approach [staff] members and the effort I put into my work, as well as with friends or other students who may be having difficulties with other professors.

Through their partnerships with academic staff, student consultants develop a more informed understanding of what is happening in classrooms, what could be happening and what is most effective in supporting learning, and this understanding multiplies their modes of engagement in their own classes. As one consultant explained:

> [Participating in this program] has changed the way I see myself as a student and my professors. I feel more capable and aware as a student, and I feel more connection and compassion for my professors and the type of work they do. When a class isn't working for me, instead of just resigning [myself] to the idea that it's a bad class, I work to understand why I am having a negative experience and what would need to happen to make it a positive one.

31.4.6.   Catalysing Multiple Forms of Engagement for and among Students

Complementing the forms of engagement between academic staff and students discussed above are multiplied forms of student engagement — for student consultants themselves and between student consultants and other students.

31.4.7.   Student Consultants Catalysing Multiple Forms of Engagement as Students

Several factors contribute to the multiplication of forms of engagement student consultants experience. The most salient and consistent ones are their being taken seriously as knowers, the deeper insights they gain into the complexities of teaching and learning, and the heightened awareness they develop of their own and others' learning gained through dialogue — through more complex relationships — with academic staff and one another.

Student consultants consistently talk about the empowerment they experience when they are taken seriously as knowers. As one consultant explained:

> Nothing is more powerful than seeing a professor take your ideas seriously, to have rich discussion about them and possibly see them implemented into a class. When I see a professor open to my ideas as a consultant, I feel that I am truly making a difference and becoming an important leader in this community.

Feeling respected and valued by academic staff in these ways, being part of analysing and shaping what the staff do, and thus engaging as a partner and leader not only as a learner, make students, they say, 'take my work more seriously'.

Analysing and gaining insight into how teaching works has a complement in analysing and gaining insight into how learning works. From two different angles, these insights catalyse new forms of engagement. In one consultant's words:

> You really don't understand the way you learn and how others learn until you can step back from it and are not in the class with the main aim to learn the material of the class but more to understand what is going on in the class and what is going through people's minds as they relate with that material.

These insights lead students to conceptualize teaching and learning as a shared responsibility between teachers and students:

> I no longer think that professors are responsible for having all the answers and making a class perfect and wonderful to suit my own needs. It is up to the entire community to make learning spaces function, so that means students have just as much responsibility as professors.

They also prompt students to rethink how they might differently engage in classrooms:

> I am a much more conscientious student in general now; I ask myself what I could do differently to improve my own classroom experience, rather than complaining about the professor or the course in general.

One form this greater consciousness and conscientiousness takes is more active engagement with course material. One consultant described the way she adapted the form of note taking required for observations of her staff partner's classroom through the SaLT program to her note taking for her own classes: 'Now in my classes, the way I take notes is to split my page in two. I have a column for the content and then a column for reflections — questions, connections, interpretations'.

Each of these student reflections offers a different example of a new form of engagement — transformations of their ways of being, of their sense of capacity and responsibility — that they embody in their larger lives as students.

31.4.8. *Student Consultants Catalysing Multiple Forms of Engagement with and for Other Students*

The complement to student consultants feeling more engaged, capable and responsible themselves as learners is a desire and a capacity to help other students feel more engaged and empowered. This commitment has several aspects.

One is recognition of what others can contribute to learning: 'My work as a student consultant has helped me appreciate the contributions of others. I can remove myself from the competitive atmosphere within the classroom to see other students' assets'. Another is recognition of how student consultants themselves affect others' learning. This recognition informs both how student consultants hold back, suspending judgement or participation when they see that others need to engage more, or, alternatively, modelling more engaged participation for other students. About the former, one consultant wrote:

> I'm a lot more aware of the dynamics of learning now. I feel a major issue for me now as a student is thinking before I speak and being more considerate of others and their learning styles and expectations of the course and maybe in a way it makes me a bit more patient.

Addressing the latter form of recognition, another consultant explained:

> [Participating in this program] makes you much more aware of yourself, your presence in the class. You don't think about yourself and the impact you'll have just by what you say and how you say it. It's easy to not say what you want to say for the fear of how it will be perceived. [But] just putting yourself out there might make the difference in the way the class goes and the way people think. I have been inspired [through my work with my staff partner] to be not as cautious if I have something to say – I say it but frame it in a way that I try not to alienate people.

And finally, consultants talk about the responsibility they take outside of classrooms for the engagement of fellow students. They describe how they bring their classmates and friends into dialogue to explore ways in which those students could be more empowered, more connected, more reflective:

> Instead of simply agreeing or disagreeing, a constructive conversation can come out of a comment about a class. We can ask questions of our classmates—Why do you think that? What would make it better?—instead of leaving their ideas to literally fester. We can share the possibility that another way of thinking exists.

31.5. Implications

Through partnerships between students and academic staff 'as a form of radical collegiality' (Fielding, 2011, p. 9), staff members, student consultants and other students experience both engagement and empowerment. Working as partners, participants in the SaLT program initiate, change and transform their attitude toward and participation in teaching and learning.

Particularly important about these multiple forms of engagement is the way in which they break down traditional power hierarchies and counter the forms of alienation that Mann (2001) enumerates, which are antithetical to engagement. When academics partner with students, sharing the power and responsibility for how a course unfolds, students gain some relief from the experience of alienation that 'arises from being in a place where those in power have the potential to impose their particular ways of perceiving and understanding the world — in other words, a kind of colonising process' (Mann, 2001, p. 11). Bringing students and staff into dialogue counters the alienation that comes from being dismissed, not heard, not recognized, not legitimated. As Mann (2001) explains: 'When the learner asks a question and this question is not heard, is brushed aside or is ridiculed, it may be difficult for the student to gain a sense of themselves, to experience and work from their desire and their creativity' (Mann, 2001, p. 13). Academic staff can experience these forms of alienation as well, but through partnership and dialogue, they too multiply their forms of engagement.

The multiple forms of engagement catalysed by participants in the SaLT program could be taken up by staff and students in various contexts. Individual staff members or staff developers could create supportive structures and processes through which academic staff and students can communicate about and collaborate on the work of teaching and learning. Such a practical and social revision of the ways that staff and students interact would move us toward 'a person-centred education for democratic fellowship' (Fielding, 2011, p. 1). More research into the experiences of academic staff and students in pedagogical partnership in other higher education contexts could further illuminate the potential of reciprocal teaching and learning built on solidarity and shared responsibility.

References

Ahlfeldt, S., Mehta, S., & Sellinow, T. (2005). Measurement and analysis of student engagement where varying levels of PBL methods of instruction were is use. *Higher Education Research and Development*, *24*(1), 5−20.

Bovill, C. (2013). *An investigation of co-created curricula within higher education in the UK, Ireland and the USA*. Innovations in Education and Teaching International. Retrieved from http://www.tandfonline.com/doi/abs/10.1080/14703297.2013.770264. Accessed on 30 May 2013.

Bovill, C., Cook-Sather, A., & Felten, P. (2011). Students as co-creators of teaching approaches, course design, and curricula: Implications for academic developers. *International Journal for Academic Development*, *16*(2), 133−145.

Bryson, C., & Hand, L. (2007). The role of engagement in inspiring teaching and learning. *Innovations in Education and Teaching International*, *44*(4), 349−362.

Clouder, L., Broughan, C., Jewell, S., & Steventon, G. (Eds.). (2012). *Improving student engagement and development through assessment: Theory and practice in higher education*. London: Routledge, Taylor & Francis Group.

Cook-Sather, A. (2006). Sound, presence, and power: Exploring 'student voice' in educational research and reform. *Curriculum Inquiry*, *36*(4), 359−390.

Cook-Sather, A. (2008). "What you get is looking in a mirror, only better": Inviting students to reflect (on) college teaching. *Reflective Practice, 9*(4), 473–483.

Cook-Sather, A. (2009a). *Learning from the student's perspective: A sourcebook for effective teaching.* Boulder, CO: Paradigm Publishers.

Cook-Sather, A. (2009b). From traditional accountability to shared responsibility: The benefits and challenges of student consultants gathering midcourse feedback in college classrooms. *Assessment & Evaluation in Higher Education, 34*(2), 231–241.

Cook-Sather, A. (2010). Teaching and learning together: College faculty and undergraduates co-create a professional development model. *To Improve the Academy, 29*, 219–232.

Cook-Sather, A. (2011a). Layered learning: Student consultants deepening classroom and life lessons. *Educational Action Research, 19*(1), 41–57.

Cook-Sather, A. (2011b). Lessons in higher education: Five pedagogical practices that promote active learning for faculty and students. *Journal of Faculty Development, 25*(3), 33–39.

Cook-Sather, A. (2012). *Amplifying student voices in higher education: Democratizing teaching and learning through changing the acoustic on a college campus* (La amplificación de las voces del alumnado en la Educación Superior: Democratización de la enseñanza y el aprendizaje en un centro universitario a través del cambio de su acústica). Revista de Educación. Ministerio de Educación. Madrid, Spain. Retrieved from http://www.educacion.gob.es/revista-de-educacion/numeros-revista-educacion/ultimo-numero/re359/re359_10.html

Cook-Sather, A., & Alter, Z. (2011). What is and what can be: How a liminal position can change learning and teaching in higher education. *Anthropology & Education Quarterly, 42*, 37–53.

Cook-Sather, A., Bovill, C., & Felten, P. (in press). *Engaging students as partners in teaching & learning: A guide for faculty.* San Francisco, CA: Jossey-Bass.

Cox, M. D., & Sorenson, D. L. (2000). Student collaboration in faculty development. *To Improve the Academy, 18*, 97–106.

Creswell, J. (2006). *Qualitative inquiry and research design: Choosing among five approaches* (2nd ed.). New York: Sage Publications, Inc.

Davis, B., & Sumara, D. (2002). Constructivist discourses and the field of education. *Educational Theory, 52*(4), 409–428.

Delpish, A., Holmes, A., Knight-McKenna, M., Mihans, R., Darby, A., King, K., & Felten, P. (2010). Equalizing voices: Student-faculty partnership in course design. In C. Werder & M. M. Otis (Eds.), *Engaging student voices in the study of teaching and learning* (pp. 96–114). Sterling, VA: Stylus.

Dunne, E., & Zandstra, R. (2011). *Students as change agents. New ways of engaging with learning and teaching in higher education.* Bristol: ESCalate Higher Education Academy Subject Centre for Education / University of Exeter.

Fielding, M. (2004). 'New wave' student voice and the renewal of civic society. *London Review of Education, 2*(3), 197–217.

Fielding, M. (2006). Leadership, radical student engagement and the necessity of person-centred education. *International Journal of Leadership in Education, 9*(4), 299–314.

Fielding, M. (2011). Patterns of partnership: Student voice, intergenerational learning and democratic fellowship. In N. Mocker & J. Sachs (Eds.), *Rethinking educational practice through reflexive research: Essays in honour of Susan Groundwater-Smith*. Dordrecht, The Netherlands: Springer.

Holdsworth, R. (2000). Taking young people seriously means giving them serious things to do. In: J. Mason & M. Wilkinson (Eds.), *Taking children seriously*. Bankstown, Australia: University of Western Sydney.

hooks, b. (1994). *Teaching to transgress*. New York, NY: Routledge.

Hutchings, P., Huber, M. T., & Ciccone, A. (2011). *The scholarship of teaching and learning reconsidered: Institutional integration and impact (Jossey-Bass/Carnegie Foundation for the Advancement of Teaching)*. San Francisco, CA: Jossey-Bass.

Kemmis, S., & Wilkinson, M. (1998). Participatory action research and the study of practice. In B. Atweh, S. Kemmis, & P. Weeks (Eds.), *Action research in practice: Partnerships for social justice in education* (pp. 21−36). New York, NY: Routledge.

Kuh, G., Kinzie, J., Schuh, J. H., & Whitt, E. J. (2010). *Student success in college: creating conditions that matter*. San Francisco, CA: Jossey Bass.

Levin, B. (2000). Putting students at the centre of education reform. *Journal of Educational Change*, *1*(2), 155−172.

Mann, S. J. (2001). Alternative perspectives on the student experience: Alienation and engagement. *Studies in Higher Education*, *26*(1), 7−19.

McCulloch, A. (2009). The student as co-producer. *Studies in Higher Education*, *34*(2), 171−183.

McCutcheon, G., & Jung, B. (1990). Alternative perspectives on action research. *Theory into Practice*, *29*(3), 144−151.

Neary, M. (2010). Student as producer: A pedagogy for the avant-garde? *Learning Exchange*, *1*(1).

Rogers, C., & Freiberg, H. J. (1969). *Freedom to learn* (3rd ed.). New York, NY: Macmillan Publishing.

Rudduck, J. (2007). Student voice, student engagement and school reform. In D. Thiessen & A. Cook-Sather (Eds.), *International handbook of student experience in elementary and secondary school* (pp. 587−610). Dordrecht, The Netherlands: Springer.

Somekh, B., & Zeichner, K. (2009). Action research for educational reform: Remodelling action research theories and practices in local contexts. *Educational Action Research*, *17*(1), 5−21.

Sorenson, L. (2001). College teachers and student consultants: Collaborating about teaching and learning. In J. E. Miller, J. E. Groccia & M. S. Miller (Eds.), *Student-assisted teaching* (pp. 179−183). Bolton, MA: Anker.

Strauss, A. L. (1987). *Qualitative analysis for social scientists*. New York, NY: Cambridge University Press.

Webber, T. (2004). Orientations to learning in midcareer management students. *Studies in Higher Education*, *29*(2), 259−277.

Werder, C., & Otis, M. M. (Eds.). (2010). *Engaging student voices in the study of teaching and learning*. Sterling, VA: Stylus Publishing, LLC.

Wolf-Wendel, L., Ward, K., & Kinzie, J. (2009). A tangled web of terms: The overlap and unique contribution of involvement, engagement, and integration to understanding college student success. *Journal of College Student Development*, *50*(4), 407−428.

Wortham, S. (2004). The interdependence of social identification and learning. *American Educational Research Journal*, *41*(3), 715−750.

Chapter 32

Practical Approaches to Student Engagement through Community-Based Research and Learning

Eileen Martin and Catherine O'Mahony

Abstract

This chapter focuses on two forms of student engagement which can be used to enhance teaching, learning and the student experience: community-based research (CBR, often carried out through Science Shops) and community-based learning (CBL, also known as service learning), two approaches which exist along a continuum of experiential learning and participatory research activities. In both approaches, the student is facilitated to take responsibility for their own learning. Such approaches need to reflect the differing requirements of student and community partners; thus, they are inherently flexible in their execution, adapting to different course programmes and different institutional and community contexts. Case studies are provided of CBR and CBL initiatives involving groups of students and individual undergraduates and postgraduates. The requirement to take responsibility for delivering a useful outcome for a community organisation often encourages students to take this work more seriously than a purely theoretical piece of work and CBL/CBR projects can enthuse otherwise disengaged students. For the more enthusiastic students, this type of work can prove stimulating as they are forced to acknowledge that they are not necessarily the experts in the situation. Students often develop increased respect as the breadth of community knowledge and experience becomes evident.

32.1. Introduction

Student engagement is often considered from the perspective of the student and institution, but this perspective can be broadened or refocused to include the notion

The Student Engagement Handbook: Practice in Higher Education
Copyright © 2013 by Emerald Group Publishing Limited
All rights of reproduction in any form reserved
ISBN: 978-1-78190-423-7

of civic engagement where the student and the institution develop collaborative relationships with the wider community. The civic engagement activity of higher education is not a new endeavour; rather it has gained increased traction in recent times due in part to global initiatives such as the 'Engaged University' movement (Watson, Hollister, Stroud, & Babcock, 2011). These initiatives have proved a catalyst for the reconsideration of the role of higher education in the wider community. Higher education in Ireland is no exception and educational policy in both Northern Ireland and the Republic of Ireland emphasises the need to encourage the third mission of civic engagement in higher education (DELNI, 2010, pp. 10−11; Hunt, 2011).

There are many examples of activities in higher education that aim to address this 'civic engagement' need. Although there is a range of definitions of community-based research (CBR) and community-based learning (CBL) (Mason O'Connor & McEwen, 2012), for the purposes of this chapter, we will use the broad definitions outlined below. CBL, which is also known as service learning, is a course or discipline-based collaboration between students, lecturers and civil society partners for mutual benefit, that is meeting the students' learning needs as well as working towards community goals, through shared learning (Hunt, 2011, p. 59). CBR, also known as 'Science Shop' research, is research conducted in collaboration with communities on issues of relevance to them (Strand, Marullo, Cutforth, Stoecker, & Donohue, 2003, p. 16). This research can be undertaken in fulfilment of the student's academic requirement such as a dissertation topic, a group work project, a research skills module project, a final year project, a Masters project or as PhD research. These approaches can be distinguished from other activities such as volunteering or student placement as the beneficiaries of CBR and CBL approaches are *both* the student and the community partner. An initial step in both examples is the development of project proposals with community partners to ensure that the differing requirements and timescales of students and community partners are considered.

This chapter provides an overview of a several curriculum-linked CBR and CBL initiatives across the island of Ireland. Through case studies, the chapter provides useable examples which readers may find relevant to their own institutional context. As might be expected of non-traditional activities, there are some challenges relating to their implementation and these have been outlined in the case studies along with recommendations on how to circumvent or remove them. The case studies span disciplines as diverse as education, public relations and environmental science, and engage individual students or groups of students at both undergraduate and postgraduate levels.

The case studies are written by members of INCERL (the Irish Network for Community-Engaged Research and Learning), a recently established inter-institutional All-Ireland network of coordinators of CBL/CBR, emerging in part from the European community (EC)-funded PERARES project.[1] Each case study

---

[1]www.livingknowledge.org/livingknowledge/perares.

provides a web link to the individual initiative for further details and resources. A 'toolbox' of support materials, developed by members of the broader EC engagement network, is also available for those interested in developing these initiatives in their own institutions.

While this chapter draws a distinction between CBR and CBL, the reality is that these approaches exist along a continuum of experiential learning and participatory research activities. There is considerable cross-over in terms of how projects are organised, the community partners linked with and the pedagogical supports provided by course coordinators or project supervisors. Through engaging in CBR or CBL projects, students are enabled to integrate real-world experience with academic theory as well as becoming more aware of and responsive to local issues and concerns. These teaching and learning strategies can greatly enrich their learning experience while making them aware of their civic responsibilities and of the potential social impact of research.

For some students, this type of work presents the first opportunity in their degree programme to apply their knowledge directly to an issue of public concern or a non-academic audience. Many find this challenging and most require additional support. In providing this support, academic and mediation/coordination staff are required to have broader discussions with students around research ethics, personal safety and social responsibility, which are more meaningful to students as they see direct relevance to their own projects. As a consequence, students often take this type of work more seriously than a purely theoretical piece, although this is by no means always the case. However, this type of work can enthuse otherwise disengaged students and, for some, it is the first time in their degree programme that they fully understand the potential impact of their learning. For the more enthusiastic, this type of work can prove inspiring; there are many examples of the CBL/CBR experience influencing the students in their next steps post graduation. Taking responsibility for delivering a useful outcome for a community organisation often encourages them to take the work more seriously. They are also quickly forced to acknowledge that they are not the experts in the situation and develop increased respect as the breadth of community knowledge and experience becomes evident in the early stages of the process.

32.2.   Case Studies

32.2.1.   *Learning to Teach for Social Justice: A Service Learning Module for Student Teachers at National University of Ireland, Galway[2]*

The Learning to Teach for Social Justice service learning experience offers opportunities to pre-service teachers while responding, in a modest way, to a range of

---

[2]For further details, please visit www.nuigalwaycki.ie.

concerns of the Galway Traveller Movement regarding education, specifically relating to the participation and achievement of minority ethnic pupils. The challenge of catering for diversity in an intercultural society is a key concern in contemporary Irish society. Teacher populations are known to be quite homogeneous, generally being of the majority ethnic and social class groups. Research suggests that teachers tend to be naively egalitarian and meritocratic in their beliefs, and have little prior experience with class or ethnic diversity (Leavy, 2005). Attitudinal change is more likely to be achieved through experiential learning opportunities which necessitate engagement with core issues of concern.

Student teachers (10–15 each year) work in the Galway Traveller Movement's homework club, providing academic and other support to traveller pupils from local schools, or with an approved organisation nationwide. The module provides student teachers with critical insight into issues associated with diversity, interculturalism and educational disadvantage. It does this by meeting a specific community need identified by partner organisations, thereby fostering a sense of civic responsibility, citizenship and concern for social justice amongst student teachers, while developing their pedagogic and interpersonal skills, and their capacity for critical reflection. The work was seed funded by the Community Knowledge Initiative at the National University of Ireland, Galway.

Experiential learning is the primary mode of learning in the community-based partner organisation, and a minimum of 15–20 hours contact time is required. Preparation and training is provided by the Galway Traveller Movement, whilst special tutorials (8 hours) are provided on campus. These prepare students for, and support them during, the experience, encouraging reflection and planning on how best to communicate their learning to others. Assessment of student learning is based on three elements: (1) a reflective paper, (2) evidence generated in the course of the tutorials (both assessed by academic staff) and (3) satisfactory engagement with the community partner, assessed by the organisation.

For the university, service learning is now embedded as a credit-bearing element of the teacher education programme — the first such initiative in Ireland. For Galway Traveller Movement, parents report that traveller pupils display more enthusiasm about attending school regularly and receive more positive feedback from teachers about their engagement and progress.

> It wasn't the kids' usual classroom environment, but it was also an entirely different experience for me... I was asked 'Are you really a teacher?' It kind of broke down barriers for students and school no longer seemed so alien. The kids wanted the help and they were treated as equal. (PDE graduate)

A key challenge was finding 'space' in the curriculum to embed this as a core experience for all students. This was overcome by communicating to colleagues how the goals of the service learning module align closely with key goals of the programme. A second challenge was maintaining relationships with community organisations, especially as students are on placements in the wider region. Through working collaboratively with organisations, staff were able to strengthen the existing partnership by engaging in activities beyond the module, for example diversity training, policy development and advocacy work. Staff also encourage and support students who source community partners in their own area. A final challenge was ensuring the sustainability of this programme for academics under pressure. Every opportunity was taken to publicise the initiative and communicate the value of civic engagement as a legitimate and valued aspect of academic work within the institution.

32.2.2.   *Community-Based Research for Postgraduate Public Relations Students at Dublin Institute for Technology[3]*

The programme for 'Students Learning with Communities' at Dublin Institute of Technology (DIT) supports CBR and CBL across the institute. This programme is funded by DIT as well as through the PERARES project. Over 1,300 students participated in course-based civic engagement projects in 2011 onwards. One such example is the MA in public relations where students take an elective module entitled 'Foundations in Community-Based Research', co-delivered by students learning with communities staff and a lecturer in media studies. Participants work in small groups, each with one community partner, to design, plan, carry out and report on a piece of research which the community partners require. The module runs over 13 weeks (2 hours weekly), and academic staff assess and give feedback (together with community partners) on student presentations, as well as the final group research reports, which are combined with individual reflection on module learning.

The research focuses on reception or use of some aspect of the community partners' public relations activity; for example, they might want to know how a particular target group responds to their website/poster campaigns. Students learning with communities staff work with community partners (NGOs, charities, support groups) with a specific interest in the area of PR/marketing, and help them to conceptualise their research ideas to match the students' interests. Often in this process other projects emerge, and these are fed through to students on other courses where appropriate. Community partners then present students with their PR research interests. Students decide which issue they would like to work on, and meet with community partners to discuss the specific goals, supported by the lecturers. They sign a research agreement and are expected to keep in touch with and consult with the community partner as the research process continues. Students present their final research reports to community partners following academic assessment.

The module is in its third year and annual reviews inform its developing structure. Research reports varied in their level of usefulness to community partners and their demonstration of the required learning by students. One challenge was

---

[3]For further details, please visit www.communitylinks.ie/SLWC.

keeping community partners engaged where the results of the work were less helpful than expected. Staff followed up with such organisations to include their views in the module evaluation, and they were kept informed of resulting changes to the module. This helped to maintain relationships. For example, feedback from community partners and students indicated that communication (between all participants) was a challenge to achieving goals, so the assessment was amended to include interim and final presentations by students to peers, lecturers and community partners. In initial iterations, it became apparent that both community partners and students expected a more hands-on PR project, so the module was modified to clarify the research focus from the outset. Small group tutorials were also introduced, to guide students during their research planning and execution, and to direct them towards the most relevant readings to inform their analysis. Students reported a range of responses, from: 'Got to experience discussing with an outside organization what their issues were and how to find a way to solve them', to the more critical:

> 'There is not enough time to complete the research project with com-
> munication between the lecturers and community partners taking so
> long. Thirteen weeks is not long enough to carry out proper research.
> What we have learned about and what we can do are very different'.
> (Ward, 2012)

All community partners reported some useful outcomes from the work, despite some challenges; several participated in the project in consecutive years.

32.2.3.   *A Participatory Approach in Master's Research Projects on Older Adults at University College Cork[4]*

The Community-Academic Research Links (CARL) project at University College Cork, based on the 'Science Shop' model, is staffed largely on a volunteer basis with some funding for a part-time coordinator from the School of Applied Social Studies (see Bates & Burns, 2012). CARL invites non-profit voluntary or community organisations to suggest potential research topics that can be pursued by students across all academic disciplines. Students apply to undertake a project, but must meet the minimum standard of 60 per cent or higher in their previous year exams/projects. They also need a letter of support from their project supervisor. A total of 25 CARL-projects have been completed in UCC in the last three academic years, mainly by Master of Social Work students.

One project submitted by community partner Bandon Network of Social Groups involved assessing outdoor spaces and buildings, using the World Health

---

[4]For further details, please visit http://carl.ucc.ie.

Organisation guidelines on age-friendly cities. This involved the joint involvement of the student and community partner in the design, execution and analysis of the research. An overall work plan was agreed by the academic, community organisation and student at the start of the process and formalised in a contract. Community members took photographs of Bandon's outdoor spaces and buildings and then analysed these in focus groups facilitated by the student to discuss the impact of age-friendly features and difficulties on their daily lives. The student coordinated the process and wrote up the results in partnership with the community group members.

A central principle of CBR is working in full and equal participation with the university. This is based on the idea that local people are experts on their communities and understand the actions required to improve their quality of life (Novek, Morris-Oswald, & Menec, 2011). One student initially felt challenged by her role as the facilitator and wondered at times about the necessity of her role as her co-researchers provided considerable support. However, once communication lines were in place, the student earned the trust of the co-researchers, placed her trust in them and the research progressed well.

The result of this collaboration was a report with a number of recommendations to create a more age-friendly town. The student presented research results to the community partners, and they planned how best to implement the project recommendations and disseminate findings. The project has subsequently made local and national media headlines and was exhibited as part of age and opportunity's national festival, which aims to promote greater participation by older people in society. The study was highly commended by the external examiner and recommended for publication in a peer-reviewed journal, which the community partner and the student are jointly working on.

One challenge is that students often feel increased responsibility and pressure in terms of carrying out a piece of work on behalf of an organisation:

> It was a huge learning experience, both challenging and rewarding.
> I felt a real responsibility to the community partner and wanted to do
> the best possible project.

Academic staff helped them understand that this enabled them to engage better with their learning. Students indicated that they felt a greater level of engagement with the research but expressed concerns that this impacted on the time they had available for other work; however, they also identified that the extra effort was rewarding since they knew the work would be used:

> I engaged more with the research as it was real-life situation and
> knowing my research could have a positive impact.

It was also challenging for academic staff to manage the extra workload alongside already busy schedules and it became clear over the course of the project that the role of the part-time co-ordinator needed to be extended.

32.2.4. *Management Students Working with Communities at Queen's University of Belfast*[5]

The Science Shop is a CBR initiative at Queen's University Belfast (QUB), based in the Directorate of Academic and Student Affairs, and a core part of the community engagement activities of the university. It is funded through the Department for Employment and Learning Northern Ireland's Higher Education Innovation Fund. Science Shop staff work with community organisations to assist them to work up their research needs into projects suitable for students, either as dissertations or curriculum-based projects. This process involves both understanding community partners' needs but also making them aware of the time commitment such research may involve on their part. Students and community organisations are asked to sign agreements, enabling all parties to be clear on the nature of the research. Whilst students from all disciplines carry out research on behalf of community organisations, there has recently been an increased interest in social enterprise, leading to a rise in research requests around business and marketing issues. The QUB Science Shop has therefore developed a partnership with the school of management. Over 40 projects have been completed with groups of undergraduate students on the business analysis module in the last three years on behalf of community organisations across Northern Ireland. This includes a group of undergraduate students who worked with Upperlands Community Development Limited in a small rural village in the centre of Northern Ireland, helping the organisation to design a web-based marketing strategy for some small business units; the website has been used to generate revenue for community development.

Projects have enabled students to carry out research which benefits their local communities, requiring them to engage both with local organisations and their peers. Whilst the Science Shop sets up and attends the initial meeting to tie down details, students take responsibility for maintaining contact with the organisations to ensure that the research will meet their needs. This is not without its challenges:

> We really struggled with how difficult our sponsor ... was to get in contact with and ... It was an uphill climb to get any responses to our interview requests.

Students therefore appreciate the time and commitment required in a real research process. In some cases, where students are reliant on community partner information to proceed, projects break down: things move on in the partner organisation, or a key contact leaves or does not have sufficient time to be fully involved. This is challenging both for students and the academic supervisor. The role of the Science Shop in helping them find alternative projects in a very short timescale has been vital in underpinning the success of the module and enabling students to take on riskier and

---

[5]For further details including a short video about the Upperlands project, please visit www.qub.ac.uk/scisho.

more challenging projects. Science Shop involvement is also vital in ensuring that ethical issues are raised at an earlier stage and are fully discussed and dealt with, and in cases where they cannot be resolved, in finding suitable alternative projects.

The increased demands of a more applied project are offset against the appeal of engaging with the public. The work is assessed by the academic supervisor via presentations and reports which are presented to the commissioning organisations. Group work presents the usual challenges involved in teams in any setting; as one student commented;

> I found myself and one other team member doing all the work while others had a lack of input, poor standard of work and lack of attendance.

Students, however, often learn much from team members, some of whom may have direct personal experience of the issue being researched.

> I feel that it was a worthwhile experience as it threw us in to a real world situation … I value the experience I gained very much.

Staff make clear the responsibility of students to resolve internal disagreements, and help them understand that this is a common feature of working in groups and teams. The organisations are not themselves involved in the assessment process, though many attend the student presentations and give feedback. Some organisations have again been disappointed in the final research produced. Science Shop staff have ensured that the learning from this has been fed back into the module and appropriate action taken, and have worked to ensure that the organisation has a strong likelihood of a positive outcome in future (e.g. by promoting future projects to postgraduate students).

In terms of student learning, the challenge is in taking the skills they have learned in a business context and applying them in a sector where the aims are primarily social. A challenge for Science Shop staff is that students have not previously been exposed to community organisations and some need encouragement to take their responsibilities seriously. The tone taken by academic staff is instrumental in this process; it is critical to the success of projects and the quality of student engagement.

32.2.5.   *Community-Based Research in Environmental Science at University of Ulster[6]*

The Science Shop at the University of Ulster is part of the widening access and participation strategy of the university. Recently a final year environmental science student undertook a Science Shop project with Carntogher Community Association, which collates heritage asset data to look at the landscape of the area in terms of

---

[6]For further details, please visit http://ulster.scienceshop.org and http://www.ancarn.org/269-631/projects/envision/Pollen-analysis-at-Ballynahone-Bog.

past and present, with a view to planning for the future. This project was requested by the organisation to gather a picture of vegetation changes through time, particularly in terms of woodland composition. The student investigated the history of the vegetation of a bog which was an area of special scientific interest, collecting and analysing peat samples taken by coring on Ballynahone Bog. Coring was done incrementally 50 cm at a time from the ground surface to the base of the peat, which was defined as the boundary with the underlying lake sediments. Laboratory analyses involved the digestion of the peat to isolate pollen grains, which were then identified and counted under a microscope.

The student's academic supervisor commented:

> Community based research requires the student to engage in both fieldwork and laboratory tasks. They then have to evaluate the data collected in relation to local and regional environmental factors (climate and human impact). A Science Shop project enables the student to appreciate the nature and scale of environmental change in the past, and to develop an understanding of potential future changes and their likely impact on vegetation systems. This project in particular allowed the student to get wet, cold and dirty … and to appreciate that research sometimes involves being uncomfortable for short periods. However this is outweighed by the benefits of being able to collect primary data and to interpret it in relation to previous studies.

The project co-ordinator of ENVISION explained that:

> The student's work will inform the local community of the past roles and aspects of the bog, and offers ideas as to future roles of the bog within the landscape and for society.

The student undertook this project as the final year dissertation project and was able to access the University of Ulster laboratory resources, so there was no direct cost to the group or student. Travel costs were met by the student. Often a challenge on these types of projects is access and permission to take core samples, but access was negotiated on her behalf by the community partner. The group made the full report available on their web site and sent a copy for information to the Minister for Agriculture and Rural Development in Northern Ireland. They have also proposed further research projects for students through the Science Shop.

32.2.6. *Community Service Initiative Module for Students at the Institute of Technology, Tralee*[7]

The Community Service Initiative module is offered in the Health and Leisure Department in the Institute of Technology, Tralee. It was developed to encourage

---

[7]For further details, please visit www.ittralee.ie/en/InformationAbout/CommunityEngagement.

better student connectivity with civic society and to enhance student personal and social responsibility as active citizens, the consequences of a disconnected society having been widely researched (Putnam, 2000).

The module is funded through the mainstream programme and budgets within the Health and Leisure Department, and made available to second year students in Health and Leisure Studies, and the Medical Commencement Programme. Delivery incorporates two lectures and one tutorial per week with students committing to volunteer weekly for three months. Tutorial sessions allow for small group discussion on pertinent engagement issues, as they arise. They also incorporate personal development exercises and role plays to assist students to gain further competence in communication, decision making, conflict management and intercultural competence. Class size is typically 20 students and the community partners include sports clubs, youth centres, day-care centres, nursing homes, homework clubs, advocacy groups and the Scouts. The institute provides a list of voluntary organisations on its website, while new organisations are also welcome, once their suitability is confirmed. Students listen to what organisations need and together they formulate what the student will do and the weekly time commitment. The course lecturer meets with each organisation initially to formalise the institute/partnership agreement. Each student reads and signs the Engagement Guideline document and the host organisations complete an evaluation form at the end of the student engagement, and also attend end of semester presentations.

The module objectives are that students will develop a critical awareness of the scale and scope of volunteering in Irish society, be able to articulate the important role that volunteers play in the development of social capital and social resilience, exemplify the skills and knowledge required to work effectively as a 'civic servant' and self-reflect on their communication style, in negotiation, conflict resolution, problem solving and motivational ability.

Student assessment is largely based on a personal reflective journal, applying the DEAL model (Ash & Clayton, 2009), whereby students describe, examine and articulate learning, across learning objectives linked to personal growth, civic learning and academic enhancement. Further marks are awarded for tutorial/preparatory material and a presentation of their experience and learning to peers and staff.

The main challenges of this approach are twofold. The first relates to the cultural diversity of the student group and different attitudes to volunteerism and altruism. The second relates to resource pressures for academic staff, as this approach requires considerable time to establish and maintain sustainable host partnerships, and involves anti-social work hours. The first challenge was addressed by including a module fact sheet on the institute website with the application form, which helped focus the students on the module requirements, ethos and commitment requirement. Feedback from the organisations and students has been very positive and student experiences were such that the lecturer continued with the module despite the time commitment required, as the benefits for both students and organisations outweighed the personal demands. Articulation across the institute of the student personal development, civic and social benefits ensured that the lecturer was timetabled to reflect the delivery demands of the module.

32.2.7.   *Drama in Prison with Occupational Therapy Students — A Service Learning Project at Trinity College, Dublin*

This peer education drama project was a collaboration between Occupational Therapy at Trinity College Dublin (TCD), the Dóchas Centre at Mountjoy (Female) Prison and the Dhá Lámh Theatre. The three organisations had an established working relationship on various projects across the previous two years. Drama was selected as the occupation to work with in response to an identified need by prison staff.

As part of their first semester's group theories and peer-education module, seven third year students engaged in weekly drama sessions in the prison with prisoners who self-selected to participate. A member of university staff supported sessions weekly; students and a dramatist from the theatre company alternated their facilitation of the sessions, with the dramatist taking a directive role and students acting predominantly as peer educators. All third year students took this module, though those not included in the drama project facilitated other peer-education projects with first year students. Students' learning was assessed and credited through a group report that required them to relate their experiences to theory and included a reflective element.

Engaging and communicating with women within the prison environment over a prolonged length of time supported development of the students' civic learning — their focus shifted from seeing 'prisoners' to meeting 'individuals'. As one student said:

> They were just women who we got on with...walking in, I don't see it as a prison anymore. Like it was just...where we went in every week and did drama.

The students found operating within the prison system challenging as it could be both unpredictable and frustrating. The unannounced introduction of new security measures and security lockdowns led to cancelled or delayed sessions, which, students feared would impact on perceived professionalism and respect towards the women. Students stated: 'our...worry was...that we [were] being inconsistent'. 'We were afraid it [the reason the sessions were cancelled] wouldn't get across to them'. However, having practical experience of negotiating another system and environment enriched students' understanding and knowledge on an academic level. They stated 'it was the first time you could completely really strongly see the effect of the environment and social situation on engagement'.

The open format of the group for the first number of weeks meant that attendance was inconsistent and students thought this may be a barrier to the group process. However, they felt that they themselves were a constant in the group and across time they built rapport — 'I think there was connectiveness within the prisoners, within us ourselves and within the group'. They stressed that their relationships with the women and their roles as peers supported the women's confidence development in drama and personal growth.

The project achieved many of its service-learning goals not simply because students' learning was situated in the community, but also because the occupation demanded that the groups developed co-dependent relationships so that they could perform as a unit, and also because students and prisoners co-constructed their activity in an atmosphere where respect underpinned all engagement. As a prisoner commented:

> They made us feel like we are people, we are recognised;
> We had the highest respect for them…they had the highest respect for us.

32.3. Benefits and Challenges of CBR and CBL Approaches

32.3.1. *Challenges for Community Partners*

The principal impacts on community partners from their collaborations in CBR initiatives are improved capacity and increased access to research resources across a wide range of disciplines (Gnaiger & Martin, 2001). CBR approaches can help transform 'who produces knowledge, who influences public knowledge, and who controls the knowledge production process' (Stoecker, 2007, p. 3). CBR initiatives allow problems articulated by community partners to be brought to the attention of the higher education research community, thus enabling initiatives to influence local research agendas by changing focus within an existing research area, by acting as an incubator for new research themes, or by creating collaborative dialogues across disciplines that may not have existed previously (Hende & Jørgensen, 2001).

One criticism of CBR, however, is that despite emphasising the involvement of community or voluntary groups in research, this does not always happen in practice. The involvement of the community partner is often limited to data collection and they have less of a role to play in defining the research question or in identifying a suitable research methodology (Stoecker, 2009). This may be due to lack of training in methods of scientific enquiry or critical thinking, and is a deficit that could be addressed through facilitating training with community partners, students and project coordinators on participatory research methodologies and approaches. This can also reflect a lack of confidence around research. Often community organisations have extensive data pertinent to their particular field but need support to utilise or reflect on the data. In all of the case studies, university staff worked with community partners to help them consider and develop their research needs and shape them into projects suitable for students to complete. These relationships, if carefully mediated, can help both students and community partners to value their own knowledge and skills, whilst students and university staff can bring fresh perspectives to the work of community partners

Mediating structures, such as Science Shops, make considerable efforts to ensure that community partners play a key role in setting research questions, and also use their knowledge of university structures to inform partners of what might be achievable within an academic context. As evidenced by several of the case studies, non-academic staff with a specific CBR/CBL role can maintain a wide range of community contacts as well as working across the higher education institution, maintaining and developing relationships with both sectors over time. This is much more challenging for academic staff who have a range of other duties to fulfil.

Although the case studies focus predominantly on good practice, sometimes the outcomes do not fully meet the needs of the organisation. Problems occur for a range of reasons. Students lack commitment, underestimate the time the work will take, undervalue the knowledge of community partners or lack appropriate academic support. Community partners lack time, have other more urgent and pressing priorities, may lack experience in working with students and often operate on very limited resources. Funding pressures in community organisations mean that there can be very frequent staff changes and responsibility for the student and the research project can be passed on inappropriately or forgotten in the process. It is crucial therefore for mediating staff to maintain good relationships with community groups and this process requires time, skill and knowledge of the community context. Working with groups over time makes it easier for them to develop under-standings of the academic context and limitations of student work, and to trust that any deficits in projects/modules will be collaboratively addressed and remedied in future. Community organisations are also made aware of the limitations of the course and the students, as often organisations will have an overarching research question which needs to be broken down into manageable elements. Where possible, both academic and mediating staff should try to ensure that time committed by the organisation to supporting the student is reflected in the quality of project outcomes. A key tenet is achieving mutual benefit for all partners, through the co-creation of knowledge which reflects the shared interests of students and the communities with which they engage. However, 'this is an ambitious goal and one that is not always achieved' (Martin & McKenna, 2012), particularly in the first iteration of any module or project.

32.3.2.   Challenges in the Academic Context

The key challenge in the academic context is having enough time to understand and develop research ideas with community organisations, and maintain relationships with them, alongside supporting students (Mason O'Connor & McEwen, 2012, p. 12). Where this work is carried out by academic staff, the time demands are severe. Having a support unit in place, such as a Science Shop, helps remove some of this burden from academic staff whilst providing a broader and more accessible platform from which community partners can engage with a fuller range of academic disciplines.

Students are also challenged in this work. Through their involvement in CBR and CBL projects, students learn how to apply knowledge in context as well as becoming aware of the local social impact of research. In comparison to more theoretical modules, students are responsible not only for undertaking research but also liaising with the community partner and translating the research findings into useable information and recommendations. This ensures the broad development of student competences in areas such as communication, knowledge application, problem solving and cooperation (Teodosiu & Teleman, 2003). Such projects require students to engage with their peers, with academic staff and with community partners in a meaningful way around an issue of common concern.

Criticisms voiced by students include the time required to understand or negotiate their role and the community partner's role in the project, difficulties experienced in working with community partners due to differing expectations or requirements, and increased feelings of responsibility or pressure as the projects address real-life issues. 'It took quite a while for us to get meeting up with a representative of our organisation and when we did our research brief changed quite a bit from what we were anticipating'. However, it is exactly these challenges which help foster more engaged learning in the students and demand high-quality teaching and support from academic staff. The three-way project planning meeting is an essential first step as it helps identify what can and cannot be undertaken in the project, it enables a shared understanding of the differing needs and expectations of the student, supervisor and community partner, and provides a tool, the Research Agreement document (in the case of CBR) or Student Engagement document (in the case of CBL), which can help manage these expectations.

Students need to be made aware of what is required of them, and how the approaches differ from other student work. This is ideally achieved through formal preparatory lectures and informal mediation/mentoring. This requires both commitment and insight from academic staff, who are often supported in this by mediating organisations such as Science Shops. Projects may include some ethically sensitive issues which also need to be considered, and potentially sent to an ethics review panel, before beginning the research work. In some cases, the project will not receive ethical approval, processes can also be very time-consuming and this is sometimes used by academics as a reason for not involving students in CBR or CBL projects. Whilst students can sometimes also be disappointed if projects do not proceed after initial preparatory work, this can provide valuable learning experience in terms of future research careers as the ethics process is now a standard feature of the academic research process, particularly in Northern Ireland.

While the case studies reflect the range of activities which students undertake through CBR, a final step common to such research projects is the student presenting the results in an accessible form to the community partner, as well as discussing how recommendations might be implemented. In some cases, this process is built in to the module, where community partners get an opportunity to feed back on draft findings or reflect on recommendations, and support the student to make the work more useful. This stage of the process often provides considerable learning for students, some of whom struggle to incorporate feedback and make suggested changes in what they see as an almost completed piece of coursework. However, this process ensures that a key aim of CBR, that is that of enabling social action and effecting social change (Strand et al., 2003), may be realised. In CBL, students are often required to keep a reflective journal to document their learning during their engagement with the community group. Students can share this learning with the community partner in the form of recommendations or by highlighting to course coordinators the possibilities for increased engagement.

It is also often the case that only a small element of the students work is bringing new knowledge or insight to the community organisation. This can be a challenge for organisations which regularly support students in CBL or CBR projects. It is possible, however, to modify academic requirements and assessment to ensure that the primary focus of the module is to deliver a useful outcome for the partner organisation.

The student's academic supervisor is a critical component in these projects, ensuring that the student works appropriately with the community partner. In advance of a meeting to articulate and finalise the research question, academics need to be briefed about what support the community partner may need. Supervisor feedback in relation to these projects has been largely positive in most of the case studies, with academics taking on elements of this work on a volunteer basis. Staff also report that they felt more engaged with the research, that the students showed increased interest in the research asking more advanced questions about methodology and data collection.

> It necessitates students becoming familiar with the scientific literature and the evaluation of that information for the benefit of a community partner organisation (academic).

These positive comments were tempered by the reflection that:

> There was a bit more work involved in supervising science shop projects and these projects were probably best suited for the more capable students (academic).

It is important to acknowledge that some academic staff can be hesitant to support students undertaking applied work in collaboration with an external organisation. Many factors may influence this — the slight extra risk inherent in an applied project, and the potential for it to require additional supervision time, as well as the time involved in the mediation of a three-way relationship, are significant issues for many staff. Some are concerned that student research is unlikely to be useful to organisations, or that students may be out of their depth. More recently, the challenges of getting approval for student projects through internal ethics committees has proved a deterrent for staff as this involves additional effort and can sometimes be a lengthy process. These factors can dissuade otherwise interested staff from becoming involved.

Based on the experiences of Irish Network members, some academic areas would seem to lend themselves more readily to CBL/CBR work than others. Whilst social and environmental sciences and health have strong outreach elements embedded in the subject areas, subjects such as English and physics may find it harder to identify the community relevance of their disciplines, and may not have the same community links, although it should be noted that in the Netherlands, for example, CBR initiatives exist in academic areas from arts and humanities to physics and chemistry. Developing projects with students in different disciplines is an on-going task for staff, and international networks are particularly useful in helping staff to examine possibilities. Many academic staff value the involvement of mediating staff and are happy to trust much of the mediation process to them. Others can be reluctant to pass on their responsibilities and also reluctant to acknowledge the interest and demand for such projects from students.

32.4.   Conclusion

CBR and learning initiatives in HE offer practical approaches to engaging students through quality learning and over the last 10 years, a range of initiatives and expertise has been developed across Ireland. They provide a mechanism for universities to engage with their local communities whilst building student skills. They also enable academic staff to help students understand how their discipline relates to the real world outside the university and how they might use their academic knowledge to contribute to this. These initiatives also offer under-resourced communities a cost-effective way to engage in the research process, contributing time rather than financial resources (Martin & McKenna, 2012, pp. 27–29).

However, while there is often an explicit commitment to support community and student engagement from universities, in practice such work remains vulnerable to changes in senior management and academic staff and considerable resistance still exists to the use of resources to support this type of work. While the benefits to student engagement with communities are clearly acknowledged, the additional time, expertise and sensitivity required to support this work over time are not. However, the concept has long been supported by the European Commission, most recently through the PERARES project, which is establishing 10 new CBR initiatives across Europe, mentored by experienced partners.

Several other key issues emerge. The issue of communication between all partners, students, staff, community organisations and mediating organisations, is critical, both to the student experience and the generation of useful outcomes for the community partner. Indeed, ensuring useful outcomes for both student and community organisation can require considerable negotiation. The time involved in such negotiations puts pressure on academic staff and mediating structures, and thus challenges the sustainability of such programmes. However, the exposure of fairly homogenous student cohorts to issues beyond their own social and cultural experience is a clear benefit of this work in terms of both student learning and student engagement, and is one of the reasons why these projects tend to be positively evaluated by participants in the process, and by external bodies.

CBL and CBR mediating staff play a key role in supporting academic staff, students and community partners in this community engagement process. The on-going support offered by academics makes a notable difference to the quality of the outcomes, and the fact that all of the work takes place within the curriculum ensures an element of quality control. The incorporation of projects from community partners enriches the curriculum and therefore enhances student learning and experience. It also enriches long-term partnerships between university and community.

The value of publicly engaged learning and teaching to students is that it enables them to better appreciate the relevance of their academic learning in social, community and employer contexts. This places a premium on understanding what the community/organisation thinks and wants and students learn directly from local communities and organisations. These experiences develop student capacity to respond to social, political and economic topics of relevance to communities and organisations and can impact positively on people's lives. The case studies above provide a snapshot of some innovative projects that are on-going across Ireland and reflect the breadth of experience in overcoming challenges in this field.[8]

Acknowledgements

The case studies are written by members of INCERL (the Irish Network for Community-Engaged Research and Learning), a recently established inter-institutional All-Ireland network of coordinators of CBL/CBR involved in coordinating, supporting and developing community-based learning and research activities in higher education. Catherine Bates, coordinator of 'Students Learning with Communities' programme, Dublin Institute of Technology; Josephine Boland, Lecturer and partner in 'Community-Engaged Research in Action' project, National University of Ireland, Galway; Kenneth Burns, Lecturer and founding member of Community-Academic Research Links (Science Shop), University College Cork; Róisín McGrogan, Civic Engagement Officer, Trinity College Dublin; Emma McKenna, Coordinator of Science Shop, Queens University Belfast; Claire Mulrone, Manager of Science Shop, University of Ulster; Edel Randles, Lecturer and coordinator of Community Service Initiative module, Institute of Technology, Tralee.

References

Ash, S. L., & Clayton, P. H. (2009). *Learning through critical reflection: A tutorial for service-learning students*. Raleigh, NC: PHC Ventures.

Bates, C., & Burns, K. (2012). Community-engaged student research: online resources, real world impact. In A. M. Quinn (Ed.), *The digital learning revolution in Ireland: Case studies from the national learning resources service*. Cambridge: Cambridge Scholars Publishing.

---

[8]Further details and resources can be accessed by contacting INCERL or individual project coordinators.

Boland J. (2010). Teaching and learning through civic engagement: Prospects for sustainability in teacher education. *Issues in Educational Research: Special Issue on Service Learning*, *20*(1), 1—20. Retrieved from www.iier.org.au/iier20/boland.html. Accessed on 28 September 2012.

Department of Employment and Learning Northern Ireland. (2010). *Graduating to success HE strategy for Northern Ireland.* Retrieved from www.delni.gov.uk/graduating-to-success-he-strategy-for-ni.pdf. Accessed on 28 September 2012.

Gnaiger, A., & Martin, E. (2001). *Science Shops: Operational models.* SCIPAS Report No. 1, Utrecht University.

Hende, M., & Jørgensen M. S. (2001). *The impact of Science Shops on university curricula and research.* SCIPAS Report No. 6, Utrecht University.

Hunt, C. (2011). *National strategy for higher education to 2030: Report of the strategy group.* Dublin: Government Publications. Retrieved from www.hea.ie/files/files/DES_Higher_Ed_Main_Report.pdf. Accessed on 28 September 2012.

Leavy, A. (2005). When I meet them I talk to them': The challenges of diversity for pre-service teacher education. *Irish Educational Studies*, *24*(2—3), 159—177.

Martin, E., & McKenna, E. (2012). The science shop at Queen's University Belfast: embedding community engagement in the curriculum. In K. Mason O'Connor & L. McEwen (Eds.), *Developing community engagement.* London: SEDA.

Mason O'Connor, K. & McEwen, L. (Eds.). (2012). *Developing community engagement.* London: SEDA.

Novek, S., Morris-Oswald, T., & Menec, V. (2011). Using photo voice with older adults: some methodological strengths and issues. *Ageing and Society*, *32*(03), 451—470.

Putnam, R. (2000). *Bowling alone.* New York, NY: Simon & Schuster.

Stoecker, R. (2007). CBR and the two forms of social change. Keynote paper presented at Learn and Serve America: Higher Education National Community-Based Research Networking Initiative Subgrantee Meeting, St. Paul, MN, 25th—27th October.

Stoecker, R. (2009). Are we talking the walk of community-based research? *Action Research*, *7*, 385—404.

Strand, K., Marullo, S., Cutforth, N., Stoecker, R., & Donohue, P. (2003). *Community-based research and higher education: Principles and practices.* London: John Wiley and Sons.

Teodosiu, C., & Teleman, D. (2003). Romanian case study report: Improving interaction between NGOs, universities, and science shops: experiences and expectations. *INTERACTS Report No. 2.* Lyngby, Denmark: Technical University of Denmark.

Ward, E. (2012). Unpublished summary of CBR module evaluation focus group.

Watson, D., Hollister, R., Stroud, S. E., & Babcock, E. (2011). *The Engaged University: International perspectives on civic engagement.* London: Routledge.

Chapter 33

Student as Producer: Radicalising the Mainstream in Higher Education

Mike Neary

Abstract

Students are a largely untapped source of rich and original ideas that can all too often be overlooked when developing the experience of those very students. In contrast to the rhetoric around students being passive consumers, the University of Lincoln has, across all subjects and involving professional services and support staff, committed to empowering students as producers of their own learning and, through this commitment, as producers of their university. This philosophy is built on the traditions of higher education where universities have been communities of scholarly debate and lifelong learning, regardless of status. This chapter reviews the universities' approach with a critical appraisal of how the University's Universities systems and structures have required change as well as the practice and behaviour of students and staff.

33.1. Radicalising the Mainstream

Student as Producer was established in 2010 as the organising principle for all teaching and learning at the University of Lincoln — United Kingdom, following development work that had been on-going at the University since 2007. This means that research-engaged teaching is embedded in all courses at all levels across the University, and that students are involved in the design and development of their own educational programmes (University of Lincoln, 2010). There is nothing unique or unusual about research-engaged teaching and students being directly involved with their own teaching and learning in higher education (Bovill & Bulley, 2011; Healey & Jenkins, 2009). What is special about these activities at Lincoln is that they have been institutionalised as the default strategy for the whole University. Since 2012, Student as Producer has been extended to include student engagement

The Student Engagement Handbook: Practice in Higher Education
Copyright © 2013 by Emerald Group Publishing Limited
All rights of reproduction in any form reserved
ISBN: 978-1-78190-423-7

across all aspects of the University of Lincoln's quality assurance and enhancement activities. At the University of Lincoln the ambition is that students really will produce their own university.

As well as being a model for curriculum development and a framework for institutional change at Lincoln, Student as Producer is part of a global social movement to reinvent the University as a radical political project. Student as Producer provides a critical intellectual framework out of which to create an intelligent resistance to the notion of student as consumer and the pedagogy of debt (Geoghan, 2011; Williams, 2009). This framework is based on a recognition that the current crisis of higher education — including its meaning and purpose, 'the idea of the university' (Neary & Saunders, 2011) — is part of a much larger social, economic and political crisis based on the continuing and catastrophic failure of market-led social development (Edu-Factory Collective, 2009). Academics, administrators and students are being asked to deliver a market-based system of higher education at the moment when a market-based system is on the point of collapse, where government policies to restore economic growth are based on increasing exploitation of labour and natural resources through the imposition of austerity and debt, with devastating negative impacts beyond the human imagination (McNally, 2011). Student as Producer seeks to radicalise the mainstream by seeking alternative forms of higher education within which these on-going and intensifying human and natural catastrophes might be confronted (Neary & Hagyard, 2010). In the recent period, these radical alternatives have extended beyond research-engaged teaching and the undergraduate curriculum to look at common research education for PhD students across all subject areas at Lincoln. The focus of this work is not interdisciplinarity but, rather, a search for the 'essence' or 'spirit' of science (Neary, 2012).

33.2.   A Model for Curriculum Design

There are many examples of Student as Producer across all curriculum areas at the University of Lincoln. Each year schools and departments at Lincoln are asked to complete a self-assessment report where they identify Student as Producer activities, including developments from previous years. These activities are celebrated in an annual festival of teaching and learning where staff, including professional and support services, are invited into classrooms, lecture theatres, design studies and laboratories to share the student educational experience. Student as Producer uses its website as a platform by which to disseminate effective practice across the University. Some disciplines identify easily with Student as Producer where it is seen as the core part of their work. These disciplines include art and architecture in the Lincoln School of Performing Arts and Creative Advertising, while others find engaging with Student as Producer more challenging (Lincoln, 2011).

The University has two funds to which staff and students can apply for monies to support curriculum development and research-engaged teaching: the

Undergraduate Research Opportunities Scheme (UROS) with grants of up to £1k, to develop research projects between academics and students, as well as a Fund for Educational Development (FED), with grants of up to £3k for curriculum development by academics and students. In the recent period these funded projects have included young people researching public youth provision, focussing on citizenship, volunteering and employability; other activities include research into human animal interaction in veterinary science, investigating mentoring and personal tutor relationships in the social sciences, looking at the legality of targeted killings in law as well as research across a range of projects in forensic and biological science. The psychology programmes at Lincoln are saturated with research-based learning from level one and include student research conferences for all three undergraduate year groups. In terms of the design and development of the curriculum, work has included creating online reading lists as a resource for computer students, as well as the setting up of *pro bono* legal advice events, as well as developing multimodal communication skills using digital media platforms featuring the extensive use of open educational resources. These curriculum developments have extended to the design of employability programmes in the engineering school where employers have their expectations challenged about student readiness for the world of work, as well as quality process in the sports and exercise sciences by turning subject review committee meetings into workshop-style events, the content of which is decided after discussions with students (Bishop et al., 2012). The students union, in collaboration with the Centre for Educational Research, has run sessions for students on how to critique their programmes, with activities that go far beyond the levels of engagement required by the National Students Survey. Students and academics at Lincoln were the first to establish programmes in the United Kingdom where undergraduates, trained, supported and remunerated, run sessions for academic staff on their teaching styles, usually in subjects that are not related to the students' own subject areas (Crawford, 2011). A good deal of student research has been published, for example, in the Reinvention Journal — an international journal of student work, based at the University of Warwick in the United Kingdom and Monash University in Australia (University of Warwick, 2012). Students from Lincoln have presented their work at the recently established British Conference for Undergraduate Research at the University of Central Lancashire and Warwick (http://atp.uclan.ac.uk/buddypress/bcur/conference/). Some of these initiatives were also written up in an edition of the Higher Education Academy's (HEA) Enhancing Learning in the Social Sciences journal (HEA, 2012), which focussed on Student as Producer.

33.3.   Institutional Framework

The extent of this collaborative research is a key feature of Student as Producer at Lincoln, yet much of this sort of activity can be found in many universities in the United Kingdom and worldwide.

The unique aspect of Student as Producer is the way in which it extends beyond the classroom to be the organising principles for all teaching and learning across the whole university. This institutional approach is made possible by an interconnecting framework of infrastructural support. This support has been put in place since work began on Student as Producer in 2007, through faculty and university decision-making committee structures, working closely with academics, students and professional and support staff. This extensive process of consultation and debate has led to high levels of ownership at Lincoln for the concept of Student as Producer, including the vice chancellor and the senior management team as well as staff and students working at all levels. Student as Producer is being embedded across the University through the building of a number of institutional platforms based on the institution's bureaucratic structures, student engagement activities, teacher networks and arranging events to challenge and invite academics to engage in the intellectual ideas that underpin Student as Producer.

33.3.1. Bureaucracy

Bureaucracy has become an offensive word in the postmodern corporatised world, including the neo-liberal university. Student as Producer, following the work of Max Weber (1978), seeks to recover the practice of bureaucracy as a progressive moral and ethical organisational principle grounded in academic values, against the populist networked and sometimes amoral practices of innovation and enterprise (Kreiss, Finn, & Turner, 2011).

The current business model of the enterprise university is based on the fantasy that only organisations that become ever more entrepreneurial and innovative can survive the new economic realities (Peters, 1992). In the recent period, those realities have been dominated by the politics of austerity and precarity, making the demand for entrepreneurialism appear ever more urgent and necessary (Du Gay, 2000, pp. 63, 64). In this way, the enterprise university sets itself firmly against bureaucracy, which is characterised as red tape, procrastination, indecision, big government, the nanny state and a tendency towards indolence (Du Gay, 2000).

The attachment to academic values and ethics and the aversion to the entrepreneurial project can be substantiated by a revaluation of the values of bureaucracy as a set of protocols and processes grounded in a set of morals and ethics that are highly valued by academics. These values include democracy, fairness, equality, freedom, collaboration, commons and critique. According to this definition, for Weber (1978), bureaucracy is 'a site of substantive ethical domain' (Du Gay, 2000, p. 2) and 'a particular ethos ... not only an ensemble of purposes and ideals within a given code of conduct but also ways and means of conducting oneself ... the bureau must be assessed in its own right as a particular moral institution and the ethical attributes of the bureaucrat be viewed as the contingent and often fragile achievements of that socially organised sphere of moral existence' (Du Gay, 2000, p. 4). In this way, the bureaucratic environment contains its very own rationality and sense of radical purpose (Du Gay, 2000, p. 75).

This radicalising of bureaucratic structures at Lincoln is an organic process intended to engage administrative staff, academics and students in debate about Student as Producer (Winn & Lockwood, 2013). These bureaucratic procedures include External Examiner Reports, Annual Monitoring Reports, Subject Committees, Periodic Academic Reviews and through the protocols and processes associated with new programme validations and revalidations. During the process of programme (re)validation, academics are asked to show ways in which the courses will include research-engaged teaching, consider issues of space and spatiality in their teaching practice, describe how they will write up their teaching as a scholarly research project, illustrate the ways in which they will use appropriate web technologies, demonstrate the extent to which students are involved in the design and delivery of programs and courses, and show how the course enables students to see themselves having a role in creating their own future, in terms of employment, and to make a progressive contribution to society (University of Lincoln, 2010). External examiners are asked a series of questions relating to Student as Producer on the External Examiner Reports forms, for example, the impact of research-engaged teaching on the student learning experience. Periodic Academic Reviews offer a planned cyclical process whereby Student as Producer is considered by staff and academics for all programmes across the University. Each year, programme staff are asked to set out as part of their Annual Monitoring Report the extent to which Student as Producer is active across all courses and subject areas. These reports are reviewed by central university committees creating a sense of collective intellectual endeavour (Neary & Saunders, 2011).

33.3.2. *Student Engagement*

Student as Producer underpins all aspects of student engagement at the University of Lincoln (Lincoln, 2012a). The student engagement strategy clearly states that the principles of Student as Producer are 'transforming our community into a place of collaboration and discovery, where barriers between teaching and research are removed' where students are seen as 'a largely untapped source of rich and original ideas'. The principles of Student as Producer which inform student engagement at Lincoln include an emphasis on the 'student voice,' reflecting the ways in which Student as Producer is dedicated to developing a community of learners and teachers which is respectful of diversity and difference, allowing for the space of dissensus and disagreement, driven by engaged and participatory pedagogies; with an acknowledgement that student engagement should go beyond just involvement and consultation so as to reach towards students being producer and change agents to create a much richer and more valuable engagement. Following the ethic of Student as Producer, the student engagement policy requires that students should not just input into the system, they should be an active part of the system by working together with staff in developing and implementing solutions because students are experts in their student experience. All parts of the university should embrace and benefit from student engagement where their activity impacts upon the student experience. Student engagement must embrace Student as Producer by working in rich collaborative partnerships with staff and where support is available to students so that they are prepared and enthused about engaging (Lincoln, 2012b).

These student engagement activities are supported by the University through the appointment of a student engagement officer working out of vice chancellor's office, with strong links to the students union. This appointment of a student officer has allowed for the development of systematic schemes to embed this model of student engagement involving input into student induction, a comprehensive student representation system, the creation and support, including training, for a team of quality student advisers, student-led committees, ensuring students are full panel members on quality committees as well as having students on staff appointments panels. The University has been successfully experimenting with new committee structures based on workshop models to promote and support student involvement (Bishop et al., 2012).

Students are free to engage with Student as Producer in whatever ways suit their inclinations: as a standout item on a CV to gain an advantage in the job market (Student as Producer, 2010–2012), as a platform from which to influence higher educational policy at the national and international level (Quality Assurance Agency, 2012a, 2012b, 2013), or as a radical critique on which to design alternative and experimental forms of higher learning (Alternative Art College, 2012). While not all students appreciate the freedom that is on offer, Student as Producer can be most dynamic and effective when committed and dedicated staff work with this dissensus, in some cases to create an enriched 'rhizomic' learning environment (Coley, Lockwood, & O'Meara, 2012).

The ultimate logic of Student as Producer's framework for student engagement is a fully constituted model of co-operative education, with students involved directly in the management and leadership of the whole institution.

33.3.3. Teaching: Network of Support

The Teaching Academy at the University of Lincoln was set up in 2011 to create a critical and experimental informal space for teaching and learning within the institution, but outside formal university structures, for example, the University's Teaching and Learning Committee. At the heart of this initiative is the ambition to connect with committed and conscientious academics who might not be persuaded by trendy leftist pedagogies, or careerist academic managers, for whom all institutional programmes, whatever their claims, are just another form of managerialism.

Harney and Moten (2009) have identified a core part of this constituency of disaffected academics as 'the Undercommons', some of whom have not yet abandoned the notion of revolution:

> Maroon communities of composition teachers, mentorless graduate students, adjunct Marxist historians, or queer management

professors, state college ethnic studies departments, closed down film programmes, visa-expired Yemeni student newspaper editors, historically black college sociologists and feminist engineers. And what will the university say of them? It will say they are unprofessional. How do those who exceed the profession, who exceed and by exceeding escape, how do those maroons problematise themselves, problematise the university, force the university to consider them a problem, a danger? The Undercommons ... are always at war, always in hiding. (Harney & Moten, 2009, p. 149)

While this definition does not involve all academics who have chosen to avoid the university's institutional reforms, it is important to recognise that student engagement involves finding ways to work with academics as part of a collaborative whole university agenda.

The University has adopted more formal procedures to engage with academic staff on matters relating to teaching and learning. University policy now requires that all teachers and those involved with supporting teachers will have or be working towards a Post Graduate Certificate in Higher Education teaching qualification or HEA fellowship recognition. This policy was decided on following extensive consultation with staff and was agreed before the recommendations of the Browne Review and Report (2010). It is expected that 100% of academic staff at Lincoln will have or be working towards a teaching qualification or HEA recognition by 2016.

33.3.4. *Intellectuality*

Student as Producer is not compulsory, rather academics are challenged and invited to get involved in the debate, generating an academic discussion based on the complexity of links between teaching, learning and research in higher education. An important part of that debate is reclaiming the radical history of higher education, what Williams calls 'teaching the University' (Williams, 2009) as well as a critical debate on the effects of the pedagogy of debt on student life (Williams, 2009).

Student as Producer is based on a negative critique of the current university structure. The modern university is fundamentally dysfunctional, with its two core activities — research and teaching — working against each other (Boyer, 1990). To promote the re-engineering of the relationship between teaching and research, Student as Producer returns to the radical history of the modern university, with reference to Wilhelm von Humboldt's University of Berlin in 1810 (Humboldt, 1970), and the student protests of 1968. Humboldt's plan was to establish 'the idea of the university' as a progressive political, liberal humanist project, and the basis of civilising the population as part of the process of building the emerging nation-state. This would be done by connecting teaching and research in a programme to promote the expansive creation of new knowledge, so that the university becomes the highest level of consciousness of liberal society (Lyotard, 1979; Neary & Hagyard, 2010). The student protests of 1968 in Paris and around the world were a defining moment in the eventual failure of the liberal humanist project, when students and workers became 'the revealers of a general crisis' of capitalist society (Ross, 2002). This failure of liberal humanism was evidenced by on-going imperialist global wars, continued repression of radical leftist political projects and the alienation and anomie at the centre of everyday life. An important aspect of this revelation by students was the demystification of the elite practice of the production of knowledge with 'research becoming something that anyone can do' (Ross, 2002).

The year 1968 was a powerful example of student engagement, with students at the heart of a major political event, with significant consequences for the future of higher education, including the democratising of university life (Scott, 1995) and impact on curriculum development, for example, the idea that students are capable of carrying out research through their own independent projects (Pratt, 1997). Given the radical contribution of 1968 to current teaching methods in higher education, academics would do well to recognise what can be learned from the current wave of student protests in the United Kingdom and around the world. These include the teaching and learning activities that became a central element of student occupations at UK universities forming part of the larger occupy movement. On-going activities that came out of this moment of student protest include Tent City University, the Social Science Centre Lincoln and the Free University of Liverpool (Stanistreet, 2012).

The radicality of Student as Producer is further underlined by its affinity with the writings of Walter Benjamin, notably 'Author as Producer' (1934), in which Benjamin addressed the question to the Society of Anti-Fascists in Paris 'how do radical intellectuals act in a moment of crisis?' Following Brecht and the Russian Constructivists, Benjamin's response was to enable students to see themselves as subjects rather than objects of history, as teachers, writers and performers, rather than recipients of knowledge, and to be able to recognise themselves in a social world of their own design (Neary & Winn, 2009).

Although the concept of Student as Producer is derived from 20th century avant-garde Marxism, few teachers at Lincoln are revolutionary Marxists. Student as Producer creates a radical framework for debates and discussion about policy and strategy for teaching and learning across the university, based on a radicalised political vernacular. Given the extent to which the language of managerialism has overwhelmed the discourse of higher education, this is no mean achievement.

While students may avoid Student as Producer, no students are able to avoid the pedagogy of debt. Debt is more than a financial arrangement; it is, rather, its own peculiar form of social discipline (Williams, 2009, pp. 90–93). Debt teaches students that higher education is a consumer service, that debt involves taking out a mortgage on one's life, making waged work unavoidable, setting up oneself to be indentured. Debt teaches students that the capitalist market is a force of nature, reinforced by the violence of the capitalist state. Debt teaches fear, stress, worry and anxiety, reinforced with each monthly payment.

Student as Producer is against the pedagogy of the debt, replacing debt with the pedagogy of excess as an alternative political economy for student life (Neary &

Hagyard, 2010). At its most political the pedagogy of excess means that students become more than students through collaborative acts of intellectual enquiry, working with academics and with each other, on subjects that look beyond their own self-interest and identity as students; exploring the origins and radical responses to the general social crisis out of which the attempt to reduce students to consumers is derived; and, connecting academics and students to their own radical political history by pointing out ways in which this radical political history can be brought back to life inside and outside of the curriculum (Neary & Hagyard, 2010), or 'teaching the university' (Williams, 2012).

33.4. Evaluation — Where Are We Now?

In 2010, Student as Producer was awarded funding for three years by the HEA under the National Teacher Fellowship Project scheme. This funded project involved setting up a consortium of national and international universities to promote and develop Student as Producer. This funded part of the project is coming to an end and is undergoing an internal evaluation. Lessons learned from the evaluation include the fact that the project is fully embedded across the University with high levels of awareness among all staff; the bureaucratic processes to support research-engaged teaching across the university are in place and being operationalised, and, while academic staff are aware of Student as Producer, the concept is open to a range of interpretations. The on-going critical debate about the nature and scope of Student as Producer provides the University with a dynamic narrative through which to describe higher education at the University of Lincoln. The University was recently audited by the QAA and given a commendation for its work on supporting learning enhancements: the area of work to which Student as Producer is central. This means that Student as Producer is recognised by mainstream higher education providers as having an impact outside of its own institution, and is sector leading.

The main issue now is how to prevent Student as Producer from becoming another managerialist initiative, whose radical and critical sensibility is overwhelmed by mainstream thinking and practice. The current response to that issue is to further radicalize Student as Producer through more experimentation at the institutional level. Currently this work is focusing on postgraduate research education with the emphasis on students engaging with each other across their discipline areas.

33.4.1. *Postgraduate Student as Producer: The Future Is Revolutionary Science*

Student as Producer seeks to radicalise mainstream higher education by seeking alternative forms of higher education within which the on-going human and natural catastrophes produced by capitalist expansion might be confronted. While reconnecting research and teaching provides the opportunity to reinvent the relationship between student and teacher, the restructuring of the production of knowledge to deal with the current crisis may have to be more carefully considered.

Academics have argued that the inability to deal with social emergencies is the way in which science has been divided into the natural and the social sciences (Burkett, 1999; Foster, 2000). This separation is seen as the result of of the preponderance of the instrumental and functionalist rationality that underpins the productive forces of industrial society (Habermas & Blazek, 1987). This issue was a real concern for Wilhelm Von Humboldt and the German idealist philosophers who created the University of Berlin in 1810. They consciously attempted to design a university that could deal with their own social and political catastrophes, not least the failure of the French Revolution and the emergence of the Thermidor. This group of idealist philosophers sought to do this through the recovery of the University not simply as an empirical project but as a metaphysical idea:

> ... the intimate connection between science and truth - to something universal, something prior to the pluralism of social life forms. The idea of the university points to principles of formation according to which all forms of objective spirit are structured. (Habermas & Blazec, 1987, p. 10)

These idealistic philosophers looked for the solution in the unity of the sciences, reconciled by the power of reason and the 'totalising power of idealism' (Habermas & Blazek, 1987, p. 10). The project failed because of

> the spectacular success of empirical science... [together with]... a favoriting of practically useful knowledge under the political instruction of the state [sealing]...the destruction of metaphysical world views in favour of economy and administration. (Habermas & Blazek, 1987, pp. 10–12)

Writers in the Marxist tradition recognize this separation as something that is based not on idealism against empiricism, but, rather on the capitalist process of production, expressed as the alienation of (wo)man from each other and the alienation of humanity from the natural world (Burkett, 1999; Foster, 2000). Marx argued this 'metabolic' rift between humanity and the earth will be fixed when 'Natural science ...subsumes the science of man just as the science of man will subsume natural science: there will be _one_ science. (Marx, quoted in Foster, 2000, p. 77). This one science does not rely on speculative or philosophical solutions, but is a scientific method of enquiry and reason based on an awareness of the historical development of humanity as the alienation from nature (Foster, 2000, p. 114). This alienation can only be overcome through 'the significance of revolutionary practical critical activity' (Marx's theses on Feuerbach, quoted in Foster, 2000, p. 112), or the struggle for life against death.

The key issue for Student as Producer is how the natural and social sciences might be reconnected as a curriculum for critical practical activity. The University of

Lincoln has taken a small step to reconnect the natural with the social sciences together with arts and humanities through the development of a postgraduate researcher education programme. The programme provides a unique opportunity for PhD students to join a community of researchers by raising awareness of the wide range of methodologies and practical strategies to foster an appreciation of academic diversity and to offer a relaxed environment for networking and personal development. During the programme, a variety of research approaches and specific methods are introduced along with a consideration of issues such as criticality, ethics and the dissemination of research outcomes. Although the course is non-credit bearing, new PhD students are encouraged to participate in the programme to get to know other researchers in an atmosphere of mutual learning. The themes explored are the philosophy of research, epistemological frameworks, reflexivity and criticality, research design, qualitative and quantitative research methods and research ethics. Visits across the city of Lincoln make the link between natural science and the social sciences and humanities by focusing on the cultural and scientific history of Lincolnshire, and have included visits to the Tennyson Research Centre in Lincoln Central Library and the Joseph Banks Conservatory. A key question of this postgraduate research programme is what is the 'spirit' or 'essence' of research.

The Researcher Education Programme draws inspiration from another revolutionary scientist, Robert Grosseteste (1170–1253), a former Bishop of Lincoln as well as first vice-chancellor of Oxford University. While Robert Grosseteste is not well known or much discussed in studies on the development of higher education, he is regarded by medieval historians as a key figure in the development of the method of experimental science through practical applications and as being central to the creation of the modern university (McEvoy, 2000; Neary, 2012; Southern, 1992).

Medieval historians argue that Robert Grosseteste's writings 'constitute the beginnings of modern science' (Hendrix, 2011, p. 4), not 'standing on shoulders of giants' but as a disruptive and subversive influence (Southern, 1992, pp. 36, 37):

> it opens up the limitless possibility of new knowledge quite independent of statements by earlier writers and only to be tested by further observations of which the greater part are still in the future … it does not lead to order and consolidation but to change and disarray. (Southern, 1992, p. 169)

It is this aspect of disruptive subversion through his experimental activities that forms the basis of Grosseteste's scientific enterprise, and confirms what we already know and what we already do not know: science, by its very nature, is an inherently radical activity.

This work to connect the natural and the social sciences at the postgraduate level is still very much in the early stage of development. Up to this point, the level of postgraduate student engagement has been very positive. The theme, 'what is the spirit' or 'essence' of science, formed the theme for the university's postgraduate research conference in 2013. The conference recognised that research is the discovery of something unknown through the methods of experimental science, as well as the application of this new knowledge for the benefit of humanity and the natural world. The conference included discoveries being made and applied by postgraduate research students at the University of Lincoln, as well as the ways in which these discoveries are represented and critiqued through the arts and the humanities. The conference demonstrated that the spirit of research is not the preserve of any particular subject or discipline, but is what all researchers share in common and constitutes what is essential about higher education, 'the idea of the university' (Lincoln, 2013).

33.5.   Conclusion

Student as Producer has had a significant impact on teaching and learning at the University of Lincoln and across the sector. It has sought to operate within the mainstream institutional frameworks of an English university, while at the same time developing a radical discursive framework within which to conceptualise and challenge the dominant marketised ideologies within which higher education is currently being designed: student as consumer and the pedagogy of debt. The ultimate success of Student as Producer will be the extent to which higher education in Lincoln and beyond can be reinvented as a radical political project. While the evaluation of Student as Producer has shown that much has been achieved, it still feels as if this work, in the context of an intensifying social, economic and political crisis, has only just begun.

References

Alternative Art College. (2012). Retrieved from http://alternativeartcollege.co.uk/

Benjamin, W. (1934). The author as producer. In: M. W. Jennings, H. Eiland & G. Smith (Eds.), (2004) *Walter Benjamin: Selected writings, Volume 2, 1927–1934*. Massachusetts: Harvard University Press.

Bishop, D., Crawford, K., Jenner, N., Liddle, N., Russell, E., & Woollard, M. (2012). Engaging students in quality processes, enhancing learning in the social sciences. Retrieved from http://www.heacademy.ac.uk/assets/documents/disciplines/social-sciences/ELiSS0403 Practice_paper02.pdf.

Bovill, C., & Bulley, C. J. (2011). A model of active student participation in curriculum design: Exploring desirability and possibility. In C. Rust (Ed.), *Improving student learning-global theories and local practices: Institutional, disciplinary and cultural variations*. Oxford: Oxford Brookes University.

Boyer, E. L. (1990). *Scholarship reconsidered: Priorities of the professoriate*. New Jersey: The Carnegie Foundation for the Advancement of Teaching.

Boyer Commission on Educating Undergraduates in the Research University. (1998). *Reinventing undergraduate education: A blueprint for America's research universities*, Stony

Brook, State University of New York at Stony Brook. Retrieved from http://naples.cc.sunysb.edu/pres/boyer.nsf/

Browne, E. (2010). *Independent review of higher education funding and student finance.* Retrieved from http://webarchive.nationalarchives.gov.uk/+/hereview.independent.gov.uk/hereview

Burkett, P. (1999). *Marx and nature: A red and green perspective.* New York, NY: St Martin's Press.

Coley, R., Lockwood, D., & O'Meara, A. (2012). *Deleuze and Guattari and photography education, Rhizome, 23.* Retrieved from http://rhizomes.net/issue23/coley/index.html

Crawford, K. (2011). *Students as co-producers in quality processes that inform and enhance.* Retrieved from http://spiq.blogs.lincoln.ac.uk/files/2011/09/RAISE-Conference-Presentation-20111.pdf

Du Gay, P. (2000). *In praise of bureaucracy: Weber, organisation, ethics.* Los Angeles and London: Sage.

Geoghan, P. (2011). Producers, not consumers. *Times Higher Education*, 28th April. Retrieved from http://www.timeshighereducation.co.uk/story.asp?storyCode = 415973& sectioncode = 2

Edu-Factory Collective. (2009). *Towards a global autonomous university: Cognitive labour, the production of knowledge and Exodus from the education factory.* New York, NY: Autonomedia.

Harney, S., & Moten, F. (2009). The university and the undercommons. In: *Towards a global autonomous university: Cognitive labour, the production of knowledge and Exodus from the education factory.* New York: Autonomedia.

Hendrix, J. (2011). *Architecture as cosmology: Lincoln cathedral and English Gothic architecture.* New York and Oxford: Peter Lang.

Foster, B. (2000). *Marx's ecology: Materialism and nature.* New York, NY: Monthly Review Press.

Kreiss, D., Finn, M. & Turner, F. (2011). The limits of peer production: Some reminders from max weber for the network society. *New Media and Society, 13*(2), 243−259.

Habermas, J., & Blazek, J. (1987). The idea of the University: Learning processes. *New German Critique, 41*, 3−22. Retrieved from http://forskpol-arkiv.pbworks.com/changes/f/Habermas1987NewGermanCritique-v41p3-22.pdf

HEA. (2012). *Lessons in listening: Where youth participation meets student as producer.* Retrieved from http://www.heacademy.ac.uk/resources/detail/subjects/csap/eliss/ELISS_vol4_issue3_academic_paper1

Healey, M., & Jenkins, A. (2009). *Developing undergraduate research and enquiry.* York: Higher Education Academy (HEA).

Humboldt, W. von (1970). On the spirit and organisational framework of intellectual institutions in Berlin. *Minerva, 8*, 242−267 [original 1810].

Lyotard, F. (1979). *The postmodern condition.* Manchester: Manchester University Press.

McEvoy, J. (2000). *Robert Grosseteste (great medieval thinkers).* Oxford: Oxford University Press.

McNally, D. (2011). *Global slump: The economics and politics of crisis and resistance.* Oakland, CA: PM Press.

Neary, M. (2012). Student as producer: An institution of the common [or, how to recover communist/revolutionary science]. In: *Enhancing learning in the social sciences*, Higher Education Academy (HEA). Retrieved from https://docs.google.com/document/d/1GVAZpP8n_rbnL1c4ODxG-ZOVvQGmBmn6iV54vZ4uFkE/edit

Neary, M., & Hagyard, A. (2010). Pedagogy of excess: An alternative political economy of student life. In M. Molesworth, E. Nixon & R. Scullion (Eds.), *The marketisation of higher education and the student as consumer*. Abingdon: Routledge.

Neary, M., & Saunders, G. (2011). Leadership and learning landscapes: The struggle for the idea of the university. *Higher Education Quarterly, 65*(4), 333–352.

Neary, M., & Winn, J. (2009). Student as producer: Reinventing the student experience in higher education. In L. Bell, H. Stevenson & M. Neary (Eds.), *The future of higher education: Policy, pedagogy and the student experience* (pp. 192–210). London: Continuum.

Peters, T. (1992). *Liberation management*. Basingstoke: Macmillan.

Pratt, J. (1997). *Polytechnic experiment 1965–1992*. Buckingham: Society for Research into Higher Education and Open University Press.

QAA. (2012a). *Student engagement: Students get to the heart of the issues*. Retrieved from www.qaa.ac.uk/Partners/students/student-engagement-QAA/Pages/default.aspx

QAA. (2012b). QAA Partners. Retrieved from www.qaa.ac.uk/Partners/students/student-engagementQAA/Pages/Dan-Derricott.aspx

QAA. (2013). *Good practice knowledge base*. Retrieved from http://www.qaa.ac.uk/ImprovingHigherEducation/GoodPractice/Documents/GPKB-case-study-Lincoln-2.pdf

Ross, K. (2002). *May '68 and its afterlives*. Chicago, IL, and London: The University of Chicago Press.

Southern, R. W. (1992). *Robert Grosseteste: The growth of an English mind in Medieval Europe* (2nd ed.). Oxford: Clarendon Press.

Scott, P. (1995). *The meanings of mass higher education*. Buckingham: Open University Press.

Stanistreet, P. (2012). Anyone can teach, everyone can learn. *Adult Learning*. Retrieved from http://www.niace.org.uk/sites/default/files/documents/adults-learning/Adults_Learning_2012_03_p20-p26.pdf

Student as Producer User Guide. (2011–2012). Retrieved from http://studentasproducer.lincoln.ac.uk/files/2010/11/user-guide-2012.pdf

University of Lincoln. (2010). *Student as producer*. Retrieved from http://studentasproducer.lincoln.ac.uk/

University of Lincoln. (2011). *Student as producer: Departmental self-assessments*. Retrieved from http://studentasproducer.lincoln.ac.uk/files/2010/11/Student_as_Producer_self_assessment_summary-20111.pdf

University of Lincoln. (2012a). *Launching Lincoln's first student engagement strategy*. Retrieved from http://studentengagement.blogs.lincoln.ac.uk/2012/09/25/launching-lincolns-first-student-engagement-strategy/

University of Lincoln. (2012b). *Student engagement strategy 2012–16*. Retrieved from http://studentengagement.blogs.lincoln.ac.uk/files/2012/09/Student-Engagement-Strategy-For-Consultation.pdf

University of Lincoln. (2013). *Annual postgraduate student conference 2013 –Expression of interest*. Retrieved from http://graduateschool.blogs.lincoln.ac.uk/annual-postgraduate-student-conference-2013-expression-of-interest/

University of Warwick. (2012). *The Reinvention Journal for Undergraduate Research*. Retrieved from http://www2.warwick.ac.uk/fac/cross_fac/iatl/ejournal/about/

Weber, M. (1978). *Economy and society*. Los Angeles: University of California Press.

Winn, J., & Lockwood, D. (2013). Student as producer is hacking the University. In H. Beetham & R. Sharpe (Eds.), *Rethinking pedagogy for a digital age: Designing for 21st Century Learning*. London: Routledge.

Williams, J. (2009). The pedagogy of debt. In: *Towards a global autonomous university: Cognitive labour, the production of knowledge and Exodus from the education factory.* New York: Autonomedia.

Williams, J. (2012). Deconstructing academe: The birth of critical university studies. *The Chronicle of Higher Education.* Retrieved from http://chronicle.com/article/An-Emerging-Field-Deconstructs/130791

Conclusion

So What Does It All Mean?...

34.1. Introduction

So, where has the array of chapters in this Student Engagement Handbook taken us? Have we seen it all before?[1] This remains a difficult question... Yes, in some ways, but no, in so many others. Tensions and stresses have often been apparent in the past, but the expansion of the sector, the difficult world economic conditions and the lack of jobs put more stress on young people, in large numbers, than ever before. And it is the current context, the political tensions, the economic situation, the social environment, today's theories on how knowledge is made, or disseminated, the prevailing ideas on learning and teaching and views on the purpose of a university education and how this relates to employment, that all impinge on what it means for students to engage at this moment in time.

Schwartz wrote of higher education in 2011:

> It was not always like this. Wisdom, at least in its religious version, was central to the medieval university, and its importance persisted right down to John Henry Newman's day.[2] But wisdom is no longer on the curriculum; it has been replaced with skills... Newman called such practical learning 'a deal of trash', but surely he was wrong... Yes, we must prepare graduates for what they will do, but we also have a duty to help them at least to think about what kind of people they want to be.

> ... If wisdom is the goal, then students must "walk 10,000 miles, read 10,000 books" said the 17th-century Chinese philosopher Gu Yanwu. In other words, becoming wise requires not just having adventures but a cultured mind that is open, ready and able to absorb the lessons that experience teaches.

---

[1]This refers back to Owen (Chapter 1).
[2]Cardinal Newman (1852) 'The Idea of a University', see references in Owen (Chapter 1).

Whether or not wisdom is the focus of a current-day education (and some would argue that it is not, but should be[3]), Schwartz touches on several important dimensions of student engagement — who, students believe, they are, and who they want to be (and this may include gaining skills); taking the opportunity for different experiences; gaining practical learning and being prepared to reflect and grow as a consequence. In many ways, these are the themes of this Handbook, and what a good university education should be about. The difference in the stories told in these chapters is the specific ways in which students can be encouraged to engage in taking real responsibility for their educational environment as well as their personal growth.

Less elusive than 'gaining wisdom' is the fact that student engagement — even if only for a moment in time — has become a central focus of attention across many parts of the world. What is absolutely clear is that, during the period from conceptualisation of this Handbook to end product, the focus on student engagement has been constantly and consistently growing. Student engagement activities are endlessly multiplying, in different contexts and for different reasons.

This Handbook has largely been created as a collection of reflective stories, examples of what individuals and groups are doing to improve the student experience. Through these stories, it is possible to tease out ideas about what student engagement is, and about ways for achieving engagement, with the two being intricately interwoven. Yet the many and various examples of student engagement make it difficult to gain any common or shared understanding, due to their very different contexts, perspectives, motivations, philosophies and practices. Bryson and Hardy (2011) suggest there are some common themes in the literature. Student engagement is

- multi-dimensional — a holistic perspective is needed;
- broader than the academic and university environment — students need to make sense of their whole lives;
- much more than just about doing — being and becoming is critical; and
- dynamic and fluid (Bryson & Hardy, 2011, p. 16).

Solomonides, Reid, and Petocz (2012) characterise student engagement very differently,[4] as a series of six metaphors: a dichotomous view of student engagement; engagement as a measured quality; engagement as an ordered phenomenon; a categorical view of engagement; a naïve view of engagement and the multi-dimensional view of engagement.

Hence, not only is student engagement complex but the ways that it is analysed by commentators is also complex and different in nature. However, despite the elusiveness of a simple characterisation of engagement, many of the authors of this

---

[3]See Maxwell and Barnett (2009) for discussion of this topic.
[4]From an analysis of chapters contributed to Solomonides et al. (2012): 'Engaging with Learning in Higher Education'.

Handbook come to a similar understanding of what engaged students can achieve — for themselves and for their communities — even if coming from very different rationales and starting points. Drawing on the chapters of the Handbook, several recurring themes are highly apparent and are discussed under the following headings:

1. Countering consumerism
2. Characterising student engagement
3. Developing a vision
4. Students as partners
5. Developing identity

34.2. Countering Consumerism

A focus on student engagement may have arisen in part as a response to fears of marketization and consumerism, and ensuing disenchantment and disengagement. The recent and continuing growth of higher education has led to concern about education becoming 'an assembly-line process where everyone endures the same classes and does the same monotonous tasks' (Nguyen, 2000). In addition, as stated by Wenstone (2012a) of the United Kingdom:

> ...it is surely no accident that the national focus on student engagement has occurred at the very time that the sector has faced turmoil over the costs of higher education and the tripling of undergraduate student fees.

Consumer attitudes are a concern that is specifically outlined by Popenici (Chapter 2), but is also raised repeatedly throughout this Handbook, in a variety of contexts, and across continents. However, as Owen points out (Chapter 1), consumerism is nothing new. Nonetheless, it is something that currently hits the headlines from time to time, with imagery — for example — of students as 'consumers buying a customized playlist of knowledge' (Roth, 2012). If, in addition to this, students conceive themselves, and are conceived of, as customers, then their behaviours and the ways that they engage with their education may suffer accordingly:

> If students are envisioned only or primarily as consumers, then educators assume the role of panderers, devoted more to immediate satisfaction than to offering the challenge of intellectual independence. (Schwartzman, 1995, p. 220)

Furedi (2009) claims:

> There is little doubt that encouraging students to think of themselves as customers has fostered a mood in which education is regarded as a commodity that must represent value for money.

Rivers and Willans (Chapter 7) suggest that, whilst there may not be so many obvious examples of engagement initiatives amongst the private providers, there is wide acceptance of the concept of the 'student as consumer' and a willingness to harness the power of the student voice in order to deliver change and enhancement. However, many of the chapters in the Handbook are designed to counter consumerist attitudes or to 'de-emphasise a consumerist approach' (Kay, Owen, & Dunne, 2012). Popenici (Chapter 2) suggests that sustainable models of education need to have at their core solutions to actively involve students in an academic culture focused on the profits of learning, not markets. Werder and Skogsberg (Chapter 8) echo the lack of emphasis on learning in critiquing the Bill and Melinda Gates' 'Student Voices on the Higher Education Pathway' — one of many deliberate efforts to listen to what students say about their experiences as consumers, but one in which the 'voice of learners' is not apparent, and students do not engage with change processes.

As van der Velden (Chapter 5) comments, a consumer approach can create a serious tension since academics feel they have to compromise academically to gain student satisfaction, with higher education becoming less collegial as a consequence. From a student viewpoint, Ratcliffe and Dimmock (Chapter 4) argue that student engagement 'places a responsibility on universities and students' unions to actively ensure that their students are not passive consumers. In order to "engage" with students, you have to entice and include them in their own learning and the wider university community'. Wintrup et al. (Chapter 12) specifically link to the concept of 'the student as co-researcher and co-producer of work — a far cry from the consumer in a transactional relationship with HE'. They claim: 'if the "contract" between HE and student is defined only in terms of exchange or transaction, however obliquely, engagement is at risk of being defined by the instrumental objectives of both parties. Such a reductionist interpretation is actively resisted by the following constructions of engagement, as a dynamic enacted through agency, community and partnership'. Ryan et al. (Chapter 25) suggest that 'the primary motivation for the adoption of any kind of "student as change agents" initiative seems to be the belief that students are really at the heart of learning and teaching and, rather than adopting a passive role as consumers, need to be actively and dynamically engaged as co-creators and leaders'.

Hence, an emphasis on active learning in the context of partnership and community and, in particular, engaging students in change processes, are seen as positive ways in which to counter the potential pitfalls of a mass market economy with a 'customer satisfaction' orientation. This does not mean that customer satisfaction should not be heeded seriously, but that the processes of engagement and learning are more complex than being satisfied with a product or outcome; they demand continued attention and effort from the learner.

34.3.   Characterising Student Engagement

As Felten and Bauman state (Chapter 21), students must engage to learn, and high-quality institutions support frequent, deep engaged activities by students to promote learning. This is echoed by Pittaway and Moss (Chapter 16) who state that the fundamental purpose of student engagement is engagement 'in and for learning'. There is no doubt about the centrality of learning, but the problem in accepting such phrases as representative of student engagement is that learning, as reported across this Handbook, is complex and multi-faceted. The focus of learning may be very different in each of the contexts described. Further, some of the student engagement activities outlined here have a variety of purposes other than learning — although learning of some kind is always likely to occur. The complexity is that, even as portrayed in this book alone, student engagement

- occurs in the classroom, across the institution, in the workplace, in the community, within the curriculum, outside the curriculum;
- includes learning through the academic curriculum, through volunteering, through representation activity, through work;
- relates to engaging with teachers, with peers and with those in the workplace and community;
- includes learning of disciplinary knowledge, academic skills, employability or work-related skills, or life skills;
- involves learning about learning, understanding of the processes of learning, metacognition and reflection, and how to be an effective student;
- includes student involvement in institutional change processes, enhancement or quality assurance, through representation or as promoters and creators of better learning environments for others;
- is of benefit to the student alone, to a whole class or group, to the discipline, to the institution, to the community or to the workplace; and
- can be highly structured, semi-structured or very loosely structured.

Add to this the many features, mentioned through the Handbook, that contribute to, or impinge on, engagement in learning

- the actual opportunities provided for learning or engagement;
- the ethos of the teaching environment and any student's academic progress in that environment;
- the ethos of the institution;
- the quality of social relationships;
- the quality of relationships between staff and students, and student peers, with peers being suggested as the most important influence on intellectual engagement.

Link this with individual student characteristics mentioned within this Handbook that include the cognitive, affective, social and emotional aspects of learning

- the role of intrinsic and extrinsic motivation;
- the time and effort devoted to study, which may be affected by a need to work to pay for education, or family commitments, and so on;
- confidence, self-belief, self-efficacy, the will to succeed;

- the impact of growing self-awareness, self-perception, identity and sense of being and belonging;
- imagination, aspirations, excitement in learning;
- the will to learn, resilience and the ability to persist;
- personal beliefs and values; and
- the inclination and ability to engage with others.

In discussing student engagement, Solomonides (Chapter 3) calls for more sensitivity to the 'intersections between life, learning and work', and Pittaway and Moss (Chapter 16) claim, 'if we want our students to be engaged, we must seek to engage the whole student: their minds, their bodies, their beliefs, attitudes, dispositions, and aspirations, while taking into consideration their domestic and other environmental/ contextual factors'. To add further complexity, Pittaway and Moss suggest that student engagement 'plays out in different ways at different points of the educational cycle'.

On top of this, the Handbook has highlighted numerous approaches, philosophies and schemes that capture nuanced variations in conceptualisation of student engagement. A key factor lies in the roles that students take on:

- students as partners/student—staff partnerships;
- students as co-researchers;
- students as learners and teachers;
- students as change agents;
- student as producer/co-producer;
- students as co-creators;
- students as champions; and
- students as co-constructers of knowledge.

In addition, there is reference to different environments for engagement, with different communities:

- engagement in learning/active learning/reflection/enquiry;
- engagement with the institution;
- engagement as practice;
- epistemic engagement;
- civic engagement; and
- community engagement

Further, engagement is described through particular approaches, philosophies or ways of working, such as the following:

- deliberative democracy;
- a dialogic classroom;
- a participative paradigm; and
- a teaching and learning academy.

Each of these terms characterises in some way the purpose of any specific student engagement activity; each begins to capture the vision and the philosophy behind it. Each may also have some kind of similarity, encapsulating a belief about what students can do and about how that can be achieved. Many are premised on principles of democratic participation or the collaborative, dialogic and participative nature of social constructivism (Bruner, 1996; Vygotsky, 1978), or simply the pragmatic belief that students are worth listening to and working with because of what they can bring to any context. Many of the terms above also characterise practices that are innovative, pushing at the frontiers of democratic and collaborative processes of learning and bringing about pedagogic change, but each is also different, with different expectations, different ways of thinking, acting and working.

Bovill (Chapter 26) further highlights that, through collaborative practices, staff or institutions want to achieve particular aims or satisfy beliefs about educational processes.

> These motivations include a desire for: a more democratic approach to education often underpinned by principles from critical pedagogy or ethical citizenship; enhanced student engagement in learning; enhanced student engagement in the university as a whole; enhanced learning; improved quality of teaching and learning in a currently problematic or "broken" course or programme; and constructing knowledge with students rather than simply handing over fully constructed knowledge (Cook-Sather, Bovill, & Felten, forthcoming)… There is mounting evidence of the beneficial outcomes of co-created curricula and co-created learning and teaching approaches (see for example, Bovill, Cook-Sather, & Felten, 2011; Sambell & Graham, 2011), and this evidence is likely to provide another motivating factor for some staff.

Overall, this complexity perhaps supports Solomonides (Chapter 3) in stating that a 'unifying theory' of student engagement may not be possible. It may also be worth considering whether it is even desirable. As Felten and Bauman (Chapter 21) point out, Shulman (2002) emphasizes the utility of frameworks like student engagement for helping us to think about what we are doing, giving a language for discussion, 'as long as we don't take them too seriously'. Felten and Bauman also add that heuristics act as cognitive lenses, bringing into focus certain aspects of the world while obscuring things that are outside of our line of sight, with the problem raised by Trowler and Trowler (2010) that student engagement can have a normative agenda, focusing on the generic student rather than diverse identities. Timmis and Williams (Chapter 29) also warn: 'We need to be careful of viewing engagement as an expectation and adherence to prescribed activities'.[5] Solomonides, too, is wary of the problems of measurement.

---

[5]It will be interesting to see if opinion changes with a National Survey of Student Engagement likely in the United Kingdom.

At the theoretical level, Solomonides takes the words of Meyer and Land (2005) to suggest that student engagement is a 'liquid' space, simultaneously transforming and being transformed by the learner as he or she moves through it. This will be impacted on by life and by the opportunities that education can provide and what students are provided to engage with. On a more pragmatic note, it is perhaps helpful to turn to Brand et al. (Chapter 27) who state: 'It is our belief that student engagement is a broad church that encompasses a wide range of activities from curriculum enhancement and student support to student employment. The definition of student engagement by Trowler and Trowler (2010) is one which resonates well with our approach as it signifies the inherent effort that both the University and students need to make if the student engagement partnership is going to be a success for both parties'.

> Student engagement is concerned with the interaction between the time, effort and other relevant resources invested by both students and their institutions intended to optimise the student experience and enhance the learning outcomes and development of students and the performance, and reputation of the institution. (Trowler & Trowler, 2010, p. 3)

As Brand suggests, the definition may be useful in characterising and being deliberate about an approach. Yet the words are suitable only for particular audiences: they have little use for the enthusiast wishing to change practice; they would have little practical meaning for students. Ratcliffe and Dimmock outline (Chapter 4), at the University where they studied, that 'there is no single or unifying consensus between students on where the emphasis should be placed in understanding the core meaning of the term'. Despite this, they present student responses to the meaning of student engagement that demonstrate serious and high-level conceptualisations of the term. These conceptualisations are deeply influenced by the culture, the activities and expectations of that university, because multiple forms of engagement are both explicitly and implicitly expected of students: for example, students learning through working in cooperation; students questioning and challenging the university; students getting the most out of their education and the best 'service' from the university, and also with students supporting the constant development and progression of the university; having awareness of opportunities or having real drive to go above and beyond the call of a normal student. There can be little doubt that being surrounded by an ethos of engaged students will influence other students. As Ratcliffe and Dimmock suggest, 'the sheer volume and loud presence of activities and opportunities made it hard for us not to engage'. Engagement in particular ways will become the norm if that is what students generally do. However, as highlighted by several chapters of the Handbook, the benefit of an explicitly shared vision is that it will have a deeper impact on both students and on institutional development.

34.4. Developing a Vision

Wenstone (2012b), vice president of NUS Higher Education, claims, 'Time and time again we don't adequately define exactly what we are talking about. When we don't attempt to define the terms of our discussions we risk confusion'. Although the Trowler and Trowler definition outlined above is an attempt to capture the essence of student engagement, and may be helpful in some contexts, it does not encapsulate a vision, or the energy and drive that is apparent in so many of the Handbook chapters. As highlighted above, there are numerous titles for the initiatives described here: students as partners, students as co-creators, students as change agents and so on. These terms in themselves start to capture something of a particular vision by being simple, memorable and succinctly describing how students might act and behave in a particular context. They are notably narrower in focus than student engagement as a whole, but encapsulate a particular aspect of the specific university from which they emanate.

To create a vision, Popenici (Chapter 2) suggests that, in the words of Nussbaum (1998), we need to train our 'narrative imagination' since 'We need to reconsider what a University is for... society needs imaginative and innovative citizens, capable to move forward thriving societies, venture into unfamiliar spaces with an unabated desire to explore the unknown, fitted to deal with continuous change and new challenges'. He also suggests that it is time for many universities to 'build a new narrative for themselves'. This kind of institutional narrative building can be seen in several of the chapters, most obviously in Neary (Chapter 33) with his vision of a university that is dedicated to the student as producer, established 'as the organising principle for all teaching and learning at the university, with students involved in the design and development of their own educational programmes', as he explains, 'What is special about these activities at Lincoln is that they have been institutionalised as the default strategy for the whole University... the ambition is that students really will produce their own university'. The vision is clear.

There are other such examples, at different points of maturity: Brand et al. (Chapter 27) describe how their work 'focuses around initially creating, and now enhancing, an academic learning community in which students feel they wish to belong and participate'. This imposes cultural change upon the institution, 'as the initiative continues to seek to bring student engagement alive and embed it as a 'state of mind' for students and staff'. A deliberate intention was to 'break down significant barriers between students and staff' so as to improve progression and retention of students, to enhance student satisfaction and to gain better outcomes in the National Student Survey. However, they claim to choose 'partnership rather than consumerism for the reason that we passionately believed this would make our university a better place to be for staff and students alike'. Bell et al. (Chapter 28) begin their chapter by stating, with a clear message, understandable to all audiences: 'We believe that true curriculum renewal will, in the future, rest equally in the hands of students and staff'. In each of these cases, the role of personal belief, passion and determination can be seen to drive the vision.

Senge (2006) suggests that creating a shared vision is specifically beneficial, with participants active in shaping their reality, both of the present and of the future — a process that can be uplifting and can encourage experimentation and innovation. A shared participation also implies shared understandings. This again is an important factor in student as producer, with a commitment to extensive consultation and promoting ownership. The consequence of not having a shared vision is described by

Pittaway and Moss (Chapter 16) as leading to 'a lack of direction and common purpose: it is difficult to determine how to engage students if we do not fully understand what such engagement might look like, and why it might be important'.
Ratcliffe and Dimmock (Chapter 4) argue in their context that more articulation is
needed for a commonality of understanding to develop — whilst emphasizing that
the words must not be seen as institutional jargon; 'If there are too many variances
and divergent interpretations, then it becomes confusing for not only the staff
involved but also the primary target audience: students'.

What is evident is that student engagement does not happen by accident. It is
connected to a vision of higher education, to a vision of learning, to the idea of
a university, be it that of Newman or Neary, or many of the other contributors
here. A vision is obviously not just about words, but about a way of thinking,
talking and acting. It needs to be open to all to hear and to see. Having a vision
is clearly an essential first step, but it is translation of that vision into practice
which counts, a vision that is shared in the way it is understood and practised,
so that it becomes, in the words of Brand et al. (Chapter 27), the 'institutional
state of mind'.

34.4.1. *Institutional Strategy*

Even when there is a compelling vision, progress may be difficult if institutional
strategies do not support it well enough. McIlrath and Tansy (Chapter 13) describe
the vision of the president of Ireland: 'With the privilege to pursue knowledge comes
the civic responsibility to engage and put that knowledge to work in the service of
humanity' (Higgins, 2012). Further to this, it is well evidenced that student engagement through volunteering has the potential 'to bring both the higher education
institution and the community closer together; to develop an ethos of civic engagement and social responsibility; and imbue in the student and graduate populations a
lifelong commitment to community, engagement and volunteering'. Yet an issue
remains: 'Nationally student volunteer programmes will continue to be fragile until
deeply embedded within the campus structures, represented in HEI's strategic plans
and regarded as central to the engagement agenda'. This is a different picture from
that offered by Neary (Chapter 33), outlining how student as producer is fully
embedded, extending 'beyond the classroom to be the organising principles for all
teaching and learning across the whole university'. This institutional approach is
made possible by an interconnecting framework of infrastructural support, through
faculty and university decision-making committee structures, working closely with
academics, students and professional and support staff. Neary also describes a raft
of roles that support the enactment of strategy: a student engagement officer to
embed induction and representation, a team of quality student advisers, student
committees and students on appointment panels engaging with academics as part of
a 'collaborative whole university agenda'. Ratcliffe and Dimmock (Chapter 4) suggest, as a less radical approach, that a strategy to appoint staff to explicitly work on
student engagement gives it weight and worth, and this is echoed by Rivers and

Willans (Chapter 7) who describe a series of roles to support engagement: the chief executive of students is a former student, has a role that is totally student oriented and ensures the student voice is at the heart of change; student voice representatives have quite specific roles and duties. In many of the initiatives explored in the Handbook, students are paid for their time and also have very specific roles to play, as with Cook-Sather's 'pedagogical consultants' (Chapter 31), and this again demonstrates a strategic commitment.

As highlighted in this volume, institutional documentation can also be important for encapsulating and disseminating a vision. Ody and Carey (Chapter 17) highlight how from 2008 the university's 'Personalised Learning Policy' has stated that, 'All students should have access to some form of Peer Support during their studies', and the institution now operates a Peer Support Strategy Group. Brand et al. (Chapter 27) describe how, in 2011/12, Birmingham City University reviewed its corporate plan so that it now includes an objective 'to be an exemplar for student engagement, working in partnership with students to create and deliver high levels of student satisfaction and graduate employment'. Institutional strategy is generally closely linked to the allocation of resource. Many of the activities described in the Handbook need resource, often in the form of people and time. Bols (Chapter 6) quotes a Canadian symposium report on the success of the Bologna Process: 'any successful continuing reform process requires both political will and resources from leaders in government and institutions, and engagement from students, faculty and staff' (AUCC, 2009). O'Mahoney and Martin (Chapter 32) report that volunteering remains vulnerable in part because considerable resistance still exists to the use of resource to support this type of work. 'While the benefits to student engagement with communities are clearly acknowledged, the additional time, expertise and sensitivity required to support this work over time are not'.

Apparent in several of the chapters is the warning that patience is essential; it can be a drawn-out process to change hearts and minds, even when there is a strong vision and strategy. Bols (Chapter 6) describes a long haul 'founded on one of those serendipitous moments when the aims of various countries and organisations come together' and a move over several years from a context where the word student was almost unused and students were excluded, to a context where partnership is expected and students have become a 'driving force'. Werder and Skogsberg (Chapter 8) outline how 'Our own institutional work oftentimes took many stages to complete and is still currently evolving as we welcome more converts into the fold', after 13 years. Timmis and Williams (Chapter 29) also argue that 'co-inquiry models are not quick fixes to student engagement but part of a longer term relational shift which takes time and mutual commitment to reflection on the process'.

34.4.2. *Critical Mass*

In strategy planning, ways of building capacity for change processes will need to be considered. There will always be enthusiasts and champions for any initiative, with 'easier to reach' students and early adopters' amongst staff. Initiatives to promote student engagement on a broad scale will need a critical mass of supporters and it will depend on the particular activity whether the key to progress lies with staff or student mass, or those outside the university. Gaining critical mass will be dependent on the quality of the vision and its sense of ownership and on the university policy and strategies to support it. A number of Handbook authors address particular ways of gaining further support. Bols (Chapter 6) describes the need for 'constant reinforcing of the importance, and benefits' in order to bring about widespread change. One of the ways of increasing interest is to provide institutional stories that show staff and students that any particular means of engage students, for whatever purpose, is worthwhile and has positive impact. Ody and Carey (Chapter 17) illustrate such a story: 'peer support has, at its heart, a continually growing cohort of altruistic and energetic students. These students motivate their peers and their staff, their energy and enthusiasm is infectious, driving development and fostering the community of students as partners'. Peer support is well established in this particular context and the stories (gained in part from on-going evaluation) have grown over many years. There are many such stories throughout this volume, each with stakeholder feedback gained through evaluation processes; this kind of evaluation, and gaining examples of positive feedback, is central to giving the stories power that will influence others.

Van der Meer et al. (Chapter 18), in explaining their notion of community of practice, employ the term 'legitimate peripheral participation' — 'as a way to speak about the relations between newcomers and old-timers, and about activities, identities, artefacts, and communities of knowledge and practice' (Lave & Wenger, 1991). In order to move from the position of 'newcomer' to the centre of a community, learners need to engage in group practices, and share a common language and common goal so that they are drawn into new ways of thinking and behaving. Neary (Chapter 33) highlights how an 'extensive process of consultation and debate has led to high levels of ownership', and this, too, is a major way of ensuring change. New participants need to feel a sense of ownership, which is best achieved when a vision allows for fluidity and creativity in interpretation (see the variety of examples in Dunne et al., Chapter 30) and is flexible enough to grow organically and to be reinterpreted (Neary) rather than being regulated and controlled: the concept is open to a range of interpretations and must not become 'another managerial initiative'. Trowler, Saunders, and Knight (2005) also emphasise the need for flexibility in that 'change involves change… initial plans and visions themselves change as they are implemented and adopted. Rational, linear understandings of change, often seen as 'common sense', have only limited usability' (p. 2). As implicit within student as producer (Neary, Chapter 33), initiatives need to be continuously explored so as to maintain freshness. Above all, students — if engaged and having a sense of ownership — will have ideas and will support the growth and sustainability of any project and the development of a critical mass, and they will continue to bring fresh ideas, year on year.

34.4.3. *Visibility*

A further means of developing critical mass is through ensuring that initiatives are constantly visible at different levels of an organization. Bols (Chapter 6) describes the power of 'simply witnessing the effective engagement of students' at Ministerial Summits and Policy Forums. Students, or students in collaboration with staff, can also demonstrate their talents in sharing good practice through institutional conferences or other celebrations (see, e.g., Neary, Chapter 33; van der Meer, Chapter 18; Dunne et al., Chapter 30). Neary specifically mentions using a website so as to share the student experience and disseminate good practice. Van der Meer highlights an informational brochure describing factors that contribute to successful research communities and peer groups, with findings being shared in a university forum with both staff and students. Such means of dissemination provides the qualitative evidence that is so powerful in attracting others to engage. As Owen argues of bringing students into the quality review process (Chapter 10), '…the experience retold in this chapter explains that many fears about engaging students can be allayed if challenged directly with evidence and other successful experiences', to the extent that Bols (Chapter 6) can quote the Quality Assurance Agency (QAA, 2012) saying of students that they are 'an anchor at the heart of the review process… we have never looked back'.

Ody and Carey (Chapter 17) highlight the importance of recognition and reward for all involved in peer mentoring: '…at every level of activity, it is essential to recognize and reward the committed students (and staff) without whom no activity would function as effectively. As well as showcasing activities and achievements, it provides an opportunity to engage key decision makers in further development'. For the broader and more established schemes, gaining external recognition is also perceived as cementing values and practices: 'the recognition of schemes internally and externally gave a high profile to the benefits of peer support'. The concept of a 'ripple' effect is important in bringing about change; cross-disciplinary projects are another means of establishing a wider audience and spread across students (see the postgraduate case study; Dunne et al., Chapter 30), and Timmis and Williams (Chapter 29) describe a snowball effect: 'partnerships and collaborations which have themselves generated further collaborations with others'. The concept of habit formation is also fundamental: Van der Meer et al. (Chapter 18) argue it is important that initiatives such as these become operationalised as 'business as usual'. Further, Bride et al. (Chapter 15) highlight the value to the staff: 'working alongside enthusiastic, dynamic, well-focussed students, and doing so in a creative context, cannot be underestimated, not just in terms of the deeper understandings of education that they themselves develop in the process, but also through the positive boost to their attitudes to students and to their own morale, which they carry into other aspects of their work'. This is important since visibly motivated and interested staff may be one of the key factors of promoting student engagement, in whatever form it takes. In so many of the chapters in this Handbook, the passion for engaging students shines through, working with them and alongside them as teachers, as collaborators and as partners.

34.5. Students as Partners

The following section addresses two facets of partnership; the concept of partners in learning, and of partners in development and change. Two further aspects that are outlined within this Handbook are the notion of 'equality of partnership', and of 'students as experts', each of which is discussed below.

34.5.1. Developing the Concept of Partnership

To some extent, partnership may be another potential means of countering consumerist attitudes. Streeting and Wise (2009) state:

> '...viewing students as 'co-producers', not as 'consumers', might help to tackle and resolve these problems. In such a model, students are viewed as essential partners in the production of the knowledge and skills that form the intended learning outcomes of their programmes. They are therefore given responsibility for some of the work involved, and are not passive recipients of a service'. (p. 2)

Bovill (Chapter 26) prefers the concept of co-creation: 'This contrasts with some of the capitalist market conceptualisations of learning and teaching currently predominant in higher education policy circles where students are considered to be consumers of education. It also moves away from some of the manufacturing metaphors that talk about students as co-producers (McCulloch, 2009). Co-creation implies a mutual process that is imaginative, inventive and resourceful'.

As with student engagement, partnership is multi-faceted and has a number of different meanings and purposes dependent on context. Although the two main areas discussed here are partners in learning, and partners in development and change, even these are not always simple to separate. Further, although most of the initiatives described in the Handbook relate to and are dependent on partnership, not all are described in these terms. A further complexity is the relationship with student-led research, which may relate to academic, curriculum-based research (e.g. Neary, Chapter 33) or curriculum-based research in the community for the purpose of bringing about social change (O'Mahoney and Martin, Chapter 32), or may be concerned with institutional change processes (e.g. Dunne et al., Chapter 30). Quality enhancement is also the subject of several chapters, though again not always labelled as such, and taking many different forms in relation to structures for student representation (e.g. Bols, Chapter 6; Freeman, Chapter 9; Owen, Chapter 10) to engaging in other ways with institutional change processes (Werder, Chapter 8; Bride et al., Chapter 15; Dunne, Chapter 30) or the specific improvement of learning processes and outcomes (Bovill, Chapter 26; Cook-Sather, Chapter 31).

Werder and Skogsberg (Chapter 8) pose a fundamental question: 'isn't this building of knowledge in dialogue with the voice of another really at the heart of the scholarly enterprise? However, the word 'partnership' is never used in relation to this process of dialogue, even though it is central. Bride et al. (Chapter 15), amongst others, do not mention partnership either, though the activities with students and University staff as well as with the local community could well be described as partnerships. In contrast, Ody and Carey (Chapter 17) use the word flexibly and talk about different kind of partnerships, for example: one of the institutional aims and objectives is currently 'to involve students as partners in their learning experience'; or 'The University Peer Support structures facilitate partnerships to support the schemes at all levels; between central services and the discipline, between academic and professional support staff, between students and staff, and between students in different year groups'; or 'two institutional widespread schemes gave a high profile to the benefits of peer support and resulted in strong partnerships with a variety of stakeholders across the institution'. Hence, partnership is a word and a concept deeply embedded in the ways of thinking and communicating of some individuals and some institutions, but not others, even where there is some kind of similarity in philosophy and practice.

The Higher Education Academy (HEA) has specifically focused on Students as Partners as a key aspect of student engagement, with partnership defined as

> '... a process not a product. It is a way of doing things, not an outcome in itself. We believe that working with students as partners has the potential to be successful and transformative...' (HEA, 2013)

It is suggested that the following principles should be 'adhered to' for the latter to occur:

- Authenticity: where there is a clear rationale for students — and others — to work in partnership, each partner has a stake in the agenda and in taking the work forward
- Inclusivity: the absence of barriers that prevent engagement in partnership work
- Speaking 'with', not 'for' or 'about' students
- Development of shared purpose, values and principles
- Taking time to understand perceptions of one another
- Joint decision making and accountability arrangements
- Equality of value while recognising difference
- Acknowledgement of power relationships
- Taking time to build trust
- Embracing a shared commitment to evaluation and learning
- Partnership work should be acknowledged and assented to by all parties involved.

In addition, it is stated that there should be specific resources to support partnership; an environment that encourages risk taking and the celebration of successful outcomes of and approaches. Also included is 'Being open to radical transformation, not just slotting partnership work into existing structures and processes' (HEA, 2013).

Principles are clearly important in underpinning practice, especially when working in new ways. They provide vision, a philosophy and ethos, and enable setting of targets. However, they are also difficult to get right, and to get right for different contexts and for different stakeholders. For example, it could be argued that 'slotting partnership work into existing structures and processes' may be a powerful way of working in some instances, as illustrated, for example, by the modules described by Dunne et al. (Chapter 30) where a focus on students as change agents was deliberately achieved within existing module structures, although learning processes were significantly revised.

There is an additional need for caution. Principles may inadvertently be damaging to a relationship. For example, the words 'Speaking "with", not "for" or "about" students', immediately highlight that these are principles for staff, when it might be more appropriate, in the name of partnership, that they speak to both staff and students — as shared principles.[6] Further, is someone not effective at student engagement because they are not following all the principles? How many of the principles have to be satisfied to be effective? What matters most is the real-life practice, the opportunities that are being provided and are being embraced, in whatever context, by whoever, whenever. It is about how people work, what they believe, what they believe is possible. Everyone should work in an environment that is supportive, equitable, democratic and that is steeped in learning. But this environment should also be exploratory, not necessarily following a recipe, or where it does not matter if all the ingredients are not available. Change processes in particular are often messy and challenging and ticking off a list of principles for partnership may not necessarily be helpful, and they may not all be satisfied.

In discussing collaboration between staff and students, Williams, in Little et al. (2011), states, I'm not sure we ever saw it as collaboration. We didn't set out to collaborate or set up a partnership. It was something that evolved...' (p. 222). Although she appreciates that she was engaging in partnership with students, she describes it more as 'an intricate web of players' or a community of practice (p. 223). Starting with principles might not have been the best approach. For Walton (Chapter 23), it was not so much a question of partnership, but modelling what she believes in: 'living her values-based action research approach in teaching situations'. Walton, influenced strongly by Heron (1996), describes a participative view of reality that has major implications for the way we view ourselves, and others in relation to ourselves. 'It challenges the power disparities that exist in social structures, where people are valued according to their perceived objective status in a hierarchically structured universe. A participative paradigm supports a view of human interaction which sees all people of equal importance and value in continually

---

[6]These HEA principles are currently open to consultation and revision.

evolving, co-created view of reality; participative decision making enables people to be involved in the making of decisions, which affect their flourishing in any way and a mutually informing relationship can develop'.

Indeed, what the Handbook shows is that each of the authors is committed to new ways of working, that they have deep philosophies or particular kinds of expertise and experience which enable them to work in the ways that they do. They have reflected deeply on the processes in which they are engaged; they often provide role models for others, both staff and students. The have their own, strong principles, both implicit and explicit, which guide their thinking and practice; they have a determination to change the relationships between staff and students. The HEA principles may therefore have value more for those who are not used to such ways of thinking and working, but only if they are workable, realistic and open enough for others to take ownership of them.

And there is no doubt that partnership approaches can fail, as detailed by Spowart and Tripp (Chapter 14), if there is not 'a clear commitment to agreed goals and expectations' and the 'philosophical and practical nature of the relationship'; '... successful community engagement does not just "happen" by opening up opportunities for students'. In addition, intentions do not always play out in practice. Freeman (Chapter 9) gives the example of a student who states: 'I'd say you are still reporting things to the department and then the department decide what to do with the things that are reported. So you have the power to say this is an issue but you don't have the power to do anything about it yourself'. Hence, there is a mismatch between the purported democratic ideals within an institution and the way students experience representation in practice: 'Democracy, whilst recognised as an important ideology by many respondents, was widely dismissed beyond the organisation of representation through elections and encouraging representatives to engage with peers'. Hence a vision, a deep philosophy and an adherence to principles are necessary, rather than just words, for deep-seated change or transformation to take place.

Although not addressed in this Handbook, Little et al. (2011) also highlight the potential for exploitation of students in collaborative educational research contexts where there may be little equity of workload or recognition for research output. However, they discuss how, '... once we put aside the often ingrained assumption that students would always and by default constitute the weaker or disadvantaged half of a partnership', we can 'allow for the idea that many students are entrepreneurial, enthusiastic and strategic about their education'. In this case, students could be seen as 'exploiting' opportunities, benefiting from expertise, developing skills, giving themselves an 'edge' in the employability market, rather than as being exploited themselves. Students are 'learning the trade' and staff and institutions are benefiting from this collaboration. As Little et al. point out, if there is a feeling of exploitation, then there is a problem which can be remedied: 'for all parties to have made explicit the terms of the partnership will be one of the most important aspects of collaboration' (Little et al., 2011, p. 218). Again, principles that are explicit and shared become essential for partnerships to work without friction or tension.

34.5.2. *Partners in Learning*

The European Commission on improving the quality of teaching and learning in Europe's higher education institutions (European Commission, 2013) states:

> Michael Hooker argued in 1997 that the nineteenth-century model of teaching at higher level still holds sway and teaching 'has not changed much since. Fundamentally, higher education is still a process of imparting knowledge by means of lectures to those who want to acquire it.' The last 15 years have seen progressive developments in many higher education institutions, but the basic model has not altered significantly, at least not in the majority of institutions.

Walton (Chapter 23) outlines work by Biggs and Tang (2007) that differentiates between three levels or ways of conceptualising teaching. The first suggests that the teacher is the 'expert', and transmits knowledge, normally by lecturing, as in the European Commission quote above. In level 2, the teacher develops a range of teaching methods and will take responsibility for evaluating the effectiveness of their teaching methodologies, and adapt to improve methods. In level 3, the focus centres on what the student learns, and whether that learning achieves identified outcomes. Each of these levels inherently suggests different power relationships. In the first, the teacher will hold the power; in the latter, the student can potentially be empowered through a partnership approach, with the teacher and students working together. The notion of such learning relationships has been implicit for generations within the philosophic and educational thinking about dialogic — as opposed to didactic — learning, dating back to Socrates and Rousseau, or more recently Dewey, and Piaget. This view of the teacher—learner relationship also fits well with current social constructivist views on effective learning (emanating from Bruner, 1996; Vygotsky, 1978), a vision wherein students are empowered in their learning through dialogic approaches, actively constructing and re-constructing their understandings through working alongside others, rather than being perceived as empty vessels to be filled with knowledge by a 'fount-of-all-wisdom' teacher. The student engagement agenda clearly relates to the idea that students should be active participants in the learning process, learning from others, questioning and being challenged, rather than being passive recipients of knowledge. As Barkley (2010) claims in her handbook on student engagement techniques: 'Active learning is fundamental to and underlies all aspects of student engagement'.

Many chapters, in particular in Part 4 of the Handbook, address students as active learners. 'Providing students with high quality assessment and feedback, helping students to develop metacognitive skills, and empowering students as partners in the learning process are three approaches to helping students work in their optimal challenge zone' — that is, where they will be most cognitively active (Barkley, 2010, p. 32). Similarly, the Learning Relationships Checklist (devised by Northumbria University in Partnership with Bedfordshire and Manchester universities, 2011) highlights that the prime responsibility and hallmark of good teaching is the quality of relationships, the development of metacognition and assessment and feedback processes. Each of these is explored in this volume, for example through Walton (Chapter 23, as well as many other chapters); Ody and Carey (Chapter 17) and Strivens and Ward (Chapter 19), respectively. Sambell (Chapter 22) describes a good example of the difference in outcome when learning is treated as a partnership in the context of assessment, with students moving from passive to active engagement. Student ideas were shared and co-produced in a constructive process of dialogue, negotiation and peer review. Students reported finding themselves investing personally in learning, rather than being overly preoccupied with performance goals and the alienating effects that the sense of being marked can entail: 'It was about me, which my assignments aren't normally'. This kind of active approach is of particular importance given that, as Sambell states, 'assessment powerfully frames how students learn and what students achieve'.

Pittaway and Moss (Chapter 16) highlight, in comparison, how lecturers who adopt a teaching-focused approach may not appear to demonstrate an interest in their students' existing ways of knowing or their questions and ideas about an area of study, which can reinforce a sense of exclusion and alienation. If students are largely dependent on the lecturer as authority, engagement becomes the sole responsibility of the student rather than a shared responsibility. In these circumstances, engagement may become an issue — that of getting the student to engage at all.

The Handbook also covers aspects of learning beyond the student with university staff in the classroom; this includes the student with those in the workplace. The purpose and nature of conversations between the different work-based parties will vary enormously, as will the learning. Workplace engagement in particular can provide the authentic learning experiences, the 'real' conversations and activities so valued by students, but genuine partnership approaches are less easily managed, as highlighted by Wintrup et al. (Chapter 12), Spowart and Tripp (Chapter 14), Timmis and Williams (Chapter 29) and McIlrath and Tansey (Chapter 13). Wintrup et al. suggest placing *practice* at the centre of engagement in the workplace, as the shared concern and goal of all parties. In doing so, 'the multi-faceted nature of student engagement is highlighted in a way that is coherent and has potential to bond rather than to divide', with the student explicitly conceived as an equal partner with the employer and the education provider, and engagement with practice as a shared concern.

34.5.3. *Partners in Development and Change*

As so many initiatives in this Handbook demonstrate, if partnership has been well thought through, the benefits are likely to be significant. Despite not using the word 'partner', Werder and Skogsberg (Chapter 8) have a strong philosophy and a clear sense of vision about the role of students as partners in bringing about institutional change: 'we stand to truly engage our students as active co-constructors of our institutions and larger scholarly missions' — 'We shouldn't engage students just for their tuition dollars or long enough to connect them to what *we* deem most important, but because we see them as essential partners in the important meaning making that can happen at the university'. They also state: 'Taking this approach, students are actively engaged because they are integral to the future of higher education'. This determination to engage in partnership with students is compelling. Their philosophy is also seen in their thinking that change does not need to be led by those at the top of the academic hierarchy: 'We want students to help ask the right questions and help frame the real challenges so that we don't blithely go about answering the wrong questions or solving beside-the-point problems'. This kind of thinking seems fundamental to so much of the Handbook. 'We want to engage them as they engage us — allowing all of us to be engaged *actors* in our educational institutions'.

Although Walton does not use the word partnership either, the sentiment of a participative, democratic paradigm to bring about change has many similarities, as does that of deliberative democracy (Bell et al., Chapter 28). Bovill (Chapter 26), too, describes the many motivations for engaging as partners in co-creation of curricula, including her own: 'critical theoretical perspective and desire for more democratic forms of higher education teaching and learning'. Brand et al. (Chapter 27) in their Students as Partners scheme clearly have a vision underpinned by partnership, in which they include the need to develop 'an active partnership with the Students' Union to ensure that together we meet students' wider educational, social, cultural, sporting, welfare and personal development needs'.

The impact of partnership can be powerful. Cook-Sather (Chapter 31) describes the knock-on effect of engaging students as consultants: 'After experiencing the kind of engagement that can come through partnering with a student consultant to explore teaching and learning within a particular course, many academic staff apply this transformed notion of engagement to other collaborative ventures with students: gathering feedback on and planning courses, interacting with students more as partners in that planning'. In this kind of relationship, Soeiro, Dias de Figueiredo, and Ferreira (2011) suggest that students become more critical, more engaged and more pedagogically responsible when the teacher relinquishes a significant part of their traditional decision-making power so that the students can share it and, through its use, contribute to a richer learning environment, while growing personally as more participative, responsible and democratic citizens. The descriptions of Ryan et al. (Chapter 25) highlight students who are acting as 'technology champions', taking on the role of 'active drivers, co-creators and partners'; students who can 'generate, incubate and gather support for new approaches and products, contributing to driving innovation'. They suggest that 'Institutions that encourage and promote creativity and innovative thinking amongst students that challenge previously held notions of more traditional relationships between the teacher and the taught and that shift the locus of control from the former to the latter' will have mutual gains for staff, for the institution, and for students. Hence, involvement of students in development and change is of benefit to all stakeholders.

34.5.4. *Equality of Partnership*

Discussions of partnership often suggest that equal partnership is important, assuming an equal power balance between students and staff. This is a difficult concept, given the many forms of partnership described in the Handbook. The quote from Ryan et al., above, suggests that students can take a leadership role in change. Does this mean there will be an equal partnership? A single example in the form of a student quote from Timmis and Williams (Chapter 29) illustrates the complexity of the concept, and also that this student, implicitly, sees partnership as a variety of different relationships, with different balances of power.

> I felt a strong sense of partnership with my supervisor, who as a consultant radiologist could offer the expertise and core knowledge, knowing that I was bringing an idea of what kind of information and learning experience we needed as students. Through creating learning content for the first time, becoming an active contributor rather than just a passive user, I felt a new partnership with the faculty which had previously been a distant, didactic presence in the course at Bristol. The following year many students in the year below asked me for advice on creating an e-tutorial and so I became involved in a partnership with them, sharing ideas and offering advice.

Bovill (Chapter 26) uses the words of Mann to point out that in any teaching context, 'whilst power may reside in an individual by virtue of their position as teacher, the particular dynamics of any one interaction may involve a shift and flux in the flow of power within the group, between teacher and students, and students and students' (Mann, 2008, p. 66). Power relationships are hence complex and, as this Handbook demonstrates, there are so many different forms of partnership, each with a different rhythm and sense of flux. Although changes in the balance of power are clearly central to all the initiatives described, judging how equal that power is at any one time will be difficult, and possibly not useful, dependent on the circumstances.

Nair, as a doctoral student developing a practical skills curriculum, describes a context (Nair and Plugge, Chapter 24) wherein the doctoral students were *more than partners* (authors' italics): 'they led on the curriculum development and delivery'. The two academic staff in the curriculum development group were described as taking a 'back seat' role, facilitating the initiative and monitoring its progress, whereas the doctoral students had been there at the inception, had decided what was to be delivered and how, and ensured this was carried through. Ryan et al. (Chapter 25) highlights the particular context as important by describing a prevailing culture in which there has already been recognition of the existence of the 'student voice', a willingness to listen to what is being said and a desire to act upon what has been heard. 'To enable students to act as change agents, the institution must be willing to acknowledge them as partners and ensure that they are empowered to act, to take decisions and to make a difference'. The importance of both instances above is not the equality of relationships, but the fact that students are empowered, and may take on a leadership role in managing aspects of change, as in the change agents initiative described by Dunne et al. (Chapter 30). It is the quality of the relationships that matters more than the equality of the partnership. What is perhaps most important is that the balance is constantly negotiated and open to discussion, and that empowerment of both staff and students can be mutual, as claimed by Walton (Chapter 23): 'mutual empowerment can only authentically be achieved through respecting those with whom I am working, in an environment where everyone has equal right and opportunity to participate in the decision-making'. Walton further suggests that 'Creating an ethos of respect for each other and the experience that each brings to the education process is, I consider, a prerequisite to creating a transformational learning environment'.

Bovill (Chapter 26) also questions the concept of equality: 'In using the term 'co-creation of curricula', there is an implied sharing of the design process, which may not be equal (as perhaps implied by the term partnership)... Co-creation implies a mutual process that is imaginative, inventive and resourceful. It draws on ideas from staff and from students'. Hence, the centrality of the student is reinforced, along with the importance of a dynamic interaction between staff and students. Bovill is clear in her chapter, a section of which is copied here due to its centrality to the argument:

> Fundamentally, co-creation of curricula implies a shift in the conceptualisation of the teacher-student relationship towards a more reciprocal model where students and staff have a role, a voice and agency to influence and meaningfully participate in teaching and learning processes. Students and academic staff have different expertise to bring to the process, and there will be times when staff may appropriately have more voice, and other times when students may appropriately have more voice. Co-creation is not about giving students complete control, nor is it about staff maintaining complete control over curriculum design decisions. The relative levels of control over decision making and appropriate levels of partnership are likely to depend upon the context, the level of study, the relative experience levels of the students and the staff, the attitudes of students and staff, what is being discussed, and the level of influence of professional bodies over the curriculum. (Bovill & Bulley, 2011)

Such relationships need a strong vision of how they will work, especially given Freeman's findings (Chapter 9) that so-called partnerships may actually not be so at all. Freeman (Chapter 9) warns about difficulties where student representatives are not really partners. In analysing the language used, she observes that the verbs used for students and for staff, respectively, create a 'hierarchy of responsibility': 'Students are required *to do* certain things whilst staff members are responsible for *ensuring* that things happen. This underlines subtle but important differences in the allocation of power and responsibility within the process which may inform the way in which individuals participate, and their perception of their ownership of the process'. For some teachers and other staff, relinquishing power may not be difficult, especially when the outcome of so-doing can be highly positive, but for others the change and the possible flux in the flow of power within a group may feel unfamiliar or uncomfortable to both staff and students, especially where the predominant model of classroom behaviour has been premised upon the teacher being in control. As Walton (Chapter 23) states, students often defer to the traditional authority of the teacher, so it is important to enable all students to feel empowered to fully contribute, and to encourage others in the group to do the same. Timmis and Williams (Chapter 29) explain how difficult changing relationships can be in the workplace, with the need for 'negotiation of roles and addressing power relations within co-inquiry models'; they describe how 'tensions can emerge where staff or students retain existing positions, sometimes unconsciously', where it cannot be assumed that everyone necessarily shares the same goals, and where 'time to develop new relationships is essential so that multiple roles and positions can be accommodated and adapted'.

Overall, it seems that respectful relationships with genuine listening and learning from each other for the purpose of securing educational and social change are fundamental; changing the balance of power will be central to this, but the flux of relationships may mean that the exact balance of power at any one time may not be crucial. What is more important, in the words of Werder and Skogsberg (Chapter 8), is being 'obsessive about inviting ALL STUDENT VOICES into all spheres of influence in university life, not just the high achieving, pre-designated student leaders'. But even this is complex; Felten and Bauman (Chapter 21) sounds a warning: 'Engaging students as partners is so complex because it requires attending to the intersectionalities within student identities (McLeod, 2011). A particular student, for example, might not only be deaf but also female and from a minority religious community. In different contexts, different aspects of that student's identity will be more or less salient'. Porter (Chapter 11) has a different kind of warning — that of the difference between intention and practice in relation to disabled students: 'meaningful student engagement should not limit itself to a process of ensuring appropriate documentation and consulting students about their views, but needs to provide appropriate support to action and empower those students to create change'. In similar mode, Hardy (Chapter 20) describes the need for a greater focus on intercultural competencies in classrooms with home and international students through mutual working. Recognising the 'barriers to working together' is crucial, and that these were 'mainly focused around language and culture which created negative affective effects for the international students; such as isolation, lack of confidence and a feeling of unfairness in tutor assessments'. It seems there is much work to be done, with equity of opportunity being of prime importance in partnership, perhaps over and above précises equality in the partnership itself.

34.5.5. *Students as Experts*

Equality in partnership will relate in part to the kind of expertise that students can bring to a particular context. Many of the chapters of the Handbook highlight this point; for example, Neary (Chapter 33) says, 'Students are a largely untapped source of rich and original ideas that can all too often be overlooked when developing the experience of those very students'. However, although students may have plenty of ideas, they will not be experts in all aspects of their learning, especially with regard to disciplinary knowledge and skills. Sambell (Chapter 22), building on Black and McCormick (2010), observes that oral discussion, involving interactive dialogue where the teacher can explore and steer by sensitive challenge, should be one of the main ways through which the learner is apprenticed into the world of academic discourse. Sambell uses the example of Lesley ('It's knowing what questions to ask, which somebody who knows their subject knows') to illustrate how it 'takes time, lots of active engagement with the subject and on-going participation with knowledgeable others to develop a feel for what a subject is *really* all about. Without this insight, however, it is difficult for students to form a genuine sense of academic standards and requirements and to gain a sense of expertise in their discipline'.

Gaining subject expertise is, however, different from students becoming experts at understanding the processes of learning that support them. Students can bring expertise to their learning, and they can become expert learners in higher education. In other words, they become experts in analysing, critiquing and commenting on the learning processes and environment on offer to them as well as being able to offer that expertise to others and, as highlighted in many chapters in the Handbook, can lead to bringing about changes in that environment. Pittaway and Moss (Chapter 16) suggest that students become experts in the role of university student, and this is exactly why peer mentoring programmes have so much value. In the peer context, both Ody and Carey (Chapter 17) and van der Meer et al. (Chapter 18) are clear of the benefits of working with peers who have 'been there before' and who have gained a sense of expertise from that prior experience. Werder and Skogsberg (Chapter 8) state, 'We enter into dialogue with one another because we trust in what we can know together through mutual engagement'. In this context, there is no sense of 'them and us', just a reminder to 'Consistently LISTEN to student voices, not as customers to be satisfied, but as co-inquirers who bring expertise about their own learning'.

Owen (Chapter 10) describes the concern of the QAA in inviting students to be involved in quality review, yet evidence shows that when fully engaged in the processes, students asked intelligent questions and played a full and equal role in making judgements, commendations and recommendations. In addition, they could ease lack of understandings between staff and students within the review and also propose new and additional lines of enquiry. This, in turn, gives them new expertise and 'greatly improves their ability to contribute to wider discussions about institutional policies and practices'. This is important in illustrating how obstacles are so often put in the way of change, and in shifting the relationships between staff and students and the institution as a whole, but evidence consistently highlights the value that students can bring. As Bovill (Chapter 26) highlights, it is 'extremely rewarding and valuable for both students and staff'. Bovill has a very clear view of what students can bring to the learning context: 'Start co-creation early. Many people think first years are not in a position to contribute to curricula design. Certainly, they may not be able to contribute meaningfully to curricula content on day one, but even small increases of choice in early stages of university learning experiences can communicate the message that student involvement in teaching and learning is welcome'. This kind of attitude links back to having a vision, one that is evident to all students throughout their degree programme and which lays out expectations for ways of engaging.

There are many more examples through the Handbook where student expertise is highlighted. Bell et al. (Chapter 28) show how they were able to make some immediate changes to a unit of study, based on the active engagement of students and staff. Their philosophy of deliberative democracy allowed informed discussion through genuine dialogue, and a World Café, involving students in curriculum design, where options were weighed and top-of-the-head opinions converted to opinion based on evidence, enabled a collective judgment. In this way, collective intelligence was harnessed to create a form of group expertise on the processes of learning. In the context of working in the community, Timmis and Williams (Chapter 29) describe how students work with professionals and disciplinary experts to produce new knowledge that has equal status with existing knowledge. Students are engaged in researching their own practices, harnessing research skills and expertise and producing new knowledge as part of an epistemic community: '…this approach to engagement can lead to the development of new relationships, knowledge and research expertise, where the roles of educator and educated are repositioned…'. In the context of technology, Ryan et al. (Chapter 25) support the QAA in believing that the students of today are well informed, understand the potential of the technologies they use and are creative in the ways that they think and work (QAA, 2010). Indeed they demonstrate that students can have real expertise with technology — which may not necessarily be shared by staff, such that students as technology champions and change agents may be able to have significant impact on the development of technology use in universities.[7]

However, not everyone is convinced of the potential benefits of the shift in relationships. Van der Meer (Chapter 18) quotes a supervisor talking about peer mentoring amongst postgraduates: 'It's the blind leading the blind'. There is an unspoken assumption that supervisors are best placed to offer guidance, and that students themselves are incapable of assuming any useful or knowledgeable mentoring role. There is also a timely reminder from O'Mahoney and Martin (Chapter 32) that the context of expertise should be noted. A student may have become an expert learner in the classroom, but this may change when they move as novices into a work-related context: 'They are also quickly forced to acknowledge that they are not the experts in the situation and develop increased respect as the breadth of community knowledge and experience becomes evident in the early stages of the

---

[7]To reinforce the point that students can be experts, there are six chapters in the Handbook with the author or joint authors being students, and taking a key role in describing and analysing their own behaviours and practices.

process'. However, as students come to see the relevance of their academic knowledge in the workplace, so their expertise may grow.

Overall, it is important that institutions recognise what students have to offer and how their opinions and expert knowledge can be used to better the learning experience for all involved, whether through student–staff relationships or through peer support. There needs to be sensitivity towards students and what they will be happy to engage with, and for what purpose, but — as many of these chapters show — it is also worth being courageous in trying out new approaches; and when recognised in some sense to be experts, student confidence is likely to be boosted.

34.6. Personal Identity

Growing in confidence relates in part to the development of personal identity. Two forms of identity emerge from the chapters of the Handbook: individual identity and that of a group, each being equally important in how students perceive themselves, and how they are — and how they want to be — seen by others. Pittaway and Moss (Chapter 16) suggest students have multiple identities in higher education: personal, academic, intellectual, social and professional. However, students talk more about themselves in terms of having confidence, happiness and self-knowledge. Yanagida, a highly active student from Western Washington University, describes student engagement as 'a path for leadership development and self-authorship' with higher education being:

> ...the environment for exploring and applying skills with trial and error, reflection and growth. These are lifelong experiences about finding, defining and knowing yourself, being in touch with how you feel and what you think, and being able to lead yourself. The opportunity to engage in your educational community and career enables people to take risks and be active in other areas of their lives, and to ultimately evolve into leaders of the future. (Kara Yanagida, personal email communication, 04/03/2013)

Such a statement gives credence to Solomonides' model of student engagement (Chapter 3), and in particular to the importance of a 'sense of being'. This is perhaps the most important aspect of individual identity, and one that is supported in the literature elsewhere. For example, Magolda (1999) has written of the need for higher education to actively engage in supporting student progress towards self-authorship (as mentioned by Kara), which includes identity (who I am and who I want to be) alongside cognitive development (metacognition and knowing how to know) and relationships (knowing how to make meaning with and through other people and how to share knowledge and expertise). Further, a major study of issues influencing student retention and success in higher education (Thomas, 2012) has reinforced a similar concept, that of 'belonging', as the key factor in determining students' ability to participate in and make the most of their opportunities in higher education. Similarly, Solomonides suggests that the concept of self-being is central to how and why students engage, and what they gain from it.

The development of a sense of being is clearly complex, and unique. Felten and Bauman (Chapter 21) tell a surprising story to illustrate this, using the concept of 'troublesome knowledge'.

> ... a threshold concept "is akin to a portal, opening up a new and previously inaccessible way of thinking about something" (p. 3). Crossing such a threshold often involves wrestling with what Perkins (1999) refers to as troublesome knowledge—knowledge that may seem counter-intuitive or odd when first encountered. Such trouble-some knowledge also may call into question issues of personal and social identity; as one of the co-authors of this chapter recalls, until he began working with deaf students, he never consciously understood himself to be a hearing person. That realization, like other thresholds, cannot be forgotten. Once crossed, a threshold is transformative and integrative, fundamentally and permanently changing the way a con-cept or even the world is understood.

Such a life-changing experience is suggested by Barnett (1997) as being funda-mental to higher education; he argues that, concurrent with the concept of 'critical being' that is central to academic learning, is a form of social and personal episte-mology — the belief that through higher education students can be changed as persons by their experiences. Similarly, alongside 'sense of being', Solomonides (Chapter 3) also includes 'sense of transformation'; that is, the expectation that higher education will be transformational, and there are many examples of this being the case throughout the Handbook.

However, development of identity is as complex as all the areas of engagement discussed so far, and the best of intentions can lead to negative outcomes. As Ody and Carey explain (Chapter 17), '... internal evaluation identified that target stu-dents who were not attending PASS [Peer Assisted Study Sessions] or engaging with their Peer Mentors wanted to, but chose not to, opt in for fear of labelling them-selves as struggling or not knowing what questions they would ask... the emphasis shifted and schemes were switched from an 'opt in' to an 'opt out' approach (all tar-get students being allocated a Mentor or PASS group'. Hence, no student was labelled as struggling or stupid and the identity of all could remain positive.

One aspect of identity that emerges from the chapters of this Handbook is the sense of social responsibility, alongside personal development. The World Café approach outlined by Bell et al. (Chapter 28) provides a good methodology in allowing all voices to be heard and acted upon, and demonstrates how consensus can be reached about curriculum developments even in extremely large student cohorts. In relation to extra-curricular activity, Ratcliffe and Dimmock (Chapter 4) express their self-interest; they wanted to 'get the most out of my time' and be pre-pared 'for life after graduation', but they also wanted to 'contribute something back to the University'. Bride and Naylor (Chapter 15) highlight a similar feeling from a student:

> Knowing that the work I conducted would go towards research to benefit students was such a confidence boost, and I am so proud to have been a part of it. Plus it looks great on my C.V. and is a real conversation piece!

However, perhaps surprisingly, the sense of altruism is not shared by all students; they perhaps do not perceive it as an important part of their sense of identity. As Spowart and Tripp (Chapter 14) point out, even when undergraduates engage with the community, they can be more interested in their personal development and competence in work-related skills than in any sense of helping others. The authors suggest that 'in seeking sustainability, educational institutions need to broker the relationship between students and community groups very carefully, so that everybody gains'. As with so many initiatives, the way that they are set up may strongly influence student motivations, behaviours and the extent to which they wish to identify with underpinning assumptions, such as that of a desire to support those in the community.

However, there are also many examples of how engaged students want to help transform the environment in which they are a student. Through such engagement, many will feel a sense of belonging, of having a group identity. Van der Meer et al. (Chapter 18) describes how, in the long, lonely journey of a PhD student, celebrating the academic and social milestones of their mentoring community was really beneficial, 'however, big or small — finishing a chapter; completing data collection; writing a paper; handing in a draft; getting a good mark', all of which added to the group identity. Ratcliffe and Dimmock (Chapter 4) talk about 'choosing' to engage, and 'choosing' how to engage; 'what motivated them to engage' and what they got out of it. They describe a developing sense of self in the context of all the richness of experience and opportunity that is available to them during their time at university, and how they felt involved and valued in the community they had selected to participate in. They also emphasise the importance of their group identity, that is joining a particular group was, 'one way that we could seek to define and establish ourselves' within the large mass. This satisfied a 'desire to both fit in and stand out' from the crowd. It allowed a sense of belonging, allowing them 'to access a group identity and group culture that comforts them and serves to define them within that larger group'. In addition, 'students are able to define and align themselves with a particular group of other students' and 'to mould their own identity within a group of ostensibly similar students'.

Haslam (2004, p. 58) describes leadership as a 'process of mutual influence... It is about the creation, coordination and control of a shared sense of 'we-ness'. Owen outlines how a sense of 'we-ness' and belonging has been created through often unpleasant initiation ceremonies over generations of students, as 'a means by which to socialise, induct and engage students with their new community'. Even if such rites of passage are far from a positive experience for students, they do support the development of group identity. More positively, Werder and Skogsberg (Chapter 8) describe how the Teaching-Learning Academy enables students 'to feel more connected with the University and with their own education'. They recount the story of a student who described 'the transformative influence of simply being heard', how he had 'never felt so acknowledged and appreciated'. This impacted on his sense of belonging and both individual and group identity in such a way as to empower him to behave in new ways and take on a leadership role; 'helping each other in the creation of our BIG questions...has made us a strong dialogical community...one that has the potential to create a supportive and intellectually developing community because it gives people a chance to share their thoughts fearlessly and feel truly involved'.

34.7. Conclusions

As suggested in the Introduction, the intention of this Handbook is that it should be highly practical and — as Solomonides says of his model (Chapter 3), it is for the reader to consider if and how it may apply in their own context. Strivens and Ward (Chapter 19) claim, 'Our response to the "conceptual muddiness" around reflection is to maintain a focus on the activities themselves'. Similarly, this Handbook has focused on the many ways in which student engagement is enacted, bringing together numerous vantage points and multiple ways of 'seeing' and understanding. It gives ideas and inspiration for changing practice that others can emulate, provides some of the wisdom of the authors who have been working in this area, along with pragmatic messages, starting points and a better understanding of how various forms of student engagement can be achieved, what it means for the student, the academic, the university and beyond. It has told some powerful, even transformational, stories of individual and institutional journeys.

Imagine for a moment a student journey through higher education where there is a strong induction into the academic and social activity and values of a higher education institution, supportive of all students, along with a sense of the transformational life experience of higher education as a time of personal growth and development.

Alongside this, there will be the opportunity for every student:

- to be immersed in the conversations of the discipline;
- to engage with teaching based on the social constructivist and dialogic processes that best support learning;
- to understand the processes of learning and reflection (including the role of assessment and feedback);
- to work with diverse student groups and across different disciplines;
- to be involved in peer education, engaged both as a receiver of support and as a supporter of others;
- to participate in curriculum design;

- to participate in collaborative research;
- to work in spaces that have been designed by students, for students;
- to engage with the institution as well as with the discipline;
- to lead change in the educational environment;
- to gain expertise in technology, in change, in community action or whatever — beyond any particular discipline;
- to gain experience of the workplace and skills useful to employment;
- to be involved in the local community and beyond;
- to be involved in transformational experiences;
- to gain a sense of confidence and identity, both as a student and in the context of life, as someone who is valued, who 'matters' and can add value to the lives of others; and
- to, possibly, gain a little wisdom.

These are the kinds of experiences of engagement that have been discussed throughout the Handbook. Each and every one of these experiences could be available to all students, no matter the educational context. They are all dependent on a vision of what is possible and the interpretation of that vision into practice. Sambell (Chapter 22) comments that the current economic climate places increasing pressure on the resourcing of pioneering pedagogic initiatives; but most of the initiatives described are dependent far less on funding than on a vision, and commitment and determination to make that vision work. Problematic is that many initiatives are dependent on the vision of an individual, or a few champions, and translating this into cross-institutional practice is far more difficult (though not impossible, as some of the chapters show).

'Student engagement' may well be a fad. Fads change, and move on, but the concept of student engagement, even if not continuing as the fad of the day, has to be something that underpins a worthwhile education. The ideas will not just disappear: indeed much of the thinking has been around for a long time already (see Owen, Chapter 1). Perhaps the most important factor is that reported by Bols (Chapter 6) — that student engagement is seen as a means for making 'a real difference to the experience of students' — the kind of experience that so many chapters in this Handbook refer to, of being deeply involved in university life, buffeted by real-life and workplace issues and tensions, involved and interested in learning processes, whether reflective or through complex problem solving in the community, of achieving, and of getting to know oneself. In these chapters, there is no indication that the soul of higher education is being lost through consumerism, student satisfaction or narrow performance indicators. Despite the mass industry of education, the words that stand out in these chapters are 'self', 'identity', 'being', 'participating', 'collaborating', 'sharing', 'partnership', 'belonging' and, above all, 'mattering'. It is these concepts that should characterise higher education from the students' vantage point, no matter the number of students, along with a sense of agency and empowerment. Using again the words of a Chinese student (Chapter 30): 'I will know better the difficulties and have wisdom to solve them. I am excited and looking forward for the future!' This is what every student should be able to say, in some form or other, at the end of their time in higher education; it is what student engagement is about.

Messick and Associates (1976) describe the potential of higher education for being a 'keyboard of possibilities... in this way we can create a higher education capable of playing not only major themes but endless variations' (p. 326). This musical metaphor seems appropriate for student engagement. Despite the variety in conceptualisations, there are major themes at its core. The idea of 'endless variations' also seems particularly apposite, not just because of the many interpretations found in the Handbook, but also because this encapsulates the idea of continuing creativity. This book has begun to demonstrate what can be possible, and to highlight that higher education is in our hands, as a shared responsibility — university staff and students alike — each bringing our own creativity and wisdom to create the best possible educational experience for the future.

Elisabeth Dunne
Derfel Owen

References

AUCC. (2009). *The Bologna Process and Implications for Canada's Universities*. Retrieved from http://www.aucc.ca/wp-content/uploads/2011/05/bologna-report-20091.pdf. Accessed on 4 February 2013.

Barkley, E. (2010). *Student engagement techniques: A handbook for college faculty*. San Francisco, CA: Jossey-Bass.

Barnett, R. (1997). *Higher education: A critical business*. Bristol: Open University Press/ Taylor & Francis.

Biggs, J., & Tang, C. (2007). *Teaching for quality learning at university*. Maidenhead: Open University Press.

Black, P., & McCormick, R. (2010). Reflections and new directions. *Assessment and Evaluation in Higher Education, 35*(5), 493–499.

Bovill, C., & Bulley, C. J. (2011). A model of active student participation in curriculum design: Exploring desirability and possibility. In C. Rust (Ed.), *Improving Student Learning (18) Global theories and local practices: Institutional, disciplinary and cultural variations* (pp. 176–188). Oxford: The Oxford Centre for Staff and Educational Development.

Bovill, C., Cook-Sather, A., & Felten, P. (2011). Changing participants in pedagogical planning: Students as co-creators of teaching approaches. Course design and curricula. *International Journal for Academic Development, 16*(2), 197–209.

Bryson, C., & Hardy, C. (2011). *Clarifying the concept of student of engagement: A fruitful approach to underpin policy and practice*. Paper presented at the HEA Conference, Nottingham.

Bruner, J. (1996). *The culture of education*. Cambridge, MA: Harvard University Press.

Cook-Sather, A., Bovill, C., & Felten, P. (forthcoming). *Student faculty partnerships in higher education: a practical guide to pedagogical and curricular collaboration*. San Francisco, CA: Jossey Bass.

European Commission. (2013). *Report to the European Commission on improving the quality of teaching and learning in Europe's higher education institutions*, June. Luxembourg: Publications Office of the European Union.

Furedi, F. (2009). Now is the age of the discontented, *Times Higher Education*, 4 June. Retrieved from http://www.timeshighereducation.co.uk/story.asp?storycode = 406780

Haslam, S. A. (2004). *Psychology in organizations: The social identity approach* (2nd ed.). Thousand Oaks, CA: Sage Publications.

HEA. (2013). Students as partners. Retrieved from http://www.heacademy.ac.uk/students-as-partners

Heron, J. (1996). *Co-operative Inquiry*. London: Sage.

Higgins, M. D. (2012). Remarks at the: Launch of the Irish Centre for Autism and Neurodevelopmental Research. Galway. Retrieved from http://www.president.ie/speeches/launch-of-the-irish-centre-for-autism-and-neurodevelopmental-research/

Hooker, M. (1997). The transformation of higher education. In D. Oblinger & S. C. Rush (Eds.), *The learning revolution*. Bolton, MA: Anker Publishing Company, Inc.

Kay, J., Owen, D., & Dunne, E. (2012). Students as change agents: Student engagement with quality enhancement of learning and teaching. In I. Solomonides, A. Reid & P. Petocz (Eds.), *Engaging with learning in higher education*. Libri Publishers.

Lave, J., & Wenger, E. (1991). *Situated learning: Legitimate peripheral participation*. Cambridge: Cambridge University Press.

Little, S., Sharp, H., Stanley, L., Hayward, M., Gannon-Leary, P., O'Neill, P., & Williams, J. (2011). In S. Little (Ed.), *Staff-student partnerships in higher education*. London: Continuum.

Magolda, B. (1999). *Creating contexts for learning and self-authorship: Constructive-developmental pedagogy*. Nashville: Vanderbilt University Press.

Mann, S. (2008). *Study, power and the university*. Society for Research into Higher Education. Maidenhead: Open University Press.

Maxwell, N. & Barnett, R. (Eds.). (2009). *Wisdom in the University (paperback reissue)*. Abingdon: Routledge.

McCulloch, A. (2009). The student as co-producer: Learning from public administration about the student-university relationship. *Studies in Higher Education*, *34*(2), 171–183.

McLeod, J. (2011). Student voice and the politics of listening in higher education. *Critical Studies in Education*, *52*, 179–189.

Messick, S., & Associates. (1976). *Individuality in Learning*. San Francisco and London: Jossey-Bass.

Meyer, J. H. F., & Land, R. (2005). Threshold concepts and troublesome knowledge (2): Epistemological considerations and a conceptual framework for teaching and learning. *Higher Education*, *49*(3), 373–388.

Nguyen, D. (2000). *The True Purpose of College and Higher Education Delta Winds: A Magazine of Student Essays*. A Publication of San Joaquin Delta College.

Northumbria University in Partnership with Bedfordshire and Manchester universities. (2011). A Good Practice Guide to Learning Relationships in Higher Education. Retrieved from http://www.heacademy.ac.uk/assets/documents/what-works-student-retention/Northumbria_Guide_to_Relationships_Dec_11.pdf

Nussbaum, M. C. (1998). *Cultivating humanity: A classical defense of reform in liberal education*. Cambridge, MA: Harvard University Press.

Perkins, D. (1999). The many faces of constructivism. *Educational leadership*, *57*, 3.

QAA. (2010). *Rethinking the values of higher education – students as change agents?* Retrieved from http://www.qaa.ac.uk/students/studentengagement/studentschangeagents.pdf

QAA. (2012) *QAA website*. Retrieved from http://www.qaa.ac.uk/Partners/students/reviews/Pages/Student-reviewers.aspx

Roth, M. S. (2012). Learning as Freedom. *The New York Times*, 5 September.

Sambell, K., & Graham, L. (2011). Towards and assessment partnership model? Students experiences of bring engaged as partners in assessment for learning (AfL) Enhancement activity. In S. Little (Ed.), *Staff-student partnerships in higher education*. London: Continuum.

Schwartz, S. (2011). Not by skills alone. *Times Higher Education*, 16 June.

Schwartzman, R. O. (1995). Are students consumers? The metaphoric mismatch between management and education. *Education, 116*, 215−222.

Senge, P. (2006 *The fifth discipline: The art and practice of the learning organization* (2nd ed.). London: Century.

Shulman, L. (2002). Making differences: A table of learning. *Change, 34*(6), 36−44.

Soeiro, D., Dias de Figueiredo, A., & Ferreira, J. A. G. (2011) Student Empowerment in Higher Education through Participatory Evaluation. *41st ASEE/IEEE Frontiers in Education* Conference Rapid City. Retrieved from http://www.academia.edu/1052696/Student_Empowerment_in_Higher_Education_Through_Participatory_Evaluation

Solomonides, I., Reid, A., & Petocz, P. (2012). *Engaging with learning in higher education*. Oxfordshire: Libri Publishing.

Streeting, W., & Wise, G. (2009). *Rethinking the Values of Higher Education — Consumption, partnership, community?* Retrieved from http://www.qaa.ac.uk/students/studentEngagement/Rethinking.pdf

Thomas, L. (2012). *Building student engagement and belonging in Higher Education at a time of change: Final report from the What Works? Student Retention & Success programme.* York: The Higher Education Academy.

Trowler, P., Saunders, M., & Knight, P. (2005). *Change thinking, change practices*. York: The Higher Education Academy.

Trowler, V., & Trowler, P. (2010). *Student engagement evidence summary*. York: Higher Education Academy.

Vygotsky, L. S. (1978). *Mind in society: The development of higher mental processes*. Cambridge, MA: Harvard University Press.

Wenstone, R. (2012a). Five questions we need to ask about partnership. *NUS Connect*. Retrieved from http://www.nusconnect.org.uk/blogs/blog/rachelwenstone/2012/09/04/Course-Leaders-Conference-speech/

Wenstone, R. (2012b). Rachel Wenstone launches a manifesto for partnership. *NUS Connect*. Retrieved from: http://www.nusconnect.org.uk/news/article/highereducation/Rachel-Wenstone-launches-a-Manifesto-for-Partnership/

Williams, J. (2011). Collaborating for staff-student partnerships: Experiences and observations. In S. Little (Ed.), *Staff-student partnerships in higher education*. London and New York, NY: Continuum.

About the Authors

Jackie Bagnall is currently a senior lecturer in leadership and organisational behaviour, with an academic background in social and organisational psychology and a consultancy background in action learning and leadership development. Jackie joined the Centre for Leadership Studies at the University of Exeter in 2003 from commerce where she launched 'Leadership Southwest', the Regional Development Agency's local centre for excellence. Her work focussed on leadership programmes which connected managers from across diverse sectors to explore, understand and implement better leadership practice. She has a specific interest in engaging students with their local community.

Paul Bartholomew is a professor of learning and teaching and head of curriculum design and academic staff development at Birmingham City University (BCU), UK. He is currently academic lead for BCU's MEd Learning and Teaching in Higher Education. He is a member of the JISC's Learning and Teaching Experts Group and has also worked as Consultant for e-Learning for the Health Sciences and Practice Subject Centre of the Higher Education Academy. He was awarded a National Teaching Fellowship in 2004 and has delivered workshops on 'Woven Learning' at the University of Pittsburgh, at Copenhagen Business School and at a number of UK universities. His doctoral research is in the field of co-located computer supported collaborative learning and he has a particular interest in using video methods to study collaborative learning behaviour. He has published on institutional change, curriculum design, innovation in Higher Education and quality enhancement.

H-Dirksen L. Bauman is a professor of deaf studies at Gallaudet University in Washington, DC, where he serves as department chair, co-ordinator the master's programme in deaf studies and co-ordinator for the Office of Bilingual Teaching and Learning. He is co-editor of *Signing the Body Poetic: Essays in American Sign Language* (2006), editor of *Open Your Eyes: Deaf Studies Talking* (2008) and co-author of *Transformative Conversations: A Guide to Mentoring Communities among Colleagues in Higher Education* (2013). He is also a producer and codirector of the film *Audism Unveiled* (2008) and producer of the film *Gallaudet*. He currently serves as co-editor of *Deaf Studies Digital Journal*, the world's first peer-reviewed academic and cultural arts journal to feature scholarship and creative work in both signed and written languages.

Amani Bell is a lecturer at the Institute for Teaching and Learning at the University of Sydney. As part of her academic development work, she supports Faculties with curriculum renewal processes. Her research focuses on academic development practices, such as reflection, peer observation and mentoring.

Alex Bols is executive director of the 1994 Group of research-intensive universities, prior to which he was an assistant director (research) and head of Higher Education at the National Union of Students (NUS), leading on student engagement and higher education policy. During this time he was a member of HEFCE's Teaching, Quality and Student Experience Strategic Advisory Committee. He has been a member of the UK Team of Bologna Experts since 2008. Previously he worked for Universities UK as the senior campaigns and events officer from 2004 to 2007. He was secretary general of ESIB — the National Union of Students in Europe (now European Students' Union), from 2001 to 2004. He was President of the Students' Union and Communications Officer at the University of Southampton, after graduating in history and politics. He completed an MA in higher and professional education at the Institute of Education in 2011.

Viola Borsos after travelling and working in education internationally, became a mature student herself in 2011 when she began to study BA (Hons) Fashion Design at Nottingham Trent University. She is Hungarian, speaks seven languages and is particularly interested in different cultures, languages and learning styles.

Catherine Bovill is a senior lecturer in the Academic Development Unit, Learning and Teaching Centre at the University of Glasgow. Prior to working as an academic developer, her background was in international and community development, health promotion and medical education. She has published and presented widely on students and staff co-creating curricula and she has active research interests in curriculum design definitions and processes; pedagogic research methodologies and the internationalisation of higher education. Recent projects include: a book outlining practical approaches to student and staff partnerships in pedagogical and curricular planning (Cook-Sather, Bovill, & Felten, 2014); a project to support higher education staff in Iraq to implement a student centred learning curriculum across their institution (Jordan et al., 2013) and a survey of pedagogic research in Scotland (Bovill et al., 2013).

Stuart Brand leads the Centre for Enhancement of Learning and Teaching at Birmingham City University and drives a university wide focus on student academic engagement. He has also led a strategic three year initiative for the Redesign of Learning Experience (RoLEx) across the institution. He focusses on improving the student learning experience through more effective partnership with Birmingham City Students' Union. This partnership, recognised with a Times Higher Education Award in 2010, led to development of the Student Academic Partners scheme described in this chapter. Previously, he led the University's Centre of Excellence in Teaching and Learning (CETL) — the Centre for Stakeholder Learning Partnerships. The CETL focussed initially on work with National Health Service employers and latterly on student engagement. He was awarded a National Teaching Fellowship in 2012.

Ian Bride is a senior lecturer in Biodiversity Management, in the School of Anthropology and Conservation, University of Kent. He currently teaches on the topics of guiding and interpretation, practical conservation, and ecotourism and manages a socio-cultural agroforestry project in the Western Ghats, India, funded by The Darwin Initiative. He has a varied academic background, which includes the natural and social sciences, as well as the arts, reflecting his interest in understanding the relationship between humans and their environment from a range of perspectives. He has a strong belief in the value and potential of education and training, both as a process that builds capacity in individuals and institutions, and as a specialist subject area within wildlife conservation.

William Carey is a teaching and learning adviser within The University of Manchester's central Teaching and Learning Support Office. With specific responsibility for the operational activity of the 'Student as Partners' programme, he works directly with Faculties and Schools to ensure the programme's implementation through appropriate student engagement and training and consultation and development of staff. One of the programme's flagship activities is 'Peer Support', which engages students in the learning and transition of others (and of themselves) focusing on facilitated academic discussion and social/pastoral integration. He has an excellent reputation in peer support and has contributed to many international conferences as well as being a founding member of the European First Year Experience conference Steering Group.

Lyn Carson is a professor in the Business Programmes Unit, School of Business at the University of Sydney. For the past 20 years she has taught and researched in the field of deliberative democracy, asking how the wider public can help to resolve intractable policy challenges. She is a seasoned practitioner and has been involved in designing, convening or facilitating Australia's first Consensus Conference, the first Deliberative Polls, the first Australian Citizens' Parliament, first Citizens' Juries and a Youth Jury as well as Community Summits and a host of other public deliberations at local, state and national levels.

Paul Chapman is a head of engagement at Birmingham City University Students' Union and is currently part seconded to the University's Centre for Enhancement of Learning and Teaching. This secondment looks at building meaningful staff and student relationships through academic student engagement initiatives with an aim to develop the learning community. In 2012 he was awarded the National Union of Students Staff Member of the Year for his partnership work and for the development of student representative initiatives. He has also been involved in several Higher Education Academy change programmes, the most recent being co-leading the What Works? project team looking at student retention and success. In 2012–2013 he led a joint student and staff team within the HEA Students as Partners change initiative, entitled 'New Student Conversations: From QA to QE'.

Alison Cook-Sather is the Mary Katharine Woodworth Professor of Education and co-ordinator of The Andrew W. Mellon Teaching and Learning Institute at Bryn Mawr College. Supported by grants from the Ford Foundation, The Arthur Vining Davis Foundations, and The Andrew W. Mellon Foundation, she has developed internationally recognised programmes through which students are positioned as pedagogical consultants to prospective secondary teachers and to practicing college faculty members. A leading scholar in the field of student voice, she has given more than 65 presentations around the world and published over 40 articles, 11 book chapters, and five books, including *Engaging Students as Partners in Teaching & Learning: A Guide for Faculty*, with Catherine Bovill and Peter Felten (Jossey-Bass, forthcoming) and *Education Is Translation: A Metaphor for Change in Learning and Teaching* (University of Pennsylvania Press, 2006). For the last several years, she has, in her role as the Jean Rudduck Visiting Scholar, facilitated seminars at the University of Cambridge in England.

Antony Coombs is an academic adviser for technology-enhanced learning within the Educational Development Unit at the University of Greenwich. As a key member of the project team for the JISC-funded Digital Literacies in Transition project he has worked on the recruitment of student researchers and the development of subject curricula in relation to digital literacy. He has over a decade of professional and teaching experience in visual art and design, including online design, and is particularly interested in the application of design processes and techniques within learning, teaching and assessment.

Barrie Cooper is an assistant director of education for mathematics and computer science at the University of Exeter and leads a cross-disciplinary group of lecturers specialising in Education and Scholarship in mathematics, computer science, engineering and physics. He obtained his PhD in mathematics from the University of Bath in 2007 and has since developed an interest in curriculum design and delivery. In 2011/2012, for the National HE STEM Programme, he led projects on student-led curriculum review, employer engagement and building a Community of Practice for Outreach practitioners. He works closely with the Academic Development team at the University of Exeter, teaching on two HEA-accredited staff development programmes and is part of the management team for Exeter's HEA-accredited ASPIRE scheme. He achieved senior fellowship of the Higher Eduction Academy in 2012.

Christopher Demirjian is studying BA (Hons) in fashion design at Nottingham Trent University, which he commenced in 2011. Prior to this he completed a foundation course in art and design at Nottingham Trent International College. He is from Cyprus and likes to use his Cypriot traditions and cultural values in his work.

Andrew Dimmock was an MA student on the European Politics programme at the University of Exeter for which he was awarded an Academic Excellence Scholarship at the time of writing. His BA is in politics with sociology (also at Exeter). He has been involved in academic representation at the discipline, college and faculty level; outreach work as a student ambassador; community liaison; the National Student

Survey; and selected as a student reviewer for the Quality Assurance Agency. He is now at ICM Research.

Elisabeth Dunne is a head of project development within education quality and enhancement at the University of Exeter, in the South West of England. Her career has been devoted to the promotion of innovation, change and strategic development in education. She has co-ordinated and directed many major research, development and evaluation projects on aspects of learning and teaching of national interest, bringing in external funding of around two and a half million pounds over her career, and writing dozens of books and articles. In addition, she has promoted a range of ground-breaking initiatives across the University of Exeter. A major focus has always been on the student experience, as well as on understanding the processes of change, including the development of evidence-based practice and working with students as change agents. She is a principal fellow of the Higher Education Academy (HEA) and a University of Exeter Teaching Fellow.

Peter Felten is an assistant provost for teaching and learning, executive director of the Centre for Engaged Learning and the Centre for the Advancement of Teaching and Learning, and associate professor of history at Elon University in North Carolina, USA. He has published and presented widely on engaged learning, faculty development, and the scholarship of teaching and learning, including most recently coauthoring *Transformative Conversations: A Guide to Mentoring Communities among Colleagues in Higher Education* (2013). He has served as president of the POD Network, an international association for teaching and learning centres in higher education. In 2012–2013, he served as a fellow of the Andrew W. Mellon Teaching and Learning Institute at Bryn Mawr College.

Emma Franklin was a final-year undergraduate student of the School of Law, Social Sciences and Communications (LSSC) at the University of Wolverhampton, studying English Language and Linguistics. She works as an editorial and research assistant in the Research Group in Computational Linguistics at the University of Wolverhampton, and now studies Applied Corpus Linguistics at the University of Birmingham. Her research interests lie mainly in computer-mediated communication and language and identity.

Rebecca Freeman is currently completing her PhD 'Student Voice in Higher Education' at the University of Birmingham and has published on the theme of student engagement and student governance. She has worked extensively with staff and students to enhance course evaluation at a number of universities and students' unions. As a researcher at the Centre for the Enhancement of Learning and Teaching at Birmingham City University she developed the Times Higher award winning 'Student Academic Partners' scheme, which employs students to lead on educational development projects. She also founded the national Student Learning and Teaching Network, which promotes active student engagement in learning and teaching in the UK. She works at the School of Life Sciences at the University of Warwick as an Educational Strategy Officer.

Tanbir Galsinh was an undergraduate student of the School of Law, Social Sciences and Communications (LSSC) at the University of Wolverhampton. She was in her final year of studying an english language and linguistics degree. Her future career lies within the field of training to help others with speech and language problems to speak more clearly.

Christine Hardy is a principal lecturer in the School of Art and Design, Nottingham Trent University. She has a PhD from Nottingham University in adult reading and is the author of a book *To Read or Not to Read: Adult Reading Habits and Moivations* (2008) and editor of *Writing in the Disciplines: Building Supportive Cultures for Student Writing in UK Higher Education* (2012). Her recent teaching is focused on research methods and supervision of post-graduate students, most of whom are international. Her current research interest, and the subject of national and international publications, is student engagement. This includes transitions, academic writing and internationalisation, taking a student perspective. She is co-founder of the international network RAISE (Researching, Advancing and Inspiring Student Engagement) who are currently organising their third international conference. She is a fellow of the Higher Education Academy.

Simon Hart is the Policy, Planning and Evaluation Librarian at the University of Otago Library. Prior to taking up this position he was the Learning Services Librarian where he was involved in strategic initiatives to position information skill development within wider learning support. His interests relate to building collaboration that promotes seamless and engaging learning. He is currently managing a collaborative activity based benchmarking project across an international network of academic libraries.

Elizabeth James has a background is in the areas of student persistence and engagement, as well as workplace learning and the transfer, organisation and implementation of knowledge in practice. She is currently a senior research assistant at the University of Southampton working on Cancer, Palliative and End of Life Care projects. She has previously been involved in research projects exploring screening for malnutrition by community nurses: barriers and facilitators; working with employers to develop and deliver a needs-led curriculum: a work-based pilot in health, education and care and Investigating Support Workers (SW) and Support, Time, Recovery (STR) Workers in their educational, training and development needs within two NHS Trusts in Hampshire.

Mark Kerrigan is a senior lecturer in teaching and learning at the University of Greenwich, where he is responsible for a series of cross-institutional activities around curriculum design and delivery. Drawing from a broad teaching experience ranging from Foundation to MSc/PhD, his recent work includes delivering national projects on digital literacies (DLinHE) and assessment and feedback (making assessment count). Mark works extensively with students as change agents and was part of the team that developed the first national student change agent network (HEI-Flyers). His work is focused on promoting excellence, enhancing the student/staff experience and realising opportunities to deliver a quality education.

Ji Kim commenced studying BA (Hons) in fashion design at Nottingham Trent University in 2011. After graduating high school in Korea she chose to study in the UK to learn English and discuss ideas in an open forum. She found it difficult to settle in and got involved in research to help other international students.

Eileen Martin has been manager of The Science Shop at Queen's University Belfast for 10 years. Through the Science Shop, students use their academic knowledge to benefit community organisations by carrying out curriculum-based research projects. Eileen has co-ordinated the development of the Queen's Community Outreach Strategy. She has participated in several EU funded Science Shop projects and is a member of the management team for the PERARES project. In addition she has worked on a voluntary basis on a number of community projects in the Glens of Antrim. She holds a masters degree in applied anthropology and previously held a research post at Queen's.

Lorraine McIlrath has co-ordinated the Community Knowledge Initiative (CKI) at the National University of Ireland Galway since 2004. There she is responsible for developing and supporting civic engagement activities across the university, with the CKI team, including service learning and student volunteering. She is Principal Investigator (PI) of Campus Engage, a national Irish network to support civic engagement within higher education in Ireland. Since 2010, she has been a member partner in a nine university EU Tempus Funded Project to support the introduction of service learning to five universities in Jordan and Lebanon entitled the Tawasol Project. She is co-editor of the recently published *Higher Education and Civic Engagement: International Perspectives* (2007) and *Higher Education and Civic Engagement: Comparative Perspectives* (2012).

Luke Millard is a head of learning partnerships in the Centre for Enhancement of Learning and Teaching at Birmingham City University. His interests lie in student engagement and partnership work with the Students' Union. He is responsible for the management and development of the full range of student engagement initiatives that the Centre leads. Luke also has substantial experience as project manager for the university's Centre for Excellence in Teaching and Learning: the Centre for Stakeholder partnerships (2005–2010).

Nga Mok is studying BA (Hons) in fashion design at Nottingham Trent University, which she commenced in 2011. She comes from Macau, China and, as an international student, has experienced difficulties studying in a foreign country, so is keen to improve the experience for all international students through involvement in research.

Timothy Moss is the course co-ordinator of the bachelor of education (primary) course in the Faculty of Education at the University of Tasmania. He lectures in literacy education, and reflective practice across face-to-face and fully online modes of delivery. His research interests include professional identity, pedagogy of teacher education and narrative and arts-based research approaches.

Manisha Nair is a Weidenfeld scholar doing her PhD in Public Health at the University of Oxford. She holds a masters degree in Global Health Science from Oxford and MBBS degree from Assam Medical College and Hospital in India. She was a faculty member at the Indian Institute of Public Health-Delhi part of the Public Health Foundation of India (PHFI). She was part of the team that established the Centre of Excellence for Chronic Diseases, at PHFI, New Delhi. She also worked in the routine immunisation and polio eradication programmes in India as part of the National Polio Surveillance Project of the World Health Organisation. She has published in the areas of the social determinants of health, maternal and child health, non-communicable diseases, and education. Her work in the field of education is mainly related to 'medical education in the emerging market economies'.

Louise Naylor became director of the Unit for the Enhancement of Learning and Teaching at the University of Kent in 2006. She now leads a large team that is responsible for the initial and continuing professional development of academic staff, curriculum and educational development including e-learning, and providing student advice and guidance for effective learning. She founded the Creative Campus project and has been a constant supporter of innovative and creative learning and teaching activities at the University.

Mike Neary has been the dean of teaching and learning at the University of Lincoln since 2007. Before taking up his post at Lincoln he taught political sociology at the University of Warwick (1994–2007). Prior to becoming an academic Mike worked in youth and community education in South London (1980–1994). His current research interests are academic labour and student life. Recent publications include 'Teaching Politically: Policy, Pedagogy and the New European University' and 'Occupy: A New Pedagogy of Space and Time?' with Sarah Amsler, both published in the *Journal of Critical Education Policy Studies* 2013. He jointly edited a collection of essays 'Teaching in Public: Making the Modern University' (2012), and is currently writing a book to be published by Zero Books next year: *Student as Producer: How Do Revolutionary Teachers Teach?* In 2007 he was given a national award for his teaching by the Higher Education Academy, a UK government agency that supports teaching in universities. He is a founder member of the Social Science Centre, Lincoln, a co-operative providing free higher education.

Marcia Ody is employed by the University of Manchester as a teaching and learning manager with responsibility for managing the 'Students as Partners' programme, developing institutional policy and advising strategic development. The areas of work she is currently involved in include induction and transition, developing the independent learner, peer support, HEAR, consulting with students and engaging students as partners in curriculum development. In addition as the UK Supplemental Instruction/PASS Certified Trainer, Marcia manages the UK National Centre for SI/PASS and has presented at many national and international conferences.

Catherine O'Mahony is the acting manager of the National Academy for the Integration of Research, Teaching and Learning (NAIRTL), which works across the Irish Higher Education sector to develop and implement policy and practices aimed at enhancing the student learning experience at undergraduate and graduate level. She completed a BSc in biochemistry in University College Cork and an MSc in science communication in Dublin City University. She recently completed her PhD which investigated innovative ways to broaden public input into science policy decision-making. She began work with NAIRTL in 2009. She is a founding member of the Community-Academic Research Links initiative at University College Cork and is an active participant in a four-year EU PERARES project.

Derfel Owen is head of academic policy and standards at the University of Exeter. His career has been spent in student facing roles. He studied British politics and legislative studies at the University of Hull where he went on to become President of the Students' Union and was then elected to the National Executive Committee of the NUS where he led efforts to improve students' union governance and their relationships with partner universities. Following this, he joined Goldsmiths, University of London as Student Support and Development Manager, to help improve personal and professional development opportunities for students and to oversee the development of effective advice and representation structures. In 2007, Derfel joined the Quality Assurance Agency (QAA), first as a development officer and going on to become multimedia and student engagement manager. At QAA he led efforts to improve student engagement and participation in the agency's work, but also to raise the profile of student views and expectations in shaping and developing activities. As part of his efforts to improve QAA's reach to students, he pioneered new approaches to communication and engagement, including launching the QAA podcast series, QAAtv, utilising social media, student led publications and a substantial redevelopment of QAA's website. Now at the University of Exeter, Derfel is responsible for leading the development of academic policies, working closely with students and staff to maintain academic standards and enhance student learning.

Leanne Piggott is the director of the Business Programmes Unit at The University of Sydney Business School where she teaches political risk management and related topics on the global business environment. Her research interests focus on Middle East security, and her research interests also include energy security, in particular, oil market fundamentals and the role that the geopolitics of the Middle East contribute to the supply side of the global market.

Sharon Pittaway is the director of student engagement in the Faculty of Education at the University of Tasmania. She lectures in professional studies, and children's literature, both of which are offered fully-online to students within Tasmania, across Australia and internationally. She led the development of the fully online offering of the BEd (in-service) course in 2008–2009. Her research interests include developing a pedagogy of online teacher education, and technology use to engage students in school classrooms.

Emma Plugge is the course director for the MSc Global Health Science and a senior clinical research fellow at the University of Oxford. She is a qualified doctor and an honorary consultant in public health, working overseas in Central America and Southern Africa before completing her training in general practice and public health in Europe. Her health research now focuses on the health of marginalised groups. However, she also has a keen interest in educational research, particularly inter-professional education and capacity building for public health, and is a fellow of the Higher Education Academy.

Stefan Popenici is a scholar with extensive international experience in teaching, research and leadership in higher education with universities in Europe, North America, South East Asia, New Zealand and Australia. He is currently working at The Centre for the Study of Higher Education at The University of Melbourne, and is an associate director of the Imaginative Education Research Group at Simon Fraser University, Canada. He is also a former senior advisor of the Minister of Education in Romania on educational reform and research, senior consultant of the president of De La Salle University Philippines on research and internationalisation, and consultant for international institutions such as Fulbright Commission, Council of Europe and others. For his work and strategic leadership in education he was awarded by the President of Romania with The Order 'Merit of Education' as Knight.

Aaron Porter is a higher education consultant who has worked with over 30 universities across the sector. He has also undertaken a number of research and evaluation projects for a number of bodies including the Department for Business, Innovation and Skills (BIS) and the HEFCE with CFE Research. He was previously President of the National Union of Students (NUS) and has served as a non-executive director for a number of organisations including UCAS, the Higher Education Academy (HEA), the OIA and as an observer to the HEFCE Board. As a student he graduated with a BA English from the University of Leicester and then served two terms as a trustee and executive officer of the students' union. He was the founding chair of Union94 (the students' unions of the 1994 Group) and as a student was editor of the student newspaper, 'The Ripple'. He is a honourary research fellow at the University of Winchester and a fellow of the Royal Society of the Arts.

Dale Potter co-ordinated a set of Students as Change Agents projects in 2009–10 at the University of Exeter. Since then, he has continued to work closely with students on institutional projects to develop innovative high-tech resources, and later as part of a nationally funded project to enhance the use of digital technologies as part of students' study and research. Throughout these projects and alongside his involvement in first-year undergraduate programme delivery, he has particularly embraced opportunities to reconcile his experiences as a recent student with organisational perspectives, innovation and change management within higher education.

Sean Prince is a senior lecturer on the undergraduate and postgraduate in fashion design courses in the School of Art and Design, Nottingham Trent University and at the Hong Kong Design Institute. He has an MA in fashion and textiles from Nottingham Trent University, is a fellow of the HEA and a member of RAISE.

Alex Ratcliffe is currently student engagement and employment officer for the College of Humanities at the University of Exeter. His recent MA and BA were both in classics and ancient history at the University of Exeter. He has been involved in academic representation; Students as Agents of Change; running a subject-based student society; community liaison and completing a 10 month graduate scheme within the University of Exeter.

Sue Rivers is an associate dean of learning and teaching at BPP University College, with a portfolio focussing on Student Learning and the Student Experience. She was previously acting dean at Coventry University. She has a doctorate in education from the University of Sheffield (based on research into the student experience of online learning) and an MBA in higher education management from the Institute of Education, University of London. She is a multidisciplinary professional being a barrister, chartered surveyor and chartered manager. She is a Fellow of the Higher Education Academy.

Oliver Roman-Worsley is from the UK and commenced studying BA (Hons) in fashion design at Nottingham Trent University in 2011. He was a teaching assistant in Germany and has studied in Hong Kong. Internationalisation has always been an interest and a strong focus in his design practice. He is a member of RAISE.

Malcolm Ryan is a recently retired Teaching Fellow at the University of Greenwich and Head of the Teaching and Learning Enhancement Team (TaLEnT) in the School of Education. Over 40 years he has worked with diverse students and stakeholder groups as a teacher, educational technologist, consultant and youth worker. He co-founded ELESIG, led the SEEL Pathfinder Project, is a member of the JISC Experts Panel and 'Critical Friend' to their Curriculum Delivery and now the Digital Literacy Programmes.

Kay Sambell is widely published and well-known internationally in the field of teaching, learning and assessment in higher education. She has directed number of large-scale research and development projects aimed at investigating and enhancing the student experience, and led on student engagement in Northumbria University's Centre for Excellence (CETL) in Assessment for Learning. In 2002 she was awarded a UK National Teaching Fellowship for her work on innovative assessment. Her subject area is the interdisciplinary area of childhood and youth studies. She specialises in children's literature and has a long track record of research in this field. In 2005 she became director of the MEDAL project: a large-scale funded initiative designed to develop students' academic literacy in Childhood Studies. This project brought together a number of National Teaching Fellows to establish an extensive network of university teachers with a focus on Childhood Studies to share expertise and build an online bank of open-access pedagogic resources. She is currently based in the Department of Social Work and Community Studies at Northumbria University, where she holds a personal chair as Professor of Learning and Teaching.

Erik Skogsberg is currently a doctoral student in the College of Education at Michigan State University (MSU). His research focuses on New Literacies, intertextuality, and dialogic practices and pedagogies in the secondary English classroom. At MSU, Erik teaches courses in introductory literacy and secondary English methods for pre-service teachers. Prior to his time at MSU, he taught high school English in Washington State. He holds degrees in English literature (BA) from Western Washington University (WWU), and secondary English education (MAT) from Brown University. While a student at WWU, he collaborated with Dr. Carmen Werder, and was heavily involved in Western's commitment to engaging students in the Scholarship of Teaching and Learning (SOTL). Erik regularly co-presented with Werder from 2003 to 2006 about student and faculty experiences in SOTL work, and co-authored a chapter with Werder and two former students in *Engaging Student Voices in the Study of Teaching and Learning* (Stylus, 2010). Much of his current dialogic pedagogy and research were inspired by the SOTL work at WWU with Werder.

Ian Solomonides is the Director of the Learning and Teaching Centre at Macquarie University, Sydney, Australia and has oversight of the Academic Development, Learning Technology, Learning Systems, Accessibility, Student Evaluation, and Administration functions of the Centre. He has a BEd (Hons) in Art and Design and a PhD in Engineering Education. Before emigrating in 2006, he was Learning and Teaching Coordinator in the School of Architecture, Design and the Built Environment, and Programme Leader for Furniture and Product Design at Nottingham Trent University in the UK. Ian has worked on various learning and teaching enhancement projects across many disciplines in the UK, Europe and Australia. He has a strong practical and research interest in the student experience with a particular focus on student engagement and teaching standards in higher education. He is currently Secretary and Treasurer of the Council of Australian Directors of Academic Development.

Lucy Spowart is the Teaching Development Framework Manager at Plymouth University, where she supports staff to gain accreditation of the Higher Education Academy. She also provides developmental programmes for academic staff who teach and support students. Her own teaching background is in sport management and sport development. She previously worked as a Senior Lecturer in Physical Education at the University College of St. Mark and St. John, Plymouth, where she gained a significant amount of experience in work-based learning and assessment. She has published in the areas of motherhood, sport participation and qualitative methodologies. More recently, her research interests have focused on the postgraduate student experience, and on teachers experiences of gaining professional accreditation.

Janet Strivens is the Senior Associate Director of the Centre for Recording Achievement and also an Educational Developer at the University of Liverpool. She is the programme director of the Postgraduate Diploma/Masters programme in Learning and Teaching in Higher Education at Liverpool. She also provided specialist input and is a member of the supervisory team for a fully online professional doctorate in higher education, together with Liverpool's partners Laureate Inc. Her recent international work, in Europe and Pakistan, has focused on developments in medical education. In her role as CRA Senior Associate Director she is involved in projects and consultancy relating to personal development planning and e-portfolio practice. She co-directed a recent project funded by the Higher Education Funding Council for England to analyse the value of e-portfolio technology in supporting the employer engagement agenda for higher education. She also is a National Teaching Fellow.

Lorraine Tansey is the student volunteer co-ordinator of the Community Knowledge Initiative. She has a BA in legal science and sociology and political studies and completed her LLB. As the co-ordinator of NUI Galway's student volunteering programme, ALIVE, she has developed a number of resources to support student volunteers. Her current areas of interest include student engagement, citizenship development and the role of third level institutions in active citizenship. In the past she has been a board member of Volunteering Ireland and advisory member of the National Steering Group for the European Year of Volunteering 2011.

Sue Timmis is a senior lecturer in technology enhanced learning at the Graduate School of Education, University of Bristol. She has been involved in researching how digital media can support and enhance learning since the early 1990s. Much of her recent work has focussed on student engagement in collaborative work and peer support. She has extensive experience of participatory research and engaging students as co-researchers.

Mike Tripp has been the Head of Department of Sports Development and Outdoor Learning at University College Plymouth St Mark and St John (aka Marjon), specialising in the history, politics and sociology of sport. He obtained his doctorate from the University of Exeter in 2010 and his thesis was entitled 'The persistence of difference: a history of Cornish wrestling.' He has contributed articles on wrestling for *The Oxford Companion to the Body*, *The New Dictionary of National Biography*, the *Encyclopedia of British Sport* and the *Encyclopedia of Traditional British Rural Sports*. He has also contributed articles to academic journals, the latest of which was entitled, 'Cornish wrestling in Australia' for *Sporting Traditions*, the official journal of the Australian Society of Sports History. Apart from sports history his professional interests include curriculum development, employability strategies and student engagement with the local community.

Carin Tunåker is a PhD candidate in Social Anthropology at the University of Kent, where she is researching LGBT youth homelessness, funded by a local charity (Porchlight). Her research interests include home, sexuality, gender and homelessness, and she has also undertaken research regarding matrifocal households in Cuba. She is the founder and co-director of the 'Home and Sexuality Research Network' and she was employed as a Team Leader, and subsequently as Research Supervisor for the Social Hubs project at the University of Kent.

Jacques van der Meer is the associate dean (Academic) at the University of Otago College of Education. In this capacity he is responsible, among other roles, for teaching and learning innovation. His latest project relates to the development of bite-size mobile learning. He has also worked in various other roles at the University, including in the Faculty of Education and Student Learning. His research areas relate to student transition and induction into higher education, student engagement and peer-learning. He also has an interest in student retention and achievement, especially of under-represented minorities.

Gwen van der Velden is a director of Learning and Teaching Enhancement at the University of Bath where she has led the student engagement agenda since 2006. Her research concentrates on the ways institutions engage with students and the role of the student voice in a changing policy era. She holds a number of roles at national level, including membership of the Planning Executive of the Standing Conference for Academic Practice (SCAP), chair of the Learning, Teaching and Quality Network within the 1994 Group and planning group member for the Heads of Educational Development Group. She is also a member of the QAA advisory group on student engagement and recently wrote an issue of the QAA's 'Talking about Quality' bulletins on the same topic.

Kelly Wakefield is currently working as a senior research assistant at the University of Southampton, having recently completed her PhD in academic networking for learning and teaching. Although her background is in human and cultural geography, over the past five years she has worked on multiple projects centred on the student experience and has become more interested in researching higher education. Her current research interests comprise geographies of higher education, global academic networking and technologies that support this. Recent publications have focussed on peer-to-peer teaching of NVivo and reflections of online interviewing. Presently, her research projects include an exploration of curriculum innovation and international postgraduate students' experiences of verbal feedback.

Simon Walker is a Higher Education Academy (HEA) National Teaching fellow, is the head of University of Greenwich's Educational Development Unit, responsible for developing university policy and strategy on learning and teaching. He is director of a number of nationally funded learning and change management projects, such as the Digital Literacy in Higher Education project, and the Students as Change Agents UK Network. Previously he led a number of national TEL projects working with schools and colleges to develop learning systems for study skills. His work includes establishing Compass: the *Journal of Learning & Teaching* and major contributions to the design of the original CAMEL model, which continues to be used to support the work of many innovative national projects. His research and publication lies mainly in the development and evaluation of learning design on which he supervises and examines PhD students. He is a contributor to the Larnaca Declaration on Learning Design, and a co-designer of the OLDS MOOC. He is co-director of the university's cross-university research eCentre, which hosts the annual Academic Practice and Technology (APT) conference.

Joan Walton is currently the director of the Centre for the Child, Family and Society in the education faculty at Liverpool Hope University. Her career has included social work with children and families, the professional development of social workers, and the continuing educational development of managers, leaders and practitioners in a wide range of professional contexts. Her role includes the supervision of part-time doctoral students who use action research methodologies, and who are interested in responding to the question: 'How can we, individually and collectively, integrate research and practice in order to improve the wellbeing of children and young people'? Their shared aim, through their individual studies, is to make an original contribution to knowledge about ways of knowing and action that will enhance the life chances of those for whom they have educational and professional responsibility.

Rob Ward is the Director of the Centre for Recording Achievement (CRA), a registered educational charity and network organisation and Associate Partner of the Higher Education Academy, that seeks to *promote awareness and understanding of the processes of recording achievement as an important element in improving learning and progression throughout the world of education, training and employment.* He leads work to support PDP implementation nationally and led the CRA contribution to the National Coordination Team on Student Employability (ESECT, 2002/5). He took a leading role in the revision of the sectoral Guidelines on Personal Development Planning (2009), was a member of the Scoping Group on Measuring and Recording Student Achievement (2004–2006) and has led the development of the Higher Education Achievement Report (HEAR, 2008-PD). He has worked on a wide range of projects and initiatives in the UK and with colleagues from the US and Australia in particular.

Carmen Werder directs the Teaching-Learning Academy and the Writing Instruction Support programmes, as well as the Library Learning Commons, at Western Washington University, where she also teaches civil discourse. As a 2005 Carnegie Scholar, she initiated an ongoing study of the use of personal metaphors in developing a sense of agency. She headed up both Carnegie Academy for the Scholarship of Teaching and Learning (CASTL) initiatives on partnering with students in the scholarship of teaching and learning: the Sustaining Student Voices cluster (2003–2006) and the Institutional Leadership Programme Student Voices themed group (2006–2009). She founded and co-chairs the 'Students as Co-inquirers' special interest group in the International Society for the Scholarship of Teaching and Learning (ISSOTL), and she co-edited the book *Engaging Student Voices in the Study of Teaching and Learning* (Stylus, 2010) with a former student. She has presented widely and published on the importance of working with students as co-inquirers in studying teaching and learning.

Thomas Willans is a PhD student researching into emotion within virtual worlds at the Serious Games Institute, Coventry University. He is a Senior Course Representative representing all research students in the Faculty of Engineering and Computing at both Faculty and University levels. As a Chartered IT Professional he has been a software developer and led a IT process improvement team and project introducing ISO9001 over 650 staff at the Met Office. He is a Member of the British Computer Society. Currently he is also the Managing Director of a Heritage Interpretation business, which serves the informal educational needs at heritage sites.

Jane Williams is a director of e-learning for the Faculty of Medicine and Dentistry at the University of Bristol. She has been involved in the research and development of e-learning for the past 22 years. This has included ground-breaking work with students who develop e-learning resources to support their peers in a staff-student partnership and at a national level on patient consent and open education. Since 2008, Sue Timmis and Jane have jointly led an interdisciplinary research programme: Telme — technology enhanced learning in medical education.

Julie Wintrup is a principal teaching fellow in the Faculty of Health Sciences, at the University of Southampton. Her teaching interests include workforce development, leadership, ethics and decision-making in health services. Recent funded research projects include a longitudinal, mixed method pedagogic study of Foundation degree students, a workforce investigation into developing new roles in health care, and case studies of widening access to HE, Advanced Apprenticeships and Technician roles in health services. She has reported and published regularly, and presented to health, ethics and education conferences nationally and internationally. In 2010 she was co-founder of the Researching, Advancing, Inspiring Student Engagement (RAISE) network of academics, students and education developers.

Jenny Wren was an outstanding lead tutor on a University of Exeter Business School core first year module, and considered herself as a 'lead learner' in experimenting alongside her students with using collaborative techniques and new technology to enhance and re-personalise large group teaching. Her previous experience was as a business development trainer and consultant with small groups of senior executives in large businesses in a variety of settings and countries, including working with Outward Bound, INSEAD and Cambridge University, and a charity in Vietnam and Myanmar. She supported her keenest and most capable students to become active as student learning champions, engaged passionately with the 'students as agents of change' process, contributed to University discussions regarding innovation, and showcased student learning at teaching focussed events and conferences, locally, nationally and internationally. Sadly, she passed away early in 2013.

Index

Academic review, 95, 167, 173–174, 591
Accreditation, 115, 303, 456, 536, 648
Acquisition of knowledge, 53
Activism, 6–7, 9, 19, 224
Added value, 175, 331, 471
Advocacy, 215, 421, 425, 428, 559, 571, 577
Agency, 46, 59–60, 105, 109, 112–114, 125, 146, 151, 164, 183, 202, 204, 246, 343, 362, 463, 479, 495–496, 509, 511–512, 518, 521–523, 529, 539, 546, 552, 592, 606, 615, 624, 632, 637, 641, 644–645, 651, 658
Alienation, 212, 272, 282, 383, 552, 563, 594, 596, 621
Alternative model, 43–44
Altruism, 59, 239, 577, 630
Ambassadors, 72, 233
Application, 43–45, 47, 114, 209, 230, 238, 247, 257, 278, 305, 319, 324, 385, 390, 405, 431, 446, 450–451, 453, 506, 522, 551, 577, 581, 598, 640
Aristotle, 6, 272, 291
Aspiration, 278
Assessed, 79, 120, 198, 214, 247, 284, 304, 362, 380, 382, 384–385, 403, 408, 411, 428, 431, 446, 516–517, 536, 570, 575, 578, 590, 663
Assessment, 28, 74, 82, 88, 105, 116, 119, 126, 133, 137, 169, 172, 182–186, 189, 192, 194, 247, 250–251, 260, 264, 271–273, 278–280, 284, 286–287, 305, 334, 336–337, 340–342, 379–394, 402–404, 408–411, 414, 416–417, 431–432, 435, 440, 447, 462, 467, 469–470, 478, 482, 484–485, 505, 509, 516, 522, 533, 536, 556, 570–572, 575, 577, 582, 588, 620–621, 631, 640, 642, 647–648, 656, 658, 665
Assessment for learning, 116, 273, 379–380, 382–383, 647
Attention, 7–8, 16, 18, 43–44, 78, 119, 121, 136, 139, 142, 181–182, 226, 250, 273, 280, 313–314, 317, 331, 333–335, 342, 344–346, 367, 369–370, 373–374, 379, 387–389, 470, 495, 500, 522–523, 533, 552, 555–556, 559, 579, 604, 606, 657, 662
AUSSE, 46, 48, 55
Australia, 1, 26, 30, 44–47, 51, 54, 108, 280, 283, 499–501, 552, 589, 639, 645–646, 648–649, 651, 653–655, 664
Authentic, 153, 237, 250–251, 285, 314, 318, 362, 380, 385, 391, 393, 432, 461, 486, 494, 509–514, 621
Authentic assessment, 391
Authentic learning, 251, 621
Authentic voice, 314, 318
Authenticity, 510, 521, 523, 617

Autonomy, 30, 85–87, 89, 154, 272,
    383, 385, 546
Awareness, 45, 67, 159–160, 188–189,
    191, 212, 228, 232, 234, 249, 272,
    278–279, 307, 309–310,
    332–333, 345, 362, 383, 407,
    466, 470, 496, 512, 544–545,
    552, 560, 577, 595–597, 608,
    610, 651

Barriers, 63, 150, 167, 178, 183, 191,
    193, 211, 226, 228, 268, 272, 282,
    287, 324, 344–345, 352, 358,
    361, 379, 480, 483, 489, 501, 570,
    591, 611, 617, 625, 642
Belief, 29, 45, 135–136, 139, 185, 259,
    266, 268, 278, 333, 350, 403, 456,
    478, 540, 546, 606–607,
    609–611, 629, 639
Belonging, 12, 17–18, 31, 51–52, 54,
    82–83, 118, 281, 283, 298, 313,
    316, 373, 379, 433, 480, 608, 628,
    630–632
Bologna, 6, 8, 93, 97–105, 107–109,
    240, 613, 638
Bureaucracy, 456, 590

Careers, 128, 166, 201, 207, 210–211,
    230, 233, 245, 296, 299,
    306–307, 339, 343, 421–422,
    424, 426, 430, 440, 516, 533, 581
Catalysing, 549, 551, 553–561
Champions, 272, 321, 326–327, 398,
    437–438, 440, 445–447, 478,
    608, 613, 622, 627, 632, 652
Change, 6, 10, 12, 18–19, 23–24, 29,
    33, 35–36, 38–39, 60, 63,
    65–66, 69, 81, 85, 88, 94, 97–98,
    102, 106, 108, 111, 115,
    118–120, 124–126, 129–130,
    133, 137–138, 143, 157, 169,
    177, 185–186, 190, 192–193,
    195, 202, 212, 255, 257–259,
    261, 263, 265, 267, 292, 295, 306,
    331, 343–344, 382, 397–398,
    406, 423, 434–435, 437–439,
    441–449, 451, 453, 455–458,
    464, 469, 477–478, 480–481,
    483, 487–489, 494–496,
    499–507, 513, 523, 527–543,
    545–547, 549–550, 553–554,
    556–557, 559–560, 562, 570,
    576, 581, 587–588, 591, 597,
    606–611, 613–616, 618–619,
    621–627, 632, 637, 639–642,
    646–647, 650, 652, 658,
    660–664
Change Agents, 6, 60, 63, 65, 69,
    118–119, 129, 186, 190, 398,
    437–439, 441–443, 445–449,
    451, 453, 455–458, 480,
    494–495, 499–501, 505, 507,
    527–528, 531–536, 540, 542,
    545–547, 549, 553, 591, 606,
    608, 611, 618, 623–624, 627,
    641–642, 646, 650
Change management, 81, 445, 447, 646,
    650
Charter, 6, 15–16, 85
Civic renewal, 502
Civic responsibility, 198, 221, 225–227,
    239, 570, 612
Co-creation, 45, 462–465, 467–473,
    496, 514, 536, 580, 616, 622, 624,
    626, 656
Co-creators, 442, 446, 456, 461, 494,
    530, 606, 608, 611, 622
Co-curricular, 65, 224, 293, 295, 657
Co-dependent, 579
Co-design, 215, 467, 499, 501, 650
Co-inquirers, 133, 135, 140, 142–143,
    553, 626, 651
Co-inquiry, 509, 512, 520–521, 523, 625
Co-investigators, 140
Collaboration, 38, 126, 134, 194, 199,
    223, 242, 245, 251, 259–260,
    264, 273, 309, 316, 327, 346, 352,
    390, 397, 410, 467–468, 472,
    477, 481, 483, 490, 510, 534, 539,
    550, 568, 573, 578, 582,

589–591, 615, 618–619, 642, 656–657

Collaborative, 37, 48, 160, 229, 246, 263, 265, 273, 286, 294, 301, 303, 314, 316, 327, 384, 392–393, 462–464, 469, 473, 480, 482, 486, 488–489, 495–496, 509, 512–515, 519–520, 522–523, 530, 546, 552–553, 555–557, 568, 579, 589, 592–593, 595, 609, 612, 619, 622, 632, 637, 642, 649, 652, 659, 664

Collaborative learning, 48, 294, 303, 316, 384, 469, 555, 637

Collaborator, 202, 495, 528, 553

Collegial engagement, 77, 79, 83–85, 88–89

Comfort zone, 305, 356

Commitment, 26–27, 37, 52, 71, 83, 135–136, 138, 164, 169, 175, 191, 215, 223, 227, 229–234, 243, 245–247, 327, 385, 401, 405, 417, 433, 443, 456, 509, 511, 516, 520, 523, 533–534, 538–539, 550, 552, 561, 574, 577, 580–581, 583, 587, 611–613, 617, 619, 632, 648, 656

Commodification, 13

Communication, 33, 64, 67, 81–82, 84, 102, 105, 135–139, 142, 156, 167, 178, 187–188, 231, 245, 247, 251, 258, 261, 268, 284, 296, 300–301, 304, 309, 322–323, 354, 357, 359, 369, 371–372, 425–426, 438–439, 442, 449, 455–456, 502, 514–515, 539, 544, 572–573, 577, 581, 583, 589, 628, 641, 645

Communities, 5–6, 18–19, 119, 148, 197–198, 216, 222, 227–228, 230, 232–234, 237, 241–242, 246, 248, 250, 280–281, 293, 295, 298, 301, 306–307, 313, 317, 320, 324–326, 373–375, 382, 405, 451, 496, 502, 509–512, 519, 541, 568, 571, 573–574, 580, 583–584, 587, 592, 605, 608, 613–615, 637, 641, 657

Communities of practice, 280, 313, 317, 405, 519, 541

Community, 1, 3, 6, 8, 10–13, 15–19, 26, 28, 30, 33, 38, 51, 54–55, 59, 62–63, 65, 67, 70–72, 74, 78, 84–85, 94, 108, 114, 118–119, 133, 135–138, 152, 164, 175–176, 186, 197–199, 202–203, 209, 211, 213, 215, 221–231, 233–235, 237–247, 249–251, 255, 257–259, 261, 263, 265–267, 271, 273, 282, 287, 294, 298–303, 310, 313, 317, 320–321, 323–325, 339, 369, 372–375, 383, 386, 415, 425, 443, 478–485, 489–490, 494–496, 501–502, 509–513, 519, 521–524, 533–534, 536–537, 539–540, 546, 560–561, 567–577, 579–584, 591, 597, 606–608, 611–612, 614, 616–619, 625, 627–628, 630–632, 637–640, 642–645, 647, 649, 656–658, 664–665

Community engagement, 55, 198, 229, 234–235, 237–239, 241–245, 247, 249–251, 443, 496, 539, 569, 571, 573–575, 577, 579, 581, 583, 608, 619

Competencies, 295, 349–354, 359, 361, 363, 450, 452, 625

Compulsory, 45, 59, 68, 70, 204, 248, 283, 293, 302, 359, 536, 593

Conflict management, 425, 577

Connections, 30, 61, 73, 143, 198, 204, 224, 251, 282, 285, 287, 324, 326, 331, 333, 336–338, 372, 463, 505, 515, 561

Constitution, 15–16

Consultants, 466, 495, 549–562, 613, 622, 640

Consumer, 2, 11, 14, 16, 49, 118, 120,
    122, 129, 149, 160, 216, 257, 447,
    495–496, 528, 544, 588, 594,
    598, 605–606, 663
Consumerism, 3, 6, 11, 77–82, 84,
    88–89, 122, 148–149, 480, 605,
    611, 632
Consumers, 11, 14, 45, 49, 74, 118, 134,
    139, 146–149, 151, 456, 463,
    481, 490, 587, 595, 605–606,
    616, 660, 663
Conversational principles, 136–137
Co-ownership, 81, 84
Co-producer, 6, 120, 148, 216, 463, 495,
    511, 528, 553, 606, 608, 616
Co-production, 84
Co-researchers, 461, 495, 509, 511–513,
    515, 517, 519, 521, 523, 573, 608,
    649
Course design, 189
Co-working, 486
Creative, 19, 33–34, 38–39, 49–52,
    184, 187, 191, 198, 243, 255,
    257–269, 345, 370, 392, 398,
    402, 405, 413, 425, 434, 438, 452,
    454, 471, 502, 518, 534, 539, 588,
    615, 627, 637, 644, 661
Creators, 442, 446, 456, 461, 494, 530,
    606–608, 611, 622
Cross-disciplinary, 324, 543, 545, 615,
    640
Culture change, 477, 487
Culture of dialogue, 133, 135, 141–142
Curriculum, 3, 14, 28, 32, 45, 48,
    59–62, 64, 74, 84–87, 118, 166,
    184, 188–189, 202, 215,
    237–243, 245–247, 249–252,
    264–265, 273, 281, 287, 293,
    302, 339, 341, 351, 361, 363, 371,
    383, 397–399, 401–404,
    408–409, 411, 413, 416–417,
    421–434, 436, 447, 456,
    461–471, 477–478, 482,
    484–487, 494, 499–503,
    505–506, 510, 517, 519, 528,

    530–531, 534–536, 542, 544,
    546, 568, 570, 574, 584,
    588–589, 594–596, 603, 607,
    610–611, 616, 623–624, 627,
    629, 631, 637–638, 640,
    642–644, 647, 649–650, 656,
    658–659, 663–665
Curriculum design, 188–189, 215, 250,
    341, 397–398, 403, 423, 427,
    461, 463–465, 467–471,
    477–478, 484–487, 499–500,
    506, 536, 588, 624, 627, 631,
    637–638, 640, 642, 656, 663, 665
Curriculum development, 45, 118, 189,
    202, 251, 417, 421, 423–428,
    431, 433, 500, 535–536,
    588–589, 594, 623, 629, 644, 649
Curriculum renewal, 494, 499–503, 505,
    611, 638

Debating, 61, 421, 425, 428, 430, 432,
    535
Degree Awarding Powers, 114–115,
    123, 125, 129
Deliberation, 494, 499, 501–502,
    504–506
Deliberative Democracy, 494, 499–503,
    505–506, 608, 622, 627, 639
Democracy, 11, 135, 147, 152–153, 158,
    160, 230, 494, 499–503,
    505–506, 590, 608, 619, 622,
    627, 639, 656
Development, 2, 10, 16, 19, 23, 29, 43,
    45–46, 48, 51, 67, 69, 74–75,
    83–89, 93–94, 99, 101,
    106–108, 114, 116, 118, 124,
    126–127, 133, 146, 153–154,
    159, 175–176, 181, 184–186,
    188–189, 191, 197, 202–203,
    205, 207–208, 212–213, 215,
    222–223, 226, 229–232, 234,
    238, 240, 242–244, 246–248,
    251, 258–259, 266, 271–272,
    277–278, 284, 291–292,
    294–297, 299, 301–304,

308−310, 314−316, 318−321,
323−324, 327, 332−333,
338−340, 349, 351−352, 355,
361−363, 379−380, 383, 385,
390−391, 393, 397−398, 403,
406−407, 413, 415, 417,
421−428, 431−434, 436, 438,
446−449, 456, 462−463, 468,
477−479, 481−482, 484−485,
487−489, 493, 495−496, 500,
502, 509−510, 513, 516−519,
521−523, 527−528, 530,
532−533, 535−536, 538,
543−546, 550, 552−553, 568,
571, 574, 576−578, 581,
587−589, 592, 594, 596−597,
610−611, 614−617, 621−623,
627−631, 637−645, 647−652,
657−658, 664−665
Dialogic engagement, 134, 553
Dialogue, 12, 26, 55, 100, 133−143, 171,
185, 187, 190, 192, 224,
261−262, 268, 273, 334, 357,
382, 389−392, 411, 417,
424−425, 435, 466, 468, 500,
503, 506, 516, 552−553, 560,
562−563, 616−617, 621,
626−627
Digital, 135, 398, 437−443, 445−457,
495, 509−521, 523, 527,
532−533, 542−546, 589, 637,
640, 642, 646−647, 649−650
Digital media, 495, 509−519, 521, 523,
543, 589, 649
Disability Equality Duty, 184
Disability Equality Scheme, 184
Disabled students, 95, 181−195, 273,
367, 625, 658
Discussion, 6, 36, 61, 67, 86−87,
104−105, 138, 141, 154, 158,
160, 174, 197, 201−202,
204−206, 211, 216, 234, 244,
246, 259, 275, 277, 279,
283−285, 292, 296, 298,
303−307, 325, 332, 336−337,
341, 344, 353, 361, 363, 382, 384,
387, 389−391, 404, 409, 411,
424, 440−442, 465−466,
468−469, 471, 486, 501−502,
506, 514, 516, 528, 536, 543, 545,
549, 551, 553−554, 556, 560,
577, 593−594, 604, 609, 624,
626−627, 639, 659, 663
Disenfranchisement, 137
Disengaged, 433, 500, 567, 569
Disengagement, 30, 32, 54−55, 82, 283,
471, 605, 656
Disorientation, 283
Dispositions, 275, 288, 333, 385, 608
Divergence, 60, 65, 141
Diversity, 37, 47, 142, 171, 187, 194,
221, 233, 257, 273, 295, 336, 341,
352, 360, 367, 369−375, 385,
422, 453, 570−571, 577, 591,
597, 665
Doctoral students, 320, 421, 423−434,
623, 651
Domains of engagement, 212

Effectiveness, 30, 95, 114, 119, 147, 174,
192, 198, 324, 327, 332, 336, 345,
349, 363, 381, 403, 435, 620, 659
Effort, 3, 25, 34, 36, 45, 48−49, 52, 54,
73, 80, 115, 127, 135, 143, 168,
178, 192, 260, 336, 345−346,
384, 390, 424, 478, 480, 511, 522,
533−534, 544−545, 556, 560,
573, 582, 606−607, 610, 656, 658
E-learning, 183, 238−240, 242, 247, 514,
516, 519, 521−522, 537, 542,
579, 637, 644, 652
Elite, 9, 37, 247, 342, 484, 594
Emotional, 28, 32, 43, 118, 124, 154,
156, 199, 211, 276, 291−292,
511, 552, 607, 657
Employability, 62, 67, 182, 186, 198,
201, 203−204, 216, 233, 240,
242−244, 250−251, 258, 268,
302−303, 309, 315, 340,
421−422, 425−426, 429−430,

432−436, 482, 487, 516, 533, 536, 538, 546, 589, 607, 619, 649, 651

Employable, 63, 166, 431, 433, 456

Empower, 62, 195, 625, 631

Empowered, 14, 137, 150, 186, 325, 406, 457, 494, 503, 554, 561−562, 620, 623, 625, 662

Empowerment, 61, 74, 81, 118−120, 129, 150, 186, 190, 345, 381, 406, 409, 412, 486, 495−496, 518, 523, 535, 541, 544, 547, 560, 562, 624, 632, 662

Engaged student, 1, 14, 23, 38, 59, 70−71, 78, 93, 199, 309, 567, 569, 605, 610, 630

Engagement, 1−3, 5−9, 11−13, 15−19, 23, 25−38, 43−55, 59−74, 77−90, 93−95, 97−109, 111, 113, 115−125, 127, 129, 133−141, 143, 145−160, 163, 165, 173−174, 178, 181−195, 197−198, 201−205, 207, 209, 211−216, 221−225, 227−231, 233−235, 237−239, 241−245, 247−251, 255, 265, 271−273, 275−288, 291−293, 297−298, 302−303, 305−306, 308−310, 313, 316, 327, 331−333, 335−339, 341−345, 349−351, 353, 356, 359, 363, 367−369, 371−375, 379−386, 389, 391, 394, 397, 401−402, 404−406, 408, 410, 415−418, 421, 426, 432−435, 437−438, 443, 446−447, 451, 453, 456−457, 461, 464−465, 468, 470−472, 477−478, 480−481, 483−489, 493−496, 499, 501−502, 506, 509−512, 521−523, 527−532, 534−540, 542, 546, 549−563, 567−571, 573−575, 577−579, 581−584, 587, 589−594, 597, 603−622, 625−633, 638−643, 645, 647−650, 652, 656−665

Enhancement, 53, 83, 85, 94, 115−116, 124, 126−127, 129−130, 146−147, 149, 155, 160, 164, 171−173, 176, 185−186, 255, 258, 293, 301, 319, 381, 386, 423, 447, 458, 461, 477−479, 481−483, 485, 487, 489, 528−530, 577, 588, 606−607, 610, 616, 637−639, 641, 643−644, 647−648, 650, 656, 658

Enterprise, 13, 44, 115, 137, 141, 233, 255−256, 323, 540, 574, 590, 597, 617

Enthusiasm, 66, 138, 197, 228, 260, 296, 307, 310, 344, 415, 438, 447, 458, 468, 483, 487, 489, 499, 506, 535, 552, 570, 614

Entrepreneurs, 448−449

Epistemic engagement, 495, 511, 608

Ethics, 322, 353, 515, 520, 569, 581−582, 590, 597, 652

European Higher Education Area, 93, 97, 99, 101−105, 108−109, 164

European Students' Union, 9, 98, 100, 638, 661

Evaluation, 46, 77−78, 86, 94, 145, 157, 167, 185, 192−193, 250, 273, 296−297, 300, 302, 305, 308, 310, 315, 324, 327, 334, 341, 382, 384, 386, 390, 407, 410−411, 414, 421−422, 424, 429, 432−434, 442, 458, 465−466, 470, 481, 500, 535−536, 538, 572, 577, 582, 595, 598, 614, 617, 629, 641−642, 646, 648, 650

Expectations, 6, 13−15, 17, 24, 34, 47, 61, 78−81, 84, 88−89, 93, 106, 124, 146, 150, 154, 212, 214−215, 230, 245, 247, 271, 276−278, 285, 300, 340, 343, 351−352, 368, 388, 426, 467−468, 470−471, 562, 581, 589, 609−610, 619, 627, 645

Experiential learning, 238–239, 402, 409, 411, 496, 538, 567, 569–570

Expert, 12, 101, 119, 205, 283, 342, 403, 468, 529, 539, 620, 626–628

Extra-curricular, 10, 45, 63–66, 68, 70, 74, 83, 202, 230, 245, 443, 447, 521–522, 531, 629

Facilitation, 64, 293, 304–305, 322, 578, 665

Facilitators, 119, 142, 304, 307, 642

Feedback, 47, 49–50, 63–65, 71–72, 80–82, 84–85, 89, 94, 106, 111, 116–120, 122–129, 151, 154–155, 158, 164, 167–169, 173, 175–176, 188, 197, 199, 241, 250, 259, 261, 264–265, 267–268, 272, 284, 286–287, 297, 301, 304, 308, 324, 327, 338–340, 342, 346, 350, 381–382, 384–387, 389–390, 398, 411, 417, 422–423, 428, 431–432, 440, 442, 453–455, 465–466, 468–471, 483, 494, 499–500, 503, 505–506, 517, 524, 528, 530, 533, 536–537, 546, 549, 551, 553, 555–557, 570–572, 575, 577, 581–582, 614, 620–622, 631, 642, 650, 656, 658–659, 661–662

Formative assessment, 273, 381, 384–385, 387, 411, 431–432, 440, 447

Foundation Degree, 197, 204–205, 207–209, 216–217, 652

Funding, 23, 26, 29, 34, 37, 84, 146, 148, 184, 191–192, 204–205, 208, 237, 240, 250, 255, 261–262, 264, 266–268, 297, 308–309, 315, 319, 322–323, 351, 361, 384–385, 393, 435, 478–479, 483, 486, 488, 522, 540, 542, 572, 580, 595, 632, 641, 649

Good practice, 47, 60–62, 69, 106, 111, 123, 126, 130, 171, 183–184, 192, 296, 304, 307, 398–399, 433, 448, 461–462, 467–468, 471–472, 481, 580, 615

Governance, 7, 10–12, 14–15, 23–24, 29–30, 34, 37, 60–62, 84–85, 87, 89, 94, 102–103, 108, 118, 146, 408, 641, 645

Graduate skills, 303, 458, 463

Greece, 5–7, 17, 291, 660–661

Guidelines, 105, 156, 164, 228, 515, 520, 551, 573, 651

Health practitioner, 208–210

Higher education, 2, 5–9, 11–14, 19, 23–31, 33–39, 43–49, 52–55, 59–61, 66, 72, 77–79, 82, 84–89, 93–95, 97–106, 108–109, 111–119, 121, 123, 125, 127, 129–130, 133–135, 139–140, 142–143, 145–146, 148, 152, 154–155, 163–164, 166, 181–186, 191, 193, 198, 201–205, 207, 209, 211, 213, 215, 221–224, 226–227, 229, 231, 233, 237–238, 240, 242, 250, 255, 258, 263, 265, 271, 273, 275–277, 280–282, 291–293, 295, 309, 313, 331–334, 342, 349, 351, 361–362, 367–368, 371–372, 374–375, 379–380, 382, 384, 389, 393, 401, 405, 416–417, 421–423, 426, 434–435, 437–438, 447–448, 450, 461–465, 468, 477–480, 483, 493–494, 499–500, 502, 509–510, 512, 514, 519, 521, 527–528, 532–533, 549, 552–553, 563, 567–568, 574, 579–580, 584, 587–589, 591–595, 597–598, 603–606, 610, 612, 616–617, 620, 622, 626, 628–629, 631–633,

637–639, 641–651, 654,
656–660, 662–665

Hippocrates, 6

History, 7, 12–13, 19, 25, 43, 67–68,
114, 121, 129, 139, 143, 166, 225,
238, 242, 359, 371–372, 380,
406, 506, 576, 593–595, 597,
638, 641, 647, 649

Humboldt, 494, 593, 596

Identity, 46, 49, 52, 54, 70–72, 74, 118,
153–154, 241, 256, 276, 278,
281–283, 286, 334, 343, 368,
375, 383, 393, 539–541, 595,
605, 608, 625, 628–632, 641,
643, 656

Identity expectation, 70

Ideologies, 94, 141, 145–148, 152, 154,
158–160, 541, 598

Impact, 2, 18, 23–24, 26–30, 33–35,
37–38, 55, 74, 93–95, 97–98,
101–102, 106, 108–109,
126–127, 147, 154, 157,
174–177, 181, 185, 187,
192–194, 225–227, 230, 233,
249, 251, 260, 280–281, 283,
291–292, 303, 307, 310, 320, 327,
356, 362–363, 371–372, 380,
394, 398, 413–414, 426, 429, 431,
437, 443, 445, 447, 458, 470, 472,
477, 487, 489–490, 494–496,
504–505, 534–535, 537, 540,
543–546, 554, 562, 569, 573, 576,
578, 580, 584, 591, 594–595, 598,
608, 610, 614, 622, 627, 660, 664

Implementation, 69, 104, 106, 139, 147,
184, 186, 255, 272, 296, 310, 326,
403, 410, 417, 424, 427, 444, 447,
463, 477, 529, 568, 639, 642, 651

Improvement, 27, 49, 55, 65, 67, 85,
94–95, 115, 117, 124, 126–129,
149, 163, 170, 175, 182,
186–187, 190, 192–194, 255,
327, 341–342, 398, 422, 482,
536, 546, 616, 652, 656, 658

Incentive, 70, 72, 74, 188, 202, 438, 442

Inclusion, 29, 70, 73, 104–106, 109,
185, 230, 249, 332, 425, 434,
486–487, 489, 494, 502, 522

Inclusive assessment, 189

Inclusivity, 183, 520, 617

Influence, 9, 14, 28–30, 32, 77–78, 81,
85, 87, 97, 103–105, 137–139,
143, 146, 150–152, 154–155,
215, 229, 239, 260, 271, 292, 334,
350, 354, 373, 393–394, 408,
416, 450, 463–464, 473, 494,
502, 513–515, 530, 553, 579,
582, 592, 597, 607, 610, 614,
624–625, 630–631, 665

Informing engagement, 159

Initiation ceremony, 16–17

Innovation, 5, 38, 264, 393, 397–398,
434, 447–448, 517, 546, 574, 590,
611, 622, 637, 641, 646, 650, 652

Integrity, 80, 458

Interaction, 6, 38, 47–48, 67, 82, 115,
224, 238, 273, 279, 293–295,
297, 299, 301, 304, 314, 316, 319,
325, 361, 384–385, 390, 403,
447, 463–464, 478, 511, 546,
589, 610, 618, 623–624

Interactions, 2, 26, 30–31, 107, 157,
292–294, 314, 318, 323, 383,
390, 414, 659

Interactive, 268, 299, 384, 390–391,
402, 413, 463, 517–518, 537, 626

Intercultural, 232, 349–353, 359,
361–363, 570, 577, 625

International students, 107, 123–124,
232, 349–350, 352–363,
433–435, 540, 543, 625, 643

Involvement, 3, 26, 30–31, 33, 45, 48,
50, 61–63, 67–69, 71, 85–88,
98–102, 104–105, 116–119, 123,
129, 158, 163, 171–172, 182,
184, 186, 190, 193–194, 202,
211, 226, 241, 243–244, 247,
249, 251, 260, 265, 271, 276, 280,
308, 319, 326–327, 390,

397−398, 404−405, 407, 415,
417, 429, 440, 442−443,
446−448, 467, 470−471, 473,
484−485, 487, 499, 509, 511,
520−521, 523, 530, 532,
537−538, 550, 552, 573, 575,
579−580, 583, 591−592, 607,
622, 627, 643, 646, 656, 664

Judgment, 627

Knowing, 12, 52−53, 138−139, 193,
215, 241, 268−269, 282−284,
300, 308, 367, 369−370, 383,
391, 402, 518, 573, 621, 623, 626,
628−630, 651
Knowledge, 2, 8, 11−14, 31, 34, 36−38,
45, 49, 51−54, 61, 67, 81, 116,
119−120, 135, 138−139,
141−143, 152, 155, 159, 166,
171, 198, 210−212, 214−215,
221, 223−225, 227, 231,
238−242, 248−249, 266, 272,
275, 277−278, 280, 282,
284−285, 288, 298, 300, 304,
306, 317−318, 325, 333,
340−341, 345, 351−353, 360,
371, 375, 384−385, 388−389,
391−392, 403, 405−409,
411−412, 414, 417, 422−423,
426−427, 432, 434, 450,
462−464, 466, 469−471,
493−496, 502, 509, 511−514,
518−519, 521−523, 530, 535,
538, 540−541, 545−546, 550,
554, 567, 569−570, 577−583,
593−594, 596−598, 603, 605,
607−609, 612, 614, 616, 620,
623, 626−629, 642−643, 649,
651, 660, 662
Knowledge production, 119, 141, 509,
521, 579

Leaders, 7, 26, 63, 65, 82, 108, 111, 143,
228, 267, 269, 293, 297,

301−303, 305, 307−310, 318,
321−327, 425, 446, 456, 533,
539−540, 606, 613, 625, 628,
651, 660, 662
Leadership, 6−10, 16, 35, 63, 65, 70, 81,
108, 123, 130, 137, 167, 231, 242,
260, 266−267, 291−293, 300,
309−310, 313, 319, 321, 323,
325, 327, 421−422, 424−425,
433−435, 443, 447, 482, 496,
502, 529−530, 533, 535,
539−540, 592, 623−624, 628,
630−631, 637, 646, 651−652, 656
Learning, 2−3, 6, 11−12, 15, 25−26, 28,
30−38, 44−54, 60−63, 66, 74,
77−86, 88, 94, 98, 103, 109,
114−120, 122, 124−127,
129−130, 133−138, 140,
142−143, 145, 148, 150, 153,
156, 163−164, 168, 170−171,
174, 176−177, 182−189,
192−194, 197, 199, 202−205,
208, 210−216, 222−225,
229−232, 234, 237−244,
246−251, 255−256, 258−263,
266, 268, 271−273, 276−281,
283−285, 287−288, 291−296,
298−299, 301−304, 306−309,
313−321, 323, 326−327,
331−337, 339−345, 350−352,
354−363, 367−368, 370−375,
379−386, 389−390, 392−394,
401−417, 421−425, 427, 429,
431−439, 443, 445−447,
456−457, 461−471, 473,
478−485, 488−490, 493−496,
499−501, 506, 509−514,
516−519, 521−522, 528−533,
536−539, 541−546, 549−550,
552−557, 559−563, 567−571,
573−575, 577−579, 581−584,
587−595, 597−598, 603−604,
606−613, 616−629, 631−632,
637−645, 647−652, 654,
656−660, 662−665

Learning communities, 119, 148, 293,
    298, 306
Learning experience, 33, 50, 60–62, 77,
    81–82, 94, 117–120, 145, 153,
    168, 170, 174, 176–177,
    185–186, 197, 199, 210–211,
    247, 250–251, 263, 271, 283,
    291–292, 295, 301, 303, 334,
    370, 383, 401, 404, 407, 415,
    422–424, 433, 462–464,
    468–469, 473, 479, 482, 485,
    488, 494, 510, 513, 517–518,
    530, 537, 550, 556, 559, 569, 573,
    581, 591, 617, 621, 623,
    627–628, 638, 645, 662,
    664–665
Learning journey, 136, 462, 543
Legitimacy, 94, 151, 176
Libanius, 14
Liberal arts, 140, 550
Lifelong learning, 205, 212, 231, 280,
    316, 467, 587
Literacy, 28, 31, 265, 267, 278, 282, 284,
    287, 321, 382, 385–387,
    389–390, 393, 454, 533,
    543–546, 640, 643, 647–648, 650

Market, 2, 12, 17, 24, 27, 29–30,
    33–35, 37–38, 49, 62–63, 69,
    88, 121, 202, 240, 244, 263, 292,
    463, 510, 588, 592, 594, 606, 616,
    619, 644–645, 660
Marketisation, 6, 19, 49, 118
Masters, 16, 568, 643–644, 648
Meaningful engagement, 181, 183, 185,
    187, 189, 191, 193
Mentor, 208, 211, 215, 292, 296,
    299–300, 305, 308, 314, 318,
    335, 629
Mentor training, 300, 305, 314
Metacognitive strategies, 331, 333, 345
Ministerial Declaration, 98, 100
Model, 1–2, 9, 25, 32, 37–38, 43–47,
    49–54, 63, 65, 67, 69, 81, 85,
    106–107, 117–118, 134–135,
    138, 140, 142–143, 147, 183,
    215–216, 247, 271–272, 287,
    291–292, 294–295, 299–302,
    309, 319–320, 332–336, 338,
    341–342, 345, 371, 382,
    384–385, 398–399, 406, 411,
    413, 437, 443–444, 446, 449,
    457, 463–464, 487, 494, 496,
    500, 503, 505–506, 509, 512,
    517, 519, 528–530, 536, 572,
    577, 588, 590, 592, 616, 620,
    624–625, 628, 631, 650
Monitoring, 93, 117, 151, 185–186, 204,
    278, 287, 297, 310, 315, 352, 433,
    512, 591, 623
Motivation, 2–3, 25–28, 30–32, 59,
    70, 72–73, 78, 101, 115, 251,
    271, 296, 331, 336, 344–346,
    368, 375, 403, 415, 449–450,
    456, 468–470, 509, 511, 522,
    531, 535, 538, 546, 606–607,
    656
Motivations, 27–29, 31–33, 37, 70, 73,
    222, 226–227, 237, 240, 244,
    250, 280, 286, 464–465, 471,
    473, 521, 604, 609, 622, 630

National Health Service (NHS),
    207–210, 212, 479, 517, 638, 642
National Student Survey, 47, 116–117,
    146, 151, 181, 470, 480, 489, 611
Negotiation, 79, 89, 164, 251, 392, 425,
    462, 468, 473, 509, 517, 523, 577,
    583, 621, 625
Newman, 6, 8, 13, 115, 184, 603, 612
Non-compulsory, 68, 283, 293
Non-traditional, 281, 285, 433, 568
NSSE, 43–49, 55, 658

Observation, 256, 261, 267, 286, 310,
    386, 389, 402, 411, 551, 638
Occupational, 578
Olympics, 238, 246–247, 249, 251
Online, 26, 55, 157, 188, 194, 202,
    228–230, 233–234, 276, 279,

282–288, 304, 307, 325–326,
337, 339, 362, 371, 422,
438–441, 450–451, 453, 499,
503, 506, 511, 514, 516–519,
543, 589, 640, 643, 645, 647,
649–650, 660

Open dialogue, 500

Organisation, 7–9, 23, 60–61, 64, 74,
81–82, 86, 88, 97, 100, 104, 107,
152–153, 156, 204, 208, 224,
230, 232–233, 238–239,
242–243, 245, 252, 263,
325–326, 338, 421, 425, 427,
430, 443, 446–447, 458,
478–479, 483, 496, 505, 567,
569–570, 573–577, 580–584,
619, 642, 644, 651

Organising, 49, 63, 126, 243–244, 250,
279, 297, 324, 344, 426, 429, 458,
533, 587, 590, 611–612, 642

Orientation, 221, 242, 271–272,
275–277, 279, 281, 283–288,
292, 294, 298–299, 301,
305–306, 368, 370, 374, 406,
412, 422, 502, 533, 551, 606

Ownership, 13, 78, 80–81, 84–85, 136,
153, 155–156, 194, 262, 266,
268, 299, 310, 320, 411,
433–434, 466, 495–496, 511,
513, 520, 523, 535, 590, 611, 614,
619, 624, 662

Oxford, 9, 112, 116, 421–425, 428–429,
431–436, 597, 644, 646, 649, 654

Paid, 18, 25, 30, 70, 72, 80, 136, 139,
169, 198, 201, 203–204, 212,
214, 243, 256, 258, 264,
281–282, 293, 451, 482, 495,
503, 531, 542, 550–551, 613

Paralympics, 247, 248, 249, 266

Part time working, 201–216

Part-time students, 66, 114, 147,
201–216, 225

Participation, 5, 10–12, 16, 23, 27–28,
33, 45–46, 54, 64, 66, 68–69, 72,

84–85, 87, 102–104, 107–108,
111, 115, 118, 136, 138, 147,
153–154, 157, 172, 175–176,
185, 194, 199, 202, 213, 215,
223–227, 229–232, 238–239,
242, 247, 251, 264, 280–281,
284, 288, 308–309, 317, 319,
321, 350, 353, 381–383, 391,
401–403, 405–413, 415–418,
423, 431, 440, 446, 453, 465, 467,
471–472, 479, 484, 488, 499,
506, 511–512, 516, 543, 549,
551–554, 562, 570, 573, 575,
609, 611, 614, 626, 645, 648, 656,
663, 665

Participatory research and action, 502

Partners, 6, 26, 38, 61–63, 74, 85, 94,
97–98, 101, 103–104, 118, 125,
141, 175, 182, 185, 188, 246, 295,
310, 375, 421, 423, 435, 442, 457,
461, 467, 477, 479, 481,
483–485, 487–489, 494–496,
509–512, 527, 529–532,
549–550, 552–559, 562,
567–569, 571–574, 577,
579–581, 583–584, 605, 608,
611, 614–617, 620–625,
638–641, 644, 649, 662

Partnership, 66, 83–85, 87, 89, 116,
124, 126, 129, 160, 181,
185–186, 190, 192, 194, 202,
227, 233–234, 242, 244,
291–292, 296, 300, 398–399,
426, 432–433, 438, 445, 462,
464–465, 467–468, 472,
477–484, 487–490, 495,
499–500, 510, 514, 518–519,
523, 528, 538, 546, 549, 551,
554, 558, 563, 571, 573–574,
577, 606, 610–611, 613,
616–625, 632, 638–639, 643,
652, 656, 665

Payment, 70, 72, 146, 208, 239, 297,
319, 482, 522, 531–532,
542–543, 594

Pedagogy, 118, 212, 216, 224, 316, 352, 374, 426, 429−430, 432, 435, 462, 464, 466, 494−495, 546, 559, 588, 593−595, 598, 609, 643−645, 648, 662

Peer assisted study, 293, 298, 629

Peer counselor, 318

Peer education, 272, 291−293, 295, 297−301, 303, 305, 307, 309−310, 578, 631

Peer feedback, 339, 384

Peer group, 27, 292, 324, 331, 335−336, 343, 346, 446, 615

Peer leaders, 293, 308−309, 318−319, 321−327

Peer leadership, 293, 319

Peer mentoring, 233, 293, 298−300, 304, 314−315, 317−318, 320, 327, 483, 488, 615, 626−627

Peer review, 94, 105, 119, 141, 164, 217, 273, 385, 390, 392, 621

Peer support, 228, 271−272, 292−298, 302, 304, 307−310, 313−317, 319−321, 323−327, 350, 456, 613−615, 617, 628, 639, 644, 649, 665

Peers, 1, 16−17, 67, 70−71, 74, 95, 105, 153, 158, 164, 210, 257, 273, 279, 281−282, 291−293, 295, 300, 304, 310, 313−314, 323, 325, 327, 338−339, 341, 343, 350−351, 383, 390, 398, 421, 426−427, 431, 434−435, 437, 439, 441, 449, 469, 496, 517−518, 527, 532, 536, 543, 546, 572, 574, 577−578, 581, 607, 614, 619, 626, 652, 656−657

Perceptions, 3, 66, 77−79, 81, 83, 85, 87, 89−90, 95, 151, 154, 157, 182, 208, 226, 241, 244, 248, 272, 337, 350, 352, 359, 381, 402, 435, 470, 485, 506, 617, 659−660

Periodic review, 163, 167, 170−172, 176

Personal development planning, 332−333, 649, 651

Personalisation, 149−150

Personalised, 81, 192, 291−292, 308, 613

Perspectives on engagement, 383

Philosophy, 6, 30, 45, 94, 150, 231, 318, 381, 385, 402, 482, 487, 533, 587, 597, 609, 617−619, 621−622, 627, 663

Placement, 198, 204, 208, 210, 213, 232, 238, 247−250, 335, 340, 409−410, 482, 568

Plato, 6, 272

Policy analysis, 425

Policymakers, 288, 462, 473

Post-92 University, 147, 151

Post graduate, 593

Postgraduate, 60, 66, 68, 86, 116, 123, 182, 198, 256−258, 269, 272, 276, 298, 313−327, 424, 433−434, 451, 471, 503, 527, 532, 542−543, 546, 568, 571, 575, 595, 597−598, 615, 646, 648, 650

Power, 2, 10, 14, 16, 26, 28, 31, 33−34, 74, 79, 81, 85, 94, 122, 129, 145, 147, 153−160, 181−182, 189−190, 194, 215, 239, 242, 346, 372, 383, 385, 402, 464, 469, 471, 494−495, 503, 509−510, 513, 522−523, 535, 552, 554, 558, 563, 596, 606, 614−615, 617−620, 622−625, 656, 658, 660

Presentation, 44, 202, 242, 247, 249, 266, 285, 307, 309, 357−359, 362, 390, 405, 414, 416, 421, 425, 428−429, 432, 440, 442, 452−453, 482, 522, 538, 577

Prison, 35, 578

Private Provider, 112, 114−115, 121, 606

Private sector, 111−117, 119−125, 127, 129−130

Process, 2, 10, 12, 28−29, 47, 50, 52, 60, 79−83, 85, 88−89, 93, 97−109,

114–118, 120, 128, 135–136, 138–142, 148, 155–157, 159–160, 163, 166–168, 171–178, 183, 185, 187–189, 191–192, 194–195, 199, 207–209, 238, 245, 247, 250–251, 255, 258–260, 262, 264–267, 269, 271, 282, 285, 294, 310, 317–318, 320–321, 327, 334–336, 338–341, 344–346, 351–352, 354–355, 372, 380–383, 385, 389–390, 392–393, 397–399, 401–409, 411–413, 415–417, 424, 427–428, 430, 432–433, 437–438, 444–451, 453–455, 458, 462–464, 466–470, 473, 477–479, 481, 484–487, 495–496, 499–503, 505–506, 509, 514, 517–519, 521, 523, 528, 534–535, 538–541, 546, 549, 551–552, 556–557, 559, 563, 569, 571, 573–575, 578–583, 589–591, 593, 596, 605, 611, 613–617, 620–621, 624–625, 628, 630, 639, 652, 662, 665

Producers, 6, 118, 148, 461, 463, 496, 510–511, 587, 616

Product, 45, 122, 260, 381, 389, 477, 485–486, 544, 604, 606, 617, 648

Professional practice, 242, 384, 421–423, 425, 427, 429, 431, 433, 435, 482

Programme approval, 86, 486

Project, 65, 82, 103, 134, 181, 184–185, 188–192, 194–195, 201, 203, 205, 213–214, 216, 232–233, 246, 248, 255–256, 258–268, 304, 309, 313–315, 317–319, 322–324, 326–327, 339, 349–350, 352, 359, 361–363, 374, 433, 435, 438–442, 444, 446–457, 477–478, 481–489, 500–502, 507, 512–515, 517,

519–521, 527, 532–545, 568–569, 571–576, 578–584, 588, 590–591, 593–596, 598, 614, 638–647, 649–650, 652

Promoting, 7, 46, 61, 63, 103, 112, 135, 142, 160, 211, 231, 243, 258, 265, 297, 316, 362, 381, 404, 432, 542, 546, 575, 611, 615, 642

Protest, 7, 9–10, 105, 157, 594

Protest, 7, 9–10, 105, 157, 594

Providers, 23, 37, 93–94, 112–115, 121, 213, 222, 237, 241, 310, 595, 606

Public Health, 422–425, 429, 433, 435, 644, 646

QAA, 60–62, 84, 94, 105–106, 114–117, 123–125, 127–128, 130, 146, 155, 160, 164–165, 170, 183, 191–192, 204–205, 332, 438, 479, 529, 533, 595, 615, 626–627, 645, 650, 658

Qualification, 123, 205, 208, 240, 392, 593

Quality assurance, 5, 25–26, 44, 46, 55, 59–61, 94, 98, 105–106, 109, 114–115, 124, 146, 151, 160, 163–164, 167–173, 176–177, 183, 295, 297, 300, 422–423, 448, 461, 479, 517, 529, 588, 592, 607, 615, 641, 645, 658

Quality Assurance Agency, 59–60, 105, 109, 114, 146, 151, 164, 183, 479, 529, 592, 615, 641, 645, 658

Quality of learning, 35, 37, 47–48, 61, 88, 462

Radicalism, 10

Recognition, 9, 16, 86, 97, 99–100, 102, 108, 140, 151, 158, 192, 229, 234, 260, 291, 296–297, 309–310, 314, 316, 340, 342, 361, 370–371, 381, 405, 456–457, 462, 479, 495, 527, 530–531, 535, 537, 562, 588, 593, 615, 619, 623, 661

Recruitment, 84, 170, 178, 187, 214,
    296, 310, 321, 352, 398, 437,
    448−450, 453−454, 456,
    482, 640
Reflection, 34, 94, 109, 139, 205, 211,
    215, 229, 247, 250−251, 265,
    272−273, 314, 331−341, 343,
    345−346, 390, 402, 406, 409,
    415−417, 523, 540, 544,
    570−571, 582, 607−608, 613,
    628, 631, 638
Reflective, 138, 170, 198, 203, 205, 213,
    230, 232, 238, 250, 271−273,
    299, 316, 322−323, 334−335,
    338, 341−342, 344, 404, 407,
    409−412, 414−417, 504−505,
    517−518, 521, 540, 543,
    553−554, 562, 570, 577−578,
    582, 604, 632, 643
Regional co-operation, xxi
Relational learning, 53
Relationship, 6, 13−14, 19, 28, 32, 35,
    44, 46, 49, 51−54, 79−82, 84,
    88−89, 94, 134, 140−141, 143,
    158, 171, 182, 197, 201−202,
    214−216, 224, 226, 233, 238,
    246, 251, 272, 293, 304−305,
    308−309, 314−315, 317, 320,
    371−372, 382, 399, 402−404,
    406, 417, 463−464, 466,
    468−469, 480−481, 484, 487,
    495, 511, 513, 528, 530, 541,
    554−555, 558, 578, 582, 593,
    595, 606, 616, 618−620, 622,
    624, 630, 639, 659, 663
Remuneration, 224, 456, 527, 532
Reporting, 126, 153, 169−170, 178,
    509, 619
Resourcing, 297, 326, 393, 632
Respect, 12, 31, 139, 260, 351, 360,
    405−406, 409, 412, 424, 439,
    545, 558−559, 567, 569,
    578−579, 624, 627, 659, 661
Respect, 12, 31, 139, 260, 351, 360,
    405−406, 409, 412, 424, 439,

    545, 558−559, 567, 569,
    578−579, 624, 627, 659, 661
Responsibility, 12, 14, 16, 36−38, 47,
    71, 74, 79−80, 82, 85, 102,
    124−125, 134, 156−157, 167,
    170−171, 178, 198, 204−205,
    214−216, 221, 223, 225−227,
    239, 246, 262, 271−273,
    277−278, 281, 295−298,
    306−307, 310, 383, 397, 403,
    408−410, 415, 417, 433−434,
    461, 468−469, 494, 496, 529,
    534−535, 537, 549, 552, 560−563,
    567, 569−570, 573−575, 577,
    580−581, 604, 606, 612, 616,
    620−621, 624, 629, 633, 639,
    644, 651, 656, 658, 661−662
Retention, 27−28, 45, 65, 83, 117, 126,
    139, 186, 192−194, 202, 226,
    291−292, 301, 314, 456, 480,
    611, 628, 639, 650, 656−658
Reward, 74, 221−222, 296−297,
    309−310, 344−345, 384, 398,
    458, 479, 482, 486, 495, 527,
    530−532, 615
Rite of passage, 16, 18−19
Russell Group, 60, 147

Satisfaction, 3, 25, 34, 45, 60, 62, 65,
    72−73, 78−79, 81−82, 84, 88,
    119, 139−140, 146, 148−149,
    151, 154, 182, 193−194, 198,
    279, 291−292, 341, 343, 381,
    422, 435, 448, 480−481, 489,
    528, 531, 537, 546, 605−606,
    611, 613, 632, 656−658
Scholarship, 6, 31, 35, 37, 135−136,
    140−141, 277, 308, 367, 373,
    379, 402, 405−406, 425, 451,
    455, 501, 509, 511, 542, 553, 637,
    640−641, 648, 651
Selection, 14, 46, 148, 170, 178, 232,
    257, 310, 341, 352, 438,
    450−452, 455−456, 467, 484,
    502, 506

Self-efficacy, 278, 282, 284−285, 375, 607

Self-esteem, 153−154, 281, 350, 362, 415, 429

Self-interest, 59, 71, 216, 227, 595, 629

Sense of being, 2−3, 43−44, 51−54, 344−345, 392, 404, 479, 608, 621, 628−629

Service-learning, 238−240, 242, 247, 579

Skills, 28, 36, 50, 54, 66, 70, 72−73, 83, 121, 142, 155, 166, 171, 173, 186, 197, 201, 203−204, 209, 211, 224, 228, 230−232, 237, 241, 243−244, 246, 248, 250−251, 256, 261−265, 267−268, 273, 275, 277−280, 282, 284−285, 288, 291−292, 297, 299−300, 302−305, 307, 314−315, 321−322, 324−325, 333, 337, 339−342, 345, 350−352, 354, 358, 362−363, 367−368, 371, 382, 384−385, 389, 404, 412−413, 415−416, 421−436, 446−448, 450, 454−456, 458, 463, 467, 471, 473, 482−483, 502, 513, 517−518, 521, 531−533, 535−536, 539−546, 568, 570, 575, 577, 579, 583, 589, 603−604, 607, 616, 619−620, 623, 626−628, 630, 632, 646, 650

Social belonging, 83

Social class, 203, 570

Social hubs, 256, 258−259, 261, 264, 268−269, 649

Social justice, 35, 135, 142, 152, 228, 237, 250, 569−570

Social model of disability, 183

Social networking, 325, 439−442, 542

Society, 6, 8, 13−14, 17, 25−27, 29, 32, 34, 36, 64−65, 71, 74, 86, 107, 182, 221−223, 225, 228−233, 240, 248, 260−262, 353, 367, 428, 435, 512, 534−535, 539, 541, 544, 568, 570, 573,

576−577, 591, 593−594, 596, 611, 646−647, 649, 651−652, 659, 661

Sport, 17, 64, 198, 227, 237, 239−251, 265, 342, 469, 648−649

Staff engagement, 277, 308

Staff perceptions, 3, 77−79, 81, 83, 85, 87, 89, 151

Stakeholder engagement, 501

Strategy, 46, 59, 61−67, 69, 72−74, 101, 119, 163−164, 184, 186, 188−190, 222, 242, 272, 308−309, 321, 331, 333−335, 337, 339, 341, 343, 345, 385, 393, 435, 438, 477, 479−480, 494, 496, 536, 574−575, 587, 591, 594, 611−613, 641, 643, 650, 657−658, 665

Student as producer, 62, 119−120, 496, 510, 587−596, 598, 608, 611−612, 614, 644

Student charter, 15, 84, 182

Student coach, 292

Student engagement, 1−3, 5−7, 9, 11, 13, 15, 17, 19, 23, 25−26, 28−34, 36−38, 43−55, 59−74, 77−79, 81−89, 93−95, 97−109, 111, 113, 115−125, 127, 129, 133, 135, 138, 143, 145−149, 151−155, 157−159, 163, 165, 173−174, 178, 181−188, 190−195, 197, 201−204, 213, 215−216, 221, 223, 225, 227, 229, 231, 233, 237, 245, 255, 271−273, 275−277, 279−281, 283−285, 287−288, 291−292, 303, 308−310, 313, 316, 327, 331−332, 336, 344−345, 349, 351, 363, 367−369, 371, 373−374, 379, 381−382, 394, 397, 401−402, 404−405, 417−418, 421, 426, 432−435, 437, 443, 446−447, 461, 464−465, 468, 472, 477−478, 480, 483−486, 488−489,

493–496, 499, 502, 509–511,
    523, 527–531, 534, 536–537,
    546, 549–550, 552, 554,
    559–560, 567, 575, 577, 581,
    583, 587, 590–594, 597,
    603–618, 620–621, 625, 628,
    631–633, 638–639, 641–643,
    645, 647–650, 652, 656–659,
    661–665
Student handbook, 155–156
Student liaison committee, 118, 122, 187
Student movement, 7, 98, 104
Student perceptions, 66, 90, 272, 352,
    470
Student representation, 7, 87, 98, 100,
    108–109, 116–117, 120, 123,
    127, 129, 148, 150–152, 155,
    157, 159–160, 181, 187, 191,
    193, 202, 215, 488, 533, 592, 616
Student reviewers, 106, 166, 168,
    172–173, 176–177
Student satisfaction, 34, 45, 60, 62,
    73, 78–79, 82, 84, 88, 146, 149,
    151, 154, 182, 193–194, 422,
    435, 448, 480–481, 489, 528,
    546, 606, 611, 613, 632,
    656–657
Student voice, 67, 77, 82, 87, 111,
    117–120, 127–129, 134, 136,
    139, 142–143, 145, 147, 149,
    152–153, 155, 164, 181, 189,
    191, 202, 375, 404, 438, 443, 446,
    448–449, 457, 480, 486, 495,
    500, 528, 530, 552–554, 591,
    606, 613, 623, 625–626,
    640–641, 648, 650–651,
    656–658, 661
Student volunteering, 19, 70, 221–229,
    233–235, 241, 243–246, 250,
    533, 643, 649
Student-led, 10, 182, 222, 227, 229, 262,
    279, 293, 298, 303, 398, 412, 432,
    437, 443, 445, 448–449, 456,
    479, 489, 501–502, 517, 521,
    527, 532–533, 536, 592, 616

Students as Learners and Teachers,
    549–550, 608
Students as partners, 118, 125, 175, 182,
    185, 295, 310, 375, 423, 435, 477,
    479, 481, 483, 485, 487–489,
    509, 530, 552–553, 605, 608,
    611, 614, 616–617, 620–622,
    625, 639–640, 644, 662
Students' guild, 62–70, 72–73, 528
Students' union, 9, 74, 84–85, 87, 98,
    100, 107–108, 120, 129,
    146–148, 152, 155–156, 160,
    167, 169, 172, 176, 181–182,
    187–188, 190–192, 423, 477,
    479–482, 490, 606, 622,
    638–639, 641, 643, 645–646, 661
Study groups, 293, 303–304, 307, 521
Study skills, 83, 302, 305, 368, 389, 650
Subject review, 163, 165, 167, 169, 171,
    173, 175, 177, 589
Summative assessment, 86, 88, 380,
    384–385, 392
Supplemental instruction, 293, 298, 300,
    644
Supplyism, 77–78, 81–82
Survey, 32, 37, 43, 45–48, 55, 79,
    81–82, 88, 112–114, 116–117,
    140, 146, 151, 181–182, 188,
    223, 225–226, 234, 256–257,
    282–283, 315–316, 325, 386,
    435, 470, 480, 482, 484, 489, 500,
    589, 609, 611, 638, 641, 658

Teaching, 3, 6, 11–12, 23, 26, 30–31,
    33–34, 37–38, 44, 48–49, 55,
    60–62, 65–66, 78–88, 94, 114,
    116, 119, 121, 126, 130,
    133–137, 140, 142, 149, 153,
    163–164, 171, 177, 182–183,
    185–189, 192–194, 202, 222,
    229, 234, 255–256, 258–259,
    261, 268, 271, 276–279, 282,
    286–287, 291, 293, 295–296,
    301, 303, 307–310, 333–334,
    339, 350–351, 354, 372–374,

380–387, 389–394, 401–403,
405–407, 410, 415–417,
421–424, 426–427, 431,
433–435, 438, 443, 445–447,
456, 462–471, 473, 478–483,
493–496, 499–501, 503,
505–506, 510, 512–514,
517–521, 527, 529, 532–534,
542, 549–563, 567, 569, 581,
584, 587–595, 598, 603,
606–609, 611–612, 616, 618,
620–624, 627, 631, 637–652,
654, 656, 659, 663

Technology, 26, 34, 114, 229–230, 234,
259, 284, 370, 398, 426, 435,
437–438, 443–446, 457, 486,
509, 516–517, 531, 533,
536–537, 544–545, 571, 576,
584, 622, 627, 632, 640, 645,
648–650, 652, 656

Technology enhanced learning, 457,
516, 649, 652

The whole student, 288, 386, 502, 608

Threshold concept, 323, 374, 629

Training, 12–13, 26, 66, 88, 93, 115,
123–124, 126–127, 142,
154–157, 165, 169, 171–174,
178, 187–189, 191–194, 209,
228, 230–232, 240, 242,
245–246, 293, 296–297,
299–300, 302, 305, 308, 310,
314–315, 319, 321, 323–324,
362, 421, 423–434, 436, 522,
570–571, 579, 592, 639, 642,
646, 651

Transactional, 3, 14, 45, 52, 55, 77–78,
88–89, 216, 606

Transform, 48, 135, 199, 222, 243, 375,
550, 557, 562, 579, 630

Transformation, 2–3, 43–44, 51–54,
89, 256, 334, 471, 528, 553–554,
559, 617, 619, 629

Transformational, 3, 45, 77–78, 88–89,
160, 406, 457, 496, 624, 629,
631–632

Transformative, 50, 52–53, 55, 137,
203, 223, 323, 375, 406–407,
413, 466, 617, 629, 631, 637, 641

Transition, 275–276, 282, 286, 288,
291–293, 295, 297–300, 337,
422–423, 425, 448, 543,
639–640, 644, 650, 656

Transition mentoring, 293

Transmission, 273, 382, 390, 403

Trust, 15, 133–136, 139–140, 142–143,
164, 208, 268, 351, 358, 362, 412,
415, 573, 580, 583, 617, 626

Usual suspects, 484, 501

Voice, 2, 7, 49, 60, 64, 67, 72, 77, 82,
85–87, 95, 100–101, 108, 111,
115, 117–120, 126–129, 141,
145, 147, 149, 152–153, 155,
164, 181, 189, 191, 202, 266, 300,
314, 318, 375, 404, 437–438,
443, 448–449, 457–458,
463–464, 480, 486, 495,
499–500, 502, 513, 528, 530,
545, 552–553, 591, 606, 613,
616, 623–624, 640–641, 650,
656–658, 661

Voluntary, 19, 37, 55, 68, 71, 198, 204,
224, 228–231, 234, 240, 243,
246, 250, 264, 293, 482, 516,
531–532, 542, 551, 572, 577,
579, 643

Volunteering, 19, 63, 70, 73, 198, 215,
221–235, 237, 239–241,
243–246, 250, 306, 309, 447,
533, 568, 577, 589, 607,
612–613, 643, 649, 665

Widening participation, 72, 223, 229,
231, 280–281, 288, 308–309

Work integrated learning, 48

Work placements, 203, 213, 215, 252,
336, 340

Workplace learning, 642

Workplace Management, 340–341

Workshops, 188, 228, 233, 256,
    283–284, 297, 299, 307,
    315, 317, 321–322, 336,
    349, 354, 360, 362–363,
    430, 454, 483, 487–488, 517,
    637, 658
World Café, 494, 502, 503, 504, 505,
    506, 627, 629

Writing, 13, 28, 46, 54–55, 61, 104,
    233, 244, 278, 284–285, 299,
    315, 322, 326–327, 334–335,
    339, 342, 346, 352, 383,
    387–389, 391–393, 411,
    413, 417, 421, 425–426, 428,
    444, 453, 483, 486, 519, 533,
    540, 551, 630, 640–642, 644,
    651, 659